"Things worthwhile generally don't just happen. Luck is a fact, but should not be a factor. Good luck is what is left over after intelligence and effort have combined at their best. Negligence or indifference are usually reviewed from an unlucky seat. The law of cause and effect and causality both work the same with inexorable exactitudes. Luck is the residue of design."

--- Branch Rickey

"I don't care if I was a ditch-digger at a dollar a day, I'd want to do my job better than the fellow next to me. I'd want to be the best at whatever I do."
-- Branch Rickey

A Letter to My Children

To Avery, Shay, & Baby Werner,

There isn't a day that passes that I don't thank God for the three of you. Being your father has taught me so many important things in life – unconditional love, limitless happiness, and – of course – the patience of a saint – but the most important take away for me, personally, is how nothing else matters. Every moment I spend with you is one that I try to never forget: the laughing and giggling, the cries from a boo-boo, the "dad will you 'nug with me?" I live for those. I cherish those. They are the greatest times of my life.

Love,

Daddy

Julianne,
Thank you for being wonderfully you.

Cal,
My best friend, my late-night writing partner, my companion. I don't know what I'd do without you.

Author Bio: Joseph Werner provides further evidence that Jim Bouton was right when he wrote, "You spend your life gripping a baseball, and in the end it turns out that it was the other way around all the time."

As a lifelong Indians fan, Werner's lived and died multiple times over. First with the original revival of Cleveland baseball in the mid-1990s, then languishing through the lean years before having his life reinvigorated by their fantastically wonderful 2016 post-season run and continued success.

All along the way, though, he's heard two of the greatest radio voices in the game: Herb Score and Tom Hamilton. Despite his youth at the time, he proudly — and somewhat embarrassingly — remembers falling asleep with his arms clutched around a portable radio as Score made his last radio call during Game 7 of 1997 World Series.

Werner has been fortunate — and incredibly blessed — to have some of his work published and mentioned on several major media outlets, including: ESPN, Yahoo! Sports, Cleveland.com, The Baseball Research Journal, and Beyond the Box Score.

A Note from the Author: As I mentioned in every book, my continued goal is to provide the reader with the best product that I can. I want it to be something that not only is informative but also enjoyable to read. My hope is that I've achieved that goal with this year's Prospect Digest Handbook. Thank you for reading – as always.

I apologize about the delay in this year's edition. Life happily, wonderfully gets in the way.

I would just like to tip my hat to the following websites because without their invaluable data, none of this would have been possible:

- fangraphs.com
- baseballreference.com
- thebaseballcube.com
- claydavenport.com
- baseballprospectus.com

Another special thank you goes out to Josh Stollings for his help on this year's cover.

I would like to thank you, the reader, once again. I enjoy hearing from you guys – be it before or after the book comes out. Please feel free to reach me at the following email address: JosephMWerner@yahoo.com. I absolutely love hearing everyone's thoughts/comments/concerns/feedback.

I'd also like to thank Michael Salfino. I appreciate you always championing my book. I'm forever indebted.

One final note: Because the book is self-published, I do not control the price of the Handbook; I wish I did, though. The price is based on the total amount of pages.

All the best,

JOE

Table of Contents

The Top 300 Prospects

Ranking the Top 300 Prospects (1-100)

Rank	Name	Team	Age	Pos	Rank	Name	Team	Age	Pos
1	Julio Rodriguez	Seattle Mariners	21	OF	51	Alek Thomas	Arizona Diamondbacks	22	CF
2	Bobby Witt Jr.	Kansas City Royals	22	3B/SS	52	Liover Peguero	Pittsburgh Pirates	21	SS
3	Adley Rutschman	Baltimore Orioles	24	C	53	Nick Gonzales	Pittsburgh Pirates	23	2B/SS
4	Spencer Torkelson	Detroit Tigers	22	1B/3B	54	Kahlil Watson	Miami Marlins	19	SS
5	Grayson Rodriguez	Baltimore Orioles	22	RHP	55	Cristian Pache	Atlanta Braves	23	CF
6	Riley Greene	Detroit Tigers	21	CF	56	Joey Bart	San Francisco Giants	25	C
7	Gabriel Moreno	Toronto Blue Jays	22	C	57	Luis Campusano	San Diego Padres	23	C
8	Anthony Volpe	New York Yankees	21	SS	58	Asa Lacy	Kansas City Royals	23	LHP
9	Jack Leiter	Texas Rangers	22	RHP	59	Tyler Soderstrom	Oakland Athletics	20	C/1B
10	George Kirby	Seattle Mariners	24	RHP	60	Cristian Hernandez	Chicago Cubs	18	SS
11	Francisco Alvarez	New York Mets	20	C	61	Nick Lodolo	Cincinnati Reds	24	LHP
12	Diego Cartaya	Los Angeles Dodgers	20	C	62	Quinn Priester	Pittsburgh Pirates	21	RHP
13	Marco Luciano	San Francisco Giants	20	SS	63	Freddy Tarnok	Atlanta Braves	23	RHP
14	George Valera	Cleveland Guardians	21	OF	64	Nick Allen	Oakland Athletics	23	2B/SS
15	Nolan Gorman	St. Louis Cardinals	22	2B/3B	65	Orelvis Martinez	Toronto Blue Jays	19	3B/SS
16	CJ Abrams	San Diego Padres	21	SS	66	Michael Harris II	Atlanta Braves	21	OF
17	Corbin Carroll	Arizona Diamondbacks	21	CF	67	Jordan Groshans	Toronto Blue Jays	22	3B/SS
18	Miguel Vargas	Los Angeles Dodgers	21	3B	68	Cole Winn	Texas Rangers	22	RHP
19	Keibert Ruiz	Washington Nationals	23	C	69	Brady House	Washington Nationals	19	SS
20	Nick Yorke	Boston Red Sox	20	2B	70	Jordan Lawlar	Arizona Diamondbacks	19	SS
21	Oneil Cruz	Pittsburgh Pirates	23	SS	71	Jasson Dominguez	New York Yankees	19	CF
22	Shane Baz	Tampa Bay Rays	23	RHP	72	Geraldo Perdomo	Arizona Diamondbacks	22	SS
23	Brett Baty	New York Mets	22	3B/LF	73	Colton Cowser	Baltimore Orioles	22	CF
24	Jordan Walker	St. Louis Cardinals	20	3B	74	Andrew Painter	Philadelphia Phillies	19	RHP
25	Robert Hassell III	San Diego Padres	20	CF	75	James Triantos	Chicago Cubs	19	2B/SS
26	Marcelo Mayer	Boston Red Sox	19	SS	76	Tyler Freeman	Cleveland Guardians	23	IF
27	Zac Veen	Colorado Rockies	20	RF	77	Elly De La Cruz	Cincinnati Reds	20	3B/SS
28	Brayan Rocchio	Cleveland Guardians	21	2B/SS	78	Austin Martin	Minnesota Twins	23	SS/CF
29	Noelvi Marte	Seattle Mariners	20	SS	79	Cole Wilcox	Tampa Bay Rays	22	RHP
30	Henry Davis	Pittsburgh Pirates	22	C	80	Matthew Liberatore	St. Louis Cardinals	22	LHP
31	Josh Jung	Texas Rangers	24	3B	81	Kristian Robinson	Arizona Diamondbacks	21	CF
32	Reid Detmers	Los Angeles Angels	22	LHP	82	D.L. Hall	Baltimore Orioles	23	LHP
33	Hunter Greene	Cincinnati Reds	22	RHP	83	Josh Lowe	Tampa Bay Rays	24	OF
34	Bobby Miller	Los Angeles Dodgers	23	RHP	84	Andy Pages	Los Angeles Dodgers	21	RF
35	MJ Melendez	Kansas City Royals	23	C	85	Gabriel Arias	Cleveland Guardians	22	3B/SS
36	Luis Matos	San Francisco Giants	20	CF	86	Oswald Peraza	New York Yankees	22	SS
37	Cade Cavalli	Washington Nationals	23	RHP	87	Jordan Balazovic	Minnesota Twins	23	RHP
38	Jackson Jobe	Detroit Tigers	19	RHP	88	Emerson Hancock	Seattle Mariners	23	RHP
39	Nick Pratto	Kansas City Royals	23	1B	89	Mick Abel	Philadelphia Phillies	20	RHP
40	Brayan Bello	Boston Red Sox	23	RHP	90	Jose Miranda	Minnesota Twins	24	IF
41	Brennen Davis	Chicago Cubs	22	OF	91	Coby Mayo	Baltimore Orioles	20	3B
42	Edward Cabrera	Miami Marlins	24	RHP	92	Jairo Pomares	San Francisco Giants	21	OF
43	Pete Crow-Armstrong	Chicago Cubs	20	CF	93	Curtis Mead	Tampa Bay Rays	21	1B/3B
44	Aaron Ashby	Milwaukee Brewers	24	LHP	94	Benny Montgomery	Colorado Rockies	19	CF
45	Max Meyer	Miami Marlins	23	RHP	95	Shea Langeliers	Atlanta Braves	24	C
46	Daniel Espino	Cleveland Guardians	21	RHP	96	Jeremy Pena	Houston Astros	24	SS
47	Roansy Contreras	Pittsburgh Pirates	22	RHP	97	Drew Romo	Colorado Rockies	20	C
48	Kevin Alcantara	Chicago Cubs	19	CF	98	Luis Gil	New York Yankees	24	RHP
49	Eury Perez	Miami Marlins	19	RHP	99	Royce Lewis	Minnesota Twins	23	SS
50	Triston Casas	Boston Red Sox	22	1B	100	Michael Burrows	Pittsburgh Pirates	22	RHP

Ranking the Top 300 Prospects (101-200)

Rank	Name	Team	Age	Pos	Rank	Name	Team	Age	Pos
101	Brailyn Marquez	Chicago Cubs	23	LHP	151	Vaughn Grissom	Atlanta Braves	21	IF
102	Nate Pearson	Toronto Blue Jays	25	RHP	152	Euribiel Angeles	San Diego Padres	20	IF
103	Ronny Mauricio	New York Mets	21	SS	153	Arol Vera	Los Angeles Angels	19	SS
104	Johan Rojas	Philadelphia Phillies	22	CF	154	Freddy Zamora	Milwaukee Brewers	23	SS
105	Sixto Sanchez	Miami Marlins	23	RHP	155	Reese Olson	Detroit Tigers	22	RHP
106	Michael Busch	Los Angeles Dodgers	24	2B	156	Michael McGreevy	St. Louis Cardinals	21	RHP
107	Joe Perez	Houston Astros	22	3B	157	Cole Henry	Washington Nationals	22	RHP
108	Gunnar Henderson	Baltimore Orioles	21	3B/SS	158	Jared Jones	Pittsburgh Pirates	20	RHP
109	Gilberto Jimenez	Boston Red Sox	21	CF	159	Jackson Rutledge	Washington Nationals	23	RHP
110	Matt McLain	Cincinnati Reds	22	SS	160	Colson Montgomery	Chicago White Sox	19	SS
111	Kyle Harrison	San Francisco Giants	20	LHP	161	Maddux Bruns	Los Angeles Dodgers	20	LHP
112	Taj Bradley	Tampa Bay Rays	21	RHP	162	Jose Rodriguez	Chicago White Sox	21	SS
113	Vidal Brujan	Tampa Bay Rays	24	IF/OF	163	Matthew Thompson	Chicago White Sox	21	RHP
114	Ivan Herrera	St. Louis Cardinals	22	C	164	Ty Madden	Detroit Tigers	22	RHP
115	Reginald Preciado	Chicago Cubs	19	3B/SS	165	Ezequiel Tovar	Colorado Rockies	20	SS
116	Chase Petty	Minnesota Twins	19	RHP	166	Bryan Ramos	Chicago White Sox	20	2B/3B
117	Sam Bachman	Los Angeles Angels	22	RHP	167	Ky Bush	Los Angeles Angels	22	LHP
118	Harry Ford	Seattle Mariners	19	C	168	Alexander Ramirez	Los Angeles Angels	19	CF
119	Garrett Mitchell	Milwaukee Brewers	23	CF	169	Armando Cruz	Washington Nationals	18	SS
120	Heston Kjerstad	Baltimore Orioles	23	OF	170	Seth Johnson	Tampa Bay Rays	23	RHP
121	S. Woods Richardson	Minnesota Twins	21	RHP	171	Joey Wiemer	Milwaukee Brewers	23	OF
122	Sal Frelick	Milwaukee Brewers	22	CF	172	Brendan McKay	Tampa Bay Rays	26	1B/LHP
123	Drey Jameson	Arizona Diamondbacks	23	RHP	173	Matt Allan	New York Mets	21	RHP
124	Blake Walston	Arizona Diamondbacks	21	LHP	174	Jhoan Duran	Minnesota Twins	24	RHP
125	Jay Allen II	Cincinnati Reds	19	CF	175	Kyle Muller	Atlanta Braves	24	LHP
126	Tahnaj Thomas	Pittsburgh Pirates	23	RHP	176	Brice Turang	Milwaukee Brewers	22	SS
127	Zack Gelof	Oakland Athletics	22	3B	177	Adam Macko	Seattle Mariners	21	LHP
128	Pedro Pineda	Oakland Athletics	18	CF	178	Carlos Duran	Los Angeles Dodgers	20	RHP
129	Kyle Isbel	Kansas City Royals	25	CF	179	Bryce Bonnin	Cincinnati Reds	23	RHP
130	Will Bednar	San Francisco Giants	22	RHP	180	Luisangel Acuna	Texas Rangers	20	2B/SS
131	Ryan Rolison	Colorado Rockies	24	LHP	181	Clayton Beeter	Los Angeles Dodgers	23	RHP
132	Hans Crouse	Philadelphia Phillies	23	RHP	182	Bryan Mata	Boston Red Sox	23	RHP
133	Mark Vientos	New York Mets	22	3B/LF	183	Victor Vodnik	Atlanta Braves	22	RHP
134	MacKenzie Gore	San Diego Padres	23	LHP	184	Matt Canterino	Minnesota Twins	24	RHP
135	Gunnar Hoglund	Toronto Blue Jays	22	RHP	185	Clarke Schmidt	New York Yankees	26	RHP
136	Deyvison De Los Santos	Arizona Diamondbacks	19	1B/3B	186	Everson Pereira	New York Yankees	21	CF
137	Hunter Brown	Houston Astros	23	RHP	187	Samuel Zavala	San Diego Padres	17	CF
138	Wilkelman Gonzalez	Boston Red Sox	20	RHP	188	JJ Bleday	Miami Marlins	24	RF
139	Owen Caissie	Chicago Cubs	19	LF	189	Drew Waters	Atlanta Braves	23	OF
140	Nolan Jones	Cleveland Guardians	24	3B/RF	190	Jackson Kowar	Kansas City Royals	25	RHP
141	Jarren Duran	Boston Red Sox	25	CF	191	Justin Foscue	Texas Rangers	23	2B
142	Jhonkensy Noel	Cleveland Guardians	20	1B/3B	192	Xavier Edwards	Tampa Bay Rays	22	IF
143	Jose Tena	Cleveland Guardians	21	SS	193	Heliot Ramos	San Francisco Giants	22	CF
144	Pedro Leon	Houston Astros	24	CF	194	Vinnie Pasquantino	Kansas City Royals	24	1B
145	Eddys Leonard	Los Angeles Dodgers	21	IF	195	Miguel Amaya	Chicago Cubs	23	C
146	Gavin Williams	Cleveland Guardians	22	RHP	196	Bubba Chandler	Pittsburgh Pirates	19	RHP
147	Ben Kudrna	Kansas City Royals	19	RHP	197	Carson Williams	Tampa Bay Rays	19	SS
148	Frank Mozzicato	Kansas City Royals	19	LHP	198	Max Muncy	Oakland Athletics	19	SS
149	A.J. Puk	Oakland Athletics	27	LHP	199	Bryson Stott	Philadelphia Phillies	24	SS
150	Landon Knack	Los Angeles Dodgers	24	RHP	200	Ethan Small	Milwaukee Brewers	25	LHP

Ranking the Top 300 Prospects (201-300)

Rank	Name	Team	Age	Pos
201	Bryce Jarvis	Arizona Diamondbacks	24	RHP
202	Khalil Lee	New York Mets	24	OF
203	Patrick Bailey	San Francisco Giants	23	C
204	Jake Burger	Chicago White Sox	26	30
205	Alec Burleson	St. Louis Cardinals	22	LF/RF
206	Cooper Kinney	Tampa Bay Rays	19	2B/3B
207	Aaron Zavala	Texas Rangers	22	3B/RF
208	Logan O'Hoppe	Philadelphia Phillies	22	C
209	Dillon Dingler	Detroit Tigers	23	C
210	Angel Zerpa	Kansas City Royals	22	LHP
211	Jackson Merrill	San Diego Padres	19	SS
212	Drew Rom	Baltimore Orioles	23	LHP
213	DJ Herz	Chicago Cubs	21	LHP
214	Alexander Canario	Chicago Cubs	22	OF
215	Carlos Colmenarez	Tampa Bay Rays	18	SS
216	Alex De Jesus	Los Angeles Dodgers	20	SS
217	Yunior Severino	Minnesota Twins	22	2B/3B
218	Jeremiah Jackson	Los Angeles Angels	22	SS
219	Joe Mack	Miami Marlins	19	C
220	Jeferson Quero	Milwaukee Brewers	19	C
221	Tyler Black	Milwaukee Brewers	21	2B
222	Hedbert Perez	Milwaukee Brewers	19	CF
223	Jordan Westburg	Baltimore Orioles	23	3B/SS
224	Kyren Paris	Los Angeles Angels	20	2B/SS
225	Jose Salas	Miami Marlins	19	SS
226	Norge Vera	Chicago White Sox	22	RHP
227	Edgar Quero	Los Angeles Angels	19	C
228	Joe Ryan	Minnesota Twins	26	RHP
229	Noah Song	Boston Red Sox	25	RHP
230	Braden Shewmake	Atlanta Braves	24	SS
231	Bryan Lavastida	Cleveland Guardians	23	C
232	Petey Halpin	Cleveland Guardians	20	OF
233	Evan Carter	Texas Rangers	20	CF
234	Korey Lee	Houston Astros	23	C
235	Deivi Garcia	New York Yankees	23	RHP
236	Anthony Solometo	Pittsburgh Pirates	19	LHP
237	Gabriel Gonzalez	Seattle Mariners	18	RF
238	Ryan Cusick	Atlanta Braves	22	RHP
239	Joey Estes	Atlanta Braves	20	RHP
240	Jose Torres	Cincinnati Reds	22	SS
241	Ryan Vilade	Colorado Rockies	23	1B/OF
242	Elehuris Montero	Colorado Rockies	23	1B/3B
243	Ben Hernandez	Kansas City Royals	20	RHP
244	Eduardo Garcia	Milwaukee Brewers	19	SS
245	Jaden Hill	Colorado Rockies	22	RHP
246	Michael Siani	Cincinnati Reds	22	CF
247	Ryne Nelson	Arizona Diamondbacks	24	RHP
248	Jack Blomgren	Colorado Rockies	23	2B/SS
249	Slade Cecconi	Arizona Diamondbacks	23	RHP
250	Ryan Bliss	Arizona Diamondbacks	22	SS
251	Steven Kwan	Cleveland Guardians	24	CF
252	Seth Beer	Arizona Diamondbacks	25	1B
253	Tucker Davidson	Atlanta Braves	26	LHP
254	Otto Lopez	Toronto Blue Jays	23	IF/OF
255	Zach McCambley	Miami Marlins	23	RHP
256	Braxton Garrett	Miami Marlins	24	LHP
257	Cody Bolton	Pittsburgh Pirates	24	RHP
258	Ian Lewis	Miami Marlins	19	2B/SS
259	JJ Goss	Tampa Bay Rays	21	RHP
260	James Wood	San Diego Padres	19	CF
261	Brayan Buelvas	Oakland Athletics	20	OF
262	Nick Loftin	Kansas City Royals	23	IF
263	Ryan Pepiot	Los Angeles Dodgers	24	RHP
264	Blaze Jordan	Boston Red Sox	19	1B/3B
265	Jeter Downs	Boston Red Sox	23	2B/SS
266	Kevin Made	Chicago Cubs	19	3B/SS
267	Cody Morris	Cleveland Guardians	25	RHP
268	Bo Naylor	Cleveland Guardians	22	C
269	Ed Howard	Chicago Cubs	20	2B/SS
270	Kyle Stowers	Baltimore Orioles	24	LF/RF
271	Jordan Wicks	Chicago Cubs	22	LHP
272	Angel Martinez	Cleveland Guardians	20	2B/SS
273	Tanner Burns	Cleveland Guardians	23	RHP
274	Ji-hwan Bae	Pittsburgh Pirates	22	2B/CF
275	Carmen Mlodzinski	Pittsburgh Pirates	23	RHP
276	Jay Groome	Boston Red Sox	23	LHP
277	Masyn Winn	St. Louis Cardinals	20	SS
278	Malcom Nunez	St. Louis Cardinals	21	3B
279	Francisco Morales	Philadelphia Phillies	22	RHP
280	Zavier Warren	Milwaukee Brewers	23	C/IF
281	Noah Miller	Minnesota Twins	19	SS
282	J.T. Ginn	New York Mets	23	RHP
283	Ethan Wilson	Philadelphia Phillies	22	OF
284	Indigo Diaz	Atlanta Braves	23	RHP
285	Eguy Rosario	San Diego Padres	22	IF
286	Nick Swiney	San Francisco Giants	23	LHP
287	Cristian Santana	Detroit Tigers	18	3B/SS
288	Ezequiel Duran	Texas Rangers	23	IF
289	Trey Sweeney	New York Yankees	22	SS
290	Luis Medina	New York Yankees	22	RHP
291	Daulton Jefferies	Oakland Athletics	26	RHP
292	Diego Rincones	San Francisco Giants	23	LF/RF
293	Thomas Saggese	Texas Rangers	23	IF
294	Dax Fulton	Miami Marlins	20	LHP
295	Connor Norby	Baltimore Orioles	22	2B
296	Ken Waldichuk	New York Yankees	24	LHP
297	Austin Wells	New York Yankees	22	C
298	Matthew Lugo	Boston Red Sox	21	SS
299	Sean Hjelle	San Francisco Giants	25	RHP
300	Brandon Williamson	Seattle Mariners	24	LHP

The Top 10 Prospects by Position

The Top 10 Prospects By Position

	Catchers	
1.	Adley Rutschman	Baltimore Orioles
2.	Gabriel Moreno	Toronto Blue Jays
3.	Francisco Alvarez	New York Mets
4.	Diego Cartaya	Los Angeles Dodgers
5.	Keibert Ruiz	Washington Nationals
6.	Henry Davis	Pittsburgh Pirates
7.	MJ Melendez	Kansas City Royals
8.	Joey Bart	San Francisco Giants
9.	Luis Campusano	San Diego Padres
10.	Tyler Soderstrom	Oakland Athletics

	Shortstop	
1.	Bobby Witt Jr.	Kansas City Royals
2.	Anthony Volpe	New York Yankees
3.	Marco Luciano	San Francisco Giants
4.	CJ Abrams	San Diego Padres
5.	Oneil Cruz	Pittsburgh Pirates
6.	Marcelo Mayer	Boston Red Sox
7.	Brayan Rocchio	Cleveland Guardians
8.	Noelvi Marte	Seattle Mariners
9.	Liover Peguero	Pittsburgh Pirates
10.	Nick Gonzales	Pittsburgh Pirates

	First Base	
1.	Spencer Torkelson	Detroit Tigers
2.	Nick Pratto	Kansas City Royals
3.	Triston Casas	Boston Red Sox
4.	Curtis Mead	Tampa Bay Rays
5.	Deyvison De Los Santos	Arizona Diamondbacks
6.	Jhonkensy Noel	Cleveland Guardians
7.	Brendan McKay	Tampa Bay Rays
8.	Vinnie Pasquantino	Kansas City Royals
9.	Ryan Vilade	Colorado Rockies
10.	Elehuris Montero	Colorado Rockies

	Outfield	
1.	Julio Rodriguez	Seattle Mariners
2.	Riley Greene	Detroit Tigers
3.	George Valera	Cleveland Guardians
4.	Corbin Carroll	Arizona Diamondbacks
5.	Brett Baty	New York Mets
6.	Robert Hassell III	San Diego Padres
7.	Zac Veen	Colorado Rockies
8.	Luis Matos	San Francisco Giants
9.	Brennen Davis	Chicago Cubs
10.	P. Crow-Armstrong	Chicago Cubs

	Second Base	
1.	Nolan Gorman	St. Louis Cardinals
2.	Nick Yorke	Boston Red Sox
3.	Brayan Rocchio	Cleveland Guardians
4.	Nick Gonzales	Pittsburgh Pirates
5.	Nick Allen	Oakland Athletics
6.	James Triantos	Chicago Cubs
7.	Tyler Freeman	Cleveland Guardians
8.	Jose Miranda	Minnesota Twins
9.	Michael Busch	Los Angeles Dodgers
10.	Vidal Brujan	Tampa Bay Rays

	Left-Handed Pitchers	
1.	Reid Detmers	Los Angeles Angels
2.	Aaron Ashby	Milwaukee Brewers
3.	Asa Lacy	Kansas City Royals
4.	Nick Lodolo	Cincinnati Reds
5.	Matthew Liberatore	St. Louis Cardinals
6.	D.L. Hall	Baltimore Orioles
7.	Brailyn Marquez	Chicago Cubs
8.	Kyle Harrison	San Francisco Giants
9.	Blake Walston	Arizona Diamondbacks
10.	Ryan Rolison	Colorado Rockies

	Third Base	
1.	Bobby Witt Jr.	Kansas City Royals
2.	Spencer Torkelson	Detroit Tigers
3.	Nolan Gorman	St. Louis Cardinals
4.	Miguel Vargas	Los Angeles Dodgers
5.	Brett Baty	New York Mets
6.	Jordan Walker	St. Louis Cardinals
7.	Josh Jung	Texas Rangers
8.	Orelvis Martinez	Toronto Blue Jays
9.	Jordan Groshans	Toronto Blue Jays
10.	Tyler Freeman	Cleveland Guardians

	Right-Handed Pitchers	
1.	Grayson Rodriguez	Baltimore Orioles
2.	Jack Leiter	Texas Rangers
3.	George Kirby	Seattle Mariners
4.	Shane Baz	Tampa Bay Rays
5.	Hunter Greene	Cincinnati Reds
6.	Bobby Miller	Los Angeles Dodgers
7.	Cade Cavalli	Washington Nationals
8.	Jackson Jobe	Detroit Tigers
9.	Brayan Bello	Boston Red Sox
10.	Edward Cabrera	Miami Marlins

Ranking the 2022 Farm Systems

Ranking the 2022 Farm Systems

Rank	Team
#1	Pittsburgh Pirates
#2	Cleveland Indians
#3	Baltimore Orioles
#4	Kansas City Royals
#5	Chicago Cubs
#6	Arizona Diamondbacks
#7	Los Angeles Dodgers
#8	Tampa Bay Rays
#9	Boston Red Sox
#10	San Francisco Giants
#11	Miami Marlins
#12	Seattle Mariners
#13	Atlanta Braves
#14	New York Yankees
#15	Detroit Tigers
#16	Cincinnati Reds
#17	Toronto Blue Jays
#18	San Diego Padres
#19	Minnesota Twins
#20	Milwaukee Brewers
#21	New York Mets
#22	St. Louis Cardinals
#23	Colorado Rockies
#24	Washington Nationals
#25	Oakland Athletics
#26	Texas Rangers
#27	Philadelphia Phillies
#28	Los Angeles Angels
#29	Chicago White Sox
#30	Houston Astros

Organizational Analysis

Arizona Diamondbacks

Top Prospects

1. Corbin Carroll, CF

	Hit	Power	SB	Patience	Glove	Overall
	55/60	40/45	60	60	55	60

Born: 08/21/00	Age: 21	Bats: L	Top Comp: Adam Eaton
Height: 5-10	Weight: 165	Throws: L	

Season	Team	Age	Level	PA	1B	2B	3B	HR	SB	CS	BB%	K%	AVG	OBP	SLG	ISO
2019	ARI	18	A-	49	7	3	4	0	2	0	10.20%	24.49%	0.326	0.408	0.581	0.256
2019	ARI	18	R	137	21	6	3	2	16	1	17.52%	21.17%	0.288	0.409	0.450	0.162
2021	ARI	20	A+	29	5	1	2	2	3	1	20.69%	24.14%	0.435	0.552	0.913	0.478

Background: In the classic baseball movie *The Natural*, Roy Hobbs, with a twinge of blood seeping through the front of his jersey, connects for one of the most memorable (fictional) homeruns in history, smashing the lights well above the upper deck.

And in a moment of pure Hollywood, the baseball wunderkind circles the bases with sparks raining down in the background. Taking a page out of Hobbs' playbook, Carroll had his own "Roy Hobbs" moment. In the second game of a double header against The Eugene Emeralds in High-A West, Carroll connected for a tape measure dinger on a ferocious swing that subsequently shredded his right shoulder last season. The result: tears in his labrum and his posterior capsule, serious injuries that required surgery several days later and consequently knocked him out for the remainder of the season. The 16th overall pick in 2019, the pint-sized mighty mite – and consensus Top 100 pick – was off to a potentially historic start the 2021 season, slugging .435/.552/.913 with a double, two triples, two homeruns, and a trio of stolen bases. For his young career, the 5-foot-10, 165-pound center fielder is sporting a .316/.428/.542 triple-slash line in just 49 games.

Snippet from The 2020 Prospect Digest Handbook: Surprising power thank to his elite bat speed and natural loft in a silky smooth left-handed swing. Carroll's a legitimate five-tool prospect, showcasing above-average tools across the board. He has a tendency to expand the strike zone at times, especially against fastballs up. Carroll's very reminiscent of an early career Adam Eaton.

Scouting Report: For the most part, Carroll's been a consensus Top 100 prospect since signing his first professional contract. He's on the smaller side and physically maxed out, but he's a gamer, a ballplayer that does everything right and maximizes his ability to the Nth-degree. Plus speed that shows up out of the batter's box, on the base paths, and in center fielder. Carroll is still oozing loud five and figures to be a franchise cornerstone for the next 10 to 12 years – assuming the shoulder issue doesn't hamper that pretty swing in any way. In terms of big league ceiling, think: .300/.390/.440.

Ceiling: 5.5-win player
Risk: Moderate
MLB ETA: 2023

2. Alek Thomas, CF

	Hit	Power	SB	Patience	Glove	Overall
	55	50	55	50	50	60

Born: 04/28/00	Age: 22	Bats: L	Top Comp: Coco Crisp
Height: 5-11	Weight: 175	Throws: L	

Season	Team	Age	Level	PA	1B	2B	3B	HR	SB	CS	BB%	K%	AVG	OBP	SLG	ISO
2018	ARI	18	R	134	28	11	1	2	4	3	8.21%	14.18%	0.341	0.396	0.496	0.154
2018	ARI	18	R	138	32	3	5	0	8	2	9.42%	13.04%	0.325	0.394	0.431	0.106
2019	ARI	19	A	402	74	21	7	8	11	6	10.70%	17.91%	0.312	0.393	0.479	0.167
2019	ARI	19	A+	104	20	2	0	2	4	5	8.65%	31.73%	0.255	0.327	0.340	0.085
2021	ARI	21	AA	329	45	18	8	10	8	5	11.25%	19.76%	0.283	0.374	0.507	0.224
2021	ARI	21	AAA	166	32	11	4	8	5	4	9.04%	20.48%	0.369	0.434	0.658	0.289

Background: There aren't too many teams – or any at all – that can boast the sheer talent level sprinkled throughout the Arizona's farm system. The DBacks snagged Alek Thomas in the second round of the 2018 draft, signing him to a deal worth $1.2 million. The son of Chicago White Sox Director of Training,

Thomas has exceeded all lofty expectations that come with a high round, big bonus draft status. He split time between rookie ball and the Pioneer League during his professional debut, batting a scorching .333/.395/.463 in 56 total games. And he promptly followed that up with a .300/.379/.450 triple-slash line between Kane County and Visalia in 2019. Last season Thomas – once again – split time between two levels and looked big league-ready in the process. In 106 games with Amarillo and Reno, the rock solid 5-foot-11, 175-pound outfielder hit .313/.394/.559 with 29 doubles, a whopping 12 triples, and a career-best 18 homeruns. He also swiped 13 bags in 24 total attempts. Per *Weighted Runs Created Plus*, his overall production topped the league mark by a staggering 46%, as a 22-year-old, in the final two levels of the minor leagues.

Snippet from The 2020 Prospect Digest Handbook: Thomas offers up an incredibly well-rounded approach at the plate, showing an above-average hit tool, power that should grow into a perennial 20-homer threat, and above-average speed. Thomas does show a slight platoon split, but it barely registers a blip on his future ceiling.

Scouting Report: Consider the following:

- Since 2006, there were only three 21-year-old hitters that met the following criteria in a Double-A season with one organization (min. 300 PA): 130 to 140 wRC+ total, a double-digit walk rate, and a strikeout rate between 18% and 22%. Those three hitters: Matt Davidson, Arismendy Alcantara, and – of course – Alek Thomas.

Unlike Davidson and Alcantara, Thomas owns (A) a considerably larger track record in the minors and (B) his levels of production have been more significant as well. Consistently barreling balls mixed with solid speed, and strong contact rates. Thomas is a little miscast as a center field, but the bat will have no problem sliding over to either corner. He doesn't own the ceiling level of Corbin Carroll, but figures to provide the Robin to his counterpart's Batman. Ceiling: .290/.340/.450.

Ceiling: 4.0-win player
Risk: Moderate
MLB ETA: 2022

3. Jordan Lawlar, SS

Hit	Power	SB	Patience	Glove	Overall
40/50	55	60	50	50	60

Born: 07/17/02	**Age:** 19	**Bats:** R	**Top Comp:** N/A
Height: 6-2	**Weight:** 190	**Throws:** R	

Background: In the short – *short* – conversation for not only the best prep player in the 2021 draft class, Lawlar's name was bandied about as a potential number one overall pick. A well-built, 6-foot-2, 183-pound shortstop from Irving, Texas, Lawlar burst onto the baseball scene as a sophomore for the Rangers in 2019, slugging a healthy .409/.534/.864 with nine doubles, a trio of triples, and five homeruns in 24 starts. In a COVID-shortened junior campaign, the burgeoning star slugged .485/.561/.848 with five doubles, two triples, and a homerun in only 12 games of action. Lawlar starred in the Perfect Game All-American Classic the ensuing summer as he was named the *Jackie Robinson Perfect Game Player of the Year.* The Vanderbilt University commit continued to shine – *brightly* – during his senior campaign for the Texas private school as he batted .425/.552/.713 with five doubles, three triples, and four homeruns while sporting a tidy 19-to-16 strikeout-to-walk ratio. Arizona happily snagged the prep star with the sixth overall pick last July, signing him to a deal worth $6,713,300. Lawlar made six trips to the plate during his debut, going 2-for-5 with a double and a walk.

Scouting Report: Per the usual, here's what I wrote about the teenage star prior to the draft last July:

> "The hits came in bunches after a slow start in 2021. Lawlar, who went hitless in six of his first 12 games, put up five such contests of his remaining 24 games. Short, compact, quick swing with 20-homer potential as his body fills out. Lawlar seems to have a propensity to chase high fastballs. Patient approach; not afraid to take several pitches. He shows a willingness to take the ball the other way. Plus speed, as evidenced by his 6.45, 60-yard time. He's not as fluid as shortstop as his counterpart Marcelo Mayer, but should be no worse than solid average."

Ceiling: 4.0-win player
Risk: Moderate
MLB ETA: 2025

4. Geraldo Perdomo, SS

Hit	Power	SB	Patience	Glove	Overall
50/55	40/50	50	60	55	60

Born: 10/22/99	**Age:** 22	**Bats:** B	**Top Comp:** Stephen Drew
Height: 6-2	**Weight:** 203	**Throws:** R	

Season	Team	Age	Level	PA	1B	2B	3B	HR	SB	CS	BB%	K%	AVG	OBP	SLG	ISO
2018	ARI	18	A-	127	23	3	2	3	9	4	14.17%	18.11%	0.301	0.421	0.456	0.155
2018	ARI	18	R	29	9	0	1	0	1	1	24.14%	13.79%	0.455	0.586	0.545	0.091
2018	ARI	18	R	101	20	4	2	1	14	1	13.86%	16.83%	0.314	0.416	0.442	0.128
2019	ARI	19	A	385	63	16	3	2	20	8	14.55%	14.55%	0.268	0.394	0.357	0.089
2019	ARI	19	A+	114	22	5	0	1	6	5	12.28%	9.65%	0.301	0.407	0.387	0.086
2021	ARI	21	AA	344	47	8	5	6	8	5	13.66%	23.55%	0.231	0.351	0.357	0.126
2021	ARI	21	AAA	14	5	0	0	0	0	1	14.29%	7.14%	0.417	0.500	0.417	0.000

Background: A native of Santo Domingo, Dominican Republic, Perdomo looked to be on the precipice of a breakout season. The baby faced shortstop was coming off of back-to-back strong offensive showings against significantly older competition. He hit an aggregate .322/.438/.460 as an 18-year-old against the Arizona Summer, Pioneer, and Northwest Leagues. A year later, in 2019, Perdomo split time between Low-A and High-A, batting a solid .275/.397/.364 with 21 doubles, three triples, and three homeruns. Last season, though, the front office continued their aggressively development plan by listing him on the club's Opening Day roster. That lasted all of four games before he was bounced back down to AA – where he continued to struggle. He would eventually get his feet under him over the last couple months of the year and earn a promotion up to Triple-A. Overall, Perdomo hit an aggregate .238/.357/.359 with just eight doubles, five triples, six homeruns, and eight stolen bases in 14 total attempts.

Snippet from The 2020 Prospect Digest Handbook: The bat is looks like an above-average weapon; the speed is a game changer; and he's surprisingly patient for a teenager player squaring off against significantly older competition. The defense, alone, could be enough to carry him to the big leagues.

Scouting Report: Maybe it was the learning curve? Maybe he was dealing with a hangover effect from the big league demotion? Whatever it was, though, Perdomo looked dreadful at the dish for the first couple months of the minor league season. In fact, he hit a lowly .144/.292/.194 over his first 49 contests with Amarillo, which included missing several weeks of action. But over his next 36 MiLB contests he slugged a scorching .348/.435/.551 with 14 extra-base hits. Tremendous patience at the plate. Solid-average power that should peak in the 15-homer range. Good speed, though he wasn't running nearly as frequently last season. Fantastic glove. He's going to be Nick Ahmed's heir apparent.

Ceiling: 4.0-win player
Risk: Moderate
MLB ETA: Debuted in 2020

5. Kristian Robinson, CF

Hit	Power	SB	Patience	Glove	Overall
45/55	55/60	50	55	50	60

Born: 12/11/00	Age: 21	Bats: R	Top Comp: N/A
Height: 6-3	Weight: 190	Throws: R	

Season	Team	Age	Level	PA	1B	2B	3B	HR	SB	CS	BB%	K%	AVG	OBP	SLG	ISO
2018	ARI	17	R	74	14	1	0	3	5	3	14.86%	28.38%	0.300	0.419	0.467	0.167
2018	ARI	17	R	182	29	11	0	4	7	5	8.79%	25.27%	0.272	0.341	0.414	0.142
2019	ARI	18	A	102	11	3	1	5	3	2	7.84%	29.41%	0.217	0.294	0.435	0.217
2019	ARI	18	A-	189	32	10	1	9	14	3	12.17%	24.87%	0.319	0.407	0.558	0.239

Background: A consensus Top 100 prospect by every meaningful outlet for the last couple of years. Robinson's production seemed to reaching a crescendo of sorts during his first two seasons in professional baseball. The athletic 6-foot-3, 190-pound outfielder slugged .279/.363/.428 in 57 games between rookie ball and Missoula during his debut in 2018. He followed that up with middle-of-the-lineup thump production: he batted .282/.368/.514 with 13 doubles, two triples, 14 homeruns, and 17 stolen bases in only 69 games between Hillsboro and Kane County the next season. And with all arrows pointing skyward Robinson's career was derailed – hopefully, just temporary. During the COVID shutdown, Robinson had an altercation with a police officer in April during, what he termed, a "mental breakdown." The top prospect was sentenced to 18 months probation for punching the officer, a move that's only complicated do to his visa issues as a citizen of the Bahamas.

Snippet from The 2020 Prospect Digest Handbook: There's a lot to like about Robinson: burgeoning plus power, plus speed, strong glove in center field, and top notch production against older competition. However – and there's *always* a "however" – the strikeout rates continues to be an issue. He whiffed in a quarter of his plate appearances with Hillsboro and slightly less than 30% of his plate appearances with Kane County. He has superstar potential and I think he eventually works past the strikeout issues.

Scouting Report: Since Robinson missed the entirety of the 2021 season, there's nothing new to report on beyond the legal issues. He has as much potential as any prospect in baseball. But from a personal standpoint, hopefully he's able to get the help he needs.

Ceiling: 5.0-win player
Risk: High
MLB ETA: 2023/2024

6. Drey Jameson, RHP

FB	CB	SL	CH	Command	Overall
70	55	55	55	45/50	55

Born: 08/17/97	Age: 24	Bats: R	Top Comp: Poor Man's Walker Buehler
Height: 6-0	Weight: 165	Throws: R	

Season	Team	Age	Level	IP	TBF	K/9	K%	BB/9	BB%	K-BB%	ERA	FIP	xFIP	Pit/Bat
2019	ARI	21	A-	11.2	58	9.26	20.69%	6.94	15.52%	5.17%	6.17	5.28	5.01	4.29
2021	ARI	23	A+	64.1	270	10.77	28.52%	2.52	6.67%	21.85%	3.92	4.43	3.95	3.77
2021	ARI	23	AA	46.1	194	13.21	35.05%	3.50	9.28%	25.77%	4.08	3.65	3.23	3.72

Background: One of college baseball's elite strikeout artists during his final two seasons as an amateur. Jameson fanned a total 243 hitters in just 163.2 innings of work, or an average of 13.4 punch outs per nine innings. Arizona made the hard-throwing, though diminutive, right-hander the seventh highest drafted player in Ball State history when they selected him with the 34th overall selection three years ago. Like many of the club's other top young hurlers, Jameson split time between two different levels in 2021. The former first rounder made 13 appearances, 12 of which were starts, with the Hillsboro Hops and another eight starts with the Amarillo Sod Poodles. Across those career-high 21 appearances, the 6-foot, 165-pound flame-throwing righty averaged 11.8 strikeouts and just 2.9 walks per nine innings to go along with a 3.98 ERA and a 4.10 FIP.

Snippet from The 2020 Prospect Digest Handbook: It's easy to ticket the Ball State product for an eventual role in the bullpen, but if the command bumps up to slightly below-average he has the chops to make it as a solid #3/#4-type starting pitcher. If the club does push him into a relief role, he could be throwing some big league innings within 18 months.

Scouting Report: Consider the following:

- Since 2006, only four 23-year-old pitchers met the following criteria in a Double-A season with one organization (min. 45 IP): a strikeout percentage of at least 34% with a walk percentage between 8.5% and 10.5%. Those four hurlers: Matt Brash, Enoli Paredes, Paul Estrada, and Drey Jameson.

He's lean and powerful like Walker Buehler, though there's a small difference in height. Jameson generates some of the best velocity from a starting pitcher in the entire minor leagues. He was sitting 95- to 98-mph and bumping 99-mph in an early season start I scouted. His breaking balls showed noticeable progress, both now ranking as above-average offerings. And his changeup adds a third offspeed weapon. Arizona's honed in on lean, hard-throwing collegiate hurlers in the draft the past couple of seasons (see: Bryce Jarvis, Slade Cecconi, Ryne Nelson), but Jameson has the best odds to succeed in a big league rotation.

Ceiling: 3.0-win player
Risk: Moderate
MLB ETA: 2022

7. Blake Walston, LHP

	FB	CB	SL	CH	Command	Overall
	55/60	55/60	50	50	50/55	55

Born: 06/28/01	Age: 21	Bats: L	Top Comp: Danny Duffy
Height: 6-5	Weight: 175	Throws: L	

Season	Team	Age	Level	IP	TBF	K/9	K%	BB/9	BB%	K-BB%	ERA	FIP	xFIP	Pit/Bat
2021	ARI	20	A	43.1	180	12.46	33.33%	3.53	9.44%	23.89%	3.32	3.84	3.80	3.76
2021	ARI	20	A+	52.1	226	9.80	25.22%	2.75	7.08%	18.14%	4.13	5.76	4.88	3.82

Background: Fun Fact: North Carolina-based New Hanover High School has produced two first round pick in their history – Trot Nixon, the seventh overall selection all the way back in 1993 and, of course, Blake Walston, the 26th overall player chosen three years ago. After receiving a hefty $2.45 million bonus, Walston split his debut between rookie ball and Hillsboro, back when it was the club's Northwest League affiliate. Last season, following the return of minor league action, Walston opened the year up with the Visalia Rawhide in the Low-A West League. That stint lasted all of just eight starts before earning a promotion up to High-A for another 11 games. In total, the lanky 6-foot-5, 175-pound southpaw tossed 95.2 innings with 117 strikeouts and just 33 walks. He finished the year with an aggregate 3.76 ERA and a noticeably worse 4.89 FIP.

Snippet from The 2020 Prospect Digest Handbook: Walston's one of my favorite prep arms in the entire class. If the control / command remains strong he could move quickly.

Scouting Report: Consider the following:

- Since 2006, there have been ten 20-year-old pitchers to meet the following criteria in a High-A season with one organization (min. 50 IP): a strikeout percentage between 24% and 26% with a walk percentage between 6% and 8%. Those ten hurlers: Danny Duffy, Patrick Corbin, Noah Syndergaard, Sean Gallagher, Randall Delgado, Hector Rondon, Adalberto Mejia, Clayton Blackburn, Eric Hurley, and – last but not least – Blake Walston.

Two years ago I was postulating that Walston's low-90s heater would eventually creep up to the mid-90s, but that hasn't happened, though I still think it's a distinct possibility. Above-average curveball that flashes plus several times a game and just lacks a little bit of consistency. He'll also mix in a tightly wound slider and a decent little changeup as well. Walston's arm action is long, robotic, and stiff.

Ceiling: 3.0-win player
Risk: Moderate
MLB ETA: 2023

8. Deyvison De Los Santos, 1B/3B

Hit	Power	SB	Patience	Glove	Overall
40/50	50/60	35	50	50/55	55

Born: 06/21/03	Age: 19	Bats: R	Top Comp: N/A
Height: 6-1	Weight: 185	Throws: R	

Season	Team	Age	Level	PA	1B	2B	3B	HR	SB	CS	BB%	K%	AVG	OBP	SLG	ISO
2021	ARI	18	A	160	25	12	0	3	2	0	8.13%	26.88%	0.276	0.340	0.421	0.145
2021	ARI	18	CPX	95	16	4	2	5	1	1	13.68%	25.26%	0.329	0.421	0.610	0.280

Background: A native of Santo Domingo, Dominican Republic, Arizona signed the 6-foot-1, 185-pound corner infielder to a deal worth $200,000 during the 2019 signing period. But De Los Santos wouldn't make his professional debut post-pandemic shutdown. He began the year in the Arizona Complex League, but after slugging .329/.421/.610 with four doubles, two triples, and five homeruns in 25 games, the front office bumped the young slugger up to full season action in early August. And, surprisingly, the then-18-year-old hitter acquitted himself quite nicely (.276/.340/.421). Overall, De Los Santos batted an aggregate .295/.370/.489 with 16 doubles, two triples, and eight homeruns.. Per *Weighted Runs Created Plus*, his production was 24% better than the league average.

Scouting Report: An under-the-radar teenage hitter – at least for the time being. Good bat speed. Tremendous raw power – particularly to the opposite field. Despite never getting cheated at the plate, De Los Santos made a reasonable amount of contact, especially once he was promoted up to Low-A. In a year, we may be mentioned De Los Santos's name among the better prospects in baseball. Don't sleep on this kid.

Ceiling: 3.0-win player
Risk: Moderate to High
MLB ETA: 2024

9. Bryce Jarvis, RHP

FB	CB	SL	CH	Command	Overall
60	55	55	65	45	50

Born: 12/26/97	Age: 24	Bats: R	Top Comp: Brandon Morrow
Height: 6-2	Weight: 195	Throws: R	

Season	Team	Age	Level	IP	TBF	K/9	K%	BB/9	BB%	K-BB%	ERA	FIP	xFIP	Pit/Bat
2021	ARI	23	A+	37.1	153	10.13	27.45%	3.13	8.50%	18.95%	3.62	4.17	4.46	3.75
2021	ARI	23	AA	35.0	152	10.29	26.32%	4.37	11.18%	15.13%	5.66	5.88	4.28	3.89

Background: Fun Fact Part I: Bryce's old man, Kevin Jarvis, was a 21st round pick by the Cincinnati Reds all the way back in 1991, made it to the bigs just three seasons later, and stayed there for 12 seasons. Fun Fact Part II: The elder Jarvis, who tallied (-)4.1 wins above replacement across 187 big league games, earned nearly $9.5 million in his career. Bryce, a well-built 6-foot-2, 195-pound right-hander bested his dad's draft status by 20 rounds when the Diamondbacks plucked him out of Duke University with the 18th overall pick two years ago. A hard-throwing, sometimes erratic, hurler during his first two years with the Blue Devils, Jarvis was practically unhittable during his four starts in 2020, posting a 40-to-2 strikeout-to-walk ratio in only 27.0 innings of work. Last season the then-22-year-old righty got his first taste of professional action. And within a few months he was already squaring off against the Double-A competition. In a combined 16 starts with Hillsboro and Amarillo (plus one rehab appearance), Jarvis struck out 89, walked 30, and compiled a 4.42 ERA in 75.1 innings of work. He lost roughly six weeks dealing with a fairly severe oblique injury midseason.

Scouting Report: Above-average or better on each of his four offerings. Jarvis's heater sits in the 93- to 96-mph range. He'll mix in a pair of above-average breaking balls: a mid-80s slider and a slightly slower curveball. Last, and certainly not least, is his fantastical changeup, a true swing-and-miss plus offering that borders on plus-plus. Jarvis's command can be touch-and-go at times, which will ultimately limit his ceiling as a #3/#4-type arm.

Ceiling: 2.0-win player
Risk: Moderate
MLB ETA: 2022/2023

10. Ryne Nelson, RHP

FB	CB	SL	CH	Command	Overall
60	55	55	50	50	50

Born: 02/01/98	Age: 24	Bats: R	Top Comp: Reynaldo Lopez
Height: 6-3	Weight: 184	Throws: R	

Season	Team	Age	Level	IP	TBF	K/9	K%	BB/9	BB%	K-BB%	ERA	FIP	xFIP	Pit/Bat
2019	ARI	21	A-	18.2	77	12.54	33.77%	4.82	12.99%	20.78%	2.89	3.33	3.26	4.10
2021	ARI	23	A+	39.1	154	13.50	38.31%	3.20	9.09%	29.22%	2.52	3.27	3.99	4.07
2021	ARI	23	AA	77.0	316	12.16	32.91%	3.04	8.23%	24.68%	3.51	4.06	3.51	4.04

Background: A full-time reliever with just five starts on his resume during his time at the University of Oregon. Arizona eyed a different plan when they selected the hard-throwing right-hander in the second round three years ago. Immediately the front office began stretching the former part-time closer out as a starting pitcher. And last season Nelson, who stands a wiry 6-foot-3 and 184 pounds, tossed 116.1 innings between Hillsboro and Amarillo – nearly 10 innings more than his three-year collegiate career at the Pac 12 powerhouse. Making a combined 22 starts, eight in High-A and the other 14 coming a level up, Nelson struck out a whopping 163 and walked just 40 to go along with a 3.41 ERA and a 3.79 FIP. For those counting at home: he averaged an impressive 12.6 strikeouts and just 3.1 walks per nine innings. Not bad for a former reliever.

Snippet from The 2020 Prospect Digest Handbook: Nelson's wicked two-pitch combo screams potential late-inning, high leverage relief option. But his lack of experience on the mound should grant him a few years to develop into a starting pitcher.

Scouting Report: Arizona has really cornered the market on hard-throwing former collegiate arms. And there's quite a bit to like about the group as a whole. And the organization's player development has done a tremendous job crafting Nelson, a former reliever, into a viable starting pitching candidate. As expected, his fastball lost a tick or two as he transitioned, but it's still sitting comfortably in the mid-90s with plenty of late, explosive life. He mixes in a couple of above-average breaking balls with a workable changeup. The organization has a strong collection of these types of arms, but they need to drag their development across the finish line.

Ceiling: 1.5- to 2.0-win player
Risk: Moderate
MLB ETA: 2022

11. Slade Cecconi, RHP

FB	CB	SL	CH	Command	Overall
55	50/55	55	50	50	50

Born: 06/24/99	Age: 23	Bats: R	Top Comp: Jhoulys Chacin
Height: 6-4	Weight: 219	Throws: R	

Season	Team	Age	Level	IP	TBF	K/9	K%	BB/9	BB%	K-BB%	ERA	FIP	xFIP	Pit/Bat
2021	ARI	22	A+	59.0	248	9.61	25.40%	3.05	8.06%	17.34%	4.12	4.22	4.71	3.80

Background: Originally taken by the Orioles in the 38th round coming out of Trinity Prep School in 2018, Cecconi first headed to Seminole County Community College and then finished his collegiate career with back-to-back seasons at the University of Miami. Arizona nabbed the 6-foot-4, 219-pound righty with the their second first round selection in 2020, just 15 picks after drafting fellow college arm Bryce Jarvis. Last season, Cecconi's pro debut was rather brief: he lasted 12 – mostly good – starts with the High-A Hillsboro Hops before shutting it down with elbow discomfort. Prior to the health woes he was averaging 9.6 strikeouts and 3.1 walks per nine innings. Cecconi did return to action in the Arizona Fall League, throwing 15 innings with 14 strikeouts and seven free passes.

Scouting Report: Cut from a similar cloth as fellow 2020 first rounder Bryce Jarvis with one exception: he lacks a second plus offering. Cecconi's fastball will sit in the 91- to 94-mph range and topped as high as 97 mph last season. Cecconi, like Jarvis, feature a pair of solid breaking balls: his curveball projects to be a 55-grade pitch with some fine tuning and a present-day above-average slider. Cecconi's changeup is merely average. The hard-throwing right-hander is another backend starting pitching option in the coming years.

Ceiling: 1.5- to 2.0-win player
Risk: Moderate
MLB ETA: 2023

12. Ryan Bliss, SS

Hit	Power	SB	Patience	Glove	Overall
50/55	40+	55	50	50	50

Born: 12/13/99	Age: 22	Bats: R	Top Comp: Nick Madrigal
Height: 5-9	Weight: 165	Throws: R	

Season	Team	Age	Level	PA	1B	2B	3B	HR	SB	CS	BB%	K%	AVG	OBP	SLG	ISO
2021	ARI	21	A	175	25	9	1	6	11	4	7.43%	22.86%	0.259	0.322	0.443	0.184

Background: Hailing from Troup County High School, home to former big leaguers Jimmy Haynes and David Kelton, the small middle infielder was highly decorated during his prep career: *Perfect Game* ranked him as the 96th best player in the country; he was a 2nd Team All-American by *Rawlings-Perfect Game* in 2018; he was named a 2018 1st Team Preseason Underclass All-American by *Perfect Game*; and he played for the 2016 USA Baseball Tournament of Stars. Oh, by the way, Bliss swiped 64 bags in 66 total attempts during his high school career. The Red Sox took a late round flier on him in 2018 as well. A key cog in Auburn's lineup since day one; Bliss, a 5-foot-9 and 165-pound infielder, batted a respectable .281/.367/.369 with 11 doubles, one triple, and three homeruns as a true freshman. He also swiped 11 bags in 13 attempts. He spent the ensuing summer playing for the Brewster Whitecaps in the Cape Cod League, hitting .286/.333/.452 in 10 games. The Georgia native elevated his production to an elite level during the 2020 COVID-shortened campaign, slugging .377/.412/.597. And that proved to be a harbinger of things to come in 2021. Appearing in 50 games for the SEC-based Tigers, Bliss swatted .365/.428/.654 with career highs in doubles (14) and homeruns (15). The Diamondbacks snagged the dynamo in the second round, 42nd overall, and signed him to a deal worth $1.25 million, saving the club roughly $500,000. He batted a respectable .259/.322/.443 with nine doubles, one triple, and six homeruns in Low-A during his professional debut.

Scouting Report: Per the usual, here's my write-up immediately following his selection by the Diamondbacks:

> *"Consider the following:*
>
> - *Between 2011 and 2020, only five SEC hitters met the following criteria (min. 200 PA): .360/.420/.650. Those five hitters are Pete Alonso, Mike Zunino, Andrew Benintendi, Mikie Mahtook, and Brent Rooker.*
>
> *That's one helluva group to belong too. And Bliss, like his counterparts, should have no issue cracking a big league lineup. Silky smooth in the field. Bliss, despite his small-ish frame, has a legitimate shot at sticking to the left side of second base and profiles to be a solid-average defender. At the plate, he showcases a short, compact swing with surprising pop for a sub-six-foot middle infielder. Loose, but strong flicks of the wrists allow him to shoot the ball from gap-to-gap. Bliss shows a willingness to hit it where it's pitched. There's a lot of similarities between Bliss and Nick Madrigal."*

Ceiling: 1.5- to 2.0-win player
Risk: Moderate
MLB ETA: 2024

13. Seth Beer, 1B

Hit	Power	SB	Patience	Glove	Overall
45	50	30	50	45	45

Born: 09/18/96	Age: 25	Bats: L	Top Comp: Kole Calhoun
Height: 6-3	Weight: 213	Throws: R	

Season	Team	Age	Level	PA	1B	2B	3B	HR	SB	CS	BB%	K%	AVG	OBP	SLG	ISO
2018	HOU	21	A	132	29	7	0	3	1	0	11.36%	12.88%	0.348	0.443	0.491	0.143
2018	HOU	21	A-	51	5	3	0	4	0	0	11.76%	19.61%	0.293	0.431	0.659	0.366
2018	HOU	21	A+	114	19	4	0	5	0	1	3.51%	19.30%	0.262	0.307	0.439	0.178
2019	HOU	22	A+	152	25	8	0	9	0	3	9.21%	19.74%	0.328	0.414	0.602	0.273
2019	ARI	22	AA	101	10	7	0	1	0	1	7.92%	24.75%	0.205	0.297	0.318	0.114
2019	HOU	22	AA	280	45	9	0	16	0	0	8.57%	20.71%	0.299	0.407	0.543	0.244
2021	ARI	24	AAA	435	55	33	0	16	0	0	8.97%	17.47%	0.287	0.398	0.511	0.224

Background: He was, in the most basic of terms, Spencer Torkelson before Spencer Torkelson, the freshman collegiate slugger destined for stardom. Beer, a lefty-swinging first baseman, mashed the competition to the tune of .369/.535/.700 with 13 doubles and 18 homeruns as a 19-year-old all the way back in 2016. But unlike Torkelson, Beer's production dramatically declined down to more mortal numbers over his final two seasons. Houston would use the 28th overall pick on him in 2018 and eventually ship him to Arizona – along with Corbin Martin, J.B. Bukauskas, and Josh Rojas – for future Hall of Famer Zack Greinke and cash. Beer appeared in 100 games with the Reno Aces, batting a rock solid .287/.398/.511 with 33 doubles and 16 homeruns. His overall production, per *Weighted Runs Created Plus*, topped the league average threshold by 28%. He also appeared in five games with the Diamondbacks as well. Beer's season ended early, a result of a dislocated left shoulder that did require surgery.

Snippet from The 2020 Prospect Digest Handbook: One of the most saber-friendly hitters in the entire minor leagues. Beer does everything you'd want a middle-of-the-lineup thumper to do: make consistent contact, hit for plus-power, walk a bit, and do so without concerning platoon splits.

Scouting Report: Consider the following:

- Since 2006, only six 24-year-old hitters met the following criteria in a Triple-A season with one organization (min. 400 PA): 123 to 133 wRC+ total, an 8% to 10% walk rate, and a sub-20% strikeout rate. Those six hitters: Kole Calhoun, Ben Gamel, Chris Carter, Peter Ciofrone, Carlos Asuaje, and – of course – Seth Beer.

Let's have a little more fun. Consider the following comparison between Kole Calhoun and Seth Beer during their age-24 season in AAA:

Season	Name	Level	Age	PA	BB%	K%	AVG	OBP	SLG	ISO	wRC+
2012	Kole Calhoun	AAA	24	463	9.50%	19.01%	0.298	0.369	0.507	0.210	125
2021	Seth Beer	AAA	24	435	8.97%	17.47%	0.287	0.398	0.511	0.224	128

And just for reference: Calhoun owns a .248/.322/.427 career slash line in 10 years in the big leagues. As for Beer, a reasonable ceiling expectation would be Calhoun's 2016 season in which he batted .271/.348/.438.

Ceiling: 1.5-win player
Risk: Low to Moderate
MLB ETA: Debuted in 2020

14. Adrian Del Castillo, C

Hit	Power	SB	Patience	Glove	Overall
40/45	40/50	30	50	50	45

Born: 09/27/99	Age: 22	Bats: L	Top Comp: N/A
Height: 5-11	Weight: 208	Throws: R	

Season	Team	Age	Level	PA	1B	2B	3B	HR	SB	CS	BB%	K%	AVG	OBP	SLG	ISO
2021	ARI	21	A	91	10	6	2	1	0	0	9.89%	30.77%	0.244	0.341	0.410	0.167

Background: Fun Fact Part #1: Del Castillo's high school alma mater, Gulliver Prep, has churned out seven draft picks, including: 2012 third rounder Adrian Marin; Joe Dunand, who was taken in the second round a few years later out of North Carolina State University, and – of course – Del Castillo, a 36th round pick by the White Sox in 2018. Fun Fact Part #2: Prior to 2021, 30 catchers have been drafted out of the University of Miami. Fun Fact Part #3: Four Hurricane backstops have been chosen in the opening round: Charles Johnson, Yasmani Grandal, Zack Collins, and Frank Castro. Del Castillo burst onto the collegiate scene with a dominant, award-winning freshman campaign as he slugging a hearty .331/.418/.576 with 22 doubles and 12 homeruns to go along with a stellar 24-to-32 strikeout-to-walk ratio. Nearly every major publication named him as a Freshman All-American. He also earned All-ACC Second Team, ACC All-Freshman Team, ABCA All-Region, All-Starkville Regional, and All-ACC Academic. And Del Castillo continued to perform as he moved into the vaunted Cape Cod League that summer as well: he batted .261/.311/.420 with 12 extra-base hits. The stocky, lefty-swinging backstop upped the ante even further during his COVID-shortened sophomore showing: .358/.478/.547. Last season, though, the 5-foot-11, 208-pound Florida native scuffled a bit, cobbling together a .275/.380/.395 slash line, belting out 13 doubles, one triple, and only a trio of homeruns. He compiled a 28-to-27 strikeout-to-walk ratio. Arizona selected him in the second round, 67th overall, and signed him to a deal worth $1 million. Del Castillo hit an aggregate .265/.367/.422 during his professional debut.

Scouting Report: Per the usual, here's what I wrote about the him prior to the draft last July:

> "Let's take a look at how dominant Del Castillo's freshman campaign was. Consider the following:
>
> - Between 2011 and 2020, only eight ACC hitters have met the following criteria: .330/.410/.520 with a double digit walk rate and a single digit strikeout rate. Those eight: Colin Moran, Seth Beer, Matt Thaiss, Adam Haseley, Pavin Smith, Mike Salvatore, David Thompson, and – of course – Del Castillo.
>
> Unfortunately for the young catcher, the power's all but dissipated during his junior campaign; he's slugged just three homeruns in 54 games – just one more than he belted out in 16 games during the COVID season. Short, quick swing and makes the adjustment on offspeed offerings. Del Castillo's morphed into more of a slasher-type approach at the plate, rather than a middle of the lineup thumper. He takes pitches, consistently puts the bat on the ball, and plays a premium position. If the power comes back, Del Castillo is a potential league average starting option."

Ceiling: 1.5-win player
Risk: Moderate
MLB ETA: 2024

15. Buddy Kennedy, 2B/3B

Hit	Power	SB	Patience	Glove	Overall
45	55	30	50	55	45

Born: 10/05/98	Age: 23	Bats: R	Top Comp: Mike Carp
Height: 6-1	Weight: 190	Throws: R	

Season	Team	Age	Level	PA	1B	2B	3B	HR	SB	CS	BB%	K%	AVG	OBP	SLG	ISO
2018	ARI	19	R	255	52	17	1	4	2	0	10.20%	13.33%	0.327	0.396	0.465	0.137
2019	ARI	20	A	438	72	18	4	7	4	4	10.73%	18.49%	0.262	0.342	0.384	0.122
2021	ARI	22	A+	127	25	5	0	5	9	2	8.66%	19.69%	0.315	0.386	0.495	0.180
2021	ARI	22	AA	279	41	6	2	17	7	2	13.98%	26.16%	0.278	0.384	0.536	0.257

Background: It doesn't matter who else comes from Millville Senior High School because it's always going to be known as Mike Trout's old stomping ground. In fact, there's only been two draft picks from the New Jersey-based prep school: Mike Trout, who famously slid to the 25th pick the 2009 draft, and Buddy Kennedy, a fifth round selection by the Diamondbacks five years ago. And just for good measure: Kennedy's fifth round bonus, $550,000, is roughly 45% of the bonus Trout was given by the Angels ($1.215 million). Kennedy, a 6-foot-1, 190-pound third baseman that sometimes moonlights at the keystone, put together his finest professional season to date: splitting time between Hillsboro and Amarillo, the New Jersey native slugged .290/.384/.523 with 11 doubles, two triples, and a career best 22 dingers. His overall production, per *Weighted Runs Created Plus*, topped the league average threshold by 41%.

Scouting Report: To put Kennedy's breakout season into perspective, consider the following:

- Last season there were 377 minor league hitters that earned at least 400 plate appearances. Of those 400, Kennedy's 141 wRC+ total was tied for the 34th best.

Now let's see how his production stacks up against his peers. Consider the following:

- Since 2006, only five 22-year-old Double-A hitters posted a wRC+ between 138 and 148 with a walk rate north of 12% in a season with one organization (min. 250 PA): Josh Bell, Daniel Vogelbach, Mike Carp, Lou Marson, and Buddy Kennedy.

Ignoring the offensive production momentarily, Kennedy's defensive metrics – according to Clay Davenport's calculations – have consistently ranged from above-average to downright spectacular; last season with Amarillo he was +8 runs saved in 66 games. Kennedy consistently posts low groundball rates, so the average to slightly better than average power should be set in stone at this point. He whiffed more in his time in AA than he has in the past, though he was compensating for it with a more patient approach. Kennedy's now entering sixth year in the organization and he's yet to display any major red flags. A .250/.330/.430 slash line seems like a reasonable ceiling for Kennedy. If the defense is as good as the metrics suggest, he may develop into a viable, low end starting third baseman.

Ceiling: 1.5-win player
Risk: Moderate
MLB ETA: 2024

16. A.J. Vukovich, 3B

	Hit	Power	SB	Patience	Glove	Overall
	40/45	50	50/40	45	50	45

Born: 07/20/01	Age: 20	Bats: R	Top Comp: N/A
Height: 6-5	Weight: 210	Throws: R	

Season	Team	Age	Level	PA	1B	2B	3B	HR	SB	CS	BB%	K%	AVG	OBP	SLG	ISO
2021	ARI	19	A	276	38	15	1	10	10	1	6.88%	27.90%	0.259	0.322	0.449	0.190
2021	ARI	19	A+	124	27	4	2	3	6	3	2.42%	22.58%	0.298	0.315	0.438	0.140

Background: Arizona wasn't shy about their infatuation for the prep third baseman. After selecting him in the fourth round out of East Troy High School two years ago, the National West Division franchise handed him a deal worth $1.25 million – the second largest bonus handed out to fourth rounders that year. The massive 6-foot-5, 210-pound third baseman made his debut last season. In 62 games with Visalia, Vukovich slugged .259/.322/.449 with 15 doubles, one triple, and 10 dingers. And he upped the ante even further following his promotion to High-A (.298/.315/.438). In total, Vukovich batted a solid .272/.320/.446 with 19 doubles, three triples, 13 homers, and 16 stolen bases. His overall production, per *Weighted Runs Created Plus*, was just one percent below the league average threshold.

Scouting Report: Consider the following:

- Since 2006, only four 19-year-old hitters met the following criteria in a Low-A season with one organization (min. 275 PA): 95 to 105 wRC+, a walk rate between 6% and 8% with a strikeout rate of at least 26%. Those four hitters: Delvi Cid, Julio Morban, Denny Almonte, and – of course – A.J. Vukovich.

A nice little developmental project that shows the basic skill set to man third base for a big league team. Average hit tool, power, and glove. He'll also work the count every now and then as well. He's entering is age-20 season with quite a bit of experience in High-A. A stop in Double-A at the end of 2022 isn't out of the question either.

Ceiling: 1.0- to 1.5-win player
Risk: Moderate
MLB ETA: 2024

17. Matt Tabor, RHP

FB	SL	CH	Command	Overall
50	55	60	50	45

Born: 07/14/98	Age: 23	Bats: R	Top Comp: N/A
Height: 6-2	Weight: 180	Throws: R	

Season	Team	Age	Level	IP	TBF	K/9	K%	BB/9	BB%	K-BB%	ERA	FIP	xFIP	Pit/Bat
2018	ARI	19	A-	60.2	253	6.82	18.18%	1.93	5.14%	13.04%	3.26	3.73	4.12	3.26
2019	ARI	20	A	95.1	377	9.53	26.79%	1.51	4.24%	22.55%	2.93	2.71	2.68	3.61
2021	ARI	22	A+	24.0	97	8.63	23.71%	2.25	6.19%	17.53%	3.00	4.15	4.89	3.22
2021	ARI	22	AA	51.0	215	8.29	21.86%	3.18	8.37%	13.49%	3.88	5.03	4.87	3.57
2021	ARI	22	AAA	32.1	156	7.24	16.67%	4.18	9.62%	7.05%	11.13	9.90	6.85	3.72

Background: The lone player to be drafted out of Milton Academy. And that happened when the club selected him in the third round, 82nd overall, in the 2017 draft. Despite his baby face and youth, Tabor has also flashed poise and pitchability – at times. After spending each of his three previous seasons at one level, the 6-foot-2, 180-pound right-hander was shot out of a rocket in 2021, going from High-A all the way up to Triple-A – though the results regressed at each stop along the way. In total, the former third round pick made a career-high 22 appearances, 21 of them coming via a start, throwing 107.1 innings of work with 96 strikeouts and 39 free passes. He finished the year with 5.87 ERA.

Snippet from The 2020 Prospect Digest Handbook: Tabor's wildly successful 2019 season has only solidified his odds of becoming a viable big league starting option in the coming years.

Scouting Report: The fastball's maxed out, sitting in the low 90s and touching 94 mph on occasion. Any success he experiences will largely be built on the back of his above-average slider and plus changeup. Average command. Once upon a time Tabor looked like a potential #4-type starting pitcher with a bunch of projection. But that projection never really happened. So now Tabor is looking at #5/#6-type gig.

Ceiling: 1.0-win player
Risk: Moderate
MLB ETA: 2023

18. Jorge Barrosa, CF

Hit	Power	SB	Patience	Glove	Overall
45/50	40/45	60	45	55/60	45

Born: 02/17/01	Age: 21	Bats: B	Top Comp: N/A
Height: 5-9	Weight: 165	Throws: L	

Season	Team	Age	Level	PA	1B	2B	3B	HR	SB	CS	BB%	K%	AVG	OBP	SLG	ISO
2018	ARI	17	R	20	2	0	1	0	0	0	5.00%	25.00%	0.167	0.200	0.278	0.111
2018	ARI	17	R	241	47	8	3	3	37	6	10.37%	14.11%	0.299	0.402	0.412	0.113
2018	ARI	17	R	47	8	0	2	0	2	2	6.38%	12.77%	0.233	0.298	0.326	0.093
2019	ARI	18	A-	252	41	12	2	1	8	4	8.33%	12.70%	0.251	0.335	0.336	0.085
2021	ARI	20	A	163	38	8	0	3	9	4	4.29%	19.02%	0.333	0.389	0.449	0.116
2021	ARI	20	A+	272	37	18	3	4	20	7	8.09%	17.65%	0.256	0.332	0.405	0.149

Background: A speedy center fielder with a predisposition for a slashing approach at the plate. Barrosa, a native of Puerto Cabello, Venezuela, has been handed some aggressive assignments following his dynamic showing in the Dominican Summer League in 2018. He made additional detours that summer in the stateside rookie league, as well as the Pioneer League. The 5-foot-9, 165-pound outfielder struggled a bit in the Northwest League the following summer, hitting a punchless .251/.335/.336 – though he was only 18-years-old. Last season, Barrosa rediscovered his stroke at the plate as he moved into Low-A and he acquitted himself nicely after the move up to High-A as well. In total, Barrosa batted a respectable .285/.353/.422 with 26 doubles, three triples, and seven homeruns. He also swiped 29 bags in 40 total attempts. Per *Weighted Runs Created Plus*, his overall production was 9% better than the league average.

Scouting Report: Consider the following:

- Since 2006, there have been only four 20-year-old hitters to meet the following criteria in a High-A season with one organization (min. 250 PA): 95 to 105 wRC+ total, a walk rate between 7% and 9%, and a strikeout rate between 16.5% and 18.5%. Those four hitters: Austin Hedges, Dustin Peterson, Randy Ventura, and Jorge Barrosa.

Not overly big. Hell, he's small. But Barrosa started showing the type of pop that typically isn't associated with 5-foot-9, 165-pound, speedy center fielders. I'm not sure if it's a sustainable, repeatable skill – especially considering his groundball rates. Barrosa can run it down well in center field and he's tracking to be an above-average defender. If the power shows up continually in the field, he has a shot to – quietly – develop into a solid starting outfielder.

Ceiling: 1.0- to 1.5-win player
Risk: Moderate
MLB ETA: 2024

19. Tommy Henry, LHP

FB	CB	CH	Command	Overall
50	60	55	45	40

Born: 07/29/97	Age: 24	Bats: L	Top Comp: Brian Matusz
Height: 6-3	Weight: 205	Throws: L	

Season	Team	Age	Level	IP	TBF	K/9	K%	BB/9	BB%	K-BB%	ERA	FIP	xFIP	Pit/Bat
2021	ARI	23	AA	115.2	493	10.50	27.38%	4.12	10.75%	16.63%	5.21	5.29	4.24	4.01

Background: A second round pick out of the University of Michigan (Go Bucks!) three years ago. Henry morphed from a regular reliever to a solid, though unremarkable starting pitcher into a bonafide collegiate ace throughout his . And the Diamondbacks bought in – heavily. After a brief three-inning debut in 2019, the front office aggressively assigned the lanky left-hander to the minors' toughest challenge, Double-A, and he passed the test with flying colors. Making 23 starts with the Amarillo Sod Poodles, the 6-foot-3, 205-pound southpaw posted a 135-to-53 strikeout-to-walk ratio in 115.2 innings of work. He compiled a 5.21 ERA, a nearly matching 5.29 FIP, and a 4.24 xFIP.

Snippet from The 2020 Prospect Digest Handbook: Big10 arms have typically struggled in the professional ranks, so this pick looks like a bit of a stretch. Strictly a backend option, and just as likely to slide into a multi-inning reliever.

Scouting Report: First, let's right a wrong: Henry's breaking ball, according to a variety of reports (previously myself as well), is actually a knuckle-curveball. And it's nasty. Average fastball that continues to play up because of his long limbs and deception. And he'll mix in an above-average fading changeup as well. With respect to his production in 2021, consider the following:

- Since 2006, only four 23-year-old pitchers met the following criteria in a Double-A season with one organization (min. 100 IP): 26.5% to 28.5% strikeout percentage with a walk percentage between 10% and 12%. Those four hurlers: David Hernandez, Radhames Liz, Tucker Davidson, and Tommy Henry.

The command needs to tick up to at least average in the next 12 months because his fastball velocity – regardless of the deception – doesn't leave a whole lot of room for error. He's currently staring down a fork in the road: backend starter vs. multi-inning relief arm. I'm inclined to think it'll be the latter option.

Ceiling: 1.0-win player
Risk: Moderate
MLB ETA: 2022

20. Jacob Steinmetz, RHP

FB	CB	CH	Command	Overall
50/55	50/55	45/50	45	40

Born: 07/19/03	Age: 18	Bats: R	Top Comp: N/A
Height: 6-5	Weight: 220	Throws: R	

Background: Taken straight from their website, Elev8 Sports Academy "specializes in providing quality training programs for the betterment of young athletes." Whatever their training regime includes, it was enough to push Steinmetz into the third round last July. Taken by the Diamondbacks with the 77th overall pick and signed to a well below slot deal worth $500,000, the 6-foot-5, 220-pound right-hander made just one brief – and quite unsuccessful – start with the organization's Arizona Complex League affiliate, coughing up three runs (one earned) while walking four in only 1.1 innings of work.

Scouting Report: The 6-foot-5, 220-pound right-hander made some headlines when the organization drafted him, making him the first Orthodox Jew to be drafted in Major League history. From a scouting standpoint: he's raw. Projectable, but very raw. He sports an average fastball that should see a few additional ticks on the radar gun. The curveball's…well…raw. It shows pretty good shape at times, but it's inconsistent. The changeup shows a little bit of fade, not a ton though. File his name away under the heading: Project.

Ceiling: 0.5- to 1.0-win player
Risk: Moderate
MLB ETA: 2025

Atlanta Braves

Top Prospects

1. Cristian Pache, CF

Hit	Power	SB	Patience	Glove	Overall
50	50	50	50	50	60

Born: 11/19/98	Age: 23	Bats: R	
Height: 6-2	Weight: 215	Throws: R	Top Comp: Melvin Upton Jr.

Season	Team	Age	Level	PA	1B	2B	3B	HR	SB	CS	BB%	K%	AVG	OBP	SLG	ISO
2018	ATL	19	A+	387	72	20	5	8	7	6	3.88%	17.83%	0.285	0.311	0.431	0.146
2018	ATL	19	AA	109	22	3	1	1	0	2	4.59%	25.69%	0.260	0.294	0.337	0.077
2019	ATL	20	AA	433	62	28	8	11	8	11	7.85%	24.02%	0.278	0.340	0.474	0.196
2019	ATL	20	AAA	105	16	8	1	1	0	0	8.57%	17.14%	0.274	0.337	0.411	0.137
2021	ATL	22	AAA	353	59	15	0	11	9	7	8.50%	27.48%	0.265	0.330	0.414	0.150

Background: A high profile free agent signing out of Santo Domingo Centro, Dominican Republic, in July 2015. Atlanta handed the toolsy center fielder a nice seven-figure bonus, $1.7 million to be exact, and pushed him directly to the stateside rookie leagues the following season for his highly anticipated debut. And Pache passed with flying colors. Splitting time between the Gulf Coast and Appalachian Leagues, he batted an aggregate .309/.349/.391 with four doubles and seven triples. A year later the then-18-year-old looked quite comfortable in the South Atlantic League testing grounds: he hit .281/.335/.343 with 21 extra-base hits in 119 games with the Rome Braves. The front office accelerated Pache's development schedule even further in 2018 as he blitzed through High-A and got his first taste of Double-A – the most important test for a prospect – before he turned 20-years-old. Pache responded with a .285/.311/.431 showing with Florida and a decent .260/.294/.337 slash line with Mississippi. Not shockingly, the club had him spend the majority of 2019 back in Mississippi for additional seasoning before bumping him up to the final minor league stop. During the 2020 COVID lockdown / shutdown, the 6-foot-2, 215-pound outfielder was on the big league club's taxi squad and he eventually appeared in a pair of games with Atlanta. Last season, Pache appeared in 89 games with Gwinnett in Triple-A East, batting .265/.330/.414 with 15 doubles and 11 dingers. He also swiped nine bags, though he was thrown out seven times. Per *Weighted Runs Created Plus*, his overall production was exactly the league average. Pache also appeared in 22 games with the Braves, hitting a paltry .111/.152/.206.

Snippet from The 2020 Prospect Digest Handbook: A plus glove with the offensive tools to settle in atop – or in the middle – of championship big league team. But the most exciting aspect for Pache's development: his blossoming power.

Scouting Report: A lot's changed in the past couple years. So let's start with the physical appearance. Namely, his weight: in 2019 Pache was measuring in at 185 pounds; last season, according to his bio, he's tipping the scales at 215 pounds. It's not necessarily bad weight, per se, but he's definitely bulkier than the lean body composition in years past. Now let's talk about production. Consider the following:

- Since 2006, only three 22-year-old hitters posted a wRC+ total between 95 and 105 with a strikeout rate of at least 25% in a Triple-A season with one organization (min. 350 PA): Nick Williams, Alex Liddi, and – of course – Cristian Pache. Williams, a former top prospect, owns a career 93 wRC+. And Liddi checks in with a 78 wRC+ across parts of three seasons with Seattle.

Well, that's not encouraging. Let's dive deeper.

- Pache was beyond useless the first couple months of the season. Including his time with Atlanta at the start of the year, he hit .166/.222/.285 over 47 games. However, over his final 64 games, he slugged a healthy .288/.352/.442. His strikeout rate over those two periods: 35.4% and 24.9%.

Now that's better. The second half numbers are more in line with the expectations. Now let's take a look at how the elite defender's numbers stacked up last season:

- Per Clay Davenport's defensive metrics, Pache was a staggering 10 runs saved below the average.

Defensive metrics tend to be unreliable in single year snapshots. Pache was incredibly valuable running the ball down in center field the first couple of seasons. But he's been a below average defender in 2019 and now 2021. And his limited work in the big league (read: extremely limited) has been average-ish. I'm betting on his offensive numbers over the final several months. But remain skeptical on his ability to provide elite levels of defensive value. In terms of ceiling, think: .250/.335/.450. One final thought: if the defense comes screaming back, he's perennial All-Star caliber talent and Gold Glover. Best case scenario: Mike Cameron.

Ceiling: 4.0-win player
Risk: Moderate
MLB ETA: Debuted in 2020

2. Freddy Tarnok, RHP

FB	CB	SL	CH	Command	Overall
60	60	55	50	50/55	60

Born: 11/24/98	Age: 23	Bats: R	Top Comp: Luis Castillo
Height: 6-3	Weight: 185	Throws: R	

Season	Team	Age	Level	IP	TBF	K/9	K%	BB/9	BB%	K-BB%	ERA	FIP	xFIP	Pit/Bat
2018	ATL	19	A	77.1	356	9.66	23.31%	4.77	11.52%	11.80%	3.96	4.03	4.64	3.97
2019	ATL	20	A+	98.0	431	7.53	19.03%	3.31	8.35%	10.67%	4.87	3.72	3.95	3.89
2021	ATL	22	A+	28.1	118	15.25	40.68%	4.13	11.02%	29.66%	4.76	4.72	3.72	4.21
2021	ATL	22	AA	45.0	181	12.20	33.70%	3.00	8.29%	25.41%	2.60	2.27	3.45	4.20

Background: The fifth pick in third round of the 2017 draft. Tarnok, a product of Riverview High School, has been on a slow, methodical development path. The 6-foot-3, 185-pound right-hander spent his first full season of action in the South Atlantic League, posting an 83-to-41 strikeout-to-walk ratio in 77.1 innings of work. An injury shortened campaign in 2019 limited him to just 19 starts with the club's High-A affiliate: he tossed 98 innings, averaging 7.5 strikeouts and 3.3 walks per nine innings. Last season, as minor league life returned to normal, Tarnok was bounced back down to High-A for additional seasoning. After seven starts he was finally promoted up to Double-A for another nine appearances. In total, the hard-throwing right-hander averaged an impressive 13.4 strikeouts and just 3.4 walks per nine innings. He finished the year with an aggregate 3.44 ERA and a slightly better 3.21 FIP.

Snippet from The 2020 Prospect Digest Handbook: I'm not certain the wiry right-hander is ready for the minors' toughest challenge, Class AA, so a return to the Florida State League is a possibility. [T] there's a chance he develops into a #5/#6-type arm.

Scouting Report: Steady progress for the young right-hander, so much so, that he may have one of the more underrated repertoire / ceiling's among all minor league arms. When he was drafted Tarnok showed a solid feel for the strike zone with a couple pitches that projected to be 55-grade offerings. Last season Tarnok's weaponry was blowing the doors off the competition. Mid- to upper-90s fastball that he commands exceptionally well. I had Tarnok upwards of 97 mph during a mid-July start. It shows exceptional late life and the Double-A hitters had a hard time catching up to it at times. His curveball is one of the better Uncle Charlie's in the minor leagues, showing the big 12-6 break with hard downward tilt that's reminiscent of a former Braves Top Prospect (Adam Wainwright). Tarnok's also added a hard, very underrated slider that may get even better with additional seasoning. He'll also mix in a decent changeup with some arm side run. There's legitimate #2/#3-type potential here. And in a system chock full of interesting arms, it's Tarnok, the former third round pick that didn't start pitching until his sophomore season in high school, that owns the highest ceiling. If you're not on the bandwagon yet, it's probably too late. The lone red flag: he's only surpassed 80 innings once his professional career (2019, 106.0 IP).

Ceiling: 4.0-win player
Risk: Moderate
MLB ETA: 2022

3. Michael Harris II, CF

Hit	Power	SB	Patience	Glove	Overall
50/50	40/45	60	50	55	60

Born: 03/07/01	Age: 21	Bats: B	Top Comp: Austin Jackson
Height: 6-0	Weight: 195	Throws: L	

Season	Team	Age	Level	PA	1B	2B	3B	HR	SB	CS	BB%	K%	AVG	OBP	SLG	ISO
2019	ATL	18	R	119	27	6	3	2	5	2	7.56%	16.81%	0.349	0.403	0.514	0.165
2019	ATL	18	A	93	12	2	1	0	3	0	9.68%	23.66%	0.183	0.269	0.232	0.049
2021	ATL	20	A+	420	74	26	3	7	27	4	8.33%	18.10%	0.294	0.362	0.436	0.142

Background: Dipping back into the prep pool that once produced Kyle Davis, a fourth round pick by the organization all the way back in 2001, Atlanta selected Michael Harris II in the third round out of Stockbridge High School three years ago. The 6-foot, 195-pound switch-hitting outfielder turned in a solid overall debut – though he torched the Gulf Coast League (.349/.403/.514) and struggled mightily after a promotion up to Low-A (.183/.269/.232). Last season, though, Harris II rediscovered his stroke – and, likely, his confidence – as he turned in a solid showing in High-A with the Rome Braves. In 101 games, he slugged .294/.362/.436 with 26 doubles, three triples, seven homeruns, and 27 stolen bases (in 31 attempts). His production topped the league average mark by 14%, per *Weighted Runs Created Plus*.

Snippet from The 2020 Prospect Digest Handbook: The raw athleticism is off the charts. Harris could prove to be one of the better value picks.

Scouting Report: Consider the following:

- Since 2006, only five 20-year-old hitters met the following criteria in a High-A season with one organization (min. 350 PA): 110 to 120 wRC+ total, a sub-20% strikeout rate, and a walk rate between 7.5% and 9.5%. Those five hitters: Franmil Reyes, Tyler Wade, Thairo Estrada, Marcus Lemon, and Michael Harris II.

Like a lot of the club's other top young outfielders, Harris is jacked with tools and can provide value on both sides of the ball. The big differentiator, at least thus far, is his modest strikeout rate. Harris fanned in only 18.1% of his plate appearances last season. On the other hand, though, Harris is similar to someone like Drew Waters due to the problematic groundball rates; the former third round posted a 50.3% mark last season. Beyond that, there are no major red flags.

Ceiling: 4.0-win player
Risk: Moderate
MLB ETA: 2023

4. Shea Langeliers, C

Hit	Power	SB	Patience	Glove	Overall
45	55	30	50	70	60

Born: 11/18/97	Age: 24	Bats: R	Top Comp: Matt Wieters
Height: 6-0	Weight: 205	Throws: R	

Season	Team	Age	Level	PA	1B	2B	3B	HR	SB	CS	BB%	K%	AVG	OBP	SLG	ISO
2019	ATL	21	A	239	40	13	0	2	0	0	7.11%	23.01%	0.255	0.310	0.343	0.088
2021	ATL	23	AA	370	50	13	0	22	1	0	9.73%	26.22%	0.258	0.338	0.498	0.240
2021	ATL	23	AAA	14	0	2	0	0	0	0	21.43%	42.86%	0.182	0.357	0.364	0.182

Background: Between 1965 and 2018, Baylor University produced a total of seven first round selections. Between 2019 and 2020, the Big 12 school produced three of them: Shea Langeliers (2019), Davis Wendzel (2019), and Nick Loftin (2020).

Langeliers was a bit of a surprise pick – at least I thought so – when the Braves called his name with the ninth overall selection three years ago. After the two sides agreed to a deal worth slightly less than $4 million, the highest bonus in school history by the way, the 6-foot, 205-pound backstop hit a respectable .255/.310/.343 in 54 games in Low-A. Last season, as minor league ball returned to action, Langeliers spent 92 games with the Mississippi Braves in Double-A South, hitting .258/.338/.498 with 13 doubles and 22 homeruns. His overall production, per *Weighted Runs Created Plus*, topped the league average mark by 28%. He also appeared in five games in AAA as well.

Snippet from The 2020 Prospect Digest Handbook: I still believe that the former Baylor slugger went about a round too early. But he profiles as a low end, capable starter at the MLB level.

Scouting Report: Consider the following:

- Since 2006, only four 23-year-old hitters posted a wRC+ total between 123 and 133 with a strikeout rate between 24% and 27% and a walk rate between 9% and 11% in a Triple-A season with one organization (min. 350 PA): Brent Rooker, Christin Stewart, Corey Toups, and Shea Langeliers.

Langeliers is an extreme flyball hitter, posting a groundball rate of just 30.7%. He owns above-average, 20- to 25-homer power potential. Decent walk rates. A below-average hit tool. And a 70-grade glove with a howitzer for an arm. The offensive ceiling isn't going to be overly large, something along the lines of .250/.320/.440, but if you thrown in great defense he becomes one of the better, more rounded backstops at the major league level. If that's the case, the front office clearly made the right move selecting Langeliers when they did.

Ceiling: 3.5-win player
Risk: Moderate
MLB ETA: 2022

5. Kyle Muller, LHP

FB	CB	SL	CH	Command	Overall
60	60	55	45	40/45	50

Born: 10/07/97	Age: 24	Bats: R	Top Comp: Sean Newcomb
Height: 6-7	Weight: 250	Throws: L	

Season	Team	Age	Level	IP	TBF	K/9	K%	BB/9	BB%	K-BB%	ERA	FIP	xFIP	Pit/Bat
2018	ATL	20	A	30.0	119	6.90	19.33%	2.40	6.72%	12.61%	2.40	4.24	3.76	3.87
2018	ATL	20	A+	80.2	337	8.81	23.44%	3.57	9.50%	13.95%	3.24	3.07	3.58	3.77
2018	ATL	20	AA	29.0	116	8.38	23.28%	1.86	5.17%	18.10%	3.10	3.68	3.65	4.18
2019	ATL	21	AA	111.2	468	9.67	25.64%	5.48	14.53%	11.11%	3.14	3.75	4.19	4.14
2021	ATL	23	AAA	79.2	345	10.51	26.96%	4.74	12.17%	14.78%	3.39	4.12	4.30	4.10

Background: The front office honed in on high ceiling prep arms early in the 2016 draft, selecting teenage hurlers Ian Anderson (3rd overall), Joey Wentz (40th overall), and Kyle Muller (44th overall) with their first three selections. The cost for the trio of pitchers: $9,550,000.

While Anderson's ascended to the upper portion of the Braves' rotation and Wentz moved to the Detroit franchise as part of the Shane Greene deal, Muller has continued to his slow, methodical march which culminated in the big left-hander making to separate stints with the big league club in 2021. Last season, Muller made 17 starts with the Gwinnett Stripers in AAA East, averaging 10.5 strikeouts and 4.7 walks per nine innings to go along with a 3.39 ERA. He also made an additional nine appearances, eight of which were starts, with Atlanta, posting a 37-to-20 strikeout-to-walk ratio and a 4.17 ERA in 36.2 innings of work.

Snippet from The 2020 Prospect Digest Handbook: He never showed a solid feel for zone, but there's no reason to think the control/command won't bounce back up to a 45-grade. There's some league average starting caliber potential, especially if the changeup is as good as it's looked in practice (assuming the control/command comes back).

Scouting Report: Two years ago Muller was working diligently on developing a third pitch. More specifically: improving his lackluster, below-average changeup. According to videos he was tweeting during the offseason, the pitch showed some serious potential as a viable third offering. Fast forward to last season and Muller's all but scrapped the changeup, opting instead for a new weapon in his arsenal: an upper 80s cutter-like slider. The big 6-foot-7, 250-pound southpaw is still working out the kinks, but it does flash above-average occasionally. Plus fastball. Plus curveball. And every once-in-a-blue-moon he'll throw a "show me" changeup. The command, which I was expecting to bounce back to 45-grade, never really did. Muller has a chance to be a viable league average starting pitcher. But there's a lot more in the tank he can somehow figure out how to get his walk rate under 4.0 BB/9.

Ceiling: 2.0-win player
Risk: Low to Moderate
MLB ETA: Debuted in 2020

6. Vaughn Grissom, IF

	Hit	Power	SB	Patience	Glove	Overall
	50/55	35/40	50	55	45/50	50

Born: 01/05/01	Age: 21	Bats: R	Top Comp: Tommy Edman
Height: 6-3	Weight: 180	Throws: R	

Season	Team	Age	Level	PA	1B	2B	3B	HR	SB	CS	BB%	K%	AVG	OBP	SLG	ISO
2019	ATL	18	R	184	35	7	1	3	3	0	8.70%	14.67%	0.288	0.361	0.400	0.113
2021	ATL	20	A	328	63	15	4	5	13	3	10.37%	14.94%	0.311	0.402	0.446	0.136
2021	ATL	20	A+	52	10	2	0	2	3	0	21.15%	9.62%	0.378	0.519	0.595	0.216

Background: Florida-based high school Paul J. Hagerty has an interesting, relatively new baseball history – at least in terms of draft picks. The prep school has produced a total of six drafts picks, all occurring since 2011 and each signing for at least $347,500. Of those six, three have been first rounders (Riley Greene, Ryan Mountcastle, and Zach Eflin), one is a fifth rounder (Tyler Marlette), and two coming in the 11th (Travis Hosterman and Vaughn Grissom). Taken with the 337th overall pick in 2019, Grissom showed a lot of offensive promise during his impressive debut that season, hitting .288/.361/.400 in 44 games with the club's Gulf Coast League affiliate. Last season Grissom shredded the Low-A competition to the tune of .311/.402/.446 with 15 doubles, four triples, five homeruns, and 13 stolen bases His overall production with Augusta topped the league average threshold by 35%. He spent the final few weeks in High-A – where he continued to swing a hot stick (.311/.402/.446).

Scouting Report: Consider the following:

- Since 2006, only five 20-year-old hitters met the following criteria in a Low-A season with one organization (min. 300 PA): 130 to 140 wRC+ total, a walk rate between 9% and 12%, and a sub-16.0% strikeout rate. Those five hitters: Desmond Jennings, Vidal Brujan, Corban Joseph, Jake Smolinski, and – of course – Mr. 11th Rounder, Vaughn Grissom.
- For those counting at home:
  - Jennings spent parts of seven seasons in the big leagues, posting a career 103 wRC+.
  - Brujan has been a consensus Top 100 prospect for several years now, and made his highly anticipated – albeit abbreviated – debut with Tampa Bay last season.
  - Joseph has parts of three years on his big league resume.
  - Smolinski, a former second round pick, has five big league seasons on his resume, hitting .235/.299/.363 in 235 games.

So excluding Grissom, the other four hitters have made it to the big leagues; two were/are top prospects; and one was an above-average, near borderline All-Star player. As for Grissom, all the evidence is pointing to a potential big league career. Strong bat-to-ball skills. Good patience. Above-average speed. And enough power to keep defenses/pitchers honest. He's likely going to shift over to second base permanently at some point. This was a tremendous job of scouting by the Braves' front office.

Ceiling: 2.5-win player
Risk: Moderate
MLB ETA: 2023/2024

7. Victor Vodnik, RHP

	FB	SL	CH	Command	Overall
	65	50/55	55	40/45	55

Born: 10/09/99	Age: 22	Bats: R	Top Comp: Mike Foltynewicz
Height: 6-0	Weight: 200	Throws: R	

Season	Team	Age	Level	IP	TBF	K/9	K%	BB/9	BB%	K-BB%	ERA	FIP	xFIP	Pit/Bat
2019	ATL	19	A	67.1	274	9.22	25.18%	3.21	8.76%	16.42%	2.94	2.79	3.39	3.93
2021	ATL	21	AA	33.2	150	10.96	27.33%	5.88	14.67%	12.67%	5.35	4.86	4.03	4.24

Background: Yet another example of organization's ability to unearth tremendous value well beyond the opening rounds of the draft. Atlanta selected the firebolt-slinging, smoke-throwing right-hander in the 14th round in 2018. Vodnik, the 412th player chosen that year, received a rather modest $200,000 bonus. The thick 6-foot, 200-pound youngster spent the 2019 season mostly working out of Rome's bullpen, throwing just 67.1 innings across 23 appearances, averaging 9.2 strikeouts and just 3.2 walks per nine innings. And last season the front office completely took the baby bumpers off of Vodnik and unleashed him onto Double-A South. In between multiple stints on the disabled list, Vodnik was able to squeeze in 11 mostly brief appearances with Mississippi: he posted a 25-to-14 strikeout-to-walk ratio in 23.2 innings of work. He finished the year with a 5.35 ERA, a 4.86 FIP, and a 4.03 xFIP.

Snippet from The 2020 Prospect Digest Handbook: He's poised to be one of the bigger breakout prospects in 2020. And he's one of my favorite arms in the minor leagues.

Scouting Report: One of the best fastballs in all of the minor leagues. Vodnik uncorks his high octane gas in the mid- to upper-90s and actually touched 101 mph at one point during the middle of the summer. And while it's easy to peg the former prep draft pick as a future reliever, he's matured a lot in the last couple of years. Vodnik is not only open to changing speeds, but he prefers too. His changeup is an above-average pitch, despite the velocity. There's some sink and fade to it with enough velocity separation. He'll also mix in a slider that flashes above-average a couple times a game. The floor of a closer definitely exists. But the Braves seem content to groom him as a starter. There's legitimate mid-rotation caliber potential. One more final thought:

- Vodnik allowed 20 earned runs in 33.2 innings. 14 of those earned runs occurred just 3.2 innings. Ignoring those, he posted a 1.80 ERA over the other eight appearances.

Ceiling: 2.5-win player
Risk: Moderate to High
MLB ETA: 2022/2023

8. Drew Waters, OF

	Hit	Power	SB	Patience	Glove	Overall
	45	45/50	50	50	55	50

Born: 12/30/98	Age: 23	Bats: B	Top Comp: Drew Stubbs
Height: 6-2	Weight: 185	Throws: R	

Season	Team	Age	Level	PA	1B	2B	3B	HR	SB	CS	BB%	K%	AVG	OBP	SLG	ISO
2018	ATL	19	A	365	55	32	6	9	20	5	5.75%	19.73%	0.303	0.353	0.513	0.211
2018	ATL	19	A+	133	23	7	3	0	3	0	6.02%	24.81%	0.268	0.316	0.374	0.106
2019	ATL	20	AA	454	85	35	9	5	13	6	6.17%	26.65%	0.319	0.366	0.481	0.162
2019	ATL	20	AAA	119	22	5	0	2	3	0	9.24%	36.13%	0.271	0.336	0.374	0.103
2021	ATL	22	AAA	459	63	22	1	11	28	9	10.24%	30.94%	0.240	0.329	0.381	0.141

Background: A product of Etowah High School, Atlanta snagged the toolsy, sometimes free-swinging outfielder in the second round, 41st overall, in the 2017 draft. Waters was part of the draft class that added Kyle Wright, Freddy Tarnok, and Bruce Zimmerman to the fold. Prior to the 2021 season, the 6-foot-2, 185-pound outfielder was coming off of three impressive campaigns: He batted .278/.362/.429 between the Gulf Coast and Appalachian Leagues during his debut; he followed that up with a .293/.343.476 showing between Low-A and High-A; and he blitzed through the minors' toughest challenge, AA, and looked comfortable in a late season promotion up to AAA. So, all signs were pointing towards bigger and better things for the former high round selection. But things don't necessarily work out the way they're supposed to. In 103 games as he returned to Gwinnett, Water hit a disappointing .240/.329/.381 with 22 doubles, one triple, 11 homeruns, and 28 stolen bases (in 37 attempts). Per *Weighted Runs Created Plus*, his overall production was 6% below the league average threshold.

Snippet from The 2020 Prospect Digest Handbook: Waters is still showing some borderline concerning swing-and-miss numbers; he whiffed in nearly 27% of his Class AA plate appearances and that number ballooned by nearly 10-percentage points during his 26-game cameo in the International League. And there's some solid raw power, though he's still putting the ball on the ground too frequently. He looks like .280/.320/.420 type hitter.

Scouting Report: Consider the following:

- Since 2006, only two 22-year-old hitters posted a wRC+ total between 90 and 100 with a strikeout rate north of 26% in a Triple-A season with one organization (min. 350 PA): Alex Liddi and Drew Waters.

The strikeout rate has been steadily climbing at each minor league stop over the past couple of seasons: 19.7% (2018 A), 24.8% (2018 A+), 26.7% (2019 AA), 36.1% (2019 AAA) and, finally, 30.0% (AAA, 2021). He did walk an above-average amount last season (10.2%), but it doesn't compensate for his lack of power or massive swing-and-miss issues. Waters is giving off some major Drew Stubbs vibes. But for that happen, though, he's going to have to show more power and cut down on his 56% groundball rate.

Ceiling: 2.0-win player
Risk: Moderate
MLB ETA: 2022

9. Braden Shewmake, SS

Hit	Power	SB	Patience	Glove	Overall
45	50	40	45	55	50

Born: 11/19/97	Age: 24	Bats: L	Top Comp: Freddy Galvis
Height: 6-4	Weight: 190	Throws: R	

Season	Team	Age	Level	PA	1B	2B	3B	HR	SB	CS	BB%	K%	AVG	OBP	SLG	ISO
2019	ATL	21	A	226	41	18	2	3	11	3	9.29%	12.83%	0.318	0.389	0.473	0.154
2019	ATL	21	AA	52	10	0	0	0	2	0	7.69%	21.15%	0.217	0.288	0.217	0.000
2021	ATL	23	AA	344	45	14	3	12	4	2	4.94%	21.80%	0.228	0.271	0.401	0.173

Background: A solid, eerily consistent contributor in Texas A&M's lineup for three seasons. Shewmake posted OPS totals of: .903, .848, and .848 beginning with his freshman season in 2017. Atlanta selected the well-rounded shortstop in the opening round, 21st overall, and signed him to a deal worth $3,129,800. And Atlanta immediately placed him on the fast track to the big leagues: he handled the transition to A-ball with aplomb, hitting .318/.389/.473, and spent the final couple weeks of his debut in AA, the minors' most challenging level for a prospect. With the return of minor league ball in 2021, Shewmake appeared back with the Mississippi Braves in the newly aligned Double-A South. The results, though, left a lot to be desired. In 83 games, the 6-foot-4, 190-pound shortstop hit a disappointingly low .228/.271/.401 with just 14 doubles, three triples, and 12 homeruns. His overall production, as measured by *Weighted Runs Created Plus*, was 16% below the league average threshold.

Snippet from The 2020 Prospect Digest Handbook: Shewmake's stellar debut – particularly in the Sally – like suggests that I may have shot a little too low on the young shortstop. I'd bump his ceiling up for a low-end starting caliber shortstop to a potentially league average one. Solid hit tool and power with a smattering of speed.

Scouting Report: OK. Well, that's some pretty poor production from a supposed top prospect. Now let's dive deeper. Consider the following:

- The former Aggie got off to a laughably bad start to the year, hitting a paltry .094/.144/.165 with just three extra-base knocks across his fist 22 games, spanning 90 plate appearances. He posted a 25-to-5 strikeout-to-walk rate.
- Between June 5th and August 20th Shewmake slugged a scorching .303/.342/.527 with 11 doubles, two triples, and nine homeruns. He also whiffed in 15.5% of his plate appearances during this stretch. He posted a 31-to-20 strikeout-to-walk rate.
- He capped off his season in another extended lull, batting .155/.189/.268 over his final 18 games, posting a 22-to-2 strikeout-to-walk ratio in 74 plate appearances.

So...which is the real Shewmake? The bookend terribleness that lasted a total of 40 games or the hot swinging shortstop over the middle 48 games? Well, it depends how frequently he's making contact. It's not a coincidence that the low points see a spike in K-rate and it declined during the hot period. The truth is, he's probably somewhere in between. 45-grade bat. 50-grade power. He'll steal a base once or so a month. The above-average defense pushes him in to that low-end starting gig, which was my initial pre-draft thought.

Ceiling: 1.5- to 2.0-win player
Risk: Moderate
MLB ETA: 2022/2023

10. Ryan Cusick, RHP

	FB	CB	CH	Command	Overall
	70	60	50	40/45	50

Born: 11/12/99	Age: 22	Bats: R	Top Comp:
Height: 6-6	Weight: 235	Throws: R	

Season	Team	Age	Level	IP	TBF	K/9	K%	BB/9	BB%	K-BB%	ERA	FIP	xFIP	Pit/Bat
2021	ATL	21	A	16.1	67	18.73	50.75%	2.20	5.97%	44.78%	2.76	1.53	1.23	4.61

Background: A highly touted prospect coming out of Avon Old Farms School, *Perfect Game* ranked the behemoth right-hander as the 115th best prospect in the country and *Baseball America* had the young gun as the 235th prospect as well. The Cincinnati Reds took a late, late round flier on Cusick following his final season in high school, nabbing him with the 1,189th selection. Obviously, the promising youngster bypassed any offers to jump into pro ball and headed directly to Wake Forest. And to put it lightly: Cusick was abysmal during his freshman season with the Demon Deacons. Splitting time between the club's rotation and bullpen, the 6-foot-6, 235-pound right-hander tallied a 6.44 ERA across 65.2 innings, recording 55 strikeouts and 29 walks. However, the Connecticut native blossomed in the Cape Cod League that summer, posting a 33-to-7 strikeout-to-walk ratio in seven starts for the Bourne Braves. Cusick had an interesting 2020 season: through four starts, he averaged a whopping 17.3 strikeouts and an equally whopping 7.3 walks per nine innings. And during his final season with the ACC squad, he tallied a 4.24 ERA with 108 strikeouts and 32 free passes in a career high 70.0 innings of work. Projected to be a Top 10 selection, Atlanta happily snagged the flame-throwing hurler in the opening round, 24th overall, and signed him to a deal worth $2.7 million. Cusick made six brief starts with Augusta during his debut, posting a dominating 34-to-4 strikeout-to-walk ratio in 16.1 innings of work.

Scouting Report: Per the usual, here's what I wrote about Cusick heading into the draft last July:

"Consider the following:

- *Between 2011 and 2020, there were 11 instances of an ACC pitcher averaging at least 12 strikeout per nine innings in a season (min. 60 IP): Marcus Stroman (who accomplished the feat twice), Carlos Rodon, Danny Hultzen, Brendan McKay, J.B. Bukauskas, Reid Detmers, Griffin Roberts, Graeme Stinson, Drew Parrish, and Jared Shuster. Only Stinson and Parrish were not taken in the first round.*
- *Among the group, only Shuster – like Cusick – averaged more than four walks per nine innings.*

Plus-plus fastball that will touch upwards of triple digits and sits comfortably in the mid-90s. Cusick also features a low to mid-80s curveball and a firm, though workable changeup. The question – of course – is whether he can consistently find the strike zone enough in the professional ranks. There's some real concern about whether he winds up in the bullpen as a two-pitch power arm. There's some risk, but a team with limited [or multiple] picks would likely be willing to gamble late in the opening round."

Ceiling: 2.0-win player
Risk: Moderate to High
MLB ETA: 2024

11. Joey Estes, RHP

	FB	SL	CH	Command	Overall
	60	50	45/50	55	50

Born: 10/08/01	Age: 20	Bats: R	Top Comp: N/A
Height: 6-2	Weight: 190	Throws: R	

Season	Team	Age	Level	IP	TBF	K/9	K%	BB/9	BB%	K-BB%	ERA	FIP	xFIP	Pit/Bat
2019	ATL	17	R	10.0	46	7.20	17.39%	6.30	15.22%	2.17%	8.10	4.01	5.18	1.89
2021	ATL	19	A	99.0	396	11.55	32.07%	2.64	7.32%	24.75%	2.91	3.30	3.78	3.85

Background: The 2019 draft class was supposed to about the two first round picks the front office held, which were eventually used on Shea Langeliers and shortstop Braden Shewmake, but it may eventually become known as the year of the late round selection. The organization selected infielder Vaughn Grissom in the 11th round, 337th overall, and went even deeper to snag hard-throwing right-hander Joey Estes. A product of Paraclete High School, Estes received a hefty bonus just shy of $500,000 as the 487th overall selection. After a brief, disastrous debut in the rookie league that summer, he posted an 8-to-7 strikeout-to-walk ratio in only 10 innings, Estes sparkled as a 19-year-old in Low-A East in 2021. Making 20 starts with the Augusta GreenJackets, the 6-foot-2, 190-pound youngster averaged an impressive 11.5 strikeouts and just 2.6 walks per nine innings. He finished the year with a 2.91 ERA, a 3.30 FIP, and a 3.78 xFIP.

Scouting Report: Consider the following:

- Since 2006, only five 19-year-old arms met the following criteria in a High-A season with one organization (min. 75 IP): post a strikeout percentage between 31% and 33%. Those five arms: Clayton Kershaw, Danny Duffy, Shelby Miller, Will Inman, and – of course – Mr. 16th round pick, Joey Estes.
- A few additional notes:
  - For those counting at home: Kershaw is a surefire Hall of Famer; Duffy's been a competent, sometimes All-Star caliber southpaw for the Royals; Miller has (famously) struggled the past several seasons, but he's topped 2.0 WAR in a season on two separate occasions; and Inman was once viewed as a Top 100 prospect by *Baseball America* and *Baseball Prospectus.*
  - Estes' walk percentage, 7.32%, was the second best among the group, trailing only Will Inman.

Big time fastball, sitting in the 95-mph range and reaching as high as 98 mph during a late-July start. Estes' secondary offerings need some work, and the same can be said for his mechanics too. Estes shows a slow, loopy slurvy-type slider and a changeup that will flash average at times. Mechanically, he has a weak front side and needs that cleaned up. The production has him on track for a league average starter, but he needs to continue developing his offspeed. But 19-year-old hurlers with big time strikeout rates combined with a strong feel for the strike zone are in short supply. Don't sleep on this kid either.

Ceiling: 2.0-win player
Risk: High
MLB ETA: 2024/2025

12. Tucker Davidson, LHP

FB	CB	SL	CH	Command	Overall
55	55	55	45	50	45

Born: 03/25/96	Age: 26	Bats: L	Top Comp: Drew Smyly
Height: 6-2	Weight: 215	Throws: L	

Season	Team	Age	Level	IP	TBF	K/9	K%	BB/9	BB%	K-BB%	ERA	FIP	xFIP	Pit/Bat
2018	ATL	22	A+	118.1	514	7.53	19.26%	4.41	11.28%	7.98%	4.18	3.98	4.27	4.12
2019	ATL	23	AA	110.2	449	9.92	27.17%	3.66	10.02%	17.15%	2.03	3.01	3.13	4.03
2019	ATL	23	AAA	19.0	82	5.68	14.63%	4.26	10.98%	3.66%	2.84	4.10	5.82	4.32
2021	ATL	25	AAA	23.0	84	10.96	33.33%	1.96	5.95%	27.38%	1.17	2.71	2.74	3.70

Background: There may have not been a more rollercoaster season than what Davidson went through in 2021. A late round pick out of Midland College all the way back in 2016, Davidson opened his sixth professional season with the Gwinnett Stripers. After two dominant starts with the AAA club, Atlanta recalled him back to the big leagues – where he would make a dominant six-inning start against the Mets. He was bounced back down to AAA for (another dominant start) before getting promoted back up to The Show. After three starts – two of them were fantastic – Davison hit the disabled list for roughly four months with a forearm strain. He made one final three-inning start with Gwinnett to end his regular season. Pretty wild, right? It gets better. Davidson, who wasn't rostered for the National League Division *or* Championship Series, replaced veteran ace Charlie Morton on the club's World Series roster and got the nod for Game 5. That game did not go so well for the big lefty: 2.0 IP, 4 R, 2 ER, 3 BB, 1K.

Snippet from The 2020 Prospect Digest Handbook: Davidson has the ceiling as a #4-type arm with the floor of a as a hard-throwing lefty reliever. The command need some work.

Scouting Report: Lefties with three above-average pitches with average command don't exactly grow on trees. And Davidson looked really to be coming into his own prior to the forearm issue last season. Combining his work with Atlanta and Gwinnett, the 6-foot-2, 215-pound southpaw posted a 2.30 ERA with 46 strikeouts and just 13 walks in 43.0 innings of work. Davidson's heater will sit in the 93 mph range. He'll mix in a late sweeping curveball in the upper 70s, and a harder mid-80s slider. He'll rarely throw his mid-80s changeup. Davidson still has the look of a solid #4-type starting pitcher – assuming he doesn't get pigeonholed into a multi-inning reliever.

Ceiling: 1.5-win player
Risk: Low to Moderate
MLB ETA: Debuted in 2020

13. Indigo Diaz, RHP

FB	CB	Command	Overall
65	50/55	50	45

Born: 10/14/98	Age: 23	Bats: R	Top Comp: Cody Allen
Height: 6-5	Weight: 250	Throws: R	

Season	Team	Age	Level	IP	TBF	K/9	K%	BB/9	BB%	K-BB%	ERA	FIP	xFIP	Pit/Bat
2019	ATL	20	R	10.1	42	13.06	35.71%	1.74	4.76%	30.95%	3.48	1.47	2.04	1.93
2021	ATL	22	A+	27.0	102	18.00	52.94%	2.33	6.86%	46.08%	1.00	0.65	1.61	4.19
2021	ATL	22	AA	18.0	73	14.50	39.73%	4.50	12.33%	27.40%	1.50	2.57	3.37	4.11

Background: Keeping with the general theme for the entire farm system – or at least some of my favorite players in the farm system. Atlanta unearthed the big boned right-hander in the 27th round of the 2019 draft after an up-and-down year at Michigan State. A member of the Spartans' squad for just the one season, courtesy of a stop-through at Iowa Western Community College, Diaz put on a meteoric rise through the club's system in 2021, just his second season in professional ball. Listed at 6-foot-5 and (perhaps) a generous 250 pounds, Diaz split time between Rome and Mississippi, averaging a mind-warping 16.6 strikeouts and just 3.2 walks per nine innings to go along with a laughably tidy 1.20 ERA and an almost impossible 1.42 FIP.

Scouting Report: A throwback type of pitcher cut from the Kenny Powers mold. Diaz rears backs and unleashes a heavy mid- to upper-90s fastball that plays up incredible well, almost making it a plus-plus pitch. He'll complement the offering with a mid-80s curveball, which flashes above-average. He's a potential closer-in-the-making and should do no worse than a dominant relief arm. Last year there were 1,677 minor leagues to surpass the 40-inning threshold:

- His strikeout percentage, 47.4%, ranked first.
- His K-rate, 16.6 K/9, ranked first.
- His K/BB%, 38.5%, ranked second.

Hitters looked very, very uncomfortable squaring off against the behemoth right-hander. He's the type of guy that will shine bright, but burnout quickly – unfortunately.

Ceiling: 1.5-win player
Risk: Moderate
MLB ETA: 2022

14. Spencer Schwellenbach, SS/RHP

Hit	Power	SB	Field	Overall
45	40	50	50	45

FB	CU	CH	Control	Overall
60	60	55/60	50	50

Born: 05/31/00	Age: 22	Bats: R	Top Comp: N/A
Height: 6-1	Weight: 200	Throws: R	

Background: A two-way star throughout the duration of his amateur years. Schwellenbach, who was drafted by Cleveland in the 34th round coming out of Heritage High School in 2018, left the Saginaw, Michigan, school with a career .416 batting; he belted out 36 total doubles, eight triples, and six dingers. Gatorade named the infielder / hard-throwing right-hander as the 2018 Michigan Baseball Player of the Year. And Collegiate Baseball listed him as a First-Team All-American that season as well. Attending the University of Nebraska-Lincoln, the 6-foot-1, 200-pound athlete more than held his own at the plate: in 107 career games, spanning 493 plate appearances, Schwellenbach batted .282/.405/.423 with 19 doubles, one triple, and 12 homeruns. He also swiped 16 bags in 20 total attempts. His work on the mound, though, is what vaulted him up the draft charts. Appearing in just 18 games in his collegiate career, all coming during his final campaign, Schwellenbach struck out 34, walked just 8, and tallied a miniscule 0.57 ERA while saving 10 games for the Big10 squad. Atlanta drafted him in the second round, 59th overall, and signed him to a below-slot deal worth $1 million – which saved the organization slightly less than $200,000. Schwellenbach was named the John Olerud Award winner, which is given to the nation's top two-way player. After joining the World Series-winning organization, Schwellenbach underwent the knife for Tommy John surgery. He'll likely miss a significant portion of 2022 – if the plan is to keep him as a hurler.

Scouting Report: Per the usual, here's what I wrote about Schwellenbach immediately after the 2021 draft:

"A late-rising prospect because Schwellenbach was a virtual unknown on the mound prior to the 2021 season. The 6-foot-1, 200-pound right-hander features a mid-90s fastball, which averaged in excess of 2300 RPM. His plus slider sits in low- to mid-80s with wipeout movement that will miss plenty of bats and averaged more than 2500 RPM. Schwellenbach will mix

in an incredibly underrated low 80s change with hard downward movement as well. As a hitter, Schwellenbach shows a 45-grade bat, tremendous on-base ability and decent power. Atlanta will likely look to stretch Schwellenbach out as a starting pitcher."

Ceiling: 2.0-win player
Risk: High
MLB ETA: 2024/2025

15. Jared Shuster, LHP

FB	SL	CH	Command	Overall
50	50	70	55	45

Born: 08/03/98	Age: 23	Bats: L	Top Comp: Jason Vargas
Height: 6-3	Weight: 210	Throws: L	

Season	Team	Age	Level	IP	TBF	K/9	K%	BB/9	BB%	K-BB%	ERA	FIP	xFIP	Pit/Bat
2021	ATL	22	A+	58.1	235	11.26	31.06%	2.31	6.38%	24.68%	3.70	4.26	4.09	3.73
2021	ATL	22	AA	14.2	68	10.43	25.00%	3.07	7.35%	17.65%	7.36	6.54	4.53	3.69

Background: Between 1965 and 2019, the Atlanta Braves selected five players out of Wake Forest University: Stephen Wrenn, Ken Zarski, Craig Gourlay, Scott Stice, and Connor Johnstone. None of the aforementioned group was taken earlier than the 15th round. Over the past two drafts, however, the franchise selected not one, but *two* Demon Deacons in the first round – Jared Schuster and Ryan Cusick, the 25th and 24th overall selections in their respective years. Shuster, a 6-foot-3, 210-pound southpaw, was rather abysmal during his first two seasons with the ACC Conference school, posting ERAs north of 6.49. Things seems to click for the crafty left-hander during the summer of 2019, though, as he ripped through the Cape Cod League competition: he posted a 35-to-5 strikeout-to-walk ratio with a sparkling 1.41 ERA in 32.0 innings of work. Shuster continued that torrid pace the following season before the COVID shutdown: he averaged 14.7 K/9 and 1.4 BB/9 through four starts. He made the his professional debut last season, making 18 appearances between Rome and Mississippi, throwing 73.0 innings with 90 punch outs and 20 walks. He finished the year with a 4.44 ERA and a 4.72 ERA.

Scouting Report: Consider the following:

- Since 2006, only six 22-year-old hurlers posted a strikeout percentage between 30% and 32% with a walk percentage between 5% and 7% in a High-A season with one organization (min. 50 IP): Dellin Betances, Tarik Skubal, James McDonald, Brett Conine, Paul Fry, and – of course – Jared Shuster.

A bit of a unicorn, of sorts, in today's game. Shuster falls into the category of "crafty lefty". His fastball sits in the 90- to 91-mph range. His slider won't shatter many bats. But his changeup is – likely – the best in the entire minor leagues. It's a straight changeup with tremendous velocity separation and deception – a bonafide swing-and-miss, legitimate out pitch. His once problematic 40-grade command and control has improved to an above-average, repeatable skill nowadays. He's a low ceiling / high floor hurler. Extreme short-arm that adds much needed deception. He's reminiscent of former lefty reliever Ron Mahay, though Shuster looks to have the chops to start until the heater fades. One final note: prior to the draft, Shuster fastball was up into the mid-90s; last season it was down several ticks when I saw him.

Ceiling: 1.5-win player
Risk: Moderate
MLB ETA: 2022

16. Spencer Strider, RHP

FB	SL	CH	Command	Overall
65	50/55	N/A	40/45	45

Born: 10/28/98	Age: 23	Bats: R	Top Comp: Matt Barnes
Height: 6-0	Weight: 195	Throws: R	

Season	Team	Age	Level	IP	TBF	K/9	K%	BB/9	BB%	K-BB%	ERA	FIP	xFIP	Pit/Bat
2021	ATL	22	A	15.1	57	18.78	56.14%	2.93	8.77%	47.37%	0.59	0.78	1.49	4.14
2021	ATL	22	A+	14.2	62	14.73	38.71%	3.68	9.68%	29.03%	2.45	3.02	3.51	3.89
2021	ATL	22	AA	63.0	266	13.43	35.34%	4.14	10.90%	24.44%	4.71	3.32	3.78	4.28

Background: Cleveland made the hard-throwing right-hander the first player drafted out of Christian Academy of Knoxville, a prep school based out of Tennessee, though Strider would bypass the opportunity to join the organization as a 35th round pick. The 6-foot, 195-pound hurler spent his freshman season working as a long reliever / spot starter at Clemson University and would miss the entirety of 2019 recovering from Tommy John surgery. Strider would make it back to the mound for the ACC Conference school the following season, throwing just 12.0 innings while racking up 19 punch outs and allowing just a trio of walks. The production was enough to get the Braves' attention, who would burn a fourth round pick on the returning right arm. Last year Strider blitzed through five separate levels, going from Low-A all the way up to the big leagues by the end of the season. In total, he made 22 minor league appearances, 21 of them coming via the start, throwing 94.0 innings with a whopping 153 strikeouts and 40 free pass to go along with a 3.64 ERA. He made two brief appearances with Atlanta as well, spanning just 2.1 innings of work.

Scouting Report: Well, that's one helluva calculated gamble by the Braves, though it's far from the first time that the club grabbed an injured collegiate arm early in the draft. Strider is mainly a two-pitch pitcher: an upper 90s fastball that can simply overpower hitters and a decent power slider with vertical movement. His slider has the look and feel of an above-average offering, but it wasn't missing many bats in the couple games I scouted last year. Strider reportedly mixes in a changeup according to a variety of reports, though I never saw one. The arsenal is best suited for a seventh, maybe an eighth inning gig.

Ceiling: 1.0- to 1.5-win player
Risk: Low to Moderate
MLB ETA: Debuted in 2020

17. Bryce Elder, RHP

	FB	SL	CH	Command	Overall
	50	60	50/55	50	45

Born: 05/19/99	Age: 23	Bats: R	Top Comp: Josh Collmenter
Height: 6-2	Weight: 220	Throws: R	

Season	Team	Age	Level	IP	TBF	K/9	K%	BB/9	BB%	K-BB%	ERA	FIP	xFIP	Pit/Bat
2021	ATL	22	A+	45.0	194	11.00	28.35%	4.00	10.31%	18.04%	2.60	3.43	4.04	3.47
2021	ATL	22	AA	56.0	218	9.64	27.52%	2.73	7.80%	19.72%	3.21	3.95	3.17	3.61
2021	ATL	22	AAA	36.2	147	9.82	27.21%	4.91	13.61%	13.61%	2.21	3.25	4.06	3.97

Background: Fun Fact: Prior to the club's selection of Elder in the fifth round in 2020, the last time Atlanta drafted a Texas Longhorn earlier in the draft was all the way back in 1990 when they nabbed outfielder John Walker with the 102nd pick. The well-built right-hander shot through three separate levels last season, his first in professional ball. Between the 25 starts with Rome, Mississippi, and Gwinnett, Elder tossed 137.2 innings of work, recording 155 punch outs and 57 walks to go along with a 2.75 ERA and a 3.60 FIP. One final note: his 155 punch outs were the tenth most among all qualified minor league arms last season.

Scouting Report: Not an overpowering arsenal by any stretch of the imagination. Elder, though, will efficiently change speeds and will typically hover around the strike zone for the majority of the game. Low 90s heat, an average offering, complemented by a hard, tightly wound slider with vertical drop and little horizontal movement. He'll also mix in a splitter-like changeup. Elder has a high arm slot/release point. There's some backend, innings eater-type potential. Nothing more.

Ceiling: 1.0- to 1.5-win player
Risk: Moderate
MLB ETA: 2022

18. Jesse Franklin, OF

	Hit	Power	SB	Patience	Glove	Overall
	40	55/60	55	50	45	40

Born: 12/01/98	Age: 23	Bats: L	Top Comp: N/A
Height: 6-1	Weight: 215	Throws: L	

Season	Team	Age	Level	PA	1B	2B	3B	HR	SB	CS	BB%	K%	AVG	OBP	SLG	ISO
2021	ATL	22	A+	406	38	24	2	24	19	4	8.37%	28.33%	0.244	0.320	0.522	0.278

Background: The University of Michigan (Go Bucks!) has proven to be a bit of baseball hotbed over the better part of the last decade. But more specifically: since 2019, the Big 10 school produced four pitchers taken before the fourth round and three hitters taken in third round. One of those bats: Jesse Franklin, a hulking 6-foot-1, 215-pound outfielder who batted a respectable .287/.385/.520 in 115 collegiate games. Atlanta drafted him in the third round, 97th overall, and signed him to a deal worth slightly less than $500,000 in 2020. The Seattle, Washington, native made his professional debut last season, spending the entirety of the year with the Rome Braves in High-A. In 191 games, Franklin batted .244/.320/.522 with 24 doubles, two triples, and 24 homeruns. He also swiped 19 bags in 23 total attempts. Per *Weighted Runs Created Plus*, his overall production was 18% better than the league average mark. Franklin spent the fall playing for – and struggling with – the Peoria Javelinas, hitting a putrid .098/.303/.176 in 66 plate appearances.

Scouting Report: Consider the following:

- Since 2006, only two 22-year-old hitters met the following criteria in a High-A season with one organization (min. 350 PA): 113 to 123 wRC+ total, a walk rate between 7.5% and 9.5% and a strikeout rate north of 26%. Those two hitters: Ibandel Isabel and Jesse Franklin.

It was an aggressive assignment, sending Franklin straight into High-A from the Big 10 Conference. And, for the most part, he handled it well – especially after a slow couple weeks to start his tenure (he hit .202/.244/.298 over his first 22 games). The power is a legitimate, above-average and may even peak as a plus skill. The actual hit tool may never creep over a 40-grade, though. His value takes a hit if he can't stay in center field. And he likely shouldn't stay there, either. If the walk rates were above-average or better he could encroach on Gorman Thomas territory. And if I were smarter, I could work in professional baseball.

Ceiling: 1.0-win player
Risk: Moderate
MLB ETA: 2024

19. Alan Rangel, RHP

	FB	CB	CH	Command	Overall
	55	50	55	55	40

Born: 08/21/97	Age: 24	Bats: R	Top Comp: Keury Mella
Height: 6-2	Weight: 170	Throws: R	

Season	Team	Age	Level	IP	TBF	K/9	K%	BB/9	BB%	K-BB%	ERA	FIP	xFIP	Pit/Bat
2018	ATL	20	A	125.1	533	7.54	19.70%	2.23	5.82%	13.88%	4.09	4.02	4.04	3.53
2019	ATL	21	A	131.2	581	8.27	20.83%	3.21	8.09%	12.74%	4.51	3.82	3.93	3.82
2021	ATL	23	A+	70.2	293	12.10	32.42%	2.67	7.17%	25.26%	3.57	3.61	3.78	4.04
2021	ATL	23	AA	34.0	132	10.85	31.06%	1.32	3.79%	27.27%	4.50	2.58	3.09	4.09

Background: One of the longest tenured notable prospects in the Atlanta system. Rangel made his professional debut in 2015, as a 17-year-old squaring off against the Gulf Coast League. The wiry right-hander spent another year in the rookie and followed it up with three separate full season stints with Rome in the old South Atlantic League. Last season, his seventh in the Atlanta farm system, Rangel made it up to High-A. And that tenure only lasted a couple of months before the front office bumped him up to Double-A for the last several weeks of the year. In total, the 6-foot-2, 170-pound right-hander tossed 104.0 innings – his third consecutive year topping the 100-inning threshold – with 136 punch outs and just 26 free passes to go along with a 3.87 ERA.

Scouting Report: Rangel's a bit of an enigma of sorts. His fastball sits in the 94- to 96-mph range. It's a bit straight and doesn't necessarily play up to its velocity, but he commands it well enough to make up for any shortcomings. He'll miss plenty of bats, or generate a solid amount of weak contact, with his hard tumbling, above-average changeup. He'll also mix in a solid-average curveball as well. He throws strikes, has a history of strong peripherals. And he's coming off of his finest professional season to date, averaging 11.7 K/9 and just 2.2 BB/9. He's eerily similar to right-hander Keury Mella, who had the potential and repertoire but just never stood out.

Ceiling: 1.0-win player
Risk: Moderate
MLB ETA: 2022

20. Dylan Dodd, LHP

	FB	CB	SL	CH	Command	Overall
	50/55	45	50	55	50	40

Born: 06/06/98	Age: 24	Bats: L	Top Comp: N/A
Height: 6-3	Weight: 210	Throws: L	

Season	Team	Age	Level	IP	TBF	K/9	K%	BB/9	BB%	K-BB%	ERA	FIP	xFIP	Pit/Bat
2021	ATL	23	A	11.0	43	11.45	32.56%	2.45	6.98%	25.58%	4.91	2.25	3.11	3.79

Background: Fun Fact Part I: Since their first draft selection in 1966, Southeast Missouri State University has had a total of 29 players selected in the amateur draft (including James Klocke, who was taken twice). Fun Fact Part II: The Braves made left-hander Dylan Dodd the earliest draft pick in school history, surpassing the previous title holder, fellow southpaw Joey Lucchesi, by 18 picks. Taken with the 96th overall selection last July, Dodd, who received a scant $122,000 bonus, turned in a remarkable senior season at the Ohio Valley Conference school: in 96.2 innings of work, the 6-foot-3, 210-pound southpaw struck out 120 and walked just 17 to go along with a 3.17 ERA. Dodd made four brief appearances between Augusta and Rome during his debut, fanning 20 and walking three in 14.0 innings of work.

Scouting Report: A well below-slot signing last summer. Dodd, who's already entering his age-24 season, attacks hitters with a standard four-pitch mix: fastball, curveball, slider, and changeup. His heater will sit in the 92-94 mph range and touched 95 mph during one his abbreviated debut appearances. His pair of breaking balls is pretty vanilla, nothing to write home about; the slider being the better of the two options. His changeup, though, is a firm 55-grade and his best offspeed weapon. Dodd is tracking like a #6-type arm, maybe some type of relief floor.

Ceiling: 1.0-win player
Risk: Moderate
MLB ETA: 2023

Baltimore Orioles

Top Prospects

1. Adley Rutschman, C

	Hit	Power	SB	Patience	Glove	Overall
	55	55/60	30	60	65	70

Born: 02/06/98	Age: 24	Bats: B	Top Comp: Buster Posey
Height: 6-2	Weight: 220	Throws: R	

Season	Team	Age	Level	PA	1B	2B	3B	HR	SB	CS	BB%	K%	AVG	OBP	SLG	ISO
2019	BAL	21	R	16	1	0	0	1	1	0	12.50%	12.50%	0.143	0.250	0.357	0.214
2019	BAL	21	A-	92	16	7	1	1	0	0	13.04%	17.39%	0.325	0.413	0.481	0.156
2019	BAL	21	A	47	3	1	0	2	0	0	12.77%	19.15%	0.154	0.261	0.333	0.179
2021	BAL	23	AA	358	46	16	0	18	1	2	15.36%	15.92%	0.271	0.392	0.508	0.237
2021	BAL	23	AAA	185	33	9	2	5	2	2	12.97%	17.84%	0.312	0.405	0.490	0.178

Background: Fun Fact Part I: The Baltimore Orioles have owned the top pick in the amateur draft twice in team history – in 1989 when the front office selected LSU ace right-hander Ben McDonald and – of course – three years ago when they nabbed Oregon State University backstop Adley Rutschman. Fun Fact Part II: Baltimore's selected collegiate backstops just twice in the opening round in their storied history – Matt Wieters, the #5 overall pick in 2007, and Rutschman. Fun Fact Part III: The franchise has selected two players from Oregon State University in the first round – Cadyn Grenier (2018) and Rutschman. Originally taken in the 40th round by the Seattle Mariners coming out of Sherwood High School in 2016, Rutschman – obviously – bypassed the late round opportunity and headed to Pac12 powerhouse OSU. But it wasn't all roses for the eventual top pick. The 6-foot-2, 220-pound switch-hitter looked overwhelmed at the plate during his freshman season with the Beavers, hitting a paltry .234/.322/.306 in 61 games. And he fared even *worse* during his trot through the Cape Cod that summer as well: in 20 games with the Falmouth Commodores – a roster, by the way, that featured Grenier, Nick Madrigal, and Trevor Larnach – he batted .164/.282/.179. Like a radioactive spider biting Peter Parker, Rutschman morphed into a superhero by the time his sophomore season rolled around. In a career best 67 games for legendary coach Pat Casey, the young catcher slugged a Ted Williams-esque .408/.505/.628 with 22 doubles, three triples, and nine homeruns. Unbelievably so, he was actually *more lethal* during his final campaign against the mere mortals of college baseball: he battered the competition to the tune of .411/.575/.751 with 10 doubles, one triple, and 17 homeruns. After Baltimore selected him atop the 2019 draft, they handed him a massive $8.1 million bonus – the largest given out to a draft pick in team history. Rutschman appeared at three separate levels during his debut (Gulf Coast, New York-Penn and South Atlantic Leagues), batting an aggregate .254/.351/.423. Last season, after minor league ball returned to action after the COVID-imposed shutdown, the former Beaver was sent straight up to Double-A , the largest test for a prospect, and he passed with flying colors. He spent the last third of the year in AAA, passing that level with relative ease as well. In total, Rutschman slugged .285/.397/.502 with 25 doubles, two triples, and 23 homeruns. Per *Weighted Runs Created Plus*, his overall production topped the league average mark by a whopping 44%.

Snippet from The 2020 Prospect Digest Handbook: Rutschman shows a smooth, easy swing without much effort that generates above-average bat speed. There's no such thing as a lock for superstardom when it comes to prospects, but Rutschman looks like a strong possibility to get there.

Scouting Report: If there was a perfect catching prospect, it might look like Adley Rutschman. And it doesn't look like him, it'd be an awfully close facsimile. Switch-hitter. Plus power. Elite bat-to-ball skills. Above-average bat. Elite eye at the plate. Elite defensive ability. During his brief minor league tenure he's basically been the offensive equivalent of Rickey Henderson without the speed. It's all impressive, but *the* most impressive aspect of Rutschman's first full season in professional baseball: he made the leapt up to the upper minors (A) with just 12 games in Low-A and (B) he finished his tenure in Double-A, the make-it-or-break-it level, with a 57-to-55 strikeout-to-walk ratio. In terms of big league ceiling, think: .290/.370/.500. One more final thought: there's no way Baltimore promotes him before the Super-2 deadline passes.

Ceiling: 7.0-win player
Risk: Moderate
MLB ETA: 2022

2. Grayson Rodriguez, RHP

	FB	CB	SL	CH	Command	Overall
	70	60	70	55	60	70

Born: 11/16/99	Age: 22	Bats: R	Top Comp: Jose Fernandez
Height: 6-5	Weight: 220	Throws: R	

Season	Team	Age	Level	IP	TBF	K/9	K%	BB/9	BB%	K-BB%	ERA	FIP	xFIP	Pit/Bat
2018	BAL	18	R	19.1	80	9.31	25.00%	3.26	8.75%	16.25%	1.40	2.68	3.43	1.81
2019	BAL	19	A	94.0	377	12.35	34.22%	3.45	9.55%	24.67%	2.68	2.64	2.94	4.10
2021	BAL	21	A+	23.1	88	15.43	45.45%	1.93	5.68%	39.77%	1.54	2.48	2.47	3.75
2021	BAL	21	AA	79.2	310	13.67	39.03%	2.49	7.10%	31.94%	2.60	2.72	2.72	4.05

Background: As much as some would like to dismiss it, there's a lot of luck involved in the summer amateur draft. Not only do organizations spend countless hours and seemingly limitless amounts of money scouting players, hoping they can correctly predict human behavior, but they have to project where players will go. Will a player be available at pick 10? What about pick 50? Did an organization catch a player during a good stretch or was he mired in an unusual slump? In a lot of ways, though, it's often better to be lucky than good – like the Los Angeles Angels selecting Mike Trout, the greatest player of his generation, who was inexplicably bypassed until the 25th pick in the 2009 draft. There may be a point in the future – perhaps as soon as 2022 or maybe even in 10 years – when we look back and question how Grayson Rodriguez wasn't the first pitcher chosen in the 2018 draft class, let alone why he wasn't the first player chosen overall. Standing an imposing 6-foot-5 and 220-pounds, Rodriguez was seemingly born to front the rotation of a big league club. And he made that abundantly clear as soon as he toed a professional rubber. The hard-throwing right-hander ripped through the Gulf Coast League during his debut and didn't stop as he moved into the South Atlantic League a year later. He would make 20 starts with the Delmarva Shorebirds that season, averaging 12.4 strikeouts and only 3.4 walks per nine innings. That dominance was just a harbinger of things to come. Rodriguez opened the 2021 season up with Aberdeen, but after toasting the mere mortals of High-A, he moved onto the proving grounds of Double-A. Again, the competition proved to be no match for Rodriguez and his elite four-pitch mix. In total, Rodriguez made 23 starts between the two affiliates, throwing 103 innings with a whopping 161 starts with 27 walks. He finished the year with an aggregate 2.36 ERA and a 2.67 FIP.

Snippet from The 2020 Prospect Digest Handbook: There's no question about it: he's an ace-in-the-making and there are few – if any – minor league pitchers I would taken over Rodriguez.

Scouting Report: Just how good was Grayson Rodriguez, not even a top 10 pick in the 2018 draft, last season? Consider the following:

- Since 2006, only two 21-year-old pitchers posted a strikeout percentage of at least 36% in Double-A with one organization (min. 50 IP): Reid Detmers, the top prospect in the Angels system, former big league reliever Carter Capps, and Grayson Rodriguez – who threw at least 25 innings more than the former duo.

In the conversation for the best overall arsenal in the minor leagues – personally, I think it's between Miami's Edward Cabrera and Grayson Rodriguez – Baltimore's budding ace owns four above-average or better offerings. His fastball sits in the mid- to upper-90s with as much life as a meteor screaming towards earth. His hellacious curveball, merely a plus pitch, isn't even his best breaking ball. His plus-plus slider is, simply put, death to hitters – especially right-handed hitters. He'll also mix in a deceptively good, plus changeup. Throw in plus command and there's a recipe for an elite, premium ceiling. Four legitimate swing-and-miss, sit down on the bench offerings.

Ceiling: 7.0-win player
Risk: Moderate
MLB ETA: 2022

3. Colton Cowser, CF

Hit	Power	SB	Patience	Glove	Overall
50/55	30/40	50	55	50	60

Born: 03/20/00	Age: 22	Bats: L	Top Comp: N/A
Height: 6-3	Weight: 195	Throws: R	

Season	Team	Age	Level	PA	1B	2B	3B	HR	SB	CS	BB%	K%	AVG	OBP	SLG	ISO
2021	BAL	21	CPX	25	7	3	0	1	3	2	12.00%	16.00%	0.500	0.560	0.773	0.273
2021	BAL	21	A	124	28	5	0	1	4	2	17.74%	15.32%	0.347	0.476	0.429	0.082

Background: Hailing from the same alma mater, Cypress Ranch High School, as Diamondbacks prospect Corbin Martin, Cowser batted .411 while driving in 38 runs and swiping 30 stolen bases en route to earning all-state honors during his senior prep campaign. A toolsy Texas-born outfielder, Cowser turned in one of the more dynamic freshman showings for Sam Houston State three years ago: appearing in 56 games for Manager Jay Sirianni, he belted out 17 doubles, seven triples, and seven homeruns while swiping nine bases to go along with a .361/.450/.602 triple-slash line. The 6-foot-3, 195-pound lefty-swinging center fielder spent the following summer playing alongside the likes of Spencer Torkelson, future Orioles prospect Heston Kjerstad, and Austin Martin for Team USA. Cowser finished his time for the national team with a .273/.390/.303 slash line. His production stumbled a bit during the COVID-shortened 2020 season: in 14 games he hit .255/.379/.364. But his numbers came roaring back in his third season for the Bearkats, slugging .374/.490/.680 with career highs in doubles (10), homeruns (16), and stolen bases (17). Baltimore snagged him fifth overall last July, signing him to a deal worth $4.9 million. After ripping through the Complex League competition, Cowser made quick work of the Low-A competition as well, slugging .347/.476/.429 with five doubles and one homeruns in 25 games.

Scouting Report: Per the usual, here's my pre-draft write-up:

"Consider the following:

- *Between 2011 and 2020, only three Southland Conference hitters have batted at least .350/.475/.650 in a season (min. 225 PA): Hunter Dozier, Jameson Fisher, and Luis Trevino.*

While it's a less than stellar collection of players – with only Dozier making an impact at the big league level – it's important to point out that Cowser, unlike his counterparts, played against premium collegiate-aged talent (Team USA) and had some level of success. And he did it as a true freshman. Simple swing from a complete upright stance, he's short and quick to the zone. Cowser doesn't project to hit from more than 10 or so homeruns during a full professional season. But he owns an above-average hit tool, enough speed to swipe 15 bags, and play a passable defense. He's low ceiling / high floor prospect and should be selected between picks 15 and 20."

Ceiling: 4.0-win player
Risk: Moderate
MLB ETA: 2023/2024

4. D.L. Hall, LHP

	FB	CB	SL	CH	Command	Overall
	N/A	N/A	N/A	N/A	N/A	60

Born: 09/19/98	Age: 23	Bats: L	Top Comp: Blake Snell
Height: 6-2	Weight: 195	Throws: L	

Season	Team	Age	Level	IP	TBF	K/9	K%	BB/9	BB%	K-BB%	ERA	FIP	xFIP	Pit/Bat
2018	BAL	19	A	94.1	391	9.54	25.58%	4.01	10.74%	14.83%	2.10	3.67	3.84	3.98
2019	BAL	20	A+	80.2	346	12.94	33.53%	6.02	15.61%	17.92%	3.46	3.22	3.55	4.29
2021	BAL	22	AA	31.2	128	15.92	43.75%	4.55	12.50%	31.25%	3.13	3.33	2.33	4.12

Background: It lasted just ten days, but it was beautiful, glorious ten days, nonetheless. For a brief fleeting moment last season the Bowie Baysox not only rostered two of the best pitching prospects in baseball, the lineup sported the best hitting prospect in the game as well. It provided the type of hope the Orioles' fans thirsted for. Grayson Rodriguez, Adley Rutschman, D.L. Hall. Just seven starts into the 2021 season, his fifth in Baltimore's organization, D.L. Hall hit the disabled list with a wonky left elbow – essentially breaking up the perfect triumvirate. The specific cause: per *The Baltimore Sun*, Hall suffered a "stress reaction in the bone in his left elbow." Those seven starts before he hit the disabled list, though, were mostly of the dominant variety: he tossed 31.2 innings, recording a staggering 56 punch outs versus 16 free passes to go along with a 3.13 ERA, a 3.33 FIP, and a 2.33 xFIP. For his brief career, the young left-hander sported a 2.99 ERA while averaging 11.8 strikeouts and 5.1 walks per nine innings. It marked the second season in a row (2019 and 2021) that Hall spent considerable time on the injured list.

Snippet from The 2020 Prospect Digest Handbook: He has the potential to develop into a Blake Snell-type lefty; he just has to throw more strikes. Snell, by the way, battled severe control issues early in his career too.

Scouting Report: Prior to the injury, Hall's arsenal was dominating and he was throwing strikes more frequently that he did in years past. During an early May outing the 6-foot-2, 195-pound left-hander's heater was sitting 93- to 94-mph and touched 98- and 99-mph on numerous occasions. It's explosive with riding life and a lot natural cutting action. He complemented the plus offering with a trio of above-average offspeed pitches: an upper 70s curveball, a quality slider, and a sneaky good changeup. Hall's a lot of arms and legs, which adds some deception to his delivery. Barring any setbacks from the stress reaction in his elbow, Hall could ascend to a mid-rotation arm – maybe even higher if the command ticks up closer to average.

Ceiling: 4.0-win player
Risk: Moderate to High
MLB ETA: 2023

5. Coby Mayo, 3B

	Hit	Power	SB	Patience	Glove	Overall
	50	50/60	40/30	55	45/50	60

Born: 12/10/01	Age: 20	Bats: R	Top Comp: Todd Frazier
Height: 6-5	Weight: 215	Throws: R	

Season	Team	Age	Level	PA	1B	2B	3B	HR	SB	CS	BB%	K%	AVG	OBP	SLG	ISO
2021	BAL	19	CPX	84	14	6	0	3	6	0	13.10%	15.48%	0.324	0.429	0.535	0.211
2021	BAL	19	A	125	19	8	1	5	5	0	12.80%	20.80%	0.311	0.416	0.547	0.236

Background: Parkland, Florida-based Stoneman-Douglas High School has had several notable ballplayers walked through their halls, including Anthony Rizzo and Jesus Luzardo, but neither were the highest drafted prospect, though. That distinction belongs to former White Sox shortstop Mike Caruso, the 42nd pick in the draft all the way back in 1996. The recipient of the largest bonus in the prep school's history, though, is Coby Mayo. Taken in the fourth round, 103rd overall, two years ago, Baltimore signed the massive 6-foot-5, 215-pound teenager to an over-slot deal worth $1.75 million. Mayo made his debut last season, ripping through the Complex League competition to the tune of .329/.440/.566. And he barely slowed in a 27-game cameo in Low-A East, slugging .311/.416/.547 with eight doubles, one triple, five homeruns, and five stolen bases. Per *Weighted Runs Created Plus*, his total production topped the league average mark by a whopping 62%.

Scouting Report: A University of Florida commit prior to joining Baltimore's organization, the player development program quieted Mayo's busy set position that he showed as a high schooler. The big third baseman would take an extreme weight transfer to his back foot as he readied himself. Mayo owns the best power potential of any minor league hitter not named Adley Rutschman in the Orioles' farm system. Plus bat speed, short stroke. Mayo combines the plus future power with strong contact rates and above-average patience. Defensively, he's raw, below-average. But he's incredibly athletic and projects to be an average third baseman. He'll be a consensus Top 100 pick by the start of 2023. In terms of big league ceiling, think: .270/.340/.500. I like him a lot. The ceiling is incredibly high. One of the most underrated prospects.

Ceiling: 4.0-win player
Risk: Moderate to High
MLB ETA: 2024/2025

6. Heston Kjerstad, OF

	Hit	Power	SB	Patience	Glove	Overall
	N/A	N/A	N/A	N/A	N/A	N/A

Born: 02/12/99	Age: 23	Bats: L	Top Comp: N/A
Height: 6-3	Weight: 205	Throws: R	

Background: A dominant middle-of-the-lineup thumper during his three-year tenure at the University of Arkansas. Kjerstad, a hulking 6-foot-3, 205-pound outfielder, was originally drafted by the Seattle Mariners in the 36th round coming out of Canyon Randall High School in 2017. The Texas native showed no ill effects jumping from high school competition to the elite Southeastern Conference. Kjerstad put together a tremendous true freshman season for the Razorbacks in 2018, slugging .332/.419/.553 with 30 extra-bases in 69 games. He nearly matched that production the following season as well, batting .327/.400/.573 with 31 extra-base knocks in 65 contests. Kjerstad start the 2020 campaign off like a bat out of hell too, hitting .448/.513/.791 with five doubles and six homeruns in just 16 games before the COVID-imposed shutdown. Baltimore selected him in the opening round, second overall, and signed him to a below-slot deal worth $5.2 million. Unfortunately for the former Arkansas star, he hasn't appeared in an affiliated game because of myocarditis (heart inflammation).

Scouting Report: Kjerstad remains a complete unknown at this point. During his collegiate days he owned plus power and made enough contact to alleviate any concerns about massive swing-and-miss issues as a potential professional hitter. He whiffed in 18.7% of his career plate appearances with Arkansas. Beyond baseball, here's hoping Kjerstad makes it back to the ball field so he can start to move towards his dream of making it the big leagues. Unfortunately for all parties involved, he remains a complete unknown at this time.

Ceiling: 4.0-win player
Risk: High
MLB ETA: 2023/2024

7. Gunnar Henderson, 3B/SS

	Hit	Power	SB	Patience	Glove	Overall
	40/45	50/55	55	55	55	55

Born: 06/29/01	Age: 21	Bats: L	Top Comp: N/A
Height: 6-2	Weight: 210	Throws: R	

Season	Team	Age	Level	PA	1B	2B	3B	HR	SB	CS	BB%	K%	AVG	OBP	SLG	ISO
2019	BAL	18	R	121	20	5	2	1	2	2	9.09%	23.14%	0.259	0.331	0.370	0.111
2021	BAL	20	A	157	24	11	1	8	5	1	8.92%	29.30%	0.312	0.369	0.574	0.262
2021	BAL	20	A+	289	28	16	3	9	11	1	13.84%	30.10%	0.230	0.343	0.432	0.202
2021	BAL	20	AA	17	2	1	0	0	0	0	11.76%	58.82%	0.200	0.294	0.267	0.067

Background: Armed with three selections in the top two rounds of the 2019 draft, first time General Manager Mike Elias took the easy choice with the club's first pick, nabbing generational catching prospect Adley Rutschman #1, but dipped into the prep ranks for their second selection: John T. Morgan High School product Gunnar Henderson. Signed to a hefty $2.3 million deal, the lefty-swinging infielder cobbled together a mediocre .259/.331/.370 slash line during his debut in the Gulf Coast League that summer. Last season, though, the then-20-year-old Henderson opened the year up on a tear with Delmarva: in 35 games he slugged a hearty .312/.369/.574 with 20 extra-base knocks. The front office bounced the former high school star up to High-A near the end of June. After an abysmal start with Aberdeen, Henderson got his footing under him and convinced the organization he was ready for the minors' toughest challenge: Double-A. He spent the remaining week-and-a-half with Bowie, going 3-for-15. Overall, Henderson batted an aggregate .258/.350/.476 with 28 doubles, four triples, and 17 homeruns. He also swiped 16 bags in 18 attempts. Per *Weighted Runs Created Plus*, his aggregate production topped the league average threshold by a solid 20%.

Snippet from The 2020 Prospect Digest Handbook: The toolsy shortstop didn't show any meaningful red flags during his debut: he handled left- and right-handers equally well; showed a solid approach at the plate; flashed some average-ish power; and played a competent shortstop. He's likely ticketed for a spot on the Top 100 list in 2021. One more thought: very short, quick, compact swing.

Scouting Report: With regard to his longest stint at a minor league level last season, consider the following:

- Since 2006, only two 20-year-old hitters posted a 105 to 115 wRC+ with a 27% to 32% strikeout rate and a walk rate north of 12% in High-A (min. 275 PA): Samad Taylor and Gunnar Henderson.

It's a bit interesting that the player development czars decided to shove Henderson through the low levels of the minors as quickly as they did given Henderson's massive punch out rates. The lefty-swinging infielder whiffed 29.3% of the time in Low-A, 30.1% in High-A, and a whopping 58.8% in 17 plate appearances in Double-A. That's red flag #1. Now here's red flag #2: he was *hapless* against southpaws as well, hitting a paltry .189/.293/.349 in 123 plate appearances. Henderson showed more power than expected, belting out 49 extra-base hits, with half of his games played in pitcher-friendly environments. If he can pull in the punch outs, he's poised to be a solid MLB contributor. If not, he's a bench guy.

Ceiling: 3.0-win player
Risk: Moderate to High
MLB ETA: 2023

8. Drew Rom, LHP

FB	CB	SF	Command	Overall
55	55	55	55	50

Born: 12/05/99	Age: 23	Bats: L	Top Comp: Sean Manaea
Height: 6-2	Weight: 170	Throws: L	

Season	Team	Age	Level	IP	TBF	K/9	K%	BB/9	BB%	K-BB%	ERA	FIP	xFIP	Pit/Bat
2018	BAL	18	R	30.2	121	8.22	23.14%	1.76	4.96%	18.18%	1.76	3.23	3.49	1.66
2019	BAL	19	A	95.1	402	11.52	30.35%	3.12	8.21%	22.14%	2.93	2.74	2.93	3.98
2021	BAL	21	A+	67.2	275	9.71	26.55%	2.26	6.18%	20.36%	2.79	3.65	3.72	3.77
2021	BAL	21	AA	40.0	163	10.58	28.83%	2.03	5.52%	23.31%	3.83	3.94	3.09	4.05

Background: There were a few notable prospects taken in the fourth round of the 2018 draft, including: Milwaukee's surging left-hander Aaron Ashby, righty Kyle Bradish (who would eventually join Baltimore's farm system), Stanford ace Tristan Beck, Cincinnati minor leaguer Michael Siani, and – of course – left-hander Drew Rom, the 115th overall pick that year. Standing a solid 6-foot-2 and 170 pounds, the Highlands High School product entered the 2021 season coming off of strong back-to-back showings in the low levels of the minors. Rom struck out 28-to-6 strikeout-to-walk ratio in 30.2 innings with the Gulf Coast League during his debut. The front office pushed the teenage arm up to the South Atlantic League the following year. And he sparkled. In 21 appearances, 15 of which were starts, Rom averaged 11.5 strikeouts and 3.1 walks per nine innings. Last year, as MiLB action returned to the diamond, Rom ripped through High-A East for 67.2 innings and he continued to assert himself as one of the club's better prospects during his nine-game cameo in Double-A. Rom would go on to throw 107.2 total innings last season, striking 120 against only 26 free passes. He finished 2021 with an aggregate 3.51 ERA and 3.76 xFIP.

Snippet from The 2020 Prospect Digest Handbook: Rom looks like a #3/#4-type arm if the fastball can bump a couple ticks, something in the 92- to 93-mph range.

Scouting Report: A crafty lefty, but not in the pejorative sense. It's clear to see that the young southpaw not only has the chops to pitch at the big league level, but he possesses the guile and smarts to match. As hinted at in *The 2020 Prospect Digest*, Rom's heater did see an increase in velocity over the past couple seasons, going all the way up to 94 mph during an early July start in High-A. He'll complement the newly minted above-average offering with an above-average curveball and a high quality splitter. Rom will vary the movement on the splitter, sometimes allowing it to sweep in a slider-like break, and other times showing more natural tumble. The lefty shows a solid feel for the strike zone and often throws quality pitcher's pitches. Rom – for whatever reason – remains under-the-radar.

Ceiling: 2.0-win player
Risk: Moderate
MLB ETA: 2022/2023

9. Jordan Westburg, 3B/SS

Hit	Power	SB	Patience	Glove	Overall
50	45/50	50	55	55	50

Born: 02/18/99	Age: 23	Bats: R	Top Comp: N/A
Height: 6-3	Weight: 203	Throws: R	

Season	Team	Age	Level	PA	1B	2B	3B	HR	SB	CS	BB%	K%	AVG	OBP	SLG	ISO
2021	BAL	22	A	91	17	5	1	3	5	1	13.19%	26.37%	0.366	0.484	0.592	0.225
2021	BAL	22	A+	285	43	16	2	8	9	4	12.28%	24.91%	0.286	0.389	0.469	0.183
2021	BAL	22	AA	130	14	6	2	4	3	0	10.77%	24.62%	0.232	0.323	0.429	0.196

Background: The AL East club opened the 2020 draft with four straight collegiate hitters, selecting Heston Kjerstad and Jordan Westburg in the opening round. A solid contributor in Mississippi State's potent lineup, Westburg signed with the Orioles for a smidgeon over $2.3 million as the 30th overall pick. A part-time starter for the Bulldogs as true freshman, the 6-foot-3, 203-pound infielder batted a mediocre .248/.319/.388 with 11 doubles and a pair of dingers in 139 plate appearances. After ripping through the Perfect Game Collegiate Baseball League that summer, Westburg's offensive production improved noticeably during his sophomore campaign: he batted .294/.402/.457 with 21 doubles, two triples, and six long balls. The Texas-born prospect continued to hit as he squared off against the Cape Cod League that year as well, slugging .326/.385/.516 in 25 games with the Hyannis Harbor Hawks. Westburg got off to another strong start as the 2020 season opened, batting .317/.432/.517 before the year was prematurely closed due to COVID. Baltimore put their former first round pick on the Gunnar Henderson development path last season as he made his debut, going from Low-A to High-A and finally settling in for 30 games at Double-A. Westburg slugged an aggregate .285/.389/.479 with 27 doubles, five triples, and 15 homeruns.

Scouting Report: With regard to his longest stint at a minor league level last season, High-A, consider the following:

- Since 2006, only four 22-year-old hitters met the following criteria in High-A with one organization (min. 275 PA): 128 to 138 wRC+ total, a walk rate north rate of 12%, and a strikeout rate between 24% and 26%. Those four hitters: Eric Jagielo, Kyle Kubitza, Tyler Ramirez, and Jordan Westburg.

Unlike Gunnar Henderson, Westburg's strikeout rate slowly declined along each stop last season, going from 26.4% down to 24.6% in his final stop in Double-A. There's not enough thump in the bat to profile as an everyday third baseman. The glove is certainly good enough to stay at shortstop – or even second base – but the club was experimenting with him at the hot corner. Average hit tool, below-average power that projects to 50-grade at maturity, a little bit of speed. He looks like the prototypical low ceiling / high floor collegiate bat.

Ceiling: 2.0-win player
Risk: Moderate
MLB ETA: 2023

10. Kyle Stowers, LF/RF

Hit	Power	SB	Patience	Glove	Overall
45	55	35	55	50	45

Top Comp: Preston Tucker

Born: 01/02/98	Age: 24	Bats: L
Height: 6-3	Weight: 200	Throws: L

Season	Team	Age	Level	PA	1B	2B	3B	HR	SB	CS	BB%	K%	AVG	OBP	SLG	ISO
2019	BAL	21	A-	228	24	13	1	6	5	1	8.77%	23.25%	0.216	0.289	0.377	0.162
2021	BAL	23	A+	161	22	6	1	7	3	3	16.77%	34.16%	0.275	0.404	0.496	0.221
2021	BAL	23	AA	276	35	15	0	17	4	1	12.32%	30.43%	0.283	0.377	0.561	0.278
2021	BAL	23	AAA	93	17	2	0	3	1	0	12.90%	34.41%	0.272	0.366	0.407	0.136

Background: The franchise has had quite a bit of luck taking prospects out of Stanford, including Hall of Famer Mike Mussina and veteran outfielder Jeffrey Hammonds. In fact, the last time the club took a Stanford Cardinal as early as Kyle Stowers in the amateur draft was Hammonds, who was the fourth overall pick in 1992. Stowers didn't go nearly that high, though he earned a bonus just shy of $900,000. The 6-foot-3, 200-pound corner outfielder, who was taken in the third round three years ago, saw spare playing time as a true freshman for the Pac12 conference school. He earned a starting gig the following year, 2018, and batted .286/.383/.510 with 23 homeruns. And he followed that up with an even better showing during his junior campaign, slugging .303/.369/.523with 19 doubles, one triple, and nine homeruns. After an absolutely abysmal showing in the New York-Penn League after joining the organization, Stowers rocketed through the final three stops in the minor leagues during his first full season of action. In 124 games he batted .278/.383/.514 with 23 doubles, one triple, and 27 homeruns.

Snippet from The 2020 Prospect Digest Handbook: He looked completely helpless against fellow left-handers (.143/.231/.200).

Scouting Report: Consider the following:

- Since 2006, three 23-year-old hitters posted a 147 to 157 wRC+ with a walk rate between 11% and 13% in Double-A (min. 275 PA): J.D. Martinez, Jordan Brown, and – of course – Kyle Stowers. The differentiating factor between Stowers and the former pair is quite apparent: he whiffed twice frequently as Martinez and Brown.

Stowers hardly resembled the same hitter he appeared to be during his disastrous debut in 2019, showing more power and handling southpaws with aplomb last season. The problem, like a lot of the club's other top minor league bats not named Adley Rutschman, is Stowers' punch out rate. He whiffed 171 times in only 530 plate appearances – or 32.3% of the time. One interesting note: his K-rate against southpaws was 26.1% and posted a K-rate of 34.4% against right-handers. Above-average power. 45-grade bat. Average glove. Future fourth outfielder.

Ceiling: 1.5-win player
Risk: Moderate
MLB ETA: 2022

11. Connor Norby, 2B

Hit	Power	SB	Patience	Glove	Overall
55	45	40	50	50	45

Born: 06/08/00	Age: 22	Bats: R	Top Comp: N/A
Height: 5-10	Weight: 187	Throws: R	

Season	Team	Age	Level	PA	1B	2B	3B	HR	SB	CS	BB%	K%	AVG	OBP	SLG	ISO
2021	BAL	21	CPX	24	2	2	0	0	1	0	4.17%	29.17%	0.182	0.208	0.273	0.091
2021	BAL	21	A	126	20	4	1	3	5	3	16.67%	22.22%	0.283	0.413	0.434	0.152

Background: Norby's list of accolades throughout his high school career reads like a novella: 2017 Underclass High Honorable Mention by *Perfect Game*; 2018 *Rawlings-Perfect Game* Honorable Mention All-American; Second-Team All-Atlantic Regional selection by *Perfect Game*; and Ranked as the 89th best shortstop prospect and Top 500 recruit by *Perfect Game*. After wrapping up his final season at East Forsyth High School by batting .446, Norby looked abysmal at the plate during his abbreviated freshman season for the East Carolina Pirates, batting a lowly .194/.286/.290 in 35 plate appearances. His offensive prowess exploded during the COVID-shortened campaign, slugging a hearty .403/.439/.500 with a double, a triple, and a dinger in 17 games for the American Athletic Conference squad. And he was able to carry that momentum over into a dynamic junior campaign: in a career high 61 contests, he hit .415/.481/.659 with 15 doubles, 15 homeruns, and 18 stolen bases. He finished the year with a 34-to-33 strikeout-to-walk ratio as well. Baltimore drafted the talented infielder in the second round, 41st overall, last July and signed him to a deal worth $1.7 million. Norby appeared in 33 games during his professional debut, 26 coming in Low-A, hitting an aggregate .264/.380/.405 with six doubles, one triple, three homeruns, and six stolen bases.

Scouting Report: Per the usual, here's my pre-draft write-up:

"Consider the following:

- *Between 2011 and 2020, only one AAC hitter batted at least .400 in a season (min. 200 PA): Bryant Packard, who accomplished the feat for ECU in 2018.*

Packard, didn't have the peripherals that Norby does. So let's expand it. Consider the following:

- *Between 2011 and 2020, only five Division I hitters met the following criteria (min. 200 PA): .400/.475/.650 with a strikeout and walk rate between 11% and 14%. Those five hitters: Effrey Valdez, Goose Kallunki, Kevin Kaczmarski, D.J. Peterson, and Ryan Scott.*

Again, not great company to keep. Peterson is the only prospect of note. As for Norby, well, he plays an up-the-middle position, shows an above-average hit tool, 12- to 15-homerun potential, and a can run a little bit. He has the potential to be a fringy league average starter. He seems like a prospect the Rangers would be interested in."

Ceiling: 1.5-win player
Risk: Moderate
MLB ETA: 2023/2024

12. Zac Lowther, LHP

FB	CB	SL	CH	Command	Overall
50	50	50	50	45+	45

Born: 04/30/96	Age: 26	Bats: L	Top Comp: Bruce Chen
Height: 6-2	Weight: 235	Throws: L	

Season	Team	Age	Level	IP	TBF	K/9	K%	BB/9	BB%	K-BB%	ERA	FIP	xFIP	Pit/Bat
2018	BAL	22	A	31.0	115	14.81	44.35%	2.61	7.83%	36.52%	1.16	1.99	2.20	4.30
2018	BAL	22	A+	92.2	372	9.71	26.88%	2.53	6.99%	19.89%	2.53	3.01	3.11	4.01
2019	BAL	23	AA	148.0	593	9.36	25.97%	3.83	10.62%	15.35%	2.55	3.17	3.49	3.91
2021	BAL	25	AAA	30.1	144	9.79	22.92%	4.75	11.11%	11.81%	6.53	4.78	4.76	4.01

Background: Part of the 2017 draft class that added fellow southpaw D.L. Hall and middle infielder / center fielder Adam Hall to the organization. Baltimore selected the hefty lefty in the second round that year after a stellar junior campaign for the Xavier Musketeers. Billed as a safe, low ceiling / high floor, fast moving collegiate arm, Lowther made quick work of the New York-Penn League, blitzed through Low-A, and he spent the entire 2019 season squaring off against the Eastern League competition. Last season, though, Lowther struggled with inconsistency and injuries as he yo-yoed between the big leagues and nearly every minor league level. He would finish the year with 39.1 innings in the minors, striking out 45 and walking 18 to go along with a 5.49 ERA. He tossed another 29.2 innings of work with the Orioles, averaging 9.1 strikeouts and 3.9 walks per nine innings.

Snippet from The 2020 Prospect Digest Handbook: Lowther is what Lowther's always been: a safe, low ceiling, fast moving pitching prospect. He's going to be a backend starting pitcher for a long time, hovering near league average status. The command, by the way, wavered at points with Bowie last season. And he's the type of pitcher where that can't happen too often.

Scouting Report: Lowther is like bad pizza. You'll still go back for a second or third slice, but there are tons of better options. Four average, unremarkable offerings: a 90- to 91-mph heater, a laterally darting slider that's typically tough on southpaws, a loopy curveball that will occasionally flash above-average, and low- to mid-80s changeup. Lowther was always more of a strike-thrower than a command guy, and that's just been exposed as he moved up the ladder. Bad body pitcher, but he'll continue to get looks as a crafty lefty on non-contending teams as an innings-eater backend starting pitcher.

Ceiling: 1.0- to 1.5-win player
Risk: Low to Moderate
MLB ETA: Debuted in 2021

13. Hudson Haskin, CF

Hit	Power	SB	Patience	Glove	Overall
50	40	55	50	50	45

Born: 12/31/98	Age: 23	Bats: R	Top Comp: N/A
Height: 6-2	Weight: 200	Throws: R	

Season	Team	Age	Level	PA	1B	2B	3B	HR	SB	CS	BB%	K%	AVG	OBP	SLG	ISO
2021	BAL	22	A	254	41	13	1	5	17	5	8.66%	23.62%	0.276	0.377	0.415	0.138
2021	BAL	22	A+	109	17	6	2	0	5	2	9.17%	16.51%	0.275	0.389	0.385	0.110

Background: Fun Fact Part I: The most successful big league player to come out of Tulane University is lefty reliever Aaron Loup, who just signed a two-year deal with the New York Metropolitans for $17 million. Fun Fact Part II: Tulane University has produced 10 players chosen in the first two rounds of the amateur draft. The 39th overall player taken two years ago, Haskin, who signed with the Orioles for $1,906,800, was a revelation during his first collegiate season with the Green Wave: he slugged a scorching .372/.459/.647 with 19 doubles, four triples, 10 homeruns, and four stolen bases. Haskin got off to a solid start to 2020, batting .333/.452/.500 before COVID prematurely ended the season. Last season the 6-foot-2, 200-pound outfielder split time between Delmarva and Aberdeen, batting an aggregate .276/.381/.406 with 19 doubles, three triples, and five homeruns. He also swiped 22 bags in 29 attempts. Per *Weighted Runs Created Plus*, Haskin's overall production topped the league average mark by a solid 20%.

Scouting Report: Fairing much better in the minor leagues than his former teammate Kody Hoese, who's sporting a career .233/.297/.334 minor league slash line. Haskin is a well-rounded prospect with a low ceiling and moderately high floor. 50-grade hit tool. 40-grade power. Above-average speed. Passable glove in center field. There's a lot of movement in Haskin's swing. Standing from nearly a perfect upright position, Haskin's take a massive stride to the ball – larger than nearly everyone I can think of – which causes a lot of movement in his head (north / south direction). He just "feels" like a fourth outfielder.

Ceiling: 1.0- to 1.5-win player
Risk: Moderate
MLB ETA: 2022

14. Darell Hernaiz, IF

Hit	Power	SB	Patience	Glove	Overall
40/45	35/45	55	50	55	45

Born: 08/03/01	Age: 20	Bats: R	Top Comp: N/A
Height: 6-1	Weight: 170	Throws: R	

Season	Team	Age	Level	PA	1B	2B	3B	HR	SB	CS	BB%	K%	AVG	OBP	SLG	ISO
2019	BAL	17	R	116	21	2	1	2	5	0	14.66%	22.41%	0.263	0.371	0.364	0.101
2021	BAL	19	A	410	85	12	0	6	22	6	6.83%	17.07%	0.277	0.333	0.358	0.081

Background: Fun Fact: Darell Hernaiz's old man, Juan, was a 12th round pick by the Dodgers in 1992 and spent parts of eight seasons in the minor leagues but petered out in Double-A. Taken in the fifth round and signed for $400,000 three years ago, the younger Hernaiz turned in a solid debut showing in the Gulf Coast League that year, batting .263/.371/.364 with five extra-base knocks in 29 games in the Gulf Coast League. Last season the front office bounced the then-19-year-old up to Low-A for his first taste of full season action. The 6-foot-1, 170-pound infielder responded with a solid .277/.333/.358 slash line, belting out 12 doubles and six homeruns to go along with 22 stolen bases in 28 total attempts. Per *Weighted Runs Created Plus,* his overall production was 8% *below* the league average.

Scouting Report: As consistent an offensive performer as you'll see in 2021. Hernaiz's monthly OPS totals throughout the year (beginning in May): .645, .682, .687, and .667. Above-average speed with solid instincts on the base paths. Hernaiz owns a strong glove at either middle infielder position. And despite slamming six dingers, the Puerto Rican prospect shows very little thump in his bat – though he projects to reach

12- to 15-homeruns at full maturity. Hernaiz owns the basic building blocks for a low end starting middle infielder at the big league level. But the bat needs to uptick to average or better for him to get there. Hernaiz is only entering his age-20 season, so plenty of time of his side.

Ceiling: 1.0- to 1.5-win player
Risk: Moderate
MLB ETA: 2024/2025

15. Kyle Bradish, RHP

	FB	CB	SL	CH	Command	Overall
	50	55	55	45/50	45	40

Born: 09/12/96	Age: 25	Bats: R	Top Comp: N/A
Height: 6-4	Weight: 220	Throws: R	

Season	Team	Age	Level	IP	TBF	K/9	K%	BB/9	BB%	K-BB%	ERA	FIP	xFIP	Pit/Bat
2019	LAA	22	A+	101.0	444	10.69	27.03%	4.72	11.94%	15.09%	4.28	4.08	3.87	3.95
2021	BAL	24	AA	13.2	52	17.12	50.00%	3.29	9.62%	40.38%	0.00	0.81	1.61	4.29
2021	BAL	24	AAA	86.2	378	10.90	27.78%	4.05	10.32%	17.46%	4.26	3.79	4.07	4.10

Background: Taken by the Los Angeles Angels in the fourth round of the 2018 draft, just six picks after the Orioles snagged lefty Drew Rom. Roughly a year-and-a-half later Baltimore acquired the New Mexico State University hurler, along with Kyle Brnovich, Zach Peek, and Isaac Mattson in exchange for former Orioles top prospect Dylan Bundy. Bradish opened the 2021 campaign up with three incredibly dominant starts with Bowie in Double-A, posting a 0.00 ERA while averaging 17.1 strikeouts and just 3.3 walks per nine innings of work. The Arizona native was promptly promoted up to Triple-A – where he more than held his own. In 86.2 innings with the Norfolk Tide, the 6-foot-4, 220-pound right-hander struck out 131 and walked 44 to go along with a 4.26 ERA, a 3.79 FIP, and a 4.07 xFIP.

Scouting Report: Consider the following:

- Since 2006, only three 24-year-old arms posted a 26.5% to 28.5% strikeout percentage with a walk percentage between 9% and 12% in Triple-A (min. 75 IP): Alex Meyer, Rogelio Armenteros, and – of course – Kyle Bradish.

Bradish became the soup du jour after his phenomenal start to the year last season. After all, who the hell *wouldn't?* But the production, repertoire, and command all paint a different story. In a late July start, Bradish's heater was sitting in the 91- to 93-mph range. A few starts later it touched 94-mph. But either way, it's too hittable, too average. The big righty will mix in a pair of above-average breaking balls that sometimes seem to blend together and a fringy changeup. Throw in 45-grade command and his age – he's entering his age-25 season – and Bradish's ceiling is somewhere between a middle relief arm and/or an up-and-down starting pitcher.

Ceiling: 1.0-win player
Risk: Low to Moderate
MLB ETA: 2022

16. Yusniel Diaz, OF

	Hit	Power	SB	Patience	Glove	Overall
	45	45	35	50	50	45

Born: 10/07/96	Age: 25	Bats: R	Top Comp: N/A
Height: 6-1	Weight: 215	Throws: R	

Season	Team	Age	Level	PA	1B	2B	3B	HR	SB	CS	BB%	K%	AVG	OBP	SLG	ISO
2018	LAD	21	AA	264	49	10	4	6	8	8	15.53%	14.77%	0.314	0.428	0.477	0.164
2018	BAL	21	AA	152	21	5	1	5	4	5	11.84%	18.42%	0.239	0.329	0.403	0.164
2019	BAL	22	A-	11	0	3	0	0	0	0	9.09%	9.09%	0.333	0.455	0.667	0.333
2019	BAL	22	A+	25	6	0	0	0	0	0	12.00%	28.00%	0.273	0.360	0.273	0.000
2019	BAL	22	AA	322	41	19	4	11	0	3	9.94%	20.81%	0.262	0.335	0.472	0.210
2021	BAL	24	AA	44	3	3	0	1	1	0	9.09%	29.55%	0.179	0.273	0.333	0.154
2021	BAL	24	AAA	209	21	4	1	4	1	2	6.70%	33.01%	0.157	0.225	0.251	0.094

Background: The Dodgers dominated the amateur international scene in 2015, signing a trio of high profile Cuban prospects: Yadier Alvarez, Omar Estevez, and Yusniel Diaz. Measuring 6-foot-1 and 215 pounds, Diaz earned a massive bonus totaling more than $15 million from the National League West powerhouse. Less than three years later the Dodgers dealt the young outfielder – along with Dean Kremer, Rylan Bannon, Zach Pop, and Breyvic Valera – to the Orioles in exchange for future Hall of Famer Manny Machado. Diaz looked to be on the precipice on cracking a big league roster following his solid showing in Double-A in 2019: he batted a respectable .262/.335/.472 as a 22-year-old in the minors' toughest level. But his 2021 season was an unmitigated disaster as he dealt with severe quad and toes issues which limited him to just 65 games. He finished the year with a vomitous .161/.233/.265 slash line, belting out only seven doubles, one triple, and five long balls.

Snippet from The 2020 Prospect Digest Handbook: Above-average or better tools across the board: plus bat, above-average pop, solid eye and contact skills at the plate, and he can play a solid center and right fields. Diaz is at an interesting precipice in his career as he enters his age-23 season. He's either going to take that next step forward into stardom, which could very well happen under the new guidance of the player development engine, or he simply stays very good.

Scouting Report: Just how poorly did Diaz perform during his 54-game stint in Triple-A last season? His production, per *Weighted Runs Created Plus*, was a laughably craptastic 73% *below* the league average mark. Diaz's once steady bat wilted with Norfolk as his strikeout rate skyrocketed to a career worst 33%. He showed no power or any underlying skills. The most damning statistical oddity from his season: he only had multiple-hit games just five times. That's it. The Cuban import has an extensive track record of solid or better offensive performances, so he'll earn a mulligan.

Ceiling: 1.5-win player
Risk: High
MLB ETA: 2022

17. Reed Trimble, CF

	Hit	Power	SB	Patience	Glove	Overall
	40/45	50	55	45	50	40

Born: 06/06/00	Age: 22	Bats: B	Top Comp: N/A
Height: 6-0	Weight: 180	Throws: R	

Season	Team	Age	Level	PA	1B	2B	3B	HR	SB	CS	BB%	K%	AVG	OBP	SLG	ISO
2021	BAL	21	CPX	18	4	1	0	0	2	0	16.67%	22.22%	0.333	0.444	0.400	0.067
2021	BAL	21	A	76	10	1	0	0	1	0	11.84%	27.63%	0.169	0.276	0.185	0.015

Background: A stellar First-Team All-State ballplayer at Northwest Rankin High School during his senior season, Trimble torched the competition by batting .469 with 15 doubles, five triples, and nine homeruns while scoring 50 runs and driving in another 51. The 6-foot, 180-pound center fielder began his collegiate career with a solid showing in 2020, hitting .275/.318/.400 for Southern Mississippi before COVID prematurely ended the season. Last year, the switch-hitting Trimble opened quite a few eyes as he slugged .345/.414/.638 with 14 doubles, two triples, 17 homeruns, and 12 stolen bases. His 17 long balls trailed just six behind the nation's leaders, South Carolina's Wes Clarke and Florida State's Matheu Nelson. Baltimore selected the Mississippi-born Trimble in the second round, 65th overall, and signed him to below-slot bonus worth $800,000. He appeared in 22 games between the Complex League and Delmarva, hitting .200/.309/.225 with a pair of doubles in 94 trips to the plate.

Scouting Report: The University of Southern Mississippi's churned out a lot of baseball talent throughout the years, including Brian Dozier and Chad Bradford. Behind the Twins' selection of Matt Wallner in the first round in 2019, Trimble is the earliest pick from the Conference USA team since the Brandon Parker, the 55th pick in 1997 by the Mariners. With regard to his production last season, consider the following:

- Between 2011 and 2020, only one Division I hitter – in any conference – met the following criteria in a season (min. 250 PA): hit .340/.400/.630 with a walk rate between 6% and 8% and strikeout rate between 16% and 18%. That hitter: Seattle's Kyle Lewis, the 11th overall pick in 2016. Obviously, Trimble's production in 2021 places him in the aforementioned criteria.

Solid power from a smaller frame thanks to great bat speed and a short compact swing. Trimble runs well and should be able to stay in center field. His lack of a collegiate track record, as well as success against a lower tiered conference raise a few red flags. Trimble looks a like a potential fourth outfielder, a poor man's Johnny Damon.

Ceiling: 1.0-win player
Risk: Moderate
MLB ETA: 2024/2025

18. Adam Hall, 2B/SS/CF

	Hit	Power	SB	Patience	Glove	Overall
	50/55	40	60	45	50	40

Born: 05/22/99	Age: 23	Bats: R	Top Comp: N/A
Height: 5-11	Weight: 165	Throws: R	

Season	Team	Age	Level	PA	1B	2B	3B	HR	SB	CS	BB%	K%	AVG	OBP	SLG	ISO
2018	BAL	19	A-	256	52	9	3	1	22	5	6.64%	22.66%	0.293	0.368	0.374	0.081
2019	BAL	20	A	534	107	22	4	5	33	9	8.43%	21.91%	0.298	0.385	0.395	0.097
2021	BAL	22	A+	338	55	13	2	3	26	1	7.10%	29.59%	0.248	0.335	0.337	0.088

Background: Born in Hamilton, Bermuda, the Orioles selected Hall in the second round in 2017 out of A B Lucas Secondary School – which is located in London, Ontario, Canada. The 5-foot-11, 165-pound middle infielder / center fielder put together solid showings in 2018 and 2019, as he batted .293/.368/.374 and .298/.385/.395 in the New York-Penn and South Atlantic Leagues. Last season, though, Hall stumbled for the first time in his professional career as he squared off against the High-A competition. In 81 games with the

Aberdeen IronBirds, he batted a disappointing .248/.335/.337 with just 13 doubles, a pair of triples, three homeruns, and 26 stolen bases (in only 27 total attempts). His production, per *Weighted Runs Created Plus*, was 11% below the league average.

Snippet from The 2020 Prospect Digest Handbook: The power is still below-average, but it's trending in the right direction. The hit tool has a chance – albeit a bit of a long shot – to become a plus weapon. The speed is already there. Defensively, he grades out between average and slightly better than average at either up the middle position. Hall is very reminiscent of Tampa Bay Rays infielder – and former top prospect – Daniel Robertson with a little less pop.

Scouting Report: Consider the following:

- Since 2006, only five 22-year-old hitters posted an 85 to 95 wRC+ with a strikeout rate between 28.5% and 30.5% in High-A with one organization (min. 300 PA): Josh Sale, Denny Almonte, Daniel Rams, Will Swanner, and – of course – Adam Hall.

In several ways Hall remained the smae: plus speed, little power, average patience, and a solid glove at a few up-the-middle positions. The big change, though, was his massive swing-and-miss tendencies in 2021. He whiffed in nearly 30% of his plate appearances with Aberdeen, up from his typical 22% K-rates in his first three seasons. Things seemed to be clicking for Hall after an abysmal first two months, but he missed roughly three weeks due to a quad injury. He did bat a Hall-esque .274/.363/.384 over his final 40 games.

Ceiling: 1.0-win player
Risk: Moderate
MLB ETA: 2023/2024

19. John Rhodes, 1B/RF

Hit	Power	SB	Patience	Glove	Overall
45/50	45/50	30	55	50	40

Born: 08/15/00	Age: 21	Bats: R	Top Comp: Jordan Luplow.
Height: 6-0	Weight: 200	Throws: R	

Season	Team	Age	Level	PA	1B	2B	3B	HR	SB	CS	BB%	K%	AVG	OBP	SLG	ISO
2021	BAL	20	CPX	16	2	0	0	0	0	0	18.75%	18.75%	0.154	0.313	0.154	0.000
2021	BAL	20	A	105	19	4	0	2	6	0	8.57%	15.24%	0.266	0.343	0.372	0.106

Background: Undrafted as he left Chattanooga Christian High School – despite being named as a 20119 MaxPreps Second-Team Medium Schools All-American – the 6-foot, 200-pound prospect made an immediate impression and forced the nation take note during his abbreviated, COVID-shortened freshman campaign at the University of Kentucky. Appearing in 17 games with the Wildcats, Rhoades slugged a Hornsby-esque .426/.485/.672 with 10 doubles, one triple, and one homerun. Then the awards and recognitions started to roll in, including: National Co-Freshman of the Year (*Collegiate Baseball News*) and Third-Team All-America (*Collegiate Baseball News*). Heading into his first full season of college action in 2021, Rhodes was a consensus Top 65 MLB draft prospect. Then he struggled. In 52 games with the SEC squad, he batted .251/.397/.508 with 15 doubles and 11 homers. Baltimore selected him in the third round, 76th overall, and signed him to a deal worth $1,375,000 – roughly $500,000 above the recommended slot value. Rhodes appeared in 23 games with Delmarva last season, hitting a mediocre .266/.343/.372 with four doubles and a pair of homeruns.

Scouting Report: Young for the draft class thanks to the reclassification, Rhodes is only entering his age-21 season and has a chance as a solid, saber-slanted offensive performer. 50-grade power, solid contact skills, above-average patience at the plate. Thanks to his age and lack of experience in college, there's more projection with Rhodes compared to most collegiate third rounders. He used to be a former high school catcher, but he broke his back as a freshman and had to permanently move away from the position.

Ceiling: 1.0-win player
Risk: Moderate
MLB ETA: 2024

20. Brandon Young, RHP

FB	CB	SL	CH	Command	Overall
50	55/60	50	45	45	40

Born: 08/19/98	Age: 23	Bats: R	Top Comp: Peter Solomon
Height: 6-6	Weight: 210	Throws: R	

Season	Team	Age	Level	IP	TBF	K/9	K%	BB/9	BB%	K-BB%	ERA	FIP	xFIP	Pit/Bat
2021	BAL	22	A	47.1	198	11.41	30.30%	4.18	11.11%	19.19%	3.23	4.00	4.19	3.97
2021	BAL	22	A+	37.0	153	13.14	35.29%	3.65	9.80%	25.49%	3.89	3.71	3.25	3.97

Background: A bit of a swing-man during his first season at Louisiana-Lafayette in 2019, making nine starts and seven relief appearances. The results: 54.1 innings, 72 strikeouts, and 34 free passes. The massive 6-foot-6, 210-pound right-hander got off to a blistering start the following year, averaging 13.5 strikeouts and just 3.3 walks per nine innings while compiling a 1.09 ERA before the COVID-imposed shutdown. Baltimore offered the undrafted a hurler a contract. And after his debut season in 2021, it's looking like a tremendous scouting job by the front office. Splitting time between Delmarva and Aberdeen, Young posted a 114-to-37 strikeout-to-walk ratio with a 3.52 ERA in only 84.1 innings of work.

Scouting Report: Standard four-pitch mix: fastball, curveball, slider, and changeup. Young's heater sits in the low 90s with a little bit of life up in the zone. His deuce, his best offspeed offering, is a hammer with 12-6 downward bite that occasionally flashes plus. His slider is erratic; the changeup is below-average. During Orioles GM Mike Elias' career with Houston, the Astros were home to several intriguing older-ish hurlers with gaudy strikeout numbers like Tyler Ivey and Peter Solomon. Expect Brandon Young to follow a similar career path.

Ceiling: 1.0-win player
Risk: Moderate
MLB ETA: 2024

Boston Red Sox

Top Prospects

1. Nick Yorke, 2B

	Hit	Power	SB	Patience	Glove	Overall
	55/65	50/55	50	55	55	60

Born: 04/02/02	Age: 20	Bats: R	Top Comp: Jose Altuve
Height: 6-0	Weight: 200	Throws: R	

Season	Team	Age	Level	PA	1B	2B	3B	HR	SB	CS	BB%	K%	AVG	OBP	SLG	ISO
2021	BOS	19	A	346	67	14	4	10	11	8	11.85%	13.58%	0.323	0.413	0.500	0.177
2021	BOS	19	A+	96	17	6	1	4	2	1	11.46%	22.92%	0.333	0.406	0.571	0.238

Background: A prep shortstop that was almost immediately identified as a professional keystone manager. Boston snagged the well-built middle infielder in the opening round, 17th overall, two years ago. The two sides came in agreement on a bonus worth $2.7 million. And that hefty seven-figure bonus looks like a smashing team-friendly deal for the Red Sox just one season later. Debuting in Low-A East, the 6-foot, 200-pound second baseman slugged a healthy .323/.413/.500 with 14 doubles, four triples, and 10 homeruns against the significantly older competition. But Yorke wasn't done. The front office bounced him up to High-A in late August for another 21 contests. His slash line maintained status quo: .333/.406/.571. When the dust finally settled, the Red Sox named their 2020 first rounder their Minor League Player of the Year after hitting an aggregate .325/.412/.516 with 20 doubles, five triples, and 14 homeruns to go along with 13 stolen bases. His overall production, per *Weighted Runs Created Plus*, topped the league average mark by a whopping 49%.

Scouting Report: Consider the following:

- Since 2006, only four 19-year-old hitters met the following criteria in a Low-A season with one organization (min. 300 PA): 140 to 150 wRC+ total and a sub-15% strikeout rate. Those four hitters: Jose Ramirez, Luis Arraez, Royce Lewis, and – of course – Mr. Red Sox Nick Yorke.
- Ramirez, of course, is one of the best players on the planet who is on a Hall of Fame trajectory. Arraez is sporting an impressive .313/.374/.403 slash line through his first three big league seasons. And Lewis, before the injuries, was a consensus Top 10 prospect in baseball.

The easy comparison is throw Yorke's way is the heir apparent to Dustin Pedroia's (future Hall of Fame) throne. And, to be honest, it seems kind of fitting. Yorke has a chance for a plus (maybe even plus-plus) hit tool, average power, average speed, and a nose for first base that will only further pump up his value. There's really nothing to not like with the skill set. He plays above-average defense and may win a few Gold Gloves. He's just…really good. In terms of big league ceiling, think: .300/.370/.440.

Oh, yeah, one more note: after a slow start to the year Yorke, who batted .177/.250/.190 over his first 20 games, slugged a scorching .365/.452/.602 the remainder of the way. I think Yorke's in the conversation for best prospect in the game.

Ceiling: 5.0-win player
Risk: Moderate
MLB ETA: 2023/2024

2. Marcelo Mayer, SS

	Hit	Power	SB	Patience	Glove	Overall
	40/55	40/50	50	55	55	60

Born: 12/12/02	Age: 19	Bats: L	Top Comp: N/A
Height: 6-3	Weight: 188	Throws: R	

Season	Team	Age	Level	PA	1B	2B	3B	HR	SB	CS	BB%	K%	AVG	OBP	SLG	ISO
2021	BOS	18	CPX	107	17	4	1	3	7	1	14.02%	25.23%	0.275	0.377	0.440	0.165

Background: Eastlake High School in Chula Vista, California, has a rich baseball history. The high school has graduated 12 players to the professional ranks in the 21st century, including: four-time All-Star and multiple Gold Glove winning first baseman Adrian Gonzalez, the first player chosen in the 2000 draft, and Twins minor leaguer Keoni Cavaco, the 13th overall selection three years ago. Enter: Marcelo Mayer, a 6-foot-3, 195-pound, lefty-swinging shortstop. A four-year starter for the Titans' vaunted high school program, Mayer verbally committed to play for the USC Trojans after his first high school season. The burgeoning star followed that up by hitting a respectable .261 while making five appearances on the bump. In a COVID-shortened junior campaign Mayer batted .294 with a pair of doubles, three homeruns, and six RBIs. The Californian spent some time on the West Roster of the Perfect Game All-American Classic. Last season Mayer vaulted his Eastlake squad to the third best team in country en route to batting .437 with 13 long balls, 40 RBIs, and 16 stolen bases. Perhaps the best news: the sweet-swinging middle infielder sported an impeccable 25-to-3 strikeout-to-walk ratio through his first 25 high school games. Long thought of to be the frontrunner for the #1 overall pick, Mayer slide to Boston with the fourth selection and signed a massive $6,664,000 deal. The lefty-swinging middle infielder held his own during his debut in the Florida Complex League, slugging .275/.377/.440 with four doubles, one triple, and three homeruns to go along with seven stolen bases. His overall production during his debut, according to *Weighted Runs Created Plus*, topped the league average threshold by 21%.

Scouting Report: Per the usual, here's what I wrote about Mayer prior to the draft last July:

"Typical shortstop build with twitchy movements. Mayer not only looks like a capable professional shortstop, but one that should provide added value on the defensive side of the spectrum. Solid arm with body control that allows him to make difficult, on-the-move throws with relative ease. Mayer is also comfortable ranging to either of his body. The Eastlake, California, native owns a short, quick, compact swing with natural loft. He has surprisingly thump for his lean build. He adjusts to breaking balls well. In terms of ceiling comps, think: Andrelton Simmons' 2018 season for the Angels when he slugged .278/.331/.421."

Ceiling: 5.0-win player
Risk: Moderate
MLB ETA: 2025

3. Brayan Bello, RHP

FB	SL	CH	Command	Overall
70	55	50/55	55	60

Born: 05/17/99	Age: 23	Bats: R	Top Comp: Luis Severino
Height: 6-1	Weight: 170	Throws: R	

Season	Team	Age	Level	IP	TBF	K/9	K%	BB/9	BB%	K-BB%	ERA	FIP	xFIP	Pit/Bat
2018	BOS	19	R	64.1	242	9.51	28.10%	1.40	4.13%	23.97%	1.68	1.94	2.33	1.76
2019	BOS	20	A	117.2	526	9.10	22.62%	2.91	7.22%	15.40%	5.43	3.66	3.52	3.75
2021	BOS	22	A+	31.2	122	12.79	36.89%	1.99	5.74%	31.15%	2.27	2.82	2.81	3.93
2021	BOS	22	AA	63.2	280	12.30	31.07%	3.39	8.57%	22.50%	4.66	3.12	3.33	4.01

Background: In terms of age as an amateur free agent, by the time the Red Sox signed the righty out of the Dominican Republic he was practically a geriatric. Nearly 18-years-old and handed a small pittance of $28,000, the return on the franchise's investment would put most people into retirement. Bello dominated – as expected – the Dominican Summer League as a 19-year-old in 2018. He posted an impressive 119-to-38 strikeout-to-walk ratio in 117.2 innings with Greenville the following year. And last season, as minor league ball returned to action, he made quick work of High-A before spending the last several months of action squaring off – and dominating – the toughest level as a prospect, Double-A. The wiry, lightning bolt-slinging right-hander tossed 95.1 innings, recording an ace-in-the-waiting-esque 132-to-31 strikeout-to-walk ratio. He finished the year with an aggregate 3.87 ERA and a 3.02 FIP. The Red Sox named him their Minor League Pitcher of the Year in 2021.

Snippet from The 2020 Prospect Digest Handbook: Bello, showing a lightning-quick arm, has an explosive above-average fastball that has a solid chance of bumping up to plus territory as he fills out. It was hovering in the 93- to 94-mph range with relative ease. He has the makings of a #4-type arm, maybe more. There's a lot to like.

Scouting Report: As I prognosticated two years ago, Bello's fastball bumped up – though no one would have surmised just how much he had in the tank. The young right-hander was pumping triple-digits – with little effort – during the summer. He combined that plus-plus offering with an above-average power slider and a low 90s tumbling changeup. Throw in above-average command and Bello's sporting a #2, maybe even bonafide #1-type potential. With regard to his work in Double-A, consider the following:

- Since 2006, only four 22-year-old pitchers posted a strikeout percentage between 30% and 32% with a walk percentage between 7% and 10% in Double-A with one organization (min. 60 IP): Mike Minor, Reynaldo Lopez, A.J. Puk, and – of course – Brayan Bello.

Ceiling: 5.0-win player
Risk: Moderate
MLB ETA: 2022

4. Triston Casas, 1B

Hit	Power	SB	Patience	Glove	Overall
45/55	55/60	45/30	60	45	60

Born: 01/15/00	Age: 22	Bats: L	Top Comp: Anthony Rizzo
Height: 6-4	Weight: 252	Throws: R	

Season	Team	Age	Level	PA	1B	2B	3B	HR	SB	CS	BB%	K%	AVG	OBP	SLG	ISO
2019	BOS	19	A	493	58	25	5	19	3	2	11.76%	23.53%	0.254	0.349	0.472	0.218
2021	BOS	21	AA	329	51	12	2	13	6	3	14.89%	19.15%	0.284	0.395	0.484	0.200
2021	BOS	21	AAA	42	3	3	1	1	1	0	19.05%	19.05%	0.242	0.381	0.485	0.242

Background: One of the prep players that got overexposed during the scouting process simply due to his notoriety. A result, simply, based upon how long the hulking infielder had been a known commodity. Casas, a massive 6-foot-4, 252-pound prospect, fell to the Red Sox with the 26th overall pick in the 2018. After the sides agreed to a deal worth a smidgeon over $2.5 million, the front office set him loose on the Gulf Coast League with ill intentions. But after five plate appearances, spanning just two games, Casas hit the disabled list with a UCL issue in his thumb. The lefty-swinging corner infielder, who is now relegated to first base (as everyone expected), got pushed up to the South Atlantic League testing grounds the following year. And he shined. Brightly. Appearing in 118 games with the Greenville Drive, Casas slugged a hearty, stick-to-your-bones .254/.349/.472 with 25 doubles, five triples, and 19 dingers. He also appeared in a pair of games in the old Carolina League to cap off his successful first full season. Last season, as minor league ball returned to a normal way of life, Red Sox management decided to accelerate their aggressive development schedule for Casas and shoved him directly into the minors' toughest level, Double-A, at the ripe old age of 21-year-old. The Florida-native responded in kind, batting .284/.395/.484 with 12 doubles, two triples, and 13 homeruns in only 77 games of action. His overall production, as measured by *Weighted Runs Created Plus*, topped the league average mark by 42%. Casas also spent nine games in AAA too, hitting .242/.381/.485.

Snippet from The 2020 Prospect Digest Handbook: With respect to Casas's peripherals: they're all quite promising – a strong eye, plus in-game power, and a solid enough hit tool. He did struggle against fellow southpaws, so that needs to be monitored closely (he batted .213/.317/.416 vs. LHP).

Scouting Report: Consider the following:

- Since 2006, only two 21-year-old hitters met the following criteria in a Double-A season with one organization (min. 300 PA): 137 to 147 wRC+ total, a double-digit walk rate and a sub-20% strikeout rate. Those hitters: Logan Morrison and – of course – Triston Casas.

The good news: on the whole, Casas passed the Double-A test with flying colors as he hit for average, power, walked a ton, and made consistent contact. The bad news: he is still struggling – mightily – against left-handers. After cobbling together a lowly .213/.317/.416 showing against them in 2019, Double-A southpaws treated him even worse in 2021 as they held him to a lowly .219/.289/.301. Further cause for concern: Casas posted a 52-to-51 strikeout-to-walk ratio vs. RHP in 2021, but a 20-to-6 mark vs. LHP. All the ingredients to be an Anthony Rizzo-type cornerstone are sitting in the pot, the only thing from stopping it is the left-handed stove knob is broken. One more thought: Rizzo eventually learned how to handle lefties. And Casas has plenty of time on his side.

Ceiling: 4.0-win player
Risk: Moderate
MLB ETA: 2022/2023

5. Gilberto Jimenez, CF

	Hit	Power	SB	Patience	Glove	Overall
	50/60	35/45	50/60	40/45	40/55	55

Born: 07/08/00	Age: 21	Bats: B	Top Comp: Denard Span
Height: 5-11	Weight: 212	Throws: R	

Season	Team	Age	Level	PA	1B	2B	3B	HR	SB	CS	BB%	K%	AVG	OBP	SLG	ISO
2018	BOS	17	R	284	64	10	8	0	16	14	6.69%	14.08%	0.319	0.384	0.420	0.101
2019	BOS	18	A-	254	67	11	3	3	14	6	5.12%	14.96%	0.359	0.393	0.470	0.111
2021	BOS	20	A	408	89	16	6	3	13	8	4.66%	21.08%	0.306	0.346	0.405	0.099

Background: Chad Jennings, over at *The Athletic*, has a fascinating article around the Sox's acquisition of Gilberto Jimenez and right-hander Brayan Bello. The speedy switch-hitting center fielder opened the club's eyes after a blazing 60-yard dash time, 6.5 seconds, in the rain, on a wet track. A little while later the storied organization ponied up a rather paltry $100,000 bonus to sign the Dominican-born prospect. A year later they let him loose on the foreign rookie league competition. He responded by batting .319/.384/.420 with 10 doubles and eight triples to go along with 16 stolen bases. Jimenez spent the next season, 2019, absolutely dominating the New York-Penn League pitching: in 59 games with the Lowell Spinners, the well-built 5-foot-11, 212-pound outfielder slugged a hearty .359/.393/.470 with 11 doubles, three triples, and three homeruns to go along with 14 stolen bases. Last season the then-20-year-old moved up to full season action for the first time. And the results remain quite promising. In a career best 94 games, Jimenez hit .306/.346/.405 with 16 doubles, six triples, three homeruns, and 13 stolen bases. Per *Weighted Runs Created Plus*, his production topped the league average threshold by 5%.

Snippet from The 2020 Prospect Digest Handbook: Jimenez is a rare five-tool athlete with the potential for above-average to plus tools across the board. As a young switch-hitter, he handles lefties and righties well, plays an up-the-middle position (albeit incredibly raw), and shows an incredible knack for consistently barreling up the baseball. The lone knock on Jimenez: he's not overly patient, but it should improve with time.

Scouting Report: Consider the following:

- Since 2006, only three 20-year-old hitters met the following criteria in a Low-A season with one organization (min. 350 PA): 100 to 110 wRC+ total, a sub-6.0% walk rate, and a strikeout rate between 19% and 22%. Those three hitters: Miguel Aparicio, Ulrich Bojarski, and – of course – Gilberto Jimenez.

Raw, but plenty of intriguing talent and athleticism. As noted by Jennings in his article for *The Athletic*, Jimenez had only been playing baseball for three years when he signed his professional contract. *And* – it's a big "ánd", by the way – he just started switch-hitting once he got into the Red Sox's organization. Now his .324/.370/.427 slash line through 220 minor league games seems all that more impressive, doesn't it? There's plenty more in the tank, in every facet of Jimenez's game. He's an elite runner, though it hasn't translated to defensive value yet. But it will. He's showing some platoon splits, as expected given his inexperience as a switch-hitter, but that's going to improve too. My only question is whether he'll hit for enough power to push him into a full time gig. He's very much projection over production at this point.

Ceiling: 3.0-win player
Risk: Moderate
MLB ETA: 2024

6. Wilkelman Gonzalez, RHP

	FB	CB	CH	Command	Overall
	60	60	55	50/55	55

Born: 03/25/02	Age: 20	Bats: R	Top Comp: Jose Berrios
Height: 6-0	Weight: 167	Throws: R	

Season	Team	Age	Level	IP	TBF	K/9	K%	BB/9	BB%	K-BB%	ERA	FIP	xFIP	Pit/Bat
2019	BOS	17	R	46.1	191	8.55	23.04%	4.66	12.57%	10.47%	3.30	4.33	4.08	1.96
2021	BOS	19	CPX	35.0	141	11.83	32.62%	2.06	5.67%	26.95%	3.60	2.83	3.84	1.90
2021	BOS	19	A	17.2	75	10.19	26.67%	4.08	10.67%	16.00%	1.53	3.98	4.47	4.03

Background: Discovered out of Maracay, Venezuela, by scouts Wilder Lobo and Rolando Pino during the summer of 2018. Boston signed the wiry right-hander to a quarter-million dollar deal. Gonzalez made his professional debut the following summer in the foreign rookie league: he tossed 46.1 innings of work, recording a 44-to-24 strikeout-to-walk ratio with a 3.30 ERA. Last season Boston pushed the intriguing righty to the Florida Complex League to begin the year. After eight overpowering appearances he was green-lighted for full-season competition. He would make four brief starts with Salem to wrap up his second season. In total, Gonzalez pitched 52.2 innings, averaging 11.3 punch outs and just 2.7 walks per nine innings to go along with a 2.91 ERA and a slightly higher 3.22 FIP.

Scouting Report: If there was one arm brewing in the low levels that could match the arsenal and potential of top prospect Brayan Bellow, its Wilkelman Gonzalez. Bar none. And there's not even a debate. Uncorking a fastball that will reach the mid-90s, Gonzalez will complement the plus offering with a wicked snapdragon of a curveball and a very, very good changeup with plenty of deception and velocity separation. He's poised to be the club's biggest breakout minor leaguer and should be on the list for biggest breakout prospect in all of baseball. It wouldn't shock me to see Gonzalez as a consensus Top 100 pick within the next 12 to 18 months. Remember this kid's name. One more thought: I think there's some added velo in his right arm that's just waiting to be tapped. He's got some Jose Berrios aura about him.

Ceiling: 3.0-win player
Risk: High
MLB ETA: 2024/2025

7. Jarren Duran, CF

	Hit	Power	SB	Patience	Glove	Overall
	45	55	60	50	50	50

Born: 09/05/96	Age: 25	Bats: L	Top Comp: poor man's Shane Victorino
Height: 6-2	Weight: 212	Throws: R	

Season	Team	Age	Level	PA	1B	2B	3B	HR	SB	CS	BB%	K%	AVG	OBP	SLG	ISO
2018	BOS	21	A	134	36	9	1	1	12	6	3.73%	16.42%	0.367	0.396	0.477	0.109
2018	BOS	21	A-	168	37	5	10	2	12	4	6.55%	15.48%	0.348	0.393	0.548	0.200
2019	BOS	22	A+	226	57	19	3	4	18	5	10.18%	19.47%	0.387	0.456	0.543	0.156
2019	BOS	22	AA	352	63	11	5	1	28	8	6.53%	23.86%	0.250	0.309	0.325	0.075
2021	BOS	24	AAA	283	34	11	2	16	16	3	10.60%	23.32%	0.258	0.357	0.516	0.258

Background: A seventh round pick out of Long Beach State in 2017 after a decent, unspectacular collegiate career with the Dirt Bags. Duran left the school as a .294/.376/.377 hitter. But the front office saw something a bit more. And that became readily apparent as soon as Duran stepped onto a minor league field. He slugged a scorching .357/.394/.516 between Lowell and Greenville during his debut. The lefty-swinging speedster continued his assault on minor league pitching the following season, 2019, as he moved into High-A (.387/.456/.543). His bat, though, slowed considerably upon his promotion up to Double-A (.250/.309/.325). Last season, the front office decided to push the then-24-year-old up to Triple-A to begin the year. And Duran's responded by batting .258/.357/.516 with 11 doubles, two triples, and 16 homeruns. He also swiped 16 bags in 19 attempts. His overall production, per *Weighted Runs Created Plus*, was 32% better than the league average. Duran also appeared in 33 games with the Sox, hitting a lowly .215/.241/.336 in 112 plate appearances.

Snippet from The 2020 Prospect Digest Handbook: The hit tool looks like it has a chance to be a plus skill and speed is already bordering on plus-plus. But the power has ways to go still, though it's flashed double-digit homer potential. The defense is still raw, but the combination of elite speed and lack of center field experience bodes well for the future. He could be a dynamic table setter if everything breaks the right way.

Scouting Report: With respect to his work in AAA, consider the following:

- Since 2006, only four 24-year-old hitters met the following criteria in a Triple-A season with one organization (min. 275 PA): 127 to 137 wRC+ total, a strikeout rate between 22.5% and 24.5%, and a walk rate between 8% and 12%. Those four hitters: Chris Davis, Rymer Liriano, Jordan Patterson, and Jarren Duran.

An easy plus runner, but the speed hasn't translated into tangible defensive value over the past couple of seasons. Duran isn't bad, per say, he's just…average. He has the basic Shane Victorino toolkit in place, but it's not likely he ascends anywhere close to the level of the two-time All-Star. He could very well be 80% of that though.

Ceiling: 2.5-win player
Risk: Moderate
MLB ETA: Debuted in 2021

8. Bryan Mata, RHP

	FB	CB	SL	CH	Command	Overall
	N/A	N/A	N/A	N/A	N/A	50

Born: 05/05/99	Age: 23	Bats: R	Top Comp: N/A
Height: 6-3	Weight: 238	Throws: R	

Season	Team	Age	Level	IP	TBF	K/9	K%	BB/9	BB%	K-BB%	ERA	FIP	xFIP	Pit/Bat
2018	BOS	19	A+	72.0	327	7.63	18.65%	7.25	17.74%	0.92%	3.50	4.76	5.04	4.00
2019	BOS	20	A+	51.1	216	9.12	24.07%	3.16	8.33%	15.74%	1.75	3.07	3.23	3.61
2019	BOS	20	AA	53.2	234	9.89	25.21%	4.02	10.26%	14.96%	5.03	3.99	3.27	4.06

Background: Slogging through the low levels of the minors leagues is difficult enough, but the odds of reaching Double-A, the largest challenge for a prospect, at the age of 20 is downright improbable. In fact, only four 20-year-old pitchers tossed 50 or more innings at the level in 2019. Bryan Mata was one of them. And he did so by averaging nearly 10 strikeouts per nine innings. But as life returned back to normal in 2021, Mata's right elbow started creaking in March last year. And before he knew, he was undergoing the knife for Tommy John surgery – an injury that, obviously, knocked him out for the entirety of 2021. Assuming the typical recovery timeline, he should be ready to return to normal action near the start of 2022. For his minor league career, the 6-foot-3, 238-pound right-hander is averaging 8.8 strikeouts and 4.1 walks per nine innings across 69 appearances (all of which were starts).

Snippet from The 2020 Prospect Digest Handbook: From painful to watch to a pure joy. Mata's on the cusp on putting everything together. The young right-hander's fastball was up to 97 mph during his final start of the year, a seven-inning, nine-strikeout performance against the New Hampshire Fisher Cats. His curveball, which previously flashed plus, has become a consistent swing-and-miss weapon. His changeup is a fine above-average offering. And he's added a hard slider/cutter that shows late, hard bite. The command can waver a bit at times, but he continues to show the mental fortitude to move beyond the brief hiccups.

Scouting Report: Looking forward to Mata's return to the mound in 2022. Fingers crossed that there won't be any speed bumps or setbacks.

Ceiling: 2.5-win player
Risk: Moderate to High
MLB ETA: 2023

9. Noah Song, RHP

	FB	CB	SL	CH	Command	Overall
	N/A	N/A	N/A	N/A	N/A	60

Born: 05/28/97	Age: 25	Bats: R	Top Comp: N/A
Height: 6-4	Weight: 200	Throws: R	

Season	Team	Age	Level	IP	TBF	K/9	K%	BB/9	BB%	K-BB%	ERA	FIP	xFIP	Pit/Bat
2019	BOS	22	A-	17.0	65	10.06	29.23%	2.65	7.69%	21.54%	1.06	2.05	2.80	4.12

Background: The hard-throwing right-hander shot up draft boards during his dominating junior campaign at the United States Naval Academy. And if not for his impending two-year post-grad service commitment, the 6-foot-4, 200-pound hurler would've been a lock an early- to mid-first round selection. Song's service commitment began in 2020, so – tentatively – he could return to organized ball as soon as 2022 – though it's to be determined if, or how, the time away has impacted his potential. Either way, thank you for your service and prolonging your professional career.

Scouting Report: With nothing new to report on, here's what I wrote about him in The 2020 Prospect Digest Handbook:

"Straight filth. His fastball was kissing 98 or 99 mph during his recent appearance for Team USA in the WBSC Premier 12. He'll also mix in a hard, oft-times absurdly good slider, a mid-70s curveball tha might just be better than the slider with

hard downward tilt, and an average changeup. To go along with the plus- to plus-plus velocity; his fastball shows impressive arm side run at times. He also commands the zone surprising well. He has the potential to be an upper-rotation-caliber arm."

Ceiling: 3.5-win player
Risk: Extremely High
MLB ETA: 2023?

10. Blaze Jordan, 3B

Hit	Power	SB	Patience	Glove	Overall
40/45	55/60	30	45	50	45

Born: 12/19/02	Age: 19	Bats: R	Top Comp: N/A
Height: 6-2	Weight: 220	Throws: R	

Season	Team	Age	Level	PA	1B	2B	3B	HR	SB	CS	BB%	K%	AVG	OBP	SLG	ISO
2021	BOS	18	CPX	76	13	7	1	4	1	0	7.89%	17.11%	0.362	0.408	0.667	0.304
2021	BOS	18	A	38	6	1	0	2	0	0	5.26%	21.05%	0.250	0.289	0.444	0.194

Background: With respect to baseball card collectors, there's probably never – in the history of the hobby – been a more hyped *third round pick that did not make their debut* than Blaze Jordan heading into last season. In three words: it was bonkers. The hype had reached a Ruthian crescendo amongst some collectors. Boston snagged the 6-foot-2, 220-pound corner infielder with the 89th overall pick two years and handed him a hefty $1.75 million (which, by the way, was only the third highest bonus given in the round). Jordan made his debut last summer as he shredded the rookie league (.362/.408/.667) for 19 games and looked mediocre in a nine-game cameo with Salem in Low-A East. He finished the year with an aggregate .324/.368/.590 slash line.

Scouting Report: Known on the high school circuits as a prolific homerun hitter, especially in derby contests, Jordan was quick to showcase his above-average bat speed, natural swing loft, and plus in-game power. I have concerns about how his hit tool will responded several times through Low-A in 2022. And his approach doesn't offer up a lot of hope for bloated OBPs in the future either. Some of that will improve through maturation (he was one of the youngest players in the draft class in 2020). Best case scenario is Nolan Gorman. Worst case: .290 OBP percentage with 25 homeruns. The outcomes are quite vast at this point.

Ceiling: 1.5-win player
Risk: Moderate
MLB ETA: 2024/2025

11. Jay Groome, LHP

FB	CB	SL	CH	Command	Overall
60	60	50	50/55	50	45

Born: 08/23/98	Age: 23	Bats: L	Top Comp: Will Smith
Height: 6-6	Weight: 262	Throws: L	

Season	Team	Age	Level	IP	TBF	K/9	K%	BB/9	BB%	K-BB%	ERA	FIP	xFIP	Pit/Bat
2021	BOS	22	A+	81.2	351	11.90	30.77%	3.53	9.12%	21.65%	5.29	4.35	3.96	3.75
2021	BOS	22	AA	15.2	64	14.94	40.63%	2.30	6.25%	34.38%	2.30	1.15	2.66	3.95

Background: Gifted with the size and raw talent of a generational prospect. Groome looked every bit the part of a potential ace-in-the-making. He's a behemoth, checking in at 6-foot-6 and a rotund 262 pounds. His fastball will top out at 96 mph. And his curveball looked like a gift from the baseball gods. Oh, yeah, he's left-handed too. But there are some things that tend to get in the way. Some are self-inflicted, like makeup issues, off-the-field problems (say, like, a father accused of distributing cocaine, heroin, and methamphetamine), and conditioning woes. Others are just an unfortunate series of circumstances, like arm procedures, or lat flare ups, or a world pandemic. Whatever the cause, though, Groome tossed just four innings between 2018 and 2020. And that's not including being limited to only 55.1 innings of work in 2017 either. Finally healthy, at least for the time being, the big southpaw put together his finest professional season to date. Making 21 starts between Greenville and Portland, Groome tossed a career best 97.1 innings, recording 134 punch outs and issuing 34 free passes to go along with a 4.81 aggregate ERA.

Snippet from The 2020 Prospect Digest Handbook: He's now lost the better part of two years of development and pitchers tend to struggle commanding the zone after Tommy John surgery – so it's not a promising recipe. His curveball is very reminiscent of fellow southpaw Rich Hill's.

Scouting Report: Consider the following:

- Since 2006, only three 22-year-old pitchers posted a strikeout percentage between 30% and 32% with a walk percentage between 9% and 11% in a High-A season with one organization (min. 75 IP): Drew Pomeranz, Jose Arredondo, and Jay Groome.

The basic building blocks for a solid, league-average starting option are in place: two above-average or better offerings with a third viable weapon in his arsenal and improving command/control. But he just has the "feel" of an eventual reliever, some of it just based on his portly appearance. At times Groome's heater will sit 94 mph with relative ease and touch 96 with barely any additional effort. Other times, he seems content on pitching at 89- to 91-mph. He still owns – and commands – a superlative curveball. And his changeup is sneaky good as well. It looked like he would mix in a rare slider too. Between 2017 and 2021, though, he put on 40 pounds to his already large frame.

Ceiling: 1.5-win player
Risk: Moderate
MLB ETA: 2022

12. Jeter Downs, 2B/SS

Hit	Power	SB	Patience	Glove	Overall
40	50	55	50	55	50

Born: 07/27/98	Age: 23	Bats: R	Top Comp: N/A
Height: 5-11	Weight: 195	Throws: R	

Season	Team	Age	Level	PA	1B	2B	3B	HR	SB	CS	BB%	K%	AVG	OBP	SLG	ISO
2018	CIN	19	A	524	79	23	2	13	37	10	9.92%	19.66%	0.257	0.351	0.402	0.145
2019	LAD	20	A+	479	55	33	4	19	23	8	11.27%	20.25%	0.269	0.354	0.507	0.238
2019	LAD	20	AA	56	9	2	0	5	1	0	10.71%	17.86%	0.333	0.429	0.688	0.354
2021	BOS	22	AAA	405	45	9	0	14	18	3	9.38%	32.35%	0.190	0.272	0.333	0.143

Background: Well, that's not how to assuage the yelling and screaming about the Mookie Betts deal with the Dodgers. Not when you're viewed as one of the two major pieces in the return package. While Alex Verdugo was busy regressing from an above-average, almost borderline All-Star performer, to literally a 2.0-win player last season, Downs morphed from a Top 100 prospect into a junior varsity talent. The 32nd overall pick in 2017, Downs appeared in 99 games with the Worcester Red Sox, cobbling together a putrid .190/.272/.333 triple-slash line. He belted out only 23 extra-base hits (nine doubles and 14 dingers) in 405 trips to the plate. Per *Weighted Runs Created Plus*, his overall production was a staggering 38% *below* the league average mark. Boston sent the struggling middle infielder to the Arizona Fall League for additional reps and the results were largely mixed; he hit .228/.389/.491 in 16 games with the Scottsdale Scorpions.

Snippet from The 2020 Prospect Digest Handbook: Downs' power – and his glove work – took a development leap. He's not going to be a star, but he could anchor Boston's infield for the better part of a decade or so.

Scouting Report: Just how poor was Downs' performance in 2021? Consider the following:

- Among 208 minor league hitters that received at least 400 plate appearances in 2021, Downs' production, 62 wRC+, was the third worst.
- Since 2006, there have been more than 7,700 hitters that surpassed the 400-plate appearance threshold. Downs' 62 wRC+ ranks as the 168th worst.
- It's the 38th worst performance in AAA since 2006, and the second worst at the level last season.

So what went wrong? The former first rounder's offensive production was always boosted by his bat-to-ball skills, only surpassing a 20% K-rate (barely) once – which happened as a 20-year-old in High-A. Last season, though, he whiffed in roughly a third of his plate appearances with Worcester. That number did regress some in the Fall League (25%), but it's still not close to his career norms. Mechanically, there isn't anything notable from his 2019 and 2021 game tape, but he just looked "off" during last season, almost as if he were guessing and always guessing incorrectly. Downs is only entering his age-23 season, but it's difficult imagining a complete bounce back after the awful showing in 2021.

Ceiling: 2.0-win player
Risk: High
MLB ETA: 2022

13. Matthew Lugo, SS

Hit	Power	SB	Patience	Glove	Overall
45/50	35/45	50	50	45/50	45

Born: 05/09/01	Age: 21	Bats: R	Top Comp: N/A
Height: 6-1	Weight: 187	Throws: R	

Season	Team	Age	Level	PA	1B	2B	3B	HR	SB	CS	BB%	K%	AVG	OBP	SLG	ISO
2019	BOS	18	R	157	28	5	1	1	3	0	9.55%	22.93%	0.257	0.342	0.331	0.074
2021	BOS	20	A	469	85	21	3	4	15	4	8.10%	20.04%	0.270	0.338	0.364	0.093

Background: Fun Fact Part I: Since their first draft pick in 2013, the Carlos Beltran Baseball Academy has churned out a total of 24 selections – an average of nearly three picks per year. Fun Fact Part II: Of those 24 selected players, 13 of them received at least a six-figure bonus and three signing for more than $500,000. Fun Fact Part III: When the Red Sox selected Matthew Lugo in the second round, 69th overall, in 2019 he (A) became the highest drafted player and (B) earned the academy's largest bonus at $1.1 million. A twitchy 6-foot-1, 187-pound shortstop, Lugo spent last season developing with the Salem Red Sox in Low-A East. In 105 games, he batted a respectable .270/.338/.365 with 21 doubles, three triples, and four homeruns. He also swiped 15 bags in 19 attempts. Per *Weighted Runs Created Plus*, his overall production was 5% below the league average line.

Snippet from The 2020 Prospect Digest Handbook: Impressive bat speed that suggests he'll develop at least 50-grade power. Lugo owns a short, compact swing and a solid approach at the plate. Defensively, he was better than average. If he's able to tap into the power, he could be a solid starting shortstop. If not, his gap-to-gap approach could make him a lower-end starter on a non-championship caliber quad.

Scouting Report: Consider the following:

- Since 2006, only five 20-year-old hitters met the following criteria in Low-A with one organization (min. 400 PA): 90 to 100 wRC+ total, a 7% to 9% walk rate, and a strikeout rate between 19% and 21%. Those five hitters: Argenis Diaz, Tyler Goeddel, Henry Ramos, Connor Oliver, and Matthew Lugo.

The nephew of potential Hall of Famer Carlos Beltran, Lugo shows a well-rounded approach on both sides of the ball without a true standout tool. He'll walk a little, run a little, shoot balls gap-to-gap, run into the occasional four-bagger, and play a little defense. It's not a mixture for stardom, let alone superstardom, but he's still tracking as a low end starting shortstop. One more note: after struggling through his first 34 games (.216/.262/.269), he hit .296/.372/.408 over his remaining 71 contests. That should be the baseline as he moves into High-A in 2022.

Ceiling: 1.5-win player
Risk: Moderate
MLB ETA: 2024

14. Alex Binelas, 3B

Hit	Power	SB	Patience	Glove	Overall
40/45	50	35	50	50	45

Born: 05/26/00	Age: 22	Bats: L	Top Comp: N/A
Height: 6-3	Weight: 225	Throws: R	

Season	Team	Age	Level	PA	1B	2B	3B	HR	SB	CS	BB%	K%	AVG	OBP	SLG	ISO
2021	MIL	21	CPX	27	6	0	0	0	1	1	18.52%	22.22%	0.286	0.444	0.286	0.000
2021	MIL	21	A	132	17	11	0	9	0	0	9.09%	25.00%	0.314	0.379	0.636	0.322

Background: Selected in the 35th round by the Washington Nationals coming out of Oak Creek High School in 2018. The lefty-swinging infielder, instead, packed his bags and shipped out to Louisville to begin a solid tenure with the Cardinals. Binelas, a stout 6-foot-3 and 225 pounds, turned in a dynamic showing as a true freshman for the ACC powerhouse: he slugged .291/.383/.612 with 14 doubles, five triples, and 14 dingers. His sophomore campaign was wrecked by a broken hamate bone after just a pair of games. Considering the rest of the country locked down after a dozen or so games, Binelas' development likely didn't take that significant of a hit. Finally healthy, Binelas returned close to his pre-injury production level by batting .256/.348/.621 with 10 doubles, two triples, and a career best 19 homeruns. Milwaukee selected the Louisville star in the third round, 86th overall, and signed him to a deal worth $700,000. Binelas ripped through the Complex League for a week before moving up to Low-A for another 29 games. He finished his debut with an aggregate .309/.390/.583 line. The Brewers, just months after drafting him, shipped him off to Boston with Jackie Bradley Jr., and minor leaguer David Hamilton for a resurgent Hunter Renfroe.

Scouting Report: Consider the following:

- Between 2011 and 2020, only three ACC hitters batted at least .250/.340/.600 with a strikeout percentage north of 20% and a walk rate between 8% and 12% (min. 200 PA): Daniel Palka, Johnny Aiello, and Andrew Rash.

Hamate issues typically sap a hitter's power well beyond their stints on the disabled list, but Binelas's thump showed no ill effects. There was a bit of a swing-and-miss slant to his game during his final season as he whiffed in more than 22% of his PAs and that mark isn't likely to improve as he moves into the minor leagues. It's a 45-grade hit tool, 20-homer thump, and decent defense. Low end starter / bench bat.

Ceiling: 1.0- to 1.5-win player
Risk: Moderate
MLB ETA: 2024

15. Tyler McDonough, 2B/CF

Hit	Power	SB	Patience	Glove	Overall
50	40	50	55	50	40

Born: 04/02/99	Age: 23	Bats: B	Top Comp: N/A
Height: 5-10	Weight: 180	Throws: R	

Season	Team	Age	Level	PA	1B	2B	3B	HR	SB	CS	BB%	K%	AVG	OBP	SLG	ISO
2021	BOS	22	CPX	13	1	3	0	0	0	0	0.00%	30.77%	0.308	0.308	0.538	0.231
2021	BOS	22	A	126	21	4	4	3	3	1	13.49%	19.05%	0.296	0.397	0.491	0.194

Background: An All-American during his tenure at Ohio prep powerhouse Moeller High School, McDonough batted a respectable .328 with 80 hits and 84 runs scored during his fantastic prep career. And the switch-hitting infielder/outfielder didn't miss a beat as he transitioned into collegiate ball. A key cog to the Wolfpack's offensive firepower as a true freshman, McDonough hit an impressive .320/.392/.452 with 14 doubles, two triples, five homeruns, and 10 stolen bases. The triumvirate of media dynamos – *Baseball America, Collegiate Baseball,* and *Perfect Game* – listed him as a Freshman All-American. The Cincinnati, Ohio, native also garnered All-ACC Second Team and ACC All-Freshman Team honors as well. McDonough upped the ante during his abbreviated, COVID-shortened campaign the following year, batting .354/.457/.554 with seven extra-base knocks in only 17 games. Last season, he continued his assault on the opposition: appearing in 55 games for the ACC squad, he slugged .339/.423/.631 with career bests in doubles (21), homeruns (15), and stolen bases (13). The Red Sox drafted McDonough in the third round, 75th overall, and signed him to a deal with $828,000, a smidgeon below the recommended slot. McDonough appeared in 31 games during his professional debut, the majority of them in Low-A, hitting a solid .298/.388/.496.

Scouting Report: Per the usual, here's my draft write up for McDonough:

> *"Consider the following:*
>
> - *Since 2011 only one N.C. State player has slugged out at least 20 doubles and ten homeruns in a single season: Tyler McDonough.*
>
> *Let's continue:*
>
> - *Between 2011 and 2020, only two ACC hitters have batted at least .330/.410/.620 with a walk rate between 10% and 14% and K-rate between 17% and 22% in a season (min. 250PA): Daniel Palka, a third rounder in 2013, and Stuart Fairchild, a second round pick in 2017.*
>
> *McDonough is cut from the same cloth as former Wake Forest center fielder Stuart Fairchild. A semi-toolsy prospect without a true, dominant standout. And the Red Sox's minor leaguer looks like a fourth/fifth outfielder at his peak. He'll run a little bit, flash gap-to-gap power, and take the occasional walk.*

I listed him as a potential third/fourth rounder.

Ceiling: 1.0-win player
Risk: Moderate
MLB ETA: 2024

16. Ronaldo Hernandez, C

Hit	Power	SB	Patience	Glove	Overall
45	50	30	30	50	40

Born: 11/11/97	Age: 24	Bats: R	Top Comp: Jesus Montero
Height: 6-1	Weight: 230	Throws: R	

Season	Team	Age	Level	PA	1B	2B	3B	HR	SB	CS	BB%	K%	AVG	OBP	SLG	ISO
2018	TBR	20	A	449	73	20	1	21	10	4	6.90%	15.37%	0.284	0.339	0.494	0.210
2019	TBR	21	A+	427	73	19	3	9	7	0	3.98%	15.22%	0.265	0.299	0.397	0.132
2021	BOS	23	AA	357	51	26	1	16	0	2	3.08%	19.61%	0.280	0.319	0.506	0.226
2021	BOS	23	AAA	30	6	3	0	0	0	0	3.33%	23.33%	0.333	0.400	0.444	0.111

Background: The stocky 6-foot-1, 230-pound backstop entered the 2019 season riding the high of a career-best showing in the Low-A. But Hernandez, a native of Arjona, Colombia, took a noticeable step backward as he struggled to the tune of .265/.299/.397. Tampa Bay sent Hernandez, along with infielder Nick Sogard, to the Red Sox in exchange for relievers Chris Mazza and Jeffrey Springs in mid-February last year. The Red Sox sent the young backstop to the minors' toughest proving ground, Double-A, and he rediscovered his offensive prowess. In 92 games with the Portland Sea Dogs, the bulky catcher slugged .280/.319/.506 with 26 doubles, one triple, and 16 homeruns. His overall production, per *Weighted Runs Created Plus*, was 21% above the league average mark. Hernandez spent the last seven games of the year mashing in AAA to cap off his rebound season.

Snippet from The 2020 Prospect Digest Handbook: Everything seemingly backed up on Hernandez last season: his power regressed, his walk rate declined all the way down to a laughably poor 4.0%, and his power dried up as well. The young backstop showed some flashes of his former offensive thump as he tallied OPS totals north of .800 during the months of May and July. But the season's other three months caused his stat line to crumble. The track record is long enough to suggest that a rebound is more than likely, but he's also – likely – headed to the minors' toughest challenge, Class AA, at some point in 2020.

Scouting Report: Consider the following:

- Since 2006, only two 23-year-old hitters posted a wRC+ between 115 and 125 with a sub-5.0% walk rate in Double-A with one organization (min. 350 PA): Jordany Valdespin and Ronaldo Hernandez.

A decent glove behind the dish, Hernandez's lack of patience severely cripples his future big league value – no matter how many fastballs he runs into. Still, though, the dearth of catching talent at the big league level almost assures him a future big league backup role. In terms of big league production, think: .250/.290/.390.

Ceiling: 1.0-win player
Risk: Moderate
MLB ETA: 2022

17. Chris Murphy, LHP

FB	CB	SL	CH	Command	Overall
50	50	50	55	50	40

Born: 06/05/98	Age: 24	Bats: L	Top Comp: N/A
Height: 6-1	Weight: 175	Throws: L	

Season	Team	Age	Level	IP	TBF	K/9	K%	BB/9	BB%	K-BB%	ERA	FIP	xFIP	Pit/Bat
2019	BOS	21	A-	33.1	127	9.18	26.77%	1.89	5.51%	21.26%	1.08	2.65	2.98	3.85
2021	BOS	23	A+	68.1	286	10.67	28.32%	3.03	8.04%	20.28%	4.21	5.81	4.58	3.99
2021	BOS	23	AA	33.0	138	12.82	34.06%	3.55	9.42%	24.64%	5.45	3.52	3.56	3.94

Background: Only three pitchers from the University of San Diego were selected earlier than Murphy over the past decade: Dylan Covey (4th round, 2013), David Hill (4th round, 2015), and Paul Richan (2nd round, 2018). Boston called the string-bean left-hander's name in the sixth round of the 2019 draft after an erratic junior campaign in the West Coast Conference. Murphy tallied both a bunch of strikeouts and a bunch of walks as he averaged 12.2 K/9 and 6.0 BB/9 for the Toreros. But something clicked for the southpaw as soon as he toed a minor league rubber: he walked just seven hitters in 33.1 innings with the Lowell Spinners during his debut. Last season Murphy made 14 starts with Greenville and another seven appearances with Portland during his first full season of action. In total he pitched 101.1 innings of work, averaging an impressive 11.4 strikeouts and 3.2 walks per nine innings to go along with a 4.62 ERA and a 5.07 FIP.

Scouting Report: Standard four-pitch mix: fastball, curveball, slider, and changeup. The first three are vanilla 50-grades and the changeup, the lone outlier, is an above-average offering. Fastball sits in the 91- to 93-mph range. The curveball is slow with depth and hook. The slider is mediocre, though probably the better option in terms of breaking balls. The changeup has some nice velocity separation. #6-type ceiling, maybe some middle relief value as a crafty lefty that can chew innings.

Ceiling: 1.0-win player
Risk: Moderate
MLB ETA: 2022/2023

18. Brainer Bonaci, 2B/SS

Hit	Power	SB	Patience	Glove	Overall
30/50	30/40	55	45	55	40

Born: 07/09/02	Age: 19	Bats: B	Top Comp: N/A
Height: 5-10	Weight: 164	Throws: R	

Season	Team	Age	Level	PA	1B	2B	3B	HR	SB	CS	BB%	K%	AVG	OBP	SLG	ISO
2019	BOS	16	R	262	45	14	2	3	18	10	8.78%	15.27%	0.279	0.356	0.397	0.118
2021	BOS	18	CPX	162	19	13	1	2	12	0	12.96%	22.84%	0.252	0.358	0.403	0.151
2021	BOS	18	A	52	7	3	1	0	0	0	5.77%	15.38%	0.224	0.269	0.327	0.102

Background: A notable signing out of Catia La Mar, Venezuela, during 2018, Boston and Bonaci's representatives inked a deal worth $280,000. He made his professional debut in the Dominican Summer League the following year, batting a respectable .279/.356/.397 with 14 doubles, two triples, and three homeruns. He also swiped 18 bags in 28 total attempts. Last season, despite losing the 2020 year due to COVID, the player development engine cautiously pushed the young middle infielder into the Complex League – which looked to be the correct call. Bonaci batted a solid .252/.358/.403 in 36 games. He also hit .224/.29/.327 in 13 games in Low-A as well.

Scouting Report: First impression watching Bonaci in the Complex League last summer: he needs to get stronger. There were swings that were reminiscent of your kid brother grabbing the oversized lumber in a pickup game at the park. The swing, though, shows some potential as an above-average hit tool. It's good looking. I'm not sure how much power his 5-foot-10, 160-ish-pound frame will allow, but his above-average speed will compensate for some of that. He's tracking like an average infielder. There's some Erick Aybar vibes here.

Ceiling: 1.0-win player
Risk: Moderate
MLB ETA: 202

19. Jeisson Rosario, CF

Hit	Power	SB	Patience	Glove	Overall
35/40	30	55	60	45/55	40

Born: 10/22/99	Age: 22	Bats: L	Top Comp: N/A
Height: 6-1	Weight: 191	Throws: L	

Season	Team	Age	Level	PA	1B	2B	3B	HR	SB	CS	BB%	K%	AVG	OBP	SLG	ISO
2018	SDP	18	A	521	93	17	5	3	18	12	12.67%	20.73%	0.271	0.368	0.353	0.083
2019	SDP	19	A+	525	83	14	4	3	11	4	16.57%	21.71%	0.242	0.372	0.314	0.072
2021	BOS	21	AA	405	61	15	1	3	11	7	12.35%	27.90%	0.232	0.335	0.307	0.075

Background: Enamored by the speedy center fielder's tools, the Padres coughed up a cool $1.85 million to convince the Dominican prospect to join their still-rebuilding farm system in 2016. And the Friars immediately placed Rosario on an accelerated development path as they pushed him directly into the stateside rookie leagues the following year for his debut. The then-17-year-old proved up to the task by batting .299/.404/.369 in 52 games. The next season, 2018, Rosario found himself as one of the youngest players in the Midwest League – though he handled himself well by hitting .271/.368/.353 in 117 games with Fort Wayne. And then the struggles started. San Diego pushed the teenager up to High-A and Rosario, simply, looked overmatched as he cobbled together a .242/.372/.314 slash line in 120 games with Lake Elsinore. Boston acquired the young outfielder, along with Hudson Potts, for veteran first baseman Mitch Moreland in late-August 2020. Undeterred by his previous struggles in the California League, his new organization pushed him up to Double-A and the results were…predictably poor: he put together a .232/.335/.307 production line, belting out just 15 doubles, one triple, and three homeruns. He also swiped only 11 bags in 18 attempts. Per *Weighted Runs Created Plus*, his overall production was 16% below the league average mark.

Snippet from The 2020 Prospect Digest Handbook: Extreme patience at the plate – which is where he generates the majority of his value. Although he's only entering his age-20 season, he's quickly heading down the path of a fourth/fifth outfielder.

Scouting Report: OBP is the name of the game for Rosario, who gobbles up walks like the Cookie Monster chases Oreos. The then-20-year-old walked in 12.3% of his plate appearances in Double-A last season – which is *astounding* given the fact that he couldn't hit his way out of the wet paper bag. Rosario owns above-average speed, which *seems* like a valuable skill set given (A) his position and (B) his ability to sniff out first base. But his defense is still disappointingly below-average and he's incredibly inefficient on the base paths. The lefty-swinging outfielder is still only entering his age-22 season, but he's years removed from putting together a serviceable production line.

Ceiling: 1.0-win player
Risk: Moderate
MLB ETA: 2023

20. Nathan Hickey, C

Hit	Power	SB	Patience	Glove	Overall
40/45	50	30	60	40/45	40

Born: 11/23/99	Age: 22	Bats: L	Top Comp: N/A
Height: 6-0	Weight: 210	Throws: R	

Season	Team	Age	Level	PA	1B	2B	3B	HR	SB	CS	BB%	K%	AVG	OBP	SLG	ISO
2021	BOS	21	CPX	28	3	2	0	0	0	0	21.43%	28.57%	0.250	0.429	0.350	0.100
2021	BOS	21	A	12	1	0	0	0	0	0	25.00%	16.67%	0.125	0.333	0.125	0.000

Background: A key member of the Florida Gators offense over the past two seasons – well, at least the past season-plus because of the COVID shutdown. The lefty-swinging backstop got off to a strong start to the 2020 season, hitting .311/.439/.622 with a pair of doubles and four homeruns through 15 games. And once college baseball returned for the 2021 season, Hickey was able to maintain a similar level of production throughout a full schedule. In 60 games for the SEC powerhouse, the 6-foot, 210-pound catcher slugged .317/.435/.522 with 15 doubles, two triples, and nine homeruns. Boston selected the offensive-minded backstop in the fifth round last July, 136th overall, and signed him to round-high $1 million bonus; the front office used some of the money from the failed Jud Fabian pick to secure Hickey's rights. Ironic they were teammates with the Gators, no? Hickey appeared in 11 games between the Florida Complex League and Low-A, batting .214/.400/.286.

Scouting Report: Consider the following:

- Between 2011 and 2020, only three SEC hitters met the following criteria in a season (min. 250 PA): .310/.425/.510 with a walk rate of at least 14% with a strikeout rate between 10% and 15%. Those three hitters: Andrew Benintendi, Kyle Martin, and Will Toffey.

A bat first backstop that's only as valuable as the damage he does at the dish. Hickey, though, proved himself against the elite SEC competition in 75 games. He shows a tremendous eye at the plate and what should be workable punch out rates. Average power. He could be a poor man's Yasmani Grandal at his peak with a poor man's Zack Collins as his floor.

Ceiling: 1.0-win player
Risk: Moderate
MLB ETA: 2024

Chicago Cubs

Top Prospects

1. Brennen Davis, OF

	Hit	Power	SB	Patience	Glove	Overall
	50/55	55	45	55	55	60

Born: 11/02/99	Age: 22	Bats: R	Top Comp: Cedric Mullins
Height: 6-4	Weight: 210	Throws: R	

Season	Team	Age	Level	PA	1B	2B	3B	HR	SB	CS	BB%	K%	AVG	OBP	SLG	ISO
2018	CHC	18	R	72	15	2	0	0	6	1	13.89%	16.67%	0.298	0.431	0.333	0.035
2019	CHC	19	A	204	34	9	3	8	4	1	8.82%	18.63%	0.305	0.381	0.525	0.220
2021	CHC	21	A+	32	5	2	0	2	2	0	9.38%	18.75%	0.321	0.406	0.607	0.286
2021	CHC	21	AA	316	34	20	0	13	6	4	11.39%	30.70%	0.252	0.367	0.474	0.222
2021	CHC	21	AAA	68	8	3	0	4	0	0	16.18%	22.06%	0.268	0.397	0.536	0.268

Background: The Cubs made their bones – and built their World Series championship – around young hitters, either acquired through the draft or via trade. And then for some reason, the front office decided to veer off course. Pitchers, and not even hard-throwing, high-ceiling ones, became en vogue for the front office. Then the fire sale happened. During that sell off last season the front office – once again – started targeting young, high upside hitters like Pete Crow-Armstrong and Kevin Alcantara while some of their own young hitters took massive strides forward. Like Brennen Davis. A second round pick out of Basha High School, 62nd overall, in 2018, Davis's production *exploded* as he rocketed through three levels, going from High-A to Double-A, and then onto Triple-A. In total, the 6-foot-4, 210-pound outfielder slugged a hearty .260/.375/.494 with 25 doubles, 19 homeruns, and eight stolen bases (in 12 attempts). Per *Weighted Runs Created Plus*, Davis's overall production topped the average mark by a whopping 44% - the best showing in the organization by any stateside player, by a *wide margin*.

Snippet from The 2020 Prospect Digest Handbook: As for Davis, he has the potential to be a special, special talent: blossoming power that should settle in as an above-average weapon, above-average hit tool, solid speed, a decent glove, phenomenal contact rates, and a willingness to walk a bit.

Scouting Report: The good news:

- Since 2006, only six 21-year-old hitters met the following criteria in a Double-A season with one organization (min. 300 PA): 130 to 140 wRC+ with a walk rate between 10.5% and 12.5%. Those six hitters: Alek Thomas, Brandon Marsh, Matt Davidson, Chance Sisco, Arismendy Alcantara, and – of course – Brennen Davis.
- The problem for Davis, though, and what separates him from the rest of the group is his massive K-rate during his Double-A stint: he whiffed in 30.7% of his plate appearances, considerably more than any other hitter in the group.

A few reasons to not fret over Davis's "concerning" 30+% strikeout rate in Double-A:

1. Age. He was just 21-years-old playing against the most difficult minor league level.
2. Track Record: Beyond the stint in Double-A last season, Davis's strikeout numbers in rookie ball, Low-A, High-A, and Triple-A have been no greater than 22.1%.

There's a chance the bat develops into an above-average tool, though it's certainly no worse than average – even on bad days. Blossoming power that could peak in the 30-homer territory. Enough speed to keep pitchers and catchers honest. And a good enough glove to man center.

Ceiling: 4.5-win player
Risk: Moderate
MLB ETA: 2022

2. Pete Crow-Armstrong, CF

	Hit	Power	SB	Patience	Glove	Overall
	50/60	50/55	50	55	50	60

Born: 03/25/02	Age: 20	Bats: L	Top Comp: N/A
Height: 6-1	Weight: 180	Throws: L	

Season	Team	Age	Level	PA	1B	2B	3B	HR	SB	CS	BB%	K%	AVG	OBP	SLG	ISO
2021	NYM	19	A	32	8	2	0	0	2	3	21.88%	18.75%	0.417	0.563	0.500	0.083

Background: Rebuilding their farm system after years of mostly failed draft classes. Chicago got together with the Mets on a big mid-year deal last season, agreeing to send All-Star fan favorite Javier Baez and veteran right-handed starting pitcher Trevor Williams in exchange for Pete Crow-Armstrong. The Cubs also sent cash to the wealthy wallet of the Mets to complete the deal as well. A toolsy 6-foot-1, 180-pound center fielder, New York selected Crow-Armstrong in the opening round two years ago, 19th overall, and handed him a hefty $3,359,000 bonus. The Harvard-Westlake High School product, like all minor leaguers, lost a season of development time due to COVID-19, and – unfortunately – his 2021 season was cut short because of a torn right labrum and cartilage injury. Prior to hitting the DL, he was slugging a healthy .417/.563/.500 through six games and 32 plate appearances.

Scouting Report: Still an unknown after two years of professional ball. With limited game tape and no reliable numbers to work off of. But what I did find from 2021 leaves no doubt that (A) the Cubs have a franchise cornerstone bat and (B) the Mets' failure to make the playoffs will only exacerbate their failings in the trade. Short, sweet stroke with gobs of bat speed. The simplicity of the swing reminds me of a young Joey Votto. I'm really impressed by his willingness to take outside pitches the opposite way. The sky could be the limit for Crow-Armstrong. And the only reason I'm ranking him second behind Davis is simply little information to go off of.

Ceiling: 4.5-win player
Risk: Moderate
MLB ETA: 2022

3. Kevin Alcantara, CF

Hit	Power	SB	Patience	Glove	Overall
50	50/60	50/40	50	55	60

Born: 07/12/02	Age: 19	Bats: R	Top Comp: N/A
Height: 6-6	Weight: 188	Throws: R	

Season	Team	Age	Level	PA	1B	2B	3B	HR	SB	CS	BB%	K%	AVG	OBP	SLG	ISO
2019	NYY	16	R	128	24	5	2	1	3	3	2.34%	21.09%	0.260	0.289	0.358	0.098
2019	NYY	16	R	46	5	3	1	0	2	0	10.87%	19.57%	0.237	0.348	0.368	0.132
2021	CHC	18	CPX	107	19	3	5	4	3	0	12.15%	26.17%	0.337	0.415	0.609	0.272
2021	NYY	18	CPX	31	8	1	0	1	2	0	12.90%	25.81%	0.370	0.452	0.519	0.148

Background: Not that the Javier Baez deal was a particularly easy pill to swallow, but for me the deals of Anthony Rizzo and Kris Bryant were incredibly difficult as a baseball fan. Rizzo and Bryant were the faces of the Cubs' resurgence in a lot of way. But at the end of last July Chicago dealt their former first baseman to the Yankees for a two-player package: right-hander Alexander Vizcaino and center fielder Kevin Alcantara. Signed out of the Dominican Republic for a million dollars in early July 2018, Alcantara split time between both organizations' Complex League affiliates. In 34 total games, the 6-foot-6, 188-pound man-child slugged .345/.423/.588 with four doubles, five triples, and five homeruns. His overall production topped the league average by 60%, per *Weighted Runs Created Plus*.

Scouting Report: A nice, easy swing that generates plenty of loft and pure power. The ball just flies off of Alcantara's bat. He's the type of prospect where things appear to come quite easy for him. Very, very projectable. The batted ball data, according to *FanGraphs*, is solid too: his average exit velocity was already at an MLB average (88 mph) with a peak of 106 mph. There's the potential for superstardom, but I'm hesitant to fully commit until he gets a year in Low-A, which will happen in 2022. He could be an impact player on both sides of the ball.

Ceiling: 5.0-win player
Risk: Moderate to High
MLB ETA: 2024/2025

4. Cristian Hernandez, SS

Hit	Power	SB	Patience	Glove	Overall
45/50	50/60	55/50	50	50	60

Born: 12/13/03	Age: 18	Bats: R	Top Comp: Carlos Correa
Height: 6-2	Weight: 175	Throws: R	

Season	Team	Age	Level	PA	1B	2B	3B	HR	SB	CS	BB%	K%	AVG	OBP	SLG	ISO
2021	CHC	17	DSL	191	34	5	1	5	21	3	15.71%	20.42%	0.285	0.398	0.424	0.139

Background: Ranked as the sixth best prospect on the international market by MLB.com last season. Chicago pulled out all the stops and signed 6-foot-2, 175-pound shortstop to a massive $3 million on January 15, 2021. Hailing from Santo Domingo, Dominican Republic, Hernandez spent last season in the hitter-friendly confines of the Dominican Summer League. Appearing in 47 games, the then-17-year-old put together a solid .285/.398/.424 slash line, belting out five doubles, one triple, and five homeruns. He also swiped 21 bags. His overall production, per *Weighted Runs Created Plus*, topped the league average mark by 32%.

Scouting Report: A very natural feel for hitting. Hernandez is big, wiry, and projectable. And the Dominican-born shortstop already owns average power with the potential to develop plus thump at a premium position. Despite being big for his age, the soon-to-be 18-year-old is incredibly smooth at shortstop as well. And as long as he doesn't get too big he should have no problems manning the position. In terms of big league lines think: .280/.350/.475.

Ceiling: 4.0-win player
Risk: Moderate
MLB ETA: 2025

5. James Triantos, 2B/SS

	Hit	Power	SB	Patience	Glove	Overall
	50/55	50/60	50	50	50	60

Born: 01/29/03	Age: 19	Bats: R	Top Comp: N/A
Height: 6-1	Weight: 195	Throws: R	

Season	Team	Age	Level	PA	1B	2B	3B	HR	SB	CS	BB%	K%	AVG	OBP	SLG	ISO
2021	CHC	18	CPX	109	19	7	1	6	3	3	6.42%	16.51%	0.327	0.376	0.594	0.267

Background: Benefiting from the change – or tweak – in draft eligibility rules, Triantos was originally part of the high school class of 2022. But, as MLB.com points out, he reclassified and became eligible for last year's July draft. A two-way star for James Madison High School in Vienna, Virginia, Chicago went well-above draft slot to sign their second round pick. Triantos, the 56th overall player chosen, received a hefty $2.1 million bonus – nearly a million dollars more than slotted. He spent the summer with the organization's Arizona Complex League affiliate, batting an impressive .327/.376/.594 with seven doubles, one triple, and six homeruns. His overall production, according to *Weighted Runs Created Plus*, topped the league average mark by 43%.

Scouting Report: Consider the following:

- There were 140 hitters to reach the 100-plate appearance mark in the Arizona Complex League last summer. Triantos' 143 wRC+ is tied for the 15th best showing.

The Cubs' front office hasn't been shy about praising the type and quality of contact Triantos makes as a professional hitter. And it's easy to see why, too. The swing is a beautiful mix of strength, explosiveness, and controlled chaos. He's going to be the biggest prospect riser in the 2022 season. And he has a chance to develop into a bonafide middle-of-the-lineup thumper. In terms of big league lines, think: .280/.340/.540. He also flashed a 96-mph fastball on the mound and ran a 6.60 60-yard dash. Elite athlete.

Ceiling: 4.0-win player
Risk: Moderate
MLB ETA: 2024

6. Brailyn Marquez, LHP

	FB	SL	CH	Command	Overall
	N/A	N/A	N/A	N/A	55

Born: 01/30/99	Age: 23	Bats: L	Top Comp: N/A
Height: 6-4	Weight: 185	Throws: L	

Season	Team	Age	Level	IP	TBF	K/9	K%	BB/9	BB%	K-BB%	ERA	FIP	xFIP	Pit/Bat
2018	CHC	19	A-	47.2	197	9.82	26.40%	2.64	7.11%	19.29%	3.21	3.80	3.34	3.52
2019	CHC	20	A	77.1	332	11.87	30.72%	5.00	12.95%	17.77%	3.61	3.30	3.28	3.77
2019	CHC	20	A+	26.1	106	8.89	24.53%	2.39	6.60%	17.92%	1.71	2.81	3.40	4.15

Background: Poised for big things in the 2021. Marquez, a big left-hander out of Santo Domingo, Dominican Republic, was spectacular in 2019, the year before the lost COVID season. Making 22 starts between South Bend and Myrtle Beach, the then-21-year-old struck out 128 and walked 50 to go along with a 3.13 ERA in 103.2 innings of work. Chicago placed Marquez on the Taxi Squad two years ago and he eventually made his – brief – big league debut. Marquez made a late September relief appearance against the cross town rival White Sox, throwing just two-thirds of an inning while allowing five runs. Last season, with a ton of momentum moving towards a potentially large role with the big league squad, Marquez missed the entire year with a problematic shoulder. According to Jordan Bastian of MLB.com, the big lefty was working through a throwing program in November.

Snippet from The 2020 Prospect Digest Handbook: The potential is there to be one of the game's premier southpaws, but more work has to be done. As Major League Baseball and their organizations continue to buy into the pitch design / pitch development by Driveline Baseball and the like, the odds of Marquez taking that elite step forward increase dramatically.

Scouting Report: There's nothing new to report on. Marquez's arsenal was impressive during his abbreviated stint with the Cubs in 2020: his fastball averaged nearly 98 mph; his slider was in the mid 80s, and his changeup was in the 90 mph range. There's the potential to be a mid-rotation caliber starter, perhaps even higher – though that depends on two big *ifs*: #1: If he's healthy and #2: If he can throw enough strikes. If he comes back healthy, he's an easy lock for a Top 50 prospect in the game, the risk knocks him down significantly though.

Ceiling: 3.0-win player
Risk: Moderate to High
MLB ETA: Debuted in 2020

7. Reginald Preciado, 3B/SS

Hit	Power	SB	Patience	Glove	Overall
50	45/50	50/45	50	55	55

Born: 05/16/03	Age: 19	Bats: B	Top Comp: N/A
Height: 6-4	Weight: 185	Throws: R	

Season	Team	Age	Level	PA	1B	2B	3B	HR	SB	CS	BB%	K%	AVG	OBP	SLG	ISO
2021	CHC	18	CPX	154	31	10	3	3	7	1	7.14%	22.73%	0.333	0.383	0.511	0.177

Background: Almost lost in a system that's quickly becoming one of the better ones in baseball. The Cubs acquired veteran hurler Zach Davies and a quartet of prospects from the Padres for ace righty Yu Darvish and backstop / infielder Victor Caratini in December 2020. As noted by an article on MLB.com, San Diego handed the 6-foot-4, 185-pound infielder a hefty $1.3 million bonus a couple years, a Panamanian-record. Preciado, whose father played professionally in the Yankees organization once upon a time, made his debut in 2021. Spending the entirety of the year with the club's Arizona Complex League affiliate, the young shortstop / third baseman batted a scorching .333/.383/.511 with 10 doubles, three triples, and three homeruns. He also swiped sevens bags in eight attempts as well. Per *Weighted Runs Created Plus*, Preciado's overall production topped the league average mark by 32%.

Scouting Report: Last season there were 53 hitters to receive at least 150 plate appearances in the Arizona Complex League. Of those 53, Preciado's overall production, 132 wRC+, ranked as the eighth best and only three 18-year-olds (Wilfred Veras, Alexander Ramirez, and Yerlin Confidan) were better overall hitters. The young switch-hitter has a wide base at the plate with limited movement. Line drive swing that may not allow him to generate ton of homeruns, though he looks like a doubles machine. Defensively, he was incredible last season, per Clay Davenport's metrics (he was +7 at third base and +3 at shortstop). If Preciado makes the transition into full season action without too many speed bumps he's a contender to be a mid-season Top 100 prospect.

Ceiling: 3.0-win player
Risk: Moderate
MLB ETA: 2024

8. Owen Caissie, LF

Hit	Power	SB	Patience	Glove	Overall
40/45	50/60	35	55	50	55

Born: 07/08/02	Age: 19	Bats: L	Top Comp: N/A
Height: 6-4	Weight: 190	Throws: R	

Season	Team	Age	Level	PA	1B	2B	3B	HR	SB	CS	BB%	K%	AVG	OBP	SLG	ISO
2021	CHC	18	CPX	136	24	7	1	6	1	2	19.12%	28.68%	0.349	0.478	0.596	0.248
2021	CHC	18	A	90	12	4	0	1	0	0	17.78%	31.11%	0.233	0.367	0.329	0.096

Background: Prior to 2020, Notre Dame High School, located in Burlington, Ontario, has produced two MLB draft picks: Craig Hawkins, a 35th round pick by the Twins in 1997, and Jamie Lehman, a 29th round pick by the Expos in 2003. Caissie, a projectable 6-foot-4, 190-pound left fielder, crushed those previous draft status when the Padres selected him in the second round, 45th overall, two years ago. The Ontatio-native signed for a $1,200,004 bonus. Chicago acquired him in the Yu Darvish deal. Last season Caissie split time between Chicago's Arizona Complex League and Low-A affiliates, hitting an aggregate .302/.434/.489 with 11 doubles, one triple, and seven homeruns. His overall production, per *Weighted Runs Created Plus*, topped the league average mark by a hefty 48%.

Scouting Report: Consider the following:

- Last season there 140 hitters that received at least 100 plate appearances in the Arizona Complex League. Caissie's overall production at the level, 179 wRC+, topped them all.

Physically he reminds of a young Joey Gallo or Jason Botts. Big. Strong. Muscular. Caissie, like those counterparts, doesn't get cheated at the plate, never taking anything less than a massive hack. There's the potential to develop plus power, as well as turn into a Three True Outcomes-type hitter. He's the type of left-hander hitter that may show some platoon splits and eventually push him into platoon role. He's entering his age-19 season, with already some Low-A experience on his resume.

Ceiling: 3.0-win player
Risk: Moderate to High
MLB ETA: 2024

9. Miguel Amaya, C

Hit	Power	SB	Patience	Glove	Overall
40	50/55	30	60	50	50

Born: 03/09/99	Age: 23	Bats: R	Top Comp: Alex Avila
Height: 6-2	Weight: 230	Throws: R	

Season	Team	Age	Level	PA	1B	2B	3B	HR	SB	CS	BB%	K%	AVG	OBP	SLG	ISO
2018	CHC	19	A	479	71	21	2	12	1	0	10.44%	19.00%	0.256	0.349	0.403	0.147
2019	CHC	20	A+	410	45	24	0	11	2	0	13.17%	16.83%	0.235	0.351	0.402	0.167
2021	CHC	22	AA	106	12	4	0	1	2	0	19.81%	20.75%	0.215	0.406	0.304	0.089

Background: Before The Great Sell Off the Cubs' farm system looked an awful lot like Old Mother Hubbard's Cupboard. It was largely built around a small group of prospects: Brennen Davis, Brailyn Marquez, Ed Howard, and Miguel Amaya with little to spare. Quietly developing into one of the more saber-friendly backstops in the minor leagues, Amaya continued to sniff out first base with nearly unparalleled frequency. Through 23 games, the 6-foot-2, 230-pound catcher hit .215/.406/.304 with four doubles and a homerun before succumbing to an elbow injury that eventually forced him under the knife for Tommy John surgery. Per *Weighted Runs Created Plus*, Amaya's overall production topped the league average mark by 17%.

Snippet from The 2020 Prospect Digest Handbook: He may not be a star, but he has the potential to be an above-average starter.

Scouting Report: Prior to their reemergence as a perennial powerhouse in baseball, the Astros' farm system sported a young middle infielder by the name of Nolan Fontana. Possessing one of the elite eyes at the plate, the former second round pick would routinely put together walk rates north of 15% and sometimes cresting over in the 20% territory. The problem, of course, is that he couldn't hit all that well or for much power. While Amaya isn't *exactly* the type of player Fontana was, he's definitely cut from the same cloth. He'll walk well above the average amount, last season he walked 19.8% of the time, and he doesn't profile to hit for much of an average. But he'll flash 20-homer pop, though. There's such a dearth of catching at the big league level that Amaya should have no problem developing into a league average or better player – depending how the BABIP bounces.

Ceiling: 2.0-win player
Risk: Moderate
MLB ETA: 2022/2023

10. DJ Herz, LHP

FB	CB	SL	CH	Command	Overall
60	60	50	55	40/45	50

Born: 01/04/01	Age: 21	Bats: R	Top Comp: N/A
Height: 6-2	Weight: 175	Throws: L	

Season	Team	Age	Level	IP	TBF	K/9	K%	BB/9	BB%	K-BB%	ERA	FIP	xFIP	Pit/Bat
2019	CHC	18	R	10.1	50	6.97	16.00%	6.97	16.00%	0.00%	2.61	5.04	5.91	1.86
2021	CHC	20	A	65.2	260	14.39	40.38%	5.21	14.62%	25.77%	3.43	4.02	3.89	4.39
2021	CHC	20	A+	16.0	64	14.63	40.63%	3.38	9.38%	31.25%	2.81	2.65	3.07	4.00

Background: Terry Sanford High School's produced a total of three draft picks, all of which happened since 2018. The Orioles and Diamondbacks burned a couple late round selections on Andrew Jayne, who signed with Baltimore for $125,000, and Christian Jayne, who's at UNC Pembroke currently. A year later Chicago unearthed their big lefty in the eighth round, signing him to a $500,000 deal. Last year, Herz made a total of 20 starts – 17 with Myrtle Beach and three with South Bend. He threw 81.2 innings, averaging a whopping 14.4 strikeouts and 4.8 walks per nine innings. He finished the year with a 3.31 ERA.

Scouting Report: Consider the following:

- Since 2006, only six 20-year-old hurlers posted a 33% strikeout percentage in Low-A with one organization (min. 60 IP): Matt Moore, Trevor May, Seth Corry, Max Lazar, Pedro Avila, and DJ Herz. Here's the list of 20-year-old Low-A pitchers to post a strikeout percentage of at least 35% (min. 60 IP): DJ Herz, who posted a 40% strikeout percentage.

Mechanically speaking, he's a hybrid between Chris Sale / MacKenzie Gore / Josh Hader. Herz owns an explosive plus fastball, a plus curveball, a solid tightly-wound slider, and a very good changeup. The young lefty trusts his change-of-pace as much as any young arm I can recall. He's a crossfire thrower and that needs to be cleaned up. There's some promising mid-rotation upside here.

Ceiling: 2.0-win player
Risk: Moderate
MLB ETA: 2024

11. Alexander Canario, OF

Hit	Power	SB	Patience	Glove	Overall
40/45	50	60	50	50	50

Born: 05/07/00	Age: 22	Bats: R	Top Comp: Manuel Margot
Height: 6-1	Weight: 165	Throws: R	

Season	Team	Age	Level	PA	1B	2B	3B	HR	SB	CS	BB%	K%	AVG	OBP	SLG	ISO
2018	SFG	18	R	208	31	5	2	6	8	5	12.98%	24.52%	0.250	0.357	0.403	0.153
2019	SFG	19	R	46	6	3	1	7	1	0	4.35%	19.57%	0.395	0.435	1.000	0.605
2019	SFG	19	A-	219	31	17	1	9	3	1	8.22%	32.42%	0.301	0.365	0.539	0.238
2021	SFG	21	A	274	30	14	3	9	15	3	12.04%	28.83%	0.235	0.325	0.433	0.197
2021	CHC	21	A+	182	22	6	1	9	6	5	5.49%	25.27%	0.224	0.264	0.429	0.206

Background: Good bye Joc Pederson. Adios Anthony Rizzo. See ya' later Javier Baez. Have a good one, Craig Kimbrel. Thanks for your service Trevor Williams, Jake Marisnick, and Ryan Tepera. And for you, Kris Bryant, thanks for the memories. A particular hard trade to deal with, Chicago dealt the middle-of-the-lineup thumper to the Giants a days before the trade deadline, receiving right-hander Caleb Kilian and outfielder Alexander Canario. Originally signed by San Francisco for a scant five-figure sum six years ago. The 6-foot-1, 165-pound center / right fielder split time between Low-A and High-A last season, hitting an aggregate .230/.300/.431 with 20 doubles, four triples, 18 homeruns, and 21 stolen bases (in 29 attempts). His overall production was 8% *below* the league average threshold.

Snippet from The 2020 Prospect Digest Handbook: Not great odds. Loud tools that can be an impact – if he can make enough contact.

Scouting Report: Looking at the basic, "old fashioned" stats it's easy to see the attraction to Canario: he flashed intriguing power potential, belting out 42 extra-base hits in only 107 total games *and* he showed above-average or better speed, swiping 21 bags. The problem, of course, is that more advanced metrics are pretty muddled. He whiffed in more than 27% of his plate appearances. *Weighted Runs Created Plus* measures his overall production below the league average mark, and *Baseball Prospectus' DRC+* had him at league average – roughly. The batted ball data is very good – his peak exit velocity was 109 mph – and the glove can play at any position in the outfield. The question is whether he's going to put it all together, have a season where it "clicks". He's shown glimpses of it. For example: he slugged .271/.333/.495 between June 3 and September 3. High risk / high reward lottery ticket.

Ceiling: 2.0-win player
Risk: Moderate
MLB ETA: 2024

12. Jordan Wicks, LHP

FB	CB	SL	CH	Command	Overall
55	N/A	50	60	5	45

Born: 09/01/99	Age: 22	Bats: L	Top Comp:
Height: 6-3	Weight: 220	Throws: L	

Background: Fun Fact Part I: No Kansas State player has been taken in the first round of the June draft. Fun Fact Part II: It's been over fifty years since a Kansas State product has been selected before the third round of the June amateur draft (Jack Woolsey, second round, 1969). Fun Fact Part III: the most successful big leaguer to don a Wildcats uniform is right-hander Ted Power, who once led the National League in appearances in 1984. Enter: Jordan Wicks, who was drafted by the Cubs with the 21st overall selection in the opening round last July. A 6-foot-3, 220-pound southpaw out of Conway High School, Wicks left his former alma mater on a high note: he posted an 11-1 win-loss record to go along with a 0.86 ERA during his senior season and parted the school as the record holder for lowest career ERA (1.39). The Arkansas native made 15 starts for Kansas State during his freshman season, throwing 84.2 innings with 86 punch outs and just 26 walks. And he was nearly unhittable during his pandemic-shortened 2020 campaign: he tallied a 0.35 ERA across 26.0 innings with 26 strikeouts and just four walks. Wicks tied a career high in starts during the 2021 season, tossing a career high 92.1 innings while averaging 11.5 strikeouts and just 2.7 walks per nine innings. He compiled a 3.70 ERA while winning just six contests. After signing with the club for $3.1 million, the big lefty made four brief appearances in High-A, fanning five and walking three in seven innings.

Scouting Report: Per the usual, here's what I wrote about the southpaw heading into the 2021 draft:

> "With respect to his junior season, consider the following:

- *Between 2011 and 2020, only six Big12 pitchers have averaged at least 11 strikeouts per nine innings in a season (min. 80 IP): Alex Manoah, Nick Lodolo, Brandon Finnegan, Ryan Zeferjahn, Morgan Cooper, and Trey Cobb.*
- *Of those six, only two averaged less than 3.0 walks per nine innings: Manoah and Lodolo, the seventh and eleventh picks in the 2019 draft.*

- *Reminder: Wicks averaged 11.5 strikeouts and 2.7 walks per nine innings in 2021.*

Wicks attacks hitters with a 92- to 94-mph heater, an above-average offering for a southpaw. But his bread-and-butter, go-to pitch is a devastating, low 80s changeup – easily a plus pitch and likely the best one in the draft class. He reportedly throws a curveball, though I didn't see one in game play. Wicks looks like a backend starter, perhaps peaking as a #4 if everything breaks the right way. He could easily go the route of Tim Cate and Anthony Kay."

Ceiling: 1.5-win player
Risk: Moderate
MLB ETA: 2023/2024

13. Kevin Made, 3B/SS

Hit	Power	SB	Patience	Glove	Overall
45/55	30/40	40	30/40	50	45

Born: 09/10/02	Age: 19	Bats: R	Top Comp: N/A
Height: 5-10	Weight: 160	Throws: R	

Season	Team	Age	Level	PA	1B	2B	3B	HR	SB	CS	BB%	K%	AVG	OBP	SLG	ISO
2021	CHC	18	A	243	47	13	3	1	2	0	2.47%	23.46%	0.272	0.296	0.366	0.094

Background: With the club's window of contention actively closing and the draft classes failing to add a ton of upside talent to a depleted farm system, the Cubbies began spending *big* on the international free agent market a couple years ago. Back in 2019 the front office pushed their collective chips to the center of the table and signed a couple of high profile teenage prospects: backstop Ronnie Quintero, who spent last season mostly struggling in the Complex League, and infielder Kevin Made. Signed to a $1.7 million deal, the 5-foot-10, 160-pound shortstop / third baseman made his debut in Low-A – at the ripe ol' age of 18. And he more than held his own. Appearing in 58 games with the Myrtle Beach Pelicans, Made batted a respectable .272/.296/.366 with 13 doubles, three triples, and one homerun. His overall production, according to *Weighted Runs Created Plus*, was 20% below the league average mark.

Scouting Report: The overall numbers are a bit underwhelming, but let's add some context. Consider the following little tidbits:

- Last season Made was just one of six 18-year-old hitters to earn at least 200 plate appearances in Low-A.
- While is overall production ranks as the fifth in the group – largely because he refuses to take a walk – his strikeout rate, 23.5%, was the best – by three full percentage points.
- Made's first game of the year May 27th. Less than a week later he hit the injured list for a month.
- After a bit of a slow start once he returned to the Pelicans Made slugged a healthy .303/.322/.421.

For those counting at home: From July 14th through the rest of the year his overall production he posted a 101 wRC+. On the flip side, though, he walked just three times in 183 plate appearances (1.6% of the time). And that's the crux of argument against Made's long term value. Here's a list of player to post a walk rate less than 4.0% and tally more than two wins above replacement in a season in the big leagues since 2015: Tim Anderson (2019), Rougned Odor (2016), Didi Gregorius (2016), Jonathan Schoop (2016), Kevin Pillar (2018), Dee Gordon (2015, 2017), Corey Dickerson (2018). It's reasonable to expect Made to show increased patience as he matures, after all it's not going to get any worse, but he's only going to go as far as his hit tool and power will take him.

Ceiling: 1.5-win player
Risk: Moderate
MLB ETA: 2024/2025

14. Ed Howard, 2B/SS

Hit	Power	SB	Patience	Glove	Overall
40/45	45/50	40	45	50	45

Born: 01/28/02	Age: 20	Bats: R	Top Comp: N/A
Height: 6-2	Weight: 185	Throws: R	

Season	Team	Age	Level	PA	1B	2B	3B	HR	SB	CS	BB%	K%	AVG	OBP	SLG	ISO
2021	CHC	19	A	326	52	9	3	4	7	2	5.52%	30.06%	0.225	0.277	0.315	0.089

Background: Fun Fact Part I: the Cubs have drafted just 10 shortstops in the first round. Fun Fact Part II: Only two of those players went on to establish themselves as above-average big leaguers – Shawon Dunston and Javier Baez – and the jury is still out on a third (Nico Hoerner). The initial results for Ed Howard, the 16th overall pick in 2020, don't appear to be promising. A product of Mount Carmel High School, the 6-foot-2, 185-pound middle infielder batted a lowly .225/.277/.315 with nine doubles, three triples, and four homeruns. He swiped seven bags in nine attempts. Per *Weighted Runs Created Plus*, Howard's overall production is 36% *below* the league average threshold.

Scouting Report: Consider the following:

- Since 2006, only four 19-year-old hitters met the following criteria in Low-A with one organization (min. 300 PA): a *Weighted Runs Created Plus* total of 70 or less, a strikeout rate of at least 28%, and a walk rate below 7%. Those four hitters: Steven Moya, D.J. Davis, Julian Leon, and Ed Howard.

So it's not all doom-and-gloom for the former first round selection. Howard got off to a *horrible* start to the year, batting a pathetic .184/.239/.251 with a 32% strikeout rate through his first 55 games. But something seemed to click for the middle infielder in mid-August and he hit .316/.359/.453 with a 25.9% strikeout rate over his remaining 27 games. Solid pop. Solid glove. A little bit of speed. But Howard's going to need to prove that the late season surge was a harbinger of things to come and not an aberration.

Ceiling: 1.5-win player
Risk: Moderate
MLB ETA: 2025

15. Anderson Espinoza, RHP

	FB	CB	SL	CH	Command	Overall
	60	55/60	55/60	50	40/45	50

Born: 03/09/98	Age: 24	Bats: R	Top Comp: N/A
Height: 6-0	Weight: 190	Throws: R	

Season	Team	Age	Level	IP	TBF	K/9	K%	BB/9	BB%	K-BB%	ERA	FIP	xFIP	Pit/Bat
2021	CHC	23	A+	16.0	68	15.19	39.71%	6.19	16.18%	23.53%	5.06	3.46	3.80	4.49
2021	SDP	23	A+	28.2	126	11.62	29.37%	4.08	10.32%	19.05%	5.02	4.12	4.09	4.37
2021	CHC	23	AA	13.1	57	10.80	28.07%	5.40	14.04%	14.04%	1.35	3.25	4.22	4.51

Background: It feels like forever ago that Espinoza was once one of the darlings of pitching prospects. A true, bonafide ace-in-waiting type of arm that looked like a young Pedro Martinez. Then Tommy John surgery hit. Then a second Tommy John surgery happened. And, all of sudden, the baseball world had passed the lanky, once-projectable right-hander by. In fact, he went five years in between professional appearances. Espinoza reemerged last season as a dominant, albeit erratic, 23-year-old. Splitting time between two levels (High-A and Double-A), as well as two separate organizations, the 6-foot, 190-pound hurler averaged 12.4 K/9 and 5.0 BB/9 in 58.0 innings of work. Chicago acquired Espinoza from the Padres near the trade deadline last July for outfielder Jake Marisnick.

Scouting Report: Espinoza's still showed an explosive heater, an easy plus offering. His curveball and slider were inconsistent, which is to be expected, but they both flashed plus at times. Average changeup. The command, of course, was spotty. If you squint hard enough you can see a dominant starting pitcher deep at his core. But, again, that comes with such an incredible risk already built in, courtesy of two Tommy John surgeries. Hell, the fact that he's bounced back to his current state just shows how far medical advances have come.

Ceiling: 2.0-win player
Risk: High
MLB ETA: 2022

16. Nelson Velazquez, OF

	Hit	Power	SB	Patience	Glove	Overall
	45	50	50	45	55	45

Born: 12/26/98	Age: 23	Bats: R	Top Comp: Dylan Moore
Height: 6-0	Weight: 190	Throws: R	

Season	Team	Age	Level	PA	1B	2B	3B	HR	SB	CS	BB%	K%	AVG	OBP	SLG	ISO
2018	CHC	19	A-	293	35	18	2	11	12	4	7.85%	27.65%	0.250	0.322	0.458	0.208
2018	CHC	19	A	120	20	1	0	0	3	0	5.83%	35.83%	0.188	0.242	0.196	0.009
2019	CHC	20	R	21	3	1	0	2	0	0	9.52%	23.81%	0.316	0.381	0.684	0.368
2019	CHC	20	A	285	51	16	4	4	5	3	7.37%	27.02%	0.286	0.338	0.424	0.137
2021	CHC	22	A+	288	42	13	1	12	12	2	6.94%	33.68%	0.261	0.321	0.456	0.195
2021	CHC	22	AA	137	17	10	1	8	5	0	7.30%	25.55%	0.290	0.358	0.581	0.290

Background: Born the day after Christmas in 1998. The Cubbies drafted the Puerto Rican-born outfielder in the fifth round all the way back in 2017. And after a lackluster first two seasons in professional ball, things seemed to click for Velazquez in Low-A in 2019: he batted .286/.338/.424 with 24 extra-base hits in only 72 contests. Last season, the 6-foot, 190-pound outfielder split time between High-A and Double-A, slugging an aggregate .270/.333/.496 with 23 doubles, two triples, and 20 homeruns. He also swiped 17 bags in 19 total attempts. Per *Weighted Runs Created Plus*, Velazquez's overall production topped the league average threshold by 22%.

Snippet from The 2020 Prospect Digest Handbook: Glimpses of solid-average, maybe even a touch better, power are visible. Velazquez looks like a fourth outfielder, maybe squeaking out a 50-grade if everything breaks the right way.

Scouting Report: Consider the following:

- Since 2006, only four 22-year-old hitters met the following criteria in a High-A season with one organization (min. 250 PA): a WRC+ total between 100 and 110, a strikeout rate of at least 30%, and a walk rate between 6% and 8%. Those four hitters: Geraldo Rodriguez, Jan Hernandez, Trey Cabbage, and – of course – Nelson Velazquez.

Velazquez's numbers are a bit misleading because he caught fire after his promotion to Double-A. He's still profiling as a fourth outfielder, though now it's more on the lower end of the spectrum. The power's really coming through, but the K-rate has climbed back into red flag territory. There's a power / speed combo that will tantalize some clubs – maybe the Cubs – to give him long looks, but he's the type that's going to get exposed by multiple looks around the league. Above-average glove.

Ceiling: 1.0- to 1.5-win player
Risk: Moderate
MLB ETA: 2023

17. Caleb Kilian, RHP

	FB	CB	SL	CH	Command	Overall
	55	50	50	50	60	45

Born: 06/02/97	Age: 25	Bats: R	Top Comp: Kendall Graveman
Height: 6-4	Weight: 180	Throws: R	

Season	Team	Age	Level	IP	TBF	K/9	K%	BB/9	BB%	K-BB%	ERA	FIP	xFIP	Pit/Bat
2019	SFG	22	R	12.0	42	8.25	26.19%	1.50	4.76%	21.43%	0.00	3.19	3.52	2.21
2021	SFG	24	A+	21.2	75	13.29	42.67%	0.42	1.33%	41.33%	1.25	1.16	2.18	3.84
2021	SFG	24	AA	63.0	244	9.14	26.23%	1.14	3.28%	22.95%	2.43	2.37	3.13	3.61
2021	CHC	24	AA	15.2	64	9.19	25.00%	2.30	6.25%	18.75%	4.02	4.61	4.09	3.39

Background: The lesser known prospect the organization received from San Francisco in the Kris Bryant trade last July. The Giants originally drafted the lanky 6-foot-4, 180-pound right-hander in the eighth round out of Texas Tech in 2019. After a dominating –

albeit brief – debut in the lower rungs of the minor leagues, Kilian began the 2021 season off on a tear: he struck out 32, walked one, and compiled a 1.25 ERA through 21.2 innings in High-A. He spent the remainder of the year – 15 starts between both organizations – battling the minors' most difficult challenge: Double-A. In total, Kilian tossed 100.1 innings, recording 112 strikeouts and just 13 walks.

Scouting Report: Consider the following:

- Since 2006, only three 24-year-old pitchers met the following criteria in a Double-A season with one organization (min. 75 IP): a strikeout percentage between 25% and 27% and a walk percentage below 6%. Those three hurlers: Luis Castillo, Matt Strahm, and Michael Plassmeyer.

Kilian's production puts him in the same group had he spent the year with one organization. Mid-90s cheddar. A solid average curveball / slider / changeup combination. Kilian lacks a sit-'em-down type of secondary offering, but his strong feel for the strike zone helps compensate. These types of guys typically make successful relief arms, some graduating to high leverage outings, but it's not a strong profile for a starting pitcher. The Cubs are in full rebuild mode, so Kilian's likely to get a few opportunities to prove himself as a grab-the-ball-every-fifth-day type.

Ceiling: 1.0-win player
Risk: Low to Moderate
MLB ETA: 2022

18. Ryan Jensen, RHP

	FB	CB	SL	CH	Command	Overall
	70	50	55	45	50	40

Born: 11/23/97	Age: 24	Bats: R	Top Comp: Brandon Bailey
Height: 6-0	Weight: 190	Throws: R	

Season	Team	Age	Level	IP	TBF	K/9	K%	BB/9	BB%	K-BB%	ERA	FIP	xFIP	Pit/Bat
2019	CHC	21	A-	12.0	57	14.25	33.33%	10.50	24.56%	8.77%	2.25	4.49	4.71	4.19
2021	CHC	23	A+	62.0	256	10.89	29.30%	3.48	9.38%	19.92%	4.50	4.53	4.02	4.17
2021	CHC	23	AA	18.0	70	7.50	21.43%	3.50	10.00%	11.43%	3.00	4.35	3.80	3.77

Background: After a debacle of a freshman season at Fresno State – he walked more than he struck out – Jensen's command improved in each of his final remaining years with the Mountain West Conference school. And after a dominating junior campaign, in which he

averaged 9.6 strikeouts and just 2.4 walks per nine innings, the Cubs selected the flame-throwing right-hander in the opening round, 27th overall, in 2019 and signed him to a deal worth $2 million. Last season Jensen made 20 stops between South Bend and Tennessee, throwing just 80.0 innings with 90 punch outs and 31 free passes. He compiled an aggregate 4.16 ERA. Jensen also made an additional six appearances in with the Mesa Solar Sox in the Arizona Fall League, posting a 20-to-12 strikeout-to-walk ratio.

Scouting Report: Consider the following:

- Since 2006, only seven 23-year-old hurlers posted a 28% to 30% strikeout percentage with a walk percentage between 9% and 11% in a High-A season with one organization (min. 60 IP): Brandon Bailey and Ryan Jensen.

Very similar profile as Brandon Bailey. Jensen, like his counterpart, is trending as a multi-inning or high-leverage reliever – despite some minor league success as a starting pitcher. Jensen's fastball is an easy plus-offering, often times letting him pitch off of it exclusively in the lower levels of the minor leagues. He'll complement the mid- to upper-90s heater with a pair of breaking balls: an average curveball and an above-average slider with cutter-like depth and movement. His changeup is a 45 and may bump up to average in time.

Ceiling: 1.0-win player
Risk: Moderate
MLB ETA: 2022

19. Christian Franklin, OF

Hit	Power	SB	Patience	Glove	Overall
40	50	55	55	50	40

Born: 11/30/99	Age: 22	Bats: R	Top Comp: N/A
Height: 5-11	Weight: 195	Throws: R	

Season	Team	Age	Level	PA	1B	2B	3B	HR	SB	CS	BB%	K%	AVG	OBP	SLG	ISO
2021	CHC	21	CPX	14	5	0	0	0	3	0	21.43%	14.29%	0.455	0.571	0.455	0.000
2021	CHC	21	A	87	9	3	0	1	1	4	19.54%	26.44%	0.200	0.402	0.292	0.092

Background: The University of Arkansas has churned out – perhaps, quietly – an impressive amount of talent throughout the years – especially over the past decade-plus, including: the second overall pick in 2020 Heston Kjerstad, Trevor Stephan, Andrew Benintendi, Brian Anderson, Jalen Beeks, Ryne Stanek, James McCann, Brett Eibner, Drew Smyly, Andy Wilkins, Mike Bolsinger, and Dallas Keuchel. And three Razorbacks have been taken within the opening two rounds of the draft since 2019: Kjerstad, Dominic Fletcher, and Isaiah Campbell. A highly touted prep bat coming out of high hchool, Franklin was rated as (1) the top player in the state of Missouri and (2) the #29 outfielder in the country by Perfect Game. He turned in a solid, sometimes dominant, freshman season, hitting .274/.361/.413 with eight doubles, one triple, six homeruns, and 12 stolen bases. His potentially explosive sophomore campaign – he batted .381/.467/.619 with eight extra-base hits through 16 games – was, of course, interrupted by COVID. Franklin's numbers during his final season with the Razorbacks were somewhere in-between: in a career high 274 plate appearances, Franklin slugged .274/.420/.544 with 15 doubles, two triples, and 13 homeruns. He also swiped 11 bags in 14 attempts. Chicago drafted the Razorback outfielder in the fourth round, 123rd overall, and signed him to a deal worth $425, 000. He batted .237/.426/.316 in 24 games between rookie ball and Low-A.

Scouting Report: Per the usual, here's my pre-draft write-up:

"Consider the following:

- *Between 2011 and 2020, there were only six instances in which a SEC hitter fanned in more than 25% of his plate appearances in a season (min. 250 PA): Jeren Kendall, Tanner English, Luke Jarvis, Harrison Ray, and Julien Edouard (who accomplished the feat in 2018 and 2019). Kendall turned out to be a first round bust. The remaining players were drafted after the 10th round. And Ray was undrafted.*
- *Again, Franklin has whiffed in 28% of his plate appearances. The tools are loud, especially the power/speed/patience, but they're all useless unless he can make contact more frequently. And his K-rate was only slightly better during the 2019 and 2020 seasons: 26%.*

Again, Franklin has whiffed in 28% of his plate appearances. The tools are loud, especially the power/speed/patience, but they're all useless unless he can make contact more frequently. And his K-rate was only slightly better during the 2019 and 2020 seasons: 26%."

I originally pegged Franklin as a late third, early fourth round talent.

Ceiling: 1.0-win player
Risk: Moderate
MLB ETA: 2024

20. Drew Gray, LHP

	FB	CB	SL	CH	Command	Overall
	55	55	50	50	45	40

Born: 05/10/03	Age: 19	Bats: L	Top Comp: N/A
Height: 6-3	Weight: 190	Throws: L	

Background: Over the past six or so years Florida-base high school IMG Academy has been a hotbed of legitimate baseball talent. The Bradenton area school has produced 19 draft picks since 2015, including two first round selections, three second round picks, and two third rounders. Last season Gray was the second player taken from IMG Academy, coming one round after the selection of outfielder James Woods by the Padres. Gray, the 93rd overall pick, signed with the National League Central Division organization for $900,000. He pitched four innings across two appearances in the Arizona Complex League, fanning nine and walking just one to go with a 0.00 ERA.

Scouting Report: Quality four-pitch mix highlighted by an above-average low-90s fastball. He'll also showcase a late-tilting, above-average curveball, an average slider and a decent changeup. Gray's solid arsenal plays up due to his long limbs. There's some sneaky upside here, but he's raw, a developmental project. One more note: he averaged an impressive 19.8 K/9 during his senior season on the mound.

Ceiling: 1.0-win player
Risk: Moderate
MLB ETA: 2025

Chicago White Sox

Top Prospects

1. Colson Montgomery, SS

Hit	Power	SB	Patience	Glove	Overall
50	40/55	50	50	50	50

Born: 02/27/02	Age: 20	Bats: L	Top Comp: N/A
Height: 6-4	Weight: 205	Throws: R	

Season	Team	Age	Level	PA	1B	2B	3B	HR	SB	CS	BB%	K%	AVG	OBP	SLG	ISO
2021	CHW	19	CPX	111	20	7	0	0	0	1	11.71%	19.82%	0.287	0.396	0.362	0.074

Background: Montgomery was a prolific prep athlete coming out of Southridge High School. So much so, in fact, the 6-foot-4, 205-pound shortstop was being pursued by some of college basketball's heavyweights as a freshman and sophomore, including: Indiana University, Purdue University, and the University of Louisville. But Montgomery blossomed on the diamond for the Raiders: he batted .333 with seven dingers and 24 stolen bases during his final campaign, leading the school to its first ever Indiana High School Athletic Association State Championship. Chicago drafted Montgomery with the 22nd overall pick last June and signed him to a deal worth a smidgeon over $3 million. He appeared in 26 contests with the organization's Arizona Summer League affiliate, batting a solid .287/.396/.362 with seven doubles. His overall production, per *Weighted Runs Created Plus*, topped the league average mark by 12%.

Scouting Report: Per the usual, here's my pre-draft write-up:

> *"Lean, athletic frame that figures to add several pounds of muscle as he matures. Montgomery is surprising fluid in the field, showing some hands a strong arm to make difficult throws look easy. The swing is controlled violence, though it tends to get a little long at times. There's 25-homerun power lurking in the bat. He consistently saw a bevy of offspeed pitches during the showcases and showed no discernible red flags."*

Ceiling: 2.5-win player
Risk: Moderate
MLB ETA: 2025

2. Jose Rodriguez, SS

Hit	Power	SB	Patience	Glove	Overall
55/60	50	60	40	50	50

Born: 05/13/01	Age: 21	Bats: R	Top Comp: Tim Anderson
Height: 5-11	Weight: 175	Throws: R	

Season	Team	Age	Level	PA	1B	2B	3B	HR	SB	CS	BB%	K%	AVG	OBP	SLG	ISO
2018	CHW	17	R	240	48	13	3	2	16	4	3.75%	12.08%	0.291	0.318	0.401	0.110
2019	CHW	18	R	200	36	7	3	9	7	1	4.50%	22.50%	0.293	0.328	0.505	0.213
2021	CHW	20	A	361	60	22	4	9	20	5	5.82%	15.79%	0.283	0.328	0.452	0.170
2021	CHW	20	A+	126	33	4	1	5	10	5	3.97%	10.32%	0.361	0.381	0.538	0.176
2021	CHW	20	AA	14	2	1	0	0	0	1	0.00%	14.29%	0.214	0.214	0.286	0.071

Background: Talk about doing their due diligence on the international free agent market. Added during the 2017-18 signing period for a paltry sum of $50,000, Rodriguez continues to show flashes of brilliance. The 5-foot-11, 175-pound middle-infielder acquitted himself nicely during his professional debut in the Dominican Summer League, hitting a solid .291/.318/.401 with 13 doubles, three triples, two homeruns, and 16 stolen bases. The front office bounced the emerging top prospect up to the Arizona Summer League the following year. And Rodriguez maintained status quo as an 18-year-old: in 44 games, he hit .293/.328/.505 with 19 extra-base hits. Last season the organization removed the developmental governor as he blitzed through three separate levels. Rodriguez opened the year by slugging .283/.328/.452 in 78 contests in Low-A. He continued to hit following his promotion up to High-A (.361/.381/.538). And his bat only slowed during his four-game cameo in the minors' toughest challenge, Double-A. In total, Rodriguez batted an impressive .301/.338/.469 with 27 doubles, five triples, 14 homeruns, and 30 stolen bases. Per *Weighted Runs Created Plus*, his overall production topped the league average mark by 15%.

Snippet from The 2020 Prospect Digest Handbook: Rodriguez's unwillingness to walk mitigates some of his overall production, despite flashing some impressive power potential at an up-the-middle position. His ability to make consistent contact may be an issuing as he moves up the ladder, so that bears watching. A potential 55-grade glove at either position.

Scouting Report: Consider the following:

- Since 2006, only three 20-year-old hitters in Low-A met the following criteria in a season for one organization (min. 350 PA): 105 to 115 wRC+, sub-6.0% walk rate, sub-16% strikeout rate, and an Isolated Power north of .150. Those three players Lewin Diaz, Jose Miranda, and – of course – Mr. Jose Rodriguez. And it should be noted that Diaz and Miranda are both first baseman.

Incredible bat-to-ball skills that are offset by his abhorrence to take a free pass. Rodriguez has the makings of an solid big league shortstop. The bat could be an a plus tool, which would match the speed. Throw in some surprising pop for a 5-foot-11, 175-pound middle infielder and the defensive chops to stay at the position, and that's a recipe for success. In fact, it's a nearly identical toolkit at the club's current All-Star shortstop. One more item to note: per FanGraphs, Rodriguez's average exit velocity was 88 mph with a peak of 106.

Ceiling: 2.5-win player
Risk: Moderate
MLB ETA: 2023/2024

3. Matthew Thompson, RHP

FB	CB	CH	Command	Overall
65	60	50	45	50

Born: 08/11/00	Age: 21	Bats: R	Top Comp: Ubaldo Jimenez
Height: 6-3	Weight: 195	Throws: R	

Season	Team	Age	Level	IP	TBF	K/9	K%	BB/9	BB%	K-BB%	ERA	FIP	xFIP	Pit/Bat
2021	CHW	20	A	71.2	324	9.67	23.77%	4.77	11.73%	12.04%	5.90	4.85	4.89	3.92

Background: Cypress Ranch High School has been witness to some impressive pitching prospects over the past four seasons Ty Madden, a 2021 first round pick from the University of Texas, graduated from the prep school back in 2018. Right-hander JJ Goss was taken with the 36th overall pick in 2019 by the Rays. And, of course, Matthew Thompson, a teammate of the duo, was taken in the second round three years ago as well. Snagged with the 45th overall pick and signed to a deal worth $2.1 million, Thompson tossed only a pair of innings in rookie ball during his debut in 2019, fanning two and walking none. Given the lack of a minor league season in 2020, last year was basically the 6-foot-3, 195-pound right-hander's debut – all things considered. Making 19 starts for Low Kannapolis Cannon Ballers, Thompson struck out 77 and issued 38 walks in 71.2 innings of work. He compiled an unsightly 5.90 ERA and a 4.89 xFIP.

Snippet from The 2020 Prospect Digest Handbook: Thompson's raw, but has the potential to develop into a backend starting pitcher. He seems confident in his ability to spin the breaking ball.

Scouting Report: Consider the following:

- Since 2006, only four 20-year-old Low-A pitchers met the following criteria in a season with one organization (min. 70 IP): post a strikeout percentage 23% and 25% with a walk percentage between 11% and 13%. Those four pitchers: Fabian Williamson, Yennsy Diaz, Yeliar Castro, and Matthew Thompson.

The best arm in a system bereft of top pitching talent. Thompson, though, has the potential to develop into a viable big league starting option. Featuring a fastball sitting in the 96-97 mph range, he continues to show a ton of promise in his ability to spin a curveball. He has trouble commanding it at times, but it's a late-breaking bender that's going to generate a ton of swing-and-misses in the future. He'll also mix in a fringy average changeup that's a bit firm, but shows some arm-side run to it. Thompson's not the typical power-based young arm. He approaches at bats with a plan and a willingness to change speeds. The command – in general – needs to see an uptick.

Ceiling: 2.5-win player
Risk: Moderate
MLB ETA: 2024

4. Bryan Ramos, 2B/3B

Hit	Power	SB	Patience	Glove	Overall
45/50	50/55	50/40	50+	50	50

Born: 03/12/02	Age: 20	Bats: R	Top Comp: David Freese
Height: 6-2	Weight: 190	Throws: R	

Season	Team	Age	Level	PA	1B	2B	3B	HR	SB	CS	BB%	K%	AVG	OBP	SLG	ISO
2019	CHW	17	R	218	36	10	2	4	3	4	8.72%	20.18%	0.277	0.353	0.415	0.138
2021	CHW	19	A	504	63	23	6	13	13	4	10.12%	21.83%	0.244	0.345	0.415	0.172

Background: Another one of the club's expenditures from the Cuban free agent market. The White Sox signed the second / third baseman for a rather sizeable fee, $300,000, four years ago. As MLB.com notes, Ramos began opening eyes as a potential serious big league prospect several years earlier as he was starring for in the 15U league in his homeland. Ramos acquitted himself nicely during his stateside debut in 2019, hitting a respectable .277/.353/.415 with 10 doubles, two triples, four homeruns, and a trio of stolen bases in 51 games in the Arizona Summer League. And despite missing development time during the 2020 COVID-interrupted season, the front office bounced the 6-foot-2, 190-pound teenage infielder straight up to Kannapolis last season. And he continued to hold his own. In 115 games with the club's Low-A affiliate, Ramos batted .244/.345/.415 with 23 doubles, six triples, 13 homeruns, and 13 stolen bases (in 17 attempts). Per *Weighted Runs Created Plus*, his overall production topped the league average mark by 9%.

Snippet from The 2020 Prospect Digest Handbook: The bat speed; raw, muscular power, and natural loft all scream future above-average power. I really, really like the upside in Ramos. There's starting potential here, possibly more. He could be one of the bigger breakouts in the minor leagues in 2020.

Scouting Report: Consider the following:

- Since 2006, only four 19-year-old Low-A hitters have met the following criteria in a season with one organization (min. 400 PA): 105 to 115 wRC+, 21% to 23% strikeout percentage, and a walk rate between 9% and 12%. Those four players: Bo Naylor, one of the top prospects in the Indians system; Jordyn Adams, an intriguing prospect in the Angels' system, and Bobby Borchering, a former first round pick.

One of the highest ceilings in Chicago's farm system. Ramos, unlike a lot of the club's other better minor league at bats, takes a well-rounded approach to the plate: strong contact skills, above-average patience, average power with the potential to be above-average, and a smattering of speed. Throw in a solid glove at second or third bases, and Ramos could blossom into a Top 100 prospect. There's a lot of boom-bust potential here, but I'm betting bat speed and power potential.

Ceiling: 2.5-win player
Risk: Moderate
MLB ETA: 2023

5. Jake Burger, 3B

Hit	Power	SB	Patience	Glove	Overall
45	55	30	50	50	50

Born: 04/10/96	Age: 26	Bats: R	Top Comp: Mark Trumbo
Height: 6-2	Weight: 230	Throws: R	

Season	Team	Age	Level	PA	1B	2B	3B	HR	SB	CS	BB%	K%	AVG	OBP	SLG	ISO
2021	CHW	25	AAA	340	49	16	2	18	0	0	7.06%	26.76%	0.274	0.332	0.513	0.239

Background: The definition of persistence. The White Sox selected the former Missouri State University star with the 11th overall pick in the 2017 – Burger was sandwiched between Jo Adell and Shane Baz, by the way. And the power-hitting third baseman had the look and potential to move quickly through the minor leagues. Then he shredded his Achilles tendon in 2018. Finally healthy, he re-injured the same Achilles tendon during a rehab assignment. He missed all of 2019 due to a heal issue. Then COVID happened and cancelled the 2020 minor league season. So the level of production Burger displayed in Triple-A last year is…basically unparalleled. Appearing in 82 games with the Charlotte Knights, the 6-foot-2, 230-pound medical wonder batted .274/.332/.513 with 16 doubles, two triples, and 18 homeruns. His overall production, per *Weighted Runs Created Plus*, topped the league average mark by 22%. Burger also appeared in 15 games with the White Sox, hitting a respectable .263/.333/.474.

Scouting Report: Consider the following:

- Since 2006, only two 25-year-old AAA hitters posted a wRC+ between 117 and 127, a walk rate below 10%, and strikeout rate between 26% and 28% in a season with one team (min. 300 PA): John Mayberry Jr. and Jake Burger.

Throw out all the traditional analysis in this instance, because it doesn't apply. Burger's a wild stallion of unpredictability. After appearing in only 47 games above rookie ball during his debut *in 2017*, he reemerged as a similar hitter four years later *in Triple-A*. It really is an unbelievable story. And the fact that he's somehow managed to remain at the hot corner is mind blowing. Never mind that he's somehow a competent, average glove at the position so *he'll likely remain there*. Oh…and by the way…Burger smoked a ball at 115.2 mph during his tenure with the Sox. He's got a legitimate shot at being a league average starter. And I'm all for it.

Ceiling: 2.0-win player
Risk: Moderate
MLB ETA: Debuted in 2021

6. Norge Vera, RHP

FB	CB	SL	CH	Command	Overall
55	55	55	50	45/50	50

Born: 06/01/00	Age: 22	Bats: R	Top Comp: N/A
Height: 6-4	Weight: 185	Throws: R	

Season	Team	Age	Level	IP	TBF	K/9	K%	BB/9	BB%	K-BB%	ERA	FIP	xFIP	Pit/Bat
2021	CHW	21	DSL	19.0	69	16.11	49.28%	2.37	7.25%	42.03%	0.00	0.94	0.97	1.87

Background: Tell me if you've ever heard this one before: The White Sox signed the Cuban prospect on the international free agent market. Signed for a hefty $1.5 million last February, the 6-foot-4, 185-pound right-hander spent a year in the premier Cuban National Series as an 18-year-old; he struck out 37 and walked 32 in 54.2 innings of work. Last season, just months after signing with Chicago, Vera made eight impressive appearances with the organization's Dominican Summer League squad, posting a 34-to-5 strikeout-to-walk ratio in only 19 innings of work. He compiled a miniscule 0.95 ERA, a 0.94 FIP, and a 0.97 xFIP.

Scouting Report: Long and wiry with a weirdly robotic arm swing in his delivery. Physically, Vera's cut from the Matthew Thompson-mold. Three above-average pitches – fastball, curveball, and slider – with a solid complementary fourth option in his changeup. Vera isn't maxed out physically yet, so there's some projection left. He's raw, but I keep coming back to the arm swing. It's going to cause some issues down the line unless it gets cleaned up. Sneaky athleticism.

Ceiling: 2.0-win player
Risk: Moderate
MLB ETA: 2024/2025

7. Lenyn Sosa, 2B/SS

Hit	Power	SB	Patience	Glove	Overall
50	45	40	40	55	45

Born: 01/25/00	Age: 22	Bats: R	Top Comp: Nick Ahmed
Height: 6-0	Weight: 180	Throws: R	

Season	Team	Age	Level	PA	1B	2B	3B	HR	SB	CS	BB%	K%	AVG	OBP	SLG	ISO
2018	CHW	18	R	291	61	13	3	4	2	2	2.41%	12.37%	0.293	0.317	0.406	0.112
2019	CHW	19	A	536	82	35	2	7	6	6	5.04%	19.03%	0.251	0.292	0.371	0.120
2021	CHW	21	A+	353	67	19	1	10	3	4	3.97%	21.81%	0.290	0.321	0.443	0.153
2021	CHW	21	AA	121	19	5	0	1	0	1	1.65%	23.14%	0.214	0.240	0.282	0.068

Background: Hailing from Puerto Ordaz, Venezuela, the White Sox placed the middle infielder on an aggressive development plan since his debut in the Arizona Summer League as a 17-year-old. And Sosa responded well enough: he hit .270/.330/.358. He upped the ante even further the following season, 2018, in the Pioneer League, batting .293/.317/.406. And he looked decent enough as a teenager with Kannapolis in Low-A in 2019. Last season the front office decided to pump the brakes for a second and pushed then-21-year-old to High-A. But after slugging .290/.321/.443 in 82 contests, he found himself – struggling – in Double-A. In total, Sosa hit an aggregate .271/.300/.401 with 24 doubles, one triple, 11 homeruns, and a trio of stolen bases.

Scouting Report: Consider the following:

- Since 2006, five 21-year-old High-A hitters met the following criteria with one organization in a season (min. 350 PA): 98 to 108 wRC+, sub-5.0% walk rate, a strikeout rate north of 20%. Those five hitters: Steven Moya, Ryan Harvey, Carlos Peguero, Jalen Miller, and Lenyn Sosa.

Cut from the same cloth as the club's other more notable minor league bats. Sosa (A) doesn't walk frequently, or ever, (B) flashes decent power, and (C) plays an up-the-middle position. Except he doesn't really showcase a true standout offensive tool – a la Leury Garcia, who happens to be the very definition of low end starting caliber bat. However, Sosa can pick it. So much so, in fact, that he could be a serviceable starting shortstop on a second-tier team.

Ceiling: 1.5-win player
Risk: Moderate
MLB ETA: 2022

8. Yoelkis Cespedes, OF

Hit	Power	SB	Patience	Glove	Overall
50	50	50	45	50	45

Born: 09/24/97	Age: 24	Bats: R	Top Comp: Danny Santana
Height: 5-9	Weight: 209	Throws: R	

Season	Team	Age	Level	PA	1B	2B	3B	HR	SB	CS	BB%	K%	AVG	OBP	SLG	ISO
2021	CHW	23	A+	199	25	17	0	7	10	2	6.53%	28.14%	0.278	0.355	0.494	0.216
2021	CHW	23	AA	100	22	3	2	1	8	4	3.00%	27.00%	0.298	0.340	0.404	0.106

Background: Without doing significant research, the White Sox have to have the strongest ties to Cuban ballplayers in recent history – perhaps, even in baseball history. Some of the more recognizable Cubans to don Chicago's pinstriped uniform include: Luis Robert, Jose Abreu, Minnie Minoso, Alexei Ramirez, Jose Contreras, Yasmani Grandal, Orlando Hernandez, Dayan Viciedo, Yonder Alonso, Jose Canseco, and – perhaps – most recently Yoelkis Cespedes. Hailing from Yara, Cuba, the Sox handed the 5-foot-9, 205-pound rock-solid outfielder a hefty deal worth a touch over $2 million last January. And with four years of time in the Cuban National Series on his resume, the front office bumped the dynamo up to High-A to begin his stateside professional career. After slugging a solid .278/.355/.494 in 45 contests, Cespedes was promoted up to AA for his remaining 27 contests. In total, Cespedes batted .285/.350/.463 with 20 doubles, two triples, eight homeruns, and 18 stolen bases.

Scouting Report: Does not get cheated. Period. Cespedes' small fame size – he's just 5-foot-9 but a tank-like 209 pounds – belies his surprising thump in his bat. Natural loft and enough power to belt out 20 or so long balls in a season. The problem, of course, is that he walks about as often as a senior citizen coming off of hip surgery and the strikeout rates are borderline red flag territory. He's not the type of prospect whose production will remain steady throughout the duration of their career. His skill set (low patience, lots of swinging) will make him susceptible to peaks and valleys.

Ceiling: 1.5-win player
Risk: Moderate
MLB ETA: 2022

9. Wes Krath, 3B

Hit	Power	SB	Patience	Glove	Overall
40/50	50/55	45	50	50	45

Born: 08/03/02	Age: 19	Bats: L	Top Comp: N/A
Height: 6-3	Weight: 200	Throws: R	

Background: Kath capped off one helluva prep career by capturing Gatorade's Arizona High School Player of the Year after belting out a state-best 11 round trippers. He finished the season by batting a scorching .486 with 29 RBIs and scoring 34 runs during the school's 24 games. Kath, a 6-foot-3, 200-pound infielder, was originally committed to Arizona State University, but the Sox selected him in the second round, 57th overall, and signed him to a deal worth $1.8 million. Like his high round draft counterpart Colson Montgomery, Kath spent his entire debut in the Complex League, batting a disappointing .212/.287/.337 with five extra-base knocks.

Scouting Report: Per the usual, here's my pre-draft write-up:

"The swing can get a little long at times, but it's certainly not lacking in loft; Kath has the power potential to belt out 20 homeruns in a professional season. A little awkward on the defensive side of the game, he's lacking fluidity from other high school infielders, though the hands are soft enough. His arm is above-average and should have no issues moving over to third base."

Ceiling: 1.5-win player
Risk: Moderate
MLB ETA: 2025

10. Jonathan Stiever, RHP

FB	CB	SL	CH	Command	Overall
55	55	50	55	45	45

Born: 05/12/97	Age: 25	Bats: R	Top Comp: Dakota Hudson
Height: 6-3	Weight: 210	Throws: R	

Season	Team	Age	Level	IP	TBF	K/9	K%	BB/9	BB%	K-BB%	ERA	FIP	xFIP	Pit/Bat
2018	CHW	21	R	28.0	116	12.54	33.62%	2.89	7.76%	25.86%	4.18	4.23	3.99	3.88
2019	CHW	22	A	74.0	320	9.36	24.06%	1.70	4.38%	19.69%	4.74	3.85	3.24	3.71
2019	CHW	22	A+	71.0	275	9.76	28.00%	1.65	4.73%	23.27%	2.15	3.13	2.89	3.50
2021	CHW	24	AAA	74.0	335	10.70	26.27%	3.41	8.36%	17.91%	5.84	4.52	4.45	4.12

Background: A steady mainstay in the University of Indiana's rotation between 2016 and 2018, Stiever left the Big 10 conference school with a career 3.56 ERA across 217.2 innings, averaging 7.6 strikeouts and 1.9 walks per nine innings. The White Sox selected the 6-foot-3, 210-pound right-hander in the fifth round four years ago. Stiever, of course, carved up the Pioneer League competition during his professional debut that year, posting a 39-to-9 strikeout-to-walk ratio in 28.0 innings of work. He split time between Kannapolis and Winston-Salem the following year. Chicago called him up to the big leagues for a two-game stint during the 2020 COVID campaign. Last year Stiever made 17 starts for the Charlotte Knights in Triple-A, fanning 88 and walking 28 in 74.0 innings of work. He made another appearance – albeit one in which he failed to make an out – with the White Sox as well.

Snippet from The 2020 Prospect Digest Handbook: Stiever has the potential to develop into a nice, innings-eater type backend starting pitcher with the floor of a solid 8th inning arm.

Scouting Report: Consider the following:

- Since 2006, only seven 24-year-old Triple-A arms have met the following criteria in a season with one organization (min. 70 IP): strikeout between 25% and 27% and walk between 7.5% and 9.5% of the hitters they faced. Those seven pitchers: Drew Pomeranz, Steven Matz, Tyler Thornburg, John Lamb, Joan Gregorio, Mike Belfiore, and Jonathan Stiever.

Stiever has a quality arsenal: 92- to 94-mph fastball, an above-average curveball, a decent little cutter-like slider, and an above-average changeup. The command isn't overly impressive – he's a strike-thrower but not a quality strike-thrower – but there are plenty of successful big league arms that compete with less. The White Sox's rotation is chalk full of quality hurlers and the club has a bevy of solid backup options, so Stiever's likely going to be forced into that eighth inning arm.

Ceiling: 1.5-win player
Risk: Moderate
MLB ETA: Debuted in 2020

11. Jason Bilous, RHP

	FB	CB	SL	CH	Command	Overall
	55	55	55	50	45	45

Born: 08/11/97	Age: 24	Bats: R	Top Comp: Rafael Montero
Height: 6-1	Weight: 185	Throws: R	

Season	Team	Age	Level	IP	TBF	K/9	K%	BB/9	BB%	K-BB%	ERA	FIP	xFIP	Pit/Bat
2018	CHW	20	R	36.2	173	7.61	17.92%	5.89	13.87%	4.05%	7.85	5.56	5.88	3.71
2019	CHW	21	A	104.2	461	9.72	24.51%	5.25	13.23%	11.28%	3.70	4.83	4.31	3.87
2021	CHW	23	A+	14.2	56	15.95	46.43%	1.23	3.57%	42.86%	2.45	0.63	1.51	3.71
2021	CHW	23	AA	65.0	295	11.08	27.12%	4.15	10.17%	16.95%	6.51	4.29	4.14	3.96

Background: The club's 2018 draft isn't spectacular by any stretch of the imagination. Beyond their top selection, Nick Madrigal, who was traded to their cross-town rivals, the draft isn't noteworthy. However, they've had four players make it to the big leagues already: Madrigal, Jonathan Stiever, Codi Heuer, and Romy Gonzalez. Chicago selected Bilous that year with the 378th selection. A starting pitcher for the Coastal Carolina, despite some bloated walk rates that might have been the worst in the country, Bilous has made tremendous strides in his feel for the strike zone since entering the Sox's organization. And last year's campaign with Winston-Salem and Birmingham was his finest season to date. Making 20 starts between the club's High-A and Double-A affiliates, he struck out 106, walked just 32, and posted a 5.76 ERA.

Scouting Report: Consider the following:

- Since 2006, eight 23-year-old pitchers in Double-A met the following criteria with an organization (min. 60 IP): K% between 26% and 28% with a BB% between 9% and 11%. Those eight arms: J.A. Happ, Jeff Niemann, Tucker Davidson, Tommy Henry, Angel Baez, Jakob Hernandez, Bowden Francis, and Jason Bilous.

To really appreciate how far Bilous's command has come in a relatively short time frame, it's important to point out just how bad it was during his collegiate days: he walked a staggering 143 in 180.2 innings, or an average of 7.1 walks per nine innings. Last season he averaged 3.6 walks per nine innings. The 6-foot-1, 185-pound emerging prospect features a trio of above-average pitches: a lively fastball that sits in the low 90s and can touch a tick or three higher; a 12-6 yacker of a curveball, and a tremendous slider. His changeup, while lacking a ton of movement, may eventually get into the 55-grade territory, and is thrown with tremendous arm speed. There's some potential to develop into a backend starter, but he's likely going to slide into a multi-inning relief arm.

Ceiling: 1.0- to 1.5-win player
Risk: Moderate
MLB ETA: 2022

12. Jimmy Lambert, RHP

	FB	CB	SL	CH	Command	Overall
	55	60	50	50	45	40

Born: 11/18/94	Age: 27	Bats: R	Top Comp: David Bednar
Height: 6-2	Weight: 190	Throws: R	

Season	Team	Age	Level	IP	TBF	K/9	K%	BB/9	BB%	K-BB%	ERA	FIP	xFIP	Pit/Bat
2018	CHW	23	A+	70.2	286	10.19	27.97%	2.67	7.34%	20.63%	3.95	2.99	3.00	3.71
2018	CHW	23	AA	25.0	101	10.80	29.70%	2.16	5.94%	23.76%	2.88	2.73	2.68	3.77
2019	CHW	24	AA	59.1	259	10.62	27.03%	4.10	10.42%	16.60%	4.55	4.71	3.34	3.92
2021	CHW	26	AAA	64.1	269	11.47	30.48%	4.48	11.90%	18.59%	4.76	4.62	4.25	4.19

Background: A fifth round pick by the Sox out of Fresno State all the way back in 2016. Just to put that into context: Mickey Moniak, Nick Senzel, and Ian Anderson were the top three selections that year. Lambert, on the other hand, was the 146th overall pick. And last season, his fifth professional campaign, was spent shuttling between Charlotte and Chicago. In 19 starts with the club's AAA affiliate, Lambert tossed 64.1 innings with 82 strikeouts and 32 free passes. He compiled a 4.76 ERA. He made an additional four appearances in the big leagues, posting a 10-to-6 strikeout-to-walk ratio with a 6.23 ERA. For his big league career, he's thrown just 15.0 innings over parts of two seasons.

Snippet from The 2020 Prospect Digest Handbook: He's likely going to be converted into a relief option after his return to action.

Scouting Report: After dealing with an elbow flare up in 2019, Lambert's return to the mound post-COVID last year didn't happen in a relief role. But that's his ultimate big league destination. As a starter his fastball was sitting in the 95 mph range, likely a tick or two high in shorter stints. He'll compliment that above-average option with a hellacious plus breaking ball and a couple of average pitches (slider and change). The command gets exposed in longer stints. He has the potential to be a very reliable setup arm. The White Sox just haven't realized that yet.

Ceiling: 1.0-win player
Risk: Low to Moderate
MLB ETA: Debuted in 2020

13. Luis Mieses, LF/RF

	Hit	Power	SB	Patience	Glove	Overall
	50	50	50/45	40	50	40

Born: 05/31/00	Age: 22	Bats: L	Top Comp: Cornelius Randolph
Height: 6-3	Weight: 209	Throws: L	

Season	Team	Age	Level	PA	1B	2B	3B	HR	SB	CS	BB%	K%	AVG	OBP	SLG	ISO
2018	CHW	18	R	204	30	10	2	2	3	0	1.96%	17.16%	0.226	0.236	0.328	0.103
2019	CHW	19	R	231	35	14	0	4	0	1	3.03%	19.91%	0.241	0.264	0.359	0.118
2021	CHW	21	A	225	43	12	1	6	0	0	5.78%	14.67%	0.305	0.347	0.463	0.158
2021	CHW	21	A+	234	22	19	2	9	0	1	4.70%	20.51%	0.236	0.278	0.464	0.227

Background: Last year started out well enough for the Dominican outfielder: he was aggressively assigned to High-A Winston-Salem and went 2-for-5 with a triple, a homerun, and 3 RBI in his first game. But by the end May, however, he was hitting just .155/.189/.366 through first 19 games and earned himself a demotion down to Low-A. After finding his stroke with Kannapolis – he batted an impressive .305/.347/.463 with 12 doubles, one triple, and six homeruns in 52 games – the front office bumped the 6-foot-3, 209-pound corner outfielder back up to High-A for a do-over. He responded by slugging .275/.319/.510 during his second stint with the Dash.

Scouting Report: Mieses is another one of these Sox prospects that don't whiff or walk all that much. It's worked for Tim Anderson well enough. But Mieses isn't Tim Anderson. He hasn't flashed the type of power that corner outfielders are associated with. And his batted ball data, per *FanGraphs*, is mediocre: his average exit velocity was a run-of-the-mill 85 mph with a peak exit velocity of 106. There really isn't a true standout tool in place, nor does one project to be so either.

Ceiling: 1.0-win player
Risk: Moderate
MLB ETA: 2024

14. Romy Gonzalez, IF/OF

	Hit	Power	SB	Patience	Glove	Overall
	45	55	55	50	50	40

Born: 09/06/96	Age: 25	Bats: R	Top Comp: Renato Nunez
Height: 6-1	Weight: 215	Throws: R	

Season	Team	Age	Level	PA	1B	2B	3B	HR	SB	CS	BB%	K%	AVG	OBP	SLG	ISO
2018	CHW	21	R	223	24	15	2	10	10	1	8.07%	29.15%	0.254	0.323	0.498	0.244
2019	CHW	22	A	405	56	22	4	4	11	3	9.38%	26.67%	0.244	0.329	0.364	0.119
2021	CHW	24	AA	344	50	11	0	20	21	6	11.05%	28.20%	0.267	0.355	0.502	0.234
2021	CHW	24	AAA	60	10	6	0	4	3	0	8.33%	25.00%	0.370	0.417	0.704	0.333

Background: One of the bigger surprises in the White Sox's paper thin farm system last season. Gonzalez, a defensive jack of all trades, developed from a late-round prospect with decent power into a prolific homerun hitting bopper in 2021. In 78 games with the Birmingham Barons, the 6-foot-1, 215-pound infielder/outfielder slugged .267/.355/.502 with 11 doubles, 20 homeruns, and 21 stolen bases. His overall production with the Double-A squad, per *Weighted Runs Created Plus*, was 36% better than the league average. Gonzalez also ripped through AAA and appeared in 10 contests with the big league squad as well.

Scouting Report: There's the potential to be a low-end super-sub type of guy. Gonzalez offers up an intriguing blend of power and speed with the ability to play practically every position on the diamond. The former Miami Hurricane appeared at second and third bases, shortstop, both corner outfield spots, and even pitched a third of an inning for the big league club. Gonzalez has the ceiling of a .240/.315/.440-type hitter.

Ceiling: 1.0-win player
Risk: Moderate
MLB ETA: Debuted in 2021

15. Yolbert Sanchez, 2B/SS

Hit	Power	SB	Patience	Glove	Overall
45	45	35	40	50	40

Born: 03/03/97	Age: 25	Bats: R	Top Comp: Yu Chang
Height: 5-11	Weight: 176	Throws: R	

Season	Team	Age	Level	PA	1B	2B	3B	HR	SB	CS	BB%	K%	AVG	OBP	SLG	ISO
2019	CHW	22	R	127	22	8	1	2	3	3	11.81%	9.45%	0.297	0.386	0.441	0.144
2021	CHW	24	A+	239	50	7	0	5	2	1	7.53%	13.81%	0.286	0.340	0.387	0.101
2021	CHW	24	AA	155	39	6	0	4	3	0	3.23%	10.32%	0.343	0.369	0.469	0.126

Background: If the White Sox haven't officially cornered the market on free agents from Cuba, then they're *really* close to doing so. And Sanchez, a 5-foot-11, 176-pound middle infielder from La Habana, is just another example.

Signed for a cool $2.5 million in early July 2019, Sanchez was a three-year mainstay in the Cuban National Series, spending a year with Isla de la Juventud and a pair of campaigns with the Industriales. Sanchez was a career .288/.331/.347 hitter prior to defecting. The Sox took the uncharacteristically conservative approach and sent the then-22-year-old down to the Dominican Summer League for his debut. And, of course, Sanchez performed well by hitting .297/.386/.441. Last season the Cuban infielder split time between Winston-Salem and Birmingham, hitting an aggregate .308/.352/.419 with 13 doubles, nine triples, and five stolen bases. He also appeared in 10 games with Glendale in the Arizona Fall League as well, slugging .393/.528/.536.

Scouting Report: He was way too old for the Dominican Summer League a couple years ago. And he was too old, at least to be taken seriously, last season in High-A as well. And while the numbers in Double-A scream of luck – he slugged .343/.369/.469 – it does help buoy his prospect status. Tell me if you've heard this one before: hates to walk and owns strong contact skills. He's a fallback option at the big league level.

Ceiling: 1.0-win player
Risk: Moderate
MLB ETA: 2022

16. Micker Adolfo, RF

Hit	Power	SB	Patience	Glove	Overall
45	60	35	45	50	40

Born: 09/11/96	Age: 25	Bats: R	Top Comp: Scott Schebler
Height: 6-4	Weight: 230	Throws: R	

Season	Team	Age	Level	PA	1B	2B	3B	HR	SB	CS	BB%	K%	AVG	OBP	SLG	ISO
2018	CHW	21	A+	336	52	18	1	11	2	1	10.12%	27.38%	0.282	0.369	0.464	0.182
2019	CHW	22	AA	95	9	7	0	0	0	3	14.74%	37.89%	0.205	0.337	0.295	0.090
2021	CHW	24	AA	242	24	15	0	15	1	0	7.85%	35.12%	0.249	0.318	0.525	0.276
2021	CHW	24	AAA	163	16	9	1	10	3	0	7.36%	32.52%	0.240	0.301	0.513	0.273

Background: Seemingly a member of the Sox's top prospect list for nearly a decade. Adolfo was originally signed by the AL Central ballclub for a hefty seven-figure bonus all the way back in 2013. And since then the results have been...like a roller coaster.

He was abysmal during his debut in rookie, but rebounded in a return to the Arizona Summer League the following year. He looked awful in Low-A as a 19-year-old, hitting .219/.269/.340. But, of course, looked significantly better – .264/.331/.453 – in a return to the level in 2017. High-A treated him nicely a year later, but Double-A treated him miserably in 2019. So it's not surprising that Adolfo bounced back down to Birmingham to start the post-COVID campaign before earning a promotion up to the minors' last stop. In total he batted .245/.311/.520 with 24 doubles, one triple, and 25 homeruns in 101 games.

Snippet from The 2020 Prospect Digest Handbook: After showing some progress in his problematic swing-and-miss rates in 2018, Adolfo fanned in nearly 38% of his Class AA plate appearances last season.

Scouting Report: Well...the numbers are pretty solid. Except...when his strikeout rate is taken into account. He fanned in more than 34% of his plate appearances last season. He's now entering his age-25 season, with a spotty track record, multiple stints at most levels, and a massive strikeout rate. Massive improvements in cratered-sized holes in a swing don't occur at this point. He's a low average, low-OBP, high homer guy.

Ceiling: 1.0-win player
Risk: Moderate
MLB ETA: 2022

17. Andrew Dalquist, RHP

	FB	CB	SL	CH	Command	Overall
	55	55	45/50	50	40	40

Born: 11/13/00	Age: 21	Bats: R	Top Comp: Tom Koehler
Height: 6-1	Weight: 175	Throws: R	

Season	Team	Age	Level	IP	TBF	K/9	K%	BB/9	BB%	K-BB%	ERA	FIP	xFIP	Pit/Bat
2021	CHW	20	A	83.0	394	8.57	20.05%	6.07	14.21%	5.84%	4.99	4.54	5.94	4.07

Background: After selecting Andrew Vaughn with the third overall pick in the draft three years ago, the Sox snagged a pair of prep arms with their next two selections: Matthew Thompson, the club's top young arm, and Andrew Dalquist, a 6-foot-1, 175-pound right-hander from California. Graduating from Union High School, Dalquist tossed just three innings in rookie ball during his professional debut. So like Thompson, Dalquist's 2021 campaign was his true debut, for all intents and purposes. Making 23 starts for the Kannapolis Cannon Ballers, the wiry righty posted a 79-to-56 strikeout-to-walk ratio in 83.0 innings of work. He finished the year with a 4.99 ERA and a 5.94 xFIP.

Snippet from The 2020 Prospect Digest Handbook: The control, like his curveball, is still raw. Dalquist has the makings of a #4/#5-type pitcher.

Scouting Report: Consider the following:

- Since 2006, only a trio of Low-A arms met the following criteria in a season with one organization (min. 75 IP): a strikeout percentage between 19% and 21% with a walk percentage north of 12%. Those three pitchers: Tim Berry, Juan Minaya, and Andrew Dalquist.

The good news: Dalquist's curveball is a verifiable above-average offering, a true swing-and-miss pitch. The bad news: his command never ticked up and still remains a 40, at best. In fact: of Dalquist's 23 starts, he walked more hitters than he struck out five times. His fastball was kissing 94 during a late-season start. His slider is sketchy but projects to be an average, vanilla offering. And he'll mix in a decent changeup. He still has the making of a #4/#5-type arm. But the command is definitely beyond concerning.

Ceiling: 1.0-win player
Risk: Moderate
MLB ETA: 2025

18. Sean Burke, RHP

	FB	CB	SL	CH	Command	Overall
	55	55	50	50	40/45	40

Born: 12/18/99	Age: 22	Bats: R	Top Comp: N/A
Height: 6-6	Weight: 230	Throws: R	

Season	Team	Age	Level	IP	TBF	K/9	K%	BB/9	BB%	K-BB%	ERA	FIP	xFIP	Pit/Bat
2021	CHW	21	A	14.0	62	12.86	32.26%	6.43	16.13%	16.13%	3.21	3.69	4.66	4.35

Background: Burke was racking up the awards and recognitions before the 2021 season even began: the 6-foot-6, 230-pound right-hander was named Preseason Big Ten Pitcher of the Year and All-Big Ten by *Perfect Game*. Burke made a career-high 14 appearances for the Maryland Terrapins, 13 of which were starts, last season. He struck out 107, walked 42, and posted a 3.27 ERA. The White Sox drafted him in the third round last June, 94th overall, signing him to a $900,000 deal. Burke tossed another 17 innings between the Complex League and Low-A during his debut, posting a 25-to-11 strikeout-to-walk ratio with a 2.65.

Scouting Report: Easy above-average velocity that plays up even further given his big frame. He compliments it with a pair of breaking balls – an above-average curveball and an average slider – and a fringy average changeup that shows some arm-side run at times. Burke has a history of subpar command, though some of that can be attributed to his lack of development time; he missed his true freshman season recovering from Tommy John surgery. He's raw. There's reliever risk here.

Ceiling: 1.0-win player
Risk: Moderate
MLB ETA: 2024

19. Tanner McDougal, RHP

FB	CB	SL	CH	Command	Overall
55/60	N/A	N/A	N/A	45	40

Born: 04/03/03	Age: 19	Bats: R	Top Comp: N/A
Height: 6-5	Weight: 185	Throws: R	

Background: Tanner's old man, Mike, turned in a nice little professional career all things considered. A 31st round selection out of California-based Taft College in 1994 by the St. Louis Cardinals, McDougal beat the odds and got close enough to the big leagues to sniff it without actually suiting up. He made 14 appearances for the Rochester Red Wings in 2000, throwing 30 innings with 25 strikeouts and six walks. The younger McDougal surpassed his father's draft status by 26th rounds and earned a hefty $850,000 bonus, tied for the second highest amount given to a fifth rounder last June. McDougal made six brief appearances in the Arizona Complex League, throwing 9.2 innings with a whopping 17 strikeouts and five free passes to go along with a horrific 9.31 ERA.

Scouting Report: There's limited game tape on McDougal, but MLB.com lists his curveball / slider combination reaching upwards of 3,000 RPMs – I didn't personally see them, likewise his changeup. The fastball's lively and has a chance to creep into plus territory.

Ceiling: N/A
Risk: N/A
MLB ETA: 2025

20. Jared Kelley, RHP

FB	SL	CH	Command	Overall
65	45/50	60	35	35

Born: 10/03/01	Age: 20	Bats: R	Top Comp: N/A
Height: 6-3	Weight: 230	Throws: R	

Season	Team	Age	Level	IP	TBF	K/9	K%	BB/9	BB%	K-BB%	ERA	FIP	xFIP	Pit/Bat
2021	CHW	19	A	21.0	112	10.71	22.32%	9.43	19.64%	2.68%	6.86	5.64	6.25	4.52

Background: The front office went all in on their selection of Kelley in the second round two years ago, signing the highly touted prep arm to a hefty $3 million bonus – the highest bonus given to any player in the round that June. The lone professional player produced by Refugio High, Kelley has provided little return on the club's big investment. The 6-foot-3, 230-pound right-hander made his debut last season in the Sox's system, throwing 23.2 innings between rookie ball and Low-A, fanning 27 and walking an incredible 26. He finished the season with a 7.61 ERA, a 5.64 FIP, and a 6.25 xFIP.

Scouting Report: Similar body type as former White Sox reliever Bobby Jenks. Kelly showcases a pair of plus pitches: a lively mid- to upper-90s fastball that touched as high as 98 in an early August start, and a swing-and-miss changeup that's particularly impressive for a teenage power arm. His slider is fringy, on the other hand, needing a lot of fine tuning (read: improvement) to make it a viable big league offering. The collective debut was disappointing. And that's before factoring in his multiple injuries: he hit the DL for six weeks due to a wonky elbow early in the season and dealt with a "shoulder impingement" later in the year. He's barely 20 innings into his professional career, but it's rough. And he has a *long* way to go to even regain half of his draft prospect status.

Ceiling: 0.5-win player
Risk: Moderate to High
MLB ETA: 2025

Cincinnati Reds

Top Prospects

1. Hunter Greene, RHP

FB	CB	SL	CH	Command	Overall
80	N/A	60	50	55	60

Born: 08/06/99	Age: 22	Bats: R	Top Comp: Tyler Glasnow
Height: 6-5	Weight: 230	Throws: R	

Season	Team	Age	Level	IP	TBF	K/9	K%	BB/9	BB%	K-BB%	ERA	FIP	xFIP	Pit/Bat
2018	CIN	18	A	68.1	294	11.72	30.27%	3.03	7.82%	22.45%	4.48	3.29	3.13	3.85
2021	CIN	21	AA	41.0	162	13.17	37.04%	3.07	8.64%	28.40%	1.98	2.35	2.82	4.06
2021	CIN	21	AAA	65.1	276	10.88	28.62%	3.44	9.06%	19.57%	4.13	4.46	4.04	3.95

Background: It's hard – actually almost impossible – to believe that the former first rounder is only entering his age-21 season because it *feels* like Greene should be a lot older. The thunderbolt-slinging righty was the second overall selection five years ago, being nabbed after the Twins drafted shortstop Royce Lewis. This, of course, was after the teenage phenom graced the cover of *Sports Illustrated*. The 6-foot-5, 230-pound hurler immediately started making waves as one of the most exciting pitchers not only in the Reds' blossoming farm system, but in all of the minor leagues. As a wiry, baby-faced 18-year-old, the California native posted an impressive 89-to-23 strikeout-to-walk ratio in only 68.1 innings in the Midwest League in 2018. Early in 2019, prior to toeing the rubber in an official game, it was announced that the burgeoning ace would require Tommy John surgery to repair the ulnar collateral ligament in his expensive right elbow. After minor league baseball returned from the COVID-imposed shutdown, Greene showed little effects from the surgical procedure in 2021. Making a career-best 21 starts between Chattanooga and Louisville, the noticeable thicker, more muscular youngster struck out 139 versus only 39 walks in 106.1 innings of work. He compiled an aggregate 3.30 ERA and a 3.65 FIP.

Snippet from The 2018 Prospect Digest Handbook: If there's such a thing as an "easy 100 mph" Greene's name certainly belongs on the short list. Blessed with a lightning-quick arm that allows his fastball to comfortably – and easily – sit in the 97- to 99-mph range with a peak at 102, Greene's polish differentiates himself from all other hard-throwers.

Scouting Report: Consider the following:

- Since 2006, only four 21-year-old hurlers posted a strikeout percentage between 27.5% and 29.5% in Triple-A with one organization (min. 50 IP): Trevor Bauer, Jose Berrios, Michael Pineda, and – of course – Hunter Greene.
- For those counting at home: Bauer won the 2020 NL Cy Young award and has tallied nearly 21 bWAR in his career; Berrios is a two-time All-Star in six big league seasons; and Pineda's totaled nearly 13 bWAR in his career.

The best fastball from a starting pitcher in professional baseball. Greene's heater sits, like clockwork, in the upper 90s / 100-mph range. And he regularly hit 102 mph during a start in Triple-A last season. The big righty relies mainly on a pair of offspeed offerings: an upper 80s slider with varying tilt and a low 90s changeup with the former being plus, the latter being average. Based on signs relayed from the catcher, Greene also throws a curveball, though I never saw it. Unlike a lot of other hard-throwing phenoms, Green shows an uncanny ability to harness his lightning and generally works around the plate. For now he remains very fastball heavy, so he'll need to continue to evolve as a pitcher that will challenge hitters early in the count with offspeed pitches.

Ceiling: 5.0-win player
Risk: Moderate
MLB ETA: 2022

2. Nick Lodolo, LHP

FB	CB	SL	CH	Command	Overall
60	60	50	50/55	60	60

Born: 02/05/98	Age: 24	Bats: L	Top Comp: Chris Sale
Height: 6-6	Weight: 205	Throws: L	

Season	Team	Age	Level	IP	TBF	K/9	K%	BB/9	BB%	K-BB%	ERA	FIP	xFIP	Pit/Bat
2019	CIN	21	R	11.1	46	16.68	45.65%	0.00	0.00%	45.65%	2.38	1.50	1.52	3.57
2021	CIN	23	AA	44.0	173	13.91	39.31%	1.84	5.20%	34.10%	1.84	1.63	2.25	3.90

Background: Fun Fact Part I: Since 2010, there have been 72 players drafted out of Texas Christian University. Fun Fact Part II: Of those aforementioned 72 instances, only two of them – Brandon Bailey and Nick Lodolo – were selected in the opening round.

Fun Fact Part III: When the Cincinnati Reds drafted Lodolo with the seventh overall pick three years ago, he became (A) the highest drafted player and (B) handed the largest bonus, $5,432,400, in the school's lengthy history. Standing an imposing 6-foot-6 an 205-pounds, the young left-hander immediately slid into the Horned Frogs' rotation as a true freshman, showing not only that he belong as a Division I hurler but that he had one of the brightest amateur futures in the country. He would make 17 appearances for the Big12 Conference school that year, throwing 78.2 innings with 72 strikeouts and 28 free passes to go along with a 4.35 ERA. Lodolo raised the ante a bit during his sophomore campaign, averaging 10.9 strikeouts and just 3.3 walks per nine innings in 77.0 innings of work. But he was practically unhittable during his final collegiate season: 103.0 IP, 131 strikeouts, just 25 free passes, and a sparkling 2.36 ERA. After joining the Reds' farm system, Lodolo ripped through eight brief low-level starts during his debut, posting an unbelievable 30-to-1 strikeout-to-walk ratio in only 18.1 innings. Last season –

just his first full season in professional ball, Lodolo made 13 starts as left shoulder fatigue plagued him. The results, none the less, were immaculate. He struck out 78, walked just 11, and compiled an aggregate 2.31 ERA in 50.2 innings of action.

Snippet from The 2020 Prospect Digest Handbook: Lodolo looks like a potential #2/#3-type arm at his peak. A few things to note: During his debut last season, [his] fastball ticked up a bit as it hit – consistently – 95 mph; his slider was 80- to 82 mph; and his changeup was filthy. There's a nonzero chance he develops three plus pitches.

Scouting Report: Consider the following:

- Since 2006, only four 23-year-old hurlers posted a strikeout percentage north of 38% with a sub-6.0% walk percentage in Double-A (min. 40 IP): Brendan McKay, Jonathan Holder, Tommy Romero, and Nick Lodolo.

As loose and easy an arm that's currently in the minor leagues. Lodolo attacks hitters with an explosive mid-90s fastball that will touch upward of 97 mph on occasion. He'll complement the plus offering with a plus-slurvy type curveball, an average-ish slider, and a hard, firm changeup that flashes above-average at times. Lodolo's a fast working, strike-thrower. He's a slinger like Chris Sale that adds some deception to his already quality arsenal. There's still quite a bit of projection left considering his brief debut, loss of 2020 due to COVID, and his injury-marred 2021 season.

Ceiling: 4.0-win player
Risk: Moderate
MLB ETA: 2022

3. Elly De La Cruz, 3B/SS

	Hit	Power	SB	Patience	Glove	Overall
	40/55	45/60	55	40	55	60

Born: 01/11/02	Age: 20	Bats: B	Top Comp: Ozzie Albies
Height: 6-2	Weight: 150	Throws: R	

Season	Team	Age	Level	PA	1B	2B	3B	HR	SB	CS	BB%	K%	AVG	OBP	SLG	ISO
2019	CIN	17	R	186	34	11	1	1	3	6	7.53%	24.19%	0.285	0.351	0.382	0.097
2021	CIN	19	CPX	55	9	6	2	3	2	0	7.27%	27.27%	0.400	0.455	0.780	0.380
2021	CIN	19	A	210	29	12	7	5	8	5	4.76%	30.95%	0.269	0.305	0.477	0.208

Background: The club's signing of the talented teenage infielder barely registered a blip on most radars – or across baseball – but Cincinnati appears to have hit a homerun with their free agent deal with De La Cruz. Inked for only $65,000, a small pittance on the international scene, out of Sabana Grande de Boya, Dominican Republic, the 6-foot-2, 150-pound prospect looked comfortable – if not unremarkable – during his debut in the foreign rookie league three years ago: he batted .285/.351/.382 with 11 doubles, one triple, and a dinger in 43 games. But in one of the more notable breakouts in the 2021 season, De La Cruz ripped through two separate levels. First, he torched the Complex League competition to the tune of .400/.455/.780 for 11 games. Then, he batted .269/.305/.477 with 12 doubles, seven triples, five homeruns, and eight stolen bases in 50 games with Daytona. His overall production in Low-A, per *Weighted Runs Created Plus*, topped the league average mark by a solid 6%.

Scouting Report: The good news:

- Since 2006, only two 19-year-old hitters posted a wRC+ total between 100 and 110 with a sub-6.0% walk rate and a strikeout rate above 28% in Low-A with one organization (min. 200 PA): Jorge Alfaro and Elly De La Cruz.

Long, twitchy, and filled with plenty of projectable tools. De La Cruz is a free-swinger who (A) doesn't get cheated at the plate and (B) won't walk much at any point in his professional career. The young Dominican is a premium athlete that's already providing value on both sides of the ball. The problem, though, is his already problematic swing-and-miss totals; he whiffed in 31.0% of his plate appearances in Low-A. But when he does connect, *watch out*. Per *FanGraphs*, his average exit velocity was a stellar 90 mph and his max exit velocity, 112 mph, tied for the sixth highest. There's superstar potential with a high level of risk. One more thought: Tremendous bat speed with just a flick of the wrist. In terms of big league ceiling, think: .280/.335/.500.

Ceiling: 4.5-win player
Risk: Moderate to High
MLB ETA: 2024

4. Matt McLain, SS

	Hit	Power	SB	Patience	Glove	Overall
	50	45	55	55	50	55

Born: 08/06/99		Age: 22		Bats: R		Top Comp: N/A			
Height: 5-11		Weight: 180		Throws: R					

Season	Team	Age	Level	PA	1B	2B	3B	HR	SB	CS	BB%	K%	AVG	OBP	SLG	ISO
2021	CIN	21	A+	119	18	6	0	3	10	2	14.29%	20.17%	0.273	0.387	0.424	0.152

Background: In the ultimate example of betting on oneself, the shortstop spurned the Diamondbacks' multimillion dollar offer following his selection as the 25th overall pick four years ago, opting to take the collegiate route instead. McLain, a native of Orange, California, vaulted up the drafted charts during his senior prep season in 2018 when he batted .369/.467/.604. And he continued to swing a hot stick as he transitioned into the West Coast League that summer. In 23 games with the Bellingham Bells, the 5-foot-10, 175-pound infielder slugged .291/.370/.442 with six extra-base hits and a 15-to-12 strikeout-to-walk ratio. Unfortunately, for McLain, though, he struggled mightily during his freshman campaign for UCLA. In 61 games for the PAC12 powerhouse, he hit a lowly .203/.276/.355 with just nine doubles, six triples, and four homeruns. The thump in his bat returned the ensuing summer in the Cape Cod League, slugging .274/.394/.425 in 34 games with the Wareham Gatemen. McLain followed that up with an explosive sophomore campaign during the COVID-shortened campaign: .397/.422/.621. Last season, the junior Bruin sported a .333/.434/.579 slash line with 14 doubles, two triples, nine homeruns, and nine stolen bases. Cincinnati called McLain's name in the opening round, 17th overall, and signed him to a deal worth $4,625,000. The front office – after a two-game cameo in the Complex League – pushed the former Bruin into High-A. He responded by batting .273/.387/.424 with six doubles and three triples. Per *Weighted Runs Created Plus*, his production in High-A topped the league average mark by a solid 27%.

Scouting Report: Per the usual, here's my pre-draft write-up:

> "Consider the following:
>
> - Since 2012, only four PAC12 hitters met the following criteria: 200+ plate appearances, an OPS between .900 and 1.100, a walk rate between 14% and 18%, and a strikeout rate between 12% and 16%. Those four players are Mitchell Tolman, Alfonso Rivas, Matt Winaker, and Austin Wells. Tolman, Rivas, and Winaker were all selected between the fourth and seventh rounds; and the Yankees selected Wells in the first round, 28th overall, last year.
>
> Fundamentally sound in the field, McLain is more sturdy than flashy – though his arm is an above-average tool, allowing him to make difficult throws in the hole or on the move. Offensively, it's a similar story. McLain is an advanced college bat without a true standout. There's a little bit of thump, enough to belt out eight to 12 homeruns in a full season. He runs well. And he profiles as a .270/.280-type hitter. In a college class lacking premium bats, McLain's likely to hear his name in the opening half of the draft, though he's a high floor/low ceiling type prospect."

Ceiling: 3.0-win player
Risk: Moderate
MLB ETA: 2023

6. Jay Allen, CF

	Hit	Power	SB	Patience	Glove	Overall
	45/50	45/50	55	50	50/55	55

Born: 11/22/02		Age: 19		Bats: R		Top Comp: N/A			
Height: 6-3		Weight: 190		Throws: R					

Season	Team	Age	Level	PA	1B	2B	3B	HR	SB	CS	BB%	K%	AVG	OBP	SLG	ISO
2021	CIN	18	CPX	75	13	3	1	3	14	1	10.67%	16.00%	0.328	0.440	0.557	0.230

Background: A dynamic three-sport athlete during his tenure at Florida-based John Carroll High School. *Perfect Game* ranked the 6-foot-3, 190-pound outfielder as the 5th best outfielder and 20th best high school prospect in the country in 2021. A University of Florida commit, Allen was snagged by the Cincinnati Reds with the 30th overall selection last June, agreeing to a deal with the NL Central Division franchise for a slightly above-slot deal worth $2.4 million. The speedy center fielder batted .363/.500/.588 during his final prep campaign, belting out eight doubles, two triples, and a pair of homeruns. He also went a perfect 22-for-22 in the stolen base department as well. The teenage outfielder appeared in 19 games with the Reds' Arizona Complex League affiliate, slugging .328/.440/.557 with three doubles, one triple, three homeruns, and 14 stolen bases (in 15 attempts). Per *Weighted Runs Created Plus*, Allen overall production topped the league average threshold by a staggering 59%.

Scouting Report: Per the usual, here's my post-draft write-up:

> *"Cincinnati hasn't shied away from premium high school talent in the opening round of the draft in recent years; the front office has used six of their 12 first round selections on prep players since 2016. Defensively, Allen has all the skills to remain in center field: plus speed, above-average arm, and a strong glove. Quick bat but not a lot of current thump. The power grades out as a 45 now, but should blossom into a solid average offering. Allen shows an underrated ability to fight off tough pitches and puts together solid at bats. He has an inconsistent hitch in his swing that needs to be cleaned up."*

Ceiling: 3.0-win player
Risk: Moderate
MLB ETA: 2025

6. Bryce Bonnin, RHP

	FB	SL	CH	Command	Overall
	60	60	N/A	50	55

Born: 10/11/98	Age: 23	Bats: R	Top Comp: N/A
Height: 6-2	Weight: 190	Throws: R	

Season	Team	Age	Level	IP	TBF	K/9	K%	BB/9	BB%	K-BB%	ERA	FIP	xFIP	Pit/Bat
2021	CIN	22	A	32.0	120	12.38	36.67%	2.25	6.67%	30.00%	1.41	1.90	2.89	3.87
2021	CIN	22	A+	11.0	48	16.36	41.67%	6.55	16.67%	25.00%	7.36	7.04	3.22	4.75

Background: Coming from an athletic family, Bonnin's father and two brothers were collegiate athletes. The Cubs selected Bonnin in the 26th round coming out of Barbers Hill High School in 2017. The hard-throwing right-hander, though, opted to take the collegiate route and headed to the SEC to play for the Arkansas Razorbacks. The 6-foot-2, 190-pound hurler would make just 11 appearances as a true freshman, throwing 19.0 innings with 16 strikeouts and 12 free passes. Bonnin would pop up briefly in the Cape Cod League and then reappear on the mound the following season throwing seeds for Texas Tech. The Texas native, who transferred to be closer to home, immediately moved in the Red Raiders' rotation – though he continued to battle some control demons. He averaged 9.1 strikeouts and 6.3 walks per nine innings across 13 starts and a pair of relief outings. Bonnin's 2020 season got off to an interesting start: he struck out 27, walked just six, but put together a 7.36 ERA in 14.2 innings before the COVID shutdown. Cincinnati selected him in the third round, 84th overall, and signed him to a deal worth $700,000. Last season the righty blitzed through three separate levels, starting in the Complex League for a quick start and finishing the season off with a three-game cameo in High-A. In total, he tossed 47 innings with a whopping 71 strikeouts and just 17 free passes. He compiled an aggregate 2.87 ERA and a sparkling 3.15 FIP.

Scouting Report: My immediate thought when I watched Bonnin carve up the lower levels of the minor leagues: "Oh, man, he looks like Kevin Brown during his Padres and Marlins heyday." Lean, but muscular with 75% of his weight carried in his lower half. Bonnin, like Brown or nowadays Johnny Cueto, twists his lower half before moving toward the plate. Two plus pitches: a mid- to upper-90s heater that sits 96 and touches 99 and a hellacious, knee-buckling, bowel-locking slider. The problem for the now-strike-throwing right-hander: he's primarily a two-pitch pitcher. Reports indicate he'll mix in a changeup, but I never saw one. After averaging more than 13 punch outs per nine innings last year, that should tell you all you need to know about the quality of his fastball / slider combo. There's legitimate mid-rotation caliber potential here, but it's *imperative* that he learns to lean on a third option – be it a curveball, cutter, or changeup. With that being said, there's definite reliever risk, but outside of Hunter Greene and Nick Lodolo, he has the highest ceiling of any arm in the system.

Ceiling: 3.0-win player
Risk: High
MLB ETA: 2024

7. Jose Torres, SS

	Hit	Power	SB	Patience	Glove	Overall
	45	50	40	45	60	50

Born: 09/28/99	Age: 22	Bats: R	Top Comp: N/A
Height: 6-0	Weight: 171	Throws: R	

Season	Team	Age	Level	PA	1B	2B	3B	HR	SB	CS	BB%	K%	AVG	OBP	SLG	ISO
2021	CIN	21	CPX	12	1	0	1	1	1	0	16.67%	16.67%	0.300	0.417	0.800	0.500
2021	CIN	21	A	107	21	4	3	4	6	2	7.48%	15.89%	0.337	0.383	0.568	0.232

Background: A native of Guayubin, Dominican Republic, Torres opened quite a few eyes during his prep career at Calvert Hall College High School: after batting .402 and knocking in 44 runs, the Brewers took a late round flier on the toolsy shortstop three years ago – though he would eventually head to N.C. State. Torres, who joined former Brewers top prospect Troy Stokes Jr. as the two most recent picks from the prep school, got off to an impressive start to his collegiate career. In 17 games, prior to the pandemic-induced shutdown, the 6-foot, 171-pound shortstop slugged .333/.369/.533 with three doubles and three homeruns – though he managed to walk just three times against 20 punch outs. Last year, just his first full season in college baseball, Torres cobbled together a .289/.343/.533 slash line, belting out 12 doubles, three triples, and 10 homeruns to go along with five stolen bases. He finished the year with a 39-to-13 strikeout-to-walk ratio. Cincinnati selected him in the third round, 89th overall, and signed him to a below slot deal worth $622,500. He appeared in 28 professional games, 25 of which were in Low-A, hitting an aggregate .333/.387/.590 with four doubles, four triples, and five homeruns. He also swiped seven bags in nine total attempts.

Scouting Report: Per the usual, here's my pre-draft write-up:

"Consider the following:

- *Between 2011 and 2020, here's the list of ACC hitters to hit between .280/.330/.500 and .300/.360/.520 with a strikeout rate north of 16% and a walk rate below 6.5% in a season (min. 200 PA): Willie Abreu, a 2016 sixth rounder out of the University of Miami.*

A below-average hit tool and surprising pop from a middle infield position. Torres' inability to work the count is also a limiting factor in his projected ceiling – though his defensive ability will help buoy his future. Soft, quick hands, an above-average or better throwing arm, and cat-like agility at shortstop, Torres could – potentially – develop into a perennial Gold Glove winner. At the plate, his swing is a bit long and the bat speed isn't overwhelming. In terms of ceiling think: Nick Ahmed's 2019 season with the Diamondbacks when he hit .254/.316/.437 and tallied 2.3 fWAR."

Ceiling: 1.5- to 2.0-win player
Risk: Moderate
MLB ETA: 2024

8. Michael Siani, CF

	Hit	Power	SB	Patience	Glove	Overall
	40/45	35/45	60	55	60	50

Born: 07/16/99	Age: 22	Bats: L	Top Comp: N/A
Height: 6-1	Weight: 188	Throws: L	

Season	Team	Age	Level	PA	1B	2B	3B	HR	SB	CS	BB%	K%	AVG	OBP	SLG	ISO
2018	CIN	18	R	205	42	6	3	2	6	4	7.80%	17.07%	0.288	0.351	0.386	0.098
2019	CIN	19	A	531	96	10	6	6	45	15	8.66%	20.53%	0.253	0.333	0.339	0.086
2021	CIN	21	A+	408	53	13	4	6	30	10	12.25%	25.25%	0.216	0.321	0.327	0.111

Background: The front office looked around at each other, collectively shrugged, and pushed their proverbially chips to the center of the table in the fourth round of the 2018 draft. The cost? Two million big ones. Cincinnati signed prep center fielder Michael Siani to the hefty seven-figure bonus, the largest amount handed to a fourth rounder since the Nationals paid the same amount to convince A.J. Cole to bypass his collegiate opportunities in 2010. Siani, for his part, turned in a promising debut in the Appalachian League that summer, hitting a league average-esque .288/.351/.386 with six doubles, a trio of three-baggers, and a pair of long balls. The club sent the baby-faced teenager to the Midwest League the following year and the results were…a bit disappointing. He batted .253/.333/.339. Last season, as minor league action returned to normal, Siani was pushed up to High-A – where the numbers continued to disappoint. In 97 games with the Dayton Dragons, the 6-foot-1, 188-pound outfielder cobbled together a .216/.321/.327 with just 23 extra-base knocks. His overall production was 15% *below* the league average threshold, per *Weighted Runs Created Plus*. Siani also appeared in 14 games with the Surprise Saguaros in the Arizona Fall League, slugging .300/.451/.450 in 51 plate appearances.

Snippet from The 2020 Prospect Digest Handbook: He's so damn good [defensively], in fact, that he could hit .220 and still carve out a starting gig in center field for a championship contending big league team.

Scouting Report: Depending on the month, Siani looked like a top prospect or a fringe minor leaguer. He batted .273/.375/.509 and .258/.337/.427 during the months of June and August, but cobbled together slash lines of .177/.293/.190, .173/.295/.235/, and .208/.321/.313 the other three months of the year. And a deep dive into his peripherals doesn't help clear the cloudy waters either. He walked at career best 12.3% of the time, but whiffed a career worst 25.2% of his plate appearances. He swiped a ton of bases, 30 in 40 attempts, but his trademark defense seemed to regress. Then during the Fall League he (A) walked more than he struck out, (B) consistently barreled the ball, and (C) handled himself against some of the better pitching prospects in the minor leagues. Physically, Siani looks thicker, more muscular. He has the tools to be an average or better big league center fielder, but he lacks the consistently. It's like his baseball development is going through puberty and he's still trying to find out who he actually is.

Ceiling: 2.0-win player
Risk: Moderate to High
MLB ETA: 2024

9. Tyler Callihan, 2B

	Hit	Power	SB	Patience	Glove	Overall
	45/55	50	45/35	50	45/50	45

Born: 06/22/00	Age: 22	Bats: L	Top Comp: N/A
Height: 6-1	Weight: 205	Throws: R	

Season	Team	Age	Level	PA	1B	2B	3B	HR	SB	CS	BB%	K%	AVG	OBP	SLG	ISO
2019	CIN	19	R	217	31	10	5	5	9	3	4.15%	21.20%	0.250	0.286	0.422	0.172
2019	CIN	19	R	21	6	0	1	1	2	0	4.76%	19.05%	0.400	0.429	0.650	0.250
2021	CIN	21	A	99	18	6	0	2	5	1	8.08%	13.13%	0.299	0.351	0.437	0.138

Background: After snagging Texas Christian ace Nick Lodolo in the first round of the 2019 draft, Cincinnati selected three straight middle infielders: Rece Hinds, Tyler Callihan, and Ivan Johnson. Callihan, the 85th overall pick that year, signed quickly and got in a full season of development with the Greeneville Reds in the Appalachian League. He batted an OBP-deficient .250/.286/.422 with 10 doubles, five triples, and five homeruns. The lefty-swinging infielder also appeared in five games with the Billings Mustangs as well, going 8-for-20. Last season the Florida native began the year off on a strong note, hitting .299/.351/.437 with eight extra-base hits through his first 23 contest. But his elbow flared up and eventually succumbed to Tommy John surgery. Prior to the injury, his overall production was 13% better than the league average threshold, per *Weighted Runs Created Plus*.

Snippet from The 2020 Prospect Digest Handbook: Here's what's already apparent: impressive power, perhaps even approaching plus power down the line; decent glove; very little patience at the plate; and a the hit tool is underdeveloped.

Scouting Report: The 2021 season had the makings of a potential breakout campaign for the former prep star: he was flashing solid power, walking nearly twice as frequently as he did during his debut, and handling the transition to full season action with relative ease. Simple, smooth left-handed stroke that's reminiscent of former first baseman Mark Grace. If the progress Callihan showed during his abbreviated 2021 season carries over into 2022, as well as no major injury setbacks, it's not out of the question for him to start the year in High-A. Defensively, after splitting time between the hot corner and the keystone during his debut, Callihan showed a lot of promise and improvement as he played solely at second base. He's got the feel as a late blooming type, like D.J. LeMahieu.

Ceiling: 1.5-win player
Risk: Moderate
MLB ETA: 2024

10. Austin Hendrick, RF

	Hit	Power	SB	Patience	Glove	Overall
	35	50/60	40	60	50	45

Born: 06/15/01	Age: 21	Bats: L	Top Comp: N/A
Height: 6-0	Weight: 195	Throws: L	

Season	Team	Age	Level	PA	1B	2B	3B	HR	SB	CS	BB%	K%	AVG	OBP	SLG	ISO
2021	CIN	20	A	266	21	16	0	7	4	2	19.17%	37.59%	0.211	0.380	0.388	0.177

Background: The opening portion of the 2020 draft was chock full of high end talent with the likes of Spencer Torkelson, Max Meyer, Asa Lacy, Emerson Hancock, Nick Gonzales, Robert Hassell, Zac Veen, Reid Detmers, and Garrett Crochet all hearing their names within the top 11 selections. And that doesn't include #2 overall pick Heston Kjerstad, who's battled myocarditis since entering the minor leagues. The 12th pick two years ago, Austin Hendrick, has been beyond abysmal as a professional. A product of West Allegheny High School, located in Imperial, Pennsylvania, Hendrick made his debut last season with the Daytona Tortugas, hitting a paltry .211/.380/.388 with 16 doubles, seven homeruns, and four stolen bases in 63 games. His overall production, per *Weighted Runs Created Plus*, still managed to top the league average threshold by a shockingly solid 19%.

Scouting Report: Consider the following:

- Only three-year-old hitters posted a 115 to 125 wRC+ total with a strikeout rate north of 33% in Low-A with one organization (min. 250 PA): Lawrence Butler, Trenton Kemp, and – of course – Austin Hendrick.

In terms of overall production, Hendrick was quite valuable for the club's Low-A East affiliate thanks to his otherworldly 19% walk rate. But where there's good, there's typically bad. And a 1970s era Cadillac could be driven through the hole in Hendrick's swing – *sideways.* He whiffed in nearly 38% of his plate appearances last season. His overall production was torpedoed by an awful showing in June when he batted .122/.308/.244. But even during May, July, and August, he was whiffing 36% of the time. You look at the swing and see plus power and matching bat speed, something along the lines of a young Clint Frazier, but the swing-and-miss issues are practically insurmountable.

Ceiling: 1.5-win player
Risk: Moderate
MLB ETA: 2025

11. Graham Ashcraft, RHP

FB	CU	SL	CH	Command	Overall
60	55	55	N/A	50	45

Born: 02/11/98	Age: 24	Bats: L	Top Comp: Ian Kennedy
Height: 6-2	Weight: 240	Throws: R	

Season	Team	Age	Level	IP	TBF	K/9	K%	BB/9	BB%	K-BB%	ERA	FIP	xFIP	Pit/Bat
2019	CIN	21	R	53.2	240	10.06	25.00%	3.52	8.75%	16.25%	4.53	3.59	3.80	3.56
2021	CIN	23	A+	38.2	161	12.80	34.16%	3.03	8.07%	26.09%	2.33	2.25	3.02	3.86
2021	CIN	23	AA	72.1	293	9.21	25.26%	2.99	8.19%	17.06%	3.36	3.19	3.46	4.04

Background: The burly right-hander took an atypical path to the minor leagues. Originally taken by the Los Angeles Dodgers in the 12th round coming out of Huntsville High School, Ashcraft opted to attend SEC powerhouse Mississippi State University. The 6-foot-2, 240-pound right-hander made 10 appearances – five coming as a starter – for the Bulldogs in 2017, averaging 9.4 strikeouts and a whopping 6.0 walks per nine innings. His freshman season, though, ended prematurely with a hip injury. The hefty hurler would miss the 2018 season due to another hip injury. This one, though, required him to undergo the knife for a surgical procedure. Finally healthy, the Alabama native transferred to University of Alabama-Birmingham, a Conference USA school, for the 2019 season. Limited to just 56.0 innings between the Blazers rotation and pen, Ashcraft struck out 53 and walked 39 in 56.0 innings of work. Cincinnati would take mid-round flier on the hard-throwing, oft-injured righty, snagging him in the sixth round that year. After throwing another 53.2 innings with the club's Appalachian League affiliate during his debut, the club bumped him up to High-A to start his first full season of action. Ashcraft would ultimately make eight starts Dayton and another 14 with Chattanooga, postings a 129-to-37 strikeout-to-walk ratio with a 3.00 ERA.

Scouting Report: Consider the following:

- Since 2006, seven 23-year-old hurlers posted a 24.5% to 26.5% strikeout percentage with a 7% to 9% walk rate in Double-A (min. 70 IP): Glen Perkins, Dean Kremer, Taylor Hearn, Carlos Pimentel, Robert Dugger, Travis Foley, and Graham Ashcraft.

A body that Kenny Powers would be proud of – or potentially use as a stunt double in a cheesy, "straight-to-VHS" B-movie. Ashcraft, who tips the scales at 240 pounds, attacks hitters with a four-pitch repertoire: a lively, plus fastball that sits in the mid- to upper-90s, a hard-tilting, 12-6 bending power slider, a late darting, slightly wrinkled cutter, and a rare changeup (one that's so rare, in fact, that I actually never saw it). Ashcraft couldn't hit the broadside of a barn during his collegiate years, but immediately honed in on the strike zone as soon as he entered the Reds' farm system. Everything about him, though, screams reliever: power pitcher, max effort mechanics, and throws nothing slow. But he's got a puncher's chance at stick in the rotation – though he's now entering his age-24 season.

Ceiling: 1.5-win player
Risk: Moderate
MLB ETA: 2022

12. Lyon Richardson, RHP

FB	CB	SL	CH	Command	Overall
60	55	55	55	40	45

Born: 01/18/00	Age: 22	Bats: R	Top Comp: N/A
Height: 6-2	Weight: 192	Throws: R	

Season	Team	Age	Level	IP	TBF	K/9	K%	BB/9	BB%	K-BB%	ERA	FIP	xFIP	Pit/Bat
2018	CIN	18	R	29.0	139	7.45	17.27%	4.97	11.51%	5.76%	7.14	5.54	5.51	3.82
2019	CIN	19	A	112.2	497	8.47	21.33%	2.64	6.64%	14.69%	4.15	3.76	3.65	3.78
2021	CIN	21	A+	76.0	346	10.78	26.30%	4.50	10.98%	15.32%	5.09	4.69	4.44	3.79

Background: A product of Jensen Beach High School, Cincinnati plucked the hard-throwing right-hander out of the Florida-based prep school in the second round four years ago – exactly one selection before the Mets snagged eventual Top 100 prospect Simeon Woods Richardson. Richardson, the 47th overall pick that year, turned in a mediocre debut in the Appalachian League as he averaged just 7.4 strikeouts and 5.0 walks per nine innings with the Greeneville Reds. The front office bumped the switch-hitting hurler up to the Midwest League for the 2019 season. This time, though, the results were far more indicative of his lofty draft status. Making 26 starts for Dayton, Richardson posted a 106-to-38 strikeout-to-walk ratio in 112.2 innings of work. Last season the organization erred on the side of caution and sent to him to High-A – which would ultimately prove to be the right call. In 19 games with the newly relocated Dayton Dragons, formerly of Low-A, Richardson fanned 91 and struck out 38. He finished the year with a 5.09 ERA, 4.69 FIP, and a 4.44 xFIP.

Snippet from The 2018 Prospect Digest Handbook: Richardson's control/command was far better than advertised in 2019. In fact, he only walked more than two hitters just twice last season. And in both instances, he handed out just three free passes in six-inning starts. He's poised to become one of the bigger breakout prospects in 2020.

Scouting Report: Consider the following:

- Since 2006, only three 21-year-old hurlers posted a 25.5% to 27.5% strikeout percentage with a walk percentage between 10% and 12% in High-A (min. 75 IP): Luis Pena, Jose Almonte, and Lyon Richardson.

Richardson's an interesting arm. When you sit and watch the arsenal, ignoring everything else, it's easy to come away impressed. His fastball was sitting in the 95- to 96-mph range; his loopy curveball tumbles off of the side of a table; his slider flashed plus fairly regularly; and his changeup is significantly underrated. One plus pitch (the heater) and the remaining three are either above-average (CB and CH) or project to be above-average (SL). But Richardson certainly has his flaws: he struggles commanding the zone, frequently deals with bouts of wildness, and runs hot-and-cold. Richardson's overall production was torpedoed by an awful three-game stint in July (he coughed up 13 ER in 9.0 IP). Otherwise, he posted a 4.15 ERA. He's tracking like a multi-inning reliever. But he's only entering his age-22 season, so there's plenty of time to harness his repertoire. One more final thought: he seemed to scrap his curveball later in the year.

Ceiling: 1.5-win player
Risk: Moderate
MLB ETA: 2024

13. Allan Cerda, CF

Hit	Power	SB	Patience	Glove	Overall
40/45	50/60	35	55	45	45

Born: 11/24/99	Age: 22	Bats: R	Top Comp: N/A
Height: 6-3	Weight: 170	Throws: R	

Season	Team	Age	Level	PA	1B	2B	3B	HR	SB	CS	BB%	K%	AVG	OBP	SLG	ISO
2018	CIN	18	R	214	30	11	0	6	3	2	11.68%	21.03%	0.272	0.402	0.439	0.168
2019	CIN	19	R	165	14	6	0	9	2	2	12.12%	33.94%	0.220	0.360	0.470	0.250
2021	CIN	21	A	276	23	14	4	14	1	7	11.23%	30.80%	0.242	0.362	0.524	0.282
2021	CIN	21	A+	87	9	8	1	3	1	1	11.49%	22.99%	0.273	0.356	0.519	0.247

Background: Born in the Bronx, New York, Cerda eventually made his way to the international free agency market and was signed by the Reds for $100,000 in mid-July 2017. Cerda, who was added to the club's 40-man roster this offseason, put together a decent, though far from dominant, debut in the Dominican Summer in 2018. He batted .272/.402/.439 with 11 doubles and six triples in 51 games – though he was already 18-years-old. The 6-foot-3, 170-pound center fielder was bumped up to the Appalachian League the following year, but the results were mixed – at best. In 39 games with Greeneville, he batted .220/.360/.470 with 15 extra-base hits. Last season the then-21-year-old outfielder split time between Low-A and High-A, battering the competition to the tune of .250/.361/.523 with 22 doubles, five triples, 17 homeruns, and a pair of stolen bases (in a whopping 10 attempts). Per *Weighted Runs Created Plus*, his overall production topped the league average mark by 36%.

Scouting Report: Three years ago Cerda struggled with the transition from the hitter-friendly Dominican Summer League to the more advanced Appalachian League. He was still showing plenty of power potential, but his contact rate cratered as he posted a 33.9% whiff rate. Last season, though, Cerda was able to trim a few percentage points during his 66-game stint in Low-A and lowered it even further during his 21 games in High-A (23.0%). The New York-born center fielder also got off to an abysmal start to the year, hitting .174/.297/.388 though his first 36 games (which included a stint on the disabled list). But beginning on July 17th through the rest of the year, Cerda slugged .301/.404/.612 with a more manageable 26.6% K-rate. Below-average glove. Very quick bat that projects for 25-homeruns. Again, it's all going to come down to his ability to make consistent contact. Right now, I'm betting that he will. I'm also betting he shifts over to left field too.

Ceiling: 1.5-win player
Risk: Moderate
MLB ETA: 2024

14. Andrew Abbott, LHP

FB	CU	CH	Command	Overall
50	60	55	50	45

Born: 06/01/99	Age: 23	Bats: L	Top Comp: N/A
Height: 6-0	Weight: 180	Throws: L	

Season	Team	Age	Level	IP	TBF	K/9	K%	BB/9	BB%	K-BB%	ERA	FIP	xFIP	Pit/Bat
2021	CIN	22	A	11.0	49	15.55	38.78%	3.27	8.16%	30.61%	4.91	4.07	2.71	3.88

Background: It took the slight-framed lefty longer than expected, but Abbott, who stands a wispy 6 feet and 180 pounds, made the conversion from oft-dominant reliever to light's out starting pitcher – finally. The 2017 Virginia Gatorade State Player of the Year following his final season at Halifax County High School, Abbott made 24 appearances during his freshman campaign for the University of Virginia, 23 of them coming out of the bullpen. He finished the year with a 3.18 ERA across 50.0 innings of work, averaging 13.8 strikeouts and just 2.8 walks per nine innings. The following season, 2019, the Virginia native made 24 more appearances, just two of them starts, tossing 44 innings with 59 punch outs, 25 free passes, and a 3.89 ERA. Abbott continued to miss an extraordinary amount of bats during his COVID-shortened campaign two years ago, averaging nearly 19.0 punch outs per nine innings in nine relief appearances. Last season, though, the coaching staff finally took off the reins on the southpaw and he flourished in the school's rotation: in 19 appearances, 17 of them via the start, he tossed a career high 106.2 innings with a 162-to-32 strikeout-to-walk ratio. Cincinnati drafted him in the second round, 53rd overall, and signed to a slightly below slot deal worth $1.3 million. He tossed 13.0 innings during his debut, posting a 22-to-4 strikeout-to-walk ratio, most of which coming with Daytona.

Scouting Report: Per the usual, here's my pre-draft write-up:

"Consider the following:

- *Between 2011 and 2020, only three ACC pitchers have averaged at least 12 strikeouts and fewer than 3.0 walks per nine innings in a season (min. 100 IP): Reid Detmers, Brendan McKay, and Danny Hultzen – all of whom were not only first round picks, but Top 10 selections as well.*

Despite a diminutive frame, at least in terms of today's baseball world, Abbott unfurls an average, low 90s fastball that he moves around to all quadrants of the strike zone. And he's particularly fond of elevating the offering when he's ahead in the count. But what separates the lefty from the pack is his quality offspeed: his tightly wound curveball is a plus pitch and his mid-80s changeup shows arm side fade and missed bats. As long as Abbott continues to pound the zone with the same regularity, he has the potential move quickly and settle in as a #4-type arm."

Ceiling: 1.5-win player
Risk: Moderate
MLB ETA: 2022

15. Mat Nelson, C

	Hit	Power	SB	Patience	Glove	Overall
	40	55	30	55	45	45

Born: 01/14/99	Age: 23	Bats: R	Top Comp: N/A
Height: 5-11	Weight: 209	Throws: R	

Season	Team	Age	Level	PA	1B	2B	3B	HR	SB	CS	BB%	K%	AVG	OBP	SLG	ISO
2021	CIN	22	A+	29	2	2	1	0	0	1	13.79%	51.72%	0.208	0.345	0.375	0.167

Background: A late round flier by the Phillies in 2018 coming out of Calvary Christian High School, Nelson was ranked as the 13th best prep backstop according to *Perfect Game*. And *Baseball America* listed the young power hitter as the 260th best prospect in the 2018 draft class. He was a key cog in leading Calvary Christian to 60 consecutive wins, a Florida high school record. Nelson looked comfortable digging in against the ACC competition during his true freshman season at Florida State University: he slugged .282/.442/.442 with seven doubles, six homeruns, and a quartet of stolen bases. Unfortunately, though, Nelson struggled – *mightily* – during his 14-game foray into the Cape Cod League that following summer, cobbling together a lowly .163/.280/.233 in 50 plate appearances. His production took a noticeable step backward during the abbreviated 2020 campaign, batting .250/.410/.383 in 17 contests. And then he *exploded*. Making a career high 237 trips to the plate in 2021, Nelson slugged.330/.436/.773 with 17 doubles and 23 homeruns, which tied for the NCAA lead. He finished the year with a concerning 58-to-31 K-to-BB ratio. Cincinnati drafted the slugging backstop in the opening round, 35th overall, and signed him to a deal worth $2,093,300. He appeared in 10 games between the Complex League and High-A.

Scouting Report: Per the usual, here's my pre-draft write-up:

"Consider the following:

- *Between 2011 and 2020, there were four instances in which an ACC hitter slugged at least .325/.425/.700 in a season (min. 200 PA): Will Craig (who accomplished the feat twice), Drew Ellis, and Tristin English.*

Less than stellar company, Nelson's strikeout rate in 2021, 24.5%, was more than 10-percentage points higher than the aforementioned trio. Catcher with above-average power and a matching arm will always be noteworthy. Ones that combine that skill set with some below-average defense and some questionable contact rates are further down the list. Guys that punch out in a quarter of their plate appearances during their best collegiate season just don't "figure it out" in the minor leagues."

Ceiling: 1.5-win player
Risk: Moderate
MLB ETA: 2024

16. Rece Hinds, 3B

Hit	Power	SB	Patience	Glove	Overall
40	55/60	40/35	45	50	40

Born: 9/05/00	Age: 21	Bats: R	Top Comp: N/A
Height: 6-4	Weight: 215	Throws: R	

Season	Team	Age	Level	PA	1B	2B	3B	HR	SB	CS	BB%	K%	AVG	OBP	SLG	ISO
2019	CIN	18	R	10	0	0	0	0	0	0	20.00%	30.00%	0.000	0.200	0.000	0.000
2021	CIN	20	CPX	41	3	3	2	2	1	1	9.76%	31.71%	0.294	0.390	0.676	0.382
2021	CIN	20	A	185	20	10	2	10	6	2	7.03%	28.11%	0.251	0.319	0.515	0.263

Background: A product of IMG Academy, quickly becoming *the* baseball hotbed for prep prospects, Cincinnati selected the 6-foot-4, 215-pound third baseman in the second round, 49th overall, three years ago. Hinds, who signed with the club for $1,797,500, made a brief 10-plate appearance cameo in the Appalachian League during his professional debut, going hitless with a pair of walks. Last season the front office sent the then-20-year-old up to Daytona. In 43 games with the Tortugas, the Florida native slugged .251/.319/.515 with 10 doubles, two triples, and 10 homeruns. He also swiped six bags in eight attempts. His overall production topped the league average threshold by 20%, per *Weighted Runs Created Plus*. He missed two months of action due to torn meniscus in his left knee.

Snippet from The 2020 Prospect Digest Handbook: Big time plus power potential that helped him capture the Under Armour All-America homerun derby two years ago. Hinds has terrific size and some of the draft class's best, pure bat speed. He looks solid enough to remain at third, though his athleticism would allow him to slide into a corner outfielder position.

Scouting Report: Consider the following:

- Since 2006, only four 20-year-old hitters posted a 115 to 125 wRC+ with a walk rate between 6% and 8% and a strikeout rate between 27% and 29% in Low-A (min. 175 PA): Nelson Velazquez, Osvaldo Duarte, Omar Meregildo, and Rece Hinds.

His batting stance, from a physical appearance standpoint, is reminiscent of Yankees' star outfielder Aaron Judge. Hinds owns impressive plus-power potential that's only amplified by his massive uppercut swing and impressive bat speed. The young infielder was plagued with questions about his hit tool coming into the draft and he's done nothing to assuage those concerns after whiffing in more than 28% of his plate appearances with Daytona. In the brief looks I saw of Hinds he seemed quite susceptible to offspeed pitches, both in and out of the strike zone. Defensively he was average and should remain at the hot corner for the time being. A move to first base isn't out of the question either.

Ceiling: 1.0-win player
Risk: Moderate
MLB ETA: 2024

17. Ivan Johnson, 2B/SS

Hit	Power	SB	Patience	Glove	Overall
40	45/50	50	55	50	40

Born: 10/11/98	Age: 23	Bats: B	Top Comp: N/A
Height: 6-0	Weight: 190	Throws: R	

Season	Team	Age	Level	PA	1B	2B	3B	HR	SB	CS	BB%	K%	AVG	OBP	SLG	ISO
2019	CIN	20	R	210	31	10	1	6	11	4	8.57%	21.90%	0.255	0.327	0.415	0.160
2021	CIN	22	A	216	27	14	2	6	8	5	12.50%	28.24%	0.263	0.366	0.457	0.194
2021	CIN	22	A+	114	17	5	0	4	3	2	12.28%	34.21%	0.265	0.368	0.439	0.173

Background: Throughout its history, Chipola College has produced several notable big leaguers, including: Jose Bautista, Russell Martin, Patrick Corbin, and, to a lesser extent, Tyler Flowers. Cincinnati tried their hands at the JuCo lottery three years ago when they selected switch-hitting middle infielder Ivan Johnson from the Marianna, Florida, based school in the fourth round, 114th overall, and signed him to a deal worth a smidgeon under $400,000. The Georgia native slugged a hearty .381/.491/.587 with 20 extra-base hits for the junior college prior to the draft. Johnson signed early and was able to get nearly a full season in with the Greeneville Reds in the Appalachian League during his debut, hitting .255/.327/.415 with 10 doubles, one triple, and six homeruns. Last season, he split time between Daytona and Dayton, the club's Low-A and High-A affiliates, batting an aggregate .264/.367/.451 with 19 doubles, two triples, 10 homeruns, and 11 stolen bases (in 18 attempts). Johnson also appeared in 17 games with the Surprise Saguaros in the Arizona Fall League, hitting .250/.343/.617 in 70 plate appearances.

Snippet from The 2020 Prospect Digest Handbook: After a start to his debut – he hit a horrible .221/.302/.319 through his first 27 games – Johnson rebounded to slug .307/.366/.560 over his remaining 19 contests. Defensively, he's incredible fluid – though he may end up shifting over to second base. There's a little bit of Brandon Phillips here.

Scouting Report: Taking a page out of his debut performance in 2019, Johnson got off to another slow start to the year in 2021. He hit an underwhelming .156/.325/.313 during his first 18 games. But he righted the ship in late June and slugged a hearty .295/.380/.491 over his final 61 games, including his time in High-A. Simple, easy, silky smooth swing with solid tools: above-average speed, burgeoning power, and solid average glove. The lone knock on Johnson: can he make enough contact as he ascends through the minor league ladder? He whiffed 30% of the time last year, including 32% K-rate during his final 61-game hot stretch. Johnson is now entering his age-23 season, so it's he needs to make some adjustments in the next 12 to 18 months.

Ceiling: 1.0-win player
Risk: Moderate
MLB ETA: 2023/2024

18. Christian Roa, RHP

FB	CU	SL	CH	Command	Overall
50	55	50	50	45	40

Born: 04/02/99	Age: 23	Bats: R	Top Comp: N/A
Height: 6-4	Weight: 220	Throws: R	

Season	Team	Age	Level	IP	TBF	K/9	K%	BB/9	BB%	K-BB%	ERA	FIP	xFIP	Pit/Bat
2021	CIN	22	A	17.2	78	10.70	26.92%	4.58	11.54%	15.38%	3.57	4.42	4.20	4.04
2021	CIN	22	A+	34.2	147	9.61	25.17%	3.89	10.20%	14.97%	4.15	4.52	4.37	3.92

Background: A little used reliever during his freshman season at Texas A&M, Roa tossed just 14.2 innings with 12 punch outs and a quartet of free passes. After a jaunt through the Northwoods League the following summer, the Aggies' coaching staff eased the reins on the 6-foot-4, 220-pound hurler during his sophomore campaign as he made 10 starts and seven relief appearances for the SEC Conference squad, posting a 46-to-11 strikeout ratio to go along with a 3.56 ERA. Roa's brief 2020 COVID-impacted season was dominant: he struck out 35 and walked nine in only 20.0 innings of work. Cincinnati selected the surging right-hander in the second round that year, 48th overall, and signed him to a deal worth $1,543,600. During Roa's first professional start, he lasted one inning before he hit the disabled list for two months due to a hernia. Finally healthy in early July, Roa shredded the Complex League for two tune-up starts and manhandled Low-A for four starts before moving up to High-A, a more appropriate level of competition. Including the two rookie league starts, Roa tossed 58.2 innings with 67 strikeouts and 26 free passes. He finished the year with a 3.53 ERA and a 4.28 FIP.

Scouting Report: I'll say this with the caveat that Roa was working his way back from an injury that put him on the DL for a couple months, but: he did not look all that impressive. An average fastball that plays up high in the zone, a spot he loves to live, due to its backspin. He throws two separate breaking balls: an above-average, late darting, wrinkle-of-a-cutter, and an average slider. He'll also mix in a 50-grade changeup as well. Along with a middling repertoire Roa battled command demons as well. Again, was it a regression to his early college days, or a result of facing better competition, or the layoff? I just didn't see him as a recent second round pick.

Ceiling: 1.0-win player
Risk: Moderate
MLB ETA: 2023/2024

19. Ariel Almonte, RF

Hit	Power	SB	Patience	Glove	Overall
35/50	40/55	50/40	50	50	40

Born: 12/01/03	Age: 18	Bats: L	Top Comp: N/A
Height: 6-1	Weight: 170	Throws: L	

Season	Team	Age	Level	PA	1B	2B	3B	HR	SB	CS	BB%	K%	AVG	OBP	SLG	ISO
2021	CIN	17	DSL	196	30	9	1	5	15	6	13.27%	26.53%	0.278	0.398	0.438	0.160

Background: Ranked as the #26 prospect on the international market by MLB.com, the Reds pulled out all the stops to sign the 6-foot-1, 170-pound corner outfielder last season. Hailing from the Dominican Republic, Almonte came to an agreement with the NL Central Division club on a nice $1.85 million deal. The left-handed throwing / hitting right fielder made his professional debut in the Dominican Summer League last season, hitting .278/.398/.438 with nine doubles, one triple, five homeruns, and 15 stolen bases. Per *Weighted Runs Created Plus*, his overall production was 37% better than the league average threshold.

Scouting Report: Raw, but the toolsy are there. They just need to be polished and cleaned up a bit. Above-average arm. Good bat speed with solid rotation during his swing. Almonte's lower mechanics need cleaned up as he's not utilizing his legs much – or at all. The young Dominican struggled a bit with consistently making contact, but his foundation is strong enough to push him stateside to the Complex League for the start of 2022.

Ceiling: 1.0-win player
Risk: Moderate
MLB ETA: 2025

20. Jared Solomon, RHP

	FB	SL	CH	Command	Overall
	N/A	N/A	N/A	N/A	35

Born: 06/10/97	Age: 25	Bats: R	Top Comp: N/A
Height: 6-2	Weight: 200	Throws: R	

Season	Team	Age	Level	IP	TBF	K/9	K%	BB/9	BB%	K-BB%	ERA	FIP	xFIP	Pit/Bat
2018	CIN	21	R	47.2	191	10.20	28.27%	2.64	7.33%	20.94%	2.27	4.42	4.39	3.62
2018	CIN	21	A	25.0	126	4.68	10.32%	6.48	14.29%	-3.97%	5.40	5.36	6.00	3.63
2019	CIN	22	A	42.0	193	9.86	23.83%	5.79	13.99%	9.84%	3.43	3.26	4.06	4.08
2019	CIN	22	A+	73.1	327	7.98	19.88%	4.17	10.40%	9.48%	4.30	4.18	4.13	3.71

Background: "Uh huh, Kenneth Road, born and raise. Spent my whole life right here in Lackawanna County and I do not intend on movin'." – Michael Scott, Regional Manager, Dunder Mifflin. Scott was from Lackawanna County. Jared Solomon, the hard-throwing right-hander, *went* to Lackawanna College in Scranton, Pennsylvania. A late round pick by the Reds in 2017, the 6-foot-2, 200-pound hurler, who was taken with the 317th overall pick, came into his own in 2019. Splitting time between Dayton and Daytona that year, Solomon posted a decent 111-to-61 strikeout-to-walk ratio in 115.1 innings of work. COVID forced a lost season of important development in 2020. And, *then*, he missed the entire 2021 season as he recovered from Tommy John surgery.

Scouting Report: Reports indicate that Solomon was showcasing a solid two-pitch mix, featuring a plus fastball and an above-average slider. His changeup, according to MLB.com, was well below-average. Even before the TJ surgery he was quickly starring down the path of relief-dom. Now he's entering his age-25 with just 73.1 innings above Low-A on his resume. Solomon is profiling as a solid middle relief option – barring any type of injury setbacks or blips.

Ceiling: 0.5- to 1.0-win player
Risk: Moderate to High
MLB ETA: 2023

Cleveland Guardians

Top Prospects

1. George Valera, OF

	Hit	Power	SB	Patience	Glove	Overall
	45/55	55/65	50	70	55	60

Born: 11/13/00	Age: 21	Bats: L	
Height: 5-11	Weight: 185	Throws: L	Top Comp: Cody Bellinger

Season	Team	Age	Level	PA	1B	2B	3B	HR	SB	CS	BB%	K%	AVG	OBP	SLG	ISO
2018	CLE	17	R	22	4	1	0	1	1	1	13.64%	13.64%	0.333	0.409	0.556	0.222
2019	CLE	18	A	26	1	0	1	0	0	2	7.69%	34.62%	0.087	0.192	0.174	0.087
2019	CLE	18	A-	188	21	7	1	8	6	2	15.43%	27.66%	0.236	0.356	0.446	0.210
2021	CLE	20	A+	263	29	2	4	16	10	5	20.91%	22.05%	0.256	0.430	0.548	0.291
2021	CLE	20	AA	100	17	3	0	3	1	0	11.00%	30.00%	0.267	0.340	0.407	0.140

Background: Born in Queens, New York, Valera and his family moved to the Dominican Republic during his early teenage years. A short while later Cleveland signed their eventual top prospect to a hefty $1.3 million deal. After a brief six-game debut in the Arizona Summer League in 2018, Valera looked battled through an up-and-down showing with the Mahoning Valley Scrappers in the New York-Penn League the following season. He hit .236/.354/.446 with seven doubles, one triple, and eight homeruns in 46 games as an 18-year-old. He also appeared in six games with the Lake County Captains in Low-A as well, going 2-for-23 with a triple. Last season, with the return of minor league ball from their COVID-imposed shutdown, the 5-foot-11, 185-pound outfielder burst out in a massive way. In an atypical move, at least for the normally conservative front office, the organization's development program pushed the now-20-year-old straight up to High-A to begin the season. In 63 games he slugged .256/.430/.548 with two doubles, four triples, and 16 homeruns. Valera was bumped up to the minors' toughest proving ground, Double-A, in late August. And he continued to rake. In 23 games with the Akron RubberDucks, the former international free agent batted .267/.340/.407. After the dust had finally settled on his breakout season, one which many were predicting, Valera hit an aggregate .260/.405/.505 with five doubles, four triples, and 19 homeruns. He also swiped 11 bags in 16 attempts. Per *Weighted Runs Created Plus*, Valera's production topped the league average threshold by a staggering 48%.

Snippet from The 2020 Prospect Digest Handbook: That loud audible crack I mentioned in [The 2018] Handbook turned out to be some *phenomenal* exit velocities in 2019: it averaged a whopping 91 mph with a peak of 107 mph. That's as an 18-year-old squaring off against competition that averaged three years his senior. There's some big time, plus power potential and well above-average patience mix in. And his strikeout rate last season in the NYPL, 27.7%, barely moves the needle in terms of concern. He was (A) 18-years-old, (B) coming off of a semi-serious injury, (C) limited to six games in rookie ball, and (D) jumped an entire level. There's some massive, *massive* upside here. He's going to be one of the biggest breakout prospects in 2020. Remember the name.

Scouting Report: Consider the following:

- Since 2006, only four 20-year-old hitters met the following criteria in High-A with one organization (min. 250 PA): at least a 160 wRC+ total and a strikeout rate between 19% and 23%. Those four hitters: Christian Yelich, Corey Seager, Jay Bruce, and – of course – Mr. Breakout George Valera.
- For those counting at home: Yelich, winner of the 2018 NL MVP award, owns a career 132 wRC+; Seager, the 2016 ML Rookie of the Year, also owns a 132 wRC+ mark in his career; and Bruce, the consensus #1 prospect in baseball heading into the 2008 season, retired with a 106 wRC+ mark.

Something, something, something – you're only as good as the company you keep, right? And if that's the case, George Valera is really, *really* good. And just for fun, here's his numbers prorated for a full 162-game campaign: nine doubles, eight triples, 36 homeruns, and 21 stolen bases. Again, he was playing against vastly older competition. And he did so while (A) improving his strikeout rate tremendously, (B) leaping up from short-season ball, and (C) spent roughly a month in the minors' true proving ground, Double-A. Valera handles lefties and righties equally well, owns one of best eyes / approaches at the plate in the minor leagues, and is just tapping into what should be plus in-game power. He hits laser beams as well and as hard as any prospect. Throw in an above-average glove in a corner outfield spot and Valera has the makings of the best homegrown everyday player since Francisco Lindor. And he could develop into the best homegrown bat since, dare I say, Manny Ramirez. In terms of big league ceiling, think .280/.420/.600.

Ceiling: 6.0-win player
Risk: Moderate
MLB ETA: 2022/2023

2. Brayan Rocchio, 2B/SS

Hit	Power	SB	Patience	Glove	Overall
55	50	55	45	60	60

Born: 01/13/01	Age: 21	Bats: B	Top Comp: Jimmy Rollins
Height: 5-10	Weight: 170	Throws: R	

Season	Team	Age	Level	PA	1B	2B	3B	HR	SB	CS	BB%	K%	AVG	OBP	SLG	ISO
2018	CLE	17	R	111	26	2	3	1	8	5	4.50%	12.61%	0.323	0.391	0.434	0.111
2018	CLE	17	R	158	37	10	1	1	14	8	6.33%	10.76%	0.343	0.389	0.448	0.105
2019	CLE	18	A-	295	47	12	3	5	14	8	6.78%	13.56%	0.250	0.310	0.373	0.123
2021	CLE	20	A+	288	45	13	1	9	14	6	6.94%	22.57%	0.265	0.337	0.428	0.163
2021	CLE	20	AA	203	31	13	4	6	7	4	6.40%	20.20%	0.293	0.360	0.505	0.212

Background: Apparently talent comes in bunches when it comes to the Guardians. By now, it's all but cemented that their 2016 draft class is historic, at least in terms of the franchise, but their 2017 international free agent class could be special as well. As noted by MLB Pipeline, the front office added the likes of George Valera, the club's best prospect, Brayan Rocchio, Aaron Bracho, Jhonkensy Noel, and emerging infielder Jose Tena as part of their *massive* haul. Hailing from Caracas, Venezuela, Cleveland signed the young switch-hitting Rocchio to a deal that barely spilled over into six figures. And it's proving to be quite the bargain. The 5-foot-10, 170-pound middle infielder ripped through the foreign and domestic rookie leagues during his debut, batting .335/.390/.442, and he spent the entire 2019 season battling the New York-Penn League as an 18-year-old. Last season, despite appearing in just 69 games above rookie ball, Rocchio opened up with Lake County and finished it with Akron. In total, he slugged .277/.346/.460 with 26 doubles, five triples, 15 homeruns, and 21 stolen bases. Per *Weighted Runs Created Plus*, his production topped the average mark by 20% – not bad for a 20-year-old squaring off against older pitching.

Snippet from The 2020 Prospect Digest Handbook: A slow start to his year, which isn't surprising, put a damper on his overall numbers. But it's important to point out that he hit a respectable .271/.329/.403 with five doubles and four homeruns over his 32 games. Short compact swing with the same lightning quickness he displayed the previous year. Very twitchy. A year later, though, I'm not certain on how the power will develop. He's more of a slasher. His potential plus-glove pushes him up to starter status.

Scouting Report: Consider the following:

- Since 2006, only two 20-year-old hitters posted a 130 to 140 wRC+ total with a 6% to 8% walk rate and a 19.5% to 24.5% strikeout rate in Double-A with one organization (min. 200 PA): Cristian Pache and, of course, Brayan Rocchio.

One of the club's biggest risers up the prospect charts in 2021. There's a chance for an above-average bat, average power, above-average speed, and a Gold Glove at the infield's most important position. Beyond Valera, Rocchio represent the highest ceiling bat in the entire farm system. He's not a lock of superstardom, but he could be a perennial All-Star.

Ceiling: 5.0-win player
Risk: Moderate
MLB ETA: 2022/2023

3. Daniel Espino, RHP

FB	CB	SL	CH	Command	Overall
70	50	60	50	50	60

Born: 01/05/01	Age: 21	Bats: R	Top Comp: Zack Wheeler
Height: 6-2	Weight: 205	Throws: R	

Season	Team	Age	Level	IP	TBF	K/9	K%	BB/9	BB%	K-BB%	ERA	FIP	xFIP	Pit/Bat
2019	CLE	18	A-	10.0	45	16.20	40.00%	4.50	11.11%	28.89%	6.30	2.60	2.43	4.27
2019	CLE	18	R	13.2	53	10.54	30.19%	3.29	9.43%	20.75%	1.98	4.20	3.84	2.53
2021	CLE	20	A	42.2	180	13.50	35.56%	4.85	12.78%	22.78%	3.37	3.20	3.29	4.00
2021	CLE	20	A+	49.0	195	16.16	45.13%	2.94	8.21%	36.92%	4.04	3.08	2.41	4.05

Background: One of the better known high school arms available in the 2019 draft class thanks in large part to social media. The hard-throwing, wickedly talented right-hander was regularly showcased on Rob Friedman's Twitter account, @PitchingNinja. Born in Panama, Panama, Espino moved to the U.S. and attended Georgia Premier Academy. Long projected as a potential #1 pick, Espino's stock tumbled as the draft neared with concerns of his long arm action – and, perhaps, from overexposure – and Cleveland happily snagged him with the 24th overall pick three years ago. The AL Central club signed him to a slightly below slot deal worth $2.5 million, saving the club roughly $300,000. The 6-foot-2, 205-pound righty made nine brief appearances between the Arizona Summer and New York-Penn Leagues during his debut, posting a 34-to-10 strikeout-to-walk ratio in 23.2 innings of work. Cleveland sent their top arm up to Low-A to start the 2021 season. And he dominated. In 10 starts with the Lynchburg Hillcats, he fanned 64 and walked 23 in 42.2 innings of work. And he actually *improved* during his second half promotion up to High-A Central. In total, Espino finished his first full professional season with a whopping 152 punch outs, the 15th highest mark in the minors, and just 39 free passes. For those counting at home: he averaged 14.9 strikeouts and 3.8 walks per nine innings.

Snippet from The 2020 Prospect Digest Handbook: Easy plus-plus velocity with a wipeout slider, and a knee-buckling curveball. Espino's fastball shows incredible late action and both breaking balls grade out as plus. He'll also mix in a rare below-average changeup, though I only witnessed the upper 80s offering once. He shows solid feel for pitching, especially considering his ability to overpower his peers with one pitch. The major knock on the wiry hurler – seemingly – is his long arm action. But his mechanical fluidity, athleticism, and flexibility alleviate a lot of my concerns, personally. Espino's the best pitching prospect in a weak class – by a wide margin. Of course, there's concern and risk associated with any hard-throwing youngster but Espino's ceiling is incredibly high.

Scouting Report: Consider the following:

- Since 2006, only five 20-year-old hurlers posted a strikeout percentage of at least 35% in High-A with one organization (min. 45 IP): Michael Kopech, MacKenzie Gore, Alex Reyes, Shelby Miller, and – of course – Daniel Espino.
- Espino's 45.1% K% leads the pack by a WIDE margin; Kopech, the runner-up, posted a 40% mark. Espino also posted the second lowest walk percentage among the group.
- Kopech, Gore, Reyes, and Miller were – at one point – recognized, almost universally, as some of the best prospects in the game.

Insanely talented. Espino attacks hitters with a genuine 80-grade fastball that sits – with ease – in the 96- to 98-mph range and will regularly touch triple-digits during the course of the game. His slider is unfairly good, sitting in the mid-80s but will pump 90 mph when he's loose and easy. He'll also mix in a rare, above-average curveball. And his changeup, which was in the 91-mph range, showed improved sink and fade. Espino owns one of the best arsenals in the game. There's bonafide ace potential, but he'll need a third option uptick to get there.

Ceiling: 4.5-win player
Risk: Moderate
MLB ETA: 2023

4. Tyler Freeman, IF

Hit	Power	SB	Patience	Glove	Overall
60/70	35	50	40	55	55

Born: 05/21/99	Age: 23	Bats: R	Top Comp: Josh Harrison
Height: 6-0	Weight: 190	Throws: R	

Season	Team	Age	Level	PA	1B	2B	3B	HR	SB	CS	BB%	K%	AVG	OBP	SLG	ISO
2018	CLE	19	A-	301	60	29	4	2	14	3	2.66%	7.31%	0.352	0.405	0.511	0.159
2019	CLE	20	A	272	47	16	3	3	11	4	6.62%	10.29%	0.292	0.382	0.424	0.131
2019	CLE	20	A+	275	64	16	2	0	8	1	2.91%	9.09%	0.319	0.354	0.397	0.078
2021	CLE	22	AA	180	35	14	2	2	4	2	4.44%	11.67%	0.323	0.372	0.470	0.146

Background: Cleveland's 2017 draft class is pretty fascinating. The savvy front office lost their first round pick as a result of signing Edwin Encarnacion. They missed on their first selection, Quentin Holmes, and their third through seventh round picks have produced zilch other than mostly flameouts. But the team formerly known as the Indians hit big it with their second pick in the second round, Tyler Freeman, as well as their ninth round pick, James Karinchak. And though the jury's still out on Eli Morgan, he looks to be a solid backend arm. A product of Etiwanda High School, Freeman, who was chosen with the 71st overall pick, put together an impressive debut showing in the Arizona Summer League, batting .297/.364/.414 in 36 games. And that was just a harbinger of things to come. Freeman torched the New York-Penn League the following season, slugging .352/.405/.511 with 35 extra-base hits in only 72 games. And he made quick work of the Midwest and Carolina Leagues in 2019 as well. Last season, as minor league action returned to its work, Freeman opened the year up in the minors' toughest level, Double-A, and he continued to rake. In an injury-shortened season, the 6-foot, 190-pound infielder batted .323/.372/.470 with 14 doubles, two triples, two homeruns, and four stolen bases in 41 games. Left shoulder surgery curtailed his campaign, though all reports indicate he'll be back to full health in time for Spring Training.

Snippet from The 2020 Prospect Digest Handbook: The hit tool is going to determine whether he develops into an above-average starter or a super-sub type of player. There's a chance it develops into a 70-grade and he's currently profiling as a Kevin Newman-type bat: .310/.350/.430 with double-digit stolen bases.

Scouting Report: Freeman is one of the few current minor league prospects that could develop a 70-grade hit tool. Surprisingly, though, his ceiling is largely predicated on his ability to consistently hit for a high average as his other tools lack standout potential. His patience at the plate will oscillate between laughably poor to below-average. But his ability to consistently get plunked with pitches – he's been hit 56 times in 272 games or roughly once every five games – helps buoy his OBPs. He's slugged just nine homeruns in 272 career minor league games. And while he has above-average speed, he projects to steal fewer than 20 bags in a season. Defensively, he could very easily get caught in a numbers game with the organization having a bevy of interesting shortstop prospects and Freeman's always seemed destined for the keystone. In terms of a big line slash line, think: .310/.350/.420.

Ceiling: 3.5-win player
Risk: Low to Moderate
MLB ETA: 2022

5. Gabriel Arias, 3B/SS

	Hit	Power	SB	Patience	Glove	Overall
	50	50	40	50	55	55

Born: 02/27/00	Age: 22	Bats: R	Top Comp: Jhonny Peralta
Height: 6-1	Weight: 217	Throws: R	

Season	Team	Age	Level	PA	1B	2B	3B	HR	SB	CS	BB%	K%	AVG	OBP	SLG	ISO
2018	SDP	18	A	504	73	27	3	6	3	3	8.13%	29.56%	0.240	0.302	0.352	0.112
2019	SDP	19	A+	511	102	21	4	17	8	4	4.89%	25.05%	0.302	0.339	0.470	0.168
2021	CLE	21	AAA	483	79	29	3	13	5	1	8.07%	22.77%	0.284	0.348	0.454	0.170

Background: In one of the bigger selloffs in franchise history, Cleveland shipped away Corey Kluber, Trevor Bauer, and Mike Clevinger. With each deal adding valuable pieces towards Cleveland's rebuild. The franchise acquired Gabriel Arias, along with the supremely underrated Cal Quantrill, Joey Cantillo, Austin Hedges, and Owen Miller, from the Padres in exchange for Clevinger, outfielder Greg Allen, and minor leaguer Matt Waldron. Originally signed by the Friars out of La Victoria, Venezuela, for a hefty $1.9 million, Arias was instantaneously placed on the fast track to the big leagues. He debuted in 2017 as a spry, baby-faced 17-year-old, and spent a couple weeks in the Midwest League. He spent all of the following season back in Low-A, though he mainly struggled as he compiled a .240/.302/.352 slash line. But the Padres continued to challenge him and sent him up to High-A for the entirety of 2019. And he raked. In 120 games with Lake Elsinore, the still-teenaged shortstop slugged .302/.339/.470 with 21 doubles, four triples, 17 long balls, and eight stolen bases. Last season, Cleveland had Arias bypass Double-A and sent him directly to Columbus. And he continued to impress. In 115 games with the Clippers, Arias, who can now legally drink, hit .284/.348/.454 with a career best 29 doubles, three triples, 13 homeruns, and five stolen bases (in six attempts). Per *Weighted Runs Created Plus*, his overall production topped the league average mark by 15%.

Snippet from The 2020 Prospect Digest Handbook: He's quite raw and incredibly athletic, so I wouldn't rule out a move to the outfield or third base if the power continues to grow. League average, maybe more depending upon how the BABIPs bounce.

Scouting Report: Consider the following:

- Since 2006, only two 21-year-old hitters met the following criteria in Triple-A with one organization (min. 350 PA): 110 to 120 wRC+, a strikeout percentage between 20% and 23%, and a walk percentage between 7% and 9%. Those two hitters: Joel Guzman and, of course, Gabriel Arias.

As with a lot of prospects last season, especially ones that bypassed an entire level, there was an adjustment period (e.g. slow start) for Arias. He batted a putrid .196/.318/.299 over his first 31 games. But beginning on June 12th through the rest of the season, the 6-foot-1, 217-pound infielder slugged an impressive .313/.359/.505 with 27 doubles, three triples, and 10 homeruns. He has always shown an advanced feel at the plate, but last season he displayed a more patient approach as well, something that he's only hinted at in the past. There's 20-homer thump brewing in the bat. Average speed which will result in double-digit stolen bases. And, perhaps the best news, he's continued to improve his once problematic strikeout rate down to a meager 22% in 2021. Defensively, he's average at shortstop. Big league ceiling, think: .270/.330/.440.

Ceiling: 3.5-win player
Risk: Moderate
MLB ETA: 2022

6. Nolan Jones, 3B/RF

	Hit	Power	SB	Patience	Glove	Overall
	45	50/60	40/35	60	50	50

Born: 05/07/98	Age: 24	Bats: L	Top Comp: Jay Bruce
Height: 6-4	Weight: 195	Throws: R	

Season	Team	Age	Level	PA	1B	2B	3B	HR	SB	CS	BB%	K%	AVG	OBP	SLG	ISO
2018	CLE	20	A	389	62	12	0	16	2	1	16.20%	24.94%	0.279	0.393	0.464	0.186
2018	CLE	20	A+	130	19	9	0	3	0	0	20.00%	26.15%	0.298	0.438	0.471	0.173
2019	CLE	21	A+	324	52	12	1	7	5	3	20.06%	26.23%	0.286	0.435	0.425	0.139
2019	CLE	21	AA	211	25	10	2	8	2	0	14.69%	29.86%	0.253	0.370	0.466	0.213
2021	CLE	23	AAA	407	42	25	1	13	10	2	14.50%	29.98%	0.238	0.356	0.431	0.194

Background: The club's 2016 draft class will *forever* be known for adding Aaron Civale (third round), Shane Bieber (fourth), and Zach Plesac (12th) into the fold. But it wasn't initially recognized as such. In fact, the storyline was largely built around the club's first round gamble of Will

Benson, who signed a below-slow deal, and the addition of Nolan Jones in the second round, who immediately became one of the club's better minor league hitters. A consensus Top 100 prospect for several years, Jones looked poised to play a major role in the club's 2020 or 2021 seasons. Instead, Jones – like the majority of minor leaguers – lost a year of development due to the 2020 COVID-imposed shutdown. And he struggled, for the first time in his career, in Triple-A in 2021. In 99 games with the Columbus Clippers, the lefty-swinging third baseman / right fielder hit a mediocre .238/.356/.431 with 25 doubles, one triple, 13 homeruns, and 10 stolen bases. Per *Weighted Runs Created Plus*, his overall production topped the league average mark by 13%.

Snippet from The 2020 Prospect Digest Handbook: Jones' lengthy, red flag raising history of platoon splits continued once again and, frankly, it showed zero signs of improvement in 2019. The former second round pick slashed a scorching .312/.439/.497 vs. right-handers, but cobbled together a paltry .151/.324/.274 against southpaws. And what's more concerning: he whiffed in 35.3% of his plate appearances against lefties.

Scouting Report: Consider the following:

- Since 2006, only four 23-year-old hitters posted a 108 to 118 wRC+ with a strikeout percentage between 29% and 31% in Triple-A with one organization (min. 350 PA): Chris Shaw, Deivy Grullon, Wilkin Ramirez, and Nolan Jones.

Jones has always flirted with concerning strikeout rates throughout his career, but it's largely been overlooked because he's consistently hit – and hit well. Last season, though, he didn't – at all. Or did he? Jones got off to a slow start to the year, batting a paltry .172/.310/.269 over his first 28 games. He also whiffed in nearly 39% of his plate appearances. But after making some adjustments, the former second rounder rebounded to slug .262/.374/.492 over his remaining 71 contests – including a more manageable 26.5% K-rate. He also posted a strong 132 wRC+ during that time as well. And for the first time in forever, the lefty-swinging Jones didn't struggle against southpaws either. Most will glance at his final line and chalk it up as a disappointment campaign. But it wasn't. Defensively, he plays third base like a right fielder. He's still a dark horse candidate for a breakout at the big league level in 2022. Big league line: .260/.360/.450.

Ceiling: 2.5-win player
Risk: Moderate
MLB ETA: 2022

7. Jhonkensy Noel, 1B/3B	Hit	Power	SB	Patience	Glove	Overall
	50	60	30	45	45/50	50

Born: 07/15/01	Age: 20	Bats: R	Top Comp: N/A
Height: 6-1	Weight: 180	Throws: R	

Season	Team	Age	Level	PA	1B	2B	3B	HR	SB	CS	BB%	K%	AVG	OBP	SLG	ISO
2018	CLE	16	R	260	32	11	0	10	6	4	9.62%	22.31%	0.243	0.357	0.431	0.188
2019	CLE	17	R	209	33	12	0	6	5	1	8.61%	18.66%	0.287	0.349	0.455	0.169
2021	CLE	19	CPX	17	2	1	0	0	0	1	5.88%	23.53%	0.200	0.294	0.267	0.067
2021	CLE	19	A	162	37	10	1	11	2	1	4.32%	16.67%	0.393	0.426	0.693	0.300
2021	CLE	19	A+	111	17	3	0	8	3	1	8.11%	27.93%	0.280	0.351	0.550	0.270

Background: Oh, you know, just another one of the club's international free agents signed during the 2017 period that's starting to pay big dividends. Thanks to a later birthday, Noel would make his organizational debut the following season at just 16-years-old. And he held his own by batting .243/.357/.431 with 11 doubles and 10 homeruns in 64 games in the foreign rookie league. Noel would spend the following season, 2019, in the stateside rookie league and he continued to hit: .287/.349/.455. Last year, with the return to minor league action, Noel opened the year up hotter than Pete Rose's gasoline suit trouncing through hell. In 38 games with the Lynchburg Hillcats, the 6-foot-1, 180-pound corner infielder bashed the competition to tune of .393/.426/.693 with 10 doubles, one triple, and 11 homeruns. The club bounced him up to High-A in mid-August for another 26 games, most of which involved Noel hitting. Overall, the Dominican-born slugger put together an aggregate .340/.390/.615 with 14 doubles, one triple, and 19 homeruns. His production topped the league average mark by a whopping 61%, per *Weighted Runs Created Plus*. An ankle sprain knocked him out of commission from more than a month.

Scouting Report: In the running for the single most underrated prospect in baseball entering the 2022 season. Noel was incredibly dominant during his breakout campaign last year, showing tremendous power potential, a future 55-grade hit tool, and the ability to absolutely annihilate baseballs. But perhaps the most impressive part of his season: a fair number of his long balls were hit off of offspeed pitches, allowing him to put on full display his ability to adjust mid-pitch. He might own some of the best pure raw power in the game; it's on the same level of Franmil Reyes. Defensively, he's still seeing significant time at the hot corner, but once he fills out he's all but destined to slide over to first base. One more strong showing in 2022 and Noel will be a consensus Top 100 prospect. Big lower half. Big time helium potential.

Ceiling: 2.5-win player
Risk: Moderate
MLB ETA: 2024

8. Jose Tena, SS

Hit	Power	SB	Patience	Glove	Overall
50	40/45	50	45	50	50

Born: 03/20/01	Age: 21	Bats: L	Top Comp: N/A
Height: 5-10	Weight: 160	Throws: R	

Season	Team	Age	Level	PA	1B	2B	3B	HR	SB	CS	BB%	K%	AVG	OBP	SLG	ISO
2018	CLE	17	R	218	48	8	4	1	10	7	6.88%	13.30%	0.313	0.367	0.410	0.097
2019	CLE	18	R	199	48	7	6	1	6	2	3.02%	22.11%	0.325	0.352	0.440	0.115
2021	CLE	20	A+	447	73	25	2	16	10	5	6.04%	26.17%	0.281	0.331	0.467	0.186

Background: Part of the same international draft class that added George Valera and Brayan Rocchio to the fold. Tena, who signed with Cleveland for $400,000, continued to his steady march through the low levels of the minor leagues. The lefty-swinging infielder performed well during his professional debut in the foreign rookie league in 2018, batting .313/.367/.410 as a 17-year-old. The organization pushed the San Cristobal, Dominican Republic, native stateside the following year. And the more advanced, mostly teenage, pitching proved to be little competition for Tena as well; he slugged .325/.352/.440 with 14 extra-base hits in only 44 games. Last season, Tena leapt over Low-A and landed comfortably in High-A Central, where the average pitcher was three years his senior. In a career best 107 games with the Captains of Lake County, the 5-foot-10, 160-pound shortstop hit .281/.331/.467 with 25 doubles, two triples, and 16 homeruns. He also swiped 10 bags in 15 attempts. His overall production topped the league average mark by 15%, per *Weighted Runs Created Plus*. Tena spent the weeks after the season dominating the Arizona Fall League pitching to the tune of .387/.467/.516.

Scouting Report: Consider the following:

- Since 2006, only three 20-year-old hitters posted a 110 to 120 wRC+ with a strikeout percentage between 24% and 28% and a single digit walk rate in High-A with one organization (min. 350 PA): Anderson Tejeda, Charlie Fermaint, and Jose Tena.

The power surge last season was unexpected. After all, Tena slugged two homeruns in 95 games between 2018-19 and belted out 16 in 107 games with Lake County. But don't buy into that just yet, though. Per *Baseball America's* ballpark factors, Lake County's home field, Classic Park, is the single most homer-friendly place in High-A Central. And that's only backed up by the fact that he hit 11 homeruns in 56 games at home vs. five dingers in 54 games on the road. The lefty-swinging Tena hits lefties and righties equally well. He doesn't walk a lot, shows above-average speed, and plays an average shortstop.

Ceiling: 2.5-win player
Risk: Moderate
MLB ETA: 2023

9. Gavin Williams, RHP

FB	CB	SL	CH	Command	Overall
70	55	50	N/A	50	50

Born: 07/26/99	Age: 22	Bats: L	Top Comp: N/A
Height: 6-6	Weight: 238	Throws: R	

Background: Impressive career statistics coming out of Cape Fear High School in 2017, Williams, a four-year letterman, threw a total of 132.0 innings for the North Carolina high school, tallying a tidy 1.06 ERA with 212 strikeouts against 74 walks and a 18-1 win-loss record. The Rays drafted the behemoth right-hander in the 30th round, 889th overall, in the 2017 draft. Williams, of course, opted to take the collegiate route, heading to the American Athletic Conference to play for East Carolina. He spent the entirety of his freshman season working out of the Pirates' bullpen, throwing 15.2 innings of 1.15 ERA-ball. And he also appeared in four disastrous – albeit brief – games in the Cape Cod League that summer as well. ECU stretched the 6-foot-6, 238-pound hurler out during his sophomore season as he tossed 49.1 innings between the rotation and pen. And he was only able to add a couple of appearances to his collegiate resume during the COVID-shortened campaign in 2020 as well. Fast forward to the 2021 season and Williams, the former late round pick, emerged as a Day 1 draft selection as he averaged 14.4 strikeouts against just 2.3 walks per nine innings in 15 appearances. Cleveland selected him in the first round, 23rd overall, and signed him to a deal worth $2.25 million, saving the club roughly $700,000. He did not appear in an affiliated game after signing.

Scouting Report: Per the usual, here's my pre-draft write-up:

"Consider the following:

- *Between 2011 and 2020, here's the list of Division I pitchers to average at least 13 strikeouts and fewer than three walks per nine innings (min. 75 IP): Trevor Bauer, Reid Detmers, Ethan Small, Logan Gilbert, Noah Song, J.P. Sears, Dan Altavilla, Phil Bickford, Ben Braymer, and Kyle Kinman.*

Not bad company. Not. At. All.

Big, big time heater that can touch triple digits on occasion – an easy 70-grade offering. An above-average mid- to upper-70s curveball, a decent little slider that shows some sweeping depth. And he'll mix in a solid changeup, according to reports (the changeup is the only offering I didn't see). Williams showed a surprising amount of strikes during his final season with ECU. And even though he's now in his fourth collegiate season, he's still only 21. There's some reliever risk here, but there's also some mid-rotation caliber potential."

Ceiling: 2.5-win player
Risk: Moderate
MLB ETA: 2023/2024

10. Bryan Lavastida, C

	Hit	Power	SB	Patience	Glove	Overall
	55	45/50	50/40	50	50	50

Born: 11/27/98	Age: 23	Bats: R	Top Comp: N/A
Height: 6-0	Weight: 200	Throws: R	

Season	Team	Age	Level	PA	1B	2B	3B	HR	SB	CS	BB%	K%	AVG	OBP	SLG	ISO
2018	CLE	19	R	149	29	4	1	1	5	5	14.77%	15.44%	0.292	0.415	0.367	0.075
2019	CLE	20	A-	240	46	19	3	2	3	3	10.42%	11.25%	0.335	0.408	0.483	0.148
2021	CLE	22	A+	198	33	12	0	5	14	5	13.13%	15.15%	0.303	0.399	0.467	0.164
2021	CLE	22	AA	119	19	7	1	3	2	3	10.08%	23.53%	0.291	0.373	0.466	0.175
2021	CLE	22	AAA	21	2	0	0	1	0	0	9.52%	47.62%	0.158	0.238	0.316	0.158

Background: Another example of the club's tremendous scouting – and development – acumen. Cleveland unearthed the blossoming backstop in the 15th round out of Hillsborough Community College four years ago. After moonlighting as a backstop in college, the Guardians immediately converted the 6-foot, 200-pound JuCo star into a full time backstop and, as they say, the rest is history. Lavastida put together a solid showing in the Arizona Summer League in 2018, batting .292/.415/.367, and shredded the New York-Penn League competition the following year (.335/.408/.483). Last season, the Florida-born prospect continued his assault on minor league pitching as he moved through High-A, passed the Double-A test, and even spent a few weeks in Triple-A. Lavastida finished the year with an aggregate .289/.380/.456 slash line, belting out 19 doubles, one triple, nine homeruns, and 16 stolen bases (in 24 attempts). His overall production, per *Weighted Runs Created Plus*, topped the league average mark by 29%.

Scouting Report: An advanced bat that has a long tracked of well above-average offensive performances in the minor leagues. Lavastida owns an above-average hit tool and a solid eye at the plate. His power is currently a 45-grade, though it's likely to bump up into average territory in the coming year(s). Above-average bat speed with incredibly quick hands, Lavastida needs to elevate the ball more frequently to take advantage of his raw power. His defense, according to Clay Davenport's metrics, is average – though he's never going to be mistaken for Ivan Rodriguez when it comes to controlling the running game. He looks like a low end starting backstop, but there may be more in the tank.

Ceiling: 1.5- to 2.0-win player
Risk: Moderate
MLB ETA: 2022

11. Petey Halpin, OF

	Hit	Power	SB	Patience	Glove	Overall
	55	30/45	50	50	55	50

Born: 05/26/02	Age: 20	Bats: L	Top Comp: N/A
Height: 6-0	Weight: 185	Throws: R	

Season	Team	Age	Level	PA	1B	2B	3B	HR	SB	CS	BB%	K%	AVG	OBP	SLG	ISO
2021	CLE	19	A	246	44	14	6	1	11	9	8.54%	20.33%	0.294	0.363	0.425	0.131

Background: In a draft year filled with a lot of uncertainty swirling about because of the COVID-imposed shutdown, the Guardians zigged when the rest of baseball seemed to zag. The front office tossed caution to the wind and selected a trio of high school players – who lacked a senior season of development and scouting – in their six selections. The organization went well above the $610,800 recommended slot value and signed Halpin to a deal worth $1,525,000. Committed to the University of Texas before joining the G-Men, Halpin made his debut with the Hillcats of Lynchburg last season. In 54 games with the organization's Low-A East affiliate, the 6-foot, 185-pound outfielder batted a rock solid .294/.363/.425 with 14 doubles, six triples, one homeruns, and 11 stolen bases – though he managed to get thrown out nine times. His overall production topped the league average threshold by 17%, per *Weighted Runs Created Plus*.

Scouting Report: Consider the following:

- Since 2006, only a pair of 19-year-old hitters posted a 112 to 122 wRC+ total with a 19% to 21% strikeout rate and a 7% to 10% walk rate in Low-A with one organization (min. 225 PA): Jeter Downs, the former Top 100 prospect who struggled mightily in 2021, and Petey Halpin.

A smooth, sweet-swinging outfielder with a well-rounded toolkit that lacks any red flags at the current time. He handles lefties and righties equally solid, runs well, shows developing power, and can absolutely chase down anything in the outfield. Halpin doesn't try to do too much at the plate, shooting balls all over the field based on where the pitch is thrown. He's listed at 6-foot and 185-pounds, but he needs to get stronger; he looks on the thin side. He's very Michael Brantley-esque. The glove and hit tool alone may push him into a low end starting gig.

Ceiling: 1.5- to 2.0-win player
Risk: Moderate
MLB ETA: 2024

12. Steven Kwan, CF

	Hit	Power	SB	Patience	Glove	Overall
	60	40	40	55	50	45

Born: 09/05/97	Age: 24	Bats: L	Top Comp: Norichika Aoki
Height: 5-9	Weight: 175	Throws: L	

Season	Team	Age	Level	PA	1B	2B	3B	HR	SB	CS	BB%	K%	AVG	OBP	SLG	ISO
2018	CLE	20	A-	14	3	1	0	0	1	0	14.29%	14.29%	0.333	0.429	0.417	0.083
2018	CLE	20	R	50	11	2	1	0	2	0	18.00%	6.00%	0.350	0.480	0.450	0.100
2019	CLE	21	A+	542	98	26	7	3	11	7	9.78%	9.41%	0.280	0.353	0.382	0.102
2021	CLE	23	AA	221	43	12	3	7	4	2	9.95%	10.41%	0.337	0.411	0.539	0.202
2021	CLE	23	AAA	120	23	3	1	5	2	0	11.67%	6.67%	0.311	0.398	0.505	0.194

Background: A sparsely used backup during his freshman season at Oregon State University, Kwan blossomed into a bonafide prospect during his follow up campaign for the Pac 12 powerhouse: in 55 games for Head Coach Pat Casey, the diminutive center fielder batted a solid .331/.440/.400 with eight extra-base hits and eight stolen bases. After a quick – and successful – jaunt through the Cape Cod League that summer, Kwan returned with a vengeance for his final go-round in college baseball. In a career best 66 games, the California native slugged .356/.463/.457 with plenty of speed and gap power to convince the Guardians to use a fifth round pick on him in 2018. And Kwan continued to do what Kwan's always done: hit. The then-21-year-old outfielder handled an aggressive promotion up to High-A in 2019, his first full season in the minors, and he responded with a solid Kwan-like .280/.353/.382. Last season the sparkplug center fielder upped the ante even further as he split time between Akron and Columbus, slugging .328/.407/.527 with 15 doubles, four triples, 12 homeruns, and six stolen bases. Per *Weighted Runs Created Plus*, his overall production topped the league average mark by a whopping 54%.

Scouting Report: Another really intriguing prospect that's been mostly overlooked – including by yours truly – throughout the majority of his collegiate and professional career. Kwan has always tracked like a fifth outfielder-type, showing an above-average hit tool, solid patience, a little bit of base thievery, and good defense – which is exactly what he showed in 2021. Except he began to hit for power. And it's likely going to prove to be a repeatable skill moving forward. Well, as much as 40-grade power can be, of course. Cleveland's outfield, at least for the time being, is as unsettled as the American political scene nowadays, so Kwan has a shot at capturing a starting gig. There's fringy starting potential here, not much more unless he proves to be a .300 hitter day-in-and-day-out at the big league level.

Ceiling: 1.5-win player
Risk: Low to Moderate
MLB ETA: 2022

13. Cody Morris, RHP

FB	CB	SL	CH	Command	Overall
60	55	50	50/55	50	45

Born: 11/04/96	Age: 25	Bats: R	Top Comp: James McDonald
Height: 6-4	Weight: 205	Throws: R	

Season	Team	Age	Level	IP	TBF	K/9	K%	BB/9	BB%	K-BB%	ERA	FIP	xFIP	Pit/Bat
2019	CLE	22	A	45.0	185	11.20	30.27%	2.00	5.41%	24.86%	3.20	2.11	2.46	4.10
2019	CLE	22	A+	44.0	203	11.25	27.09%	3.48	8.37%	18.72%	5.52	3.95	3.23	4.04
2021	CLE	24	AA	20.0	80	13.05	36.25%	3.15	8.75%	27.50%	1.35	2.62	3.14	4.18
2021	CLE	24	AAA	36.2	144	12.76	36.11%	2.95	8.33%	27.78%	1.72	1.86	3.06	4.15

Background: While the jury is still out on the return from their 2018 draft class, it's safe to say Cleveland added a lot of minor league talent and depth to their farm system in June four years ago. One of the club's better value picks: seventh rounder Cody Morris. A product of the University of South Carolina, Morris put together a dynamic, albeit limited, showing with the Gamecocks in 2017. He tossed just 39.1 innings in his return from Tommy John surgery, averaging 10.8 strikeouts and 1.8 walks per nine innings. He followed that up with a strong showing during his redshirt sophomore season for the SEC conference school, convincing the Guardians to take a mid-round gamble on him. Morris wouldn't make his debut until the following season, 2019, but saw considerable time in High-A. The 6-foot-4, 205-pound hurler missed the first few months of 2021 recovering from a stiff right shoulder, but after a tune-up rehab appearance in the Complex League he moved quickly through Double-A before settling in with Columbus. Morris would throw 61.0 innings of work, recording 93 strikeouts and 20 free passes to go along with a sparkling 1.62 ERA.

Snippet from The 2020 Prospect Digest Handbook: One of the more underrated arms in the entire minor leagues. And he's exactly the type of pitcher the Indians have excelled at developing. Sneaky, sneaky upside. #4-type ceiling.

Scouting Report: One of my favorite arms in the entire minor leagues. Morris is reminiscent of former multi-Cy Young award winning right-hander Corey Kluber: he's tall, lean but muscular, and shows no emotion whatsoever. The former Gamecock works exclusively from the stretch, showing a solid four-pitch mix, including a mid-90s fastball, an above-average curveball, a solid slider, and an improved changeup that flashed above-average at times. Despite throwing just 150.0 minor league innings, Morris is nearing big league-readiness. He's a strike-thrower, but seems prone to bouts of wildness.

Ceiling: 1.5-win player
Risk: Moderate
MLB ETA: 2022

14. Bo Naylor, C

Hit	Power	SB	Patience	Glove	Overall
35/45	45	50/40	50	60	45

Born: 02/21/00	Age: 22	Bats: L	Top Comp: N/A
Height: 5-10	Weight: 195	Throws: R	

Season	Team	Age	Level	PA	1B	2B	3B	HR	SB	CS	BB%	K%	AVG	OBP	SLG	ISO
2018	CLE	18	R	139	24	3	3	2	5	1	15.11%	20.14%	0.274	0.381	0.402	0.128
2019	CLE	19	A	453	58	18	10	11	7	5	9.49%	22.96%	0.243	0.313	0.421	0.178
2021	CLE	21	AA	356	35	13	1	10	10	0	10.39%	31.46%	0.188	0.280	0.332	0.144

Background: The Cleveland franchise has a long, storied history. And during that history there's been a sextuple of brothers to don the club's uniform at the same time: George and Patsy Tebeau (1894-95, Cleveland Spiders), Bill and Harry Hinchman (1907, Cleveland Naps), Dave and Vean Gregg (1913, Cleveland Naps), Joe and Luke Sewell (1921-30, Cleveland Indians), Jim and Gaylord Perry (1974-75, Cleveland Indians), and, more recently, Roberto and Sandy Alomar Jr. (1999-2000, Cleveland Indians). The Naylor brothers, Josh and Bo, could become the seventh set to play for the big league club at the same time. Cleveland selected the younger Naylor in the opening round, 29th overall, four years ago, making him just the fourth backstop drafted by the club in the first round. The lefty-swinging catcher began his career on solid footing as he batted a respectable .274/.381/.402 in 33 games with the club's rookie league affiliate. The Canadian-born prospect stumbled a bit as he spent the entirety of sophomore season in the Midwest League, though he did cobble together a .243/.313/.421 slash line while learning the game's most challenging position against vastly older competition. Last season, though, the front office made the calculated move to send Naylor up to the proving grounds of Double-A, a true test for prospects. And he failed. Miserably. In 87 games with the RubberDucks, Naylor hit a putrid .189/.280/.332 with 13 doubles, one triple, and 10 homeruns. Per *Weighted Runs Created Plus*, his overall production was a disappointing 31% *below* the league average threshold.

Snippet from The 2020 Prospect Digest Handbook: The foundation is in place to develop into a better-than-average backstop: above power with the potential to jump into 55-grade territory, a surprising amount of speed, solid hit tool, and a slightly better-than-average glove at a premium position.

Scouting Report: It's not unheard of for a 21-year-old prospect to step into Double-A, struggle as much as Naylor did in 2021, and eventually carve out of a successful big league career. But it is exceptionally rare. The notable guys to do so include Cedric Hunter, Marwin Gonzalez, and Austin Hedges. The differentiating factor between those three and Naylor: swing-and-miss rates. Naylor posted a 31% K-rate last season, more than 50% higher than any of the three. The most troubling aspect about Naylor's disastrous 2021 campaign: he showed no signs of month-to-month progress. He's still a quality receiver behind the dish: *Baseball Prospectus* has him at +5.6 Framing Runs and Clay Davenport's metrics have him +4 overall on defense. He's still young enough to rebound, but it's likely going to come down to his ability to make consistent contact – which he *was* doing *prior* to 2021.

Ceiling: 1.5-win player
Risk: Moderate
MLB ETA: 2023

15. Angel Martinez, 2B/SS

Hit	Power	SB	Patience	Glove	Overall
40/50	40/45	50	50	50/55	45

Born: 01/27/02	Age: 20	Bats: B	Top Comp: N/A
Height: 6-0	Weight: 165	Throws: R	

Season	Team	Age	Level	PA	1B	2B	3B	HR	SB	CS	BB%	K%	AVG	OBP	SLG	ISO
2019	CLE	17	R	261	50	10	7	1	11	5	11.11%	11.11%	0.306	0.402	0.428	0.122
2021	CLE	19	A	424	58	20	6	7	13	6	10.14%	20.75%	0.241	0.319	0.382	0.141

Background: Let me know if you've heard this one recently: the Guardians have this young shortstop developing in the minor leagues. And if you haven't heard, let's just say that it's a continuing trend for one of the game's more savvy organizations. Signed out of Santo Domingo, Dominican Republic, for $500,000 four years ago, the switch-hitting infielder showed plenty of offensive promise during his debut in the foreign rookie leagues three years ago: he batted .306/.402/.428 with 18 extra-base knocks in 56 games. Last season, the front office aggressively challenged – another theme for the organization, by the way – and sent the then-19-year-old middle infielder up to Low-A East. Martinez responded with a mediocre .241/.319/.382 slash line, belting out 20 doubles, six triples, and seven homeruns. He swiped 13 bags in 19 attempts. Per *Weighted Runs Created Plus*, his overall production was 8% *below* the league average mark.

Scouting Report: Consider the following:

- Since 2006, only a pair of 20-year-old hitters posted an 87 to 97 wRC+ with a 20% to 22% strikeout rate and a 9% to 11% walk rate (min. 350 PA): Abraham Almonte and Angel Martinez.

Unlike a lot of the club's other more recognizable prospects, Martinez actually hit the ground running at the start of 2021. *Then* he faded down the stretch – which isn't overly concerning given his (A) age, (B) level of competition, and (C) never having experienced the rigors of full season action. Martinez slugged .301/.367/.495 over his first 51 games, but cobbled together a lowly a .177/.268/.260 over his final 46 contests. On the other hand, Martinez had the advantage of playing half of his games in a hitter-friendly park (.257/.348/.391 at home vs. .227/.292/.374 away). He could be one of the bigger breakouts in the G-Men's system in 2022.

Ceiling: 1.5-win player
Risk: Moderate
MLB ETA: 2024

16. Tanner Burns, RHP

FB	CB	SL	CH	Command	Overall
50	55	55	50	50/55	45

Born: 12/28/98	Age: 23	Bats: R	Top Comp: N/A
Height: 6-0	Weight: 180	Throws: R	

Season	Team	Age	Level	IP	TBF	K/9	K%	BB/9	BB%	K-BB%	ERA	FIP	xFIP	Pit/Bat
2021	CLE	22	A+	75.2	315	10.82	28.89%	3.45	9.21%	19.68%	3.57	4.35	4.21	4.04

Background: A sturdy, reliable, oft-dominant hurler throughout his three-year tenure at Auburn University. Burns, who was originally taken by the Yankees in the 37th round in 2017, immediately stepped into the Tigers' rotation as a freshman and he never looked back. After averaging 8.0 strikeouts and 3.8 walks per nine innings as a baby-faced 19-year-old, Burns progressed into one of the country's best arms as a sophomore the following season. In 16 appearances in 2019, 15 of which were starts, the 6-foot, 180-pound righty posted a 101-to-23 strikeout-to-walk ratio in only 79.2 innings of work. And he continued to improve during his abbreviated 2020 campaign as well, averaging 12.9 K's and just 2.8 BB's per nine innings across four starts prior to the COVID-imposed shutdown. Cleveland snagged the low ceiling / high floor right-hander in the opening round and signed him to a deal worth $1.6 million. He tossed 75.2 innings with 91 strikeouts and 29 walks. He missed a handful of weeks during the middle of the season courtesy of a sore elbow.

Scouting Report: Consider the following:

- Since 2006, only two 22-year-old pitchers posted a 28% to 30% strikeout percentage with an 8% to 10% walk percentage in High-A with one organization (min. 75 IP): Wilfredo Pereira and Tanner Burns.

Another Cleveland-like pitching prospect that falls into the Aaron Civale-type category. Burns won't blow his low-90s fastball by many hitters, but he moves it around the strike zone and generally commands it well. He'll mix in two above-average breaking balls: a 12-6 deuce and a cutter-like slider that he likes to bust in on the hands of lefties. He'll also show a rare average changeup. The arsenal is solid, yet unremarkable, but everything plays up due to his above-average command.

Ceiling: 1.5-win player
Risk: Moderate
MLB ETA: 2022

17. Doug Nikhazy, LHP

FB	CB	SL	CH	Command	Overall
50	55	55	50	50	45

Born: 08/11/99	Age: 22	Bats: L	Top Comp: N/A
Height: 6-0	Weight: 205	Throws: L	

Background: A well decorated prep athlete coming out of Florida-based West Orange High School, Nikhazy, who lettered all four years, immediately made an impact at Ole' Miss. As a true freshman, the 6-foot, 205-pound lefty posted an impressive 86-to-33 strikeout-to-walk ratio to go along with a 9-3 win-loss record and a 3.31 ERA. Nikhazy continued his dominant work with the Rebels during the abbreviated 2020 season, averaging 12.1 strikeouts and 3.5 walks per nine innings across four starts. Last season, though, Nikhazy raised the bar even higher. In a career best 92.0 innings of work, the young southpaw averaged a whopping 13.9 strikeouts and just 3.0 walks per nine innings. Cleveland drafted him in the second round, 58th overall, and signed him to a deal worth $1.2 million, roughly $14,000 below the recommended slot value. He did not appear in an affiliated game after signing.

Scouting Report: Consider the following:

- Between 2011 and 2020, only three SEC hurlers averaged at least 13 punch outs per nine innings in a season (min. 75 IP): Asa Lacy, Ethan Small, and Zach Thompson.
- Obviously, Nikhazy's production would place him on the list as well.
- Interestingly enough: all three of the listed pitchers, as well as Nikhazy, are all left-handed.

A throwback pitcher that would dominate in the 1980s and early 1990s. Nikhazy is the very definition of a crafty lefty: his fastball sits in the 88- to 92-mph range. He complements the average offering with an assortment of solid secondary weapons: two above-average breaking balls, a mid-70s curveball and a horizontally darting slider, as well as an average changeup. High floor / low ceiling arm.

Ceiling: 1.0- to 1.5-win player
Risk: Moderate
MLB ETA: 2023/2024

18. Richie Palacios, 2B/CF

Hit	Power	SB	Patience	Glove	Overall
55	40	50	55	55	40

Born: 05/16/97	Age: 25	Bats: L	Top Comp: N/A
Height: 5-11	Weight: 180	Throws: R	

Season	Team	Age	Level	PA	1B	2B	3B	HR	SB	CS	BB%	K%	AVG	OBP	SLG	ISO
2018	CLE	21	A	82	19	2	1	2	3	0	2.44%	15.85%	0.300	0.317	0.425	0.125
2018	CLE	21	A-	86	22	5	1	2	2	1	12.79%	13.95%	0.411	0.477	0.589	0.178
2018	CLE	21	R	22	4	1	0	2	2	0	27.27%	9.09%	0.438	0.591	0.875	0.438
2021	CLE	24	AA	283	40	24	3	6	10	3	11.66%	14.84%	0.299	0.389	0.496	0.197
2021	CLE	24	AAA	145	22	9	1	1	10	0	17.24%	19.31%	0.292	0.434	0.416	0.124

Background: Palacios's selection in 2018 marks the first time the Cleveland organization drafted a player out of Towson University – which seems shocking until it's considered that the school produced just 22 draft picks in its history. The 103rd overall player chosen four years ago, making him the third highest pick in school history, Palacios got off to an impressive start to his professional career as he slugged .361/.421/.539 between rookie ball, Mahoning Valley, and Lake County. Unfortunately for the former Towson Tiger star, he would miss the entire 2019 season with an injury and then wouldn't pop up in a game until 2021. But the 5-foot-11, 180-pound second baseman / center fielder made up for lost time with his impressive 2021 season. Splitting time between Akron and Columbus, Palacios slugged an aggregate

.297/.404/.471 with 33 doubles, four triples, seven homeruns, and 20 stolen bases. His overall production, according to *Weighted Runs Created Plus*, topped the league average mark by 41%. The Brooklyn, New York, native spent the fall with the Scottsdale Scorpions, where he continued to hit: .269/.387/.513 with 12 extra-base hits in 20 games.

Scouting Report: Palacios' career may not extend back very long or barely span more than 140 games, but he's consistently hit – and hit well – at each of his abbreviated stops. He's a patient hitter, willing to work the count until he finds a pitch that allows him to spray line drives all over the diamond with his above-average hit tool. But the problem with Palacio is his lack of thunder in the stick. If Cleveland were a rebuilding team, like the Pirates or Orioles, Palacios would be all but guaranteed to open 2022 up with a starting gig. And while Cleveland doesn't have their second base – or center field – gig written in concrete, there are simply better options available. One more final (contradictive) thought: he does have the feel as a potential late-blooming player like Jeff McNeil, though.

Ceiling: 1.0-win player
Risk: Low to Moderate
MLB ETA: 2022

19. Tobias Myers, RHP

FB	CB	SL	CH	Command	Overall
50	55	50	55	55	40

Born: 08/05/98	Age: 23	Bats: R	Top Comp: N/A
Height: 6-0	Weight: 193	Throws: R	

Background: Myers has been passed around like a piece of stale holiday fruitcake. A sixth round pick coming out of Winter Haven High School in 2016, Baltimore would deal the young right-hander to Tampa Bay roughly a year later for a surging Tim Beckham. Myers would chug along in their farm system for parts of four seasons before being shipped off to Cleveland for foreign rookie league slugger Junior Caminero in November 2021. Last season, Myers split time between Tampa Bay's Double-A and Triple-A affiliates, the Montgomery Biscuits and Durham Bulls, throwing 117.2 innings with a spectacular 146-to-28 strikeout-to-walk ratio.

Scouting Report: Consider the following:

- Since 2006, only two 22-year-old pitchers posted a 26% to 28% strikeout percentage with a 7% to 9% walk percentage in Triple-A with one organization (min. 50 IP): Sean Reid-Foley, the hyphenated assassin, and Tobias Myers, the funky stale holiday dish.

Myers attacks hitters with a standard four-pitch mix: a low-90s fastball that touched 94 during a late-July start; a 12-6 curveball with solid depth; a cutter / slider that's more of a wrinkle rather than a bite; and a low-80s heavy tumbling above-average changeup that he doesn't throw nearly frequently enough. He is a consistent strike-thrower with innings eater potential. He's projecting like a backend arm with a high probability he ends up as a multi-inning reliever. He doesn't get the "Cleveland Bump" in development since the Rays churn out arms as well.

Ceiling: 1.0-win player
Risk: Moderate
MLB ETA: 2022

20. Xzavion Curry, RHP

FB	CB	SL	CH	Command	Overall
50	50/55	N/A	50/55	60	40

Born: 07/27/98	Age: 23	Bats: R	Top Comp: Eli Morgan
Height: 5-11	Weight: 190	Throws: R	

Season	Team	Age	Level	IP	TBF	K/9	K%	BB/9	BB%	K-BB%	ERA	FIP	xFIP	Pit/Bat
2021	CLE	22	A	25.1	94	13.50	40.43%	1.42	4.26%	36.17%	1.07	2.08	2.90	3.93
2021	CLE	22	A+	67.2	270	10.64	29.63%	1.60	4.44%	25.19%	2.66	3.99	3.91	3.82

Background: The franchise went nearly a decade between selections from Georgia Tech. Prior to choosing Curry in the seventh round three years ago, the previous time the club grabbed a Yellow Jacket was Chase Burnette back in 2010. The 220th overall pick that year, Curry wouldn't make his professional debut until last year, thanks in part to shoulder woes and the COVID-imposed shutdown the following season. But the undersized right-hander quickly made up any lost developmental time as he pitched at three separate levels. Opening the year in dominant fashion in Low-A, Curry continued to confound High-A hitters for 13 starts before finishing the year with a start in Akron. In total, the South Carolina native tossed 97.2 innings – which exceed his career high in college – while racking up plenty of strikeouts (123) and very few walks (16). He averaged 11.3 K/9 and just 1.5 BB/9 to go along with a sparkling 2.30 ERA.

Scouting Report: Consider the following:

- Since 2006, only four 22-year-old hurlers posted a strikeout percentage between 28.5% to 30.5% with a sub-5.0% walk percentage in High-A with one organization (min. 60 IP): Logan Gilbert, Kevin Slowey, Ljay Newsome, and, of course, Xzavion Curry.

A very intriguing, Cleveland-like pitching prospect. Curry hits a lot of the organizational check boxes: he consistently throws pitcher's pitches, hurls a heavy, riding fastball that he elevates with regularity, and can spin an above-average breaking ball. Curry's fastball sits in the 92 mph range, but in spite of the average-ish velocity, hitters were consistently late. His curveball is slow, perhaps a tick or three too slow, but shows good shape and spin – even though it'll range from the low- to mid-70s. He'll also mix in a deceptive changeup that flashes above-average. In all reality, there's not a whole lot of separation between Curry and, say, Eli Morgan. But you can never discount the organization's ability to maximize a pitcher's potential. One more thing: he reportedly throws a slider, though I never saw one.

Ceiling: 1.0-win player
Risk: Moderate
MLB ETA: 2022/2023

Colorado Rockies

Top Prospects

1. Zac Veen, RF

	Hit	Power	SB	Patience	Glove	Overall
	50/55	50/60	60	60	55	60

Born: 12/12/01	Age: 20	Bats: L	Top Comp: Bobby Abreu
Height: 6-4	Weight: 190	Throws: R	

Season	Team	Age	Level	PA	1B	2B	3B	HR	SB	CS	BB%	K%	AVG	OBP	SLG	ISO
2021	COL	19	A	479	74	27	4	15	36	17	13.36%	26.30%	0.301	0.399	0.501	0.201

Background: In a draft class loaded with awesome high school-aged hitters it's Zac Veen, 6-foot-4, 190-pound corner outfielder, that owns the highest ceiling. A product of Spruce Creek High School, Veen was the second high school teenager player that year, ninth player overall, and signed to a massive $5 million by the Rockies. Like every other minor league player chosen two years ago, the COVID-interrupted 2020 season forced his professional debut to be delayed until last season. And it was 100% worth the wait. Appearing in 106 games with the Fresno Grizzlies in Low-A West, the Florida-born outfielder slugged hearty .301/.399/.501 with 27 doubles, four triples, 15 homeruns, and 36 stolen bases (in 51 total attempts). Among all qualified Low-A hitters Veen's batting average ranked 10th, on-base percentage was third, slugging percentage was fifth, his 27 doubles ranked sixth, his four triples tied for the 10th highest total, his 15 homeruns tied for fifth, and his 36 stolen bases was good enough for second. Per *Weighted Runs Created Plus*, his overall production topped the league average mark by 35%, fourth best in the league.

Scouting Report: Consider the following:

- Since 2006, only two 19-year-old hitters met the following criteria in a Low-A season with one organization (min. 300 PA): 130 to 140 wRC+, a double-digit walk rate, and a strikeout rate north of 25%. Those two hitters: Kevin Padlo and, of course, Zac Veen.

A supremely gifted ballplayer whose numbers get even better if his slow start to the year is ignored; he batted .317/.406/.526 from May 21st through the end of the year. Veen did spend half of his time playing in a slightly favorable home ballpark, but still slugged an impressive .290/.402/.441 on the road. Plus speed and the power potential to match it in the coming years. Incredibly patient at the plate, though his K-rate (26.3%) is a little on the high side – though not overly concerning. The lefty-swinging Veen also showed no discernible platoon splits, either. In terms of big league production, think something along the lines of .320/.440/.560.

Ceiling: 5.0-win player
Risk: Moderate
MLB ETA: 2023/2024

2. Benny Montgomery, CF

	Hit	Power	SB	Patience	Glove	Overall
	45	40/50	70	50	60	60

Born: 09/09/02	Age: 19	Bats: R	Top Comp: N/A
Height: 6-4	Weight: 200	Throws: R	

Season	Team	Age	Level	PA	1B	2B	3B	HR	SB	CS	BB%	K%	AVG	OBP	SLG	ISO
2021	COL	18	CPX	52	15	0	1	0	5	1	9.62%	17.31%	0.340	0.404	0.383	0.043

Background: A native of Lewisberry, Pennsylvania, Montgomery was regarded as one of the top prep bats in the 2021 draft class. Standing 6-foot-4 and 200-pounds, Montgomery burst onto the scene as a sophomore in 2019 as he slugged .359/.418/.487 with four doubles, a pair of homeruns, and an 8-to-9 strikeout-to-walk ratio. And after a COVID-shortened junior campaign, Montgomery continued to make noise on the national circuit as he captured the Perfect Game Homerun Derby Crown. Last season, the speedy – albeit raw – prospect hit .426 with seven homeruns, 22 RBIs, and 44 runs scored. He also walked in 18 of his 117 plate appearances. Colorado selected the University of Virginia commit with the 8th overall pick last July, signing him to a hefty $5,000,000 deal. And the immediate return on their investment was promising. In 14 games with the club's Arizona Complex League affiliate, Montgomery batted .340/.404/.383.

Scouting Report: Per the usual, here's my pre-draft write-up:

> "Speed to burn. Montgomery's been clocked at a 6.45-second 60-yard dash. And he has an arm to match: he's been clocked as high as 96 mph as well. The question with Montgomery isn't athleticism or tools, it's whether he's going to hit enough in the professional ranks. Above-average or better bat speed. But...Montgomery's developed a timing hitch with his hands that might make him vulnerable to mid-level minor league breaking balls. He's long and gangly, like Hunter Pence. There's some Bradley Zimmer-type potential.

Ceiling: 3.5-win player
Risk: Moderate
MLB ETA: 2023

3. Drew Romo, C

	Hit	Power	SB	Patience	Glove	Overall
	50/55	40/45	60/45	45	55/60	55

Born: 08/29/01	Age: 20	Bats: B	Top Comp: Paul Lo Duca
Height: 6-1	Weight: 205	Throws: R	

Season	Team	Age	Level	PA	1B	2B	3B	HR	SB	CS	BB%	K%	AVG	OBP	SLG	ISO
2021	COL	19	A	339	73	17	2	6	23	6	5.60%	14.75%	0.314	0.345	0.439	0.125

Background: The fourth — and final — backstop taken in the opening round two years ago. The Rockies, with the second first round selection, grabbed the switch-hitting catcher with the 35th overall pick and signed him to a deal worth just a shade over $2 million. The 6-foot-1, 205-pound prospect teamed with fellow 2020 first rounder Zac Veen and Ezequiel Tovar to form a triumvirate of teenager thump in the heart of the Fresno Grizzlies lineup last season. In 79 contests with Colorado's Low-A affiliate, Romo batted an impressive .314/.345/.439 with 17 doubles, a pair of triples, six homeruns, and 23 stolen bases (in 29 total attempts). His overall production, according to *Weighted Runs Created Plus*, topped the league average mark by 4%.

Scouting Report: Consider the following:

- Since 2006, only seven 19-year-old hitters met the following criteria in a Low-A season with one organization (min. 300 PA): 100 to 110 wRC+, a sub-7.0% walk rate, and a sub-16% strikeout rate. Those seven hitters: Alex Verdugo, Odubel Herrera, Jose Peraza, Tyrone Taylor, Gorkys Hernandez, Lorenzo Cedrola, and — of course — Drew Romo.

Romo has the quiet potential to develop into one of the better catching prospects in baseball. A sweet-swinging switch-hitter with strong contact skills and a line drive approach to shoot balls from foul line to foul line. His defense falls into the above-average, maybe even plus category. He also threw out 35% of would-be base stealers in a run-heavy environment. Add it up and it's a recipe for All-Star success. And like his counterpart Zac Veen, Romo showed some impressive offensive chops away from hitter-friendly Fresno as well, batting .325/.346/.391.

Ceiling: 3.0- to 3.5-win player
Risk: Moderate
MLB ETA: 2024

4. Ezequiel Tovar, SS

	Hit	Power	SB	Patience	Glove	Overall
	50	45	55	40	70	55

Born: 08/01/01	Age: 20	Bats: B	Top Comp: Placido Polanco
Height: 6-0	Weight: 162	Throws: R	

Season	Team	Age	Level	PA	1B	2B	3B	HR	SB	CS	BB%	K%	AVG	OBP	SLG	ISO
2018	COL	16	R	158	26	4	4	0	16	9	13.92%	20.89%	0.262	0.369	0.354	0.092
2019	COL	17	R	86	15	2	2	0	4	1	11.63%	19.77%	0.264	0.357	0.347	0.083
2019	COL	17	A-	243	46	4	2	2	13	0	6.58%	21.40%	0.249	0.304	0.313	0.065
2021	COL	19	A	326	57	21	3	11	21	4	4.29%	11.66%	0.309	0.346	0.510	0.201
2021	COL	19	A+	143	19	9	0	4	3	2	2.10%	13.29%	0.239	0.266	0.396	0.157

Background: The third and final piece of the Fresno Grizzlies' vaunted trio of baby-faced 19-year-old bashers. Tover teamed with 2020 first round picks Zac Veen and Drew Romo to offer plenty of hope and promise to one of baseball's more disorganized franchises / ownership groups. Signed out of Maracay, Venezuela, the 6-foot, 162-pound switch-hitting infielder put together a pair of lackluster showings during his first two seasons in professional baseball. But that all changed as soon as he dug in against full season pitching for the first time in 2021. Appearing in 72 games with the Grizzlies, Tovar slugged .309/.346/.510 with plenty of speed and thump to dream upon. And unlike Veen and Romo, Colorado's front office opted to challenge the teenager with a promotion up to High-A in early August. After a rough adjustment period, the young shortstop got his feet under him for the last several weeks of the year. In total, Tovar hit an aggregate .287/.322/.475 with 30 doubles, three triples, 15 homeruns, and 24 stolen bases. His overall production was 5% better than the league average.

Snippet from The 2020 Prospect Digest Handbook: One of my favorite prospects in the entire minor leagues. Tovar's an absolute wizard at shortstop. So much so, in fact, if he could post production lines within 10% of the league average mark he'd be a 2.5- to 3.0-win player. Very young, very, very raw.

Scouting Report: Still one of my favorite prospects in all of baseball. And this year he was raw — just less raw. He's in the conversation as one of the best defensive shortstops in the minor leagues. It's likely an argument between Tovar and Oakland's Nick Allen. Either way, Colorado's defensive wizard is an elite defender. Per Clay Davenport's defensive metrics, he saved 12 runs more than the average in only 64 games with Fresno. That's otherworldly. And last year his offense decided to lurch forward as well. His production is going to be capped by subpar walk rates, but he doesn't swing-and-miss much, shows some thump, and runs well. Consider the following:

- Since 2006, only four 19-year-old hitters in Low-A met the following criteria with one organization (min. 300 PA): 115 to 125 wRC+, a sub-6.0% walk rate, and a strikeout rate below 13%. Those four hitters: Austin Romine, Luis Matos, Erwin Almonte, and Ezequiel Tovar.

In terms of offensive ceiling, think: .265/.320/.420.

Ceiling: 3.0-win player
Risk: Moderate
MLB ETA: 2024

5. Ryan Rolison, LHP

	FB	CB	SL	CH	Command	Overall
	55	60	50	50	60	50

Born: 07/11/97	Age: 24	Bats: R	Top Comp: JA Happ
Height: 6-2	Weight: 213	Throws: L	

Season	Team	Age	Level	IP	TBF	K/9	K%	BB/9	BB%	K-BB%	ERA	FIP	xFIP	Pit/Bat
2018	COL	20	R	29.0	109	10.55	31.19%	2.48	7.34%	23.85%	1.86	3.71	3.35	3.58
2019	COL	21	A	14.2	53	8.59	26.42%	1.23	3.77%	22.64%	0.61	1.99	3.13	3.64
2019	COL	21	A+	116.1	509	9.13	23.18%	2.94	7.47%	15.72%	4.87	5.12	4.05	3.65
2021	COL	23	AA	14.2	57	12.27	35.09%	1.23	3.51%	31.58%	3.07	2.29	2.90	3.84
2021	COL	23	AAA	45.2	202	8.87	22.28%	3.15	7.92%	14.36%	5.91	5.20	5.37	3.75

Background: Health issues interrupted Rolison's third professional campaign in the Rockies' farm system – though it wasn't a baseball injury. The 2018 first rounder missed more than two months in middle of the year recovering from appendicitis surgery – an issue that, more than likely, cost him a shot at making his big league debut. The 22nd overall pick out of Ole' Miss, Rolison made a total of 16 starts between Triple-A and the various rehab stints last year. He tossed 71.2 innings of work, posting a 5.27 ERA while averaging 9.7 strikeouts and just 2.8 walks per nine innings. The 6-foot-2, 213-pound southpaw popped up with the Tigres del Licey in the Dominican Winter League following the year as well, throwing an additional 20.0 innings with 24 strikeouts and five walks to go along with a 3.15 ERA.

Snippet from The 2020 Prospect Digest Handbook: Rolison is looking like a strong candidate to develop into a #3-type starting pitcher.

Scouting Report: Not only a consistent strike-thrower, but a consistent quality strike-thrower. Rolison has a quality four-pitch mix showcased by an above-average low-90s fastball and a plus-curveball. He'll also mix in a slider and a changeup – both of them earning 50 grades. Unfortunately, though, Rolison and Colorado are – and have always been – a poor match. I still think he ends up a quality mid-rotation arm – though it's likely not going to be with the Rockies.

Ceiling: 2.5-win player
Risk: Low to Moderate
MLB ETA: 2022

6. Jaden Hill, RHP

	FB	SL	CH	Command	Overall
	60	55	70	45	50

Born: 12/22/99	Age: 22	Bats: R	Top Comp: N/A
Height: 6-4	Weight: 234	Throws: R	

Background: Fun Fact: Ashdown High School in Ashdown, Arkansas, has produced four professional baseball players: Cedrick Harris, Kentrell Hill, Dugan Ward, and Harry Young. Fun Fact Part II: Harris (cousin) and Hill (brother) are related to the hard-throwing right-hander. Fun Fact Part III: Kentrell Hill was the starting center fielder on LSU's College World Championship team in 2000 – which also featured Ryan Theriot, Brian Tallet, Brad Hawpe, Mike Fontenot, and Shane Youman. The younger Hill, who stands a rock-solid 6-foot-4 and 234 pounds, was a two-way monster during his prep career: he .540 with 11 homeruns and sported a 0.51 ERA with a 7-1 record on the mound. The Cardinals took a late, late round flier on him in the 2018 draft. Hill's collegiate career got off to an impressive start as he fanned 11 and walked just three in 10.0 innings of work, but it was cut short due to two separate injuries: #1 he had surgery to repair of a collarbone issue he sustained playing football in high school and #2 the UCL ligament in his right elbow was barking. His sophomore season – like the rest of the country – was shutdown due to COVID, limiting him to just 11.2 innings of work. And, unfortunately, for the mercurial, snake-bitten right-hander his junior campaign was halted after just seven starts due to Tommy John surgery. He finished his 2021 season with a 25-to-12 strikeout-to-walk ratio and an unsightly 6.67 ERA in 29.2 innings of action. The Rockies took a calculated gamble on the Hill and selected him in the second round, 44th overall, and signed him to a deal worth $1,689,000.

Scouting Report: Per the usual, here's my pre-draft write-up:

"Well, it's not too often that you'll see a projected first round pick coming off a career with a major elbow injury (Tommy John surgery), another season lost to a wonky elbow and a preexisting health issue, and limited to just 51.1 career innings. But here we are. At his best – which was not often in 2021 – Hill will flash a dominant plus fastball, an above-average tightly spun slider, and the best changeup in the entire draft class. The control's been mediocre throughout his three abbreviated collegiate years with the command slightly worse. It's easy to see Hill and dream upon a bonafide frontline ace. But there's a lot of Dillon Tate to his projection. Tate, of course, was the fourth overall pick in the 2015 draft who (A) was traded a year later to the Yankees and then later dealt to Baltimore and (B) is a mediocre reliever. Best case scenario if his body doesn't cooperate – or if the control/command doesn't uptick – is Milwaukee's Devin Williams, owner of a plus fastball and vaunted changeup (which is really a screwball)."

Ceiling: 2.0-win player
Risk: Moderate to High
MLB ETA: 2024/2025

7. Ryan Vilade, OF

	Hit	Power	SB	Patience	Glove	Overall
	50	40/45	50	50	45	50

Born: 02/18/99	Age: 23	Bats: R	Top Comp: Neil Walker
Height: 6-2	Weight: 226	Throws: R	

Season	Team	Age	Level	PA	1B	2B	3B	HR	SB	CS	BB%	K%	AVG	OBP	SLG	ISO
2018	COL	19	A	533	96	20	4	5	17	13	9.19%	18.01%	0.274	0.353	0.368	0.094
2019	COL	20	A+	587	105	27	10	12	24	7	9.54%	16.18%	0.303	0.367	0.466	0.163
2021	COL	22	AAA	518	93	28	5	7	12	5	7.34%	17.76%	0.284	0.339	0.410	0.126

Background: The defensive evolution of Ryan Vilade has been an oddity over the past couple of years. Drafted as a shortstop out of Stillwater High School in 2017, Vilade spent the first two seasons of his career at the position. He split time, however, between shortstop and third base during the 2019 year. And last season he moved to more traditional run producing positions: first base, left field, right field, and a smattering of center field too. Vilade appeared in 117 games with the Albuquerque Isotopes in AAA, hitting .284/.339/.410 with 28 doubles, five triples, and seven homeruns. He swiped 12 bags in 17 attempts too. Vilade appeared in 23 games with the Salt River Rafters in the Arizona Fall League following the season as well, hitting .253/.344/.304. Colorado also – briefly – called him up during the regular season too.

Snippet from The 2020 Prospect Digest Handbook: Strong bat-to-ball skills with developing power to belt out 12- to 15-homeruns and a solid willingness to walk. The biggest improvement in Vilade's game last season was his work with the leather: he was abysmal at shortstop two years ago, but graded out as slightly below-average last season.

Scouting Report: Consider the following:

- Since 2006, only three 22-year-old hitters met the following criteria in a Triple-A season with one organization (min. 400 PA): 82to 92 wRC+, a walk rate between 5% and 8%, and a strikeout rate below 20%. Those three hitters: Neil Walker, Billy Hamilton, and Ryan Vilade.

Vilade The Shortstop would have had a decent offensive season in 2021. Vilade The Run Producer, not so much. The majority of his time was spent at first base or either corner outfield spot. He lacks the power or patience at the plate that are typically requisite of those positions. Vilade still puts the ball on the ground too frequently (45.1% in AAA), so swing/approach adjustments will need to be done. Right now Vilade is profiling as a .270/.340/.430-type hitter.

Ceiling: 1.5- to 2.0-win player
Risk: Low to Moderate
MLB ETA: Debuted in 2021

8. Elehuris Montero, 1B/3B

Hit	Power	SB	Patience	Glove	Overall
45	55	30	55	45	50

Born: 08/17/98	Age: 23	Bats: R	Top Comp: Brandon Moss
Height: 6-3	Weight: 235	Throws: R	

Season	Team	Age	Level	PA	1B	2B	3B	HR	SB	CS	BB%	K%	AVG	OBP	SLG	ISO
2018	STL	19	A	425	77	28	3	15	2	0	7.76%	19.06%	0.322	0.381	0.529	0.207
2018	STL	19	A+	106	18	9	0	1	1	0	4.72%	20.75%	0.286	0.330	0.408	0.122
2019	STL	20	R	15	4	0	0	0	0	0	6.67%	13.33%	0.308	0.400	0.308	0.000
2019	STL	20	AA	238	27	8	0	7	0	1	5.88%	31.09%	0.188	0.235	0.317	0.129
2021	COL	22	AA	379	56	11	1	22	0	0	11.35%	23.75%	0.279	0.361	0.523	0.245
2021	COL	22	AAA	121	14	9	1	6	0	0	8.26%	16.53%	0.278	0.355	0.546	0.269

Background: Caught up in one of the more widely criticized trades in recent memory – which is really saying something. Colorado dealt away franchise icon and future Hall of Fame third baseman Nolan Arenado to St. Louis for, what most deemed, pieces and parts: Austin Gomber, a quality big league arm; Jake Sommers, who spent last season as (A) a 24-year-old in (B) a relief role for (C) a High-A ballclub; Tony Locey, a 2019 third round pick with massive control issues; Mateo Gil, a light-hitting shortstop; and – of course – Elehuris Montero. Like Gomber, Montero tried to make the case that the deal wasn't total robbery. In 120 games between Hartford and Albuquerque, the 6-foot-3, 235-pound hulking corner infielder slugged .278/.329/.889 with 20 doubles, two triples, and a career best 28 homeruns. His overall production, per *Weighted Runs Created Plus*, topped the league average mark by 32%.

Snippet from The 2020 Prospect Digest Handbook: I told you I was president of the Montero fan club. His status has taken a (significant) hit, but I'm still betting on a rebound in 2020 – particularly the second half.

Scouting Report: Consider the following:

- Since 2006, only three 22-year-old hitters met the following criteria in a Double-A season with one organization (min. 350 PA): 132 to 142 wRC+, a double-digit walk rate, and a strikeout rate between 23% and 25%. Those three hitters: Scott Moore, Trayvon Robinson, and Elehuris Montero.

I'm still a big believer in Montero. He's not going to be a superstar. But there's potential to be a low end starting corner infielder – nearly guaranteed to be first base. A lot of his overall production, though, was buoyed by a scorching month of July (.429/.477/.879) and a strong September (.274/.349/.505). Otherwise, he batted .218/.354/.410 in May, .229/.288/.438 in June, and .233/.324/.350 in August. He's still quite young and still needs some additional seasoning. In term of big league hitting, think .260/.340/.500.

Ceiling: 1.5- to 2.0-win player
Risk: Moderate
MLB ETA: 2023

9. Jack Blomgren, 2B/SS

Hit	Power	SB	Patience	Glove	Overall
50/55	35/40	55	60	55	50

Born: 09/27/98	Age: 23	Bats: R	Top Comp: Poor Man's Eddie Stanky
Height: 5-10	Weight: 180	Throws: R	

Season	Team	Age	Level	PA	1B	2B	3B	HR	SB	CS	BB%	K%	AVG	OBP	SLG	ISO
2021	COL	22	A+	345	59	13	4	3	30	7	13.04%	21.45%	0.284	0.406	0.392	0.108

Background: As a proud alum of The Ohio State University it pains me to refer to The School Up North as anything else, but the University of Michigan has produced a ton of talent over the past decade. In fact, 13 players from TTUN have garnered a six-figure bonus since 2017. One of those players, Jack Blomgren, signed for a nice $394,300 bonus as a fifth round pick two years ago. Blomgren made his professional debut last season with the Spokane Indians. In 86 games with the High-A ballclub, the 5-foot-10, 180-pound middle infielder batted a respectable .284/.406/.392 with 13 doubles, four triples, three homeruns, and 30 stolen bases. Per *Weighted Runs Created Plus*, his overall production topped the league average mark by an impressive 24%.

Scouting Report: Consider the following:

- Since 2006, there have been nine 22-year-old hitters that have met the follow criteria in a season in High-A with one organization (min. 300 PA): 120 to 130 wRC+, a walk rate of at least 12%, and a strikeout rate between 20.5% and 22.5%. Those nine hitters: Alfonso Rivas, Mike Costanzo, Vince Belnome, Marvin Lowrance, Karexon Sanchez, Tim Federoff, Luis Alejandro Basabe, Mark Karaviotis, and – of course – Mr. Jack Blomgren.

A fantastic little prospect that could carve out a lengthy big league career. Blomgren's abysmal month of June (.085/.236/.102) dampened his overall numbers. But he was specifically lethal from July through September, slugging .333/.438/.458. He did benefit from Spokane's bandbox home field (.293/.392/.414 vs. .267/.402/.373). He has a nose for first base, above-average speed, above-average glove. He's only lacking a lot of thump. Don't sleep on him. He's like a poor man's Eddie Stanky.

Ceiling: 1.5- to 2.0-win player
Risk: Moderate
MLB ETA: 2023

10. Helcris Olivarez, LHP

	FB	CB	CH	Command	Overall
	70	55	50	40/45	45

Born: 08/08/00	Age: 21	Bats: L	Top Comp: Sean Newcomb
Height: 6-2	Weight: 192	Throws: L	

Season	Team	Age	Level	IP	TBF	K/9	K%	BB/9	BB%	K-BB%	ERA	FIP	xFIP	Pit/Bat
2018	COL	17	R	35.2	147	9.08	24.49%	5.55	14.97%	9.52%	2.78	3.78	3.85	2.04
2018	COL	17	R	19.0	73	11.37	32.88%	1.89	5.48%	27.40%	1.42	1.76	2.20	1.90
2019	COL	18	R	14.0	55	13.50	38.18%	4.50	12.73%	25.45%	0.64	2.35	2.85	2.22
2019	COL	18	R	46.2	212	11.76	28.77%	4.63	11.32%	17.45%	4.82	5.81	4.54	4.03
2021	COL	20	A+	99.2	453	10.11	24.72%	6.14	15.01%	9.71%	6.05	5.71	5.50	4.03

Background: Now entering his sixth year in the Rockies' organization. Colorado signed the gangly left-hander to a sub-six-figure deal on August 12, 2016. Olivarez spent parts of three seasons in the Dominican Summer League before moving stateside into the Pioneer League in 2019. Last season, though, Olivarez made up for lost time – sort of – as he spent the year squaring off against the vastly older competition in the High-A West League. Making a career-high 22 appearances, only one of which came as a reliever, the 6-foot-2, 192-pound southpaw tossed 99.2 innings, recording an impressive 112 strikeouts against a whopper of a walk total (6.1 BB/9). He finished the year with an unsightly 6.05 ERA, a 5.71 FIP, and a 5.50 xFIP.

Snippet from The 2020 Prospect Digest Handbook: Big, big time fastball potential. Olivarez's heater would sit 92- to 94-mph and easily touch 97 mph at will. And it's not just the velocity that's impressive, it's the ease that he generates velocity. His curveball is loopy but shows the requisite shape. It grades out as a strong 45 now, but it could easily wind up as plus as he matures. The changeup, which was widely regarded a well below-average prior to the year, was far better than expected. It shows some arm-side run and fade with the potential to be average, maybe better if everything breaks the right way. Olivarez is raw, but there's sneaky potential brewing in his powerful arm. Had he lived stateside and eligible for the June draft, I would have put a second/third round grade on him.

Scouting Report: Consider the following:

- Since 2006, only two 20-year-old hurlers met the following criteria in High-A with one organization (min. 75 IP): 24.0 to 26.0% strikeouts percentage with a walk percentage of at least 14%. Those two arms: Victor Payano and – of course – Helcris Olivarez.

Now for the updated scouting report: The fastball is still a big, *big* time weapon for the young hurler, sitting in the mid- to upper-90s with relative ease. During a late June start he topped 98 mph multiple times. His curveball has improved from a below-average to an above-average power-breaking ball. And Olivarez showed some incredible maturity and confidence in his improving changeup, now an average offering. The change-of-pace got some awkward / weird reactions from hitters. The question is whether he can throw enough strikes moving forward. If he can keep his walk rate around four per nine innings, he's going to be nice backend arm. Reliever floor either way.

Ceiling: 1.5-win player
Risk: Moderate
MLB ETA: 2024

11. Adael Amador, SS

	Hit	Power	SB	Patience	Glove	Overall
	40/50	35/45	55	55	45/55	45

Born: 09/11/03	Age: 19	Bats: B	Top Comp: N/A
Height: 6-0	Weight: 160	Throws: R	

Season	Team	Age	Level	PA	1B	2B	3B	HR	SB	CS	BB%	K%	AVG	OBP	SLG	ISO
2021	COL	18	CPX	200	34	10	1	4	10	7	13.50%	14.50%	0.299	0.394	0.445	0.146

Background: Heading into the 2019 international free agent signing period, MLB.com ranked the then-16-year-old shortstop as the twelfth best prospect in the class. A wiry, 6-foot, 160-pound switch-hitting shortstop out of Santiago, Dominican Republic, Amador's professional debut was delayed until last season – courtesy of COVID-19. The front office started his career off by pushing him to the Arizona Complete League in 2021. In 47 games, Amador slugged a hearty .299/.394/.445 with 10 doubles, one triple, and four homeruns. He also swiped 10 bags. Per *Weighted Runs Created Plus*, his overall production topped the league average threshold by 22%.

Scouting Report: A different stance from each side of the plate. My assumption is that he's relatively new to switch-hitting. His swing looks more natural from the right-side, more loft. He's more open as a left-handed hitter – it's a short, compact, slashing type of swing a la Johnny Damon. Above-average speed, but not blazing. Reports indicated that he was an above-average defender, though he struggled mightily during his debut. Consider the following:

- Since 2006, there six 18-year-old hitters to the following criteria in a season in the complex or stateside rookie leagues with one organization (min. 175 PA: 117 to 127 wRC+, a 12.5% to 14.5% walk rate, a 13.5% to 15.5% strikeout rate, and an Isolated Power between .130 to .160. Those six hitters: Jeter Downs, Alexy Palma, Douglas Duran, Christopher Morel, Hendry Jimenez, and Adael Amador.

Ceiling: 1.5-win player
Risk: Moderate
MLB ETA: 2025

12. Michael Toglia, 1B/OF		Hit	Power	SB	Patience	Glove	Overall
		40+/45	55	40	60	50	45

Born: 08/16/98	Age: 23	Bats: B	Top Comp: Lucas Duda
Height: 6-5	Weight: 226	Throws: L	

Season	Team	Age	Level	PA	1B	2B	3B	HR	SB	CS	BB%	K%	AVG	OBP	SLG	ISO
2019	COL	20	A-	176	20	7	0	9	1	1	15.91%	25.57%	0.248	0.369	0.483	0.234
2021	COL	22	A+	330	37	10	2	17	7	3	12.73%	27.58%	0.234	0.333	0.465	0.230
2021	COL	22	AA	169	15	10	1	5	3	0	13.61%	30.18%	0.217	0.331	0.406	0.189

Background: One of the more polished collegiate bats in the 2019 draft class. The UCLA product was coming off of back-to-back stellar campaigns for the Bruins in which he hit .336/.449/.588 as a sophomore and followed that up with a .314/.392/.624 slash line as a junior. Colorado selected the 6-foot-5, 226-pound switch-hitter in the opening round, 23rd overall, and signed him to a deal worth $2,725,000. Toglia began his career on solid footing, hitting .248/.369/.483 in 41 games in the Northwest League, but struggled – mightily – as he split time between High-A and Double-A last season. In a combined 115 games, the first baseman / corner outfielder hit a lowly .228/.333/.445 with 20 doubles, three triples, and 22 homeruns. His overall production, per *Weighted Runs Created Plus*, was 8% above the league average threshold.

Snippet from The 2020 Prospect Digest Handbook: His offensive struggles in the Cape Cod in back-to-back seasons is a major red flag.

Scouting Report: The lion's share of Toglia's value is wrapped up in two separate, but related skills: above-average power and tremendous patience at the plate. The hit tool, as I suggested two years ago, but a major red flag and it's been underwhelming as pro – especially once he moved into more advanced leagues. Per *FanGraphs*, his batted ball data was pretty impressive: 90 mph average exit velocity and 107 mph peak. One more final note: Toglia looked pretty comfortable during his final 38 games with High-A, hitting a solid .273/.358/.481. There's some low end starting potential here, but he needs to come out swinging in 2022. In terms of big league line, think: .240/.350/.480.

Ceiling: 1.5-win player
Risk: Moderate
MLB ETA: 2023

13. Joe Rock, LHP		FB	SL	CH	Command	Overall
		N/A	N/A	N/A	N/A	N/A

Born: 07/29/00	Age: 21	Bats: L	Top Comp: N/A
Height: 6-6	Weight: 200	Throws: L	

Background: One of the more intriguing starters in the 2021 draft class for a variety of reasons: #1. He's big and left-handed; #2. He was incredibly dominant for Ohio University during his redshirt sophomore campaign; #3. That dominance occurred after a hugely disappointing freshman season; #4. He missed the entire 2020 season, not from injury, but from academic ineligibility. Last year the 6-foot-6, 200-pound lefty struck out 117 and walked 27 in 88.2 innings of work, compiling an 8-3 win-loss record and a 2.33 ERA in 14 starts for the Mid-American Conference school. Colorado selected Rock in the second round, 68th overall, and signed him to a deal worth $953,100. The big southpaw made four brief appearances in the Arizona Complex League, fanning 11 and walking just one in 8.0 innings.

Scouting Report: Consider the following:

- Between 2011 and 2020, only three Mid-American Conference pitchers have averaged at least 11 strikeouts in a season (min. 75 IP): Drey Jameson, Joey Murray (twice), and John Baker.

Rock's production in 2021 would include him on the list – except his walk rate, 2.7 BB/9, would be the only one under three walks per nine innings. Unfortunately, Rock's one of the few pitchers that I personally didn't watch due to lack of game tape. Reports on MLB.com indicated his fastball sat in the 93- to 96-mph with a power slider and a changeup. He throws a ton of strikes for his size and thanks to a late birthday, he's only entering his age-21 season. I look forward to watching him in Low-A next year.

Ceiling: N/A
Risk: N/A
MLB ETA: N/A

14. Chris McMahon, RHP	FB	SL	CH	Command	Overall
	45/55	55	45/50	55	45

Born: 02/04/99	Age: 23	Bats: R	Top Comp: Jakob Junis
Height: 6-2	Weight: 217	Throws: R	

Season	Team	Age	Level	IP	TBF	K/9	K%	BB/9	BB%	K-BB%	ERA	FIP	xFIP	Pit/Bat
2021	COL	22	A+	114.1	485	9.37	24.54%	2.52	6.60%	17.94%	4.17	4.32	4.56	3.62

Background: The Rockies struck gold with their first two selections in the 2020 draft, taking prep outfielder Zac Veen, who has the look of a budding superstar, and high school switch-hitting catcher Drew Romo. With their next pick Colorado selected University of Miami right-hander Chris McMahon, with the 46th overall selection. The Rockies signed the 6-foot-2, 217-pound right-hander to a deal worth slightly more than $1.6 million. A stalwart for the Hurricanes during his three-year collegiate career, McMahon looked otherworldly during his COVID-abbreviate campaign: he struck out 38 and walked just five in 25.2 innings across four starts. The righty didn't make his professional debut – again, thanks to COVID – until last season. In 22 appearances with Spokane, 20 of which were start, the Pennsylvania native fanned 119 and walked 32 in 114.1 innings. He finished the year with a 4.17 ERA, a 4.32 FIP, and a 4.56 xFIP.

Scouting Report: Consider the following:

- Since 2006, only five 22-year-old hurlers met the following criteria in High-A with on organization (min. 100 IP): 25.5 to 25.5% strikeout percentage with a walk percentage between 5.5% and 7.5%. Those five hurlers: Josh Sborz, Kendry Flores, Tyson Miller, Brendan White, and, Chris McMahon.

I caught two of McMahon's starts last season: a May 28th outing against the Eugene Emeralds and a June 26th outing against the Hillsboro Hops. The former Hurricane's fastball looked lively in the earlier start, sitting in the mid-90s. A month later he was laboring to bump 88 mph against the Hops. Maybe the stadium gun was a bit low, but it looked sickly either way. Above-Average slider that's often confused for a curveball. And a below-average changeup that projects to be workable. Based on what I saw last year, McMahon didn't have the look of a recent second round pick. But he throws strikes and has a fairly open trek to the big leagues.

Ceiling: 1.0- to 1.5-win player
Risk: Moderate
MLB ETA: 2023

15. Sam Weatherly, LHP	FB	CB	SL	CH	Command	Overall
	55	50	60	45/50	45	45

Born: 05/28/99	Age: 23	Bats: L	Top Comp: Kevin Siegrist
Height: 6-4	Weight: 205	Throws: L	

Season	Team	Age	Level	IP	TBF	K/9	K%	BB/9	BB%	K-BB%	ERA	FIP	xFIP	Pit/Bat
2021	COL	22	A	69.0	296	12.52	32.43%	4.17	10.81%	21.62%	4.83	4.59	4.71	3.96

Background: Maybe it was due to the COVID-shortened season. Maybe it was a little bit of lull in the talent on their roster. Or, more likely than not, it's a result of the draft being limited to just five rounds. But Clemson produced just a pair draft picks in the 2020 class, the fewest numbers of players selected since 2013. The two Tigers drafted: Sam Weatherly, the Rockies' third round pick, and Spencer Strider, chosen a round later by the Braves. The 6-foot-4, 205-pound southpaw with a history of well below-average command was practically unhittable during his final season with the ACC squad, posting a 0.79 ERA while averaging 17.1 K/9 and 5.6 BB/9 through 22.2 innings of work. Colorado took the cautious route and opted to have the hard-throwing lefty spend the entirety of 2021 in Low-A. And the results were…better than expected. Making 15 starts for the Fresno Grizzlies, Weatherly struck out 96 and walked 32 in 69.0 innings of action.

Scouting Report: In a word: Raw. In two words: Command Issues. In three words: Work In Progress. No matter how you slice it, the hard-throwing lefty's walk rate last season, 4.2 BB/9, is the lowest total since his pre-college days. But there's hope for continued progress on the horizon:

- Over his first 32.0 innings last season, Weatherly walked 23 hitters – or an average of 6.5 BB/9
- Over his final 37.0 innings, he walked just nine in 37.0 innings of work – or an average of 2.2 BB/9

But he needs to repeat it for more than seven starts for me to buy in. Despite the gaudy strikeout rates, Weatherly doesn't possess an elite, plus-heater. It's good, above-average, but nothing to hang your career on. His slider is, though. It's filthy – a legitimate sit-down-see-ya-later strikeout pitch. He mixed in an average curveball and a firm changeup as well. There's obvious reliever risk here – especially given the fastball/slider combo. He. Needs. To. Repeat. The. Command.

Ceiling: 1.0- to 1.5-win player
Risk: Moderate
MLB ETA: 2024

16. McCade Brown, RHP

	FB	CB	SL	CH	Command	Overall
	55/60	60	50/55	N/A	40/45	45

Born: 05/15/00	Age: 22	Bats: R	Top Comp: N/A
Height: 6-6	Weight: 225	Throws: R	

Background: Colorado went the pitching route – particularly collegiate pitching – early and often in the draft last July, selecting arms with four of their first six selections. Brown, a massive 6-foot-6, 225-pound right-hander out of Indiana University, was the club's fourth pick. Taken with the 79th overall selection in the third round, Brown missed a lot of things during his final campaign for the Big 10 school – namely bats and the strike zone. He averaged a whopping 14.3 strikeouts and 6.3 walks per nine innings, but somehow finished with a 3.39 ERA. Colorado signed him to a bonus worth $780,400. Brown made four brief appearances in in the Arizona Complex League, fanning nine and walking a trio in eight innings of work.

Scouting Report: Brown's fastball typically sits in the low- to mid-90s, touching a tick or two higher at times. It's an above-average offering with some room to grow. His best offspeed pitch is a wicked, plus, low-80s curveball with plenty of depth. His mid- to upper-80s slider has the potential to blossom into an above-average pitch thanks to the late tilt. He'll also mix in a rare changeup (though I didn't see one). Brown was basically an unknown heading into the 2021 season; a back injury limited him to less than three innings as a freshman and he made just four brief appearances during the COVID-shortened 2020 season. There's more growth here than the typical 21-year-old college arm.

Ceiling: 1.0- to 1.5-win player
Risk: Moderate
MLB ETA: 2024

17. Colton Welker, 1B/3B

	Hit	Power	SB	Patience	Glove	Overall
	45	45/50	35	50	50	40

Born: 10/09/97	Age: 24	Bats: R	Top Comp: Will Craig
Height: 6-1	Weight: 235	Throws: R	

Season	Team	Age	Level	PA	1B	2B	3B	HR	SB	CS	BB%	K%	AVG	OBP	SLG	ISO
2018	COL	20	A+	509	106	32	0	13	5	1	8.25%	20.24%	0.333	0.383	0.489	0.156
2019	COL	21	AA	394	55	23	1	10	2	1	8.12%	17.26%	0.252	0.313	0.408	0.156
2021	COL	23	A+	35	2	1	0	3	0	0	5.71%	28.57%	0.194	0.257	0.516	0.323
2021	COL	23	AAA	98	15	5	1	3	0	0	12.24%	20.41%	0.286	0.378	0.476	0.190

Background: The fourth round of the 2016 draft produced a ton of talent: Shane Bieber, Corbin Burnes, Joey Lucchesi, and Bobby Dalbec – all of whom the Rockies overlooked to snag corner infielder Colton Welker. A product of Stoneman-Douglas High School, the 6-foot-1, 235-pound slugger got popped in early May last season for a banned substance and suspended for 80 games. Disregarding his rehab / tune-up games in the lower minors, Welker batted a solid .258/.345/.483 with seven doubles, one triple, and six homeruns in 33 games in AAA. Colorado called him up on September 8th. He hit .189/.250/.216 in 19 big league games.

Snippet from The 2020 Prospect Digest Handbook: Strong contact rates, average patience, average glove at third base. The power is coming.

Scouting Report: The batted ball data, per *FanGraphs*, is average – at best. His average exit velocity is 87 mph with a peak of 104 mph. He continued to improve upon getting the ball in the air; last season his groundball rate was 34.4% in AAA – easily the best mark, albeit in an abbreviated sample size, in his career. There's just not a lot of difference between Welker and, say, former Pirates first rounder Will Craig.

Ceiling: 1.0-win player
Risk: Moderate
MLB ETA: Debuted in 2021

18. Hunter Goodman, C

Hit	Power	SB	Patience	Glove	Overall
40/45	50	30	45	45	35

Born: 10/08/99	Age: 22	Bats: R	Top Comp: N/A
Height: 6-1	Weight: 210	Throws: R	

Season	Team	Age	Level	PA	1B	2B	3B	HR	SB	CS	BB%	K%	AVG	OBP	SLG	ISO
2021	COL	21	CPX	74	9	7	0	2	1	0	12.16%	18.92%	0.300	0.419	0.517	0.217

Background: A consistent, perhaps underrated, bat throughout his tenure at the University of Memphis. Goodman, a 6-foot-1, 210-pound backstop, hit a rock solid .326/.367/.573 as the club's starter as a true freshman. He got off to a scorching start during the COVID-shortened 2020 year, slugging a red hot .357/.416/.743 through 77 plate appearances. And he – more or less – maintained status quo during his junior campaign for the AAC school: in a career best 56 games, Goodman batted .307/.401/.678 with 10 homeruns, one triple, and a career best 21 homeruns – tied for the fourth highest total among all Division I hitters. Colorado drafted him in the fourth round, 109th overall, and signed him to a deal worth $600,000. Goodman appeared in 22 games with Colorado's Arizona Complex League, hitting .300/.419/.517 with seven doubles and a pair of dingers.

Scouting Report: Consider the following:

- Between 2011 and 2020, only seven Division I hitters met the following criteria in a season (min. 200 PA): .300/.400/.650 with a walk rate between 10% and 14% with a strikeout rate between 20% and 23%. Those seven hitters: Adam Walker, Jake Adams, Jeremy Eierman, Zach Stephens, Ryan Flick, Luke Heyer, and Matt Leeds.

Never one to work the count – especially during his first two seasons at Memphis. Goodman, including his summer in the Cape Cod League, walked a total of 17 times **in 498 plate appearances.** Last season he somehow discovered the ability to work the count and walked in more than 12% of his plate appearances. Solid pop with a decent hit tool at a premium position. I'm not convinced that he's an OBP guy just yet.

Ceiling: 0.5- to 1.0-win player
Risk: Moderate
MLB ETA: 2024

19. Ryan Feltner, RHP

FB	CB	SL	CH	Command	Overall
55	50	50	50	50	35

Born: 09/02/96	Age: 25	Bats: R	Top Comp: Replaceable Joe Reliever
Height: 6-4	Weight: 190	Throws: R	

Season	Team	Age	Level	IP	TBF	K/9	K%	BB/9	BB%	K-BB%	ERA	FIP	xFIP	Pit/Bat
2018	COL	21	R	30.2	108	11.45	36.11%	1.17	3.70%	32.41%	0.88	2.80	2.93	3.96
2019	COL	22	A	119.0	532	8.77	21.80%	3.48	8.65%	13.16%	5.07	4.21	3.77	3.84
2021	COL	24	A+	37.1	156	10.85	28.85%	4.34	11.54%	17.31%	2.17	3.44	4.48	3.86
2021	COL	24	AA	72.2	298	9.91	26.85%	2.72	7.38%	19.46%	2.85	3.52	4.01	3.77

Background: The Ohio State University, my alma mater, has produced a number of arms throughout the years – though only one of real note. Taken by the Seattle Mariners in the second round of the 1987 draft, Dave Burba would go on to win 115 games and tally more than 16 wins above replacement. Beyond that, though, it's pretty meager. In fact, Feltner's not-so-great debut with the Rockies last season was worth -0.3 wins above replacement, which is tied for the ninth most successful hurler produced by the Big 10 school. Beyond the brief two starts in the big leagues last season, Feltner rocketed through the minor leagues, throwing 112.2 innings posting a 127-to-42 K/BB.

Scouting Report: A strike-thrower without superb command. The book on Feltner was that he'd uncork a mid- to upper-90s fastball. Last season, though, it was several ticks lower in the minor leagues and his heater averaged just a smidge over 92 mph during his abbreviated debut with Colorado. Average curveball, average slider, average changeup. Average. Average. Average. He's not the type of hurler to be overly successful in Denver. He may get a couple shots at a starting gig, but is better suited for a relief role – where, hopefully, he regains his heater.

Ceiling: 0.5-win player
Risk: Moderate
MLB ETA: Debuted in 2021

20. Brenton Doyle, CF

Hit	Power	SB	Patience	Glove	Overall
45	50	55	45	50	35

Born: 05/14/98	Age: 24	Bats: R	Top Comp: N/A
Height: 6-3	Weight: 200	Throws: R	

Season	Team	Age	Level	PA	1B	2B	3B	HR	SB	CS	BB%	K%	AVG	OBP	SLG	ISO
2019	COL	21	R	215	47	11	3	8	17	3	14.42%	21.86%	0.383	0.477	0.611	0.228
2021	COL	23	A+	424	75	16	2	16	21	6	7.08%	31.60%	0.279	0.336	0.454	0.174

Background: Division II school Shepherd University has produced a total of four draft picks in its history: Nathan Minnich, an eighth round pick by Boston in 2012; Josh McCauley, a 21st round pick by the Cubs a year later; Brenton Doyle, a fourth round selection in 2019; and Jared Carr, taken in the 13th round last season by the Phillies. Doyle, by the way, earned the only six-figure bonus among the group as he came to terms with the NL West organization for $500,000. Feasting off of the bandbox known as Spokane, the 6-foot-3, 200-pound center fielder slugged .279/.336/.454 with 16 doubles, two triples, 16 homeruns, and 21 stolen bases. His overall production, per *Weighted Runs Created Plus*, topped the league average threshold by 10%.

Scouting Report: Consider the following:

- Since 2006, only three 23-year-old hitters met the following criteria in a High-A season with one organization (min. 350 PA): 105 to 115 wRC+, a strikeout rate north of 30%, and a sub-8% walk rate. Those three hitters: Bobby Crocker, Tyler Frost, and – of course – Brenton Doyle.

A decent toolkit: average power, above-average speed, solid enough glove to man center field. The problem, of course, is whether Doyle's going to make consistent enough contact as he progresses up the minor league ladder. He was particularly giddy during his the last three months of the season: despite hitting .306/.345/.507, he posted an abhorrent 71-to-10 strikeout-to-walk ratio. One more final thought: even though he spent half the year playing at home, his away production was actually better (.244/.313/.417 vs. .304/.347/.498). He's a fifth outfielder unless his contact rate improves. The Rockies do have a knack for developing older prospects and that could happen with Denton in the coming years.

Ceiling: 0.5-win player
Risk: Moderate
MLB ETA: 2024

Detroit Tigers

Top Prospects

1. Spencer Torkelson, 1B/3B

Hit	Power	SB	Patience	Glove	Overall
55/60	60/70	30	70	50	70

Born: 08/26/99	Age: 22	Bats: R	Top Comp: Miguel Cabrera
Height: 6-1	Weight: 220	Throws: R	

Season	Team	Age	Level	PA	1B	2B	3B	HR	SB	CS	BB%	K%	AVG	OBP	SLG	ISO
2021	DET	21	A+	141	17	11	1	5	3	2	17.02%	19.86%	0.312	0.440	0.569	0.257
2021	DET	21	AA	212	22	10	0	14	1	1	14.15%	23.58%	0.263	0.373	0.560	0.297
2021	DET	21	AAA	177	15	8	1	11	1	0	12.99%	20.34%	0.238	0.350	0.531	0.293

Background: The draft is, at best, a gamble. Sure, front offices and organizations will make decisions to help mitigate risks, but nothing is certain. Personally, I always find it fascinating when undrafted prep players step into big time Division I baseball and dominate – a la Spencer Torkelson. A product of Casa Grande High School in Petaluma, California, the corner infielder put together a season for the ages – as a true freshman. In 55 games for the Arizona State Sun Devils, the 6-foot-1, 220-pound slugger hit .320/.440/.743 with 12 homeruns and 25 dingers – obliterating Barry Bonds' freshman homerun record at the school. He continued swinging a massive stick during the following summer in the Cape Cod League: in 25 games with the Chatham Anglers he put together a .333/.472/.704 slash line. Next season, 2019, Torkelson continued to showcase his elite talents for the Sun Devils, posting an impressive .351/.446/.707 with 17 doubles and 23 homeruns. And he was on pace for a historic junior year before COVID canceled the college season, slugging .340/.598/.780 through 17 games. Detroit, of course, made him the top pick in the draft two years ago and handed him a humungous $8,416,300 bonus – which already has the makings of a massive bargain. Last season, his debut in professional ball, he blitzed through High-A, Double-A, and Triple-A, hitting an aggregate .267/.383/.552 with 29 doubles, two triples, and 30 homeruns.

Scouting Report: This cannot be said enough: Torkelson played in a total of 17 actual games in 2020 and stepped right into the mid-levels of the minor leagues without missing so much as a beat. He rocketed through three different levels and put himself in position to make his big league debut at some point in 2022. Torkelson is going to hit for average. He's going to hit for plus power. He consistently barrels balls, all day long. He doesn't swing-and-miss a lot. And he walks a ton. Defensively, he was average at both first and third bases – potentially adding even more value if he can stick at the hot corner. Outside of the power display last season, Torkelson did a phenomenal job with his strikeout-to-walk rate, posting an aggregate 114-to-77 mark. In terms of big league ceiling, think something along the lines of .320/.420/.630.

Ceiling: 7.0-win player
Risk: Moderate
MLB ETA: 2022

2. Riley Greene, CF

Hit	Power	SB	Patience	Glove	Overall
55	55	55	55	60	60

Born: 09/28/00	Age: 21	Bats: L	Top Comp: Andrew McCutchen
Height: 6-3	Weight: 200	Throws: L	

Season	Team	Age	Level	PA	1B	2B	3B	HR	SB	CS	BB%	K%	AVG	OBP	SLG	ISO
2019	DET	18	R	43	8	3	0	2	0	0	11.63%	27.91%	0.351	0.442	0.595	0.243
2019	DET	18	A	108	15	2	2	2	4	0	5.56%	24.07%	0.219	0.278	0.344	0.125
2019	DET	18	A-	100	21	3	1	1	1	0	11.00%	25.00%	0.295	0.380	0.386	0.091
2021	DET	20	AA	373	60	16	5	16	12	1	10.99%	27.35%	0.298	0.381	0.525	0.227
2021	DET	20	AAA	185	29	9	3	8	4	0	11.89%	27.57%	0.308	0.400	0.553	0.245

Background: Looking back at the 2019 draft and it's obvious that the early portion of it has a chance to be historic: Adley Rutschman, Bobby Witt Jr., Riley Greene, C.J. Abrams, Nick Lodolo, and Josh Jung have all established themselves as legitimate top prospects. That doesn't include the likes of Andrew Vaughn and Alex Manoah, who already appeared with their respective big league teams. And there is plenty of top talent sprinkled through the rest of the round too. Greene, a product of Paul J. Hagerty High School in Oviedo, Florida, received an impressive $6,180,700 bonus from Detroit as the fifth overall pick that year. The organization immediately put the toolsy center fielder on the fast track to the big leagues, pushing him through rookie ball, short-season, and Low-A during his abbreviated professional debut. His aggressive assignments continued last season as well: he ripped through the minors' toughest challenge, Double-A, in a mere 84 games before finishing the year at Triple-A. When the dust finally settled Greene's slash line was a healthy, five-tool packed .301/.387/.534 with 25 doubles, eight triples, 24 homeruns and 16 stolen bases (in 17 attempts).

Snippet from The 2020 Prospect Digest Handbook: He has the potential to develop into an above-average big league starting outfielder.

Scouting Report: Consider the following:

- Since 2006, only five 20-year-old hitters met the following criteria in a Double-A season with one organization (min. 350 PA): 140 to 150 wRC+ and a double-digit walk rate. Those five hitters: Cody Bellinger, Dylan Carlson, Colby Rasmus, Jon Singleton, and – or course – Mr. Riley Greene.

A few additional notes and tidbits:

- Greene's strikeout rate, 27.4%, was the worst among the group, by at least four percentage points.
- Here are the career big league wRC+ totals for each of the hitters: 124 (Bellinger), 106 (Carlson), 102 (Rasmus), and 81 (Singleton).

Greene shows an impressive power-speed combo. Throw in above-average patience and defense and he has the makings of a potential perennial All-Star. The strikeout rate is a bit concerning, though not in full blown red flag territory. Assuming that it doesn't continue to bloat, Greene looks like a .275/.360/.460-type hitter.

Ceiling: 5.0-win player
Risk: Moderate
MLB ETA: 2022

3. Jackson Jobe, RHP

	FB	CB	SL	CH	Command	Overall
	60	55	70	60	50	60

Born: 07/30/02	**Age:** 19	**Bats:** R	**Top Comp:** N/A
Height: 6-2	**Weight:** 190	**Throws:** R	

Background: "He's the best high school pitcher I've ever seen. You get guys a lot of guys that can throw the ball 95, 96, 97 miles an hour, they don't always have the command, Jackson can go out there and throw a strike with any of his pitches on any count. It's just amazing to watch that kid throw the baseball. He just goes out there and he'll give us a complete game in 75 pitches." – Heritage Hall Head Coach Jordan Semore, in an interview with Fox 25. And that's just the tip of the iceberg for the hard-throwing, generationally gifted hurler. Jobe, a Perfect Game All-American, was simply unhittable during his senior campaign for the Oklahoma high school. In 10 starts in 2021, the 6-foot-2, 190-pound righty struck out a whopping 122, surrendered just 15 hits, and compiled a tidy .135 ERA in 52.1 innings of work. For those keeping track at home: that's a staggering 21 punch outs per nine innings. Or in other words: 77.7% of the outs made were recorded via the punch out. Jobe was committed to Mississippi. Detroit selected the young flame-thrower with the third overall pick last July and signed him to a massive deal worth $6.9 million. He did not appear in a game after joining the organization.

Scouting Report: Per the usual, here's what I wrote about the talented prep arm prior to the draft:

> "Silky smooth mechanics that make his mid-90s heat look almost effortless. But the conversation on Jackson begins – and will always begin – on his plus-plus slider, which, according to reports, has reached over 3,000 RPMs. His curveball is a solid above-average strikeout offering. And, according to reports, he's spent a lot of time during the offseason improving his plus changeup. Barring any injury concerns that come along with a young arm, Jobe has the potential to slide into the front of a rotation."

Ceiling: 4.5-win player
Risk: Moderate
MLB ETA: 2025

4. Ty Madden, RHP

	FB	CB	SL	CH	Command	Overall
	60	N/A	70	50	50	60

Born: 02/21/00	**Age:** 22	**Bats:** R	**Top Comp:** N/A
Height: 6-3	**Weight:** 215	**Throws:** R	

Background: Cypress Ranch High School, a Texas powerhouse, has churned out an *impressive* amount of talent over the past couple of seasons. Right-hander JJ Goss was chosen by the Rays with the 36th overall pick three years ago. And fellow righty Matthew Thompson, who earned a slightly larger signing bonus, was taken by the White Sox nine selections later. Then there's Sam Houston State center fielder Colton Cowser, the fifth overall pick in 2021. And, of course, Madden heard his name in the opening round last July as well. A massively broad-shouldered, Texas-born fireballer, Madden, who was taken by the Royals in the late rounds coming out of high school, split his freshman season between the Longhorn's bullpen and starting rotation. He tossed 42.1 innings, racking up 37 punch outs and a whopping 24 free passes. The 6-foot-3, 215-pound hurler spent the ensuing summer playing for the Chatham Anglers: he made another eight appearances, averaging 9.3 strikeouts and 4.7 walks per nine innings. Madden got off to dominant start to the COVID-shortened 2020 campaign. He posted an impressive 26-to-4 strikeout-to-walk ratio in 25 innings of work. And he was able to carry that momentum over into a dominant 2021 season. He made a career best 18 appearances, all of them coming via the start, throwing 113.2 innings with 137 strikeouts and

44 walks. He compiled a 2.45 ERA while winning seven games. He was projected to be a Top 10 selection, but fell to the Tigers with the 32nd overall pick. The club signed him to a $2.5 million deal. He did not appear in a game after signing.

Scouting Report: Per the usual, here's what I wrote about the hard-throwing Longhorn before the draft last summer:

"Consider the following:

- *Between 2011 and 2020, here's the list of Big12 pitchers that averaged at least 10 strikeouts per nine innings in a season (min. 90 IP): Nick Lodolo, Alek Manoah, Jon Gray, Steven Gingery, Brandon Finnegan, Ben Krauth, Jake Irvin, and Chad Donato. Madden, of course, averaged 10.8 K/9 in 2021.*

I have to admit, going into the games I saw Madden pitch I fully expected his command/control to be below-average. But each time, though, I was pleasantly surprised. Madden attacks hitters with one of the class's better heaters, a plus offering that can touch as high as 99 and sits comfortably in the mid-90s. His slider is one of the best secondary pitches in the class as well, showing hellacious downward tumble and sits in the mid-80s. He also features a solid-average changeup that showed some inconsistent arm-side fade when he was finishing. Madden is the rare high floor/high ceiling prospect. If his changeup fails to materialize – or if the command/control regresses – he's a dominant relief arm. But if everything clicks [Madden] looks like a #2/#3-type starting pitcher."

Ceiling: 2.5-win player
Risk: Moderate
MLB ETA: 2024

5. Reese Olson, RHP

	FB	CB	SL	CH	Command	Overall
	55+	55	55	55/60	45/50	50

Born: 07/31/99	Age: 22	Bats: R	Top Comp: Jake Odorizzi
Height: 6-1	Weight: 160	Throws: R	

Season	Team	Age	Level	IP	TBF	K/9	K%	BB/9	BB%	K-BB%	ERA	FIP	xFIP	Pit/Bat
2018	MIL	18	R	10.1	45	5.23	13.33%	3.48	8.89%	4.44%	5.23	4.65	4.92	1.60
2019	MIL	19	A	94.2	425	7.99	19.76%	4.47	11.06%	8.71%	4.66	4.45	4.26	4.09
2021	MIL	21	A+	69.0	294	10.30	26.87%	4.57	11.90%	14.97%	4.30	4.16	4.51	4.15
2021	DET	21	A+	11.0	41	11.45	34.15%	1.64	4.88%	29.27%	0.00	1.77	2.93	4.20
2021	DET	21	AA	24.2	104	7.66	20.19%	5.11	13.46%	6.73%	4.74	4.04	4.98	3.74

Background: Exactly the type of trade a rebuilding team should execute. All. Day. Long. Detroit acquired the young right-hander from the Brewers a day before the trade deadline in exchange for veteran southpaw Daniel Norris. Milwaukee's scouting and player development program have done wonders. Taken in the 13th round, 395th overall, the club signed the North Hall High School product for a sizeable $440,000 bonus, the (A) largest in the round and (B) enough to convince him to forgo his commitment to Georgia Tech. Olsen opened some eyes – including mine – during his showing in the Midwest League in 2019; the then-19-year-old posted an 84-to-47 strikeout-to-walk ratio in 94.2 innings of work. Last season he made 21 starts between High-A and Double-A, throwing 104.2 innings of work with 114 strikeout and 51 free passes. He finished the year with a 3.96 ERA.

Snippet from The 2020 Prospect Digest Handbook: The former prep arm is still quite raw, but he has the potential to help fill out the backend of a big league rotation if the control / command continues to trend in the right direction – perhaps peaking as a #4.

Scouting Report: One of my favorite arms in the minors. You don't have to squint too hard to see a viable big league starting pitcher, and one, who may eke his was into a Top 100 prospect list at some time. Borderline plus fastball that regularly sits in the 93- to 94-mph range and has peaked as high as 95 mph during an outing I scouted. Above-average mid- to upper-70s curveball. Above-average mid-80s slider. And a filthy changeup that eventually becomes a consistent plus offering. The lone thing holding him – and his ceiling – back: command. It's a 45. If it bumps up to average he's a lock to surprise a lot of people. He's entering his age-22 season with Double-A experience. Don't sleep on this guy.

Ceiling: 2.5-win player
Risk: Moderate
MLB ETA: 2022/2023

6. Dillon Dingler, C

	Hit	Power	SB	Patience	Glove	Overall
	45	50/55	30	45	55	50

Born: 09/17/98	Age: 23	Bats: R	Top Comp: Jorge Alfaro
Height: 6-3	Weight: 210	Throws: R	

Season	Team	Age	Level	PA	1B	2B	3B	HR	SB	CS	BB%	K%	AVG	OBP	SLG	ISO
2021	DET	22	A	12	3	1	0	0	0	0	0.00%	25.00%	0.333	0.333	0.417	0.083
2021	DET	22	A+	141	20	6	1	8	0	0	9.22%	25.53%	0.287	0.376	0.549	0.262
2021	DET	22	AA	208	28	3	3	4	1	0	4.33%	29.81%	0.202	0.264	0.314	0.112

Background: The last time the Tigers drafted a player out of The Ohio State University it didn't work out so well – for all parties involved. Third baseman Ronnie Bourquin was the best hitter the Buckeyes had during my tenure at the school, showcasing an impressive feel for hitting and flashing above-average thump. So Detroit burned the 50th overall pick in 2006 on the lefty-swinging infielder and it became immediately clear that Bourquin lacked the chops to be a successful professional hitter. Fourteen years later the team snagged another Buckeye in the second round: backstop Dillon Dingler. The 38th overall pick in the 2020 draft – and the first player chosen in the second round – Dingler bounced through three separate levels during his pro debut last season. In total, he hit .239/.310/.407 with 10 doubles, four triples, and 12 homeruns. Per *Weighted Runs Created Plus*, his overall production was 5% below the league average threshold.

Scouting Report: The overall slash line is a bit low, troublesome. But let's provide some important context: Like Torkelson, and many others, Dingler was limited to just a few weeks of action during his junior campaign in college, courtesy of COVID. He returns to regular action a year later and immediately steps into High-A without missing a beat: he slugged .287/.376/.549 in 32 games. Detroit bumped him up to Double-A in mid-June and he struggled then hit the injured list for three weeks. So Dingler basically went from college ball to the minors' toughest challenge, Double-A, with only a few weeks of game play in between. There's 20-homer potential with above-average defense. The hit tool will be hard pressed to post .250+ batting averages. But there's certainly everyday production here.

Ceiling: 2.0-win player
Risk: Moderate
MLB ETA: 2022/2023

7. Cristian Santana, 3B/SS

	Hit	Power	SB	Patience	Glove	Overall
	30/45	50	50/40	50	40/50	45

Born: 11/25/03	Age: 18	Bats: R	Top Comp: N/A
Height: 6-0	Weight: 165	Throws: R	

Season	Team	Age	Level	PA	1B	2B	3B	HR	SB	CS	BB%	K%	AVG	OBP	SLG	ISO
2021	DET	17	DSL	216	23	12	2	9	12	7	13.89%	21.30%	0.269	0.421	0.520	0.251

Background: One of the club's big expenditures on the international free agent scene last winter. Santana, touted as a Top 15 prospect by MLB.com, agreed to a deal worth a hefty $2.95 million bonus in January. The 6-foot, 165-pound infielder made his professional debut in the Dominican Summer League in the ensuing months, slugging .269/.421/.520 with 12 doubles, two triples, nine homers, and 12 stolen bases in 19 attempts. Per *Weighted Runs Created Plus*, Santana's overall production was a staggering 61% better the league average – a stellar showing in the offensive-friendly foreign rookie league.

Scouting Report: Consider the following:

- There were 51 hitters that made at least 200 trips to the plate in the Dominican Summer League last year. Of those 51, Santana's 161 wRC+ ranks as the third best showing – and tops for any player under the age of 18.
- His Isolated Power, .251, bested the league, as well.

Short, quick, compact swing with above-average power potential. Santana showed a bit too much swing-and-miss during his debut, fanning in more than 21% of his plate appearances. But after a strong showing as a 17-year-old, Santana's all but punched his ticket to the states for 2022.

Ceiling: 1.5-win player
Risk: Moderate
MLB ETA: 2025

8. Joey Wentz, LHP

FB	CB	SL	CH	Command	Overall
50	55	45	55	45	45

Born: 10/06/97	Age: 24	Bats: L	Top Comp: Logan Allen
Height: 6-5	Weight: 220	Throws: L	

Season	Team	Age	Level	IP	TBF	K/9	K%	BB/9	BB%	K-BB%	ERA	FIP	xFIP	Pit/Bat
2018	ATL	20	A+	67.0	266	7.12	19.92%	3.22	9.02%	10.90%	2.28	3.64	3.91	4.07
2019	ATL	21	AA	103.0	436	8.74	22.94%	3.93	10.32%	12.61%	4.72	4.40	4.08	3.97
2019	DET	21	AA	25.2	98	12.97	37.76%	1.40	4.08%	33.67%	2.10	2.27	1.86	4.57
2021	DET	23	A	18.2	84	11.57	28.57%	3.86	9.52%	19.05%	6.75	6.00	4.14	4.10
2021	DET	23	AA	53.1	233	9.79	24.89%	5.57	14.16%	10.73%	3.71	4.96	5.17	4.27

Background: It seems like a lifetime ago – maybe more – that the Braves cornered the 2016 draft class market on high upside teenage arms, grabbing the likes of Ian Anderson, Joey Wentz, and Kyle Muller within the first 44 selections. And at one point the trio cultivated dreams of another famous group of Atlanta arms. Alas, those type of things generally don't happen too frequently. Three years after handing Wentz a $3,050,000 bonus as the 40th overall pick the club dealt him – along with Travis Demeritte – to the Tigers for veteran reliever Shane Greene. The 6-foot-5, 220-pound southpaw spent the 2019 season splitting time between both organizations' Double-A affiliates and would eventually undergo Tommy John surgery in mid-March a year later. The big southpaw returned to action last season, making five starts with Lakeland before being promoted back up to Double-A. In total, Wentz made 18 starts, throwing 72.0 innings with 82 punch outs, 41 walks, and a 4.50 ERA.

Snippet from The 2020 Prospect Digest Handbook: At times he looks like a solid #4-type arm. And at other times he's looks like an up-and-down arm. I'd really like to see Wentz throw his fantastic changeup more frequently.

Scouting Report: As expected, Wentz was a bit rusty as he came back from elbow surgery: he allowed 21 earned runs across his first 29.2 innings. But he began to right the ship in mid-July and finished on a positive note: he posted a 3.19 ERA with a 51-to-26 strikeout-to-walk ratio over his final 42.1 innings. He's never been a flamethrower and his command has generally been slightly below-average. But Wentz (A) is left-handed, (B) has two above-average secondary weapons, and (C) owns a high draft pedigree. He still hasn't distinguished himself from a backend starting pitcher or an up-and-down arm. There's a lot of Logan Allen vibes going on here.

Ceiling: 1.0- to 1.5-win player
Risk: Moderate
MLB ETA: 2022

9. Ryan Kreidler, SS

Hit	Power	SB	Patience	Glove	Overall
45	50	50	50	50	45

Born: 11/12/97	Age: 24	Bats: R	Top Comp: Jordy Mercer
Height: 6-4	Weight: 208	Throws: R	

Season	Team	Age	Level	PA	1B	2B	3B	HR	SB	CS	BB%	K%	AVG	OBP	SLG	ISO
2019	DET	21	A-	257	34	13	4	2	9	4	7.78%	23.74%	0.232	0.307	0.351	0.118
2021	DET	23	AA	388	59	15	0	15	10	4	8.25%	30.67%	0.256	0.325	0.429	0.173
2021	DET	23	AAA	162	26	8	0	7	5	2	14.81%	24.07%	0.304	0.407	0.519	0.215

Background: UCLA has churned out an impressive number of shortstops throughout the years – 25 of them, to be exact. But only four of them eventually made it to the big leagues, with just one – Brandon Crawford – becoming an above-average regular. Only two of the school's shortstops – Matt McLain and Kevin Kramer – were taken earlier than the Tigers' selection of Ryan Kreidler. Selected in the fourth round, 112th overall, three years ago, the 6-foot-4, 208-pound infielder made the leap from short-season ball in 2019 all the way to Double-A – and eventually Triple-A – last season. In 129 combined games, Kreidler batted a rock solid .270/.349/.454 with 23 doubles, 22 homeruns, and 15 stolen bases. Per *Weighted Runs Created Plus*, his overall production topped the league average mark by 18%.

Scouting Report: Consider the following:

- Since 2006, only five players met the following criteria in a Double-A season with one organization (min. 300 PA): 100 to 110 wRC+ total, a strikeout rate between 28% and 30%, and a walk rate between 8% and 11%. Those five hitters: Kyle Lewis, Jose Siri, J.J. Matijevic, Matthew den Dekker, and – of course – Ryan Kreidler.

Kreidler quietly put together one of the better offensive campaigns in the Tigers' farm system last year. After a slow (read: adjustment period) start to the year, which is expected given the leap from short-season all the way up to Double-A, Kreidler slugged a healthy .290/.368/.485 with a 27.7% punch out rate. A little bit of speed and enough glove to stay at shortstop. Kreidler looks like a competent low-end starting option.

Ceiling: 1.0- to 1.5-win player
Risk: Moderate
MLB ETA: 2022

10. Gage Workman, SS

Hit	Power	SB	Patience	Glove	Overall
40/45	45/50	60	50	50+	45

Born: 10/24/99	Age: 22	Bats: B	Top Comp: N/A
Height: 6-3	Weight: 202	Throws: R	

Season	Team	Age	Level	PA	1B	2B	3B	HR	SB	CS	BB%	K%	AVG	OBP	SLG	ISO
2021	DET	21	A	228	27	16	4	3	22	3	13.16%	26.32%	0.256	0.357	0.426	0.169
2021	DET	21	A+	285	29	21	2	9	9	5	8.07%	34.04%	0.237	0.302	0.440	0.202

Background: Originally taken by the Brewers in the 14th round coming out of Basha High School. Workman, instead, opted for the college route and improved his draft status by 10 rounds. A career .298/.372/.496 hitter for Pac12 powerhouse Arizona State, Detroit selected the 6-foot-3, 202-pound switch-hitter with the 102nd overall pick, signing him to a deal worth $1 million. Workman made his professional debut in 2021, hitting an aggregate .246/.326/.434 with 37 doubles, six triples, and 12 homeruns. He also swiped 31 bags in 39 attempts. Per *Weighted Runs Created Plus*, his overall production topped the league average mark by 6%.

Scouting Report: A younger version of fellow Pac12 counterpart – and organizational mate – Ryan Kreidler. Workman flashes a decent power / speed combination with a good glove at shortstop. The problem, though, is his below-average hit tool and problematic swing-and-miss numbers; he fanned in 30.1% of his plate appearances last season. He's four-fifths the way to an above-average big league shortstop. The lacking skill, the hit tool, is pretty damning though. If he can maintain some above-average defensive metrics he may be able to carve out a low end starting gig. One final note: Workman's batted ball data was pretty solid last season, posting an average exit velocity of 91 mph with a peak of 109 mph.

Ceiling: 1.0- to 1.5-win player
Risk: Moderate to High
MLB ETA: 2024

11. Roberto Campos, OF

Hit	Power	SB	Patience	Glove	Overall
35/45	50/55	40/30	50	50	40

Born: 07/14/03	Age: 19	Bats: R	Top Comp: N/A
Height: 6-3	Weight: 200	Throws: R	

Season	Team	Age	Level	PA	1B	2B	3B	HR	SB	CS	BB%	K%	AVG	OBP	SLG	ISO
2021	DET	18	CPX	155	18	5	0	8	3	0	10.97%	26.45%	0.228	0.316	0.441	0.213

Background: The front office was willing to bet *big* on the teenage Cuban import a couple summers ago as they handed the then-16-year-old a $2.85 million bonus, a franchise record at the time. According to reports, Campos made his bones as a 13-year-old after being named MVP in the Punta Cana International Tournament. Shortly thereafter he defected. Last season the 6-foot-3, 200-pound outfielder made his stateside debut, donning the club's Florida Complex League uniform for the entirety of the year. In 38 games he hit .228/.316/.441 with five doubles and eight homeruns. He finished the year with a near-league average production line.

Scouting Report: The good news: Campos finished his debut season tied for fourth in the league in homeruns (eight). The bad news: he had trouble consistently making contact, as evidenced by his 26.5% strikeout rate. His numbers improved after the first couple weeks of the season as he batted .243/.352/.466 with a more modest 23.8% K-rate. Fast bat and does not get cheated; there's always going to be a swing-and-miss element to Campos' game. There's some potential as a lower end, power-oriented outfielder, but he's quite raw. I'm not overly optimistic that he remains in center field, either.

Ceiling: 1.0-win player
Risk: Moderate
MLB ETA: 2025

12. Keider Montero, RHP

FB	CB	CH	Command	Overall
50/55	55	45/50	55	40

Born: 07/06/00	Age: 21	Bats: R	Top Comp: N/A
Height: 6-1	Weight: 145	Throws: R	

Season	Team	Age	Level	IP	TBF	K/9	K%	BB/9	BB%	K-BB%	ERA	FIP	xFIP	Pit/Bat
2018	DET	17	R	46.1	204	7.77	19.61%	3.11	7.84%	11.76%	2.14	3.76	3.76	1.67
2019	DET	18	A-	24.2	91	9.49	28.57%	1.82	5.49%	23.08%	2.55	2.96	2.33	4.85
2019	DET	18	R	23.0	100	9.00	23.00%	4.30	11.00%	12.00%	1.57	2.94	3.42	1.85
2021	DET	20	A+	61.1	290	8.66	20.34%	2.79	6.55%	13.79%	5.28	4.44	4.67	3.61

Background: Signed out of Santa Teresa del Tuy, Venezuela, Montero spent the first two seasons of his professional career toiling away in the foreign rookie leagues, first battling the strike zone and then bouncing between the rotation and bullpen. Montero moved stateside in 2019, at the age of 18, and held his own during abbreviated stints in the Gulf Coast and the New York-Penn

Leagues: 47.2 IP, 49 strikeouts and just 16 walks. Last season the front office aggressively challenged Montero and pushed him directly into High-A. Making a career-high 15 starts, the 6-foot-1, 145-pound right-hander averaged a solid 8.7 strikeouts and just 2.8 walks per nine innings. He compiled a 5.28 ERA, 4.44 FIP, and a 4.67 xFIP.

Scouting Report: Consider the following:

- Since 2006, only five 20-year-old hurlers met the following criteria in a High-A season with one organization (min. 50 IP): 19.5% to 21.5% strikeout rate with a walk rate between 5.5% and 7.5%. Those five hurlers: Brent Honeywell Jr., Rob Kaminsky, Ryan Castellani, Lachlan Wells, and – of course Keider Montero.

An interesting developmental wild card for the Tigers, Montero adds and subtracts off his fastball. Sometimes it'll sit in the 89-91 mph. Other times it'll bump up to 92- to 93-mph. And when he really wants to he'll reach back and touch the mid-90s. Montero mixes in two offspeed pitches: a high-70s curveball with good shape and a fringy changeup that doesn't show a lot of velocity separation unless he's pumping 92- to 94-mph. Montero shows a solid feel for command the zone, especially on his fastball. Sometimes these types of arms develop into a #5.

Ceiling: 1.0-win player
Risk: Moderate
MLB ETA: 2023/2024

13. Izaac Pacheco, SS

Hit	Power	SB	Patience	Glove	Overall
40	40/60	30	55	45	40

Born: 11/18/02	Age: 19	Bats: L	Top Comp: N/A
Height: 6-4	Weight: 225	Throws: R	

Season	Team	Age	Level	PA	1B	2B	3B	HR	SB	CS	BB%	K%	AVG	OBP	SLG	ISO
2021	DET	18	CPX	125	17	4	2	1	1	0	14.40%	34.40%	0.226	0.339	0.330	0.104

Background: It was, by and large, the "high school shortstop" draft last July. There were nine prep shortstops taken in the opening round (out of 36 selections), and another three picked in the second.

Pacheco, a 6-foot-4, 225-pound product out of Friendswood High School, was the first teenage shortstop taken in the second round. The Texas native agreed to a deal worth $2.75 deal. A Texas A&M commit, Pacheco looked a bit raw during his abbreviated debut in the Florida Complex League last summer: in 30 games, 125 plate appearances, he batted a lowly .226/.339/.330 with just four doubles, a pair of triples, and one homerun. His overall production, per *Weighted Runs Created Plus*, was 12% *below* the league average threshold.

Scouting Report: Big, strong kid that will move over to third base before long – which will help to hide his lack of range. And I don't think a move across the diamond to first base is out of the question either. Pacheco owns a great looking swing, a quasi-picture-esque lefty one, but I think he's going to show some massive platoon splits, especially once southpaws start pounding him low-and-away with soft stuff. And he's already showing some massive swing-and-miss concerns; he fanned in more than 34% of his plate appearances last summer.

Ceiling: 1.0-win player
Risk: Moderate
MLB ETA: 2025

14. Colt Keith, 2B/3B

Hit	Power	SB	Patience	Glove	Overall
45/55	30/40	30	55	50+	40

Born: 08/14/01	Age: 20	Bats: L	Top Comp: Colin Moran
Height: 6-3	Weight: 211	Throws: R	

Season	Team	Age	Level	PA	1B	2B	3B	HR	SB	CS	BB%	K%	AVG	OBP	SLG	ISO
2021	DET	19	CPX	10	4	1	0	0	0	0	30.00%	0.00%	0.714	0.800	0.857	0.143
2021	DET	19	A	181	37	6	3	1	4	1	16.57%	21.55%	0.320	0.436	0.422	0.102
2021	DET	19	A+	76	8	1	1	1	0	0	10.53%	35.53%	0.162	0.250	0.250	0.088

Background: Beginning all the way back in 1969, their first pick, Biloxi High School has produced a total of 10 players hear their names called in the draft. And prior to Keith, the earliest chosen player was third baseman Joe Pomierski, a tenth round pick by the

Mariners in 1992. Gifted with a name that fits in the old Wild West, along the likes of Jesse James, the Tigers drafted Colt Keith in the fifth round, 132nd overall, in 2020 and signed him to a deal worth $500,000. The second / third baseman made his professional debut last season. After getting a late start to the year Keith, who didn't appear in a game until the second week of June, hit a solid .320/.436/.422 with six doubles, three triples, and one homerun in 44 games with Lakeland. Detroit bumped the young infielder up to High-A in late August, where he promptly struggled (.162/.250/.250).

Scouting Report: The former fifth round pick has the makings of a professional hitter, the infamous label slapped onto sweet-swinging players with little pop. He sprays line drives all over the diamond with little bias. Very patient approach, which is often lacking in young players making their debuts directly in Low-A. Throw in a solid-average glove and Keith has the makings of a decent little prospect. Cut from the Colin Moran mold, though. No platoon splits.

Ceiling: 1.0-win player
Risk: Moderate
MLB ETA: 2025

15. Dylan Smith, RHP

	FB	CB	SL	CH	Command	Overall
	50	N/A	55	N/A	50+	40

Born: 05/28/00	Age: 22	Bats: R	Top Comp: N/A
Height: 6-2	Weight: 180	Throws: R	

Background: One of the bigger risers in the draft last July. Smith went from a little-used reliever / spot-starter during his first two seasons at the University of Alabama to a bonafide collegiate ace during his junior campaign. Making a career-high 16 appearances, all of which were starts, Smith threw 98.1 innings with 113 strikeouts and just 20 free passes. He tallied a 3.84 ERA and, yet, somehow only posted a 2-8 win-loss record for the Crimson Tide. Detroit drafted the 6-foot-2, 180-pound righty in the third round, 74th overall, and signed him to a deal worth $1,115,000. Fun Fact: The Padres originally selected Smith in the 18th round coming out of high school in 2018.

Scouting Report: Consider the following:

- Between 2011 and 2020, there were only eight instances of an SEC hurler averaging at least 10 strikeouts and fewer than 2.0 walks per nine innings in a season (min. 75 IP): Kumar Rocker, Casey Mize (twice), Alex Faedo, Dane Dunning, Trevor Stephan, Michael Plassmeyer, and Michael Byrne.

Smith's production last season puts him in the same company. He reportedly features a four-pitch mix: a fastball, curveball, slider, and changeup. I saw two: fastball and slider. His heater, an average offering, sat in the low 90s with a bit of life down in the zone and his slider is a strong swing-and-miss pitch. During the brief clips I saw Smith showed a solid feel for the strike zone particularly with his best pitch, the slider. There's not a lot of room for error for Smith, so there's some reliever risk with backend upside.

Ceiling: 1.0-win player
Risk: Moderate
MLB ETA: 2024

16. Alex Faedo, RHP

	FB	SL	CH	Command	Overall
	N/A	N/A	N/A	N/A	40

Born: 11/12/95	Age: 26	Bats: R	Top Comp: N/A
Height: 6-5	Weight: 225	Throws: R	

Season	Team	Age	Level	IP	TBF	K/9	K%	BB/9	BB%	K-BB%	ERA	FIP	xFIP	Pit/Bat
2018	DET	22	A+	61.0	246	7.52	20.73%	1.92	5.28%	15.45%	3.10	3.28	3.77	3.92
2018	DET	22	AA	60.0	254	8.85	23.23%	3.30	8.66%	14.57%	4.95	5.81	4.25	3.98
2019	DET	23	AA	115.1	473	10.46	28.33%	1.95	5.29%	23.04%	3.90	3.57	2.96	3.90

Background: Each year I always return to the same thing: Faedo was a part of one of the greatest pitching staffs and most talented teams in college history. The 2016 Florida Gators pitching staff included: Alex Faedo (of course), A.J. Puk, Brady Singer, Kirby Snead, Dane Danning, Shaun Anderson, Scott Moss, and Logan Shore. The squad's lineup included: Pete Alonso, Jonathan India, JJ Schwarz, and Dalton Guthrie. Faedo, who finished second on the team that year with 17 starts, was taken with the 18th overall pick in the 2017 draft. He breezed through High-A and spent half of his 2018 debut season in Double-A. He spent the following year refining his repertoire and command in Double-A and looked poised for big things. The 2020 season was lost due to COVID and he underwent Tommy John surgery later that year in December. According to report, he should be back to action in spring 2022.

Snippet from The 2020 Prospect Digest Handbook: Faedo shows straight 55's across the board: fastball, slider, changeup, and command. He's the ideal, innings eater fourth starter type pitcher that may squeak out a few years of slightly better production.

Scouting Report: The lost COVID season coupled with the Tommy John surgery really put a damper on Faedo's prospect status. Now he's 26-years-old with zero experience above Double-A. He seems like a bit of a long shot to develop into a backend starting pitcher at this point, but there's always hope. One more thought: Faedo's heater was sitting in the 90- to 93-mph range before surgery, so it's imperative that it doesn't show any downgrades as he comes back from a major arm injury.

Ceiling: 1.0-win player
Risk: Moderate
MLB ETA: 2022

17. Daniel Cabrera, LF/RF

	Hit	Power	SB	Patience	Glove	Overall
	45	45	45	50	50	40

Born: 09/05/98	Age: 23	Bats: L	Top Comp: N/A
Height: 6-3	Weight: 200	Throws: L	

Season	Team	Age	Level	PA	1B	2B	3B	HR	SB	CS	BB%	K%	AVG	OBP	SLG	ISO
2021	DET	22	A+	422	58	19	6	9	7	4	8.06%	22.51%	0.242	0.300	0.395	0.153
2021	DET	22	AA	71	6	2	0	4	1	0	1.41%	25.35%	0.174	0.197	0.377	0.203

Background: Originally taken by the Padres in the 26th round coming out of high school in 2017. Cabrera, of course, passed on the opportunity and headed to SEC powerhouse LSU instead. A key cog in the center of the Tigers' lineup for his three seasons, Cabrera, a career .305/.392/.518 hitter, was drafted by Detroit in the second round of the 2020 COVID-shortened draft. Signed for a smidgeon over $1.2 million, the 6-foot-3, 200-pound corner outfielder made his debut last season with the West Michigan Whitecaps. After a moderately successful 99-game stint with the club's High-A affiliate he was promoted up to Double-A for the season's last few remaining weeks. He finished the year with an aggregate .232/.285/.392 triple-slash line, belting out 21 doubles, six triples, and 13 homeruns. He also swiped eight stolen bases in 12 total attempts. His overall production, per *Weighted Runs Created Plus*, was 18% *below* the league average threshold.

Scouting Report: Consider the following:

- Since 2006 only two 22-year-old High-A hitters met the following criteria in a season with one organization (min. 300 PA): 83 to 93 wRC+, a 7% to 9% walk rate, and a strikeout rate between 21.5% and 23.5%. Those two hitters: Darren Seferina and Daniel Cabrera.

A midseason slump pretty much doomed Cabrera's overall production line: he batted a respectable .277/.332/.421 through his first 49 games, but promptly batted a lowly .146/.227/.260 over his next 34 contests. Cabrera's a doing-everything-well-enough type of player without owning a true standout tool. Below-average hit tool, average-ish patience, same with the glove too.

Ceiling: 1.0-win player
Risk: Moderate
MLB ETA: 2022/2023

18. Wilmer Flores, RHP

	FB	CB	CH	Command	Overall
	55	55	N/A	45	40

Born: 02/20/01	Age: 21	Bats: R	Top Comp: N/A
Height: 6-4	Weight: 225	Throws: R	

Season	Team	Age	Level	IP	TBF	K/9	K%	BB/9	BB%	K-BB%	ERA	FIP	xFIP	Pit/Bat
2021	DET	20	CPX	13.0	57	12.46	31.58%	1.38	3.51%	28.07%	4.85	2.53	3.07	1.79
2021	DET	20	A	53.0	224	12.23	32.14%	3.74	9.82%	22.32%	3.40	2.80	3.21	3.91

Background: A virtual unknown heading into the 2021 season. The Tigers' scouting department found a potential overlooked gem, signing the Arizona Western College alum as an undrafted free agent in 2020. A year later the 6-foot-4, 225-pound right-hander opened a lot of eyes during his oft-dominant debut season. The Venezuelan-born hurler shredded the Florida Complex League competition through three brief starts to begin the year, posting an 18-to-2 strikeout-to-walk ratio in 13.0 innings of work. Detroit bumped the emerging youngster up to Low-A. And Flores continued to hold his own. In 13 starts with the Lakeland Flying Tigers, he averaged an impressive 12.2 strikeouts and 3.7 walks per nine innings. He compiled a 3.40 ERA, 2.80 FIP, and a 3.21 xFIP during his time in Low-A.

Scouting Report: Consider the following:

- Since 2006, only four 20-year-old hurlers met the following criteria in a Low-A season with one organization (min. 50 IP): 31% to 33% strikeout percentage with a walk percentage between 9% and 11%. Those four arms: Matt Manning, Hector Yan, Alexander Smit, and – of course – Mr. Unknown, Wilmer Flores.

Not only was Flores practically a mystery man heading into the year, but he remains as such at the end of the season. There's no full game tape available and I scoured the internet and found only one brief clip from last season. Above-average fastball / breaking ball, which looked like a curveball. Flores was especially dominant over his final six starts of the year, posting a 45-to-11 strikeout-to-walk ratio with a 1.39 ERA in 32.1 innings of work. He's one of the guys I'm really looking forward to scouting in 2022.

Ceiling: 1.0-win player
Risk: Moderate
MLB ETA: 2025

19. Eliezer Alfonzo, C

	Hit	Power	SB	Patience	Glove	Overall
	55	35/40	35	45	55	40

Born: 09/23/99	Age: 22	Bats: B	Top Comp: Yorvit Torrealba
Height: 5-10	Weight: 155	Throws: R	

Season	Team	Age	Level	PA	1B	2B	3B	HR	SB	CS	BB%	K%	AVG	OBP	SLG	ISO
2018	DET	18	R	136	32	10	1	0	3	1	14.71%	5.88%	0.391	0.485	0.500	0.109
2018	DET	18	R	80	13	1	0	1	3	1	11.25%	11.25%	0.217	0.300	0.275	0.058
2019	DET	19	A-	191	49	7	0	1	2	2	4.19%	8.90%	0.318	0.342	0.374	0.056
2021	DET	21	A	171	33	7	1	7	2	0	7.02%	6.43%	0.308	0.363	0.500	0.192
2021	DET	21	A+	232	46	11	0	1	1	2	6.90%	10.34%	0.272	0.319	0.338	0.066

Background: Signed out of Barcelona, Venezuela, in early July 2016. The wiry 5-foot-10, 155-pound catcher made his pro debut in the Dominican Summer League the following year, batting a respectable .305/.414/.344 in 52 games. And Alfonzo's bat hasn't slowed one iota over the following years either. He hit .324/.417/.413 in 2018 as he split time between a return to the foreign league and a stateside rookie league. Then in a 98-stint with the Connecticut Tigers the young Venezuelan batted .318/.342/.374. The front office – finally – bumped Alfonzo up to full-season action last season. And...he continued to hit. He slugged .308/.363/.500 in 39 games with Lakeland and strung together a .272/.319/.338 showing in High-A. Alfonzo hit a combined .287/.337/.407 with 18 doubles, one triple, and eight dingers. Per *Weighted Runs Created Plus*, his overall production was 4% better than the league average mark.

Scouting Report: A bat before power, strong-gloved backstop with a history of solid offensive performances. It's not a recipe for superstardom, but it is a mixture for a potential solid backup. Alfonzo's generally been in age-appropriate levels of competition for his career, so it'll be interesting to see how he handles Double-A as a 22-year-old in the second half of 2022.

Ceiling: 1.0-win player
Risk: Moderate
MLB ETA: 2024

20. Parker Meadows, CF

	Hit	Power	SB	Patience	Glove	Overall
	30/40	50	50	50	50	35

Born: 11/02/99	Age: 22	Bats: L	Top Comp: N/A
Height: 6-5	Weight: 205	Throws: R	

Season	Team	Age	Level	PA	1B	2B	3B	HR	SB	CS	BB%	K%	AVG	OBP	SLG	ISO
2018	DET	18	A-	21	5	1	0	0	0	0	9.52%	28.57%	0.316	0.381	0.368	0.053
2018	DET	18	R	85	14	2	1	4	3	1	9.41%	29.41%	0.284	0.376	0.500	0.216
2019	DET	19	A	504	74	15	2	7	14	8	9.33%	22.42%	0.221	0.296	0.312	0.090
2021	DET	21	A	12	2	1	0	0	0	0	0.00%	25.00%	0.273	0.333	0.364	0.091
2021	DET	21	A+	408	49	15	2	8	9	8	9.07%	24.26%	0.208	0.290	0.330	0.121

Background: The younger brother of Rays All-Star outfielder Austin Meadows. Parker was a highly touted prep player, like his brother, out of Grayson High School when the Tigers drafted him with the first pick in the second round, signing him to a deal worth a hearty $2.5 million. The younger Meadows began his professional career on a high note, slugging .290/.377/.473 with three doubles, one triple, and four homeruns in 28 games between the Gulf Coast and New York-Penn Leagues. The front office bumped him up to Low-A the following year, 2019, and he struggled – mightily, hitting a lowly .221/.296/.312 in 126 games. And a return to action after the COVID interrupted 2020 season was no better. Last season in 94 games with the West Michigan Whitecaps the toolsy 6-foot-5, 205-pound center fielder hit a lowly .208/.290/.330 with 15 doubles, two triples, and eight homeruns. Per *Weighted Runs Created Plus*, his overall production was 28% *below* the league average.

Snippet from The 2020 Prospect Digest Handbook: Well, he was pretty terrible.

Scouting Report: Well, he was pretty terrible – again. And, unfortunately, he showed no signs of taking any meaningful steps – or adjustments – forward during the season as well. He posted OPS total of .554 or less in three separate months (May, June, and August). And in his best two months, July and September, he tallied only mark of .744 and .753. The truth is simple: Meadows is now coming off of back-to-back seasons in which he posted wRC+ totals of 72 and 80, so there's little hope of a turnaround now. Peripheral-wise, there's little in terms of red flags: power, speed, patience, not overly large strikeout rates. He's just…not living up to the billing.

Ceiling: 0.5-win player
Risk: Moderate
MLB ETA: 2025

Houston Astros

Top Prospects

1. Jeremy Pena, SS

Hit	Power	SB	Patience	Glove	Overall
50	50	55	50	55	55

Born: 09/22/97	Age: 24	Bats: R	Top Comp: Jhonny Peralta
Height: 6-0	Weight: 202	Throws: R	

Season	Team	Age	Level	PA	1B	2B	3B	HR	SB	CS	BB%	K%	AVG	OBP	SLG	ISO
2018	HOU	20	A-	156	28	5	0	1	3	0	11.54%	12.18%	0.250	0.340	0.309	0.059
2019	HOU	21	A	289	54	8	4	5	17	6	12.11%	19.72%	0.293	0.389	0.421	0.128
2019	HOU	21	A+	185	35	13	3	2	3	4	6.49%	17.84%	0.317	0.378	0.467	0.150
2021	HOU	23	CPX	27	6	1	1	0	1	0	7.41%	22.22%	0.348	0.444	0.478	0.130
2021	HOU	23	AAA	133	19	4	2	10	5	1	4.51%	26.32%	0.287	0.346	0.598	0.311

Background: Often overlooked, the University of Maine has produced seven big leaguers, the best of which include: Bill Swift, who tallied more than 20 bWAR, and Mark Sweeney. Jeremy Lee, a third round pick by the Astros, in 2018 not only became the school's

highest selection since 1991 (Larry Thomas, White Sox), but he's on the precipice of becoming the school's eighth big leaguer. His 2021 season, however, was delayed several months as he recovered from a surgical procedure on his left wrist. Pena made his debut in AAA on August 28th. He was able to squeeze in 30 impressive games with Sugar Land, slugging a scorching .287/.346/.598 with four doubles, two triples, and 10 homeruns. He also swiped five bags in six total attempts. His overall production, according to *Weighted Runs Created Plus*, topped the league average mark by 26% - his lowest total since his debut in short-season ball in 2018.

Snippet from The 2020 Prospect Digest Handbook: The power's a 45 and will result in 10 or so homeruns. Above-average speed. Defensive versatility. And a solid glove. He's going to be a solid bench option in the next 18 months or so.

Scouting Report: The presumed heir apparent when Carlos Correa bolts Houston for greener pastures. And, to be honest Pena's offensive potential has already exceeded my modest expectations. He's consistently, from Low-A to High-A to Triple-A, been a well above-average performer at the dish. A .270/.340/.430 slash line seems like a reasonable expectation. Above-average speed and glove. Solid approach at the plate with newly added thump. He's not going to be a superstar, but he's going to be a competent big league shortstop for a long time.

Ceiling: 3.0-win player
Risk: Low to Moderate
MLB ETA: 2022

2. Joe Perez, 3B

Hit	Power	SB	Patience	Glove	Overall
50	55	35	50	50	55

Born: 08/12/99	Age: 22	Bats: R	Top Comp: Brian Anderson
Height: 6-2	Weight: 198	Throws: R	

Season	Team	Age	Level	PA	1B	2B	3B	HR	SB	CS	BB%	K%	AVG	OBP	SLG	ISO
2018	HOU	18	R	14	4	0	0	0	1	0	21.43%	7.14%	0.364	0.500	0.364	0.000
2019	HOU	19	A-	195	18	7	2	7	3	1	5.64%	27.69%	0.188	0.246	0.365	0.177
2021	HOU	21	A	59	9	4	0	2	0	2	15.25%	22.03%	0.300	0.407	0.500	0.200
2021	HOU	21	A+	109	16	11	0	8	1	1	9.17%	19.27%	0.354	0.413	0.707	0.354
2021	HOU	21	AA	307	48	19	0	8	2	1	7.82%	26.06%	0.267	0.322	0.420	0.153

Background: Archbishop High School's home to a pair of notable big leaguers, who just happen to be former teammates: All-Stars Nick Castellanos and Alex Avila. The Florida-based prep school has also produced 2012 first rounder Nick Travieso, 2014 third round selection

Brian Gonzalez, and – of course – the Astros second round pick five years ago, Joe Perez. A two-way star with a pair of plus offerings as a pitcher, upper 90s heater and a slider, Houston selected him with the 53rd overall pick and signed him to a deal worth $1.6 million. Maybe it was the Tommy John surgery or, simply, the Astros believed in Perez's bat more, but he's been strictly a hitter since entering pro ball. And at the end of 2019 it looked like that was the wrong decision: Perez hit a paltry .188/.246/.365 with 50 games with Tri-City in the New York-Penn League. But something seemed to click for the 6-foot-2, 198-pound third baseman as he jetted through Low-A, High-A, and handled Double-A with aplomb. When the dust finally settled Perez compiled an aggregate .291/.354/.495 triple-slash line, belting out 34 doubles and 18 homeruns. Per *Weighted Runs Created Plus*, his production topped the league average mark by 25%.

Scouting Report: With regard to Perez's showing in AA, his longest stint last season, consider the following:

- Since 2006, only three 21-year-old hitters met the following criteria in a Double-A season with one organization (min. 300 PA): 95 to 105 wRC+ and a strikeout rate between 25% and 28%. Those three hitters: Wladimir Balentien, Trey Michalczewski, and Joe Perez.

Obviously, it's less-than-stellar production comps. So let's dive down into Perez's tour through the minors' toughest challenge. Perez's tenure with Corpus Christi began, perhaps predictably so, on a low note: he hit a paltry .137/.211/.216 through his first 14 contests. But after the adjustment period Perez slugged .296/.348/.465 with 18 doubles and seven homeruns over his next 55 games. His overall production topped the league average mark by 17%. I'm a believer in the bat. In terms of ceiling, think along the lines: .270/.340/.470.

Ceiling: 3.0-win player
Risk: Moderate
MLB ETA: 2022

3. Hunter Brown, RHP

	FB	CB	SL	CH	Command	Overall
	60	65	60	N/A	45	55

Born: 08/29/98	Age: 23	Bats: R	Top Comp: Dylan Cease
Height: 6-2	Weight: 212	Throws: R	

Season	Team	Age	Level	IP	TBF	K/9	K%	BB/9	BB%	K-BB%	ERA	FIP	xFIP	Pit/Bat
2019	HOU	20	A-	23.2	102	12.55	32.35%	6.85	17.65%	14.71%	4.56	2.89	3.28	4.19
2021	HOU	22	AA	49.1	217	13.86	35.02%	5.29	13.36%	21.66%	4.20	3.86	3.33	4.24
2021	HOU	22	AAA	51.0	216	9.71	25.46%	3.71	9.72%	15.74%	3.88	4.60	4.59	3.86

Background: Thanks to a later birthday the hard-throwing right-hander was able to get in three full seasons of college ball – despite entering the draft as a 20-year-old. After a pair of mediocre campaigns at Wayne State, Brown blossomed into a bonafide ace during his junior year with the Great Lakes Intercollegiate Athletic Conference school. The 6-foot-2, 212-pound right-hander averaged 12.0 strikeouts and 4.0 free passes every nine innings. Houston drafted the hard-throwing hurler in the fifth round three years ago, 166th overall, and signed him to a deal worth $325,000. After debuting in the New York-Penn League in 2019, the organization aggressively challenged Brown and sent him to Double-A. And after 13 appearances with Corpus Christi, Brown earned a promotion up to AAA. He made 24 appearances, 19 of which were starts, fanning 131 and walking 50. He finished the year with a 4.04 ERA.

Scouting Report: Consider the following:

- Since 2006, five 22-year-old hurlers met the following criteria in a AAA season with one organization (min. 50 IP): 24.5% and 26.5% strikeout percentage with a walk percentage between 8% and 11%. Those five pitchers: Wade Davis, Griffin Canning, Logan Allen, Dana Eveland, and Hunter Brown.

Brown not only owns the best arsenal in the Houston system, but he's among the most lethal hurlers in all of minor league baseball. The former Division II hurler sports a mid-90s heater, a filthy yacker of a curveball, and a wipeout slider. All three offerings are plus with the curveball flashing plus-plus. He reportedly throws a below-average changeup, though I didn't see it. There's obvious reliever risk given his propensity for handing out walks. Boom-bust. Reliever or Front half of a rotation caliber starting pitcher.

Ceiling: 3.0-win player
Risk: Moderate to High
MLB ETA: 2022

4. Pedro Leon, SS/CF

	Hit	Power	SB	Patience	Glove	Overall
	50	55	60	55	50	55

Born: 05/28/98	Age: 24	Bats: R	Top Comp: Tommy Pham
Height: 5-10	Weight: 170	Throws: R	

Season	Team	Age	Level	PA	1B	2B	3B	HR	SB	CS	BB%	K%	AVG	OBP	SLG	ISO
2021	HOU	23	AA	217	29	7	1	9	13	8	11.52%	30.88%	0.249	0.359	0.443	0.195
2021	HOU	23	AAA	75	6	2	0	0	4	2	18.67%	30.67%	0.131	0.293	0.164	0.033

Background: Signed out of La Habana, Cuba, for $4 million last January. Leon first popped up on big league radars as a 19-year-old when he debuted in the Cuban National Series, hitting .333/.365/.556 for the Huracanes de Mayabeque. And he followed that up with an even better showing the next year in Cuba's premier professional league: he slugged .383/.467/.789 with seven doubles and 15 homeruns. And Houston didn't have any qualms about challenging their high priced import during his first season stateside either. In 52 games with the Corpus Christi Hooks, Houston's Double-A affiliate, Leon batted a respectable .249/.359/.443 with seven doubles, one triple, and nine homeruns. He also appeared in 17 mostly forgettable games in AAA as well.

Scouting Report: I'll be accused – I'm sure – of manipulating the data to fit a narrative, but I'll explain my argument in a minute. Let's break down Leon's season into three separate parts:

- Part I: In 13 games he bats .128/.226/.277
- Part II: In 44 games he hits .285/.402/.481
- Part III: In 12 games he hits .073/.240/.073

Part II is, by far, the most reliable baseline. Now let me explain:

- Part I: Adjustment period. Leon hadn't played official baseball in two years and Houston shoved the 23-year-old straight into the minors' toughest challenge, the make-it-or-break-it level (Double-A).
- Part II: Post-adjustment period, which is pretty self explanatory.
- Part III: Return from DL. Leon spent six weeks on the disabled list, the result of a fractured pinky.

His production during Part II, per *Weighted Runs Created Plus*, topped the league average mark by 38%. If you're into speculating on prospect baseball cards, here's one I'd be buying.

Ceiling: 2.5-win player
Risk: Moderate
MLB ETA: 2022

5. Korey Lee, C				Hit	Power	SB	Patience	Glove	Overall
				50	45	35	50	50	50

| Born: 07/25/98 | | | Age: 23 | | | Bats: R | | Top Comp: Wilson Ramos | |
| Height: 6-2 | | | Weight: 210 | | | Throws: R | | | |

Season	Team	Age	Level	PA	1B	2B	3B	HR	SB	CS	BB%	K%	AVG	OBP	SLG	ISO
2019	HOU	20	A-	259	47	6	4	3	8	5	10.81%	18.92%	0.268	0.359	0.371	0.103
2021	HOU	22	A+	121	28	5	0	3	1	0	9.92%	19.83%	0.330	0.397	0.459	0.128
2021	HOU	22	AA	203	29	9	1	8	3	1	8.37%	17.24%	0.254	0.320	0.443	0.189
2021	HOU	22	AAA	38	4	4	0	0	0	0	5.26%	23.68%	0.229	0.263	0.343	0.114

Background: Not much of an offensive threat during his first two seasons at University of California, Berkley, Lee burst onto the scene during his junior campaign: he slugged a healthy .337/.416/.619 for the Pac 12 conference school, belting out 12 doubles and 15 homeruns. Houston selected the surging backstop in the opening round, 32nd overall, in 2019 and signed him to a deal worth $1.75 million. Lee made stops at three separate levels during his 2021 season, going from High-A to Double-A and capped it off with a nine-game stint in AAA. In total, the 6-foot-2, 210-pound catcher batted a solid .277/.340/.438 with 18 doubles, one triple, and 11 homeruns. He also swiped four bags in five attempts. His overall production, per *Weighted Runs Created Plus*, topped the league average mark by 6%.

Snippet from The 2020 Prospect Digest Handbook: Lee doesn't own a true standout skill. He's similar to former University of California backstop – and 2016 second rounder – Brett Cumberland, though with less patience at the plate. Lee looks like a solid backup, perhaps peaking as a low-end starting option for a non-contending team.

Scouting Report: Average hit tool, 15-homer thump, and a solid approach at the plate. The bar for catcher production is fairly low at the big league level, so Lee's still tracking as a potential starting option within the next year or two. Consider the following:

- Since 2006, seven 22-year-old hitters met the following criteria in a Double-A season with one organization (min. 200 PA): Austin Romine, Ali Sanchez, David Winfree, Jake Cave, Engelb Vielma, Nathan Lukes, and Korey Lee.

Ceiling: 1.5- to 2.0-win player
Risk: Moderate
MLB ETA: 2022

6. Jaime Melendez, RHP

	FB	CB	SL	CH	Command	Overall
	55	55	50	50	45/55	45

Born: 09/26/01	Age: 20	Bats: L	Top Comp: Tim Collins
Height: 5-8	Weight: 190	Throws: R	

Season	Team	Age	Level	IP	TBF	K/9	K%	BB/9	BB%	K-BB%	ERA	FIP	xFIP	Pit/Bat
2019	HOU	17	R	28.1	118	12.39	33.05%	5.08	13.56%	19.49%	2.86	2.79	3.05	2.16
2021	HOU	19	A	18.1	68	18.65	55.88%	2.45	7.35%	48.53%	0.49	1.36	1.31	4.62
2021	HOU	19	A+	32.0	155	11.53	26.45%	6.75	15.48%	10.97%	4.78	4.45	5.48	3.64

Background: The franchise handed the diminutive right-hander a fairly sizeable bonus, just under $200,000, three years ago. And it looked like a questionable signing at the time. Melendez stood just 5-foot-8 and looked to be physically maxed out. And then he stepped on the mound. Melendez posted a 39-to-16 strikeout-to-walk ratio in 28.1 innings of work in the Dominican Summer League in 2019. And the front office decided to aggressively challenge the teenage right-hander last season, assigning him directly to Low-A. That lasted all of six appearances – in which he posted a 0.49 ERA – before getting bumped up to High-A and then eventually up to Double-A. By season's end Melendez, the new Mighty Mouse, averaged 14.0 strikeouts and 5.1 walks per nine innings. He tallied 11 starts, nine relief appearances, and 58.0 innings of work.

Scouting Report: Per *Baseball Reference's Stathead*, there are 123 instances in which a pitcher 5-foot-8 or less tossed at least 150 innings. The last do it: Fred Norman, all the way back in 1972. And before him: Vic Lombardi, in 1946. Both of those guys, for what it's worth, were southpaws. So, needless to say, Melendez has some pretty long shot odds to become a big league starting pitcher – though that's not for a lack of talent. Fastball peaks at 94 mph. Above-average curveball. Average slider. And an average changeup that's a bit too firm for my liking. Melendez shows a lot of confidence in his entire repertoire and he changes speeds well. He's a potential multi-inning relief arm or an opener, if Houston decides to employ that strategy. I really like him, though.

Ceiling: 1.5-win player
Risk: Moderate
MLB ETA: 2023

7. Diosmerky Taveras, RHP

	FB	CB	SL	CH	Command	Overall
	65	N/A	45/55	N/A	40	45

Born: 09/23/99	Age: 22	Bats: R	Top Comp: Dellin Betances
Height: 6-3	Weight: 248	Throws: R	

Season	Team	Age	Level	IP	TBF	K/9	K%	BB/9	BB%	K-BB%	ERA	FIP	xFIP	Pit/Bat
2018	HOU	18	R	37.0	166	8.51	21.08%	6.57	16.27%	4.82%	4.14	4.20	4.48	2.03
2019	HOU	19	R	24.2	122	10.22	22.95%	10.22	22.95%	0.00%	5.47	5.37	5.66	2.20
2021	HOU	21	A	60.2	276	10.68	26.09%	6.38	15.58%	10.51%	5.19	4.44	4.80	4.18
2021	HOU	21	A+	17.2	68	11.72	33.82%	3.06	8.82%	25.00%	1.53	3.65	3.85	4.16

Background: The news barely registered a blip in the press release. Major League Baseball announced the Astros had signed 26 international free agents on July 3, 2017, highlighted by Brazilians Heitor Tokar and Victor Coutinho, and Dominican Jose Betances. And listed at the bottom of the article, almost as if he's a footnote, was the announcement of Diosmerky Taveras' signing, for $55,000 out of the Dominican Republic. Last year Taveras, a broad-shouldered hurler who's built more like a linebacker, moved into full season action for the first time. He made 17 appearances with Fayetteville before moving up to Asheville for another four appearances. The 6-foot-3, 248-pound righty tossed 78.1 innings, recording a whopping 95 punch outs and racking up 49 free passes. He compiled an aggregate 4.37 ERA.

Scouting Report: One of the more fascinating hurlers to watch in the minor leagues. Taveras uncorks a plus to plus-plus heater – which, admittedly, a lot of guys do nowadays. But it's the way he delivers the ball that makes him fascinating. It's an extreme, funky short-arm action. One of the minor league announcers likened it to shot-putting the ball towards home plate. He throws two separate breaking balls: a curveball, which he was reluctant to throw, and a power slider that flashed above-average, maybe even better. The slider is inconsistent, raw, but it's going to become a swing-and-miss pitch with some further fine-tuning. He also throws a changeup, but he consistently shook off that pitch as well. He's heading into a full time relief role. But there's a high ceiling here as a late-inning fireman.

Ceiling: 1.0- to 1.5-win player
Risk: Moderate
MLB ETA: 2023/2024

8. Forrest Whitley, RHP

	FB	CB	SL	CU	CH	Control	Overall
	N/A	N/A	N/A	N/A	N/A	N/A	45

Born: 09/15/97	Age: 24	Bats: R	Top Comp: N/A
Height: 6-7	Weight: 238	Throws: R	

Season	Team	Age	Level	IP	TBF	K/9	K%	BB/9	BB%	K-BB%	ERA	FIP	xFIP	Pit/Bat
2018	HOU	20	AA	26.1	108	11.62	31.48%	3.76	10.19%	21.30%	3.76	3.34	3.71	4.31
2019	HOU	21	AA	22.2	103	14.29	34.95%	7.54	18.45%	16.50%	5.56	4.33	3.93	4.51
2019	HOU	21	AAA	24.1	119	10.73	24.37%	5.55	12.61%	11.76%	12.21	8.07	5.57	4.14

Background: What's the baseball equivalent of the old adage, "Always a bridesmaid, never a bride"? For Forrest Whitley it has to be something like, "Always a Top Prospect, never a Big Leaguer." It goes without saying that Whitley, the 17th overall pick in the 2016 draft, has had a rough go over it for the past several years. He dealt with an oblique and lat issue in 2018. That was followed up with right shoulder woes in 2019. And then his elbow flared up during the COVID 2020 season. Finally, he missed all of last year – wait for it – recovering from Tommy John surgery. He last toed the mound in a meaningful game on September 2, 2019.

Snippet from The 2020 Prospect Digest Handbook: The control, repertoire, and build – he's 6-foot-7 and 195-pounds – all suggest elite pitcher, but it's concerning that he's been as limited as he has been in terms of workload.

Scouting Report: Once upon a time Whitley looked like the steal of the 2016 draft. A bevy of plus pitches, solid command, a massive frame – it's literally the mold every pitcher should be cut from. At this point, though, anything the club gets out their former top prospect would be surprising. Here's hoping for a healthy return to action in 2022.

Ceiling: 1.5-win player
Risk: High
MLB ETA: 2022 /2023

9. Peter Solomon, RHP

	FB	CB	SL	CU	CH	Control	Overall
	50	55	55	55	50	45	40

Born: 08/16/96	Age: 25	Bats: R	Top Comp: Kendall Graveman
Height: 6-4	Weight: 211	Throws: R	

Season	Team	Age	Level	IP	TBF	K/9	K%	BB/9	BB%	K-BB%	ERA	FIP	xFIP	Pit/Bat
2018	HOU	21	A	77.2	317	10.20	27.76%	3.24	8.83%	18.93%	2.43	2.63	3.19	3.55
2018	HOU	21	A+	23.0	86	10.17	30.23%	1.57	4.65%	25.58%	1.96	1.62	2.26	3.91
2021	HOU	24	AAA	97.2	426	10.32	26.29%	3.87	9.86%	16.43%	4.70	5.12	5.23	3.96

Background: Just another example of the organization's ability to churn out pitching prospects. Solomon, a fourth round pick out of Notre Dame in 2017, was a little-used spot starter during his junior campaign. And one who had a history of spotty command. And just a year after entering the organization Solomon developed into one of the club's better performing minor league arms, averaging 10.2 strikeouts and 2.9 walks per nine innings in 24 appearances between Low-A and High-A. Solomon missed all of 2019 recovering from Tommy John surgery and, of course, had to sit out the 2020 COVID year as well. Last season, his first game action since June 28, 2019, Solomon tossed 97.2 innings with Sugar Land, posting a 112-to-42 strikeout-to-walk ratio. He also tossed an additional 14.0 innings with the Astros, fanning 10 and walking 8.

Scouting Report: It's all about the breaking ball for Solomon – all three of them. And they're all above-average. The 6-foot-4 right-hander relies primarily on a slider / cutter combination, particularly as his out pitches. He loves locating the cutter in on left-handed hitters' hands. And he spots the slider low-and-away to right-handers. Beyond that, his fastball sits in the low 90s, peaking a tick or two higher, and a low 80s changeup. Solomon's likely not going to get a ton of opportunities in the Astros' rotation because (A) they're trying to extend their closing window of contention and (B) it's simply a numbers game. There's some Kendall Graveman-type relief potential here.

Ceiling: 1.0-win player
Risk: Low to Moderate
MLB ETA: Debuted in 2020

10. Alex Santos II, RHP

	FB	CB	SL/CU	CH	Command	Overall
	50/55	50	50/55	N/A	40/45	40

Born: 02/10/02	Age: 20	Bats: R	Top Comp: Jordan Balazovic
Height: 6-4	Weight: 194	Throws: R	

Season	Team	Age	Level	IP	TBF	K/9	K%	BB/9	BB%	K-BB%	ERA	FIP	xFIP	Pit/Bat
2021	HOU	19	A	41.2	183	10.37	26.23%	6.48	16.39%	9.84%	3.46	4.53	5.50	4.09

Background: Surprisingly enough Mount St. Michael High, located in the Bronx, has produced a number of draft picks – seven, to be exact. None of the previous six, though, ever sniffed the big leagues during their professional career. Houston selected the 6-foot-4, 194-pound New Yorker in the second round, 72nd overall, two years ago and signed him to a deal worth $1.25 million. The young right-hander made 12 appearances, seven of which were starts, with the organization's Low-A affiliate; he struck out 48 and walked 30 in 41.2 innings of work. He compiled a 3.46 ERA, a 4.53 FIP, and a 5.50 xFIP.

Scouting Report: Consider the following:

- Since 2006, only three 19-year-old hurlers met the following criteria in a season in Low-A with one organization (min. 40 IP): a strikeout percentage between 25% and 27% with a walk percentage of at least 14%. Those three hurlers: Archie Bradley, Adys Portillo, and – of course – Alex Santos II.

It's pretty incredible that Santos was handing out walks like they were going out of style and, yet, somehow he finished the year with a 3.89 ERA. A low 90s fastball, a slurvy-type curveball, and a slider/cutter that projects to above-average. While the young pitcher is quite raw – which is to be expected coming from a cold-weather state – there's a silver lining to his command-deficient debut: Santos has back-to-back starts in early July where he walked 11 hitters in 5.1 innings of work. Ignoring those two disastrous outings, his walk rate declines from 6.5 BB/9 to 4.71 BB/9. As an organization Houston develops breaking balls as well as any. Santos is certainly a name to watch in the coming years.

Ceiling: 1.0-win player
Risk: Moderate
MLB ETA: 2025

11. Yainer Diaz, C/1B

Hit	Power	SB	Patience	Glove	Overall
50	45	30	45	50	40

Born: 09/21/98	Age: 23	Bats: R	Top Comp: N/A
Height: 6-0	Weight: 195	Throws: R	

Season	Team	Age	Level	PA	1B	2B	3B	HR	SB	CS	BB%	K%	AVG	OBP	SLG	ISO
2018	CLE	19	R	164	40	9	4	2	1	0	4.27%	10.98%	0.355	0.387	0.503	0.148
2019	CLE	20	R	88	26	6	0	5	0	0	4.55%	9.09%	0.451	0.477	0.707	0.256
2019	CLE	20	A-	140	27	6	2	2	0	0	2.86%	15.71%	0.274	0.293	0.393	0.119
2021	CLE	22	A	258	50	19	1	5	1	1	5.81%	16.28%	0.314	0.357	0.464	0.151
2021	HOU	22	A	49	8	2	0	1	1	0	0.00%	8.16%	0.229	0.224	0.333	0.104
2021	HOU	22	A+	105	23	4	0	11	2	0	7.62%	16.19%	0.396	0.438	0.781	0.385

Background: Two of the more analytically savvy organizations got together for a good ole' fashioned challenge trade. Houston agreed to send speedy but power deficient center fielder Myles Straw to Cleveland in exchange for the Spin Doctor Phil Maton and Yainer Diaz. A 6-foot-1, 195-pound backstop who will moonlight at a first baseman, Diaz has hit at every stop along his minor league journey. He batted .294/.321/.379 as an 18-year-old in the Dominican Summer League, followed that up with a scorching .355/.387/.503 showing a year later in the stateside rookie league, and punished the lower minor leagues with a .341/.364/.512 triple-slash line in 2019. Last year, believe it or not, was the first time Diaz squared off against full-season competition – and he continued to mash. Splitting time between Low-A and High-A, the Dominican-born backstop slugged .324/.362/.527 with 25 doubles, one triple, and 17 homeruns.

Scouting Report: He doesn't walk all that often, but he doesn't strikeout all that often either. Solid average power. He shows a knack for squaring the ball up. And he controls the opposition's running game relatively well too. The problem, of course, is his lack of experience against meaningful competition. He's been in professional baseball since 2017 and finally appeared in full season action in 2021, as a 22-year-old. He also puts the ball on the ground far too frequently as well.

Ceiling: 1.0-win player
Risk: Moderate
MLB ETA: 2023

12. Tyler Whitaker, 3B/CF

Hit	Power	SB	Patience	Glove	Overall
40/45	40/50	50	50	50	40

Born: 08/02/02	Age: 19	Bats: R	Top Comp: N/A
Height: 6-4	Weight: 190	Throws: R	

Season	Team	Age	Level	PA	1B	2B	3B	HR	SB	CS	BB%	K%	AVG	OBP	SLG	ISO
2021	HOU	18	CPX	114	15	2	1	3	8	1	7.89%	35.09%	0.202	0.263	0.327	0.125

Background: The Astros play the draft game as well as any organization in baseball. And despite forfeiting their top two selections in 2021 (as well as 2020), the organization came away with a first round talent. Prior to the draft MLB.com had Whitaker as the 37th best prospect. Houston selected the Las Vegas prepster with 87th overall pick and signed him to a deal worth $1.5 million – tied for the second largest bonus given in the round last July. The toolsy 6-foot-4, 190-pound outfielder turned in a disappointing debut in the Florida Complex League, hitting a scant .202/.263/.327 with just six extra-base knocks in 29 games. Per *Weighted Runs Created Plus*, his overall production was a whopping 42% *below* the league average.

Scouting Report: He just looks like a ballplayer. The stance, the build. You name it. He just looks like a damn ballplayer. But based on video, it looks like he has issues with his weight transfer. Short, quick swing with easy bat speed. Whitaker's aggressive approach, however, was exploited during his brief debut in the rookie league. Houston has a propensity to develop hitters, so we'll see how they can improve Whitaker in the coming years.

Ceiling: 1.0-win player
Risk: Moderate
MLB ETA: 2025

	FB	CB	SL	CH	Command	Overall
13. Misael Tamarez, RHP	55/60	50	55	45	45	40

Born: 01/16/00	Age: 22	Bats: R	Top Comp: N/A
Height: 6-1	Weight: 206	Throws: R	

Season	Team	Age	Level	IP	TBF	K/9	K%	BB/9	BB%	K-BB%	ERA	FIP	xFIP	Pit/Bat
2019	HOU	19	R	23.1	105	10.03	24.76%	5.01	12.38%	12.38%	2.70	3.46	3.94	1.99
2019	HOU	19	R	15.1	74	10.57	24.32%	6.46	14.86%	9.46%	2.35	4.55	4.42	1.99
2021	HOU	21	A	43.0	188	13.40	34.04%	5.86	14.89%	19.15%	3.98	4.14	4.33	4.18
2021	HOU	21	A+	33.2	137	10.43	28.47%	2.67	7.30%	21.17%	3.48	3.88	4.91	3.92

Background: Another one of the club's under-the-radar free agents off the international scene. Houston signed the wiry right-hander out of San Pedro de Macoris, Dominican Republic, for only $15,000. The 6-foot-1, 206-pound right-hander made his professional debut between the foreign and stateside rookie leagues three years ago, posting a 44-to-24 strikeout-to-walk ratio in 38.2 total innings. Last season, now that baseball returned from its COVID absence, Tamarez – once again – split time between two separate levels: he made 12 appearances in Low-A and another seven appearances in High-A. The young Dominican averaged 12.1 strikeouts and 4.5 walks per nine innings to go along with an aggregate 3.76 ERA.

Scouting Report: Wiry but with a thick lower half. Tamarez has the look of a big league pitcher. He shows an above-average fastball, which ranges from 91- to 94-mph and I expect it'll get another uptick as he continues to develop in the Astros' system. The young hurler mixes in two breaking balls – an average curveball and an above-average slider, though it's inconsistent – and a below-average changeup. Tamarez needs to develop a consistent third option otherwise he's going to get pushed into a relief role.

Ceiling: 1.0-win player
Risk: Moderate
MLB ETA: 2024

	Hit	Power	SB	Patience	Glove	Overall
14. Colin Barber, OF	40/45	40/45	35	55	50	40

Born: 12/04/00	Age: 21	Bats: L	Top Comp: Preston Tucker
Height: 6-0	Weight: 194	Throws: L	

Season	Team	Age	Level	PA	1B	2B	3B	HR	SB	CS	BB%	K%	AVG	OBP	SLG	ISO
2019	HOU	18	R	119	18	5	1	2	2	1	15.97%	24.37%	0.263	0.387	0.394	0.131
2021	HOU	20	A+	53	5	1	0	3	1	1	16.98%	41.51%	0.214	0.365	0.452	0.238

Background: They certainly weren't the first club to do so, but they seem to be the one to popularize spending significant portions of their draft budget outside of the first round. Take for example Colin Barber, an outfielder out of Pleasant Valley High School. The Astros selected the 6-foot, 194-pound prospect in the fourth round, 136th overall, and handed him the only seven-figure bonus among all players chosen in that round that year. The California-native had a solid debut in the Gulf Coast League, hitting a respectable .263/.387/.394 with five doubles, one triple, and two homeruns. And last season the organization shoved him straight into High-A East to start the year. But he hit the disabled list just 16 games into the season, courtesy of a wonky shoulder that required surgery. He finished his injury-shortened campaign with an Asheville-inflated .214/.365/.452 triple-slash line.

Scouting Report: It's tough to get a read on Barber – at least from a statistical standpoint. His affiliated career is comprised of a total of 44 games across two seasons, three years, and wildly separate levels of competition. He swings-and-misses a lot, like *A Lot, A Lot*. Among those 16 games last season he struck out at least once 12 times. And he K'd multiple times in seven games. And he failed to knock an extra-base hit away from Asheville's bandbox – again, small sample size. The swing is short, compact, and quick, but it doesn't lend itself to a ton of over-the-fence thump. He's likely going to return to High-A following his recovery from should surgery in 2022.

Ceiling: 1.0-win player
Risk: Moderate
MLB ETA: 2024/2025

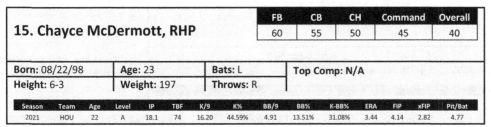

	FB	CB	CH	Command	Overall
15. Chayce McDermott, RHP	60	55	50	45	40

Born: 08/22/98	Age: 23	Bats: L	Top Comp: N/A
Height: 6-3	Weight: 197	Throws: R	

Season	Team	Age	Level	IP	TBF	K/9	K%	BB/9	BB%	K-BB%	ERA	FIP	xFIP	Pit/Bat
2021	HOU	22	A	18.1	74	16.20	44.59%	4.91	13.51%	31.08%	3.44	4.14	2.82	4.77

Background: Ball State's history is littered with high round draft selections: the Mid-American Conference university has produced eight first round selections, including 2002 #1 overall pick Bryan Bullington; a pair of second round draft choices; two thirds and three fourths as well. But despite all the notable picks, the four best players to come out of the college are Zach Plesac, Larry Bigbie, Thomas Howard, and Jeremy Hazelbaker. Last year the Astros grabbed hard-throwing 22-year-old right-hander Chayce McDermott in the fourth round, 132ⁿᵈ overall, and signed him to a deal worth $372,500 – the eleventh highest bonus given to a player in school history. McDermott put together a dominating final campaign for the Division I school, averaging 13.6 strikeouts and 3.9 walks per nine innings to go along with a 3.05 ERA. After signing with the club, he made seven brief appearances, fanning 40 and walking 11 in only 21.2 innings of work.

Scouting Report: Consider the following:

- Between 2011 and 2020, only two MAC hurlers have averaged at least 13 strikeouts per nine innings in a season (min. 75 IP): Joey Murray (twice), and former first rounder Drey Jameson, who also went to Ball State.
- Now here's the list of all Division I hurlers to average more than 13 strikeouts and between 3.5 and 4.5 walks per nine innings in a season (min. 75 IP): Joey Murray (twice), Zac Lowther, Jake Lee, Asa, and Asa Lacy.

Obviously, McDermott's production from last year puts him in the same company. Explosive mid-90s, plus fastball that sits 94- to 96-mph. An above-average, late-tilting power curveball, and a fringy-average changeup. There's some reliever risk here given his age and lack of a quality third option. There's the potential he spends a good portion of 2022 in Double-A

Ceiling: 1.0-win player
Risk: Moderate
MLB ETA: 2023/2024

	FB	CB	SL/CU	CH	Command	Overall
16. Tyler Ivey, RHP	50	50	50	50	50	40

Born: 05/12/96	Age: 26	Bats: R	Top Comp: Jordan Lyles
Height: 6-4	Weight: 195	Throws: R	

Season	Team	Age	Level	IP	TBF	K/9	K%	BB/9	BB%	K-BB%	ERA	FIP	xFIP	Pit/Bat
2018	HOU	22	A	41.2	171	11.45	30.99%	1.73	4.68%	26.32%	3.46	2.14	2.40	3.47
2018	HOU	22	A+	70.1	284	10.49	28.87%	2.69	7.39%	21.48%	2.69	2.56	2.86	4.02
2019	HOU	23	AA	46.0	184	11.93	33.15%	3.13	8.70%	24.46%	1.57	3.32	3.04	4.27
2021	HOU	25	AAA	11.0	54	10.64	24.07%	6.55	14.81%	9.26%	4.91	6.11	5.86	4.09

Background: A third round pick out of Grayson College by way of Texas A&M. Houston drafted the 6-foot-4, 195-pound crafty right-hander five years ago and immediately placed him on an accelerated path to the big leagues. He's spent time at multiple levels in each season. Last year the Texas-born hurler was limited to fewer than 20.0 innings – though 4.2 of them came with the Astros during his debut – courtesy of a nerve issue in his right elbow. He posted a 13-to-8 strikeout-to-walk ratio in 11.0 innings with Sugar Land. And coughed up four runs, struck out three, and issued one walk in 4.2 big league innings. For his minor league career, Ivey owns a 3.13 ERA, averaging an impressive 11.0 strikeouts and just 3.0 walks per nine innings across four seasons.

Snippet from The 2020 Prospect Digest Handbook: Ivey's the safest of backend minor league starting options due to a lengthier track record, arsenal, and feel for the strike zone. Good #4.

Scouting Report: Still nothing to report. Nerve issue notwithstanding, Ivey still has the look and feel of a capable backend starting pitcher, though he's going to be pressed to be a valuable member of a contending rotation. His repertoire: 90-mph fastball, low-70s curveball, 80-mph slider, and a 82-mph changeup. Ivey has a long history of solid-average command, but last season he really struggled throwing strikes, let along quality strikes – though the nerve issue likely contributed.

Ceiling: 1.5-win player

Risk: Extremely High
MLB ETA: 2024

17. Jairo Solis, RHP

	FB	CB	SL/CU	CH	Command	Overall
	50/55	50	50/55	N/A	40/45	45

Born: 12/22/99	Age: 22	Bats: R	Top Comp: N/A
Height: 6-2	Weight: 205	Throws: R	

Season	Team	Age	Level	IP	TBF	K/9	K%	BB/9	BB%	K-BB%	ERA	FIP	xFIP	Pit/Bat
2018	HOU	18	A	50.2	225	9.06	22.67%	5.68	14.22%	8.44%	3.55	3.74	4.24	4.02

Background: Queue the *Star Wars* theme song. Once upon a time – in a not so distant past – Solis had, perhaps, the highest ceiling among all the arms in the vaunted Houston Astros farm system. Well-built, wiry, projectable, and holding his own as an 18-year-old in the old Midwest League. He struck out 51 and walked 32 in 50.2 innings of work. Then the injuries hit. And they hit *hard*. Over. And over. And over. He missed the latter portion of 2018 and all of 2019 recovering from Tommy John surgery. COVID, of course, wrecked the 2020 minor league season – though, according to Eric Longenhagen, of *FanGraphs* fame, he popped up in the instructional leagues. And, if reports are correct, Solis had loose bodies removed from his right elbow in April last year. Then two months later underwent his second Tommy John surgery. Solis last toed the rubber in an actual game on August 6, 2018.

Snippet from The 2020 Prospect Digest Handbook: Obviously, there's nothing to report on. Here's hoping for a full return to health for the promising right-hander. He did battle some control/command issues in 2018, and typically a pitcher's feel for the strike zone takes a hit coming back from Tommy John surgery. Just something to watch for in 2020.

Scouting Report: Still nothing to report. I don't have the data on success rates of a second Tommy John, but my gut feeling is that Solis' career is likely done – unfortunately. Hopefully, I'm wrong. Fingers crossed for Solis.

Ceiling: 1.5-win player
Risk: Extremely High
MLB ETA: 2024

18. Shay Whitcomb, IF

	Hit	Power	SB	Patience	Glove	Overall
	50	45	60	50	45	40

Born: 09/28/98	Age: 23	Bats: R	Top Comp: Elliot Johnson
Height: 6-3	Weight: 202	Throws: R	

Season	Team	Age	Level	PA	1B	2B	3B	HR	SB	CS	BB%	K%	AVG	OBP	SLG	ISO
2021	HOU	22	A	187	36	3	0	7	14	2	10.70%	28.34%	0.282	0.369	0.429	0.147
2021	HOU	22	A+	257	32	22	0	16	16	3	7.39%	31.52%	0.300	0.358	0.601	0.300

Background: Regardless of your personal feelings on the matter, the Astros' farm system was dealt a *massive* blow when they lost their 2020 and 2021 first and second round picks. But they've put together some astute draft classes – in spite of their hands being tied. Case in point: Shay Whitcomb, a fifth round pick out of UC San Diego two years ago. And, perhaps, one of Whitcomb's biggest selling points: he signed for a paltry – or less than paltry, in baseball draft terms – sum of $56,000. To put that into proper perspective: 26 of the 29 players taken in the fifth round that year received at least $97,000 and four earned deals worth at least $800,000. Last season, Whitcomb's first in professional ball, he split time between Fayetteville and Asheville, hitting an aggregate .293/.363/.530 with 25 doubles, 23 homeruns, and 30 stolen bases. Per *Weighted Runs Created Plus*, his overall production topped the league average mark by 37%.

Scouting Report: To put Whitcomb's season into perspective, his 137 wRC+ total was the best total among all qualified hitters in the Astros' farm system. Now, some of that offensive thump is the result of playing half of his High-A games at Asheville's bandbox. He swings-and-misses *way too frequently*, so the .293 batting average is going to come crashing down as he moves up the ladder. Houston has bounced him around the infield, prepping him for a utility role.

Ceiling: 0.5- to 1.0-win player
Risk: Moderate
MLB ETA: 2023

19. Enmanuel Valdez, IF

Hit	Power	SB	Patience	Glove	Overall
45	45	45	45	50	40

Born: 12/28/98	Age: 23	Bats: L	Top Comp:
Height: 5-9	Weight: 191	Throws: R	

Season	Team	Age	Level	PA	1B	2B	3B	HR	SB	CS	BB%	K%	AVG	OBP	SLG	ISO
2018	HOU	19	A-	264	33	16	1	8	11	6	8.33%	20.08%	0.244	0.311	0.420	0.176
2019	HOU	20	A	139	19	11	0	3	2	3	11.51%	15.11%	0.275	0.374	0.442	0.167
2019	HOU	20	A+	247	32	11	1	5	6	2	5.67%	24.70%	0.215	0.264	0.338	0.123
2021	HOU	22	A+	318	34	16	1	21	5	1	7.86%	21.07%	0.254	0.313	0.541	0.286
2021	HOU	22	AA	98	10	6	0	5	0	1	13.27%	22.45%	0.256	0.367	0.512	0.256

Background: Coming off of his sixth year – and fifth professional season – in the Houston organization. The power-packed, pint-sized infielder had his finest showing to date – by a massively wide margin. Taking full advantage of the Ashville Tourists' home ballpark, the 5-foot-9, 191-pound lefty-swinging infielder slugged a hearty .254/.313/.541 with 16 doubles, one triple, and 21 homeruns in only 75 games. He continued to batter the competition following his late-season promotion up to Double-A as well, batting .256/.367/.512 with 11 extra-base hits in only 23 games. In total, Valdez hit .255/.326/.534 with 22 doubles, one triple, 26 homeruns, and five stolen bases. Per *Weighted Runs Created Plus*, his overall production topped the league average threshold by 22%.

Scouting Report: Consider the following:

- Since 2006, only four 22-year-old players met the following criteria in a High-A season with one organization (min. 300 PA): 115 to 125 wRC+, 7% to 9% walk rate, 20% and 22% strikeout rate. Those four hitters: Jared Oliva, Chad Tracy, Ryan Jeffers, and Enmanuel Valdez.

The good news: Tracy spent parts of nine years in the big leagues; Jeffers, a former second round pick, has two seasons with the Twins on his resume; and Oliva has had two brief cups of coffee with the Pirates the past two years. The bad news: Valdez, as one would expect, feasted off of Ashville's hitter-friendly confines (.278/.320/.627) and struggled massively on the road (.224/.306/.432). He's typically struggled against southpaws (though that wasn't the case last season). Low end utility guy. Unless he proves that he can hit outside of Asheville for extended periods of time.

Ceiling: 0.5- to 1.0-win player
Risk: Moderate
MLB ETA: 2023

20. Angel Macuare, RHP

FB	CB	SL	CH	Command	Overall
45/50	50	50	50	45	35

Born: 03/03/00	Age: 22	Bats: R	Top Comp: N/A
Height: 6-2	Weight: 250	Throws: R	

Season	Team	Age	Level	IP	TBF	K/9	K%	BB/9	BB%	K-BB%	ERA	FIP	xFIP	Pit/Bat
2018	HOU	18	R	39.1	181	9.15	22.10%	3.89	9.39%	12.71%	3.43	3.81	3.73	1.62
2019	HOU	19	A-	30.2	138	9.98	24.64%	6.46	15.94%	8.70%	5.87	3.96	4.17	3.98
2021	HOU	21	A	15.2	61	13.79	39.34%	2.87	8.20%	31.15%	1.15	2.70	2.73	4.00
2021	HOU	21	A+	25.1	122	11.37	26.23%	4.62	10.66%	15.57%	9.95	5.98	4.79	3.80
2021	HOU	21	AA	25.0	100	6.84	19.00%	6.12	17.00%	2.00%	1.80	4.88	5.71	3.92

Background: After slowly moving through the lower levels of the minor leagues during his first three seasons in Houston's organization, the rotund right-hander hit the ground running last season as he rocketed through Low-A, High-A, and settled in for a couple appearances in Double-A. Macuare, who signed with the organization in early July 2016, made a career-high 18 appearances between the three levels, throwing a career-high 66.0 innings, averaging an impressive 10.2 strikeouts and 4.8 walks per nine innings. He compiled an unsightly 4.77 ERA, a nearly identical 4.78 FIP, and a slightly better 4.65 xFIP.

Scouting Report: There's really nothing noteworthy about Macuare. Below-average fastball that'll sit in the upper 80s/ low 90s. He'll reach back for some above-average velocity to finish off a hitter when needed. Inconsistent slider. Blasé curveball and a matching changeup. Macuare's already tipping the scales at 250 pounds, so he's going to need to improve his diet/conditioning if he wants to give himself a shot at the big leagues. He wouldn't even make many Top 20 lists, but the Astros' system is the worst it's been since the former regime started selling off anything that wasn't nailed down.

Ceiling: 0.5-win player
Risk: Moderate
MLB ETA: 2023

Kansas City Royals

Top Prospects

1. Bobby Witt Jr., 3B/SS

Hit	Power	SB	Patience	Glove	Overall
60	60	60	50	45	80

Born: 06/14/00	Age: 22	Bats: R	Top Comp: Corey Seager
Height: 6-1	Weight: 200	Throws: R	

Season	Team	Age	Level	PA	1B	2B	3B	HR	SB	CS	BB%	K%	AVG	OBP	SLG	ISO
2019	KCR	19	R	180	35	2	5	1	9	1	7.22%	19.44%	0.262	0.317	0.354	0.091
2021	KCR	21	AA	279	41	11	4	16	14	8	8.96%	24.01%	0.295	0.369	0.570	0.275
2021	KCR	21	AAA	285	31	24	0	17	15	3	9.12%	22.46%	0.285	0.352	0.581	0.296

Background: Every time I look up Bobby Witt Jr.'s *Baseball Reference* page, which is about – oh – every other day, I inevitably wind up on his old man's page and I'm always blown away by his first couple of years in the big leagues. Witt Sr., the third overall pick in the 1985 draft, was a full-time big leaguer by the '86 season. And between his first two MLB season the hard-throwing right-hander *averaged* 8.5 BB/9 in **_300.2 innings_**. Man, the 1980s were wild time, weren't they? Anyways, when you're old man is the third overall pick in the draft, the odds are pretty small that you're going to be able to top that lofty status, but Bobby Witt Jr. did just that – barely. A product of Colleyville Heritage High School, the club signed him to a massive $7,787,400 deal – nearly a third of the earnings his dad tallied in 16 big league seasons. Junior appeared in 37 games with Kansas City's Arizona Summer League affiliate that year, batting a mediocre .262/.317/.354 with eight extra-base knocks. Last season, after minor league ball returned to action following the COVID-imposed shutdown, the front office looked almost insane as they shoved the then-21-year-old infielder with barely three dozen professional games past his high school days straight into the minors' toughest challenge, Double-A, to begin the 2021 campaign. But Dayton Moore & Co. proved to be crazy – like a fox. Witt responded by slugging an impressive .295/.369/.570 with 11 doubles, four triples, 16 homeruns, and 14 stolen bases. The front office bumped him up to Triple-A in late July and he continued to mash, posting a nearly identical .285/.352/.581 slash line. In total – again, with just 37 games beyond his high school career – Witt Jr. slugged an aggregate .290/.361/.576 with 35 doubles, four triples, 33 homeruns, and 29 stolen bases (in 40 attempts). Per *Weighted Runs Created Plus*, his overall production topped the league average mark by an astounding 43%.

Snippet from The 2020 Prospect Digest Handbook: A patient hitter with explosive bat speed, Witt Jr. possesses the rare gift of true five-tool talent. The hit tool and power look like above-average offerings. And he does a phenomenal job keeping his hands inside of the baseball.

Scouting Report: Let's have a little fun, shall we? With regard to Witt's production in Double-A, consider the following:

- Since 2006, only five 21-year-old hitters posted a 140 to 150 wRC+ total with a walk rate between 8% and 10% in Double-A with one organization (min. 275 PA): Gavin Lux, Miguel Vargas, Justin Williams, Kyle Blanks, and – of course – Bobby Witt Jr.

Now let's take a look at his production in AAA:

- Since 2006, only four 21-year-old hitters posted a 137 to 147 wRC+ total with a strikeout rate between 21% and 23% in Triple-A with one organization (min. 275 PA): Adam Jones, Wil Myers, Dilson Herrera, and – of course – Bobby Witt Jr.

Unsurprisingly, Witt got off to a wickedly slow start to the year, hitting a lowly .234/.303/.467 through his first 26 games. Beginning on June 5th through the rest of the season, he slugged .305/.376/.605. Phenomenal hit tool. Plus power. Solid patience. Above-average speed. No platoon splits. Elite production against significantly older competition. The lone knock on an otherwise perfect prospect? His below-average glove. In terms of big league ceiling, think: .300/.380/.550.

Ceiling: 7.0-win player
Risk: Moderate
MLB ETA: 2022

2. M.J. Melendez, C

Hit	Power	SB	Patience	Glove	Overall
50	60	30	60	55	60

Born: 11/29/98	Age: 23	Bats: L	Top Comp: Brian McCann
Height: 6-1	Weight: 190	Throws: R	

Season	Team	Age	Level	PA	1B	2B	3B	HR	SB	CS	BB%	K%	AVG	OBP	SLG	ISO
2018	KCR	19	A	472	51	26	9	19	4	6	9.11%	30.30%	0.251	0.322	0.492	0.241
2019	KCR	20	A+	419	25	23	2	9	7	5	10.50%	39.38%	0.163	0.260	0.311	0.149
2021	KCR	22	AA	347	39	18	0	28	2	4	12.39%	21.90%	0.285	0.372	0.628	0.342
2021	KCR	22	AAA	184	24	4	3	13	1	2	17.39%	21.20%	0.293	0.413	0.620	0.327

Background: The Royals front office led off their 2017 draft class by selecting prep first baseman Nick Pratto and followed it up by choosing another prep phenom, MJ Melendez, with their first selection in the second round – perhaps, forever linking the two top picks.

And if their draft status and age made them comparable, then their significant, almost career defining slumps in 2019 only cemented the two. After slugging .251/.322/.492 in 111 games in Low-A in 2018, the lefty-swinging backstop hit a putrid .163/.260/.311 in 110 games with Wilmington the following year. And just like – you've guessed it! – Nick Pratto, Melendez's production surged to a career best in 2021 as he split time in Double-A and Triple-A. When the dust had finally cleared on his renaissance season, the former second round pick was batting .288/.386/.625 with 22 doubles, three triples, and 41 homeruns, the highest total in the minor leagues. His overall production, per *Weighted Runs Created Plus*, topped the league average threshold by a staggering 62%.

Snippet from The 2020 Prospect Digest Handbook: If one promising hitting prospect looks lost at the plate as his production craters to sub-Mario Mendoza lines it could be a variety of things: undisclosed injury, poor conditioning, mechanical flaws, or – perhaps – a failure of talent. But if two highly drafted hitters fail at the identical subterranean levels, than it can't be a coincidence, right? Because Pratto's hit tool was superior to Melendez prior to their disastrous 2019 season, but the latter's defense adds an added dimension. But they're both fighting an uphill battle now. One final note: Melendez threw out 60% of would-be base stealers last season.

Scouting Report: Consider the following:

- Since 2006, only four 22-year-old hitters posted at least a 150 wRC+ with a walk rate north of 12% and an 18% to 22% strikeout rate in Double-A with one organization (min. 300 PA): Joey Votto, Alex Gordon, Chris Carter, and – of course – MJ Melendez.
- Now...slow down...Melendez's production was at least 10 percentage points below the next closet hitter (Gordon).

If Pratto's metamorphosis was special, than Melendez's transformation is – simply – one-in-a-million. The lefty-swinging shortstop went from posting three consecutive seasons of 30% or higher strikeout rates to – *somehow* – whiffing in less than 22% of his plate appearances at the minors' two most challenging levels. Of course, Melendez, like Pratto, made some mechanical tweaks between 2019 and 2021, such as: he lowered his hands, holding them closer to his chest/torso. Throw in his trademark stellar work behind the dish and his ability to control the running game, and Melendez – like Pratto – should become a franchise cornerstone. In terms of big league ceiling, think: .270/.370/.500.

Ceiling: 5.0-win player
Risk: Moderate
MLB ETA: 2022

3. Nick Pratto, 1B

	Hit	Power	SB	Patience	Glove	Overall
	50	60	40	60	45/50	60

Born: 10/06/98	Age: 23	Bats: L	Top Comp: Anthony Rizzo
Height: 6-1	Weight: 215	Throws: L	

Season	Team	Age	Level	PA	1B	2B	3B	HR	SB	CS	BB%	K%	AVG	OBP	SLG	ISO
2018	KCR	19	A	537	87	33	2	14	22	5	8.38%	27.93%	0.280	0.343	0.443	0.163
2019	KCR	20	A+	472	49	21	1	9	17	7	10.38%	34.75%	0.191	0.278	0.310	0.119
2021	KCR	22	AA	275	28	13	4	15	7	5	16.73%	29.09%	0.271	0.404	0.570	0.299
2021	KCR	22	AAA	270	19	15	3	21	5	0	13.70%	28.52%	0.259	0.367	0.634	0.375

Background: It might not have been the right move, but it wouldn't have been out of the question when John Sherman took control of the Kansas City franchise that he would have cleaned house in the front office. The Royals were at the start of another rebuild, many of the club's supposed top prospects had regressed *mightily* (see: Nick Pratto, MJ Melendez), and it would have given Sherman the perfect excuse to bring in his own guys. But the new captain of the Royals' ship did the prudent thing: he left Dayton Moore, who remains one of the more underrated front office members in the game (at least, in terms of the casual fan), alone. Two years later the system is flourishing, the Royals seem on track for another resurgence, and those failed top prospects have rebounded. Taken with the 14th overall pick five years ago, Pratto had the look and feel of a smooth-hitting, batting average-driven, power-deficient first baseman. He handled the tough South Atlantic League with relative ease as a 19-year-old, batting .280/.343/.443 in 2018. And then the wheels on the Pratto express just...fell off. He stopped hitting – *completely* – when he moved in High-A in 2019, cobbling together a vomitous .191/.278/.310 slash line in 124 games. The performance was so bad, that most – including myself – had all but written him off. Two years later: he's morphed into a legitimate power-hitting first baseman. In 124 games between Northwest Arkansas and Omaha, the Huntington Beach High School product mashed .265/.385/.602 with 28 doubles, seven triples, 36 homeruns, and 12 stolen bases. Per *Weighted Runs Created Plus*, his production topped the league average mark by a whopping 56%.

Snippet from The 2020 Prospect Digest Handbook: Mechanically speaking, he's made some changes. In 2018 the former first round pick kept his hands closer to his torso with his left thumb near ear level height. Last season, though, the hands were pushed back with a lot more jostling prior to the pitch. He also looked noticeably bulking in 2019 as well, and not in a good one. I ultimately think it's just going to be a mechanical flaw, so it's difficult to completely hop off Pratto's bandwagon after an abysmal season (though, you can't really blame someone for doing so). But he has a *long* road ahead of him.

Scouting Report: Consider the following:

- Since 2006, only four 22-year-old hitters posted a 150 wRC+ total with at least a 12% walk rate and a strikeout rate north of 26% in Triple-A with one organization (min. 250 PA): Kris Bryant, Joc Pederson, Domingo Santana, and Nick Pratto.

Let's go to the game tape, shall we? Reexamining his 2019 tape and it's pretty evident that Pratto was out of sync (his timing and weight transfer were off) and he did look a bit...pudgy. Last season, though, Pratto was swinging with much more authority, getting better rotation with his torso, showcasing better bat speed, and – in general – looked much better. Plus, he's walking more frequently, putting the ball on the ground less, and still showing no platoon splits (he actually hit lefties slightly better in 2021). In terms of big league ceiling, think: .280/.350/.500.

Ceiling: 5.0-win player
Risk: Moderate
MLB ETA: 2022

4. Asa Lacy, LHP

	FB	CB	SL	CH	Command	Overall
	60	60	60	70	40/45	60

Born: 06/02/99	Age: 23	Bats: L	Top Comp: Robbie Ray
Height: 6-4	Weight: 215	Throws: L	

Season	Team	Age	Level	IP	TBF	K/9	K%	BB/9	BB%	K-BB%	ERA	FIP	xFIP	Pit/Bat
2021	KCR	22	A+	52.0	237	13.67	33.33%	7.10	17.30%	16.03%	5.19	4.81	4.70	4.15

Background: Fun Fact Part I: Kansas City has selected 16 players out of Texas A&M University throughout their history. Fun Fact Part II: The organization has used two Top 5 selections on former Aggies – Jeff Granger (1993, fifth overall) and Asa Lacy (2020, fourth overall), both of whom are hurlers. A dominant, sometimes erratic pitcher throughout his tenure with the SEC Conference school, Lacy seemed to be on the precipice of one of the most dominating pitching seasons in recent memory: he posted a videogame-esque 0.75 ERA with 46 punch outs and eight free passes in 24.0 innings across four starts. Last season, though, Lacy battled a few demons as he made his highly anticipated debut within the organization: his control had completely abandoned him and he hit the disabled list with a wonky shoulder in late July. He was limited to 14 starts with the Quad Cities River Bandits, averaging an impressive 13.7 K/9 and a hugely concerning 7.1 BB/9. He finished the regular season with a 5.19 ERA, a 4.81 FIP, and a 4.70 xFIP. Lacy did pop up with the Surprise Saguaros in the Arizona Fall League, throwing another 7.2 innings with a bunch of strikeouts (15) and too many free passes (six).

Scouting Report: If one were to build a pitching prospect from the ground up, the end result may resemble Asa Lacy in a lot of ways. The former Aggies ace owns a quartet of plus offerings, each a potential dominant, swing-and-miss offering on their own. Combined, they could be one of the best repertoires in the game – at any level. Plus mid-90s fastball with incredible life and added deception from the funk in his delivery. Hard tilting, knee-buckling curveball. Late, two-plane-breaking slider that's lethal when thrown towards the back foot area of the right-hander's batter's box. And – quite simply – one of the best changeups I saw all last season. He throws it with tremendous arm, resulting in significant velocity separation. Combine that with his frame size – 6-foot-4 and 215 pounds – and the fact that he throws left-handed, and Lacy seems to have it all. Except a grasp on the strike zone. He was never a "command guy" in college, but last season's struggles are a first – which brings hope that he'll rebound in 2022.

Ceiling: 4.0-win player
Risk: Moderate
MLB ETA: 2022

5. Kyle Isbel, CF

	Hit	Power	SB	Patience	Glove	Overall
	50	45	55	50	55	50

Born: 05/03/97	Age: 25	Bats: L	Top Comp: Angel Pagan
Height: 5-11	Weight: 190	Throws: R	

Season	Team	Age	Level	PA	1B	2B	3B	HR	SB	CS	BB%	K%	AVG	OBP	SLG	ISO
2018	KCR	21	R	119	25	10	1	4	12	3	11.76%	14.29%	0.381	0.454	0.610	0.229
2018	KCR	21	A	174	30	12	1	3	12	3	6.90%	24.71%	0.289	0.345	0.434	0.145
2019	KCR	22	R	27	5	2	0	2	3	1	7.41%	18.52%	0.360	0.407	0.680	0.320
2019	KCR	22	A+	214	27	7	3	5	8	3	7.01%	20.56%	0.216	0.282	0.361	0.144
2021	KCR	24	AAA	451	70	18	3	15	22	5	9.98%	20.18%	0.269	0.357	0.444	0.175

Background: The Royals' 2018 draft class could – potentially – go down as the best in franchise history – which is saying something. And if it fails to reach that summit, than it could be the *deepest* in their history. Five of the club's first six selections – Brady Singer, Jackson Kowar, Daniel Lynch, Kris Bubic, and Kyle Isbel – have already reached the big leagues. Isbel, the first hitter taken by the organization that year, was a solid contributor in UNLV's lineup his first two seasons, but things came together for the lefty-swinging center fielder during his junior campaign as he slugged .357/.441/.643 in 59 games. And he continued to swing a hot stick as he moved into the professional ranks for his debut: he batted .326/.389/.504 in 64 games between the Pioneer and South Atlantic Leagues. Kansas City sent him directly to High-A in 2019, but he struggled to stay healthy and hit a disappointing .217/.282/.361 in only 52 games. Last season, despite the poor, limited showing in High-A, the front office aggressively showed the former Rebel directly up to Triple-A. This time, though, Isbel proved up to the challenge. In 105 games with the Omaha Storm Chasers, the 5-foot-11, 190-pound outfielder hit .269/.357/.444 with 18 doubles, three triples, 15 homeruns, and 22 stolen bases. His production, per *Weighted Runs Created Plus*, topped the league average mark by 16%. Isbel also sandwiched his season with a pair of extended stays in Kansas City, hitting an aggregate .276/.337/.434.

Scouting Report: Consider the following:

- Since 2006, only four 24-year-old hitters met the following criteria in Triple-A with one organization (min. 350 PA): 110 to 120 wRC+, a 9% to 11% walk rate, and a 19% to 21% strikeout rate. Those four hitters: Jesus Montero, Tim Federowicz, Conner Capel, and Kyle Isbel.

I've always been a huge fan of the former UNLV masher. He just seems like a gamer, the type of guy that gets the most out of his talent – like Ryan Freel. It took Isbel a couple months to get his footing underneath him, but he was able to turn it around in late June. After hitting .234/.320/.360 over his first 53 games (including his first stint in the big leagues), he batted .297/.378/.502 over his final 80 contests (including his second stint in the big leagues). Runs. Works the count. Flashes 15-homer power. Plays a solid center field.

Ceiling: 2.5-win player
Risk: Low to Moderate
MLB ETA: Debuted in 2021

6. Ben Kudrna, RHP

FB	SL	CH	Command	Overall
60	55	60	50/55	50

Born: 01/30/03	Age: 19	Bats: R	Top Comp: N/A
Height: 6-3	Weight: 175	Throws: R	

Background: As highlighted in a post-draft article on *Sports Illustrated*, the script couldn't have been written better for the young, hard-throwing right-hander. The Kansas-born teenager attended school at Blue Valley Southwest High School which – according to Google Maps – is just 31 minutes away from Kauffman Stadium. The only player drafted in Blue Valley Southwest's history, the front office went well beyond the recommended slot bonus and signed the 6-foot-3, 175-pound pitcher to a massive $2,997,500 bonus as the 43rd overall pick. The deal was roughly $1.3 million more than recommended value. Prior to the joining the organization he was committed to attend SEC powerhouse Louisiana State University. He was also named the Kansas Gatorade Player of the Year. His final senior numbers: 9-1 win-loss record with a sparkling 0.99 ERA.

Scouting Report: Long, lean, and just oozing future projection. Physically speaking, Kudrna's cut from the same cloth as Jackson Kowar. The former prep star features an impressive three-pitch mix: fastball, slider, and changeup, all of which are swing-and-miss options. The fastball's been clocked in the upper 90s, showing late zip. The slider is tight and, simply put, too good for prep hitters to not chase. And the changeup is one of the better ones you'll see from a recently signed teenager. The Royals really have a chance to make a statement with their first two picks in the draft last July – as long as they can avoid the injury nexus. It's easy to see why the club went well beyond the slot value to sign him. The more I watch, the more I like.

Ceiling: 2.5-win player
Risk: Moderate
MLB ETA: 2025

7. Frank Mozzicato, LHP

FB	CB	CH	Command	Overall
50/55	65	45/50	50	50

Born: 06/09/03	Age: 19	Bats: L	Top Comp: N/A
Height: 6-3	Weight: 175	Throws: L	

Background: The biggest surprise on the first night of the draft – easily surpassing Kumar Rocker's slide to the tenth overall selection – the Royals reached way down into their bag of tricks and selected Frank Mozzicato, a 6-foot-3, 175-pound southpaw out of East Catholic High School in Connecticut. Mozzicato rocketed up drafted charts after spending the offseason developing – and putting on ten pounds – at the Cressey Sports Performance, which created a workout regime and nutrition plan for the teenage phenom. After the extra training, the fuse for Mozzicato's explosion was lit. He struck out a whopping 135 hitters in just 55.2 innings as a senior, including a 17-strikeout, one-hitter in the Class M Connecticut State Championship. For those counting at home: Mozzicato struck out an average of 21.8 strikeouts every nine innings during his final prep campaign. He finished the season with a stellar 0.16 ERA; he also tossed four straight no-hitters during the season as well. The East Catholic High School star signed for a below slot bonus of $3.55 million, saving the Royals slightly less than $2 million.

Scouting Report: Per the usual, my draft write-up:

> "Eric Cressey, owner of Cressey Sports Performance where Mozzicato trained last offseason, was hired by the Yankees in early 2020 to oversee their strength/conditioning departments. So...it was clearly a smart move by the young left-hander. Low 90s fastball that, according to reports, touched as high as 94 mph during the 2021 season. Mozzicato's curveball is (A) his bread-and-butter pitch, (B) lethal, and (C) one of the best in the entire draft class. Sitting in the mid-70s, it's a snapdragon of a breaking ball, showing late hard, downward bite. The changeup needs some work/tweaking, but it shows some arm-side run and should develop into – at least – an average offering. There's some sneaky upside here, reminiscent of a young Cole Hamels, though the trademark offspeed pitches differ (changeup vs. curveball). "

Ceiling: 2.5-win player
Risk: Moderate
MLB ETA: 2022

8. Jackson Kowar, RHP

FB	SL	CH	Command	Overall
55	55	65	45	50

Born: 10/04/96	Age: 25	Bats: R	Top Comp: Zac Gallen
Height: 6-5	Weight: 200	Throws: R	

Season	Team	Age	Level	IP	TBF	K/9	K%	BB/9	BB%	K-BB%	ERA	FIP	xFIP	Pit/Bat
2018	KCR	21	A	26.1	107	7.52	20.56%	4.10	11.21%	9.35%	3.42	4.15	4.06	4.04
2019	KCR	22	A+	74.0	312	8.03	21.15%	2.68	7.05%	14.10%	3.53	3.60	3.78	3.71
2019	KCR	22	AA	74.1	310	9.44	25.16%	2.54	6.77%	18.39%	3.51	3.68	3.53	3.81
2021	KCR	24	AAA	80.2	338	12.83	34.02%	3.79	10.06%	23.96%	3.46	3.05	3.27	4.27

Background: Brady Singer and Jackson Kowar teamed up together to form one of the best pitching tandems in the country in 2018 as each eclipsed 100 innings and 100 strikeouts during their respective junior seasons at the University of Florida. And by happenstance the Royals were able to come away with *both* Gators in the opening round of the 2018 draft. After selecting Singer with the 18th overall selection, the rebuilding club snagged Kowar 15 picks later. The 6-foot-5, 200-pound right-hander turned in a mediocre, albeit small sample-sized debut, but reemerged as a consensus Top 100 Prospect after a stellar 2019 campaign. Last season, Kowar made 17 appearances with the Storm Chasers of Triple-A, throwing 80.2 innings with 115 punch outs and just 34 free passes. Kansas bumped the hard-throwing North Carolina native up to The Show a couple times. He would toss another 30.1 innings with the Royals, posting an 11.27 ERA while averaging 8.6 K/9 and 5.9 BB/9.

Snippet from The 2020 Prospect Digest Handbook: Prior to last year I was concerned about Kowar's being "too hittable." The uptick in command has squashed those ill feelings.

Scouting Report: At first blush, Jackson Kowar owns a tremendously impressive arsenal. His fastball sits in the 94- to 96-mph range. His mid- to upper-80s changeup sometimes looks like the game's greats from yesteryear woke from their slumber to teach him how to make the pitch dance. And his slider is a solid above-average offering. But my initial fears spelled out after his debut came back to haunt last year. He's too hittable. And, for whatever reason, the sum isn't as great as the individual pieces. His four-seam fastball, for example, doesn't generate many swings-and-misses and posted a paltry 15.2% whiff% with the Royals. To put that into perspective, that's Chi-Chi Gonzalez, Matt Harvey, Zac Gallen territory. In fact, he relies *too heavily* on his fastball and should throw his slider more frequently. There's #4 upside, definitely more, but he needs to adjust his approach on the mound for that to happen.

Ceiling: 2.0-win player
Risk: Moderate
MLB ETA: Debuted in 2020

9. Vinnie Pasquantino, 1B

Hit	Power	SB	Patience	Glove	Overall
50	55	35	55	50	50

Born: 10/10/97	Age: 24	Bats: L	Top Comp: John Jaso
Height: 6-4	Weight: 245	Throws: L	

Season	Team	Age	Level	PA	1B	2B	3B	HR	SB	CS	BB%	K%	AVG	OBP	SLG	ISO
2019	KCR	21	R	248	29	17	2	14	0	0	10.89%	16.13%	0.294	0.371	0.592	0.299
2021	KCR	23	A+	276	33	20	3	13	4	0	11.96%	13.77%	0.291	0.384	0.565	0.274
2021	KCR	23	AA	237	34	17	0	11	2	0	13.08%	10.97%	0.310	0.405	0.560	0.250

Background: Old Dominion University isn't exactly a hotbed of baseball talent. Sure, the Conference USA school has produced one surefire future Hall of Famer (Justin Verlander) and a pair of solid big league arms (Daniel Hudson and Ryan Yarbrough). But the Royals may have unearthed another potentially solid, under-the-radar prospect in first baseman Vinnie Pasquantino. A hulking 6-foot-4, 245-pound first baseman, Pasquantino was a solid middle-of-the-lineup thumper in each of his three seasons with the Monarchs as he compiled a career .309/.388/.507 slash line. Kansas City selected the Richmond, Virginia, native in the 11th round, 319th overall, and signed him to a reasonably low risk deal worth $125,000 in 2019. Pasquantino signed early enough to get in a full season with the Burlington Royals in the Appalachian League during his debut, batting a rock solid .294/.371/.592 with 33 extra-base hits in only 57 games. Last season, despite not appearing in a game above the rookie advanced league, the front office pushed him straight into High-A to begin the year. And he flourished. He hit .291/.384/.565 in 61 games with Quad Cities. And he continued to bash as he moved up to Double-A, the minors' toughest challenge: he slugged .310/.405/.560. Overall, Pasquantino, the former 11th round pick, posted an aggregate .300/.394/.563 with 37 doubles, three triples, and 24 homeruns. He also swiped six bags in as many tries – just for good measure. His overall production, per *Weighted Runs Created Plus*, topped the league average mark by 54%.

Scouting Report: Consider the following:

- Since 2006, only six 23-year-old hitters met the following criteria in Double-A with one organization (min. 225 PA): a wRC+ total of at least 145, a sub-13.0% strikeout rate, and a double-digit walk rate. Those six hitters: Willson Contreras, John Jaso, Tony Kemp, Jordan Brown, Dave Sappelt, and – of course – Vinnie Pasquantino.
- For those counting at home: Contreras owns a career 114 wRC+ mark; Jaso, always an underrated hitter during his time, finished his nine-year career with a 115 wRC+; and Kemp has been slightly better-than-average in 463 MLB games (101 wRC+).

A good bet to the "professional hitter" label slapped on him at some point in his professional career. The former Old Dominion slugger possesses the rare blend of above-average power, extreme contact rates, and above-average patience at the dish. Really good looking swing from the first baseman. Short, quick, explosive. He handles righties *and* lefties equally well. Another very savvy draft pick by the Royals.

Ceiling: 2.0-win player
Risk: Moderate
MLB ETA: 2022

10. Angel Zerpa, LHP

FB	SL	CH	Command	Overall
55	55	60	50	50

Born: 09/27/99	Age: 22	Bats: L	Top Comp: Drew Smyly
Height: 6-0	Weight: 220	Throws: L	

Season	Team	Age	Level	IP	TBF	K/9	K%	BB/9	BB%	K-BB%	ERA	FIP	xFIP	Pit/Bat
2018	KCR	18	R	48.2	203	6.29	16.75%	2.22	5.91%	10.84%	3.88	4.81	4.24	1.63
2019	KCR	19	R	51.1	203	8.94	25.12%	2.28	6.40%	18.72%	3.33	4.19	3.72	3.97
2021	KCR	21	A+	41.2	167	11.45	31.74%	1.73	4.79%	26.95%	2.59	2.57	3.00	3.78
2021	KCR	21	AA	45.1	200	10.72	27.00%	3.77	9.50%	17.50%	5.96	4.43	3.71	4.01

Background: Proving that you don't need to garner a whole lot of attention or command a massive six- or seven-figure bonus on the international market. Kansas City signed the 6-foot, 220-pound southpaw for a small pittance – just $10,000 – midsummer of 2016. Five years later, at the ripe ol' age of 21, he was donning a Royals uniform during his abbreviated big league debut. A native of Valle de la Pascua, Venezuela, Zerpa was twirling gems for the Burlington Royals for the majority of the 2019 season. After taking the COVID-imposed year off in 2020, the portly southpaw dominated High-A for eight starts, continued to impress across 13 Double-A starts, stopped for a clunker in Triple-A, and made one brief appearance with Kansas City. When it was all said and done, Zerpa posted a 108-to-28 strikeout-to-walk ratio in 88.1 minor league innings. And he baffled the Cleveland ballclub for five innings in late September.

Scouting Report: Consider the following:

- Since 2006, only four 21-year-old hurlers posted a 26% to 28% strikeout percentage with an 8.5% and 10.5% walk percentage in Double-A with one organization (min. 40 IP): Tommy Hanson, Chance Adams, Edgar Garcia, and Angel Zerpa.

Quality three-pitch mix backed up by strike-throwing ability. Zerpa's fastball sits in the 93- to 94-mph range with sneaky life. He'll complement the above-average offering with two quality offspeed pitches: a low- to mid-80s slider with impressive spin and a genuine swing-and-miss, mid-80s changeup. Kansas City governed his workload in the latter part of the season. The command needs a bit of refining, but there's definite #4-type potential here – something along the line of a Drew Smyly.

Ceiling: 2.0-win player
Risk: Moderate
MLB ETA: Debuted in 2021

11. Ben Hernandez, RHP

FB	CB	CH	Command	Overall
60	55	60	40/45	50

Born: 07/01/01	Age: 20	Bats: R	Top Comp: N/A
Height: 6-2	Weight: 205	Throws: R	

Season	Team	Age	Level	IP	TBF	K/9	K%	BB/9	BB%	K-BB%	ERA	FIP	xFIP	Pit/Bat
2021	KCR	19	A	31.1	139	8.90	22.30%	4.88	12.23%	10.07%	4.31	4.84	5.05	3.93

Background: Fun Fact Part I: Chicago-based De La Salle Institute has produced a quartet of draft picks in their history – Denny O'Toole (1967), Eric Keefner (2000), Gerardo Esquivel (2009), and Ben Hernandez (2020). Fun Fact Part II: Hernandez became the highest selected player in the school's history when the club nabbed him in the second round. The 41st overall player chosen two years ago, Kansas City signed the hard-throwing right-hander to a deal worth slightly less than $1.5 million. Last season the 6-foot-2, 205-pound righty made his professional debut with the Columbia Fireflies, throwing just 31.1 innings with 31 strikeouts and 17 free passes. He compiled a 4.31 ERA, a 4.84 FIP, and a 5.05 xFIP. Hernandez hit the disabled list for more than two months, but would pop back up in the Complex League for a trio of brief appearances at the end of the season.

Scouting Report: One of the better arsenals in a system chock full of intriguing arms. Hernandez attacks hitters with a mid- to upper-90s fastball, reaching as high as 98 mph on occasion. He'll twirl an above-average power curveball. And his phenomenal plus changeup adds a third swing-and-miss option to his repertoire. Hernandez is quite raw, often battling control/command issues and was prone to bouts of wildness during his abbreviate debut. There's a lot to like here. And Kansas City has proven that they can develop arms well. I wouldn't be shocked to see him among the club's best prospects in a year. There's legitimate Top 100 prospect potential here. Don't sleep on this guy.

Ceiling: 1.5- to 2.0-win player
Risk: Moderate
MLB ETA: 2024/2025

12. Nick Loftin, IF

Hit	Power	SB	Patience	Glove	Overall
50	45	50	50	50	45

Born: 09/25/98	Age: 23	Bats: R	Top Comp: N/A
Height: 6-1	Weight: 180	Throws: R	

Season	Team	Age	Level	PA	1B	2B	3B	HR	SB	CS	BB%	K%	AVG	OBP	SLG	ISO
2021	KCR	22	A+	410	66	22	5	10	11	2	10.24%	14.63%	0.289	0.373	0.463	0.174

Background: Back in the late 1990s and early 2000s, the Royals made a habit of dipping into the collegiate ranks and selecting a Baylor University prospect. But the club went more than a decade-and-a-half before they selected a Bear. And they did so in fashion, drafting Baylor shortstop Nick Loftin in the opening round, 32nd overall, and signed him to a deal worth $3 million – roughly $800,000 above the recommended slot bonus value. A dynamic, line-driving slapping hitter in the Big 12 Conference, Kansas City pushed the 6-foot-1, 180-pound infielder straight into High-A last season for his debut. In 90 games with the Quad Cities River Bandits, Loftin slugged a rock solid .289/.374/.464 with 22 doubles, five triples, 10 homeruns, and 11 stolen bases (in 13 attempts). Per *Weighted Runs Created Plus*, his overall production topped the league average mark by 30%.

Scouting Report: Consider the following:

- Since 2006, six 22-year-old hitters posted a 125 to 135 wRC+ with a sub-16.0% strikeout rate and a walk rate between 9% and 11% in High-A with one organization (min. 350 PA): Garrett Hampson, Tyler Collins, Jose Cardona, Chesny Young, Jordan Brown, and – of course – Nick Loftin.

Like a lot players in the 2020 draft class, Loftin struggled to get it going early on the season, batting .219/.312/.354 over his first 25 games. However, beginning on June 10th through the rest of the year, the former Baylor star slugged .313/.391/.498 with 32 extra-base knocks in only 70 games. There's an interesting speed/power blend built into a middle-infielder's role. Loftin's a throwback player in a lot of ways by making consistent hard contact. Defensively, he could stay at either middle infield spot, but the club had him experiment at the hot corner – where his bat doesn't profile nearly as well. He could be a low end starting option in 18 months.

Ceiling: 1.5-win player
Risk: Moderate
MLB ETA: 2023

13. Jonathan Bowlan, RHP

	FB	SL	CH	Command	Overall
	N/A	N/A	N/A	N/A	45

Born: 12/01/96	Age: 25	Bats: R	Top Comp: N/A
Height: 6-6	Weight: 240	Throws: R	

Season	Team	Age	Level	IP	TBF	K/9	K%	BB/9	BB%	K-BB%	ERA	FIP	xFIP	Pit/Bat
2018	KCR	21	R	35.0	165	5.91	13.94%	2.31	5.45%	8.48%	6.94	6.02	5.38	3.47
2019	KCR	22	A	69.2	278	9.56	26.62%	1.29	3.60%	23.02%	3.36	2.89	3.02	3.72
2019	KCR	22	A+	76.1	294	8.96	25.85%	1.53	4.42%	21.43%	2.95	2.75	2.75	4.07
2021	KCR	24	AA	17.0	66	13.24	37.88%	1.59	4.55%	33.33%	1.59	1.07	2.01	3.98

Background: Part of the front office's celebrated 2018 draft class. The burly right-hander was a stalwart atop the University of Memphis' rotation throughout the majority of three-year career. After posting a 104-to-18 strikeout-to-walk ratio in 85.0 innings with the Tigers, KC drafted him in the second round and signed him to a deal worth slightly less than $700,000. The Tennessee-born hurler turned in an impressive first full season in the Royals' organization in 2019, averaging 9.2 strikeouts and just 1.4 walks per nine innings between stops with Lexington and Wilmington. Last season, as minor league action returned to their regular schedule, Bowlan got off to an incredibly dominating start as he moved into Double-A, posting a 25-to-3 strikeout-to-walk ratio through 17.0 innings. Unfortunately, his right elbow flared up and he would eventually undergo the knife for Tommy John surgery.

Snippet from The 2020 Prospect Digest Handbook: Bowlan's the typical polished, crafty collegiate veteran succeeding with a decent arsenal that's backed up with pinpoint accuracy. His heater, an above-average offering, touches 94 mph on occasion. And he commands it to both sides of the plate exceptionally well. His low- to mid-80s slider is his go-to offering. It's not an overly dominating pitch, often settling in as a 50-grade with flashes of a 55. He consistently throws it for quality strikes, even when he's behind in the count. His changeup's not good, but he gets by with it. Bowlan's the typical fast moving, low ceiling arm that eventually settles in as a decent #5. One more final thought: the rotund righty has an interesting windup as he wraps his arms up and around his head.

Scouting Report: Hopefully, Bowlan makes it back to the mound in 2022.

Ceiling: 1.5-win player
Risk: Moderate to High
MLB ETA: 2022/2023

14. Alec Marsh, RHP

	FB	CB	SL	CH	Command	Overall
	60	55	60	50	40	45

Born: 05/14/98	Age: 24	Bats: R	Top Comp: N/A
Height: 6-2	Weight: 220	Throws: R	

Season	Team	Age	Level	IP	TBF	K/9	K%	BB/9	BB%	K-BB%	ERA	FIP	xFIP	Pit/Bat
2019	KCR	21	R	33.1	132	10.26	28.79%	1.08	3.03%	25.76%	4.05	4.08	3.42	3.52
2021	KCR	23	AA	25.1	106	14.92	39.62%	4.62	12.26%	27.36%	4.97	3.87	3.15	4.16

Background: After selecting a pair of shortstops with their first two picks in the draft in 2019, including some guy by the name of Bobby Witt Jr., Kansas City ripped off two straight picks of collegiate arms: Arizona State University right-hander Alec Marsh and Oregon State University hurler Grant Gambrell. Marsh turned a solid showing during his junior campaign for the Sun Devils in 2019, averaging 8.8 strikeouts and 3.2 walks per nine innings to go along with a 3.46 ERA. The Wisconsin-born hurler dominated the Pioneer League with Idaho Falls that summer too, posting a 38-to-4 strikeout-to-walk ratio in 33.1 innings of work. Last season the front office aggressively challenged Marsh and sent him directly into the boiling water of Double-A. And, for the most part, he more than held his own in an injury-interrupted campaign. In only 25.1 innings of work, Marsh struck out 42 and walked 13 to go along with a 4.87 ERA. He was shutdown with an undisclosed injury in mid-June. Marsh popped back up – briefly – with the Surprise Saguaros in the Arizona Fall League where he would throw 1.1 innings with three punch outs, one walk, and surrendered four earned runs.

Snippet from The 2020 Prospect Digest Handbook: Right now, though, he looks like a #5 / up-and-down arm.

Scouting Report: Prior to the injury shutdown, it's safe to safe I was too low on Marsh a couple years ago. Last season his heater was pumping mid- to upper-90s gas. His curveball, an above-average offering, was impressive. His plus slider with plenty of bite was even better. Marsh tossed a mediocre changeup. He was a typical power-pitcher's build – big, burly, barrel-chested. Great pickoff move. There's obvious reliever risk due to the 40-grade command – and that was before the loss of 2021. He's a name to watch though.

Ceiling: 1.5-win player
Risk: Moderate to High
MLB ETA: 2022

15. Jon Heasley, RHP

	FB	CB	CH	Command	Overall
	55	55	55	50	45

Born: 01/27/97	Age: 25	Bats: R	Top Comp: Tom Koehler
Height: 6-3	Weight: 225	Throws: R	

Season	Team	Age	Level	IP	TBF	K/9	K%	BB/9	BB%	K-BB%	ERA	FIP	xFIP	Pit/Bat
2018	KCR	21	R	50.2	227	6.22	15.42%	2.84	7.05%	8.37%	5.15	4.99	5.26	3.36
2019	KCR	22	A	112.2	467	9.59	25.70%	2.72	7.28%	18.42%	3.12	3.75	3.41	3.99
2021	KCR	24	AA	105.1	433	10.25	27.71%	2.91	7.85%	19.86%	3.33	4.59	4.24	3.86

Background: While the majority of the praise gets heaped upon the early rounds of the club's 2018 draft class, and rightfully so, the front office unearthed a few gems in the middle and later rounds as well. Case in point: Oklahoma State University right-hander Jon Heasley, the 392nd overall player taken that year. Kansas City signed the 6-foot-3, 225-pound hurler to a deal worth $247,500, the second highest bonus handed out to a player in the 13th round. The former Cowboy put together a mediocre debut showing in the Pioneer League, averaging just 6.2 strikeouts and 2.8 walks per nine innings. Heasley had a bit of a coming out party as he moved into the South Atlantic League the following year, posting a 120-to-34 strikeout-to-walk ratio in 112.2 innings of work. Last season the organization bumped him up to the minors' toughest test, Double-A, and he turned in his finest season to date – even going back to his collegiate days. In 22 appearances, 21 of which were starts, Heasley tossed 105.1 innings, fanning 120 and walking 34. He finished the year with a 3.33 ERA, a 4.59 FIP, and a 4.24 xFIP. He also made three starts in the big leagues as well, posting a 4.91 ERA with six strikeouts and three walks.

Scouting Report: Consider the following:

- Since 2006, only two 24-year-old hurlers posted a 26.5% to 28.5% strikeout percentage with a walk percentage between 7% and 10% in Double-A with one organization (min. 100 IP): Rogelio Armenteros and Jon Heasley.

A solid repertoire – particularly for a late round draft pick. Heasley sports an above-average three-pitch mix: a low-90s fastball, an 80-mph curveball, and a mid-80s diving changeup. The repertoire alone looks like a basic starter's kit for a #5 spot in the rotation. Heasley works around the plate but is more of a strike-thrower rather than a command guy.

Ceiling: 1.0- to 1.5-win player
Risk: Low to Moderate
MLB ETA: Debuted in 2021

16. Carter Jensen, C

	Hit	Power	SB	Patience	Glove	Overall
	35/45	45/55	40/30	45	50	45

Born: 07/03/03	Age: 18	Bats: L	Top Comp: N/A
Height: 6-1	Weight: 210	Throws: R	

Season	Team	Age	Level	PA	1B	2B	3B	HR	SB	CS	BB%	K%	AVG	OBP	SLG	ISO
2021	KCR	17	CPX	65	12	1	1	1	4	0	15.38%	29.23%	0.273	0.385	0.382	0.109

Background: The Royals called the names of two local kids during the 2021 draft: first the rebuilding franchise selected right-hander Ben Kudrna in the second round (and signed him to a massive over-slot deal) and then they nabbed lefty-swinging backstop Carter Jensen with the 78th overall pick, signing *him* to an over-slot bonus as well. The recommended value for that pick was $793,000. The organization blew past that mark by roughly $400,000 when they inked the Kansas City native to a contract worth $1,097,500. Like his Kudrna, Jensen was also committed to SEC powerhouse Louisiana State University. A product of Park Hill High School, Jensen was a First Team All-Conference member during his final season, batting .387 with a .578 OBP.

Scouting Report: Big time uppercut from the lefty-swinging backstop, who projects to have above-average power at full maturation. Jensen loads up by shifting his entire weight on his back leg before uncoiling his swing – almost a little Ichiro-esque. Defensively, he shows a solid-average arm that plays up because of his accuracy. There's some Mitch Moreland-type upside with the bat. One more positive note: he's only entering his age-18 season.

Ceiling: 1.0- to 1.5-win player
Risk: Moderate
MLB ETA: 2025

17. Peyton Wilson, 2B

Hit	Power	SB	Patience	Glove	Overall
45	45	55	50	50	45

Born: 11/01/99	Age: 22	Bats: B	Top Comp: N/A
Height: 5-9	Weight: 180	Throws: R	

Season	Team	Age	Level	PA	1B	2B	3B	HR	SB	CS	BB%	K%	AVG	OBP	SLG	ISO
2021	KCR	21	A	46	5	3	1	0	5	0	8.70%	21.74%	0.231	0.326	0.359	0.128
2021	KCR	21	CPX	41	2	3	1	1	2	2	12.20%	24.39%	0.219	0.366	0.469	0.250

Background: Fun Fact: Wilson's older brother, John Parker, was a quarterback for the University of Alabama before entering the NFL as an undrafted free agent; the older Wilson, who spent time with the Atlanta Falcons, Jacksonville Jaguars, and Pittsburgh Steelers, owned a significant amount of Alabama records prior to his graduation. As for the younger Wilson, Peyton was a standout prep player during his career at Hoover High School; *Perfect Game* named him the third best catcher and sixth best player in the entire state of Alabama. Wilson appeared in just 12 games during the COVID-shortened 2020 season, hitting a solid .333/.417/.433 with three doubles and a stolen base. Last season, just his first full year of action for the Crimson Tide, the 5-foot-9, 180-pound switch-hitter batted .290/.353/.460 with 13 doubles, one triple, nine homeruns, and 10 stolen bases. The Royals snagged Wilson in the second round, 66th overall, and signed the recently converted second baseman to a deal worth slightly north of a million dollars. Wilson hit an aggregate .216/.341/.392 with six doubles, two triples, one homerun in 91 games during his debut.

Scouting Report: Per the usual, my draft write-up:

"Consider the following:

- *Between 2011 and 2020, only two SEC hitters met the following criteria in a season (min. 250 PA): hit between .275/.340/.450 and .300/.375/.475. Those two hitters: Ryne Birk and Nick Banks. Birk was a 13th round pick by the Astros in 2016 and Banks was a fourth round pick by the Nationals in 2016.*

A good, not great collegiate bat during his first full season of action. Wilson did everything well without owning a true standout tool other than defensive versatility. The diminutive infielder/former backstop looks like a super sub if everything breaks the right way. But he doesn't figure to walk much, so the hit tool is going to have to carry him."

Ceiling: 1.0- to 1.5-win player
Risk: Moderate
MLB ETA: 2023/2024

18. Yefri Del Rosario, RHP

FB	CB	SL	CH	Command	Overall
50	60	55	N/A	45/50	40

Born: 09/23/99	Age: 22	Bats: R	Top Comp: N/A
Height: 6-2	Weight: 180	Throws: R	

Season	Team	Age	Level	IP	TBF	K/9	K%	BB/9	BB%	K-BB%	ERA	FIP	xFIP	Pit/Bat
2018	KCR	18	A	79.0	337	8.20	21.36%	3.30	8.61%	12.76%	3.19	4.47	4.30	3.67
2021	KCR	21	AA	70.2	325	9.93	24.00%	4.46	10.77%	13.23%	5.99	5.22	4.92	3.75

Background: Caught up – to no fault of his own – in the Atlanta Braves' international free agent scandal several years back. Del Rosario appeared in a total of 13 games in the Braves' system before being granted free agency. Kansas City swooped in and signed the 6-foot-2, 180-pound right-hander for $650,000 in early December 2017. The Miches, Dominican Republic, native turned in a tremendously promising season during his first year in the Royals' organization, posting a 72-to-29 strikeout-to-walk in 79.0 innings in the South Atlantic League – as an 18-year-old. Unfortunately for Del Rosario – as well as the Kansas City hopefuls – the hard-throwing right-hander missed the entirety of the 2019 due to a nerve issue. COVID, of course, forced all those not rostered with a big league club – or a big league club's taxi squad – to miss the 2020 season. Last year Del Rosario finally returned to a bump after essentially two full seasons of lost development. He would make 26 appearances, 11 of which were starts, with the Northwest Arkansas Travelers in Double-A, posting a 78-to-35 strikeout-to-walk ratio in 70.2 innings of work. He compiled a 5.99 ERA, 5.22 FIP, and 4.92 xFIP.

Snippet from The 2020 Prospect Digest Handbook: Prior to the injury, Del Rosario was sporting two above-average or better pitches – a low-90s fastball that had the potential to jump into plus territory and a strong slider – with a chance for an average changeup. Nerve issues can be tricky – as evidence by Brady McConnell – so Del Rosario's future is a bit cloudy. Here's hoping for a full return to heath in 2020.

Scouting Report: The good news is that Del Rosario made a triumphant return to the mound after missing two seasons, one of those due to a fairly serious nerve issue. The bad news: the fastball looked visibly slower, showing less life and oompf. By the time I caught a game of his, it was late in the year. And for those that pitched, remember the days that it felt like your arm was moving in water? That's what Del Rosario looked like. His fastball was too hittable. On the other hand, his curveball was impressive and the slider for promising. You could make the argument that he shouldn't be in the Top 20, but I find him interesting. I haven't given up all hope yet.

Ceiling: 1.0-win player
Risk: Moderate
MLB ETA: 2022

19. Drew Parrish, LHP

FB	CB	CH	Command	Overall
45	50	60	55	40

Born: 12/08/97	Age: 24	Bats: L	Top Comp: Poor Man's John Means
Height: 5-11	Weight: 200	Throws: L	

Season	Team	Age	Level	IP	TBF	K/9	K%	BB/9	BB%	K-BB%	ERA	FIP	xFIP	Pit/Bat
2019	KCR	21	R	25.0	95	14.04	41.05%	1.44	4.21%	36.84%	2.52	3.22	2.19	3.71
2021	KCR	23	A+	15.2	56	13.21	41.07%	1.72	5.36%	35.71%	0.00	1.41	2.95	3.79
2021	KCR	23	AA	83.0	336	10.30	28.27%	2.71	7.44%	20.83%	3.36	3.49	4.14	3.98

Background: A mainstay in the Florida State Seminoles rotation in each of his three seasons with the ACC Conference school. Parrish, who is generously listed at 5-foot-11 and 200-pounds, averaged an impressive 10.6 strikeouts and just 3.0 walks per nine innings in nearly 300.0 collegiate innings. Kansas City snagged the crafty left-hander in the eighth round, 229th overall, three years ago. Parrish dominated the Appalachian League competition during his abbreviated debut that season, posting a 39-to-4 strikeout-to-walk ratio in 25.0 innings of work. Parrish opened last season up on a tear with the Quad Cities River Bandits, throwing 15.2 innings of nearly perfect baseball; he gave up just five hits, fanning 23, walking a trio, and didn't surrender a run. Kansas City quickly bumped him up to Double-A in early June where he would throw another 83.0 innings – most of which were quality innings. Parrish finished the year with 118 punch outs, 28 walks, and a tidy 2.83 ERA.

Scouting Report: Consider the following:

- Since 2006, only five 23-year-old hurlers met the following criteria in Double-A with one organization (min. 75 IP): 27% to 29% strikeout percentage and a 6% to 8% walk percentage. Those five hurlers: Brandon Woodruff, Justin Dunn, Eric Surkamp, Luis Frias, and – of course – Drew Parrish.

A really fun, crafty-type pitcher to watch. A throwback to the 1980s / early 1990s, Parrish's fastball lives around the 90 mph mark, though, according to the telecast, he's touched as high as 94 mph at some point in the summer. The little lefty does a spectacular job moving the below-average heater up and down, in and out. And despite lacking a type of quality velocity, he doesn't shy away from challenging hitters in on their hands. He'll flip up an average curveball, but his plus changeup is an absolute difference maker. He's a command guy – and needs to be – but there's a puncher's chance to snag a #5-spot in a rebuilding team's rotation. Poor Man's John Means.

Ceiling: 1.0-win player
Risk: Moderate
MLB ETA: 2022

20. Erick Pena, CF

Hit	Power	SB	Patience	Glove	Overall
30/45	30/55	40	50	45	40

Born: 02/20/03	Age: 19	Bats: L	Top Comp: N/A
Height: 6-3	Weight: 200	Throws: R	

Season	Team	Age	Level	PA	1B	2B	3B	HR	SB	CS	BB%	K%	AVG	OBP	SLG	ISO
2021	KCR	18	CPX	156	8	10	1	3	4	4	9.62%	36.54%	0.161	0.256	0.314	0.153

Background: Before the ink on Pena's massive free agent contract had dried, the comparisons and mentions of Carlos Beltran were bandied about. In their write-up of the $3.8 million deal, MLB.com said that "several evaluators" were reminded of a young Beltran when gazing upon the lefty-swinging center fielder. A native of Santo Domingo, Dominican Republic, Pena rose to the fifth best available international prospect on the market three years ago, but his *highly* anticipated professional debut left a lot to be desired. In 40 games with the club's Arizona Complex League Affiliate, the 6-foot-3, 200-pound teenage outfielder cobbled together a lowly .161/.256/.314 with just 10 doubles, one triple, and a trio of homeruns in 156 trips to the plate. Per *Weighted Runs Created Plus*, his overall production was a pitiful 4% *below the league average mark.*

Snippet from The 2020 Prospect Digest Handbook: Pena didn't make his regular season stateside debut – though he spent fall putting in work in the Instructs. Loose, easy swing with strong wrists and blazing bat speed. Pena shoes above-average power potential and a willingness to shoot the ball from gap-to-gap. He has the chance for loud tools across the board. He currently employees a toe-tap timing mechanism, though the team likely moves him away from that. He could vault himself up as the best hitting prospect in the Royals system within a year or two.

Scouting Report: Clearly, I wasn't the only prognosticator that was *way* off base with Pena. For a bat-first prospect, Pena was *supposed* to show a little something at the plate. Instead, he just swung-and-missed *a lot*. Like more than 36% of his plate appearances ended in a punch out. It's like the Dominican teenager is swinging his bat under water. He looked late the majority of the time, like he was swinging an entire tree. Physically, he's like a baby fawn – all legs, wobbly, and needs to gain strength. It's too soon to jump off the Pena bandwagon, and the Royals certainly get the benefit of the doubt as talent evaluators as well as their ability to develop hitters (see: Nick Pratto and MJ Melendez), but Pena needs to show something more in 2022. If not, then I'm officially off the bandwagon.

Ceiling: 1.0-win player
Risk: Moderate to High
MLB ETA: 2025

Los Angeles Angels

Top Prospects

1. Reid Detmers, LHP

FB	CB	SL	CH	Command	Overall
55	60	60	50	50	60

Born: 07/08/99	Age: 22	Bats: L	Top Comp: David Price
Height: 6-2	Weight: 210	Throws: L	

Season	Team	Age	Level	IP	TBF	K/9	K%	BB/9	BB%	K-BB%	ERA	FIP	xFIP	Pit/Bat
2021	LAA	21	AA	54.0	225	16.17	43.11%	3.00	8.00%	35.11%	3.50	3.27	2.33	4.20

Background: The University of Louisville is on one helluva run the past several seasons: since 2016 the ACC powerhouse has had three players chosen in the Top 5 of the draft, seven total players taken in the opening round, and a whopping 15 players chosen through the first three rounds. And Detmers, the 10th overall pick in 2020, is the second highest pitcher drafted from the Cardinals – only outdone by two-way star Brendan McKay. A 6-foot-2, 210-pound southpaw, Detmers rocketed through the Angels' farm system in his first professional campaign in 2021. The consensus Top 100 prospect made quick work of the Double-A South competition, posting an absurd 97-to-18 strikeout-to-walk ratio in just 54 innings of work. He was practically unhittable in his first start in Triple-A in late July, fanning nine in only six innings of work before the Angels' front office brass promoted him up to The Show. Then, and only then, did the dominant left-hander look fallible: he got rocked for 15 runs in 19.0 innings across four starts. The organization pushed him back down to Triple-A for one brief two-inning stint before bouncing back up to LA for one more unsuccessful start.

Scouting Report: Consider the following:

- Since 2006, here's the list of 21-year-old pitchers to post a strikeout percentage of at least 35% in a season in Double-A (min. 50 IP): Carter Capps, Grayson Rodriguez, and Reid Detmers.

Taking it one step further:

- Here's the list of 21-year-old arms to fan at least 40% of the hitters they faced in Double-A (min. 50 IP): Reid Detmers.

Detmers was as dominant a pitching prospect that I've seen since writing The Prospect Digest Handbook. His fastball was hovering in the 92- to 93-mph range, and touching a tick higher at times. It may not be a "true" plus pitch, but it got a lot of late swing swings-and-misses. Both breaking balls – a mid 70s curveball and a hellacious mid-80s slider – are wicked plus offerings. And he'll mix in an average, albeit rare, changeup as well. If the command ticks up there's bonafide ace potential; otherwise he's going to settle in nicely as a very good #2 with the occasional flashes of brilliance. The best news: thanks to a later birthday, Detmers is only entering his age-22 season.

Ceiling: 5.0-win player
Risk: Moderate
MLB ETA: Debuted in 2021

2. Sam Bachman, RHP

FB	SL	CH	Command	Overall
70	60	50	55	55

Born: 09/30/99	Age: 22	Bats: R	Top Comp:
Height: 6-1	Weight: 235	Throws: R	

Season	Team	Age	Level	IP	TBF	K/9	K%	BB/9	BB%	K-BB%	ERA	FIP	xFIP	Pit/Bat
2021	LAA	21	A+	14.1	58	9.42	25.86%	2.51	6.90%	18.97%	3.77	3.84	3.70	3.55

Background: Miami University of Ohio has a few baseball claims to fame throughout its history, including: Hall of Fame manager Walt Alston, crafty left-hander Charlie Leibrandt, infielders Bill Doran and Tim Naehring, and outfielder Adam Eaton are all alums. The RedHawks have never had a player chosen in the first round. Enter: hard-throwing righty Sam Bachman. Hailing from Hamilton Southeastern High School, Bachman, a two-year letter winner, struck out an impressive 32.6% of the hitters he faced during his varsity prep career. A member of Miami's rotation as a true freshman, the 6-foot-1, 235-pound hurler made 15 appearances, 14 of which were starts, throwing 75.2 innings with 75 punch outs, 39 free passes, and a 3.93 ERA. Bachman honed in on the strike zone with an increased regularity during his COVID-shortened sophomore season: he averaged a whopping 11.8 strikeouts and 2.3 walks per nine innings across four starts. And the Indiana-native upped the ante even further during his dominant junior campaign for the Mid-American Conference squad: in 12 starts for the RedHawks, Bachman fanned 93, walked just 17, and tallied a barely-there 1.81 ERA en route to winning four games. The Angels drafted the dynamic right-hander in the first round last July, 9th overall, and signed him to a deal just north of $3.8 million. Bachman made five brief starts for the Tri-City Dust Devils in High-A, recording 15 strikeouts and four walks in 14.1 innings of work.

Scouting Report: Per the usual, my pre-draft write-up:

> *"Consider the following:*
>
> - *Between 2011 and 2020 there were only five instances of a MAC pitcher averaging more than 12 strikeouts per nine innings (min. 50 IP): Drey Jameson (twice), Joey Murray (twice), and Kyle Nicolas. Jameson was drafted in the first round. Murray was taken in the eighth. And Nicolas was a second round pick. Only Jameson averaged more punch outs than Bachman.*
>
> *Now let's look at all Division I hurlers. Consider the following:*
>
> - *Between 2011 and 2020, only six Division I hurlers averaged at least 14 K/9 and fewer than 3.0 BB/9 in a season (min. 50 IP): Jason Bahr, Graeme Stinson, Ethan Small, Aaron Ochsenbein, Noah Song, and Jonathan Holder.*
>
> *An explosive, plus-plus fastball that can touch as high as 101 mph. Bachman compliments the offering with a deadly plus slider. He'll also mix in a solid-average changeup. Bachman has a high floor/high ceiling. He has legitimate #2-type potential, though the changeup will need to see an uptick. Similar to Toronto's Nate Pearson."*

Ceiling: 3.0-win player
Risk: Moderate
MLB ETA: 2023/2024

3. Arol Vera, 2B/SS

	Hit	Power	SB	Patience	Glove	Overall
	50/55	40/55	50/45	45	50	55

Born: 09/12/02	Age: 19	Bats: B	Top Comp: Jurickson Profar
Height: 6-2	Weight: 170	Throws: R	

Season	Team	Age	Level	PA	1B	2B	3B	HR	SB	CS	BB%	K%	AVG	OBP	SLG	ISO
2021	LAA	18	A	90	23	0	0	0	9	2	6.67%	22.22%	0.280	0.344	0.280	0.000
2021	LAA	18	CPX	164	27	16	3	0	2	2	7.32%	23.78%	0.317	0.384	0.469	0.152

Background: The front office opened up their seemingly limitless pocketbook on July 2nd, 2019 and handed the switch-hitting infielder a hefty $2 million bonus. And Vera, who's listed at 6-foot-2 and 170-pounds, began his professional career like a bat of hell in 2021: he opened the campaign up with a 10-game hitting streak, slugging a hearty .419/.480/.605 with the club's Arizona Complex League. In total, the Valencia, Venezuela, native batted an aggregate .304/.370/.401 with 16 doubles, three triples, and 11 stolen bases in 57 games.

Snippet from The 2020 Prospect Digest Handbook: Vera creates a tremendous amount of torque that – barring any contact issues – will lead to 20-homer pop down the line.

Scouting Report: Wide base. Simple approach at the plate. Above-average, maybe better bat speed. And Vera doesn't get cheated either. The over-the-fence pop hasn't started to show up in games yet. But it's coming. Vera makes consistent contact, and held his own as an 18-year-old in Low-A. Vera is poised to be one of the bigger breakout prospects in 2022 and could potentially wind up a Top 100 prospect as well.

Ceiling: 3.0-win player
Risk: Moderate
MLB ETA: 2024

4. Ky Bush, LHP

	FB	CB	SL	CH	Command	Overall
	60	N/A	60	N/A	50	50

Born: 11/12/99	Age: 22	Bats: L	Top Comp:
Height: 6-6	Weight: 240	Throws: L	

Season	Team	Age	Level	IP	TBF	K/9	K%	BB/9	BB%	K-BB%	ERA	FIP	xFIP	Pit/Bat
2021	LAA	21	A+	12.0	54	15.00	37.04%	3.75	9.26%	27.78%	4.50	2.15	2.67	3.94

Background: Since the 2016 draft St. Mary's College of California, located in Moraga, has churned out a surprising amount of professional prospects: a total of 16 players have been selected from the West Coast Conference squad – including Corbin Burnes, who's blossomed into one of the best pitchers on the planet, and Tony Gonsolin, both were chosen in 2016. Bush, a massive 6-foot-6, 240-pound southpaw, is the highest drafted prospect from the school since the Athletics snagged Mark Teahen with the 39th overall pick in 2002. The 45th overall pick, Bush originally transferred to St. Mary's from Washington State – after spending a year at Central Arizona College – following an abysmal freshman campaign in which he posted a 12.69 ERA in 39.0 innings of work. Last season the big lefty made 14 starts, throwing 78.1 innings with a staggering 112 strikeouts and just 19 free passes to go along with a 2.99 ERA. After signing with Los Angeles for a smidge over $1.7 million, Bush made five brief appearances with Tri-City, posting a 20-to-5 strikeout-to-walk ratio in 12.0 innings.

Scouting Report: Consider the following:

- Between 2011 and 2020, only seven Division I pitchers averaged more than 12 strikeouts and fewer than 2.4 walks per nine innings in a season (min. 75 IP): Trevor Bauer, Logan Gilbert, Casey Mize, Marcus Stroman, David Peterson, Danny Hultzen, and Nick Sandlin. Bush's 2021 production places him among the group as well.

A plus fastball / slider combo that tends to be death on both left- and right-handers. Bush, according to reports, mixes in a pair of 45-grade offerings in his curveball and changeup – though I didn't see any prior to the draft. He'll need the development of one of the two to at least tick up to average, but there's a lot to like in the Angels' second round pick. He could move quickly in the next 12 to 18 months.

Ceiling: 2.5-win player
Risk: Moderate
MLB ETA: 2023/2024

5. Alexander Ramirez, CF

Hit	Power	SB	Patience	Glove	Overall
40/50	50/55	50/45	50	50	55

Born: 08/29/02	Age: 19	Bats: R	Top Comp: Odubel Herrera
Height: 6-2	Weight: 180	Throws: R	

Season	Team	Age	Level	PA	1B	2B	3B	HR	SB	CS	BB%	K%	AVG	OBP	SLG	ISO
2019	LAA	16	R	177	19	8	5	4	6	0	9.04%	33.33%	0.234	0.328	0.429	0.195
2021	LAA	18	A	81	5	0	1	0	1	1	8.64%	41.98%	0.083	0.185	0.111	0.028
2021	LAA	18	CPX	154	19	7	4	5	3	3	14.29%	32.47%	0.276	0.396	0.512	0.236

Background: Ranked as the 24th best prospect on the international market by MLB.com during the 2018 season. The Angels handed the raw, toolsy center fielder a hefty million bonus. The following year, 2019, Ramirez spent the summer as one of the younger players in the Dominican Summer League. And he acquitted himself well enough. In 39 games, the then-16-year-old batted .234/.328/.429 with eight doubles, five triples, four homeruns, and six stolen bases. His overall production, per *Weighted Runs Created Plus*, was 9% better than the league average. Last summer the front office bumped him up to the Arizona Complex League where he continued to show a ton of promise: .276/.396/.512 with seven doubles, four triples, five homeruns, and three stolen bases. Then his season cratered. He was promoted up to Inland Empire in late August and looked like he never played a professional game, batting a lowly 0.83/.185/.111 in 81 trips to the dish.

Scouting Report: Among all players in domestic rookie leagues last season with 150 plate appearances or more, Ramirez's 136 wRC+ ranked as the ninth best total out of the 90 qualified hitters. Only one other 18-year-old, White Sox's Wilfred Veras, topped his mark. But here's the kicker: according to FanGraphs, Ramirez's average Exit Velocity was 95 mpg and a Max of 111 mph, which is tied for 14th among the 627 players the site has data on. Big leg kick with plus bat speed and does not get cheated. Loud tools.

Ceiling: 2.5-win player
Risk: Moderate
MLB ETA: 2025

6. Jeremiah Jackson, SS

Hit	Power	SB	Patience	Glove	Overall
45	55/60	50	50	45+	50

Born: 03/26/00	Age: 22	Bats: R	Top Comp: Jazz Chisholm
Height: 6-0	Weight: 165	Throws: R	

Season	Team	Age	Level	PA	1B	2B	3B	HR	SB	CS	BB%	K%	AVG	OBP	SLG	ISO
2018	LAA	18	R	91	15	4	2	5	6	1	7.69%	27.47%	0.317	0.374	0.598	0.280
2018	LAA	18	R	100	7	6	3	2	4	1	8.00%	34.00%	0.198	0.260	0.396	0.198
2019	LAA	19	R	291	29	14	2	23	5	1	8.25%	32.99%	0.266	0.333	0.605	0.340
2021	LAA	21	CPX	22	5	1	0	2	2	0	4.55%	31.82%	0.381	0.409	0.714	0.333
2021	LAA	21	A	196	19	14	3	8	11	3	12.24%	33.16%	0.263	0.352	0.527	0.263

Background: Mobile, Alabama-based St. Luke's Episcopal High School is home to just one draft pick: Jeremiah Jackson, the Angels' second round pick in 2018. A twitchy middle-infielder, Jackson put on an impressive show during the first half of his professional debut, slugging a scorching .317/.374/.598 in 21 games in the Arizona Summer League – though that was completely undone by his lackluster production with Orem later in the year (.198/.260/.396). To no surprise, Jackson found himself back in the Advanced Rookie League the following year and he...*flourished*.

In 65 games with the Owlz, the 6-foot, 165-pound infielder slugged .266/.333/.605 with 14 doubles, two triples, and a whopping 23 dingers. Last season Jackson spent an injury-shortened year with Inland Empire in Low-A, batting a solid, Jackson-esque .263/.352/.527 with 14 doubles, three triples, and eight homeruns. He also swiped 11 bags in 14 attempts. His overall production, per *Weighted Runs Created Plus*, topped the league average threshold by 22%.

Snippet from The 2020 Prospect Digest Handbook: He's still young enough to tweak the swing / approach at the plate, but he could very easily get chewed up when he reaches Class AA. Boom or bust type prospect – just like Brandon Wood.

Scouting Report: Consider the following:

- Since 2006, only three 21-year-old hitters posted a wRC+ total between 117 and 127 with a K-rate north of 30% in Low-A (min. 175 PA): Addison Barger, Rashun Dixon, and Jeremiah Jackson.

He's intriguing the same way that 2014 first rounder Jake Gatewood was – a middle infielder with plus-power potential and a questionable hit tool. Unfortunately for the Brewers, who drafted Gatewood, the high school star had to shift away from the middle infielder. Jackson, however, has the defensive chops to at least stay on the left side of the keystone. He also walks at a significantly higher clip as well. The power and speed can be dreamed upon. But he's going to have to keep the strikeouts in check – or at least make sure they don't increase in the coming years.

Ceiling: 2.0-win player
Risk: Moderate
MLB ETA: 2023

7. Kyren Paris, 2B/SS

Hit	Power	SB	Patience	Glove	Overall
45/50	45/50	60	50	50	50

Born: 11/11/01	Age: 20	Bats: R	Top Comp: Jazz Chisholm
Height: 6-0	Weight: 165	Throws: R	

Season	Team	Age	Level	PA	1B	2B	3B	HR	SB	CS	BB%	K%	AVG	OBP	SLG	ISO
2019	LAA	17	R	13	2	1	0	0	0	0	23.08%	30.77%	0.300	0.462	0.400	0.100
2021	LAA	19	CPX	15	4	0	0	1	2	0	6.67%	20.00%	0.357	0.400	0.571	0.214
2021	LAA	19	A	136	16	5	6	2	16	4	19.85%	30.15%	0.274	0.434	0.491	0.217
2021	LAA	19	A+	55	8	2	1	1	4	0	3.64%	36.36%	0.231	0.273	0.365	0.135

Background: Freedom High School, located in Oakley, California, has produced just two minor leaguers – ever. Chris Bodishbaugh, a 38th round draft by the Marlins in 2003 who would eventually be re-drafted out of Los Medanos Community College, and Kyren Paris. On the opposite end of the draft spectrum, the Angels selected the twitchy middle infielder in the second round, 55th overall, and handed him a cool $1.5 million bonus three years ago. After a brief three-game cameo in the Arizona Summer League, which barely constitutes a professional debut, Paris appeared in 47 games between rookie ball, Low-A, and High-A in an injury-marred 2021 season. The then-19-year-old batted a collective .267/.388/.459 with seven doubles, seven triples, four homeruns, and 22 stolen bases.

Snippet from The 2020 Prospect Digest Handbook: [H]e doesn't utilize a whole lot of his legs. It's like his lower half is completely out of sync with his torso. Defensively, he's smooth with soft hands, plenty of range, and should be able to stay on the left side of the keystone. Right now, he profiles as a bit of glove-first utility guy.

Scouting Report: The swing looks improved and he's utilizing his lower half much more efficiently now. Plus speed. Developing power that looks like a potential average tool. The long red flag for Paris: there's a little too much swing-and-miss to his game, even in a couple short sample sizes. He's whiffed in 68 of his 219 total plate appearances – roughly 27% of the time. There's a utility floor with some Jazz Chisholm-type ceiling.

Ceiling: 2.0-win player
Risk: Moderate
MLB ETA: 2024

8. Edgar Quero, C

	Hit	Power	SB	Patience	Glove	Overall
	45/50	55	50/45	55	50	50

Born: 04/06/03	Age: 19	Bats: B	Top Comp: Francisco Mejia
Height: 5-11	Weight: 170	Throws: R	

Season	Team	Age	Level	PA	1B	2B	3B	HR	SB	CS	BB%	K%	AVG	OBP	SLG	ISO
2021	LAA	18	CPX	116	9	8	1	4	1	1	19.83%	24.14%	0.253	0.440	0.506	0.253
2021	LAA	18	A	42	4	2	0	1	1	0	11.90%	38.10%	0.206	0.310	0.353	0.147

Background: Signed out of Cienfuegos, Cuba, for $200,000 a couple years ago. Quero, a switch-hitting backstop, first opened eyes during his tenure with the country's 15U squad; he batted a scorching .400 with five walks and didn't strikeout. Last season the 5-foot-11, 170-pound prospect made his stateside professional debut with the organization's Arizona Complex League squad, batting a solid .253/.440/.506 with eight doubles, one triple, and four homeruns. He compiled an impressive 28-to-23 strikeout-to-walk ratio. Quero capped off his successful 2021 campaign with a 10-game cameo with Inland Empire in Low-A. He hit an aggregate .240/.405/.463 between both levels.

Scouting Report: Another of the club's better prospects that simply didn't get in a ton of playing in 2021. Really like the swing from both sides of the plate. Above-average bat speed, natural loft to belt out 15 to 20 homeruns. And, perhaps most importantly, Quero shows a strong ability to work the count and doesn't give away at bats. He's a good athlete and shows a bit of speed on the base paths as well. He's the type of athlete that would be able to move to second or third bases without much trouble.

Ceiling: 2.0-win player
Risk: Moderate
MLB ETA: 2025

9. Landon Marceaux, RHP

	FB	CB	SL	CH	Command	Overall
	50	55	55	55	50	45

Born: 10/08/99	Age: 22	Bats: R	Top Comp: Shaun Marcum
Height: 6-0	Weight: 179	Throws: R	

Background: Los Angeles went the collegiate pitching route early and often during the 2021 draft. In fact, the front office tried to corner the *entire market* on college pitching last June. They had 20 picks. They took 20 collegiate arms – the third of which was Landon Marceaux, who, perhaps aptly, played for the LSU Tigers (Geaux Tigers, get it?). The 6-foot, 179-pound right-hander led the SEC powerhouse in wins (seven), games started (17), innings pitched (102.2), strikeouts (116), and ERA (2.54). The Halos snagged the Tiger in the third round, 80th overall, and signed him to a deal worth $765,300. Marceaux made a pair of very brief, limited started in the Arizona Complex League, throwing 3.2 innings with six strikeouts, zero walks, and a hefty 14.73 ERA.

Scouting Report: Consider the following:

- Between 2011 and 2020, only five SEC pitchers met the following criteria in a season: 100+ IP, 10 K/9, and fewer than 2.5 BB/9. Those five arms: Aaron Nola, Clarke Schmidt, Casey Mize, Alex Faedo, and Chris Stratton. For those counting at home, Marceaux's production in 2021 would put him on the same list.

It's all about the offspeed, baby! The diminutive right-hander, at least by modern day standards, showcases an average fastball, but spins a couple above-average breaking balls and mixes in a matching changeup. Had his heater been two ticks higher Marceaux would've been a lock as a mid- to late-first rounder. Alas, it's not. And the Angels found a very solid pitching prospect in round three. The lack of velocity will put a strain on his average command at times, but he has the makings of a #4/#5-type arm.

Ceiling: 1.5-win player
Risk: Moderate
MLB ETA: 2023

10. Brendon Davis, Util.

	Hit	Power	SB	Patience	Glove	Overall
	45	55	50	45	50	45

Born: 07/28/97	Age: 24	Bats: R	Top Comp: Freddy Galvis
Height: 6-4	Weight: 185	Throws: R	

Season	Team	Age	Level	PA	1B	2B	3B	HR	SB	CS	BB%	K%	AVG	OBP	SLG	ISO
2018	TEX	20	A+	463	72	23	2	6	6	2	9.94%	22.68%	0.254	0.334	0.365	0.111
2019	TEX	21	AA	401	53	13	1	3	0	3	10.47%	28.18%	0.202	0.298	0.272	0.069
2021	LAA	23	A+	282	37	17	3	14	9	3	6.74%	26.60%	0.280	0.337	0.535	0.256
2021	LAA	23	AA	131	17	4	1	8	4	0	13.74%	25.95%	0.268	0.366	0.536	0.268
2021	LAA	23	AAA	133	21	8	2	8	3	1	7.52%	21.05%	0.333	0.409	0.641	0.308

Background: From minor league retread to dominating stick. Davis, perhaps, opened more eyes in the Angels' farm system outside of the club's top prospects. He's had an interesting, albeit frustrating professional career. Originally taken by the Dodgers in the fifth round in 2015, Davis' flashy tools quickly fizzled and the club packaged him up as part of the deal for Yu Darvish several years ago. The former LA farmhand had an abysmal year in High-A in 2018. And an even worse campaign in Double-A in 2019 (he batted a disgusting .202/.298/.272). The infielder / outfielder came back from the COVID-interrupted year with a vengeance, though: rocketing through High-A, Double-A, and Triple-A, as he slugged an aggregate .290/.361/.561 with 29 doubles, six triples, 30 homeruns (which is more than his previous career *TOTAL*), and 16 stolen bases. Per *Weighted Runs Created Plus*, was 38% better than the league average.

Scouting Report: What a year for the former toolsy fifth rounder. His 138 wRC+ total ranked as the 16th best tally among all minor leaguers with 500 or more plate appearances. The good news continues: his aggregate strikeout rate, 25.1%, marks the second lowest total of his professional career *and* he's flashing above-average, in-game thump for the first time as well. The only question that remains: is it repeatable – any of it, most of it, all of it? It's not unheard of for older-ish, toolsy prospects finally putting it all together. But I'm not completely sold either. Before their massive offseason, Texas wasn't remotely closing to contending – which boded well for Davis. Now, though, it remains to be seen.

Ceiling: 1.0- to 1.5-win player
Risk: Moderate
MLB ETA: 2022

12. Jack Kochanowicz, RHP

	FB	CB	SL	CH	Command	Overall
	55	60	50	45/50	50	40

Born: 12/22/00	Age: 21	Bats: L	Top Comp: Jon Rauch
Height: 6-6	Weight: 220	Throws: R	

Season	Team	Age	Level	IP	TBF	K/9	K%	BB/9	BB%	K-BB%	ERA	FIP	xFIP	Pit/Bat
2021	LAA	20	A	83.1	385	7.88	18.96%	3.78	9.09%	9.87%	6.91	5.72	5.31	3.59

Background: Harriton High School, located in Bryn Mawr, Pennsylvania, is home to one single, solitary professional ballplayer: Jack Kochanowicz. A third round pick three years ago, the Angels handed the big righty a hefty $1.25 million bonus as the 92nd overall player chosen that year – the fifth highest bonus handed out to a player in the third round, by the way. Kochanowicz didn't make his professional debut until last season, spending the entirety of it with the Inland Empire 66ers in Low-A. In 20 appearances, all but two of them coming via the start, the 6-foot-6, 220-pound righty struck out 73 and walked 35 in 83.1 innings of work. He finished his debut campaign with a 6.91 ERA and a 5.31 xFIP.

Scouting Report: Consider the following:

- Since 2006, here's the list of 20-year-old High-A pitchers to post a strikeout percentage between 18% and 20% with a walk percentage between 8% and 10% in a season (min. 75 IP): Mike Foltynewicz, Austin Franklin, Bobby Bundy, Francisco Perez, George Soriano, Josh Wall, Luis Rico, Nick Struck, Paul Demny, Ty Boyles, Zack Britton, and Jack Kochanowicz.

It's all about the curveball. Kochanowicz consistently snaps off one of the more wicked deuces in the lower minors. It's big, beautiful arcing breaking ball with late tilt that's buckled more than a few knees during his stint in Low-A. The massive 6-foot-6, 220-pound youngster doesn't throw as hard as his behemoth size would suggest. But it's an above-average offering that plays up given his long limbs. It also looks like the baby faced hurler is mixing in an undocumented slider/cutter as well. It's harder than the curve with less north-south movement and more east-west. He'll also showcase a decent changeup.

Ceiling: 1.0-win player
Risk: Moderate
MLB ETA: Debuted in 2025

12. Janson Junk, RHP

	FB	CB	SL	CH	Command	Overall
	50	55	50	50	55	40

Born: 01/15/96	Age: 26	Bats: R	Top Comp: Chad Ogea
Height: 6-1	Weight: 177	Throws: R	

Season	Team	Age	Level	IP	TBF	K/9	K%	BB/9	BB%	K-BB%	ERA	FIP	xFIP	Pit/Bat
2018	NYY	22	A	88.1	372	7.23	19.09%	3.16	8.33%	10.75%	3.77	4.38	4.12	3.72
2019	NYY	23	A+	80.2	376	8.48	20.21%	4.13	9.84%	10.37%	5.24	4.20	3.71	3.89
2021	NYY	25	AA	65.2	254	9.32	26.77%	2.74	7.87%	18.90%	1.78	3.59	4.05	3.99
2021	LAA	25	AA	27.1	121	9.55	23.97%	2.30	5.79%	18.18%	5.27	4.43	4.00	3.55

Background: Under-the-radar Seattle University has churned out a total of two big leaguers: Detroit rookie left-hander Tarik Skubal and Jason Junk. A 22nd round pick by the Yankees in 2017, the Halos acquired the crafty right-hander at the trade deadline last season as part of the return for disappointing southpaw Andrew Heaney. Los Angeles also acquired right-hander Elvis Peguero as well. For his part, Junk was phenomenal during his minor league season in 2021, particularly prior to the trade, averaging 9.4 strikeouts and just 2.6 walks per nine innings to go along with a 2.81 ERA. The Angels promoted him up to The Show for a quartet of starts, posting a 10-to-2 strikeout-to-walk ratio in 16.1 innings of work.

Scouting Report: Consider the following:

- Since 2006, here's the list of 25-year-old pitchers to post a strikeout percentage between 25% and 27%% with a walk percentage between 6% and 10% in a season in Double-A with one organization (min. 75 IP): Felix Pena, Ricky Salinas, Jacob Barnes, Austin Hyatt, Connor Sadzeck, and Janson Junk.

Janson's a throwback pitcher, someone like Chad Ogea with a track record twenty year ago. But the game's different nowadays. And velocity reigns supreme. Junk isn't exactly chucking up meatballs – his fastball sits in the 91- to 93-mph range – but he's old in terms of prospects. His curveball is his best secondary weapon, an above-average offering with hard 12-6 break. He'll also mix in decent little slider. And a sinking changeup up as well. A lot of Junk's value is simply going to reside in his ability to chew innings. If something inhibits that, he's no longer valuable.

Ceiling: 1.0-win player
Risk: Low to Moderate
MLB ETA: Debuted in 2021

13. Davis Daniel, RHP

	FB	CB	CH	Command	Overall
	55	60	55	50+	40

Born: 06/11/97	Age: 25	Bats: R	Top Comp: Brandon Bailey
Height: 6-1	Weight: 190	Throws: R	

Season	Team	Age	Level	IP	TBF	K/9	K%	BB/9	BB%	K-BB%	ERA	FIP	xFIP	Pit/Bat
2021	LAA	24	A+	46.2	183	12.34	34.97%	3.86	10.93%	24.04%	2.31	3.76	3.93	4.02
2021	LAA	24	AA	47.0	192	12.64	34.38%	1.53	4.17%	30.21%	2.68	2.53	2.97	4.20
2021	LAA	24	AAA	21.0	105	10.29	22.86%	2.57	5.71%	17.14%	10.29	6.98	5.87	3.65

Background: Thrice drafted as an amateur, the Angels finally convinced the 6-foot-1, 190-pound right-hander to turn pro following his junior campaign at Auburn University. His recent elbow procedure – Tommy John surgery – may have forced his hand, though. His 2019 season with the Tigers was cut short after just one start, which lasted all of two innings. Finally healthy, the former seventh round selection blitzed through three levels during his debut professional season, going from Tri-City to Rocket City to Salt Lake. In total Daniel tossed 114.2 innings across 23 appearances, averaging a whopping 12.1 strikeouts and just 2.7 walks per nine innings.

Scouting Report: The command, let alone the control, was far better than expected considering that (A) he was coming back from Tommy John surgery (kind of) and (B) hadn't played a meaningful game in basically three years. Two above-average offerings in his lively fastball and hard fading changeup and complemented by a plus, tightly wound curveball. He's more likely than not headed for a relief role at some point, or at least will be caught in the no man's land of quasi-starter / multi-inning relief arm. Daniel was smacked around quite a bit during his five-game cameo in Triple-A, so he's likely headed back for more minor league seasoning. Either way, it's a very savvy raft pick for an organization not known for their deft drafting ability.

Ceiling: 1.0-win player
Risk: Moderate
MLB ETA: 2022

14. Jordyn Adams, CF

Hit	Power	SB	Patience	Glove	Overall
40	40/45	60	50	55	40

Born: 10/18/99	Age: 22	Bats: R	Top Comp: D.J. Davis
Height: 6-2	Weight: 180	Throws: R	

Season	Team	Age	Level	PA	1B	2B	3B	HR	SB	CS	BB%	K%	AVG	OBP	SLG	ISO
2018	LAA	18	R	82	13	2	2	0	5	2	12.20%	28.05%	0.243	0.354	0.329	0.086
2018	LAA	18	R	40	6	4	1	0	0	1	10.00%	17.50%	0.314	0.375	0.486	0.171
2019	LAA	19	R	14	6	1	0	0	4	0	7.14%	21.43%	0.538	0.571	0.615	0.077
2019	LAA	19	A	428	69	15	2	7	12	5	11.68%	21.96%	0.250	0.346	0.358	0.108
2019	LAA	19	A+	40	5	1	1	1	0	1	12.50%	35.00%	0.229	0.325	0.400	0.171
2021	LAA	21	A+	307	46	7	2	5	18	4	9.12%	37.79%	0.217	0.290	0.310	0.094

Background: The three players chosen directly following Adams' selection in the first round four years ago have either made the big leagues (Brady Singer and Trevor Larnach) or is a consensus Top 100 prospect (Nolan Gorman). As for Adams, the 17th overall pick that year, he turned in a disappointing

showing in High-A last season. After batting a decent .250/.346/.358 in Low-A as a teenager, Adams cobbled together a lowly .217/.290/.310 slash line with just seven doubles, two triples, five homeruns, and 18 stolen bases in 71 games. His overall production, per *Weighted Runs Created Plus*, was a whopping 34% *below* the league average threshold.

Snippet from The 2020 Prospect Digest Handbook: Very raw, but making plenty of important strides to his offensive game; Adams does a lot of things well with few – correctable – flaws.

Scouting Report: Consider the following:

- Since 2006, only six 21-year-old hitters posted a sub-70 wRC+ total with a strikeout rate north of 30% in High-A (min. 300 PA). Ignoring Adams momentarily, only one of the players – Javy Guerra – made the big leagues and that one came after he transitioned to a pitcher.

Pretty damning comparison. The potential to be a plus-speed / average pop guy is still there, but Adams looked absolutely helpless against High-A pitching. And it got to the point where pitchers could have told him what was coming and he still wouldn't have done much with it. And, perhaps, even more troubling: his average exit velocity was just 86 mph with a peak of 104 mph. The glove is above-average, but it's not good enough to get him to the big leagues alone.

Ceiling: 1.0-win player
Risk: Moderate
MLB ETA: 2024

15. Robinson Pina, RHP

FB	CB	CH	Command	Overall
55	55	50	35	40

Born: 11/26/98	Age: 23	Bats: R	Top Comp: Austin Adams
Height: 6-4	Weight: 180	Throws: R	

Season	Team	Age	Level	IP	TBF	K/9	K%	BB/9	BB%	K-BB%	ERA	FIP	xFIP	Pit/Bat
2018	LAA	19	R	14.1	61	10.67	27.87%	3.14	8.20%	19.67%	3.14	2.75	3.32	1.87
2018	LAA	19	R	14.0	65	11.57	27.69%	5.14	12.31%	15.38%	3.21	5.05	5.60	3.62
2018	LAA	19	R	15.2	65	14.94	40.00%	3.45	9.23%	30.77%	4.02	1.71	1.93	1.88
2019	LAA	20	A	108.0	475	12.17	30.74%	5.08	12.84%	17.89%	3.83	3.29	3.37	3.99
2021	LAA	22	A	22.2	88	13.10	37.50%	2.38	6.82%	30.68%	1.19	3.26	3.13	3.76
2021	LAA	22	A+	57.1	246	13.34	34.55%	6.44	16.67%	17.89%	4.40	4.28	4.46	4.21
2021	LAA	22	AA	15.1	77	12.91	28.57%	5.28	11.69%	16.88%	9.39	9.01	5.08	3.79

Background: Unlike a lot of the club's other Top 20 prospects found on the international market, the Angels didn't hand the hard-throwing right-hander a hefty six-figure bonus. Instead the two sides agreed to a pact worth a paltry $50,000 in 2017. Since then the 6-foot-4, 180-pound righty has continued to miss plenty of

bats, as well as the strike zone with a high regularity. And last season was no different. Splitting time between Inland Empire, Tri-City, and Rocket City, the Dominican-born hurler tallied 95.1 innings of work, averaging a whopping 13.2 strikeouts and an equally inflated 5.3 walks per nine innings to go along with a 4.44 ERA.

Snippet from The 2020 Prospect Digest Handbook: The control's a definite 40 and it may not ever get up to a true 45 – which likely pushes him into a relief role.

Scouting Report: Same story two years later. The Angles have seemingly – and unfortunately – cornered the market on hard-throwing, erratic, strikeout machine arms that are destined to be relievers over the past several seasons. And Pina is just another example. His fastball was sitting in the 92- to 94-mph range, peaking at 95 mph during a couple midseason starts. He'll mix in above-average low-80s curveball and a mid-80s splitter, which he deploys as a changeup. He's entering his age-23 season – which likely means it's his final shot at proving some type of command for the zone before – rightfully – being pushed into a relief role.

Ceiling: 0.5- to 1.0-win player
Risk: Moderate
MLB ETA: Debuted in 2021

16. Orlando Martinez, OF

	Hit	Power	SB	Patience	Glove	Overall
	45	50	40	45	50	40

Born: 02/17/98	Age: 24	Bats: L	Top Comp: Brennan Boesch
Height: 6-0	Weight: 185	Throws: L	

Season	Team	Age	Level	PA	1B	2B	3B	HR	SB	CS	BB%	K%	AVG	OBP	SLG	ISO
2018	LAA	20	A	238	47	12	1	3	6	5	7.14%	23.53%	0.289	0.340	0.394	0.106
2018	LAA	20	R	53	11	5	0	2	3	2	7.55%	16.98%	0.375	0.415	0.604	0.229
2019	LAA	21	A+	422	63	21	4	12	5	4	8.53%	18.72%	0.263	0.325	0.434	0.171
2021	LAA	23	AA	436	62	23	2	16	5	3	6.88%	27.29%	0.258	0.313	0.445	0.188

Background: Sam Bowie to Michael Jordan. Martinez opened up a lot of eyes as a member in Cuba's 18U national league as he batted .400, capturing the hitting crown. Martinez's slugging percentage, according to various reports finished second – to only ~~Michael Jordan~~…Luis Robert. Los Angeles signed the lefty-swinging outfielder for a quarter-million dollars during the 2017 summer. After a solid debut in 2018 – he batted .305/.354/.432 between Orem and Burlington – Martinez handed an aggressive promotion up to Inland Empire well enough; in 88 games with the organization's High-A affiliate, he hit .263/.325/.434 with 21 doubles, four triples, and 12 dingers. Last season the front office bumped the 6-foot, 185-pound outfielder up to Double-A, the minors' toughest challenge, and he maintained status quo: he slugged .258/.313/.445 with 23 doubles, two triples, and 16 homeruns. He also swiped five bags in eight attempts. Per *Weighted Runs Created Plus*, his overall production topped the league average by 7%.

Snippet from The 2020 Prospect Digest Handbook: Martinez's overall skill set screams future fourth outfielder: he shows a 50-grade hit tool, enough power to keep pitchers honest, an average walk rate, solid contact skills, and the ability to play all three outfield positions above-average. Martinez was rather susceptible to fellow left-handers last season, so that bears watching.

Scouting Report: Consider the following:

- Since 2006, only three 23-year-old hitters posted a wRC+ between 102 and 112 with a strikeout rate between 27% and 30%, and a walk rate between 6% and 8% in a season in Double-A (min. 400 PA): Derek Hill, Collin DeLome, and – of course – Orlando Martinez.

The batted ball data, per *FanGraphs*, is pretty bordering between disappointing and mediocrity; his average exit velocity was 87 mph with a peak of 105. And just like in years past, lefties gave Martinez all kinds of fits. He batted a solid, albeit OBP deprived .262/.318/.479 against right-handers, but cobbled together a lowly .233/.293/.322 showing against southpaws. Average power. 45-grade hit tool against righties (worse vs. lefties). A smidgeon of speed, but not enough to matter. He's no longer a fourth outfielder option, but likely headed for a fifth outfielder/Quad-A type now.

Ceiling: 0.5- to 1.0-win player
Risk: Moderate
MLB ETA: 2022

17. D'Shawn Knowles, SS/CF

	Hit	Power	SB	Patience	Glove	Overall
	40	40	60	45	45	40

Born: 01/16/01	Age: 21	Bats: B	Top Comp: Ti'Quan Forbes
Height: 6-0	Weight: 165	Throws: R	

Season	Team	Age	Level	PA	1B	2B	3B	HR	SB	CS	BB%	K%	AVG	OBP	SLG	ISO
2018	LAA	17	R	130	28	4	1	1	7	4	11.54%	20.77%	0.301	0.385	0.381	0.080
2018	LAA	17	R	123	20	9	2	4	2	3	10.57%	30.89%	0.321	0.398	0.550	0.229
2019	LAA	18	R	290	40	11	4	6	5	4	8.97%	26.21%	0.241	0.310	0.387	0.146
2021	LAA	20	A	393	51	21	5	5	31	1	6.36%	29.01%	0.227	0.280	0.355	0.127

Background: Yet another example of one of the club's big expenditures on the international market that hasn't quite gone according to plan. The front office handed the Bahamian shortstop / center fielder a hefty $850,000 bonus several years ago. And it looked like a solid investment at the start. Knowles batted an aggregated .311/.391/.464 as a 17-year-old splitting time between the Arizona Summer and Pioneer Leagues. The organization bounced him back down to Orem to start the following year, 2019, and the results were dramatically worse: he hit a mediocre .241/.310/.387 with 11 doubles, four triples, and six homeruns in 64 games in the Advanced Rookie League. Last season Knowles spent the year with Inland Empire in Low-A West. He cobbled together a .227/.280/.355 slash line with 21 doubles, five triples, five homeruns, and 31 stolen bases (in only 32 total attempts). His overall production, per *Weighted Runs Created Plus*, was a whopping 33% *below* the league average threshold.

Snippet from The 2020 Prospect Digest Handbook: [H]e was particularly susceptible to left-handers last season as well. Throw in some borderline red flag strikeout numbers – in both stints in the Pioneer League – and Knowles' future looks pretty cloudy at this point. Right now, he's profiling as a fourth / fifth outfielder.

Scouting Report: Consider the following:

- Since 2006, only six 20-year-old Low-A hitters posted a sub-70 wRC+ with a strikeout rate between 27% and 30% in a season (min. 350 PA): Jorge Martinez, Jacob Scavuzzo, Julio Garcia, Lester Madden, Richard Pena, and D'Shawn Knowles.

Knowles didn't show any massive platoon splits. His numbers were equally poor against both left-handers and right-handers. And, perhaps, more damning: he production never increased as the season progressed, suggesting that the then-20-year-old failed to make any necessary adjustments. Per *FanGraphs*, his average exit velocity was 85 mph with a peak of 103 mph. He's still quite young, but there's little hope that he develops into anything more than an organizational player at this point.

Ceiling: 0.5- to 1.0-win player
Risk: Moderate
MLB ETA: 2025

18. Mason Albright, LHP

FB	CB	CH	Command	Overall
45/50	55	55/60	45	40

Born: 11/26/02	Age: 19	Bats: L	Top Comp: Kodi Meideros
Height: 6-0	Weight: 190	Throws: L	

Background: IMG Academy is certainly no stranger to big time draft talent over the past couple of seasons. Since 2015, the likes of Logan Allen, Brady Aiken, Jacob Nix, Kendall Williams, Rece Hinds, Brennan Malone, Drew Gray, and James Woods have all drafted. But, perhaps, it's Albright, a 12th rounder last June that might end turning the most heads. Los Angeles handed the 6-foot, 190-pound southpaw a record $1.25 million bonus. That's the highest amount of money handed out to a player past the opening 10 rounds in the bonus-pool era. And for those counting at home: that's roughly late second round money in the 2021 draft. Albright made three brief appearances with the organization's Arizona Complex League after signing, posting an impressive 8-to-2 strikeout-to-walk ratio.

Scouting Report: Kudos to the Angles for going above-and-beyond on locking up the young left-hander. But it's a risky investment. Not only because he's a young arm – which should go without saying – but Albright's arm action is ugly. And potentially career limiting. It's long and stiff. And I think it's going to make him susceptible to right-handers in the future. The fastball velocity is fringy average, and I'm not sure how much more is left in the take in terms of projection. He can spin an above-average deuce. But it's his changeup that should be a difference maker.

Ceiling: 0.5- to 1.0-win player
Risk: Moderate
MLB ETA: 2025

19. Ryan Smith, LHP

FB	SL	CH	Command	Overall
45	50	50	45	40

Born: 08/13/97	Age: 24	Bats: L	Top Comp: Alex Young
Height: 5-11	Weight: 185	Throws: L	

Background: Throughout its history Princeton University produced two noteworthy big leaguers: former All-Star right-hander Chris Young and outfielder Will Venable. Beyond that there's a bunch of up-and-down types that spent a little bit of time at the game's pinnacle level, including: Matt Bowman,

Season	Team	Age	Level	IP	TBF	K/9	K%	BB/9	BB%	K-BB%	ERA	FIP	xFIP	Pit/Bat
2019	LAA	21	R	25.2	113	12.97	32.74%	4.21	10.62%	22.12%	5.26	5.22	4.13	4.26
2021	LAA	23	A	27.2	105	14.31	41.90%	2.28	6.67%	35.24%	1.63	2.97	2.75	3.83
2021	LAA	23	A+	45.2	175	10.25	29.71%	1.38	4.00%	25.71%	3.74	4.29	3.84	3.94
2021	LAA	23	AA	33.2	146	9.62	24.66%	2.14	5.48%	19.18%	4.28	3.91	3.85	3.45
2021	LAA	23	AAA	22.1	108	8.46	19.44%	4.43	10.19%	9.26%	8.46	7.02	6.30	4.05

David Hale, Ross Ohlendorf, and Danny Barnes. Unfortunately for the Angels, as well as Smith, the 5-foot-11, 185-pound southpaw falls more into the latter category. Last season, his second in professional ball, Smith rocketed through four minor league stops: Low-A, High-A, Double-A, and Triple-A. When the dust settled he tossed a career-high 129.1 innings with 153 strikeouts and 33 walks per nine innings. He compiled an aggregate 4.24 ERA.

Scouting Report: It's not surprising that Smith's production and peripherals steadily declined at each stop along the way. He's a soft-tossing southpaw with a below-average upper-80s heater that will occasionally spill over into the 90, 91-mph range. He shows a lot of confidence in his secondary weapons: a 77- to 82-mph slider and a changeup in the same range. He's effectively wild – for now. And showcases a ton of sliders as he pitches backwards.

Ceiling: 0.5-win player
Risk: Moderate
MLB ETA: 2022

20. Hector Yan, LHP

FB	CB	SL	CH	Command	Overall
55	55	50	50	35	40

Born: 04/26/99	Age: 23	Bats: L	Top Comp: Matt Krook
Height: 5-11	Weight: 180	Throws: L	

Season	Team	Age	Level	IP	TBF	K/9	K%	BB/9	BB%	K-BB%	ERA	FIP	xFIP	Pit/Bat
2018	LAA	19	R	29.2	133	8.80	21.80%	6.07	15.04%	6.77%	4.55	6.22	5.95	3.74
2019	LAA	20	A	109.0	458	12.22	32.31%	4.29	11.35%	20.96%	3.39	3.17	3.34	4.23
2021	LAA	22	A+	82.1	381	10.28	24.67%	6.34	15.22%	9.45%	5.25	6.61	5.89	3.82

Background: Another intriguing, albeit ceiling-limited, prospect the Angels signed on the international market. Yan, who hails from La Romana, Dominican Republic, agreed to a deal with the club for a rather paltry sum of $80,000 seven years ago. Since then the 5-foot-11, 180-pound southpaw spent a full season at each minor league stop all the way up to High-A, his 2021 destination. Making 20 appearances, 16 of them coming via the start, for the Tri-City Dust Devils Yan tossed 81.1 innings of work, averaging an impressive 10.3 strikeouts and a staggering 6.3 walks per nine innings. He compiled an unsightly 5.25 ERA and an even worse 5.89 xFIP.

Snippet from The 2020 Prospect Digest Handbook: The Angels are likely to give Yan every opportunity to succeed as a starter, but unless the control / command continues to improve he's going to settle in as a Tony Sipp / Oliver Perez-type lefty reliever.

Scouting Report: Consider the following:

- Since 2006, here's the list of 22-year-old pitchers to fan between 23% and 26% and walked more than 14% of the hitters they faced in a High-A season (min. 75 IP): Jorge Guzman, Matt Krook, Raffi Vizcaino, Sam Selman, Jordan Pratt, and – of course – Hector Yan.

The more things change, the more they stay the same. Yan is still sporting an above-average fastball / curveball combo. And he's still mixing in a rare, vanilla-esque changeup. But he's also added a slider, which hasn't shown up an any scouting reports that I've seen. It'll flash 50 at times, but it's clear it's still a work in progress. The track record for 22-year-old High-A pitchers with bloated walk rates is practically nil, so beyond his diminutive size Yan has a pretty difficult march towards the big leagues.

Ceiling: 0.5-win player
Risk: Moderate
MLB ETA: 2023

Los Angeles Dodgers

Top Prospects

1. Diego Cartaya, C

	Hit	Power	SB	Patience	Glove	Overall
	50	60	30	60	55	70

Born: 09/07/01	Age: 20	Bats: R	Top Comp: Jorge Posada
Height: 6-3	Weight: 219	Throws: R	

Season	Team	Age	Level	PA	1B	2B	3B	HR	SB	CS	BB%	K%	AVG	OBP	SLG	ISO
2019	LAD	17	R	57	7	2	2	1	0	0	8.77%	19.30%	0.240	0.316	0.420	0.180
2019	LAD	17	R	150	27	10	0	3	1	0	7.33%	20.67%	0.296	0.353	0.437	0.141
2021	LAD	19	A	137	18	6	0	10	0	0	13.14%	27.01%	0.298	0.409	0.614	0.316

Background: The 2018 international free agent class is turning out to be pretty special, one of the better ones in recent memory. Marco Luciano, Orelvis Martinez, Noelvi Marte, Francisco Alvarez, Kevin Alcantara, and Alexander Ramirez were some of the notable names to be added to affiliated ball that season. The Dodgers, though, added – arguably – the best prospect on the international scene that season. Ranked by MLB.com and *Baseball America* as the first and third best prospect in the class, Los Angeles signed the big backstop for a massive $2.5 million deal that summer. Standing an imposing 6-foot-3 and 219 pounds, Cartaya debuted in 2019 as he split time between the club's foreign and stateside rookie league affiliates, batting an aggregate .281/.343/.432 with 12 doubles, two triples, and four homeruns. His overall production, per *Weighted Runs Created Plus*, topped the league average mark by a solid 11%. Last season, as minor league ball returned from its COVID-imposed shutdown, the front office pushed the then-19-year-old, baby faced teenager to Low-A West. In an injury-shortened sophomore campaign the Venezuelan-born prospect slugged a scorching .298/.409/.614 with six doubles and 10 homeruns in only 31 games. His overall production was a whopping 58% better than the league average mark.

Snippet from The 2020 Prospect Digest Handbook: Big time pull power. Cartaya shows an incredibly low maintenance swing and keeps his hands inside the well. Smooth right-handed swing. Based on foot speed alone, Cartaya's – maybe – a 35 runner. The young backstop looks like the he's going to move quickly. Plus-throwing arm, both in terms of accuracy and arm strength. He's going to break out in a big way in 2020.

Scouting Report: Just for fun, here's Cartaya's production prorated for a full 162-game season: 31 doubles and 52 homeruns. Not. Too. Shabby. On a bit of a personal note: there's only been a handful of times that I've watched a player for the first time and the hair on the back of my neck stood up and I leaned closer to the computer screen to get a better look. The first time: Joakim Soria during one of his first big league appearances. More recently, though: Diego Cartaya. As high of a ceiling as any hitter – read: not ballplayer – in the minor leagues, Cartaya put his talents on full display during his abbreviated 2021 campaign: He showed plus power, plus patience, and a decent hit tool. The lone knock on an otherwise superb, albeit shortened, season: his 27.0% K-rate. Is it high? Sure, a touch. Is it concerning? Maybe. But he was 19-years-old, playing the most rigorous defensive position, and squaring off against significantly older competition. Defensively speaking, he performed better than expected. In terms of a big league ceiling think: .280/.350/.500.

Ceiling: 6.0-win player
Risk: Moderate
MLB ETA: 2023/2024

2. Miguel Vargas, 3B

	Hit	Power	SB	Patience	Glove	Overall
	55	50/60	50/40	50	45/50	60

Born: 11/17/99	Age: 22	Bats: R	Top Comp: Anthony Rendon
Height: 6-3	Weight: 205	Throws: R	

Season	Team	Age	Level	PA	1B	2B	3B	HR	SB	CS	BB%	K%	AVG	OBP	SLG	ISO
2018	LAD	18	R	103	23	11	1	2	6	1	7.77%	12.62%	0.394	0.447	0.596	0.202
2018	LAD	18	R	37	9	3	1	0	1	0	13.51%	8.11%	0.419	0.514	0.581	0.161
2018	LAD	18	A	89	14	1	1	0	0	0	11.24%	22.47%	0.213	0.307	0.253	0.040
2019	LAD	19	A	323	64	20	2	5	5	1	10.84%	13.31%	0.325	0.399	0.464	0.139
2019	LAD	19	A+	236	39	18	1	2	4	3	8.47%	16.95%	0.284	0.353	0.408	0.123
2021	LAD	21	A+	172	30	11	1	7	4	0	5.23%	18.60%	0.314	0.366	0.532	0.218
2021	LAD	21	AA	370	72	16	1	16	7	1	9.73%	15.41%	0.321	0.386	0.523	0.202

Background: Los Angeles inked the power-hitting third baseman after defecting from Cuba in September 2017 – with much less fanfare than a lot his fellow countrymen. Vargas' old man, Lazaro, was quite the ballplayer during his prime. The elder Vargas was a dynamic hitter in the Cuban Serie Nacional: he led the league in hits during the 1983-84 season and was named Serie Nacional Most Value Player after pacing the circuit in runs and hits. Lazaro would also appear on a pair of Olympic teams, including the gold medal winning 1996 squad. He would also manage the Industriales for four seasons after his retirement. As for the younger Vargas, after signing with the perennial National League powerhouse for $300,000, he made stops at three stops during his affiliated debut in 2018, appearing in 53 games with the organization's rookie league team, Ogden, and Great Lakes. He finished the year with a .330/.404/.465 slash line. The 6-foot-3, 205-pound infielder split the 2019 season between Great Lakes and Rancho Cucamonga, hitting an aggregate .308/.380/.440 with 38 doubles, three triples, and seven homeruns. Last season, with the return of minor league ball, Vargas torched High-A for 37 games before continuing his assault on Double-A, slugging an impressive .319/.380/.526 with 27 doubles, two triples, 23 homeruns, and 11 stolen bases (in 12 total attempts). Per *Weighted Runs Created Plus*, his overall production topped the league average mark by 42%.

Snippet from The 2020 Prospect Digest Handbook: One of the more underrated prospects in the minor leagues. Vargas continues to showcase the type of skills – offensive *and* defensive – to be a perennial All-Star caliber third baseman. Solid patience, phenomenal bat-to-ball skills. And Vargas, who stands 6-foot-3 and 205 pounds, hasn't even tapped into his in-game power. There's 20-homer potential here. In terms of ceiling think .290/.350/.460.

Scouting Report: Another one of my favorite prospects in the minor leagues. With respect to Vargas' production in Double-A, consider the following:

- Since 2006, only three 21-year-old hitters posted a 135 to 145 wRC+ total with a sub-17.0% strikeout rate and a walk rate between 8% and 11% in Double-A with one organization (min. 350 PA): Kyle Blanks, Gavin Cecchini, and – of course – Miguel Vargas.

One of the more talented hitters in the minor leagues. Vargas possesses the rare ability to hit for power and consistently make contact. He's never going to be confused for Kevin Youkilis and his bloated OBPs, but the Dodgers' emerging star will post average walk rates. Defensively, the front office has experimented with him at first base and the keystone. He's passable at any of the three positions (1B, 2B, 3B) with the most value at second base. In terms of thinking, think: .300/.360/.500.

Ceiling: 5.5-win player
Risk: Moderate
MLB ETA: 2022

3. Bobby Miller, RHP

	FB	CB	SL	CH	Command	Overall
	60	55	60	55	55	60

Born: 04/05/99	Age: 23	Bats: L	Top Comp: Walker Buehler
Height: 6-5	Weight: 220	Throws: R	

Season	Team	Age	Level	IP	TBF	K/9	K%	BB/9	BB%	K-BB%	ERA	FIP	xFIP	Pit/Bat
2021	LAD	22	A+	47.0	188	10.72	29.79%	2.11	5.85%	23.94%	1.91	2.81	3.71	4.20

Background: Fun Fact Part I: in their storied history, the Los Angeles Dodgers selected five players out of the University of Louisville. Fun Fact Part II: All five of those aforementioned draft picks have come since 2011. Fun Fact Part III: of those five picks, three of them were first round selections – Kyle Funkhouser (2015), Will Smith (2016), and Bobby Miller (2020). Taken in the later parts of the opening round two years ago, Miller, the 29th overall pick, began his collegiate career with the Cardinals as a swing-man, making nine starts and eight relief appearances during his freshman season. He worked in the same capacity for Manager Dan McDonnell during his sophomore campaign, posting an 86-to-38 strikeout-to-walk ratio in 80.0 innings of work. Miller, though, was finally handed a full time starting gig during his third season – though he made just four starts before the COVID shutdown. He managed to post a 34-to-9 strikeout-to-walk ratio with a 2.31 ERA in 23.1 innings of work. After signing with the organization for $2,197,500, Miller made his professional debut last season, making 14 appearances with Great Lakes and three final ones with Tulsa. Miller compiled a 70-to-13 strikeout-to-walk ratio in 56.1 innings. Miller also made five brief appearances with the Glendale Desert Dogs in the Arizona Fall League, striking out 10 and walking seven in 10.0 innings of work.

Scouting Report: The Dodgers brought Miller along slowly last season, limiting him to four or fewer innings until early July. But despite their best efforts, the hard-throwing right-hander would eventually hit the disabled list for roughly six weeks with an undisclosed injury. Miller attacks hitters with a standard four-pitch mix: an explosive, mid- to upper-90s heater; an above-average curveball; a plus, late darting slider with hard cutter-like movement; and a diving changeup. Physically, he's built in the same mold as Dodgers ace Walker Buehler – though Miller is three inches taller. The former Louisville hurler commands the zone well. And has the potential to be a front-of-the-rotation caliber arm.

Ceiling: 5.0-win player
Risk: Moderate
MLB ETA: 2023

4. Andy Pages, RF

	Hit	Power	SB	Patience	Glove	Overall
	40/45	60	35	55	55	60

Born: 12/08/00	Age: 21	Bats: R	Top Comp: Franmil Reyes
Height: 6-1	Weight: 212	Throws: R	

Season	Team	Age	Level	PA	1B	2B	3B	HR	SB	CS	BB%	K%	AVG	OBP	SLG	ISO
2018	LAD	17	R	178	16	8	0	9	9	6	12.92%	17.42%	0.236	0.393	0.486	0.250
2018	LAD	17	R	34	3	1	0	1	1	1	17.65%	11.76%	0.192	0.382	0.346	0.154
2019	LAD	18	R	279	27	22	2	19	7	6	9.32%	28.32%	0.298	0.398	0.651	0.353
2021	LAD	20	A+	538	59	25	1	31	6	3	14.31%	24.54%	0.265	0.394	0.539	0.274

Background: Another one of the club's tremendous signings out of Cuba. Pages, like fellow countryman Miguel Vargas, earned a $300,000 bonus on the international free agency market. Hailing from La Habana, the 6-foot-1, 212-pound well-built outfielder made his organizational debut in 2018, making stops in the Dominican and Arizona Summer League. He compiled a batting average-deficient .229/.392/.464 slash line with nine doubles and 10 dingers. Pages moved up to – and completely dominated – the Pioneer League the following season; he slugged a hearty .298/.398/.651 with a staggering number of extra-base hits – 43, to be exact. Last season the front office, convinced by Pages development and production in 2019, pushed the Cuban import up to High-A. And he continued to bash. In a career best 120 games with the Great Lakes Loons, Pages posted a .265/.394/.539 with 25 doubles, one triple, and 31 four-baggers. His overall production, per *Weighted Runs Created Plus*, topped the league average mark by 52%.

Snippet from The 2020 Prospect Digest Handbook: Off the charts power thanks to his lightning fast hands. The problem for Pages, however, is his massive swing-and-miss totals; he whiffed in slightly more than 28% of his plate appearances last season. A large, untimely leg kick is clearly causing timing issues as he's struggling to get his foot back down. It's a pretty safe bet that the Dodgers' player development guys are going to eliminate it – or at least quiet it a bit. Mike Stanton type power but the hit tool needs to take several leaps forward.

Scouting Report: Consider the following:

- Since 2006, there have been five 20-year-old hitters to a wRC+ total between 147 and 157 in High-A with one organization (min. 300 PA): Gavin Lux, Logan Morrison, Luis Campusano, Clint Frazier, and – of course – Andy Pages.
- While each of the five players sports a double-digit walk rate, only two whiffed in more than 20% of their plate appearances: Frazier, 21.3%, and Pages, 24.5%.

Miscast as a center fielder, but he's more built like stout right fielder, Pages has the foundation for a Three True Outcomes hitter. Big time power, impressive walk rates, and a questionable – though, admittedly, improved – strikeout rate. His K-rate improved from 28.3% in 2019 down to a more manageable 24.5% last season. Pages made some modifications to his stance over the past couple of years, though not the one that I thought was ripe for improvement (his leg kick). Instead, he's holding his hands closer to his chest. His stance is reminiscent of former slugging right fielder Jay Buhner, though Pages' isn't open. The 21-year-old owns as much power as any player in the minor leagues. If he can keep the K-rates in the 24% to 26%, he be bashing plenty of big league dingers.

Ceiling: 3.5-win player
Risk: Moderate
MLB ETA: 2023/2024

5. Michael Busch, 2B

	Hit	Power	SB	Patience	Glove	Overall
	45	50	35	60	50	55

Born: 11/09/97	Age: 24	Bats: L	Top Comp: Brian Dozier
Height: 6-1	Weight: 210	Throws: R	

Season	Team	Age	Level	PA	1B	2B	3B	HR	SB	CS	BB%	K%	AVG	OBP	SLG	ISO
2019	LAD	21	R	16	1	0	0	0	0	0	6.25%	12.50%	0.077	0.250	0.077	0.000
2019	LAD	21	A	19	2	0	0	0	0	0	31.58%	15.79%	0.182	0.474	0.182	0.000
2021	LAD	23	AA	495	61	27	1	20	2	3	14.14%	26.06%	0.267	0.386	0.484	0.218

Background: Throughout their long, storied history the Los Angeles Dodgers have drafted just three players out of the University of North Carolina: Howie Freiling (1987, eighth round), Ron Mauer (1990, 23rd round), and – of course – Michael Busch. The 31st overall pick in the 2019 draft class, Busch put together a heavily saber-slanted career with the Tar Heels, particularly his sophomore and junior seasons when he struck out only 69 times against 116 bases-on-balls. Busch dabbled in professional ball following his signing with the club – he appeared in just 10 games – and missed all of 2020 due to the COVID shutdown, so last year's showing was, in a large part, his first full taste of minor league action. The front office aggressively shoved him up to Double-A, the minors' most challenging level. In 107 games with the Tulsa Drillers, the 6-foot-1, 210-pound infielder slugged .267/.386/.484 with 27 doubles, one triple, and 20 homeruns. He also swiped two bags in five attempts. Per *Weighted Runs Created Plus*, his production topped the league average mark by an impressive 34%.

Snippet from The 2020 Prospect Digest Handbook: Lacking the prototypical size and/or power projection for a first base or corner outfield prospect. Busch, nonetheless, owns an above-average hit tool, 15-homer power potential, and strong on-base peripherals.

Scouting Report: Consider the following:

- Since 2006, only four 23-year-old hitters met the following criteria in Double-A with one organization (min. 350 PA): 130 to 140 wRC+, a walk rate of at least 12%, and a strikeout rate north of 25%. Those four hitters: Bradley Zimmer, Drew Ward, Mike Costanzo, and Michael Busch.

The former Tar Heel started the year off without showing any ill effects due to the aggressive assignment – or the low layoff. He's still showing average power, plus walk rates, and – surprisingly – enough glove to stick at the keystone. His semi-concerning strike rate, 26.1%, improved as the year went on. And he tallied just 23.7% whiff rate over his final 63 games. The lone red flag: his ineptitude against southpaws; he posted a lowly .198/.355/.354 slash line against them (vs. a .288/.396/.524 mark against RHP). There's above-average starting material – a la Brian Dozier – but he needs to prove he can handle southpaws first.

Ceiling: 3.0-win player
Risk: Moderate
MLB ETA: 2022

6. Eddys Leonard, IF

	Hit	Power	SB	Patience	Glove	Overall
	50/55	50	45	50	50	55

Born: 11/10/00	Age: 21	Bats: R	Top Comp: Jorge Polanco
Height: 6-0	Weight: 160	Throws: R	

Season	Team	Age	Level	PA	1B	2B	3B	HR	SB	CS	BB%	K%	AVG	OBP	SLG	ISO
2018	LAD	17	R	182	23	10	0	4	13	6	15.38%	18.13%	0.248	0.385	0.396	0.148
2019	LAD	18	R	23	6	0	0	1	0	2	4.35%	39.13%	0.333	0.391	0.476	0.143
2019	LAD	18	R	200	33	7	4	3	2	4	13.50%	24.00%	0.280	0.380	0.423	0.143
2021	LAD	20	A	308	42	19	2	14	6	2	11.04%	24.03%	0.295	0.399	0.544	0.249
2021	LAD	20	A+	184	29	10	2	8	3	1	9.24%	22.83%	0.299	0.375	0.530	0.232

Background: Like a lot of the club's top bats in the farm system, Leonard, too, turned in a dynamic, breakout season in 2021. Hailing from Santo Domingo, Dominican Republic, the Dodgers signed the 6-foot, 160-pound twitchy infielder to a $200,000 bonus during the summer of 2017. The teenage Leonard would make his professional debut a year later with the organization's Dominican Summer League affiliate, batting a mediocre .248/.385/.396 with 14 extra-base hits in 45 games. Leonard would spend the majority of 2019 season in the state side rookie league, though he made brief stops in the Pioneer and Midwest Leagues. In total, the Dominican middle infielder / third baseman hit .285/.379/.425. Last season, with the return of minor league ball, Leonard torched the Low-A West competition and continued to swing a hot bat during his second half promotion up to High-A. He would finish the year with an aggregate .296/.390/.539 with career bests in doubles (29) and homeruns (22), while tying a career high with four triples. Per *Weighted Runs Created Plus*, his overall production topped the league average mark by 45% – another career best, by a wide margin.

Scouting Report: Consider the following:

- Since 2006, only four 20-year-old hitters met the following criteria in Low-A with one organization (min. 300 PA): 140 to 150 wRC+ total, a double-digit walk rate, and a 23% to 26% strikeout rate. Those four hitters: Nolan Jones, Isan Diaz, Drew Robinson, and Eddys Leonard.

Generously listed as 6-foot and 160-pounds, Leonard had shown doubles power during his first two seasons in the Dodgers' farm system. Last season, though, he cut down his batted ball rates and began driving the ball more consistently, with more authority. There are some mechanical tweaks in his swing that are still required. For example, his back foot has a tendency to disengage from the ground. Fantastic bat speed. Physically built like Mookie Betts. Leonard is still a man without a defensive position, but there's starting big league potential here. In terms of big league ceiling, think: .290/.340/.450.

Ceiling: 2.5-win player
Risk: Moderate
MLB ETA: 2024

7. Landon Knack, RHP

	FB	CB	SL	CH	Command	Overall
	60	50	55	60	60	50

Born: 07/15/97	Age: 24	Bats: L	Top Comp: Rick Porcello
Height: 6-2	Weight: 220	Throws: R	

Season	Team	Age	Level	IP	TBF	K/9	K%	BB/9	BB%	K-BB%	ERA	FIP	xFIP	Pit/Bat
2021	LAD	23	A+	39.2	154	12.48	35.71%	1.13	3.25%	32.47%	2.50	2.33	2.86	3.87
2021	LAD	23	AA	22.2	92	10.72	29.35%	1.19	3.26%	26.09%	4.37	5.20	3.64	3.82

Background: Fun Fact Part I: The Dodgers have selected just three players out East Tennessee State University throughout their history – Nathan Dunn (1992, 49th round), Clint Freeman (2014, 18th round), and – of course – Landon Knack. Fun Fact Part II: Knack is the second highest player chosen in East Tennessee State University history, trailing former All-Star left-hander Atlee Hammaker by 39 picks. Knack, like fellow Dodgers top pitching prospect Bobby Miller, is a lefty-swinging, righty-throwing hurler. Taken with the 60th pick in the 2020 draft, sandwiched between Bobby Miller and Clayton Beeter, Knack has dealt with a couple of serious injuries throughout his amateur career. As detailed by MLB.com, the 6-foot-2, 220-pound right-hander tore his labrum during a high school game and he dislocated his non-throwing shoulder in 2017. Knack was a good starting pitcher during his first season at East Tennessee State University, but looked like Greg Maddux during his final season with the Southern Conference school in 2020. Before the COVID-imposed shutdown, he posted an absolutely astronomical 51-to-1 strikeout-to-walk ratio with a 1.08 ERA in 25.0 innings of work. Last season, his first taste of minor league ball, Knack blitzed through High-A in only 10 appearances and continued to dominate Double-A for another six games. In total, he tossed 62.1 innings with 82 punch outs and just eight free passes. He tallied a 3.18 ERA and a 3.38 FIP.

Scouting Report: One of the most, in not *the most*, consistent strike-throwing machine in the minor leagues. Knack fills up the zone with quality pitches at will. And when he does miss, it's often on purpose as a chase offering. But the former East Tennessee State University ace isn't just a soft-tossing, crafty pitcher. He unfurls a plus fastball that sits in the 94- to 96-mph range. He complements it with an average curveball, a 55-grade slider, and a dominating plus changeup. And everything plays up do to his sniper-like precision. Los Angeles has a tremendously deep rotation, as well as a full bushel of arms waiting in the minor leagues, so Knack may get lost in the shuffle. Rick Porcello-type potential.

Ceiling: 2.5-win player
Risk: Moderate
MLB ETA: 2023

8. Maddux Bruns, LHP

	FB	CB	SL	CH	Command	Overall
	60	60	55	50	45/50	50

Born: 06/20/02	Age: 20	Bats: L	Top Comp: N/A
Height: 6-2	Weight: 205	Throws: L	

Background: The recipient of the Gatorade Baseball Player of the Year for the state of Alabama after a meteoric senior campaign at UMS-Wright Prep in 2021. Bruns, who was also tabbed by the Alabama Sports Writers Association as the state's Mr. Baseball, surrendered just 13 hits in 49 innings pitched during his final amateur campaign, striking out 102 against just 19 free passes. He finished the season with a 0.86 ERA (six earned runs). The 6-foot-2, 205-pound southpaw also batted a healthy .337 with a .450 on-base percentage to go along with three dingers and 17 RBIs at the dish as well. The Dodgers snagged the hard-throwing lefty in the opening round, 29th overall. The two sides came to an agreement on a deal worth $2.2 million – slightly below the recommended slot bonus of $2.4 million. Prior to the draft, Bruns was committed to SEC powerhouse Mississippi State University. On a side note: the Miami Marlins selected former UMW-Wright Prep alum – and Mississippi State University product – Tanner Allen in the fourth round of the draft as well. Bruns was named after Greg Maddux, and his middle name, John, is a hat tip to fellow Braves ace John Smoltz. Talk about pressure…

Scouting Report: Per the usual, here's my post-draft write-up:

> "Thick lower body. Bruns features a standard four pitch mix: fastball, curveball, slider, and a changeup. Bruns' heater sits in the low- to mid-90s, reportedly touching as high as 98 mph at times. He'll complement the plus offering with a high spin curveball, which averages between 2600 and 2900 RPMs, adding a second plus weapon. His slider flashes above-average. And his changeup adds a fourth weapon in his arsenal. There's some Max Fried-type potential brewing in his left arm. Very, very strong – and savvy – pick by one of baseball's best run organizations."

Ceiling: 2.5-win player
Risk: Moderate
MLB ETA: 2025

9. Carlos Duran, RHP

	FB	SL	CH	Command	Overall
	60	60	N/A	50/55	55

Born: 07/30/01	Age: 20	Bats: R	Top Comp: N/A
Height: 6-7	Weight: 230	Throws: R	

Season	Team	Age	Level	IP	TBF	K/9	K%	BB/9	BB%	K-BB%	ERA	FIP	xFIP	Pit/Bat
2018	LAD	16	R	42.0	157	6.43	19.11%	0.64	1.91%	17.20%	1.50	2.74	2.84	1.56
2019	LAD	17	R	21.0	77	9.86	29.87%	4.29	12.99%	16.88%	0.43	2.87	3.20	2.13
2019	LAD	17	R	19.1	107	7.45	14.95%	4.66	9.35%	5.61%	8.38	6.49	5.66	1.73
2021	LAD	19	A	73.2	340	13.32	32.06%	2.93	7.06%	25.00%	5.25	4.20	3.63	3.67

Background: Standing as tall as an NBA shooting guard, it's hard not to notice the 6-foot-7, 230-pound right-hander. And that's exactly what the Dodgers did when they saw him throw a baseball – they took notice. The club eventually signed him to a deal worth $300,000 in early 2018. Duran would make his professional debut a few months later in the foreign rookie league. And, as expected, the behemoth right-hander dominated the mere mortal competition as he posted a 1.50 ERA with 30 punch outs and just three free passes in 42.0 innings of work. Duran opened the following season back up in the Dominican Summer League, but after five solid starts, the front office moved him stateside for another eight appearances. Last season, the hard-throwing youngster spent the majority of the year with the Rancho Cucamonga Quakes, but manage to squeeze in a pair of games in High-A as well. He would throw 81.0 innings, averaging an impressive 12.8 strikeouts and 3.3 walks per nine innings. He finished the year with a 5.56 ERA and a 4.24 FIP.

Scouting Report: Consider the following:

- Since 2006, only four 19-year-old pitchers met the following criteria in Low-A with one organization (min. 70 IP): 31% to 33% strikeout percentage and a 6% and 8% walk rate. Those four arms: Danny Duffy, Shelby Miller, Joey Estes, and – of course – Carlos Duran.
- For those wondering: Duffy's been an above-average, though oft-injured, pitcher during his career; Shelby Miller once looked to be one of the best young pitchers in the game before crashing in his mid-20s; and Joey Estes is one of the Braves best young arms.

Duran does the one thing that gigantic pitchers *aren't* supposed to do: throw consistent strikes. What's even more impressive: he was a teenager doing so. But the young, baby-faced Dominican does just that – with a pair of plus offerings. Duran's fastball sits in the 93- to 96-mph range and touched as high as 98 mph during the summer. And his slider is a legitimate power breaking ball with severe downward tumble. Reports indicate he throws a below-average changeup, though I did not see one. With that being said, Duran may continue to dominate the low levels of the minor leagues with his fastball / slider combo, but he needs to establish at least a reliable third offering. He looks like a candidate that may succeed throwing a splitter. Reliever risk with one of the larger ceilings as a pitcher in the farm system.

Ceiling: 3.0-win player
Risk: High
MLB ETA: 2023/2024

10. Clayton Beeter, RHP

	FB	CB	SL	CH	Command	Overall
	60	60	60	N/A	50	50

Born: 10/09/98	Age: 23	Bats: R	Top Comp:
Height: 6-2	Weight: 220	Throws: R	

Season	Team	Age	Level	IP	TBF	K/9	K%	BB/9	BB%	K-BB%	ERA	FIP	xFIP	Pit/Bat
2021	LAD	22	A+	37.1	151	13.26	36.42%	3.62	9.93%	26.49%	3.13	3.24	3.41	4.12
2021	LAD	22	AA	15.0	62	13.80	37.10%	4.20	11.29%	25.81%	4.20	3.95	3.28	4.19

Background: Very rarely will there be a collegiate pitcher with 40 or so innings on their resume, across multiple seasons, hear their name called as earlier as Beeter. After redshirting his freshman season because of a pair of surgical procedures on his right elbow, the burly 6-foot-2, 220-pound right-hander spent the 2019 season in the Red Raiders' bullpen, saving eight games with 40 strikeouts and 20 walks in only 20.2 innings of work. Beeter got off to an absurdly dominating start to the 2020 season, averaging 14.1 strikeouts and just 1.7 walks per nine innings with a 2.14 ERA across four starts before COVID prematurely ended the collegiate season. Los Angeles selected the Texas-born righty in the second round, 66th overall, and signed him to a deal worth $1,196,500. The front office pushed the promising hurler straight into High-A to begin his debut last season. And after 23 brief appearances with the Loons, he wrapped up his successful first season with a five-game cameo at Double-A. Beeter tossed 52.1 innings last season, averaging 13.4 strikeouts and 3.8 walks per nine innings. He finished the year with an aggregate 3.44 ERA and a matching 3.44 FIP.

Scouting Report: Possesses some of the best pure "stuff" in the entire organization – which is saying something given the Dodgers' lengthy history of pitching development success. Beeter attacks hitters with a 95- to 97-mph plus fastball with extreme life above the belt. He consistently moves the offering around the strike zone and doesn't shy away from attacking hitters in under their hands. He complements the offering with a pair of plus breaking balls: a low-80s 12-6 hammer of a curveball, though it does lack a bit of consistency, and a wipeout, knee-buckling high-80s slider. Various reports indicate the former Texas Tech hurler will throw a changeup, though I never saw one in either game I scouted. Given Beeter's lack of innings on the mound in college, Los Angeles closely governed his workload early in the season before stretching him out to three-inning stints late in the year. There's definite reliever risk, and it remains to be seen whether Beeter can turnover a lineup without a changeup, but the Dodgers develop arms as well as any club.

Ceiling: 2.5-win player
Risk: Moderate to High
MLB ETA: 2023

11. Alex De Jesus, SS

Hit	Power	SB	Patience	Glove	Overall
40/45	45/55	30	55	45/50	50

Born: 03/22/02	Age: 20	Bats: R	Top Comp: N/A
Height: 6-2	Weight: 170	Throws: R	

Season	Team	Age	Level	PA	1B	2B	3B	HR	SB	CS	BB%	K%	AVG	OBP	SLG	ISO
2019	LAD	17	R	63	10	5	0	1	0	0	12.70%	22.22%	0.296	0.381	0.444	0.148
2019	LAD	17	R	178	34	8	1	2	5	1	6.74%	32.58%	0.276	0.326	0.374	0.098
2021	LAD	19	A	422	56	25	1	12	1	0	16.35%	30.33%	0.268	0.386	0.447	0.179

Background: Another one of the club's high profile, potential homeruns on the international market. Los Angeles inked the 6-foot-2, 170-pound shortstop to a deal worth $500,000 four years ago. De Jesus, a native of Santo Domingo, Dominican Republic, made his professional debut the following season as he split time between the foreign and stateside rookie leagues. He would bat an aggregate .281/.340/.392 with 13 doubles, one triple, and three homeruns. Last season, the then-19-year-old began to blossom as an offensive threat during his jaunt through Low-A West with Rancho Cucamonga. In 97 games with Quakes, the young middle infielder slugged .268/.386/.447 with 25 doubles, one triple, and 25 homeruns. His overall production, per *Weighted Runs Created Plus*, topped the league average mark by 23% – the fourth best mark for a 19-year-old in Low-A West in 2021, trailing only Robert Hassell, Zac Veen, and Euribiel Angeles.

Scouting Report: Consider the following:

- Since 2006, only three 19-year-old hitters posted a 118 to 128 wRC+ total with a walk rate of at least 12% and strikeout rate between 27% and 31% in Low-A with one organization (min. 350): Brendon Davis, Braxton Davidson, and – of course – Alex De Jesus.

Perhaps unsurprisingly given the missed 2020 season as well as his youth and limited track record, De Jesus got off to a dreadful start to the year in 2021; he batted a rotten .179/.294/.316 with a strikeout rate of more than 38% through his first 33 games. However, beginning on June 19th through the rest of the year, De Jesus slugged a hearty .312/430/.513 with 21 doubles, one triple, and eight homeruns in only 64 games. The best part: his 26.2% swing-and-miss rate is far less concerning. Good patience. 25-homerun potential. Defensively, he'll never be confused with Ozzie Smith, but projects as an average shortstop.

Ceiling: 2.0-win player
Risk: Moderate
MLB ETA: 2024

12. Jorbit Vivas, 2B/3B

Hit	Power	SB	Patience	Glove	Overall
50	50	40	50	55	45

Born: 03/09/01	Age: 21	Bats: L	Top Comp: Omar Infante
Height: 5-10	Weight: 171	Throws: R	

Season	Team	Age	Level	PA	1B	2B	3B	HR	SB	CS	BB%	K%	AVG	OBP	SLG	ISO
2018	LAD	17	R	217	27	11	1	0	16	4	11.98%	16.13%	0.222	0.350	0.295	0.074
2019	LAD	18	R	97	16	6	1	1	5	5	6.19%	16.49%	0.286	0.371	0.417	0.131
2019	LAD	18	R	137	27	11	2	1	5	4	9.49%	10.95%	0.357	0.438	0.513	0.157
2021	LAD	20	A	375	65	20	4	13	5	3	7.20%	11.20%	0.311	0.389	0.515	0.204
2021	LAD	20	A+	102	20	6	0	1	3	1	12.75%	12.75%	0.318	0.422	0.424	0.106

Background: Owner of – perhaps – the best name in all of professional baseball. And if it's not the best, then it's at least my *favorite* name in professional baseball. The Dodgers signed the lefty-swinging infielder out of Puerto Cabello, Venezuela, for $300,000 in 2017. After a slow, disappointing start to his career in the foreign rookie league a year later, Vivas started to his feet under him in the Arizona Summer League in 2019 and has stopped hitting as he moved up to the Pioneer League and into the first two levels of full season action in 2021. Splitting time between Rancho Cucamonga and Great Lakes, the 5-foot-10, 171-pound second / third baseman slugged an aggregate .312/.396/.496 with 26 doubles, four triples, 14 homeruns, and eight stolen bases (in 12 attempts). Per *Weighted Runs Created Plus*, his production topped the league average mark by 36%.

Scouting Report: Consider the following:

- Since 2006, there were four 20-year-old hitters that met the following criteria in Low-A with one organization (min. 350 PA): 130 to 140 wRC+, a sub-15% strikeout rate, and a walk rate between 7% and 9%. Those four hitters: Jose Altuve, Josh Reddick, Otto Lopez, and Jorbit Vivas.
- For those counting at home: Altuve owns a career 125 wRC+; Reddick is sporting a 104 wRC+ in over 1,300 big league games, and Lopez posted a 136 wRC+ in Double-A last season.

One of the more underrated prospects in the system, as well as in all of baseball. A throwback to ballplayers of yesteryear, Vivas is an extreme contact hitter, posting an aggregate K-rate of just 11.5% last season. The walk rates will never inflate his OBP, but he's a patient hitter and won't chase frequently. He profiles better at the keystone, but may hit enough to justify keep him at the hot corner as he matures.

Ceiling: 1.5-win player
Risk: Moderate
MLB ETA: 2023

13. Ryan Pepiot, RHP

FB	CB	SL	CH	Command	Overall
60	N/A	50	70	45	45

Born: 08/21/97	Age: 24	Bats: R	Top Comp: Poor Man's Lucas Giolito
Height: 6-3	Weight: 215	Throws: R	

Season	Team	Age	Level	IP	TBF	K/9	K%	BB/9	BB%	K-BB%	ERA	FIP	xFIP	Pit/Bat
2019	LAD	21	A	18.1	76	10.31	27.63%	4.42	11.84%	15.79%	2.45	2.79	3.60	4.04
2021	LAD	23	AA	59.2	233	12.22	34.76%	3.92	11.16%	23.61%	2.87	3.75	4.07	4.00
2021	LAD	23	AAA	41.2	202	9.94	22.77%	4.54	10.40%	12.38%	7.13	7.12	5.79	3.88

Background: The highest drafted player in Butler University history. The Dodgers selected the hard-throwing right-hander in the third round, 102nd overall, and signed him to a deal worth $547,500 – also the largest bonus given to a former Bulldog. The 6-foot-3, 215-pound hurler turned in a dominant debut showing in the minor leagues in 2019, posting a 31-to-13 strikeout-to-walk ratio in with a 1.93 ERA in 23.1 innings of work. Last season, after missing a year of development due to COVID, Pepiot split time between the minors' final two stops. Totaling 101.1 innings between Tulsa and Oklahoma City, averaging 11.3 strikeouts and 4.2 walks per nine innings. He compiled an aggregate 4.62 ERA and a 5.14 FIP.

Scouting Report: Consider the following:

- Since 2006, only five 23-year-old hurlers posted a strikeout percentage north of 33% and a double-digit walk percentage in Double-A with one organization (min. 50 IP): Enoli Paredes, Matt Brash, Paul Estrada, Paul Voelker, and – of course – former Butler Bulldog Ryan Pepiot.

Mainly a two-pitch pitcher, Pepiot relies heavily on his plus mid- to upper-90s fastball and wipeout plus-plus change with tremendous arm side fade and dive. Reportedly, he'll mix in a pair of breaking balls – slider and curveball – though I only witness his average-ish slider. He's prone to bouts of wildness and was particularly erratic following his promotion up to Triple-A West. Watching Pepiot dominate with his fastball / changeup combo, and it's easy to dream upon a #4-type arm. But his lack of third quality option – especially lack of an option he trusts – almost dooms him to a future role as a relief ace. White Sox ace Lucas Giolito has mainly lived off of his tremendous FB/CH combination, but he also shows above-average command.

Ceiling: 1.5-win player
Risk: Moderate
MLB ETA: 2023

14. Jose Ramos, OF

Hit	Power	SB	Patience	Glove	Overall
40/45	50/60	30	50	50	45

Born: 01/01/01	Age: 21	Bats: R	Top Comp: N/A
Height: 6-1	Weight: 200	Throws: R	

Season	Team	Age	Level	PA	1B	2B	3B	HR	SB	CS	BB%	K%	AVG	OBP	SLG	ISO
2019	LAD	18	R	243	40	15	0	2	9	3	8.23%	18.93%	0.275	0.362	0.377	0.101
2021	LAD	20	A	220	32	18	3	8	1	4	7.27%	25.91%	0.313	0.377	0.559	0.246

Background: Born on a pretty notable date: 01/01/01. The Dodgers signed the 6-foot-1, 200-pound outfielder out of Chepo, Panama, for a rather paltry sum – just $30,000 – in 2018. Ramos put together a moderately successful showing in the Dominican Summer League the following year, hitting .275/.362/.377 with 15 doubles and a pair of homeruns in 57 games. Last season, though, the club moved him stateside to the Complex League. But that stint lasted just 15 games before he earned a promotion up to Low-A (of course, batting .383/.456/.633 helps to accelerate one's path). Ramos continue to hit well during his extended look with Rancho Cucamonga as well, slugging .313/.377/.559 with 18 doubles, three triples, and eight homeruns in only 47 games. His production with the Quakes, per *Weighted Runs Created Plus*, topped the average threshold by 38%.

Scouting Report: Just for fun, his Low-A numbers prorated for a full 162-game season: 62 doubles, 10 triples, and 28 homeruns. Never one to put the ball on the ground frequently, Ramos began tapping into some of his power potential last season after showing very little thump during his professional debut in 2019. Watching Ramos take hacks and it's clear he's trying to do one thing over-and-over again: hit absolute moon shots out of any park in the country. And he doesn't even try and hide it. Extreme uppercut but it's a really good looking swing. Good bat speed. Ramos is going to be a boom-or-bust type of hitter: he's either going to make enough consistent contact to become an All-Star or his K-rates are going to bloat and he's going to flame out. I don't see it ended any other way than those two options.

Ceiling: 1.5-win player
Risk: Moderate to High
MLB ETA: 2023

15. Justin Yurchak, 1B

Hit	Power	SB	Patience	Glove	Overall
55/60	35	30	55	55	40

Born: 09/17/96	Age: 25	Bats: L	Top Comp: N/A
Height: 6-1	Weight: 204	Throws: R	

Season	Team	Age	Level	PA	1B	2B	3B	HR	SB	CS	BB%	K%	AVG	OBP	SLG	ISO
2019	LAD	22	R	123	19	8	0	8	0	0	21.14%	23.58%	0.365	0.496	0.698	0.333
2019	LAD	22	A	162	25	11	1	5	0	1	8.64%	18.52%	0.292	0.358	0.486	0.194
2018	CHW	21	A	363	61	17	1	1	0	2	12.40%	14.60%	0.256	0.348	0.326	0.070
2021	LAD	24	A+	269	64	10	1	5	2	1	14.13%	17.47%	0.356	0.446	0.476	0.120
2021	LAD	24	AA	134	34	8	0	2	0	0	9.70%	16.42%	0.383	0.436	0.504	0.122

Background: State University of New York at Birmingham (boy, that's a mouthful) has produced just 16 draft picks throughout their history. And three of those picks, Justin Yurchak, Nick Wegmann, and Ben Anderson, came in successive years (2017 through 2019). A 12th round pick by the White Sox in 2017, the Dodgers acquired the underrated prospect for former top prospect flameout Manny Banuelos immediately following the conclusion of the 2018 season. Almost as soon as he donned a Dodgers affiliate uniform Yurchak began hitting. He torched the younger competition in the Pioneer League in 2019, hitting .365/.496/.698 and handled himself well during his 38-game cameo in the Midwest League. Last season, though, was one for the ages. In a combined 92 games with Great Lakes and Tulsa, the 6-foot-1, 204-pound first baseman slugged a scorching .365/.443/.485 with 18 doubles, one triple, and seven homeruns. His overall production, per *Weighted Runs Created Plus*, topped the league average mark by a staggering 55%.

Scouting Report: The former 12th round pick paced the minor league circuit as he captured the hitting title with an aggregate .365 average. Yurchak is a throwback type of hitter, something along the lines of a Mark Grace, Wally Joyner, or Keith Hernandez as he sprays line drives but doesn't offer up much in terms of pop. One of the most amazing statistics about Yurchak's phenomenal season: after hitting a putrid .131/.289/.164 over his first 20 games, the lefty-swinging first baseman batted red hot .416/.479/.556 over his remaining 72 contests. Good glove. Above-average hit tool. Dominant production against younger competition. And middle infield power. If Yurchak is going to develop into a viable big leaguer, the Dodgers farm system and player development engine is the best place to be. If he hits in Double-A, he'll hit at the big league level. Mark it down.

Ceiling: 1.0-win player
Risk: Low to Moderate
MLB ETA: 2022

16. Pete Heubeck, RHP

FB	CB	CH	Command	Overall
55	60	N/A	45/50	45

Born: 08/21/97	Age: 24	Bats: R	Top Comp: N/A
Height: 6-3	Weight: 215	Throws: R	

Background: The Dodgers honed in on pitching like a heat-seeking missile during the draft last summer, using 17 of their 19 total selections on arms. Only two of those, though, were high schoolers – both of which were taken with their first two choices. The club nabbed left-hander Maddux Bruns with the 29th overall pick and doubled down of prep arms with their selection of right-hander Pete Heubeck, who was taken with the 101st overall pick. Signed for an above-slot bonus worth $1,269,500, the 6-foot-3, 215-pound hurler made a pair of appearances in the Arizona Complex League last summer, throwing four innings with a whopping nine punch outs and just two free passes. Heubeck surrendered just one hit – a single to Seattle's Cole Barr – and didn't surrender a run – earned or unearned.

Scouting Report: Signed for the equivalent of mid-second round money, it was enough to convince Heubeck to bypass his strong commitment to Wake Forest University. Physically reminiscent of a young Dustin May: tall, long arms, and filled with gobs of potential. Heubeck attacks hitters with a low-90s fastball that peaked in the mid-90s at various points. But his best offering is a hellacious, plus curveball with late, hard downward tilt. He'll also mix in a changeup, though I didn't see one on tape. Heubeck utilizes his lower half exceptionally well. He's very much cut from the typical Dodgers pitching prospect cloth. Very savvy pick.

Ceiling: 1.0- to 1.5-win player
Risk: Moderate to High
MLB ETA: 2025

17. Carson Taylor, C

	Hit	Power	SB	Patience	Glove	Overall
	45	50	30	55	50	40

Born: 06/06/99	Age: 23	Bats: B	Top Comp: N/A
Height: 6-2	Weight: 205	Throws: R	

Season	Team	Age	Level	PA	1B	2B	3B	HR	SB	CS	BB%	K%	AVG	OBP	SLG	ISO
2021	LAD	22	A+	342	55	16	1	9	1	0	13.16%	18.42%	0.278	0.371	0.433	0.155

Background: Yet another savvy selection during the draft process by one of the best drafting organizations in Major League Baseball. A defensive vagabond during his days at Virginia Tech, Taylor, who roved between catcher and both corner infield positions, was in the midst of a dynamic offensive performance before the COVID-imposed shutdown as he slugged a Ruthian .431/.541/.690 with seven doubles, one triple, and a pair of homeruns in 16 games. The Dodgers nabbed the young switch-hitter in the fourth round two years ago and signed him to a deal worth $397,500. Last season, as minor leaguers moved back to work, the front office aggressively challenged the Georgia-born prospect and sent him directly to High-A Central. He responded with a rock solid .278/.371/.433 with 16 doubles, one triple, and nine dingers. Per *Weighted Runs Created Plus*, his overall production topped the league average mark by 23%. Taylor also appeared in 11 games with the Glendale Desert Dogs in the Arizona Fall League, batting .297/.316/.459.

Scouting Report: Consider the following:

- Since 2006, there were four 22-year-old h`itters that met the following criteria in High-A with one organization (min. 300 PA): 118 to 128 wRC+, a walk rate north of 12%, and a 17% to 20% strikeout rate. Those four bats: Miles Mastrobuoni, Zeke DeVoss, Travis Jones, Carson Taylor.

An underrated, do-everything-well-without-a-true-standout-tool hitter. Taylor makes consistent contact, flashes solid power, and works the count incredibly well. And like many of the hitters being aggressively challenged last season, the former Virginia Tech star got off to an abysmal start to his debut, batting a lowly .182/.351/.227 over his first 15 games. But he got his feet underneath him in early June and slugged .296/.375/.470 over his final 64 games. He's built from the Austin Barnes mold: positional versatility, good patience, and pop. The lone differentiator, though, is Barnes' above-average, Gold Glove caliber defense. Taylor is merely average.

Ceiling: 1.0-win player
Risk: Moderate
MLB ETA: 2023

18. Andre Jackson, RHP

	FB	CB	SL	CH	Command	Overall
	50	45	50	55	50	40

Born: 05/01/96	Age: 26	Bats: R	Top Comp: Replacement Joe Reliever
Height: 6-3	Weight: 210	Throws: R	

Season	Team	Age	Level	IP	TBF	K/9	K%	BB/9	BB%	K-BB%	ERA	FIP	xFIP	Pit/Bat
2018	LAD	22	A	49.2	233	8.15	19.31%	7.43	17.60%	1.72%	4.35	5.05	5.03	4.08
2018	LAD	22	R	18.1	75	15.22	41.33%	1.96	5.33%	36.00%	3.44	1.34	1.75	2.01
2019	LAD	23	A	48.1	189	9.31	26.46%	3.54	10.05%	16.40%	2.23	2.83	3.29	3.98
2019	LAD	23	A+	66.1	294	12.35	30.95%	5.16	12.93%	18.03%	3.66	3.89	3.71	4.16
2021	LAD	25	AA	63.1	253	10.66	29.64%	2.84	7.91%	21.74%	3.27	4.71	4.13	3.96
2021	LAD	25	AAA	26.1	114	7.86	20.18%	3.08	7.89%	12.28%	5.13	6.17	5.64	4.02

Background: A decent bat that patrolled the outfield pastures at the University of Utah. Jackson was limited to just over 20 innings on the mound before hitting the disabled with a wonky elbow that eventually required Tommy John surgery. The Dodgers scouting gurus, though, saw enough promise in the wiry right-hander and took a 12th round flier on him in 2017. The 6-foot-3, 210-pound hurler would eventually make it back to the mound a year later as he began his slow climb through the minor leagues. Last season, Jackson began the year in Double-A, got bumped up to Triple-A, and then eventually got the call up to The Show. After a start against the Pirates he was demoted all the way down to Low-A, brought back up to Los Angeles, and spent the remainder of the year in AAA. He finished the year with a 103-to-30 strikeout-to-walk ratio in 95.1 minor league innings. And in 11.2 MLB innings he struck out 10 and walked six.

Scouting Report: Jackson's fastball, which sat in the low-90s and would reach a tick higher with noticeable effort, lacked the explosive he's shown in years past. And his offspeed offerings lacked crisp bite as well. Curveball is below-average and spins as fast as the tires on a toddler's tricycle (it averaged just 1929 RPM during his time with the Dodgers). His slider is a workable average offering, sitting in the mid-80s with late cutter-like movement. And his changeup adds the lone above-average offering to his arsenal. There was a point several years ago that Jackson may have owned as much untapped potential as any arm in the Dodgers' system, but he seems to have just plateaued. He's still an organizational win: a former over-slot 12th rounder that's cracked a big league roster a couple times.

Ceiling: 0.5 to 1.0-win player
Risk: Low to Moderate
MLB ETA: Debuted in 2021

19. Gavin Stone, RHP

	FB	CB	SL	CH	Command	Overall
	55	50	50	50/55	55	40

Born: 10/15/98	Age: 23	Bats: R	Top Comp: N/A
Height: 6-1	Weight: 175	Throws: R	

Season	Team	Age	Level	IP	TBF	K/9	K%	BB/9	BB%	K-BB%	ERA	FIP	xFIP	Pit/Bat
2021	LAD	22	A	70.0	295	12.99	34.24%	2.57	6.78%	27.46%	3.73	3.17	3.29	3.83
2021	LAD	22	A+	21.0	83	15.86	44.58%	2.14	6.02%	38.55%	3.86	2.20	1.57	3.99

Background: The University of Central Arkansas isn't exactly a well-known hotbed for baseball talent. The Southland Conference school has produced just 22 draft picks throughout its history. But the Bears have produced a whopping eight picks over the past four draft classes. The earliest pick among the group (as well as in school history): right-hander Gavin Stone, the Dodgers' final selection in the limited 2020 draft. Taken in the fifth round, 159th overall pick, Stone began to open eyes as a long reliever for Central Arkansas in 2019, posting a dominating 1.52 ERA while averaging 11.0 strikeouts and just 2.1 walks per nine innings. The school transitioned the righty into a full time starting gig in 2020. And he blossomed. Or he *was* blossoming before COVID shut it down. He finished the abbreviated campaign with a 31-to-6 strikeout-to-walk ratio and a 1.30 ERA in 27.2 innings of work. Last season, the Dodgers sent the 6-foot-1, 175-pound hurler to Low-A to begin his professional career. After 18 appearances, he was bumped up to High-A for another five starts. He finished the year with 91.0 innings, averaging 13.6 strikeouts and 2.5 walks per nine innings. He totaled an aggregate 3.76 ERA and a 2.95 FIP.

Scouting Report: Consider the following:

- Since 2006, only two 22-year-old hurlers posted a strikeout percentage north of 32% with a sub-7% walk percentage in Low-A with one organization (min. 70 IP): Jaime Arias-Bautista and Gavin Stone.

Stone does a lot things that older pitching prospects showcase in the lower levels that lead to gaudy strikeout numbers and overall production: he commands the strike zone, throws several pitches for strikes, and can throw offspeed strikes early in the count. Above-average fastball, average curveball, average slider (though it's the better of the two breaking balls), and a changeup that shows enough run and fade that it may eventually creep into above-average territory. Everything plays up, though, due to his ability to consistently throw quality strikes. There isn't enough here to be a big league starter, but the Dodgers' development program is always full of surprises.

Ceiling: 0.5 to 1.0-win player
Risk: Moderate
MLB ETA: 2023

20. Kendall Williams, RHP

	FB	CB	SL	CH	Command	Overall
	50/55	50	45/50	50	55	40

Born: 08/24/00	Age: 21	Bats: R	Top Comp: N/A
Height: 6-6	Weight: 205	Throws: R	

Season	Team	Age	Level	IP	TBF	K/9	K%	BB/9	BB%	K-BB%	ERA	FIP	xFIP	Pit/Bat
2019	TOR	18	R	16.0	63	10.69	30.16%	3.94	11.11%	19.05%	1.13	2.63	3.32	2.02
2021	LAD	20	A	93.1	413	8.39	21.07%	2.12	5.33%	15.74%	4.53	5.15	4.37	3.32

Background: A product of IMG Academy, the Bradenton, Florida, based baseball talent factory. Williams was part of IMG's massive influx of talent into the professional ranks in 2019 as the school churned out six picks, including three players chosen among the top two rounds. Toronto selected the big prep right-hander in the second round, 52nd overall, and signed him to a deal worth $1,547,500 – roughly $100,000 above the recommended slot value. A little more than a year later the Jays flipped Williams, along with Ryan Noda, to the Dodgers in exchange for veteran right-hander Ross Stripling. Last season Williams made 23 appearances with the Rancho Cucamonga Quakes, 19 of which were starts, throwing 93.1 innings with 87 punch outs and 22 free passes. He finished his first full season in minor league ball with a 4.53 ERA, 5.15 FIP, and a 4.37 xFIP.

Scouting Report: Consider the following:

- Since 2006, there have been twelve 20-year-old hurlers to post a 20% to 22% strikeout percentage with a 4% to 6% walk percentage in Low-A with one organization (min. 90 IP): Jacob Nix, Tyler Mahle, Jose Rodriguez, Jean Cosme, Brock Dykxhoorn, Will Stewart, Alejandro Requena, Jonathan Martinez, Manuel Espinoza, Marcos Frias, Zack Von Rosenberg, and Kendall Williams.

I was expecting more out of the former second round pick. The fastball was good, not great. The curveball was mediocre, not above-average. The slider was workable, but not a swing-and-miss pitch. And the changeup, which he was at least confident in, may eventually get to 55-grade territory. But, overall, I was not impressed. There are a lot of physical similarities between Dustin May and Kendall Williams: long, flowing, luscious hair, both 6-foot-6, both have massive, funky-esque leg kicks out of the windup. Williams is listed here not on production, but in hopes that the Dodgers unlock some of his remaining projection.

Ceiling: 0.5 to 1.0-win player
Risk: Moderate
MLB ETA: 2024

Miami Marlins

Top Prospects

1. Edward Cabrera, RHP

FB	CB	SL	CH	Command	Overall
70	60	70	60	55	60

Born: 04/13/98	Age: 24	Bats: R	Top Comp: Dinelson Lamet
Height: 6-5	Weight: 217	Throws: R	

Season	Team	Age	Level	IP	TBF	K/9	K%	BB/9	BB%	K-BB%	ERA	FIP	xFIP	Pit/Bat
2018	MIA	20	A	100.1	440	8.34	21.14%	3.77	9.55%	11.59%	4.22	4.51	4.13	3.60
2019	MIA	21	A+	58.0	227	11.33	32.16%	2.79	7.93%	24.23%	2.02	2.20	2.53	3.90
2019	MIA	21	AA	38.2	156	10.01	27.56%	3.03	8.33%	19.23%	2.56	4.33	3.76	3.76
2021	MIA	23	AA	26.0	97	11.42	34.02%	2.08	6.19%	27.84%	2.77	3.05	2.92	3.97
2021	MIA	23	AAA	29.1	129	14.73	37.21%	5.83	14.73%	22.48%	3.68	3.91	3.95	4.12

Background: When I was working for *Baseball Info Solutions* many, many years ago, I scouted one of the first big league games of a young right-hander – Joakim Soria. I scribbled in my notebook, "special". There was something about Soria that made me think he was destined to be a star at the big league level. During the 2018 season, as I was scouting minor league pitchers, I was struck by that same sense of potential future stardom. I was watching a wiry right-hander from Santiago, Dominican Republic, who was unfurling wipeout offering after wipeout offering. I was scouting Edward Cabrera for the first time. Since then, Cabrera has exploded up prospect charts and I've become his largest supporter. Signed by the organization for $100,000 as a 17-year-old on July 2nd, 2015, Cabrera wouldn't start to blossom for three more years. The flame-throwing right-hander spent that year twirling games for the Greensboro Grasshoppers, posting a 93-to-42 strikeout-to-walk ratio in 100.1 innings of work. Cabrera's dominance lurched forward the following season as he split time between Jupiter and Jacksonville, averaging 10.8 strikeouts and just 2.9 walks per nine innings to go along with a 2.23 ERA. After losing a season of further development due to the COVID-imposed shutdown, Cabrera did a two-game tune-up in early June with Jupiter before blitzing through Double-A and Triple-A and eventually making his big league debut with Miami at the end of August. The big righty finished the minor league season with 92 punch outs, 25 walks, and a 2.93 ERA 61.1 innings of work. Cabrera threw an additional 26.1 innings in *The Show*, averaging 9.6 strikeouts and 6.5 walks per nine innings.

Snippet from The 2020 Prospect Digest Handbook: I scouted a handful of Cabrera's games in Class AA season. The main takeaway: he's evolving from a thrower into a full-fledged pitcher. He's always possessed a plus-plus fastball and that wipeout, hard-tilting slider, and a lot his early success was simply from overpowering low level hitters. Last season, though, his changeup progressed into an above-average weapon – one that (A) he showed a significant amount of trust in and (B) adds a third swing-and-miss option to his repertoire. It's power changeup, sitting in the 91- to 92-mph range, with some dive to it. Cabrera has the look, build, and repertoire of a #2/#3-type arm. I really, *really* like him.

Scouting Report: Not only an elite arsenal, but – perhaps – *the* elite arsenal in all of the minor leagues. Cabrera's owns four *or better* offerings that individually can befuddle and dominate hitters. Cabrera's heater averages a smidgeon under 98 mph and will touch triple digits on occasion. His curveball, a low- to mid-80s offering, is a power breaking ball with late snapdragon bite. His slider is ever better, a genuine plus-plus pitch that can simply take the bat out of even the best of hitters' hands. And his changeup, with low-90s velocity, shows hard, fading, riding life. When it comes to facing him, it's pick your poison. Cabrera's evolved as player, going from a thrower into a legitimate pitcher – and one who doesn't shy away from mixing speeds in any count. He's one of the rare prospects that could ascend to the top of a big league rotation.

Ceiling: 4.5-win player
Risk: Moderate
MLB ETA: Debuted in 2021

2. Max Meyer, RHP

FB	SL	CH	Command	Overall
60	65	55/60	55	60

Born: 03/12/99	Age: 23	Bats: L	Top Comp: Walker Buehler
Height: 6-0	Weight: 196	Throws: R	

Season	Team	Age	Level	IP	TBF	K/9	K%	BB/9	BB%	K-BB%	ERA	FIP	xFIP	Pit/Bat
2021	MIA	22	AA	101.0	416	10.07	27.16%	3.56	9.62%	17.55%	2.41	3.34	3.61	3.57
2021	MIA	22	AAA	10.0	38	15.30	44.74%	1.80	5.26%	39.47%	0.90	1.86	1.98	3.97

Background: The University of Minnesota has had a couple Hall of Famers walk the hallowed halls of their school in its history: Dave Winfield was the fourth overall pick by the San Diego Padres in the 1973 draft and Paul Molitor went #3 overall by the Milwaukee Brewers just four seasons later. Other Golden Gopher notable alums include: Terry Steinbach, a three-time All-Star during his 14-year career; Denny Neagle, a two-time All-Star with the Pirates and Braves; backstop Dan Wilson, a 1996 member of the midsummer classic; and Minnesota-born lefty Glen Perkins, who also made three All-Star appearances with the Twins between 2013 and 2015. When Miami selected hard-throwing right-hander Max Meyer in the 2020 draft, he tied Molitor as the highest drafted Golden Gopher in school history. A light's out closer during his freshman season with the Big 10 Conference school, Meyer immediately transitioned into a dominant starting pitcher the following year as he averaged 10.2 strikeouts and just 2.3 walks per nine innings. And he got off to a remarkable start to the 2020 season before COVID shutdown collegiate baseball: 27.2 IP, 1.95 ERA, 46 strikeouts, and just eight walks. After signing with the Marlins for a massive $6.7 million, Meyer made his professional debut in 2021. And the organization didn't hold back as they aggressively shoved the 6-foot, 196-pound right-hander straight into the minors' toughest level – Double-A. Simply put, Meyer dominated for 20 stats and was nearly unhittable in two late-season starts in AAA. He finished the year with 130 punch outs, 42 free passes, and a 2.27 ERA in 111.0 innings of work.

Scouting Report: Consider the following:

- Since 2006, only five 22-year-old hurlers posted a strikeout percentage between 26.5% and 28.5% with a walk percentage between 8.5% and 10.5% in Double-A with one organization (min. 75 IP): Justin Dunn, Jake Faria, Matt Magill, Ronald Bolanos, and – of course – Mr. Golden Gopher, Max Meyer.

Plus, mid-90s fastball, a power breaking ball (more on that in a minute), an above-average changeup, and a strong feel for the strike zone. A variety of reports, as well as commentators, refer to Meyer's breaking ball as a slider. It certainly has the shape and velocity of a typical slider. However, his catcher signals it as a curveball. Either way it's plus- to plus-plus. And according to TrackMan data at the ballpark, it was spinning at incredible 2,800 RPMs. Meyer was essentially a two-pitch hurler in his early college days, so his above-average changeup may see a slight bump up as he continues to throw it more frequently. The lone knock on Meyer: he's a bit undersized at 6-foot and 196 pounds. There's a strong #2 vibe to his potential with a non-zero chance he ascends to ace-dom.

Ceiling: 4.5-win player
Risk: Moderate
MLB ETA: 2022

3. Eury Perez, RHP

	FB	CB	CH	Command	Overall
	60/70	55/60	50/55	55/60	60

Born: 04/15/03	Age: 19	Bats: R	Top Comp: N/A
Height: 6-8	Weight: 200	Throws: R	

Season	Team	Age	Level	IP	TBF	K/9	K%	BB/9	BB%	K-BB%	ERA	FIP	xFIP	Pit/Bat
2021	MIA	18	A	56.0	222	13.18	36.94%	3.38	9.46%	27.48%	1.61	2.73	3.33	4.20
2021	MIA	18	A+	22.0	83	10.64	31.33%	2.05	6.02%	25.30%	2.86	5.32	4.04	4.08

Background: The Marlins likely didn't know when they spotted the wiry right-hander on the open market, but they may have unearthed one of the better pitching prospects in the entire 2019 class. Signed for $200,000 in early July that year, Perez was standing a solid 6-foot-4, but weighed a wispy 155 pounds. Fast forward two seasons and he's measuring an NBA shoot guard-size 6-foot-8 and 200 pounds. But that's not even the best part. As a result of his signing and the ensuing COVID shutdown the following year, Perez made his professional debut as a baby-faced 18-year-old. In the Low-A Southeast League. And he would eventually make five final starts in High-A Central, as well. When the dust had finally settled, the previously little known hurler had completed the best teenage debut by a pitcher since in Low-A since Julio Urias in 2013. Perez tossed 78.0 innings across both levels, recording an impressive 108 strikeouts versus only 26 walks to go along with a dazzling 1.96 ERA and a 3.46 FIP. For those counting at home: he averaged 12.5 strikeouts and just 3.0 walks per nine innings.

Scouting Report: Consider the following:

- Since 2006, only four 18-year-old hurlers struck out at least 30% of the hitters they faced in Low-A with one organization (min. 50 IP): Hunter Greene, the 2nd pick in the 2017 draft; Jason Knapp, Tim Collins, and – of course – the behemoth Eury Perez.

Not only did Perez's strikeout percentage, 36.9%, lead the aforementioned group, but his walk percentage, 9.5%, was the second lowest. Perez's fastball sits – *comfortably* – in the mid-90s. His 80-mph curveball is average but projects to be plus. It already shows impressive shape and tilt. He'll also twirl a 90-mph changeup, which flashes above-average at times. Combine his age, frame size, and impressive repertoire with his ability to consistently throw *quality* strikes, and it's not unreasonable to think that Perez has a puncher's chance to develop into the minors' top pitching prospect – as long as he can navigate through the injury nexus.

Ceiling: 5.0-win player
Risk: High
MLB ETA: 2023/2024

4. Kahlil Watson, SS

	Hit	Power	SB	Patience	Glove	Overall
	40/55	40/55	60	50	55	60

Born: 04/16/03	Age: 19	Bats: L	Top Comp: N/A
Height: 5-9	Weight: 178	Throws: R	

Season	Team	Age	Level	PA	1B	2B	3B	HR	SB	CS	BB%	K%	AVG	OBP	SLG	ISO
2021	MIA	18	CPX	42	8	3	2	0	4	1	19.05%	16.67%	0.394	0.524	0.606	0.212

Background: Part of the quartet of high school shortstops that would hear their names among the top 16 picks of the 2021 draft, Watson put together a dynamic prep career for Wake Forest High School.

The 5-foot-9, 178-pound middle infielder batted .389 with a pair of homeruns and 22 RBI while swiping 17 bags during his freshman campaign.

He followed that up with an incredible sophomore season in which he slugged .578 with six long balls, 23 RBI, 26 stolen bases. And after an abysmal five-game COVID-shortened 2020, the young dynamo exploded during his final season with the North Carolina prep school: through his first 13 games of the year, Watson hit .528 with six doubles, one triple, and five homeruns. He was also sporting a spectacular 14-to-1 walk-to-strikeout ratio as well. He was committed to North Carolina State University. Miami selected the pint-sized Mighty Mite with the 16th overall pick last July, signing him to a deal worth $4,540,790. Watson appeared in nine games with the Marlins' Florida Complex League affiliate, hitting a scorching .394/.524/.606 with a pair of doubles and five stolen bases (in six attempts).

Scouting Report: Per the usual, here's my pre-draft write-up of Watson:

> *"Love the swing. Does. Not. Get. Cheated. Watson unfurls some impressive power potential despite a modest frame size. He may have some swing-and-miss issues in the professional ranks – at least initially. Phenomenal bat speed combined with a patient approach at the plate. There's some Brandon Phillips-type offensive potential here."*

Ceiling: 4.0-win player
Risk: Moderate
MLB ETA: 2025

5. Sixto Sanchez, RHP

FB	CU	SL	CH	Command	Overall
N/A	N/A	N/A	N/A	N/A	60

Born: 07/29/98	Age: 23	Bats: R	Top Comp: N/A
Height: 6-0	Weight: 234	Throws: R	

Season	Team	Age	Level	IP	TBF	K/9	K%	BB/9	BB%	K-BB%	ERA	FIP	xFIP	Pit/Bat
2018	PHI	19	A+	46.2	188	8.68	23.94%	2.12	5.85%	18.09%	2.51	2.66	3.11	3.55
2019	MIA	20	A+	11.0	46	4.91	13.04%	1.64	4.35%	8.70%	4.91	3.94	3.36	3.07
2019	MIA	20	AA	103.0	411	8.48	23.60%	1.66	4.62%	18.98%	2.53	2.69	2.92	3.54

Background: A consensus Top 100 prospect since 2018. The hard-throwing, budding ace was viewed as the key to the J.T. Realmuto deal with Philadelphia in early February 2019 – though Sanchez didn't come without several important questions: #1. The Dominican right-hander was injured at the time of the trade; a worrisome elbow prematurely ended his previous season in early June. Would he have ill effects in 2019 or later on in his career? #2. Would his 6-foot, 180-pound frame withstand the general rigors of grabbing the baseball every fifth day? The answer to the first part of question #1is, no, there weren't any ill effects from the previous elbow issue. The answer to question #2 appears – at least for the time being – to be no, as well. Sanchez, who made his big league debut with seven starts at the end of the 2020 season, missed the entirety of 2021. The cause: a new arm injury. A wonky shoulder eventually forced him under the knife to surgically repair "a capsular tear and clean out the back side of his right shoulder." He's currently on track for Spring Training 2022.

Snippet from The 2020 Prospect Digest Handbook: I have to be honest: I'm not sure I have the testicular fortitude to make the trade the Marlins did when they acquired Sixto Sanchez. He was limited to just 46.2 early season inning in 2018. And a setback with the elbow curtailed his Arizona Fall League debut before it even began. A few months later Miami's front office pegged him as the centerpiece of a deal involving one of the best backstops in professional baseball. But here we are. And it's proving to be a brilliant deal. Sanchez's repertoire just screams top-of-the-rotation caliber pitcher. His fastball was sitting mid- to upper-90s with the effort of throwing a slow pitch softball. His changeup jumped from a potential plus pitch to a plus-plus weapon. And he showed a level of confidence in the offering that's reminiscent of an in-his-prime Pedro Martinez. And his curveball falls in line with a 55-grade.

Scouting Report: Beyond the new injury, there's something else that should be addressed: Heading into the 2020 season Sanchez's weight was listed as a svelte 185 pounds. Now, he's tipping the scales 234 pounds. That's not a great sign.

Ceiling: 4.0-win player
Risk: High
MLB ETA: Debuted in 2020

6. J.J. Bleday, RF

Hit	Power	SB	Patience	Glove	Overall
45	50	30	60	50	50

Born: 11/10/97	Age: 24	Bats: L	Top Comp: Kole Calhoun
Height: 6-3	Weight: 205	Throws: L	

Season	Team	Age	Level	PA	1B	2B	3B	HR	SB	CS	BB%	K%	AVG	OBP	SLG	ISO
2019	MIA	21	A+	151	25	8	0	3	0	0	7.28%	19.21%	0.257	0.311	0.379	0.121
2021	MIA	23	AA	468	47	22	3	12	5	3	13.68%	21.58%	0.212	0.323	0.373	0.161

Background: Opening picks of the 2019 draft are saturated with not only high end talent, but some of the game's most recognizable prospects, such as: Adley Rutschman, Bobby Witt, Riley Greene,

C.J. Abrams, and Nick Lodolo. And that doesn't count Andrew Vaughn who's already spent a full year in the big leagues. The lone pockmark on the first seven selections: former Vanderbilt star J.J. Bleday. The fourth overall pick three years ago, sandwiched between Andrew Vaughn and Riley Greene, Bleday was spectacular over his final two seasons with the Commodores, slugging .368/.494/.511 and .347/.465/.701. But he's been underwhelming during his professional career as Miami – perhaps, incorrectly – shoved him aggressively through the minors. The 6-foot-3, 205-pound corner outfielder appeared in 38 games with the Jupiter Hammerheads in High-A during his debut, batting a mediocre, powerless .257/.311/.379. Last season, undeterred by the inauspicious start to his career, the organization sent Bleday to the minors' toughest challenge: Double-A. He responded with a lowly .212/.323/.373 slash line, belting out 22 doubles, three triples, and 12 homeruns. Per *Weighted Runs Created Plus*, his overall production was 3% *below* the league average mark. However, on the other hand, things seemed to click for the Vanderbilt star in the Arizona Fall League as he slugged a scorching .316/.435/.600 in 24 games with the Mesa Solar Sox.

Snippet from The 2020 Prospect Digest Handbook: Bleday shows easy nature loft in his swing which allows his plus-raw power to transition into plus-in-game power. [He] tends to be too pull happy, so he's likely going to face a plethora of defensive shifts. He looks like a capable starting outfielder, though one not destined for stardom.

Scouting Report: Bleday was *really, really* bad the majority of the season with Pensacola, hitting a vomitous .195/.310/.348 over his 83 games. His bat, though, did show some signs of life over his remaining 27 contests: he batted .263/.362/.453. Bleday's swing looked really good during the Fall League, showing plenty of bat speed, rotation, and natural loft. And it's definitely not easy to jump from college ball into High-A, miss a season, and then be thrust in Double-A either. But the fact is: he's entering his age-24 season and has been terrible for the large portion of his professional career. Assuming he can carry the late season momentum into 2022, he looks like a .250/.340/.440-type hitter.

Ceiling: 2.0-win player
Risk: Moderate
MLB ETA: 2024

7. Joe Mack, C	Hit	Power	SB	Patience	Glove	Overall
	35/45	40/55	50/40	55	55	50

Born: 12/27/02	Age: 19	Bats: L	Top Comp: N/A
Height: 6-1	Weight: 201	Throws: R	

Season	Team	Age	Level	PA	1B	2B	3B	HR	SB	CS	BB%	K%	AVG	OBP	SLG	ISO
2021	MIA	18	CPX	75	5	1	0	1	0	1	26.67%	29.33%	0.132	0.373	0.208	0.075

Background: Not know as a hotbed for premium baseball talent, western New York, though, featured one of the best catching prospects – or any prospect, for that matter – in 2021. Mack, not to be confused by the former big leaguer by the same name who earned a cup of coffee with the Boston Braves in 1945, has been making waves for a few years. A muscular, well-built backstop out of Williamsville East High School, Mack won a homerun derby in Cooperstown, belting out nine homeruns – surpassing the record previously set by a young Bryce Harper. Oh, and for good measure, the then-seventh grader batted cleanup for the Williamsville East High School squad. Miami selected the lefty-swinging backstop in the opening round, 31st overall, and signed him to a deal worth $2.5 million. He appeared in 19 Complex League games during his debut, hitting a paltry .132/.373/.208.

Scouting Report: Per the usual, here's my pre-draft write-up of Watson:

> "As expected for a projected first round pick, Mack showcases plus bat speed at the plate that combines with a natural loft to generate easy above-average power – though he looks to be a bit too pull happy. Mack starts his hands from a high position, above his ears, which causes for a lot of pre-pitch movement to get into position. Defensively, he shows an above-average arm, and he should have no problem sticking behind the plate."

Ceiling: 2.0-win player
Risk: Moderate
MLB ETA: 2025

8. Jose Salas, SS

Hit	Power	SB	Patience	Glove	Overall
40/50	30/50	50/40	50	45/50	50

Born: 04/26/03	Age: 19	Bats: B	Top Comp: N/A
Height: 6-2	Weight: 191	Throws: R	

Season	Team	Age	Level	PA	1B	2B	3B	HR	SB	CS	BB%	K%	AVG	OBP	SLG	ISO
2021	MIA	18	CPX	107	23	10	0	1	8	5	10.28%	21.50%	0.370	0.458	0.511	0.141
2021	MIA	18	A	123	22	4	0	1	6	0	8.94%	22.76%	0.250	0.333	0.315	0.065

Background: Under the new Derek Jeter-led regime, the Miami Marlins have been dogged in their pursuit of young talent, both nationally and internationally. And Salas is just another example. The headliner for the 2019 signing class, Miami handed the 6-foot-2, 191-pound middle infielder a hefty $2.8 million that summer. Salas made his organizational debut last summer: he ripped through the Florida Complex League and acquitted himself nicely as an 18-year-old in Low-A with the Jupiter Hammerheads. The Florida-born shortstop batted an aggregate .305/.391/.405 with 14 doubles, two homeruns, and 14 stolen bases (in 19 total attempts). Per *Weighted Runs Created Plus*, his combined production topped the league average mark by a solid 21%.

Scouting Report: Salas did everything the organization expected during his debut last season: he was dominating in the Complex League and didn't look too overmatched as an 18-year-old in Low-A. He ran and fielded well. And he flashed gap-to-gap pop. Above-average bat speed and showed some promise on turning on low-90s fastballs. Salas didn't show a ton of homerun thump during his debut – he belted out just a pair of long balls – but there's 50-grade power brewing in his stick. Natural loft to his swing.

Ceiling: 2.0-win player
Risk: Moderate
MLB ETA: 2024

9. Braxton Garrett, LHP

FB	CB	SL	CH	Command	Overall
50	55	55	55	45	45

Born: 08/05/97	Age: 24	Bats: L	Top Comp: Andrew Heaney
Height: 6-2	Weight: 202	Throws: L	

Season	Team	Age	Level	IP	TBF	K/9	K%	BB/9	BB%	K-BB%	ERA	FIP	xFIP	Pit/Bat
2019	MIA	21	A+	105.0	438	10.11	26.94%	3.17	8.45%	18.49%	3.34	3.73	2.71	3.77
2021	MIA	23	AAA	85.2	357	9.04	24.09%	3.36	8.96%	15.13%	3.89	4.13	4.50	3.90

Background: Pitchers were flying off the board at a fast and furious pace to start the 2017 draft. Six of the first nine selections were hurlers, and four of those were teenage high school arms. Garrett, the seventh overall pick that year, hit the operating table just four starts into his debut season in 2017. The cause: a wonky elbow that required Tommy John surgery. The 6-foot-2, 202-pound left-hander would made it back to full season action two years later, spending time between High-A and Double-A. Last season – despite only one start in Double-A on his resume – Garrett opened the year up with the Jacksonville Jumbo Shrimp in Triple-A East. The southpaw would spend the entirety of the year yo-yoing between the minor and major leagues. With the Shrimp, he tossed 85.2 innings while averaging 9.0 strikeouts and 3.4 walks per nine innings. With the Marlins: 34.0 IP, 32 K, 20 BB, and a 5.03 ERA.

Snippet from The 2020 Prospect Digest Handbook: Garrett looked like the prototypical crafty lefty in his return from injury. He looks like a nice, solid #4-type arm – a league average starting pitcher to help fill out a club's rotation.

Scouting Report: Twenty years ago the term "crafty" was like a badge of honor. Nowadays with specified training and an emphasis on weighted ball throwing regimens and lifting heavy for pitchers, the term carries more of a negative connotation. Braxton Garrett is a crafty lefty that doesn't quite own the level of command to make it work long term. In today's game, 90 mph fastballs simply don't work without Kyle Hendricks' command. Garrett owns the former without the latter. He does sport a trio of above-average secondary weapons – including a new slider – but there's not a lot of room for error. At best, he's a #5-type arm.

Ceiling: 1.5-win player
Risk: Low to Moderate
MLB ETA: Debuted in 2021

10. Zach McCambley, RHP

FB	CB	SL	CH	Command	Overall
60	60	55	50	55	45

Born: 05/04/99	Age: 23	Bats: L	Top Comp: Jason Frasor
Height: 6-2	Weight: 220	Throws: R	

Season	Team	Age	Level	IP	TBF	K/9	K%	BB/9	BB%	K-BB%	ERA	FIP	xFIP	Pit/Bat
2021	MIA	22	A+	57.0	231	11.53	31.60%	0.95	2.60%	29.00%	3.79	3.96	3.17	3.83
2021	MIA	22	AA	40.0	178	10.58	26.40%	4.50	11.24%	15.17%	5.18	6.58	5.02	4.01

Background: The third pick in the third round two years ago. McCambley was a peripherally-friendly hurler during his first two seasons at Coastal Carolina University. The 6-foot-2, 220-pound right-hander, though, really came into his own during the 2019 summer in the Cape Cod League. Working in the Cotuit Kettleers' rotation, McCambley struck out 24, walked just seven, and tallied a barely-there 1.74 ERA in 20.2 innings of work. And the New Jersey-born hurler carried that level of dominance into the COVID-shortened 2020 season. He averaged 11.5 punch outs and just 2.5 walks per nine innings through four starts. He signed with the club for $775,000. McCambley made a total of 20 starts last season, 11 in High-A and nine in Double-A, throwing 97.0 innings with 120 punch outs and just 26 free passes. He finished his debut showing with an aggregate 4.36 ERA and a 5.04 FIP.

Scouting Report: Definite reliever risk. McCambley attacks hitters with a mid-90s, plus fastball that will run upwards of 97 mph on occasion. In one of his earlier starts in Double-A the former Coastal Carolina hurler was primarily fastball / changeup with the latter showing heavy sink. A few weeks later, in early September, McCambley was showcasing a pair of breaking balls: a plus curveball and an above-average slider.

Ceiling: 1.5-win player
Risk: Low to Moderate
MLB ETA: 2022

11. Ian Lewis, IF

Hit	Power	SB	Patience	Glove	Overall
40/55	40/45	60	45	50/60	50

Born: 02/04/03	Age: 19	Bats: B	Top Comp:
Height: 5-10	Weight: 177	Throws: R	

Season	Team	Age	Level	PA	1B	2B	3B	HR	SB	CS	BB%	K%	AVG	OBP	SLG	ISO
2021	MIA	18	CPX	161	27	10	5	3	9	4	6.83%	14.91%	0.302	0.354	0.497	0.195

Background: Miami signed the Bahamian infielder to a deal worth $950,000 three years ago; it was the largest bonus handed out to a prospect from the Bahamas during that signing period. A native of Nassau, the 5-foot-10, 177-pound switch-hitting infielder made his debut in the Florida Complex League last season, slugging an impressive .302/.354/.497 with 10 doubles, five triples, and three homeruns. He also swiped nine bags in 13 attempts. Per *Weighted Runs Created Plus*, his overall production topped the league average mark by 22%. Miami named Lewis the club's Florida Complex League Most Valuable Player.

Scouting Report: Smooth defender that may win a couple Gold Gloves. Lewis is blessed with plus-plus speed that's easy to see on the base paths as well as in his agility and fluidity on defense. Offensively, he's already showing more thump than his 5-foot-10, 177-pound frame would suggest. Lewis isn't going to walk very frequently, but there's a chance for an above-average hit tool, 15 homeruns, and 25 stolen bases. Like a lot of the club's young players, he needs to get stronger though.

Ceiling: 1.5- to 2.0-win player
Risk: Moderate to High
MLB ETA: 2025

12. Dax Fulton, LHP

FB	CB	CH	Command	Overall
55/60	60	45	45	45

Born: 10/16/01	Age: 20	Bats: L	Top Comp: N/A
Height: 6-7	Weight: 225	Throws: L	

Season	Team	Age	Level	IP	TBF	K/9	K%	BB/9	BB%	K-BB%	ERA	FIP	xFIP	Pit/Bat
2021	MIA	19	A	58.2	251	10.12	26.29%	4.60	11.95%	14.34%	4.30	3.85	4.01	4.04
2021	MIA	19	A+	19.2	86	8.24	20.93%	3.66	9.30%	11.63%	5.49	5.45	4.55	3.98

Background: The Marlins' plan of attack for the 2020 draft was a simple one: pitching, pitching, and more pitching. They selected arms with all six of their picks two years ago. In fact, five of those six were collegiate arms. The only prep hurler: big southpaw Dax Fulton. Standing a towering 6-foot-7 and 225-pounds, the native Oklahoman, who received a hefty $2.4 million, made his professional debut last season. Appearing in 20 games, 19 of which were starts, between Jupiter and Beloit, Fulton tossed 78.1 innings with 84 punch outs, 38 base-on-balls, a 4.60 ERA, and a slightly better 4.25 FIP.

Scouting Report: I caught two of Fulton's starts last season: his June 25th game against the Bradenton Marauders in Low-A Southeast and his September 1st showing against the Wisconsin Timber Rattlers in High-A Central. Between the games the big southpaw looked like two completely different hurlers. In the earlier start his fastball was pumping 93- to 94-mph; his curveball was sitting in the low 80s with strong bite. In the later outing, his third to last start of the year, Fulton's fastball was downgraded to 89- to 91-mph and his deuce was 76- to 78-mph with a little less bite and more loop. Earlier in the year he looked like a potential #4 starter if the changeup improves. In the later start he looked was more polished with a lesser ceiling. Fulton's young enough that it's likely just him wearing down during his first full season in pro ball. If that assumption's correct, that's a lot of intrigue here. Command and changeup need to show an uptick, though.

Ceiling: 1.5-win player
Risk: Moderate
MLB ETA: 2023/2024

13. Cody Morissette, IF

Hit	Power	SB	Patience	Glove	Overall
45/55	40/45	35	55	50	45

Born: 01/16/00	Age: 22	Bats: L	Top Comp: N/A
Height: 6-0	Weight: 175	Throws: R	

Season	Team	Age	Level	PA	1B	2B	3B	HR	SB	CS	BB%	K%	AVG	OBP	SLG	ISO
2021	MIA	21	A	159	18	8	1	1	0	2	12.58%	23.90%	0.204	0.308	0.299	0.095

Background: Hailing from an athletic family, Morissette's mother, Kristen, played basketball and softball at Plymouth State and his father, Dave, played for the basketball team. As for Morissette: the 6-foot, 175-pounder starred on both sides of the ball for Exeter High School during his prep career: he helped lead the squad to back-to-back state titles in 2017 and 2018; batted .434 as a senior and tallied a nearly perfect 19-1 win-loss record in his career to go along with a 1.21 ERA. A key cog in Boston College's lineup for his three-year tenure, Morissette hit .320/.371/.476 with 20 doubles, two triples, four homeruns, and eight stolen bases as a true freshman. He spent the ensuing summer playing for the Bourne Braves in the Cape Cod League, cobbling together a mediocre .252/.319/.350 slash line in 38 games. Morissette looked unearthly during his 15-game 2020 campaign, slugging .448/.522/.655. His numbers came fell back to earth during his final showing for BC in 2021, hitting .321/.398/.497 with just nine doubles, one triple, six homeruns, and eight stolen bases. He finished the year with a 33-to-21 strikeout-to-walk ratio. Miami selected the lefty-swinging infielder in the second round, 52nd overall, and signed him to a deal worth $1,403,200. Morissette appeared in 34 games with Jupiter for his debut, hitting a lowly .204/.308/.299.

Scouting Report: Per the usual, here's my pre-draft write-up of Watson:

"Consider the following:

- *Between 2011 and 2020, only three ACC hitters batted between .310/.390/.490 and .330/.410/.510 with a double-digit walk rate in a season (min. 175 PA): Jackson Lueck, Brandon Riley, and Matt Vierling*

A bat first infielder without a true home. Morissette's bounced between shortstop, and second and third bases throughout his collegiate career. 45-grade power. Not a lot of speed. Morissette's a well-rounded player without a red flag or a dominant standout tool. He profiles more as a second baseman in the professional ranks."

Ceiling: 1.5-win player
Risk: Moderate
MLB ETA: 2024

14. Victor Mesa Jr., CF

Hit	Power	SB	Patience	Glove	Overall
45/50	35/40	50	45	55	45

Born: 09/08/01	Age: 20	Bats: L	Top Comp: N/A
Height: 6-0	Weight: 195	Throws: L	

Season	Team	Age	Level	PA	1B	2B	3B	HR	SB	CS	BB%	K%	AVG	OBP	SLG	ISO
2019	MIA	17	R	207	36	9	4	1	7	4	11.59%	14.01%	0.284	0.366	0.398	0.114
2021	MIA	19	A	474	77	21	11	5	12	5	6.96%	21.52%	0.266	0.316	0.402	0.136

Background: Without a doubt the lesser known – and lesser valued – commodity of the two Mesa brothers when the duo signed their contracts with Miami following the 2018 season. While the older brother, Victor Victor Mesa, inked a deal worth $5.25 million and he's failed to live up to the expectations, the younger brother, Victor Mesa Jr., signed a deal worth

$1 million and has exceed those relatively modest expectations. The young center fielder turned in a decent enough debut in the Gulf Coast League three years ago, hitting .284/.366/.398 with 14 extra-base hits in 47 games. Last season the front office pushed the then-19-year-old up to Low-A Southeast , and he held his own. In 111 games with the Jupiter Hammerheads, the 6-foot, 195-pound outfielder batted .266/.316/.402 with 21 doubles, 11 triples, five homeruns, and 12 stolen bases (in 17 attempts). His overall production was 7% *below* the league average mark.

Snippet from The 2020 Prospect Digest Handbook: Strong wrists but a slapper's mentality at the plate. Mesa Jr.'s not projected to offer up a whole lot of pop – though he should settle in with eight- to 10-homeruns. He's quick, but not fast. The teenage outfielder shows good bat control with the chance to develop an above-average hit tool. He looks like a fourth outfielder type.

Scouting Report: There's a checklist of items I run through when it comes to younger prospects in (A) the low levels of the minor leagues or (B) squaring off against significantly older competition. Mesa Jr. hits both of those. He was 19-years-old, playing against vastly older competition, and playing for the first time in full season ball. While the numbers aren't great – they're borderline mediocre, if I'm being blunt – Mesa Jr. showed something incredibly important: steady, continued progress throughout the year. His monthly OPS totals (beginning in May): .636, .622, .707, .803, and .878. Also, he batted .306/.339/.489 over his final 57 games. He's going to go as far as the batting averages will take him. Above-average speed, below-average power that project to eventually get to a 40-grade, won't walk a ton, and a good, maybe even borderline great, glove in center field.

Ceiling: 1.5-win player
Risk: Moderate
MLB ETA: 2024

15. Peyton Burdick, OF

Hit	Power	SB	Patience	Glove	Overall
40	60	40	60	50	45

Born: 02/26/97	Age: 25	Bats: R	Top Comp: Chris Carter
Height: 6-0	Weight: 205	Throws: R	

Season	Team	Age	Level	PA	1B	2B	3B	HR	SB	CS	BB%	K%	AVG	OBP	SLG	ISO
2019	MIA	22	A	288	40	20	3	10	6	6	11.11%	23.26%	0.307	0.408	0.542	0.235
2019	MIA	22	A-	25	5	0	1	1	1	1	8.00%	20.00%	0.318	0.400	0.545	0.227
2021	MIA	24	AA	460	44	17	2	23	9	5	16.52%	29.35%	0.231	0.376	0.472	0.241
2021	MIA	24	AAA	31	1	3	0	0	0	0	9.68%	35.48%	0.143	0.226	0.250	0.107

Background: One of the more pleasant surprises in the farm system heading into the lost 2020 season. Burdick, a third round pick out of Wright State University in 2019, turned in a phenomenal debut that summer – most of which was spent in the Midwest League. He would slug .308/.407/.542 with 20 doubles, four triples, 11 homeruns, and seven stolen bases. And that was enough to convince the Marlins' front office brass that the 6-foot, 205-pound outfielder was ready for the minor league prime time: Double-A. In 106 games with the Pensacola Blue Wahoos, Burdick batted a mediocre .231/.376/.472 with 17 doubles, two triples, and 23 homeruns. He also swiped nine bags in 14 attempts with the club as well. Per *Weighted Runs Created Plus*, his overall production topped the league average mark by 37%. Burdick spent the last week or so up in Triple-A with the Jacksonville Jumbo Shrimp.

Snippet from The 2020 Prospect Digest Handbook: Burdick could prove to be one of the bigger steals of last year's draft class. The power's incredible, potentially peaking as a plus in-game tool. Solid peripherals and glove in left field.

Scouting Report: Consider the following:

- Since 2006, only three 24-year-old hitters posted a 132 to 142 wRC+ total with a walk rate north of 12% and a strikeout rate north of 25% in Double-A with one organization: Keon Broxton, Allan Dykstra, and – of course – former third rounder Peyton Burdick.

Burdick was pretty abysmal for the better part of three months as he batted a putrid .193/.351/.417 over his first 73 games in Double-A. Beginning on July 30th through the remainder of his time at the level he slugged .311/.431/.588 (33 games). Burdick has the standard recipe for a Three True Outcomes hitters: he walks an enormous amount of the time (16.5% walk rate in Double-A), strikes out frequently (29.3%), and showcases light tower thunder. He's miscast as a center fielder, but handles a corner spot well. Despite his age – he's entering his age-25 season – Burdick has only accrued 183 minor league games on his resume, most of which was in Double-A, so there's a chance the hit tool may see a modest uptick with added experience.

Ceiling: 1.0- to 1.5-win player
Risk: Moderate
MLB ETA: 2023

16. Jake Eder, LHP

	FB	SL	CH	Command	Overall
	55	55	50	45	45

Born: 10/09/98	Age: 23	Bats: L	Top Comp: Jarrod Washburn
Height: 6-4	Weight: 215	Throws: L	

Season	Team	Age	Level	IP	TBF	K/9	K%	BB/9	BB%	K-BB%	ERA	FIP	xFIP	Pit/Bat
2021	MIA	22	AA	71.1	287	12.49	34.49%	3.41	9.41%	25.09%	1.77	2.48	3.18	3.87

Background: Originally drafted by the New York Mets coming out of Calvary Christian High School in 2017. Eder, instead, chose Plan B – attend Pitcher U., a.k.a. Vanderbilt University. The 6-foot-4, 215-pound southpaw had an up-and-down career with SEC powerhouse. He spent his true freshman season working out of the Commodores' rotation, tallying a 5.45 ERA with a 1-4 win-loss record. Eder spent the following season, 2019, as a full time reliever with notably better results: 2.97 ERA, 9.4 K/9, and 3.7 BB/9. The big lefty returned to Vanderbilt's rotation in 2020 and got off to a solid start – 15.0 IP, 15 K, and 4 BB – before the COVID shutdown. Miami took a fourth round flier on the Florida native, signing him to a deal worth $700,000. Eder made his professional debut last season – in Double-A. In 15 starts with the Pensacola Blue Wahoos, the southpaw struck out 99, walked just 27, and posted a barely-there 1.99 ERA. Unfortunately, the former Commodore succumbed to elbow woes and underwent the knife for Tommy John surgery in early September.

Scouting Report: Consider the following:

- Since 2006, only six arms posted a K% north of 30% with a BB% between 8.5% and 10.5% in Double-A with one organization (min. 60 IP): Mike Minor, A.J. Puk, Jose De Leon, Tony Sipp, Brayan Bello, and Jake Eder.

A fairly solid three-pitch repertoire highlighted by a 92- to 94-mph fastball. He'll complement the above-average offering with a slurvy slider, a second above-average offering. He'll also mix in a solid average changeup. Eder is more of a strike-thrower than a pure command guy and he's susceptible to bouts of wildness from time-to-time. With the recent Tommy John surgery, he will miss the entire 2022 season.

Ceiling: 1.5-win player
Risk: Moderate to High
MLB ETA: 2023/2024

17. Jose Devers, 2B/SS

	Hit	Power	SB	Patience	Glove	Overall
	40/55	30	40	45	50	40

Born: 12/07/99	Age: 22	Bats: L	Top Comp: Jamey Carroll
Height: 6-0	Weight: 174	Throws: R	

Season	Team	Age	Level	PA	1B	2B	3B	HR	SB	CS	BB%	K%	AVG	OBP	SLG	ISO
2018	MIA	18	A	362	76	12	4	0	13	6	4.14%	13.54%	0.273	0.313	0.332	0.059
2019	MIA	19	R	46	7	3	1	0	3	1	8.70%	8.70%	0.275	0.370	0.400	0.125
2019	MIA	19	A	13	3	2	0	0	0	0	15.38%	15.38%	0.455	0.538	0.636	0.182
2019	MIA	19	A+	138	37	3	1	0	5	0	5.80%	14.49%	0.325	0.384	0.365	0.040
2021	MIA	21	AAA	41	7	1	1	0	0	0	2.44%	12.20%	0.231	0.250	0.308	0.077

Background: Signed by the New York Yankees out of Samana, Dominican Republic, on July 2, 2016, for a sizeable $250,000 bonus. Devers – who, by the way, is the younger cousin of Red Sox star Rafael Devers – was traded away roughly 17 months later as part of the mega-swap that involved future Hall of Famer Giancarlo Stanton. Immediately placed on an aggressive development path to the big leagues, Devers played nearly a full season in the stateside rookie leagues at 17-years-old. He reached High-A – briefly – a year later. And turned in his finest offensive showing in 2019, as a 19-year-old, in an injury-interrupted 33-game cameo back in Jupiter as he slugged .325/.384/.365. Last season the Marlins had the 6-foot, 174-pound middle infielder skip the proving grounds of Double-A and sent him directly to the big leagues in late May for a couple weeks before bouncing him up-and-down until a posterior labrum tear in his right shoulder prematurely ended his 2021 season. He batted a lowly .244/.304/.317 in 21 big league games, and he was slightly worse in 12 games with the Jacksonville Jumbo Shrimp.

Snippet from The 2020 Prospect Digest Handbook: There's a chance for a plus-hit tool, especially considering his age and level of competition.

Scouting Report: A bit of an enigma. Devers owns plus foot speed, but hasn't run consistently since his stint in Low-A all the way back in 2018. His groundball rates have improved from awful to above-average, but he has as much power as a lawnmower motor. And he has the potential to develop an impressive hit tool, but the Miami's have pushed him so aggressively that it hasn't time to develop properly. He's twitchy, but average on defense. He's a low end backup infielder, unless the bat starts to come alive in the coming years.

Ceiling: 1.0-win player
Risk: Low to Moderate
MLB ETA: Debuted in 2020

18. Griffin Conine, RF

	Hit	Power	SB	Patience	Glove	Overall
	35/40	60	35	55	60	40

Born: 07/11/97	Age: 24	Bats: L	Top Comp: poor man's Rob Deer
Height: 6-1	Weight: 213	Throws: R	

Season	Team	Age	Level	PA	1B	2B	3B	HR	SB	CS	BB%	K%	AVG	OBP	SLG	ISO
2018	TOR	20	A-	230	26	14	2	7	5	0	8.26%	27.39%	0.238	0.309	0.427	0.189
2019	TOR	21	A	348	43	19	2	22	2	0	10.92%	35.92%	0.283	0.371	0.576	0.293
2021	MIA	23	A+	288	26	7	2	23	3	0	15.97%	35.76%	0.247	0.382	0.587	0.340
2021	MIA	23	AA	173	11	4	0	13	0	1	6.94%	47.40%	0.176	0.243	0.447	0.270

Background: In a serendipitous turn of events, the franchise acquired the son of Mr. Marlin, Jeff Conine, who was rostered for both of the organization's World Series titles. Miami originally drafted the younger Conine in the 31st round coming out of Pine Crest High School all the way back in 2015. Nothing more than a courtesy selection, Conine, instead, headed to Duke University. The 6-foot-1, 213-pound right fielder was dreadful as a true freshman, hitting a putrid .205/.306/.247 in limited action. But like a sleeping giant, he was awoken from his slumber in 2017. The then-sophomore slugged .298/.425/.546 with 11 doubles, two triples, and 13 homeruns. And he carried that momentum over to the Cape Cod League the ensuing summer as well, batting .329/.406/.537 with 15 extra-base knocks in 42 games with the Cotuit Kettleers. The son of Mr. Marlin turned in another solid showing for the Blue Devils during his junior campaign as well, slugging .286/.410/.608 with 15 doubles, two triples, and 18 homeruns. Toronto selected him in the second round four years ago. Conine showed some offensive promise as a 21-year-old in the Midwest League in 2019, batting .283/.371/.576, but the Jays would ship him south at the end of August two years ago for veteran infielder Jonathan Villar. Last season, Conine tied for the second best homerun total in the minor leagues, belting out 36 dingers though he only manage to cobble together a .218/.330/.530 slash line.

Snippet from The 2020 Prospect Digest Handbook: In all likelihood Conine's going to travel down the path of a poor man's Three True Outcomes hitter. He's going (continue) to whiff a lot. And he's already showing borderline plus-plus power.

Scouting Report: It was a tale of two seasons for the former Blue Devil:

- He topped the league production line by a massive 56% while slugging .247/.382/.587 in 66 games in High-A.
- After his promotion up to the challenging Double-A in late July, Conine hit a disgusting .176/.243/.447 in 42 games.

Regardless of how great or poor his production was last season, Conine was creating constant windstorms at the plate, fanning 185 times in only 461 plate appearances – or 40.1% of the time. Not only will he not make the big leagues with that punch out rate, but he could very well be out of affiliated ball within two years.

Ceiling: 1.0-win player
Risk: Moderate
MLB ETA: 2023

19. Jordan McCants, 2B/SS

	Hit	Power	SB	Patience	Glove	Overall
	30/50	30/40	50	50	50	40

Born: 05/21/02	Age: 20	Bats: L	Top Comp: N/A
Height: 6-1	Weight: 165	Throws: R	

Season	Team	Age	Level	PA	1B	2B	3B	HR	SB	CS	BB%	K%	AVG	OBP	SLG	ISO
2021	MIA	19	CPX	85	16	1	0	0	1	2	7.06%	25.88%	0.224	0.286	0.237	0.013

Background: Fun Fact Part I: Pensacola Catholic High School is home to 10 different draft picks. Fun Fact Part II: Before McCants' selection by the Marlins last season, the last player chosen out of Pensacola Catholic High School was all the way back in 2010 when the Cincinnati Reds selected right-hander Wes Mugarian in the fifth round. Miami nabbed the lefty-swinging middle infielder in the third round, 88th overall, and signed him to a deal worth $800,000. Committed to play ball at Mississippi State University prior to his selection, McCants appeared in 23 games with the club's Florida Complex League, hitting a light .224/.286/.237 with just one double.

Scouting Report: McCants' older brother, TJ, turned in a dynamic season for Ole' Miss in 2021 as he batted .300/.369/.433 with 10 doubles, two triples, and five homeruns. The younger McCants shows a classic inside-out swing as he consistently shoots balls the other way. It's an approach that likely won't allow much power to develop for the lefty-swinging infielder. Good bat speed. There's a surprising amount of swing-and-miss to his game, especially given his slap-tastic approach. McCants strikes me as a guy that would have been better off taking the collegiate route to get big, stronger rather than jumping into the professional ranks. Plus, he's already entering his age-20 season thanks to a late birthday.

Ceiling: 1.0-win player
Risk: Moderate
MLB ETA: 2025

20. Yiddi Cappe, SS

Hit	Power	SB	Patience	Glove	Overall
35/45	30/40	50/40	45	50	40

Born: 09/17/02	Age: 19	Bats: R	Top Comp: N/A
Height: 6-3	Weight: 175	Throws: R	

Season	Team	Age	Level	PA	1B	2B	3B	HR	SB	CS	BB%	K%	AVG	OBP	SLG	ISO
2021	MIA	18	DSL	216	31	17	1	2	9	8	8.80%	16.20%	0.270	0.329	0.402	0.132

Background: Ranked by MLB Pipeline as the 10th best prospect on the international market last year. Cappe, a native of La Habana, Cuba, was certainly paid like a top prospect: Miami handed the 6-foot-3, 175-pound shortstop a massive $3.5 million deal in early January 2021. Per the MLB.com announcement of his agreement, Cappe began playing ball at 4-years-old and would make his way up to national play 12 years later. He would eventually defect to the Dominican Republic in late 2018. The Cuban infielder made his professional debut in the foreign rookie league last summer, hitting a respectable .270/.329/.402 with 17 doubles, one triple, and a pair of homeruns to go along with nine stolen bases (in 17 attempts). Per *Weighted Runs Created Plus*, his production topped the league average mark by just 3%.

Scouting Report: Simply put: it was a bit of a disappointing debut for the Cuban import. Not only was he old for someone considered a top prospect in the Dominican Summer League, but his production was lackluster – at best. Long limbs and wiry, Cappe's bat looked slow and long. And it's clear he needs to add quite a bit of strength to be competitive in the coming years. Truthfully, I think it's already clear that the Marlins overextended themselves – quite a bit – by signing him to a big $3.5 million. On a side note: he is represented by the same agency as right-hander Edward Cabrera.

Ceiling: 1.0-win player
Risk: Moderate
MLB ETA: 2025

Milwaukee Brewers

Top Prospects

1. Aaron Ashby, LHP

FB	CB	SL	CH	Command	Overall
60	55	60	55	45	60

Born: 05/24/98	Age: 24	Bats: R	Top Comp: Gio Gonzalez
Height: 6-2	Weight: 181	Throws: L	

Season	Team	Age	Level	IP	TBF	K/9	K%	BB/9	BB%	K-BB%	ERA	FIP	xFIP	Pit/Bat
2018	MIL	20	R	20.1	87	8.41	21.84%	3.54	9.20%	12.64%	6.20	5.86	4.89	3.46
2018	MIL	20	A	37.1	155	11.33	30.32%	2.17	5.81%	24.52%	2.17	2.04	2.25	3.75
2019	MIL	21	A	61.0	252	11.80	31.75%	4.13	11.11%	20.63%	3.54	3.30	3.13	4.05
2019	MIL	21	A+	65.0	278	7.62	19.78%	4.43	11.51%	8.27%	3.46	3.50	4.10	3.67
2021	MIL	23	AAA	63.1	276	14.21	36.23%	4.55	11.59%	24.64%	4.41	2.64	2.26	3.84

Background: One of the more underrated arms in the entire minor leagues since entering the professional ranks as a fourth rounder in 2018. The nephew of big league veteran Andy Ashby, Aaron turned in a fantastic debut showing as he split time between Helena and Wisconsin that year, averaging 10.3 strikeouts and just 2.7 walks per nine innings. He followed that up with another solid showing as he opened the 2019 season back in Low-A before a mid-year promotion up Carolina: 126.0 IP, 135 strikeouts, 60 walks, and a 3.50 ERA. After minor league ball returned action in 2021, Milwaukee had the hard-throwing southpaw bypass Double-A and start the season with the Nashville Sounds in Triple-A East. And he was dominant. In 21 appearances, 12 of which were starts, the 6-foot-2, 181-pound hurler struck out 100 and walked 32 in 63.1 innings of work. Ashby made appeared in three separate stints with the Brewers throughout the year as well, averaging 11.1 strikeouts and just 3.4 walks per nine innings to go along with a 4.55 ERA.

Snippet from The 2020 Prospect Digest Handbook: Along with looking physically stronger / bulking in the lower half, Ashby's fastball gained a few ticks on the radar gun, touching – on several occasions – as high as 95 mph. It's a borderline plus pitch that may eventually move into 60-grade territory in the next year or two as he continues to get stronger. His curveball looked sharper with that same late tilt and bite. And his changeup remained in the above-average / 55-grade territory. The lanky lefty also added a fourth pitch: a low-80s slider with a lot of horizontal movement. There's some #4-type potential, maybe more if the command ticks up.

Scouting Report: Consider the following:

- Since 2006, only three 23-year-old pitchers met the following criteria in a Triple-A season with one organization (min. 50 IP): post a strikeout percentage of at least 35%. Those three pitchers: Max Scherzer, Tyler Glasnow, and – of course – Mr. Aaron Ashby.
- For those counting at home, that's (A) one surefire future Hall of Famer, (B) one of the best young arms in the game, and (C) Andy's kid nephew, a former fourth round, the 125th overall player chosen in 2018.

Ashby's heater has gained considerable velocity since entering professional ball, going from 91-mph all the way up to 98 mph last season. His curveball's wicked sharp. His changeup, still an above-average offering, is in the same velocity range that his fastball was just four years ago. And his slider, a new offering in 2019, has morphed into a knee-buckling, fall-off-the-table swing-and-miss pitch. If the command can get to an average level Ashby will ascend to a bonafide #2-type arm. And I really think there's some left-handed Corbin Burnes potential here. I really do.

Ceiling: 4.5-win player
Risk: Moderate
MLB ETA: Debuted in 2021

2. Garrett Mitchell, CF

Hit	Power	SB	Patience	Glove	Overall
45	45	60	60	55	55

Born: 09/04/98	Age: 23	Bats: L	Top Comp: Trent Grisham
Height: 6-3	Weight: 215	Throws: R	

Season	Team	Age	Level	PA	1B	2B	3B	HR	SB	CS	BB%	K%	AVG	OBP	SLG	ISO
2021	MIL	22	A+	120	21	5	2	5	12	1	23.33%	25.00%	0.359	0.508	0.620	0.261
2021	MIL	22	AA	148	20	1	0	3	5	1	12.16%	27.70%	0.186	0.291	0.264	0.078

Background: Fun Fact: Mitchell became the highest drafted outfielder from UCLA since the Padres selected Shane Mack with the 11th overall selection all the way back in 1984. (On a bit of a side note: Mack put together a very underrated career, batting .299/.364/.456 across nine big league seasons; he also spent two successful seasons with the Yomiuri Giants in the Japan Central League.) Mitchell, a toolsy 6-foot-3, 215-pound outfielder, was originally drafted by the Athletics in the 14th round coming out of Orange Lutheran High School in 2017. He bypassed the late round offer and headed to the land of the Bruins. And he immediately established himself as one of the better bats in college baseball. The California native batted a respectable .280/.337/.331 with four doubles and a pair of triples during his freshman season. He returned to the Pac12 school with a vengeance the following year: in 62 games he slugged a scorching .349/.418/.566 with 14 doubles, 12 triples, six homeruns, and 18 stolen bases. And like so many other promising seasons, Mitchell's fantastic junior campaign (.355/.425/.484) was interrupted because of COVID. The Brewers drafted him in the opening round, 20th overall, and signed him to a deal worth $3,242,900. The lefty-swinging outfielder made his professional debut in 2021. And it was a tale of two seasons. After just three games with the Wisconsin Timber Rattlers the former Bruin hit the injury list, courtesy of a strained popliteus muscle in his leg. He missed nearly a month of action. He would eventually rip through the High-A competition to the tune of .359/.508/.620 in 29 games before earning a promotion to the minors' most challenging levels, Double-A. Then his season tanked. In 35 games with Biloxi he hit .186/.291/.264.

Scouting Report: So, will the real Garrett Mitchell please stand up? Was he the Ruthian middle-of-the-lineup dreamboat that was on display during his scorching stint in High-A? Or was he simply the guy swinging a wet noodle at Double-A pitching? Truth be told – he's probably somewhere in between. Mitchell's never shown a tremendous amount of over-the-fence thump at any point since entering college, but he was on pace to swat 20 dingers in a full 162-game season last year. Is that real? No. His groundball rate at both levels was over 60%, an absurdly high mark. He also showed some swing-and-miss issues as well (26.5%) and some susceptibility to left-handers (.214/.329/.321). Now the good news: plus speed, above-average glove, and a willingness to spray the ball around the diamond. The swing-and-miss issues will likely prove to be an aberration and the hit tool has a chance to be an above-average weapon. He's not going to be a star, but he could be a solid contributing player on a championship caliber squad. In terms of big league ceiling: think Trent Grisham, something along the lines of .250/.330/.430.

Ceiling: 3.0-win player
Risk: Moderate
MLB ETA: 2022/2023

3. Sal Frelick, CF

Hit	Power	SB	Patience	Glove	Overall
55	40	60	55	55	55

Born: 04/19/00	Age: 22	Bats: L	Top Comp: Denard Span
Height: 5-9	Weight: 175	Throws: R	

Season	Team	Age	Level	PA	1B	2B	3B	HR	SB	CS	BB%	K%	AVG	OBP	SLG	ISO
2021	MIL	21	CPX	17	5	1	1	0	3	0	11.76%	11.76%	0.467	0.529	0.667	0.200
2021	MIL	21	A	81	23	6	1	1	6	2	11.11%	12.35%	0.437	0.494	0.592	0.155
2021	MIL	21	A+	71	7	1	1	1	3	0	14.08%	18.31%	0.167	0.296	0.267	0.100

Background: Frelick's high school resume reads like a novella: He was a two-time captain for the baseball, football, and hockey teams; the *Boston Globe* named him the Athlete of the Year after his senior season; he was named the Gatorade State Player of the Year for Massachusetts after his final high school season in which he tossed 30 touchdowns; and he's a two-time league MVP on the gridiron and captured the award once on the diamond. A three-sport star during his prep career, Frelick received scholarship offers to play both baseball *and* football at Boston College – though eventually choosing to stay on the diamond to focus on a potential future career. Frelick ripped through the competition during his freshman season for the Eagles, slugging a healthy .367/.447/.513 with eight doubles, one triple, and four homeruns to go along with 18 stolen bases. That production earned him a spot on the All-ACC Second Team and ACC All-Freshman Team. D1Baseball, Collegiate Baseball News, and Perfect each named him as a Freshman All-American. His production tumbled during the abbreviated 2020 season; he hit .241/.380/.414 in 71 plate appearances. But after tearing through the Futures Collegiate Baseball League during the ensuing summer, Frelick's offensive firepower came roaring back in 2021. In 48 games the 5-foot-9, 175-pound center fielder slugged .359/.443/.559 with career high in doubles (17), triples (2), and homeruns (six). He's also swiped 13 bags in 18 attempts. Milwaukee selected him with the 15th overall pick last July, signing him to a deal worth $4,000,000. Frelick split time between three separate leagues during his professional debut, hitting an aggregate .329/.414/.466 with eight doubles, three triples, and two homeruns. He also swiped 12 bags in 14 total attempts.

Scouting Report: Per the usual, here's what I wrote about Frelick prior to the draft last year:

"Consider the following:

- *Between 2011 and 2020, there just 13 instances in which an ACC hitter posted a .350/.440/.500 slash line with a double digit walk rate and a sub-14% strikeout rate in a season (min. 175 PA). Frelick's 2021 season is the second time he's accomplished the feat.*

Very simple, low maintenance swing that shoots balls to the gap. The 5-foot-9, 175-pound center fielder doesn't project to hit more than six to eight homeruns [in a season] in the professional ranks. But he consistently barrels the ball up. He's another low ceiling, high floor prospect that has the ceiling of a .280/.340/.400-type hitter with solid defense."

Ceiling: 3.0-win player
Risk: Moderate
MLB ETA: 2023

4. Freddy Zamora, SS

Hit	Power	SB	Patience	Glove	Overall
55	40	55	55	60	50

Born: 11/01/98	Age: 23	Bats: R	Top Comp: Yunel Escobar
Height: 6-1	Weight: 190	Throws: R	

Season	Team	Age	Level	PA	1B	2B	3B	HR	SB	CS	BB%	K%	AVG	OBP	SLG	ISO
2021	MIL	22	A	321	58	13	1	5	9	5	14.02%	17.76%	0.287	0.396	0.399	0.112
2021	MIL	22	A+	92	17	9	0	1	1	0	13.04%	20.65%	0.342	0.435	0.494	0.152

Background: Flashing some complete package tools from the moment Zamora stepped onto the University of Miami's campus. The 6-foot-1, 190-pound infielder batted .303/.388/.412 with 17 extra-base knocks as a true freshman. The Nicaragua-born shortstop followed that up with a slightly better showing during his sophomore campaign for the Hurricanes: appearing in 50 games for the ACC squad, Zamora slugged .296/.393/.447 with 12 doubles and six homeruns to go along with 13 stolen bases (against just being thrown out only three times). Zamora was poised to be an early first round selection heading into his junior campaign, but a suspension and knee injury forced him out the entire year. The Brewers took a second round flier on Zamora, signing him to a deal worth $1.15 million. Fast forward a year and…*BAM*…Zamora looked every bit of a potential big league shortstop. In 92 games between Carolina and Wisconsin, the now-22-year-old batted .300/.404/.421 with 22 doubles, one triple, and six homeruns. His overall production, per *Weighted Runs Created Plus*, topped the league average mark by an impressive 31%.

Scouting Report: Consider the following:

- Between 2006 and 2021, only three 22-year-old hitters met the following criteria in a Low-A season with one organization (min. 300 PA): 120 and 130 wRC+ total, a walk rate north of 12%, and a strikeout rate between 17% and 20%. Those three hitters: Allan Dykstra, Jon Karcich, and Freddy Zamora.

After a slow start to the year, Zamora, who batted .213/.337/.267 over his first 20 games, flipped the switch and slugged .324/.423/.463 over his remaining 72 games. There's a chance for three above-average or better tools: bat, speed, and glove. Zamora doesn't project for much power, but may reach 10 or so homeruns in a season. There's legitimate starting potential here. And it's another example of the Brewers' savvy drafting / developing. I'm a really big fan. A strong showing in AA in 2022 may put him in position for a late-season call up.

Ceiling: 2.5-win player
Risk: Moderate
MLB ETA: 2022/2023

5. Joey Wiemer, OF

Hit	Power	SB	Patience	Glove	Overall
45	55	55	55	55	55

Born: 02/11/99	Age: 23	Bats: R	Top Comp: N/A
Height: 6-5	Weight: 215	Throws: R	

Season	Team	Age	Level	PA	1B	2B	3B	HR	SB	CS	BB%	K%	AVG	OBP	SLG	ISO
2021	MIL	22	A	320	48	11	2	13	22	4	14.06%	21.56%	0.276	0.391	0.478	0.201
2021	MIL	22	A+	152	22	7	0	14	8	2	11.84%	23.68%	0.336	0.428	0.719	0.383

Background: The University of Cincinnati's produced three notable big leaguers in the school's history: Kevin Youkilis, Josh Harrison, and Ian Happ, the ninth overall pick in the 2015 draft. As for Wiemer, Milwaukee selected the 6-foot-5, 215-pound outfielder in the fourth round two years ago, making him the fourth highest drafted player in Cincinnati's history. Wiemer made his professional debut last season – and it was one to remember. After a 75-game tenure with the Carolina Mudcats in which he batted a healthy .276/.391/.478 with 11 doubles, two triples, and 13 homeruns, he continued his assault on low level minor league pitching with the Wisconsin Timber Rattlers. In 34 games with the club's High-A affiliate, Wiemer batted .336/.428/.719. When the dust finally settled, he finished the year with an aggregate .295/.403/.556 slash line, belting out 18 doubles, two triples, 27 homeruns, and 30 stolen bases. Per *Weighted Runs Created Plus*, his overall production topped the league average mark by 55%. The former Bobcat ripped through the Arizona Fall League as well, sporting a .467/.568/.667 mark through nine games.

Scouting Report: What. The. Actual. Hell? Wiemer went from slugging just 12 homeruns in 122 college games to belting out 27 in 109 minor league games. Clearly the Brewers' scouting / analytic department saw something no one else did. With respect to Wiemer's showing in Low-A last season, consider the following:

- Since 2006, only three 22-year-old hitters met the following criteria in a Low-A season with one organization (min. 300 PA): 130 to 140 wRC+, a walk rate north of 12%, and a strikeout rate between 20% and 23%. Those three hitters: Ryan Costello, Jermaine Mitchell, and Joey Wiemer.

It's still a touch too early to go all-in on Wiemer as a potential big league bat – after all, he was 22-years-old doing a good portion of his damage in Low-A. And he was playing half of his time in hitter-friendly confines (Carolina and Wisconsin, by the way). But there is *a lot* to like. A lot. Above-average power. Above-Average speed. Good patience / willingness to work the count. Solid contact rates. Oh, yeah, his batted ball data was absurd. Per *FanGraphs*, his average exit velocity was 94 mph, tied for the tenth best in the minor leagues, with a peak velocity of 109 mph. With another strong showing in High-A / Double-A and Wiemer, the former Cincinnati nobody, could easily find himself on the brink of Top 100 prospect. stardom.

Ceiling: 2.5- to 3.0-win player
Risk: Moderate to High
MLB ETA: 2023

6. Brice Turang, SS

Hit	Power	SB	Patience	Glove	Overall
45	40	60	60	55	50

Born: 11/21/99	Age: 22	Bats: L	Top Comp: J.P. Crawford
Height: 6-0	Weight: 173	Throws: R	

Season	Team	Age	Level	PA	1B	2B	3B	HR	SB	CS	BB%	K%	AVG	OBP	SLG	ISO
2018	MIL	18	R	57	13	2	0	0	8	1	15.79%	10.53%	0.319	0.421	0.362	0.043
2018	MIL	18	R	135	24	4	1	1	6	1	16.30%	20.74%	0.268	0.385	0.348	0.080
2019	MIL	19	A	357	68	13	4	2	21	4	13.73%	15.13%	0.287	0.384	0.376	0.089
2019	MIL	19	A+	207	25	6	2	1	9	1	16.43%	22.71%	0.200	0.338	0.276	0.076
2021	MIL	21	AA	320	54	14	3	5	11	7	8.75%	15.00%	0.264	0.329	0.385	0.122
2021	MIL	21	AAA	176	27	7	0	1	9	2	18.18%	19.89%	0.245	0.381	0.315	0.070

Background: It's difficult to believe, especially coming off of the 2021 draft class which was littered with high profile prep shortstops, but the Brewers made Turang just the third overall shortstop taken in the 2018 draft, second prep player at the position. The 21st overall selection that year, Turang was viewed as a rare low risk, high floor/low ceiling high school player. And, for the most part, he's lived up to that billing. The lefty-swinging middle infielder split time between Biloxi and Nashville last season, hitting an aggregate .258/.347/.362 with 21 doubles, three triples, six homeruns, and 20 stolen bases (in 29 total attempts). His overall production, per *Weighted Runs Created Plus*, was one percent below the league average threshold.

Snippet from The 2020 Prospect Digest Handbook: Turang began elevating the ball more frequently last year, so it wouldn't be surprising to see him belt out 12 or 15-homeruns during his peak. He's a gamer and a potential All-Star.

Scouting Report: Consider the following:

- Since 2006, only five 21-year-old hitters met the following criteria in a Double-A season with one organization (min. 300 PA): 95 to 105 wRC+, 8% to 10% walk rate, and a sub-20% strikeout rate. Those five hitters: Eugenio Suarez, Tim Beckham, Mike Carp, Hak-Ju Lee, and Brice Turang.

A grinder at the plate that sniffs out first base via a walk with a high frequency. Turang continued his trend of improved flyball rates, posting a career-low 38.5% groundball rate during his extended stint in Double-A. He's speedy, owns an above-average glove, and generally does things well without a lot of flare. There's definite big league value here. Big ceiling: something along the lines of .270/.340/.380.

Ceiling: 2.0-win player
Risk: Low to Moderate
MLB ETA: 2022

7. Ethan Small, LHP

FB	SL	CH	Command	Overall
55	50	60	45	50

Born: 02/14/97	Age: 25	Bats: L	Top Comp: Wade Miley
Height: 6-4	Weight: 215	Throws: L	

Season	Team	Age	Level	IP	TBF	K/9	K%	BB/9	BB%	K-BB%	ERA	FIP	xFIP	Pit/Bat
2019	MIL	22	A	18.0	68	15.50	45.59%	2.00	5.88%	39.71%	1.00	0.67	1.35	4.47
2021	MIL	24	AA	41.1	164	14.59	40.85%	4.57	12.80%	28.05%	1.96	2.14	2.96	4.10
2021	MIL	24	AAA	35.0	147	6.17	16.33%	5.40	14.29%	2.04%	2.06	4.99	5.86	4.03

Background: One of the most prolific strikeout artists in college baseball history. Small, a herky-jerky southpaw, averaged an impressive 13.1 strikeouts per nine innings during his three-year tenure at Mississippi State University. After a spectacular junior campaign in which he posted a 1.93 ERA while averaging nearly 15 K/9, the Brewers snatched Small with the 28th overall pick in 2019. After a wildly successful debut in the lower levels of the minor leagues, Milwaukee aggressively shoved the long-limbered hurler up to Double-A and eventually to Triple-A during his first full season in professional ball. In total, Small tossed 77.1 innings of work, striking out 92 and walking 42 to go along with a 1.98 ERA and a 3.44 FIP. He missed some action for several weeks as he was dealing with a ligament issue in his left hand.

Snippet from The 2020 Prospect Digest Handbook: Small looks like a solid #3/#4-type arm at maturity. One final thought: Love to the bulldog mentality on the mound.

Scouting Report: It really was a tale of two seasons for the big left-hander: he was incredibly dominant during his eight-start cameo in Double-A, averaging 14.6 K/9, but his swing-and-miss rate declined all the way down to a disappointing 6.2 K/9 during his nine starts in Triple-A. The fastball's going from average-ish to better-than-average; it was sitting in the 92- to 93-mph range during a start in AAA. His changeup is an elite offering, generating tons of weak contact and swings-and-misses. It's the type of pitch that's tough to hit, even if the opposition is sitting on it. It looks like he's scrapped his curveball for a more tradition slider, showing pretty solid horizontal movement. Small has consistently posted lower-than-expected, even miniscule, ERAs. He looks like a potential backend starting option.

Ceiling: 2.0-win player
Risk: Moderate
MLB ETA: Debuted in 2021

8. Jeferson Quero, C

	Hit	Power	SB	Patience	Glove	Overall
	45/55	40/45	50/40	50	55	50

Born: 10/08/02	Age: 19	Bats: R	Top Comp: N/A
Height: 5-10	Weight: 165	Throws: R	

Season	Team	Age	Level	PA	1B	2B	3B	HR	SB	CS	BB%	K%	AVG	OBP	SLG	ISO
2021	MIL	18	CPX	83	13	5	1	2	4	3	14.46%	12.05%	0.309	0.434	0.500	0.191

Background: Recognized by MLB.com as one of the better catching prospects on the international scene a couple years ago. The Brewers handed the 5-foot-10, 165-pound teenage backstop a relatively small pittance of just $200,000 – a sum that looks like quite the bargain three years later. Making his official debut last season with the organization's Arizona Complex League, Quero slugged a hearty .309/.434/.500 with five doubles, one triple, and a pair of homeruns. Per *Weighted Runs Created Plus*, his overall production topped the league average threshold by a whopping 48%. His season ended a bit prematurely, courtesy of a surgical procedure to repair a separated shoulder on his non-throwing arm.

Scouting Report: There's not a lot of information lack here: (A) Quero appeared in just 23 Complex League games last season, garnering only 83 plate appearances and (B) there's no game tape, as far as I can tell, of Quero. With that being said, he did show an interesting bat-first approach at the plate during his debut last season, shooting the ball from gap-to-gap without much bias. He also walked more times (12) then he whiffed (10). Defensively, he looked to be an above-average defender in limited action while throwing out roughly one-third of would-be base thieves.

Ceiling: 2.0-win player
Risk: Moderate
MLB ETA: 2025

9. Tyler Black, 2B

	Hit	Power	SB	Patience	Glove	Overall
	45/55	50	50	60	50	50

Born: 07/26/00	Age: 21	Bats: L	Top Comp: N/A
Height: 6-2	Weight: 190	Throws: R	

Season	Team	Age	Level	PA	1B	2B	3B	HR	SB	CS	BB%	K%	AVG	OBP	SLG	ISO
2021	MIL	20	CPX	12	2	0	0	1	2	0	50.00%	16.67%	0.500	0.750	1.000	0.500
2021	MIL	20	A	103	14	4	0	0	3	2	19.42%	28.16%	0.222	0.388	0.272	0.049

Background: A tough as nails competitor – as evidenced by his hockey and football background – Black was one of college baseball's most lethal, as well as underrated, bats since 2019. Appearing in 47 games at the keystone and another five at shortstop as a true freshman for Wright State, the 6-foot-2, 190-pound Black battered the competition to the tune of .353/.469/.600 with 11 doubles, five triples, seven homeruns, and eight stolen bases. He finished the year with an impeccable 18-to-38 strikeout-to-walk ratio. Black's production stumbled a bit during his 13-game COVID-shortened 2020 campaign; he hit .239/.340/.370. But it came roaring back during his dominant 2021 follow up. In 48 games for the raiders, Black slugged a hearty .383/.496/.683 with career highs in doubles (14), homeruns (13), and stolen bases (11). He finished the year with 39 walks and 25 punch outs. Milwaukee selected the Canadian-born infielder in the opening round last July, 33rd overall, and signed him to a deal worth $2.2 million. Black appeared in 26 games during his debut, 23 of them with Carolina in Low-A, hitting a lowly .241/.426/.322 with four doubles and a dinger.

Scouting Report: Per the usual, here's what I wrote prior to the draft last year:

"Consider the following:

- *Between 2011 and 2020, only seven Division I hitters batted at least .375/.485/.675 with a walk rate north of 15% and a strike rate below 11% (min. 200PA): Andrew Vaughn, Nick Gonzales, Will Craig, Casey Gillaspie, Patrick Causa, Luis Trevino, Frazier Hall, and Taylor Davis.*

Black, of course, fits into the aforementioned group. Above-average, perhaps even peaking with a plus-hit tool. Solid-average power. Can run a little bit. Tremendous bat-to-ball skills. Great eye. Add it all up and Black is one of the more underrated prospects in the draft class. He feels like A Tampa Bay or Oakland-type prospect."

Ceiling: 2.0-win player
Risk: Moderate
MLB ETA: 2024

10. Hedbert Perez, CF	Hit	Power	SB	Patience	Glove	Overall
	40/50	50/55	40	45	50	45

Born: 04/04/03	Age: 19	Bats: L	Top Comp: N/A
Height: 5-10	Weight: 160	Throws: L	

Season	Team	Age	Level	PA	1B	2B	3B	HR	SB	CS	BB%	K%	AVG	OBP	SLG	ISO
2021	MIL	18	CPX	132	23	11	0	6	2	0	6.06%	25.76%	0.333	0.394	0.575	0.242
2021	MIL	18	A	68	8	2	0	1	0	0	1.47%	36.76%	0.169	0.206	0.246	0.077

Background: Fun Fact Part I: Perez's old man, Robert, spent parts of six seasons at the big league level, four of them coming north of the border with the Blue Jays. Fun Fact Part II: during the 1996 season, his longest extended look at the big leagues, Robert slugged a scorching .327/.354/.406 with 10 doubles and a pair of homeruns in 86 games. Fun Fact Part III: despite the impressive slash line that years, the elder Perez's OPS+ was still below average (93). Milwaukee signed the younger Perez for a sizeable $700,000 bonus three years ago. Hedbert made his professional debut in the Complex League last summer, swinging a hot stick to the tune of .333/.394/.575 with 11 doubles and six homeruns in just 32 contests. The front office bounced him to up Low-A at the end of August for a couple – mostly disappointing – weeks to cap off his first year of action. Perez finished the year with an aggregate .276/.330/.459.

Scouting Report: There were 140 players to receive at least 100 plate appearances in the Arizona Complex League last season, Perez's overall production, 148 wRC+, was tied for the 11th best. Quick bat. Short, compact swing. Perez showed surprising power during his debut in the Complex League, but there was a semi-concerning amount of swing-and-miss to his approach as well, which was only further exploited after his promotion up to Low-A. He's a hacker, so he's not going to walk a whole lot. Loves the high pitch.

Ceiling: 1.5-win player
Risk: Moderate
MLB ETA: 2025

11. Eduardo Garcia, SS	Hit	Power	SB	Patience	Glove	Overall
	40/45	45/55	35	45	55/60	50

Born: 07/10/02	Age: 19	Bats: R	Top Comp: N/A
Height: 6-2	Weight: 160	Throws: R	

Season	Team	Age	Level	PA	1B	2B	3B	HR	SB	CS	BB%	K%	AVG	OBP	SLG	ISO
2019	MIL	16	R	40	7	2	0	1	1	1	15.00%	22.50%	0.313	0.450	0.469	0.156
2021	MIL	18	A	42	7	4	0	0	1	0	14.29%	30.95%	0.333	0.452	0.455	0.121
2021	MIL	18	CPX	136	13	10	3	3	2	2	6.62%	29.41%	0.238	0.316	0.443	0.205
2021	MIL	18	CPX	14	2	2	0	1	0	1	7.14%	14.29%	0.385	0.429	0.769	0.385

Background: Ranked among the Top 30 prospects on the international scene in 2018 by MLB Pipeline. The Brewers signed the Duaca, Venezuela, native to a deal worth slightly more than a million dollars. The 6-foot-2, 160-pound shortstop made his debut with the organization a year later, hitting a solid .313/.450/.469 in a 10-game stint in the Dominican Summer League. Then COVID shut the minors down. Milwaukee pushed the then-18-year-old to the stateside rookie leagues to begin the 2021 season. And he shined brightly – at the start. Starring for the ACL Brewer Blue squad, Garcia torched the competition to the tune of .385/.429/.769 for a trio of games before earning the nod to the Gold squad in the Complex League. There his numbers cooled dramatically: .238/.316/.443 in 33 games. Garcia capped off his sophomore professional season with a dominant 10 game stint in Low-A, slugging .333/.452/.455.

Scouting Report: A slow start with the Gold squad killed his overall production line with the team: he hit a lowly .188/.291/.438 over his first 13 games vs. the .270/.333/.446 slash line he compiled over his remaining 20 contests. The teenage shortstop was pegged for his defensive prowess as a free agent – which he's lived up to the billing as a smooth defender – so anything he contributes with the bat is a positive. And it's been *a lot*. Surprising pop. But there's too much swing-and-miss going on with him at the plate. He fanned in more than 29% of his appearances with the Gold team last year. If Garcia chews his problematic K-rate down to the lower 20% range, he's going to be a competent starter.

Ceiling: 2.0-win player
Risk: Moderate to High
MLB ETA: 2024/2025

12. Zavier Warren, C/1B/3B

Hit	Power	SB	Patience	Glove	Overall
50	45/55	40	55	50	45

Born: 01/08/99	Age: 23	Bats: B	Top Comp: N/A
Height: 6-0	Weight: 190	Throws: R	

Season	Team	Age	Level	PA	1B	2B	3B	HR	SB	CS	BB%	K%	AVG	OBP	SLG	ISO
2021	MIL	22	A	230	28	8	2	10	1	0	14.35%	21.30%	0.251	0.374	0.471	0.220
2021	MIL	22	A+	157	25	7	1	3	5	0	11.46%	20.38%	0.267	0.357	0.400	0.133

Background: While there's been a handful of players from Central Michigan University to ascend to the big leagues, there's only one that went on to a long, established, above-average career: former 1986 second round selection Kevin Tapani, a 143-game winner with five different franchises. Milwaukee drafted Zavier Warren in the third round two years ago out of Central Michigan, signing him to a deal worth $575,000 and making him the sixth highest selection in the school's history. A defensive vagabond who's spent time at catcher and both corner infield positions in the pros, Warren split time between Carolina and Wisconsin during his debut last season. In 89 total games between the organization's Low-A and High-A affiliates, he slugged .258/.367/.442 with 15 doubles, three triples, and 13 homeruns. He also went a perfect 6-for-6 in stolen bases as well. Per *Weighted Runs Created,* his overall production was 22% above the league average mark.

Scouting Report: Ignoring all the other stats that Warren put together last season – at least momentarily. The most eye-catching numbers: 96. As in: 96 mph – his exit average exit velocity, trailing only Spencer Torkelson as the second best in the minor leagues, per *FanGraphs*. Warren spent time all around the infield in college, including second base and shortstop, but he's primarily been relegated to catching and first and third bases. He's been a 50-grade glove at all the spots too. Above-average patience. Solid contact skills. Above-average power potential. There's definite super-sub potential here, especially if he can moonlight as a backstop from time-to-time.

Ceiling: 1.5-win player
Risk: Moderate
MLB ETA: 2023

13. Joe Gray Jr., CF

Hit	Power	SB	Patience	Glove	Overall
40	55	50	50	60	45

Born: 03/12/00	Age: 22	Bats: R	Top Comp: N/A
Height: 6-1	Weight: 195	Throws: R	

Season	Team	Age	Level	PA	1B	2B	3B	HR	SB	CS	BB%	K%	AVG	OBP	SLG	ISO
2018	MIL	18	R	98	7	5	0	2	6	0	18.37%	25.51%	0.182	0.347	0.325	0.143
2019	MIL	19	R	129	10	4	1	3	3	2	10.08%	27.91%	0.164	0.279	0.300	0.136
2021	MIL	21	A	231	21	15	7	12	12	0	14.29%	26.41%	0.289	0.407	0.632	0.342
2021	MIL	21	A+	248	30	7	2	8	11	3	8.06%	28.23%	0.219	0.306	0.381	0.163

Background: Mississippi-based Hattiesburg High School has a pretty high success rate for turning draft picks into eventual big leaguers. Excluding Gray, who's still making his way through the minor leagues, three of the school's 11 drafted players made it to the game's pinnacle level: Robert Carson, Jermaine Van Buren, and John Lindsey. The prep school's also produced three second rounders as well, Van Buren, the 60th overall player chosen by the Rockies in 1998; Matt Butler, the 81st player taken a year later by the Braves; and – of course – Joe Gray Jr., the 60th player chosen four years ago. The 6-foot-1, 195-pound center fielder was shot out of a cannon at the start of last season, slugging a herculean .289/.407/.632 with 15 doubles, seven triples, 12 homeruns, and 12 stolen bases in only 51 games with the Carolina Mudcats. Then his season hit the skids as he morphed into the second coming of Mario Mendoza. Gray was promoted up to High-A for good in early July. He responded by batting .219/.306/.381 in 59 contests.

Scouting Report: Just how different was Gray's production from level to level last season? Or was it really? Consider the following:

- Since 2006, only three 21-year-old hitters met the following criteria in a Low-A season with one organization (min. 200 PA): at least a 165 wRC+ total, a walk rate north of 12%, and a strikeout rate of at least 25%. Those three hitters: Max White, Will Benson, and – of course – Joe Gray Jr.

Now let's take a look at his work in High-A, as well. Consider the following:

- Since 2006, only four 21-year-old hitters met the following criteria in a High-A season with one organization (min. 200 PA): a wRC+ total between 85 and 95; a strikeout rate between 27% and 29%, and a walk rate between 7% and 9%. Those four hitters: Je'Von Ward, Victor Labrada, Chuckie Jones, and Joe Gray Jr.

Gray's a raw outfielder with loud offensive tools and an above-average, maybe even plus glove. But he's flawed. He swings-and-missed too frequently, the hit tool is, at best, a 45-grade. And he feasted off of some favorable home environments. He's certainly come a long, *long* way from the disastrous showings his first two seasons (.182/.347/.325 and .164/.279/.300) but there's a lot of work that still needs to happen. The defense and speed/power combo may be enough to compensate and push him into a reserve role at the big league level. But he's a long shot.

Ceiling: 1.5-win player
Risk: Moderate to High
MLB ETA: 2024

14. Russell Smith, LHP

FB	SL	CH	Command	Overall
55	50	55/60	50	45

Born: 09/10/98	Age: 23	Bats: L	Top Comp: N/A
Height: 6-9	Weight: 235	Throws: L	

Background: Taken by the Cubs in the 38th round coming out of Midlothian High School in 2017. Smith, instead, attended Big12 school Texas Christian University. And his collegiate career got off to a solid start through six games: he averaged 7.9 strikeouts and 4.9 walks per nine innings. Then his elbow flared up and he succumbed to Tommy John surgery – which would cost him the remainder of 2018 and all of 2019. Finally healthy Smith returned for four incredibly dominant starts in 2020 – he posted a 27-to-2 strikeout-to-walk ratio through 21.0 innings – before COVID shut the rest of the season down. Last year Smith – finally – put in a full season worth of work. Making 15 starts for the Horned Frogs, the 6-foot-9, 235-pound southpaw struck out 101 and walked just 20 en route to tallying a 3.83 ERA. Milwaukee selected him in the second round, 51st overall, and signed him to a deal worth $1 million. He did not appear in a game after signing.

Scouting Report: Consider the following:

- Between 2011 and 2020, only seven Big12 pitchers averaged at least 10 strikeouts and fewer than 2.5 walks per nine innings in a season (min. 75 IP): Alek Manoah, Nick Lodolo, Chad Donato, Brandon Finnegan, Jon Gray, and Andrew Heaney. All but Donato were first round draft picks, by the way.

Smith's 2021 production puts him in the same category. He's big – like big, *big*. Randy Johnson big. But Smith commands the strike zone incredibly well – in spite of his massive 6-foot-9 frame. He doesn't own a blazing heater; it sits in the low-90s but plays up because of his size. His changeup is borderline plus, showing tons of sink-and-fade thanks to a lot of pronation. Smith will also mix in a slurvy-type breaking ball. There's some backend starting potential, but he needs to firm up the breaking ball.

Ceiling: 1.0- to 1.5-win player
Risk: Moderate
MLB ETA: 2024

15. Alec Bettinger, RHP

FB	CB	SL/CU	CH	Command	Overall
50	55	55	45	50	40

Born: 07/13/95	Age: 26	Bats: R	Top Comp: Chase Anderson
Height: 6-2	Weight: 210	Throws: R	

Season	Team	Age	Level	IP	TBF	K/9	K%	BB/9	BB%	K-BB%	ERA	FIP	xFIP	Pit/Bat
2018	MIL	22	A	62.2	257	7.18	19.46%	2.44	6.61%	12.84%	3.73	4.04	4.09	3.88
2018	MIL	22	A+	54.2	243	9.22	23.05%	2.80	7.00%	16.05%	6.91	4.67	3.57	4.03
2019	MIL	23	AA	146.1	588	9.66	26.70%	2.15	5.95%	20.75%	3.44	3.13	3.01	3.84
2021	MIL	25	AAA	96.2	416	9.12	23.56%	2.42	6.25%	17.31%	4.75	4.25	3.98	3.91

Background: Already surpassed any modest expectations placed on late round draft picks. The Brewers selected the 6-foot-2, 210-pound right-hander in the 10th round out of the University of Virginia five years ago. His bonus: a measly $10,000. Since then, though, Bettinger has consistently posted impressive peripherals at each minor league level as he's trekked towards Milwaukee. After opening the 2021 season with the Brew Crew on a sour note – he allowed 11 earned runs in only four innings of work in early May – Bettinger bounced between the big leagues and Nashville the remainder of the season. The former Cavalier made 21 appearances, 18 of which were starts, with the Nashville Sounds, posting a 98-to-26 strikeout-to-walk ratio in 96.2 innings of work. He also tossed 10.0 innings with the Brewers, posting a lowly 5-to-3 strikeout-to-walk ratio to go along with a 13.50 ERA.

Snippet from The 2020 Prospect Digest Handbook: He has the look and feel as a #5-type arm or an ideal partner to work with an opener.

Scouting Report: At this point the book on Bettinger is not only written, but it's pretty well digested and understood. Low-90s fastball that won't miss many bats. An above-average curveball. An above-average slider / cutter, which morphs between the two depending on his liking. And a nearly non-existent changeup. As I mentioned in The 2020 Prospect Digest Handbook, Bettinger has the look and feel of a Chase Anderson-type pitcher, a late blooming arm that will sparkle for a year before trending back towards mediocrity.

Ceiling: 1.0-win player
Risk: Low to Moderate
MLB ETA: Debuted in 2021

16. Mario Feliciano, C

Hit	Power	SB	Patience	Glove	Overall
45/50	45	30	40	45	40

Born: 11/20/98	Age: 23	Bats: R	Top Comp: Dioner Navarro
Height: 6-1	Weight: 200	Throws: R	

Season	Team	Age	Level	PA	1B	2B	3B	HR	SB	CS	BB%	K%	AVG	OBP	SLG	ISO
2018	MIL	19	A+	165	19	7	1	3	2	0	7.88%	35.76%	0.205	0.282	0.329	0.123
2018	MIL	19	R	16	3	1	0	0	0	1	12.50%	18.75%	0.286	0.375	0.357	0.071
2019	MIL	20	A+	482	72	25	4	19	2	1	6.02%	28.84%	0.273	0.324	0.477	0.205
2019	MIL	20	AA	14	1	0	1	0	0	0	0.00%	28.57%	0.167	0.286	0.333	0.167
2021	MIL	22	CPX	29	5	3	1	0	0	0	3.45%	20.69%	0.360	0.448	0.560	0.200
2021	MIL	22	AAA	114	17	2	0	3	1	0	3.51%	22.81%	0.210	0.246	0.314	0.105

Background: Milwaukee added the stocky backstop in the second round out of the Carlos Beltran Baseball Academy all the way back in 2016. To put that into proper context: that was the same draft class that the Mets added Pete Alonso, the Polar Bear, into the fold. As for Feliciano, who was taken 11 selections after Alonso, the 6-foot-1, 200-pound catcher dealt with a shoulder issue that would limit his playing time to just 32 games with Nashville, a handful more on a rehab assignment, and one *large* game with the big league squad. Feliciano batted a lowly .210/.246/.314 during his stint in AAA last season. The Puerto Rican born prospect also spent the fall playing for the Salt River Rafters, slugging a scorching .318/.348/.432 with five doubles in 13 contests.

Snippet from The 2020 Prospect Digest Handbook: Early in his career Feliciano employed a high contact, no power approach at the plate – which resulted in production marks south of the league average mark. Since entering High Class A two years ago, he's morphed his approach heavily towards more power with high strikeout rates. Defensively, well, he's not good and – frankly – barely passable. The state of catching at the big league level is beyond terrible, so that opens the door – widely – for Feliciano's prospects. If the power holds firm without regressing, he has a chance to be a bat-first option but he's unlikely to ever approach league average status at the big league level.

Scouting Report: Feliciano remains an offensive enigma – again. He's walking as often as an elderly person in need of a hip replacement. But, on the other hand, he improved his swing-and-miss rates considerably, even in an injury riddled campaign. And, of course, his defense is like trying to eat spaghetti with a spoon. With that being said, the dearth of catching talent may eventually push him into a backup role.

Ceiling: 1.0-win player
Risk: Moderate
MLB ETA: Debuted in 2021

17. Carlos Rodriguez, OF

Hit	Power	SB	Patience	Glove	Overall
50/55	35/40	50	50	50	40

Born: 12/07/00	Age: 21	Bats: L	Top Comp: N/A
Height: 5-10	Weight: 150	Throws: L	

Season	Team	Age	Level	PA	1B	2B	3B	HR	SB	CS	BB%	K%	AVG	OBP	SLG	ISO
2018	MIL	17	R	22	7	0	0	0	2	1	9.09%	4.55%	0.350	0.409	0.350	0.000
2018	MIL	17	R	230	54	13	1	2	12	8	3.04%	8.26%	0.323	0.358	0.419	0.097
2019	MIL	18	R	22	6	1	0	0	1	1	0.00%	9.09%	0.318	0.318	0.364	0.045
2019	MIL	18	R	157	43	3	1	3	4	6	2.55%	12.74%	0.331	0.350	0.424	0.093
2021	MIL	20	A+	382	70	17	4	1	15	6	9.16%	19.63%	0.267	0.336	0.348	0.081

Background: Handed a large $1,355,000 bonus as part of one of the headliners in their international free agent class several years ago. Rodriguez put together a couple impressive showings to begin his professional career. He hit .323/.358/.419 in 56 games in the Dominican Summer League in 2018, and he followed that up with a .331/.350/.424 triple-slash line in 36 contests in the Pioneer League the next year. Last season the front office aggressively challenged the baby-faced, then-20-year-old and pushed him directly up to High-A, bypassing Low-A all together. And the results were…mediocre. In a career-best 94 games with the Wisconsin Timber Rattlers the 5-foot-10, 150-pound outfielder batted .267/.336/.348 with 17 doubles, four triples, and one homerun. He also swiped 15 bags in 21 total attempts. Per *Weighted Runs Created Plus*, his overall production was 7% *below* the league average threshold.

Snippet from The 2020 Prospect Digest Handbook: If the hit tool continues to perform and approach plus territory, he's a lock to become an above-average regular. If not, he could be a capable fourth outfielder on a contending team.

Scouting Report: Consider the following:

- Since 2006, only five 20-year-old hitters in High-A met the following criteria in a season with one organization (min. 300 PA): 88 to 98 wRC+, a walk rate between 8% and 10%, and a strikeout rate between 18% and 21%. Those five hitters: Brent Brewer, Dustin Peterson, Nick Noonan, Darwin Perez, and Carlos Rodriguez.

Rodriguez isn't showing a lot of hope for future power potential and at 5-foot-10 and 150 pounds he doesn't project to develop a ton either. There was a bit of a learning curve last year for Rodriguez, which is to be expected: after starting the year out by hitting .208/.321/.292 over his first 35 games, he righted the ship and batted.298/.344/.378 over his remaining 59 contests. The batted ball data is fairly low: 86 mph average exit velocity with a peak of just 97 mph. He's going to go as far as the hit tool will carry him, because the rest of the skill set is blasé.

Ceiling: 1.0-win player
Risk: Moderate
MLB ETA: 2024

18. Antoine Kelly, LHP

FB	SL	CH	Command	Overall
60	50	50	40/45	40

Born: 12/05/99	Age: 22	Bats: L	Top Comp: Taylor Hearn
Height: 6-6	Weight: 205	Throws: L	

Season	Team	Age	Level	IP	TBF	K/9	K%	BB/9	BB%	K-BB%	ERA	FIP	xFIP	Pit/Bat
2019	MIL	19	R	28.2	108	12.87	37.96%	1.57	4.63%	33.33%	1.26	1.93	2.59	2.29
2021	MIL	21	A	17.0	79	12.71	30.38%	8.47	20.25%	10.13%	6.88	4.15	5.59	4.24

Background: Not a baseball hotbed, perse, but Wabash Valley College has produced 38 draft picks in the school's history — 34 of them occurring after the year 2000. And Kelly, a big 6-foot-6, 205-pound southpaw, became the school's highest drafted player when the Brewers selected him in the second round, 65th overall, three years ago. The big lefty turned in a strong, oft-dominant debut in the Arizona Summer League that season, averaging 12.9 strikeouts and just 1.6 walks per nine innings. Last season, though, got off to a disappointing start: Kelly succumbed to Thoracic Outlet Syndrome surgery, a procedure and rehabilitation that would knock him out until mid-July. After a brief, one-inning tune-up in the Complex League, Kelly made seven starts in Low-A and one final start in High-A. In total, he tossed just 19.1 innings, recording 27 strikeouts and 19 walks. For his career he's averaging 12.7 strikeouts and 4.9 walks per nine innings.

Snippet from The 2020 Prospect Digest Handbook: Nitrous infused fastball that (A) not only regularly touches 97 mph and sits 94- to 95-mph comfortably, but (B) also has a chance to add a little bit of velocity as his wiry 6-foot-6, 205-pound frame continues to fill out. It's a plus offering that has a chance to blossom into a plus-plus weapon. As far as the secondary pitches are concerned, well, they're raw — very, very raw. I was only able to catch one of Kelly's professional games, the Low Class A contest against the Kane County Cougars. Kelly already has a big league fastball, but he could – likely will – fall into the Taylor Hearn category of one plus pitch, little secondary, perennial noteworthy prospect without making too many waves at the big league level.

Scouting Report: Thoracic Outlet Syndrome is notoriously difficult to come back from. Most notably: former ace right-hander Matt Harvey, who's never been able to recapture the previous magic that he displayed early in his career. But Kelly showed little evidence of losing anything from his repertoire. His fastball was sitting in 95 mph range. And both his second weapons – a slider and changeup – have ticked up from below-average to solid 50-grades. The command is still below-average, maybe even a 40-grade at times. And while he's only entering his age-22 season, I think he's going to head down the path to relief-dom. In order to avoid that, he needs two major transformations to occur: (1) consistently throw more quality strikes and (B) develop a legitimate secondary weapon.

Ceiling: 1.0-win player
Risk: Moderate
MLB ETA: 2024

19. Justin Bullock, RHP

	FB	CB	CH	Command	Overall
	50	55	55	50	40

Born: 05/12/99	Age: 23	Bats: R	Top Comp: N/A
Height: 6-2	Weight: 195	Throws: R	

Season	Team	Age	Level	IP	TBF	K/9	K%	BB/9	BB%	K-BB%	ERA	FIP	xFIP	Pit/Bat
2018	MIL	19	R	58.2	258	10.12	25.58%	3.53	8.91%	16.67%	5.68	5.46	4.99	3.50
2019	MIL	20	A	19.2	96	9.15	20.83%	6.41	14.58%	6.25%	7.78	7.01	4.66	3.50
2021	MIL	22	A	19.0	69	12.79	39.13%	2.37	7.25%	31.88%	1.42	1.92	2.92	4.30
2021	MIL	22	A+	44.1	176	8.73	24.43%	1.83	5.11%	19.32%	3.65	3.97	4.04	3.81
2021	MIL	22	AA	34.1	155	7.86	19.35%	3.15	7.74%	11.61%	6.55	5.99	5.41	3.79

Background: There was a lot of talent to be had in the 16th round of the 2017 draft. Four players – Kyle Dohy, Alan Trejo, Ty Tice, and Kutter Crawford have already accrued big league time on their resumes. Joey Cantillo, the 467th overall pick that year, transformed himself from a crafty prep southpaw into a legitimate big league prospect. And, quietly, Justin Bullock, a slight-framed 6-foot-2, 195-pound right-hander out of South Granville High School, began to open some eyes during the 2021 season. The 474th overall player chosen in 2017, Bullock, who received a $295,000 bonus, blew through three stops en route to his best professional season to date. Making a total of 20 starts between Low-A, High-A, and Double-A, the young righty posted a 100-to-26 strikeout-to-walk ratio en route to tallying a 4.24 ERA.

Scouting Report: A consistent strike-thrower that saw an uptick in command last season. Bullock's repertoire won't blow the doors off of anything: average fastball, above-average curveball / changeup combination. He's like Josh Tomlin without the elite command. Bullock doesn't have a ton of room for error, but he trusts his arsenal and knows how to pitch. One more thought: his flyball rates suggest homeruns may plague him as he continues to ascend up the ladder.

Ceiling: 1.0-win player
Risk: Moderate
MLB ETA: 2022/2023

20. Ernesto Martinez, 1B/CF

	Hit	Power	SB	Patience	Glove	Overall
	40/45	50/55	55	55	50	40

Born: 06/20/99	Age: 23	Bats: L	Top Comp: N/A
Height: 6-6	Weight: 229	Throws: L	

Season	Team	Age	Level	PA	1B	2B	3B	HR	SB	CS	BB%	K%	AVG	OBP	SLG	ISO
2018	MIL	19	R	146	22	5	1	0	5	3	10.96%	32.88%	0.224	0.336	0.280	0.056
2019	MIL	20	R	188	26	10	1	6	4	5	11.17%	28.72%	0.262	0.356	0.445	0.183
2021	MIL	22	A	311	42	15	5	11	30	4	10.29%	27.01%	0.274	0.370	0.492	0.218

Background: It took a bit of finagling, but the Brewers were able to scrounge up the funds to sign the Cuban import to a deal worth $800,000 in late May of 2017. Milwaukee acquired the monies courtesy of the Baltimore Orioles, who sent $885,300 for relief pitch Damien Magnifico. Since signing his professional contract, though, Martinez was largely a disappointment: he hit a lowly .232/.383/.368 in both the foreign and domestic rookie leagues during his debut; he followed that up with a lowly .224/.336/.280 in a return to the Arizona Summer League the following year; and began to show some punch during his third season (.262/.356/.445). Last season Martinez – finally – made it up to full season action. And he was able to compile his best professional season, by a *large margin*. In 79 games with the Carolina Mudcats, the 6-foot-6, 229-pound first baseman / center fielder slugged .274/.370/.492 with 15 doubles, five triples, and 11 homeruns. He also swiped 30 bags in 34 total attempts. Per *Weighted Runs Created Plus*, his overall production topped the league average mark by an impressive 32%.

Scouting Report: Injury limited Martinez's breakout season to just 79 games. So, just for fun, let's prorate his counting stats over a full 162-game campaign: 31 doubles, 10 triples, 23 homeruns, and 62 stolen bases. Not too shabby. Martinez has a bit of saber-slant flavor to his production. He works the count well, flashes above-average thump, and he'll mix in above-average speed. He's always struggled with his swing-and-miss rates, though it continues to trend in the right direction. Martinez is also showing some concerning platoon splits: he batted .280/.370/.526 against RHP and only .235/.366/.265 against fellow southpaws. He's a future platoon bat – if everything breaks the right way, which is rarely – if ever – the actual case.

Ceiling: 0.5- to 1.0-win player
Risk: Moderate
MLB ETA: 2024

Minnesota Twins

Top Prospects

1. Austin Martin, SS/CF

	Hit	Power	SB	Patience	Glove	Overall
	55/60	40/45	50	65	45/55	60

Born: 03/23/99	Age: 23	Bats: R	Top Comp: Brandon Belt (pre-2021)
Height: 6-0	Weight: 185	Throws: R	

Season	Team	Age	Level	PA	1B	2B	3B	HR	SB	CS	BB%	K%	AVG	OBP	SLG	ISO
2021	TOR	22	AA	250	41	10	2	2	9	3	14.80%	21.20%	0.281	0.424	0.383	0.102
2021	MIN	22	AA	168	23	8	0	3	5	1	13.69%	17.86%	0.254	0.399	0.381	0.127

Background: It was a deal that didn't seem like a possibility heading into the season last year. Minnesota was coming off of back-to-back playoff appearances. The organization had several players finish high in the 2020 awards, including:

Nelson Cruz coming in sixth in the MVP award voting, Kenta Maeda was the Cy Young runner-up, and after winning the AL Manager of the Year in 2019, Rocco Baldelli finished in the top 5 a year later. Yet, almost unimaginably the Twins faltered, fell out of the playoff race and were forced to deal away some of the team's veterans – and fan favorites – as the trade deadline approached. Minnesota acquired young right-hander Simeon Woods Richardson and Austin Martin from Toronto for All-Star right-hander Jose Berrios, who would eventually sign a mega-deal with his new team. Martin, the fifth overall pick and the second bat taken in the 2020 draft, was a dynamic sparkplug for one of the premier collegiate programs in the country, Vanderbilt University. The shortstop/center fielder left the school with a .368/.474/.532 triple-slash line. Last year, his professional debut, the 6-foot, 185-pound hitter spent the season with both organization's Double-A affiliates, hitting an aggregate .270/.414/.382 with 18 doubles, two triples, five homeruns, and 14 stolen bases. His overall production, according to *Weighted Runs Created Plus*, topped the league average threshold by an impressive 28% – not bad for a debut showing in the minors' most challenging level.

Scouting Report: Consider the following:

- Since 2006, only three Double-A hitters met the following criteria in a season with one organization (min. 350 PA): 123 to 133 wRC+ total, a walk rate of at least 12%, and a strikeout rate between 19% and 22%. Those three hitters: Alex Avila, Michael Reed, and Charcer Burks. Martin's production places him squarely among the group, as well.

Just one season into his career, barely removed from being considered one of the best amateur bats in the country, Martin has seemingly gathered a small – or perhaps not so small – faction of doubters. His defensive position seems to be a bit unsettled, as he continues to split time between shortstop and center fielder; he's striking out more frequently than many thought; and, of course, he's not flashing a ton of power. So let's break it down point-by-point:

1. According to Clay Davenport's defensive metrics, Martin's graded out as slightly below average at shortstop and slightly above-average at center field. Personally, he's probably more valuable at shortstop and isn't that far away from being a solid defender.
2. He's fanned in 19.9% of his plate appearances. So? Who gives a shit? We live in a time where teams live with 30+% K-rates. And he closed out the year by whiffing only five times in his final 16 games. Plus, let's not forget he went from an abbreviated college season to a delayed debut and right into the most challenging level in minor league baseball. So, again, who gives a shit? It's less than 20%.
3. He's never going to be a 20-homer guy. But I'm confident he's going to top out around 12- to 15-dingers in a full season. His average exit velocity, per *FanGraphs*, was a stellar 90 mph.

Martin may never be a star. But he's going to be a very good player on a championship caliber team.

Ceiling: 3.5-win player
Risk: Low to Moderate
MLB ETA: 2022/2023

2. Jordan Balazovic, RHP

	FB	CB	SL	CH	Command	Overall
	60	60	50	55	50/55	60

Born: 09/17/98	Age: 23	Bats: R	Top Comp: Zack Wheeler
Height: 6-5	Weight: 215	Throws: R	

Season	Team	Age	Level	IP	TBF	K/9	K%	BB/9	BB%	K-BB%	ERA	FIP	xFIP	Pit/Bat
2018	MIN	19	A	61.2	254	11.38	30.71%	2.63	7.09%	23.62%	3.94	3.03	3.03	3.81
2019	MIN	20	A	20.2	83	14.37	39.76%	1.74	4.82%	34.94%	2.18	1.61	1.97	3.92
2019	MIN	20	A+	73.0	298	11.84	32.21%	2.59	7.05%	25.17%	2.84	2.28	2.54	4.00
2021	MIN	22	AA	97.0	429	9.46	23.78%	3.53	8.86%	14.92%	3.62	3.91	4.28	3.90

Background: A tremendous find, as well as a tremendous job by the organization's player development program. The club drafted the 6-foot-5, 215-pound right-hander out of St. Martin SS prep school, located in Mississauga, Ontario, in the fifth round of the 2016 draft. Since then Balazovic has moved through the organization's minor league chain like a shark's fin through water. Last season the then-22-year-old hurler spent the entirety of the year battling – and impressing – in the minor's most challenging level, Double-A. In a career high 20 starts, Balazovic tossed 97.0 innings, averaging 9.5 strikeouts and 3.5 walks per nine innings. He finished his fifth professional season with a 3.62 ERA, 3.91 FIP, and a 4.28 xFIP.

Snippet from The 2020 Prospect Digest Handbook: After his phenomenal showing in 2019, Balazovic's ceiling now resides – comfortably – in the #3-type starting pitcher.

Scouting Report: Consider the following:

- Since 2006, only five 22-year-old hurlers met the following criteria in a Double-A season with one organization (min. 90 IP): 23% to 25% strikeout percentage with a walk percentage between 8% and 10%. Those five hurlers: Zack Wheeler, Jordan Zimmerman, Wily Peralta, Jorge Lopez, and – of course – Mr. Jordan Balazovic.
- For those counting at home: *Per FanGraphs,* Wheeler's tallied more than 21 wins above replacement in his career, Jordan Zimmerman was worth more than 25 WAR in his career, and both Peralta and Lopez have had long, slightly above replacement level careers.

I noted in the 2020 Prospect Digest Handbook that Balazovic was the prospect I most looked forward to scouting. And nothing changed over the past two years either – except the fact that he's gotten better. Plus mid-90s fastball. Hellacious, knee-buckling curveball. An average, late moving slider. And a split-change that's really, really come along way, moving from average to above. There's some genuine #2-type potential. And I think the command actually creeps into above-average territory at some point as well.

Ceiling: 3.5-win player
Risk: Moderate
MLB ETA: 2022

3. Jose Miranda, IF/OF

	Hit	Power	SB	Patience	Glove	Overall
	55	55	35	45+	50	60

Born: 06/29/98	Age: 24	Bats: R	Top Comp: Jorge Polanco
Height: 6-2	Weight: 210	Throws: R	

Season	Team	Age	Level	PA	1B	2B	3B	HR	SB	CS	BB%	K%	AVG	OBP	SLG	ISO
2018	MIN	20	A	439	75	22	1	13	0	1	5.92%	11.62%	0.277	0.326	0.434	0.157
2018	MIN	20	A+	113	14	5	0	3	0	2	4.42%	9.73%	0.216	0.292	0.353	0.137
2019	MIN	21	A+	478	75	25	1	8	0	0	5.02%	11.30%	0.248	0.299	0.364	0.116
2021	MIN	23	AA	218	46	8	0	13	4	2	7.80%	11.47%	0.345	0.408	0.588	0.242
2021	MIN	23	AAA	373	76	24	0	17	0	2	6.70%	13.14%	0.343	0.397	0.563	0.220

Background: Fun fact Part I: across all affiliated minor league levels, there were 377 hitters that received at least 400 plate appearances last season. Fun Fact Part II: Of those 377 qualified hitters, Miranda's total production, as measured by *Weighted Runs Created Plus*, was ranked as the fourth highest – at 58% *above* the league average level. Needless to say, the defensive vagabond had quite the showing in 2021. Splitting time between Wichita and St. Paul, the 6-foot-2, 210-pound infielder – and sometimes outfielder – slugged a robust .344/.401/.572 with career highs in doubles (32) and homeruns (30). He also finished the season with a solid 74-to-42 strikeout-to-walk ratio as well.

Scouting Report: Consider the following:

- Since 2006, only three hitters have met the following criteria in a Triple-A season with one organization (min. 300 PA): a total wRC+ of at least 150 wRC+ with a sub-17% strikeout rate. Those three hitters: Brandon Nimmo, Adam Eaton, and, of course, Mr. Jose Miranda.
- For those counting at home: Nimmo's been 26% better than the league average offensive line during his career and Eaton's topped the threshold by 9%, as well.

Not bad comps. The batted ball data, according to *FanGraphs*, is average. And Miranda certainly benefited from spending half the year at two different hitter-friendly confines; though he did bat a hearty .330/.389/.564 on the road. The power's a completely new skill – and one that is typically the last to develop. I watched all of Miranda's homeruns. And I'm convinced the power is legit. He was mashing some absolute bombs – all around the diamond. He uncorked an opposite field shot that looked like a jam-job against a St. Louis affiliate that might not have landed. His batted ball profile hasn't changed dramatically, so it'll be interesting to see how big leaguers pitch him. But Miranda's one of the most – if not *the most* – underrated prospect in the baseball.

Ceiling: 3.5-win player
Risk: Moderate
MLB ETA: 2022/2023

4. Royce Lewis, SS

Hit	Power	SB	Patience	Glove	Overall
40/55	45/55	55	50	50	60

Born: 06/05/99	Age: 23	Bats: R	Top Comp: Dansby Swanson
Height: 6-2	Weight: 200	Throws: R	

Season	Team	Age	Level	PA	1B	2B	3B	HR	SB	CS	BB%	K%	AVG	OBP	SLG	ISO
2018	MIN	19	A	327	61	23	0	9	22	4	7.34%	14.98%	0.315	0.368	0.485	0.169
2018	MIN	19	A+	208	34	6	3	5	6	4	9.13%	16.83%	0.255	0.327	0.399	0.144
2019	MIN	20	A+	418	61	17	3	10	16	8	6.46%	21.53%	0.238	0.289	0.376	0.138
2019	MIN	20	AA	148	19	9	1	2	6	2	7.43%	22.30%	0.231	0.291	0.358	0.127

Background: It's been a rough couple of seasons for the former top pick. Taken with the first overall selection in the 2017 draft, the JSerra Catholic High School product battled through an absurdly disappointing 2019 season in which he hit a disappointing .238/.289/.376 in 94 games in High-A and continued to flounder after the club promoted him up to Double-A as well . He finished the year with a .236/.290/.371 slash line – though he did rebound during his 22-game stint in the Arizona Fall League. Lewis, like all minor leaguers not on the taxi squad, lost a season of develop as the country reared from the pandemic. And then the 6-foot-2, 200-pound tools-laden shortstop missed the entirety of 2021 as he recovered from a torn ACL in his right knee. The injury, according to reports at the time, say it's unclear on how exactly it happened. Per an article by Do-Hyoung Park of MLB.com, "the injury only presented as slight soreness in the knee until Lewis underwent an MRI exam as part of a physical at Spring Training." Assuming the minor league season starts on time, the duration between his last stint in the Arizona Fall League will be roughly 950 days earlier.

Snippet from The 2020 Prospect Digest Handbook: The problem isn't necessarily his swing, per se. It's this massive leg kick that's creating issues. Sometimes he's late getting his foot down. Sometimes it seems as if his weight is leaning too forward. It's just…bad. I went back and watched old tape from 2018. The leg kick was still prevalent. But the competition of his talent was such that he was able to succeed in spite of it. Lewis possesses the intangibles that made him the top pick in the draft. I think he needs to alter his lower half, rather than the whole swing.

Scouting Report: There's – literally – nothing to report on at this point. Hopefully Lewis' recovery doesn't impede any of his explosiveness.

Ceiling: 3.5-win player
Risk: Moderate to High
MLB ETA: 2022/2023

5. Chase Petty, RHP

FB	CB	SL	CH	Command	Overall
70	55	55	50/55	45/50	55

Born: 04/04/03	Age: 19	Bats: R	Top Comp: N/A
Height: 6-1	Weight: 190	Throws: R	

Background: The legend of Chase Petty, as told by Joseph Santoliquito in a July 2nd, 2021, article for the *PhillyVoice*, began years ago – like when he was 12 and sitting in the mid-70s. He was bumping the low 80s two years later. And hit 88 mph, according to Santoliquito, as a 15-year-old. Fast forward to two years ago, the 6-foot-2, 190-pound thunderbolt slinging right-hander kissed 102 mph at the *Area Code Games*. With a tattoo emblazoned on his powerful right arm, Petty – without question – dominated the competition during his final season at Mainland Regional High School: the University of Florida commit tallied 99 punch outs and a 1.15 ERA in 48.2 innings of work as he led his team to the state championship round. Minnesota selected the hard-throwing righty in the opening round, 26th overall, and signed him to a deal worth $2.5 million. Petty made two brief appearances in the Florida Complex League, fanning six and walking one.

Scouting Report: Per the usual, here's what I wrote about Petty prior to the draft:

> "It all starts with a blistering plus-plus fastball for Petty, which is among the best in the entire draft class. And it may actually stand alone at the top when it's all said and done. But what separates Petty's heater from among other plus-plus offerings is the run that he'll generate on the two-seamer. A lot of scouting reports indicate the hard-throwing hurler only mixes in a slider, which was an above-average offering late last summer, but he'll also mix in a hard downward biting curveball as well. Petty will [throw] a hard, fading changeup that's deceptively good and may peak as an above-average pitch with a little more use. There's been a lot of talk about his mechanics, but they're clean, fluid, and repeatable. The arm action is a little long in the back, a la Daniel Espino. Barring injury, Petty has a chance to be a solid mid-rotation arm – something along the line of a healthy Nate Eovaldi."

Ceiling: 3.0-win player
Risk: Moderate
MLB ETA: 2024

6. Simeon Woods Richardson, RHP

FB	CB	SL	CH	Command	Overall
55	55	50	60	55	55

Born: 09/27/00	Age: 21	Bats: R	Top Comp: German Marquez
Height: 6-3	Weight: 210	Throws: R	

Season	Team	Age	Level	IP	TBF	K/9	K%	BB/9	BB%	K-BB%	ERA	FIP	xFIP	Pit/Bat
2018	NYM	17	R	11.1	47	11.91	31.91%	3.18	8.51%	23.40%	0.00	2.07	2.46	1.89
2019	NYM	18	A	78.1	325	11.14	29.85%	1.95	5.23%	24.62%	4.25	2.53	2.24	4.07
2019	TOR	18	A+	28.1	107	9.21	27.10%	2.22	6.54%	20.56%	2.54	2.46	2.93	3.88
2021	TOR	20	AA	45.1	202	13.30	33.17%	5.16	12.87%	20.30%	5.76	3.78	4.08	4.07

Background: An on-the-go top prospect over the past couple of seasons. The Mets drafted the well-built right-hander out of Kempner High School in 2018. A little more than a year later New York flipped the former second round pick, along with Anthony Kay, to the Blue Jays for All-Star right-hander Marcus Stroman. Woods Richardson made it two years in Toronto's farm system – with one of those years via the COVID-shutdown – before he was dealt away to Minnesota, along with Austin Martin, for two-time All-Star right-hander Jose Berrios. The 6-foot-3, 210-pound righty struggled through his worst professional season to date in 2021. Splitting time between both organizations' Double-A affiliates, Woods Richardson tossed only 53.1 innings of work, fanning 77 but walking a whopping 34. He finished the year with an unsightly 5.91 ERA.

Snippet from The 2020 Prospect Digest Handbook: Absolute bulldog that would make peak Orel Hershiser pause for a double take.

Scouting Report: Still intimidating hitters with his bulldog mentality; the problem for Woods Richardson was his declining command last season. The 2021 campaign started out on impressive footing – he posted a 48-to-11 strikeout-to-walk ratio in his first 30 innings – but after a disastrous start against Bowie at the end of June his season turned. Over his final eight games, split evenly between both organizations – he walked 23 and fanned 29 in 23.1 innings of work. The promising youngster has always shown a solid feel for the strike zone, so the Twins were wise to bet on the past, as opposed to the present. With regard to his repertoire, Woods Richardson's fastball sat in the 91- to 93-mph range. He complements the above-average offering with a matching mid-70s curveball, a rare average, low-80s slider, and a plus-changeup. There's #3/#4-type potential, assuming the command bounces back.

Ceiling: 3.0-win player
Risk: Moderate
MLB ETA: 2022/2023

4. Jhoan Duran, RHP

FB	CB	CH	Command	Overall
55	60	55	55	60

Born: 01/08/98	Age: 24	Bats: R	Top Comp: N/A
Height: 6-5	Weight: 230	Throws: R	

Season	Team	Age	Level	IP	TBF	K/9	K%	BB/9	BB%	K-BB%	ERA	FIP	xFIP	Pit/Bat
2018	ARI	20	A	64.2	290	9.88	24.48%	3.90	9.66%	14.83%	4.73	3.93	3.53	3.85
2018	MIN	20	A	36.0	135	11.00	32.59%	2.50	7.41%	25.19%	2.00	2.68	2.56	3.99
2019	MIN	21	A+	78.0	318	10.96	29.87%	3.58	9.75%	20.13%	3.23	3.05	2.77	4.03
2019	MIN	21	AA	37.0	153	9.97	26.80%	2.19	5.88%	20.92%	4.86	2.76	2.56	3.41
2021	MIN	23	AAA	16.0	75	12.38	29.33%	7.31	17.33%	12.00%	5.06	3.86	3.72	4.43

Background: Minnesota's system was hit pretty hard with arm injuries – particularly right elbow woes, though shoulder issues popped up as well. Most notable minor leaguers to succumb to wonky arms: Matt Canterino, Blayne Enlow, Josh Winder, and Jhoan Duran. A gas-throwing right-hander built like a tight end, Duran first tasted Double-A success two years ago – as a baby-faced 21-year-old. And he figured to play a role in the Twins 2021 plans, at least at some point in the year. But just 16 innings into his debut with the St. Paul Saints, the 6-foot-5, 230-pound hurler's season prematurely ended. He finished the year with a disappointing 22-to-13 strikeout-to-walk ratio. For his career, the former Arizona farmhand is averaging 8.9 strikeouts and 3.3 walks per nine innings with a 3.99 ERA.

Snippet from The 2020 Prospect Digest Handbook: There's some upper rotation caliber potential as long as he doesn't take the Brusdar Graterol route.

Scouting Report: Reports indicate, at least for the time being, that Duran was able to avoid any type of surgical procedure – which is ideal, of course. But call me skeptical. These things never seem to work out well in the end. Heading into the 2020 season I had Duran showing a plus-plus fastball and a pair of plus offspeed pitches: a power curveball and a devastating changeup. If he can prove the elbow is up to the task, he may find himself as a late-inning arm for the Twins in 2022.

Ceiling: 3.5-win player
Risk: High
MLB ETA: 2022

8. Matt Canterino, RHP

FB	CB	SL	CH	Command	Overall
55	60	65	55	55	50

Born: 12/14/97	Age: 24	Bats: R	Top Comp: Rich Harden
Height: 6-2	Weight: 222	Throws: R	

Season	Team	Age	Level	IP	TBF	K/9	K%	BB/9	BB%	K-BB%	ERA	FIP	xFIP	Pit/Bat
2019	MIN	21	A	20.0	75	11.25	33.33%	3.15	9.33%	24.00%	1.35	2.30	3.03	4.36
2021	MIN	23	A+	21.0	78	18.43	55.13%	1.71	5.13%	50.00%	0.86	0.87	1.12	4.17

Background: Houston-based Rice University has the stigma of chewing through arms like a tank tread over terrain. And, unfortunately for the Twins, Canterino's 2021 season looks like another cautionary tale. The 2019 second round pick got off to a blazing start to the year, posting a 35-to-3 strikeout-to-walk ratio while surrendering just a pair of earned runs over his first 18.0 innings. Then the arm issues popped up – for the first time that season. What was termed as a right-elbow strain shelved Canterino in late May and he wouldn't come off the disabled list until early August. Upon his return, the 6-foot-2, 222-pound hurler made one dominant three-inning start against the Peoria Chiefs and then hit the DL with a strained right elbow – again. He finished the year by averaging 17.6 strike outs and just 1.6 walks per nine innings to go along with a laughable 0.78 ERA in 23.0 innings of work.

Snippet from The 2020 Prospect Digest Handbook: Canterino increases his effectiveness through a lot of mechanical deception. It's difficult to describe, but there's a slight pause in his windup, very herky-jerky. Because Canterino throws strikes and sports two plus breaking balls, he's likely going to quickly chew through the low levels of the minor leagues, so his first test likely won't happen until he reaches Class AA. #4/#5-type potential.

Scouting Report: I scouted two of Canterino's six appearances. He was as dominant – if not more dominant – than any other minor league hurler I saw in 2021. The fastball's sneaky quick, a 55-grade, but what it lacks in sheer velocity, it makes up with in explosiveness. There were a *ton* of late hacks by solid minor league bats. His curveball would be the best offering for a lot of hurlers. It's an easy plus-pitch. But it's not even Canterino's best breaking ball. His late-tilting, hard-biting slider is. It's a borderline plus-plus pitch that's death to left-hander hitters. His changeup bumped up from a below-average to better-than-average offering too. There's plenty of arm-speed deception with fade and velocity difference. Canterino showed the talent to slide into the upper part of rotation. But I think the injuries are going to be a constant in his career.

Ceiling: 2.5-win player
Risk: High
MLB ETA: Debuted in 2021

9. Yunior Severino, 2B/3B

Hit	Power	SB	Patience	Glove	Overall
50	50	35	50	45	50

Born: 10/03/99	Age: 22	Bats: B	Top Comp:
Height: 6-1	Weight: 189	Throws: R	

Season	Team	Age	Level	PA	1B	2B	3B	HR	SB	CS	BB%	K%	AVG	OBP	SLG	ISO
2018	MIN	18	R	218	36	8	0	8	0	1	7.80%	23.85%	0.263	0.321	0.424	0.162
2019	MIN	19	R	22	2	1	1	1	0	0	0.00%	27.27%	0.227	0.227	0.500	0.273
2019	MIN	19	A	86	12	7	0	0	0	0	8.14%	31.40%	0.244	0.302	0.333	0.090
2021	MIN	21	A	268	33	17	1	5	2	0	11.94%	27.99%	0.245	0.347	0.393	0.148
2021	MIN	21	A+	157	27	12	1	3	1	0	12.74%	31.85%	0.321	0.414	0.493	0.172

Background: A bit of collateral damage from the Braves' international free agency scandal several years back. Severino originally signed with the Atlanta for a hefty $1.9 million, but after he was granted free agency in 2017 the Twins swooped in and offered the switch-hitting infielder an even larger bonus: $2.5 million. The 6-foot-1, 189-pound second / third baseman, who got to keep the original bonus Atlanta handed him, split time between Fort Myers and Cedar Rapids in 2021. In a combined 98 games, he batted .273/.372/.430 with 29 doubles, two triples, eight homeruns, and three stolen bases. Per *Weighted Runs Created Plus*, his overall production topped the league average production line by a solid 22%.

Scouting Report: Severino's overall numbers (.245/.347/.393) with Fort Myers in Low-A are skewed significantly by a poor May. He batted a lowly .194/.306/.290 through his first 17 games with the Mighty Mussels. From June 1st through the end of his tenure with the club he hit .263/.362/.431. And he upped the ante even further once he got to High-A (.321/.414/.493). There's the potential to develop 20-homer pop, but he needs to elevate the ball more frequently. Solid patience, but not enough to compensate for some bloated swing-and-miss tendencies. He's raw defensively, though likely better suited for third base. He could be a solid complementary player, something like a young Eduardo Escobar (.270/.335/.490).

Ceiling: 2.0-win player
Risk: Moderate
MLB ETA: 2023

10. Joe Ryan, RHP

FB	CB	SL	CH	Command	Overall
55	50	55	50	55	50

Born: 06/05/96	Age: 26	Bats: R	Top Comp: Mike Fiers
Height: 6-2	Weight: 205	Throws: R	

Season	Team	Age	Level	IP	TBF	K/9	K%	BB/9	BB%	K-BB%	ERA	FIP	xFIP	Pit/Bat
2018	TBR	22	A-	36.1	147	12.63	34.69%	3.47	9.52%	25.17%	3.72	3.15	2.73	4.08
2019	TBR	23	A	27.2	115	15.29	40.87%	3.58	9.57%	31.30%	2.93	2.29	2.21	4.24
2019	TBR	23	A+	82.2	312	12.19	35.90%	1.31	3.85%	32.05%	1.42	1.69	2.15	4.04
2019	TBR	23	AA	13.1	54	16.20	44.44%	2.70	7.41%	37.04%	3.38	2.55	1.42	4.87
2021	TBR	25	AAA	57.0	215	11.84	34.88%	1.58	4.65%	30.23%	3.63	3.24	3.41	3.93

Background: Maybe we'll look back on the summer of 2020, not as the return of minor league baseball from its COVID-induced hibernation, but as the Summer of Substance. Grip, tackiness, sticky stuff. Substance. And Joe Ryan, mid-round pick out of California State University, Stanislaus, made one hell of an observation as he pitched for Team USA last year. As quoted by Hannah Keyser of Yahoo! Sports, Ryan remarked: "It's the best ball in the world. They need this ball over in America. It is amazing. It's perfect. I love throwing with it, all the pitchers love throwing it." In terms of his on-field work stateside, the 6-foot-2, 205-pound right-hander made 14 appearances between Tampa Bay's and Minnesota's Triple-A affiliates, throwing 66.0 innings, recording an impeccable 92-to-12 strikeout-to-walk ratio. He made five starts with the Twins as well, averaging 10.1 strikeouts and just 1.7 walks per nine innings. Minnesota acquired Ryan with Drew Strotman for future Hall of Famer Nelson Cruz and Calvin Faucher.

Snippet from The 2020 Prospect Digest Handbook: If a secondary pitch – or two – ticks up or if he shows an increased level of confidence in them, Ryan has the ceiling as a #4-type arm.

Scouting Report: It takes some gumption to (A) trade with the Tampa Bay Rays, (B) acquire an arm from said trade, and (C) not get absolutely fleeced. As for Ryan, his fastball looked like it lost a bit of life, and half of a grade, during his 2021 summer of dominance. It was in the low-90s in Minnesota. But…he found the strike zone with unparalleled consistency. His curveball's a slow, loopy low-70s offering. His changeup is nothing special. But his slider does as a second above-average offering. He's 26 and destined for a #4/#5-type starting gig.

Ceiling: 1.5- to 2.0-win player
Risk: Low to Moderate
MLB ETA: Debuted in 2021

11. Noah Miller, SS

Hit	Power	SB	Patience	Glove	Overall
40/50	45	45	50	50	45

Born: 11/12/02	Age: 19	Bats: B	Top Comp: Cole Tucker
Height: 6-0	Weight: 185	Throws: R	

Season	Team	Age	Level	PA	1B	2B	3B	HR	SB	CS	BB%	K%	AVG	OBP	SLG	ISO
2021	MIN	18	CPX	96	14	3	1	2	1	1	9.38%	27.08%	0.238	0.316	0.369	0.131

Background: The younger brother of Cleveland infielder prospect Owen Miller. The younger Miller would eventually best his older brother's draft status by two rounds. Noah, a commit to the University of Alabama, was taken with the last pick in the supplemental first round, 36th overall, and signed to a deal worth $1.7 million – more than a million dollars more than Owen received from the Padres three years earlier. For his debut, the Ozaukee High School product batted a disappointing .238/.316/.369 with three doubles, one triple, and a pair of long balls in the Florida Complex League. His overall production, per *Weighted Runs Created Plus*, was 15% *below* the league average threshold.

Scouting Report: Simple, low maintenance swing from both sides of the plate. He's more geared towards shooting line drives around the diamond, but can occasionally put a jolt into one. He's not fast, but quick. He's not strong, but twitchy. He reminds me of a young Cole Tucker. Miller profiles as a low ceiling / high floor type of prospect.

Ceiling: 1.5-win player
Risk: Moderate
MLB ETA: 2025

12. Cole Sands, RHP

FB	CB	CH	Command	Overall
55	55	55	50	40

Born: 07/17/97	Age: 24	Bats: R	Top Comp: N/A
Height: 6-3	Weight: 215	Throws: R	

Season	Team	Age	Level	IP	TBF	K/9	K%	BB/9	BB%	K-BB%	ERA	FIP	xFIP	Pit/Bat
2019	MIN	21	A	41.1	174	10.67	28.16%	2.40	6.32%	21.84%	3.05	2.16	3.11	4.03
2019	MIN	21	A+	52.0	192	9.17	27.60%	1.21	3.65%	23.96%	2.25	2.79	2.70	3.91
2021	MIN	23	AA	80.1	334	10.76	28.74%	3.92	10.48%	18.26%	2.46	3.55	4.42	4.13

Background: Originally taken by the Houston Astros in the 22nd round coming out of North Florida Christian High School in 2015, Sands improved his draft stock 17 rounds following his three years at Florida State and a pair of summers with the Falmouth Commodores in vaunted Cape Cod League. Last season, his second in professional ball, Sands returned back to Double-A after making a start to cap off his wildly successful debut in 2019. In a career-high 19 appearances, Sands struck out an impressive 96 and walked 35 in just 80.1 innings of work. He compiled a tidy 2.46 ERA, a 3.55 FIP, and a 4.42 xFIP.

Snippet from The 2020 Prospect Digest Handbook: Sands' repertoire and command suggests a capable backend starting pitcher. But I have doubts as to whether he'll reach that ceiling. He's a low three-quarter slinger that, I believe, will eventually leave him susceptible to left-handed hitters. His likely landing spot is a multi-inning relief-type workhorse with the occasional spot-start thrown his way.

Scouting Report: Consider the following:

- Since 2006, only two 23-year-old pitchers met the following criteria in a Double-A season with one organization (min. 75 IP): 27.5% to 29.5% strikeout percentage with a 9.5% to 11.5% walk percentage. Those two arms: Matt Barnes and – of course – Cole Sands.

As I speculated two years ago, left-handers did, in fact, cause all kinds of issues for Sands in 2021. Righties hit .185/.277/.292 against him. Lefties, on the other hand, slugged .269/.377/.444. Low 90s fastball that'll peak in the mid-90s on a rare occasion. His curveball is an above-average pitch. And his changeup got noticeably better, going from average to above. It's a heavy offering. He's a strike-thrower and will eventually slide into a relief role. But there's definite MLB value here.

Ceiling: 1.0-win player
Risk: Low to Moderate
MLB ETA: 2022

13. Blayne Enlow, RHP

FB	CB	SL	CH	Command	Overall
N/A	N/A	N/A	N/A	N/A	40

Born: 03/21/99	Age: 23	Bats: R	Top Comp: Boof Bonser
Height: 6-3	Weight: 170	Throws: R	

Season	Team	Age	Level	IP	TBF	K/9	K%	BB/9	BB%	K-BB%	ERA	FIP	xFIP	Pit/Bat
2018	MIN	19	A	94.0	408	6.80	17.40%	3.35	8.58%	8.82%	3.26	3.99	4.52	3.41
2019	MIN	20	A	41.1	185	9.58	23.78%	3.27	8.11%	15.68%	4.57	3.81	3.32	3.74
2019	MIN	20	A+	69.1	291	6.62	17.53%	2.99	7.90%	9.62%	3.38	3.84	3.98	3.37
2021	MIN	22	A+	14.2	59	14.11	38.98%	3.68	10.17%	28.81%	1.84	2.75	2.83	4.00

Background: After finishing the 2019 season with 13 games in High-A, it was bit surprising the front office would bounce the former 2017 third rounder back down to the level two years later. But that's exactly what happened. And, of course, Enlow got off to a tremendously dominant start to the year: he struck out 23, walked just 6, and tallied 1.84 ERA before hitting the injured list. The cause: a barking right elbow, which would eventually force the St. Amant High School product under the knife for Tommy John surgery. For his professional career, Enlow is averaging 7.8 strikeouts and 3.1 walks per nine innings to go along with a 3.27 ERA.

Snippet from The 2020 Prospect Digest Handbook: The stuff's ticked up. His fastball was sitting in the 94- to 95-mph range and touching as high as 97 mph on occasions. His curveball continued to flash above-average. His slider, which either (A) I didn't see in 2018 or (B) is a new offering, is a solid 55-grade as it sits in the 88-mph to 90-mph territory. His changeup also showed the makings of peaking as above-average too. Command-wise, he's more of a strike-thrower, rather than a quality pitcher-thrower.

Scouting Report: Losing back-to-back development years is a killer. Assuming there are no setbacks in his recovery, Enlow's going to be 23-years-old and will have zero experience above High-A. He's going to have to hit the ground running. He's tracking like a backend starter with the floor of a multi-inning reliever.

Ceiling: 1.0-win player
Risk: Moderate
MLB ETA: 2023

14. Steve Hajjar, LHP

	FB	CB	CH	Command	Overall
	50	50	60	45	40

Born: 08/07/00	Age: 21	Bats: R	Top Comp: N/A
Height: 6-5	Weight: 215	Throws: L	

Background: The University of Michigan (Go Bucks!) has churned out a ton of professional talent over the past several seasons. But Hajjar, a 6-foot-5, 215-pound southpaw, was the second highest selection from the Big10 school in nearly two decades. The big southpaw was quite dominant for the Wolverines last season. Making a career-high 14 starts, he posted an impressive 110-to-29 strikeout-to-walk ratio in just 81.2 innings of work. After Minnesota drafted him in the second round, 61st overall, the club signed him to a deal worth a smidgeon over $1.1 million. He did not appear in an affiliated game after leaving the collegiate ranks.

Scouting Report: Consider the following:

- Between 2011 and 2020, only three Big10 pitchers have averaged at least 11 strikeouts per nine innings in a season (min. 75 IP): Oliver Jaskie, Seth Lonsway, and Brett Adcock.

Now let's expand it a bit:

- Here's the list of Division I hurlers to average at least 12 K/9 with a walk rate between 3.0 BB/9 and 3.4 BB/9: Carlos Rodon, J.B. Bukauskas, Joey Lucchesi, Kyle Brnovich, Zach Thompson, Drew Parrish, Drey Jameson, Matt Brash, and Matt Hall

A bit of an overreach – unless he was a below-slot signing, which he wasn't. Average fastball that plays up due to a funky arm slot that allows the ball to stay hidden longer than normal. Hajjar's curveball is a 50-grade as well. The great divider for him, though, is his plus, deep-diving, almost screwball-like changeup. Low ceiling/moderate floor. There's not a lot of room for error for Hajjar to make it as a #5-type hurler.

Ceiling: 1.0-win player
Risk: Moderate
MLB ETA: 2023/2024

15. Matt Wallner, LF/RF

	Hit	Power	SB	Patience	Glove	Overall
	45	55	30	50	40	40

Born: 12/12/97	Age: 24	Bats: L	Top Comp: Brent Rooker
Height: 6-5	Weight: 220	Throws: R	

Season	Team	Age	Level	PA	1B	2B	3B	HR	SB	CS	BB%	K%	AVG	OBP	SLG	ISO
2019	MIN	21	R	238	31	18	1	6	1	1	7.98%	27.73%	0.269	0.361	0.452	0.183
2019	MIN	21	A	53	3	3	1	2	0	0	9.43%	26.42%	0.205	0.340	0.455	0.250
2021	MIN	23	A+	294	37	14	2	15	0	1	9.52%	33.33%	0.264	0.350	0.508	0.244

Background: The University of Southern Mississippi's churned out a handful of notable big leaguers in their history, including: Brian Dozier, Chad Bradford, Patt Rapp, and Kevin Young. But the Conference USA-based school's produced only one first round selection: Matt Wallner. A 6-foot-5, 220-pound corner outfielder, Wallner was a dynamic middle-of-the-order bat in each of his three seasons as he compiled a career .337/.461/.652 triple-slash line. The Twins drafted him with the 39th overall pick three years ago, signing him to a deal worth $1.8 million. After a solid debut in the lower levels, Wallner spent the – albeit injury-interrupted – year with Cedar Rapids. In 66 games, he hit .264/.350/.508 with 14 doubles, two triples, and 15 homeruns. His production, per *Weighted Runs Created Plus*, topped the league average threshold by 31%.

Snippet from The 2020 Prospect Digest Handbook: Remarkably consistent during his three-year collegiate career. Wallner posted OPS totals between 1.093 and 1.127 and nearly three identical strikeout-to-walk ratios. Wallner fanned more frequently during his professional debut, which (A) wasn't expected given his track record and (B) needs to be monitored moving forward. Twenty-five homer power potential, average walk, solid glove, and a strong arm – as evidenced by his work on the mound during his freshman and sophomore seasons. Wallner has the makings of a .245/.315/.450-type hitter.

Scouting Report: Just for fun, here's Wallner's numbers prorated for a full 162-game season: 34 doubles, five triples, and 37 homeruns. Not too shabby. With regard to his production and peripherals, though, consider the following:

- Since 2006, only five 23-year-old hitters met the following criteria in a High-A season with one organization (min. 250 PA): 126 to 136 wRC+ total with a strikeout rate north of 30%. Those five hitters: Donovan Casey, Dylan Busby, Chandler Taylor, Anthony Miller, and Matt Wallner.

As I intimated two years ago, Wallner's unexpected surge in strikeouts needed to be monitored. And last year's 33.3% rate showed exactly why. Here are the facts: above-average power, decent patience, below-average – perhaps even – unplayable glove in the outfield. I expect him to eventually shift into a full time designated hitter role. He shows no platoon splits. But he's a one dimensional hitter that provides one dimensional value. Those guys tend to be a dime a dozen.

Ceiling: 1.0-win player
Risk: Moderate
MLB ETA: 2023

16. Chris Vallimont, RHP

	FB	CB	SL	CH	Command	Overall
	55	55	55	50	40/45	40

Born: 03/18/97	Age: 25	Bats: R	Top Comp:
Height: 6-5	Weight: 220	Throws: R	

Season	Team	Age	Level	IP	TBF	K/9	K%	BB/9	BB%	K-BB%	ERA	FIP	xFIP	Pit/Bat
2018	MIA	21	A-	29.0	132	6.21	15.15%	7.14	17.42%	-2.27%	6.21	5.83	5.51	3.76
2019	MIA	22	A	69.1	271	10.38	29.52%	3.38	9.59%	19.93%	2.99	3.01	3.05	3.89
2019	MIA	22	A+	36.0	147	10.50	28.57%	2.75	7.48%	21.09%	3.50	2.97	2.96	3.82
2019	MIN	22	A+	22.1	85	11.28	32.94%	1.61	4.71%	28.24%	3.63	1.34	2.26	3.72
2021	MIN	24	AA	91.0	418	12.86	31.10%	6.03	14.59%	16.51%	6.03	4.84	4.85	4.05

Background: Pennsylvania-based Mercyhurst University produced 22 draft picks during the school's history. Four of those 22 players have made it to the big leagues: John Costello, David Lee, David Lough, and Dan Altavilla. But only one player, Altavilla, was drafted earlier than Chris Vallimont – by just six selections. Taken with the 147th overall pick in the 2018 draft, Minnesota acquired the 6-foot-5, 220-pound right-hander along with Sergio Romo and a Player To Be Named Later for first baseman Lewin Diaz. After a dominant, dominant showing between Low-A and High-A in 2019, Vallimont spent the year toiling away against the minors' toughest challenge, AA, with some varying degrees of success. The good: he averaged 12.9 strikeouts per nine innings. The bad: he tallied a horrible 6.03 ERA. The ugly: he posted a massive 6.0 walk rates.

Snippet from The 2020 Prospect Digest Handbook: I wouldn't be shocked to see him move into several Top 100 lists within a year.

Scouting Report: Definitely not the same pitcher I saw during the 2019 season. The fastball, while an above-average offering, didn't have the same explosive life that he showed previous. The curveball, again, looks a half-a-grade lower. And the changeup remained unremarkably average. Throw in some horrible command issues, and Vallimont's ceiling is a lot lower than what I originally thought. Consider the following:

- Since 2006, only two 24-year-old hurlers met the following criteria in Double-A with one organization (min. 75 IP): a strikeout percentage north of 30% with a walk percentage of at least 12%. Those two hurlers: Marquis Fleming and Chris Vallimont.

Ceiling: 1.0-win player
Risk: Moderate
MLB ETA: 2022

17. Josh Winder, RHP

	FB	CB	SL	CH	Command	Overall
	N/A	N/A	N/A	N/A	N/A	40

Born: 10/11/96	Age: 25	Bats: R	Top Comp: N/A
Height: 6-5	Weight: 210	Throws: R	

Season	Team	Age	Level	IP	TBF	K/9	K%	BB/9	BB%	K-BB%	ERA	FIP	xFIP	Pit/Bat
2018	MIN	21	R	38.2	157	9.78	26.75%	1.40	3.82%	22.93%	3.72	2.62	3.60	3.71
2019	MIN	22	A	125.2	494	8.45	23.89%	2.15	6.07%	17.81%	2.65	3.44	3.56	3.70
2021	MIN	24	AA	54.2	208	10.70	31.25%	1.65	4.81%	26.44%	1.98	2.84	3.18	4.00
2021	MIN	24	AAA	17.1	67	7.79	22.39%	1.56	4.48%	17.91%	4.67	5.15	4.30	3.55

Background: A mid-round pick out of Virginia Military Institute in 2018. Winder, the 214th overall pick who signed for $198,700, was – coincidentally - taken five selections after newly added Joe Ryan. The 6-foot-5, 210-pound right-hander absolutely shredded the Double-A competition during his first 10 starts of the year, posting a 1.98 ERA while averaging 10.7 strikeouts and just 1.6 walks per nine innings. Minnesota bounced the big righty up to the minors' final stop, AAA, in early July. That stint, unfortunately, only lasted four starts before a wonky right shoulder, eventually deemed a shoulder impingement, prematurely ended his season. He finished the year with 80 strikeouts and just 13 walks in 72.0 innings.

Scouting Report: Consider the following:

- Since 2006, only three 24-year-olds met the following criteria in a Double-A season with one organization (min. 50 IP): 30% to 32% strikeout percentage and a walk percentage of 5% or less. Those three hurlers: Jhonathan Diaz, Robert Manuel, and Josh Winder.

I don't grade repertoires of pitchers currently on the injured list with serous woes – or at least, I typically don't. He's now entering his age-25 season, coming off of an abbreviated year in which he dealt with a shoulder issue. That's typically not a recipe for success.

Ceiling: 1.0-win player
Risk: Moderate
MLB ETA: 2024

18. Cade Povich, LHP

	FB	CB	SL	CH	Command	Overall
	50	50	N/A	50	55	40

Born: 04/12/00	Age: 22	Bats: L	Top Comp: N/A
Height: 6-3	Weight: 185	Throws: L	

Background: The University of Nebraska has churned out some impressive baseball talent over the years, including: Alex Gordon, the second overall pick in 2005; Darin Erstad, the top pick in 1995 and one of that generation's most underrated players; shortstop Roy Smalley, first baseman Pete O'Brien, and pitchers Joba Chamberlain, Tony Watson, Stan Bahnsen, and Brian Duensing. But the 2021 draft was a bit of milestone of sorts for the Cornhuskers: it was the first time the school's had two players chosen in the top three rounds since 2005. Atlanta drafted two-way player Spencer Schwellenbach in the second round and, of course, a round later the Twins selected Povich. A slight-framed southpaw, Povich was brilliant during his final season for the Big10 school in 2021, averaging 9.8 strikeouts and just 2.4 walks per nine innings in 15 starts. The Twins signed the lefty, the 98th overall player chosen, to a deal worth $500,000. Povich made four brief appearances in the lower levels for his debut, fanning 16 and walking a pair in 10 innings.

Scouting Report: A couple decades ago, like the mid-90s to early 2000s, Povich would have been a lock to be a first round selection. Solid repertoire. Above-average command. Strong showing during his last season in college. Left-handed. Instead, these types of pitchers – like Steve Hajjar as well – simply are not as coveted as they used to be. 89- to 92-mph fastball. Slow loopy curveball. Mid-80s changeup. Povich, according to reports, also mixes in a slider – though I didn't see one. #5/#6-type arm. He does have the potential to move quickly.

Ceiling: 1.0-win player
Risk: Moderate
MLB ETA: 2024

19. Cody Laweryson, RHP

	FB	SL	CH	Command	Overall
	55	50	60	50	40

Born: 01/01/99	Age: 23	Bats: L	Top Comp: N/A
Height: 6-4	Weight: 205	Throws: R	

Season	Team	Age	Level	IP	TBF	K/9	K%	BB/9	BB%	K-BB%	ERA	FIP	xFIP	Pit/Bat
2019	MIN	20	R	41.0	154	12.95	38.31%	1.98	5.84%	32.47%	1.76	2.27	2.60	4.02
2021	MIN	22	A+	58.2	259	11.20	28.19%	2.91	7.34%	20.85%	4.91	3.84	4.25	3.90

Background: The University of Maine is far from a baseball hotbed, producing just one notable big leaguer in its history – right-hander Bill Swift, who tallied more than 20 wins above replacement in his career (*Baseball Reference*). And Cody Laweryson, a 6-foot-4, 205-pound right-hander who was selected in the 14th round three years ago, became only the fifth highest player drafted from the school since 2004. The big righty spent last season battling against – and sometimes dominating – the High-A competition: in 15 appearances, 14 of which were starts, he averaged a stellar 11.2 strikeouts and just 2.9 walks per nine innings. He compiled a 4.91 ERA. Laweryson made eight additional appearances with the Scottsdale Scorpions, fanning 18 and walking seven in 14.0 innings of work.

Scouting Report: Sneaky low 90s heater, a pretty bland slider, but a phenomenal changeup. His shorter arm action allows Laweryson to hide the ball as well. It's doubtful that the Maine product develops into anything more than a middle relief arm. And he's going to have to hold his own against the Double-A competition next year.

Ceiling: 0.5- to 1.0-win player
Risk: Moderate
MLB ETA: 2023

20. Keoni Cavaco, SS

Hit	Power	SB	Patience	Glove	Overall
35/40	35	35	50	45	40

Born: 06/02/01	Age: 21	Bats: R	Top Comp: N/A
Height: 6-2	Weight: 195	Throws: R	

Season	Team	Age	Level	PA	1B	2B	3B	HR	SB	CS	BB%	K%	AVG	OBP	SLG	ISO
2019	MIN	18	R	92	10	4	0	1	1	1	4.35%	38.04%	0.172	0.217	0.253	0.080
2021	MIN	20	CPX	10	1	1	0	0	1	0	10.00%	30.00%	0.222	0.300	0.333	0.111
2021	MIN	20	A	260	45	6	2	2	5	2	6.92%	34.23%	0.233	0.296	0.301	0.068

Background: The club has a rather spotty track record with their first round selections in recent years. They've certainly hit on guys like Byron Buxton and Jose Berrios. And they *look* like they've made fine selections with Alex Kirilloff and Royce Lewis. But they've missed on the likes of Levi Michael, Travis Harrison, Hudson Boyd, Alex Wimmers, Luke Bard, Kohl Stewart, Nick Gordon, Tyler Jay, and – almost guaranteed at this point – Keoni Cavaco. Taken with the 13th overall pick in the 2019 draft – and in front of several notable players like Corbin Carroll, Quinn Priester, and George Kirby – Cavaco was beyond abysmal during his abbreviated 25-game debut in the Gulf Coast League, hitting a lowly .172/.217/.253. The front office bumped him up to A-ball to start the 2021 season. And the results were.shitty. In 60 games with Fort Myers, the 6-foot-2, 195-pound middle infielder hit a lowly .233/.296/.301. His overall production, per *Weighted Runs Created Plus*, was a whopping 33% *below* the league average threshold.

Snippet from The 2020 Prospect Digest Handbook: There's bad debuts. Then there's awful debut. And there there's Cavaco's showing in the Gulf Coast League last season. Not only was his bat as limp as a wet noodle, but he barely walked – 4.3% – and whiffed way too frequently (38.0%).

Scouting Report: There's two ways to approach this: the traditional scouting measure or the analytical side. But it doesn't really matter because they both add up to the same thing: Cavaco can't hit. And his defense is just as abysmal. His swing looks...awful. It lacks explosion and he seems to be battling balance issues. That's backed up by his 34.2% strikeout rate too. No power. He rarely runs. And per Clay Davenport's defensive metrics, he was seven runs worse than the average in only 60 games. Yikes.

Ceiling: 0.5-win player
Risk: Moderate
MLB ETA: 2025

New York Mets

Top Prospects

1. Francisco Alvarez, C

Hit	Power	SB	Patience	Glove	Overall
50/60	55	35	55	50	70

Born: 11/19/01	Age: 20	Bats: R	Top Comp: Victor Martinez
Height: 5-11	Weight: 233	Throws: R	

Season	Team	Age	Level	PA	1B	2B	3B	HR	SB	CS	BB%	K%	AVG	OBP	SLG	ISO
2019	NYM	17	R	31	6	4	0	2	0	1	12.90%	12.90%	0.462	0.548	0.846	0.385
2019	NYM	17	R	151	26	6	0	5	1	1	11.26%	21.85%	0.282	0.377	0.443	0.160
2021	NYM	19	A	67	13	5	0	2	2	2	22.39%	10.45%	0.417	0.567	0.646	0.229
2021	NYM	19	A+	333	33	13	1	22	6	3	12.01%	24.62%	0.247	0.351	0.538	0.290

Background: The Mets — perhaps unsurprisingly — have a lengthy list of strong backstops through the club's history: Mike Piazza's Hall of Fame plaque is adorned with New York's hat; Gary Carter, the Kid, spent four All-Star seasons with the organization beginning in the 80s; Todd Hundley's two midsummer classic appearances happened in 1996-97; Jerry Grote was a two-time All-Star and a key member of the Miracle Mets in '69 and John Stearns was a four-time All-Star between 1977 and 1982. That doesn't include solid seasons by Paul LoDuca, Mackey Sasser, and Ron Hodges either. And Francisco Alvarez, a wunderkind at the plate, is poised to become the next great Metropolitan backstop. Signed by the club for a hefty $2.7 million in early July, 2018, Alvarez ripped through both stateside rookie leagues during his debut the following year, slugging an aggregate .312/.407/.510 with 10 doubles and seven homeruns in only 42 games. Last season, despite the lost 2020 campaign, Alvarez continued to impressive in Low-A for 15 games before earning a promotion up to Brooklyn. In total, the 5-foot-11, 233-pound backstop batted .272/.388/.554 with 18 doubles, one triple, 24 homeruns, and eight stolen bases. His overall production, per *Weighted Runs Created Plus*, topped the league average mark by a staggering 48%.

Snippet from The 2020 Prospect Digest Handbook: It remains to be seen if Alvarez's stocky frame will eventually push him from behind the plate, but the bat looks like it'll play at any position on the diamond.

Scouting Report: Consider the following little tidbits:

- Since 2006, only four 19-year-old hitters met the following criteria in a season for one organization (min. 300 PA): 127 to 137 wRC+ and a walk rate of at least 9%. Those four hitters: Cody Bellinger, Addison Russell, Domingo Santana, and – of course – Francisco Alvarez.
- Last year there were 84 minor league catchers that received at least 300 plate appearances. Alvarez's offensive explosion, as measured by wRC+, was the second best in the group, trailing only Kansas City's M.J. Melendez.
- Since 2006, Alvarez's 132 wRC+ ranks as 137th out 1,250 backstops with at least 300 plate appearances at any level, at any age.
- Alvarez's 132 wRC+ in High-A is the best offensive showing for a teenage backstop at the level since 2006.

Above-average thump that could creep into plus territory in a couple years. Solid contact skills. Above-average patience at the plate. Not a terrible runner. Elite production against significantly older competition. And a solid enough glove so that he can stay behind the dish. After starting slowly in High-A last season – he batted .218/.342/.452 over his first 39 games – Alvarez slugged .271/.359/.606 over his remaining 45 contests. Elite catching prospect that closed the gap on Adley Rutschman's status as the best in baseball.

Ceiling: 6.0-win player
Risk: Moderate
MLB ETA: 2023

2. Brett Baty, 3B/LF

Hit	Power	SB	Patience	Glove	Overall
50	50/60	35	55	50	60

Born: 11/13/99	Age: 22	Bats: L	Top Comp: Kyle Seager
Height: 6-3	Weight: 210	Throws: R	

Season	Team	Age	Level	PA	1B	2B	3B	HR	SB	CS	BB%	K%	AVG	OBP	SLG	ISO
2019	NYM	19	R	25	3	3	0	1	0	0	20.00%	24.00%	0.350	0.480	0.650	0.300
2019	NYM	19	R	186	15	12	2	6	0	0	12.90%	30.11%	0.222	0.339	0.437	0.215
2019	NYM	19	A-	17	1	1	0	0	0	0	35.29%	17.65%	0.200	0.529	0.300	0.100
2021	NYM	21	A+	209	34	14	1	7	4	3	11.48%	25.36%	0.309	0.397	0.514	0.204
2021	NYM	21	AA	176	28	8	0	5	2	0	12.50%	25.57%	0.272	0.364	0.424	0.152

Background: Fun Fact Part I: Lake Travis High School in Austin, Texas, has been home to just five professional ballplayers — Brett Baty, Jim Lewis, Cohl Walla, Brad Dydalewicz, Denny McDaniel, and Doug Rummel. Fun Fact Part II: Baty and Lewis went in the first two rounds of the 2019 draft, both signing seven-figure deals. Baty, part of the loaded 2019 first round, was the 12th overall selection. The Mets bounced the sweet lefty-swinging third baseman through three separate levels during his debut that year, hitting an aggregate .234/.368/.452 with 16 doubles, two triples, and seven homeruns. Last season Baty upped his offensive game to elite levels. Splitting time between High-A and the minors' toughest challenge, AA, the 6-foot-3, 210-pound prospect slugged an impressive .292/.382/.473 with 22 doubles, one triple, 12 homeruns, and six stolen bases. His overall production, per *Weighted Runs Created Plus*, topped the league average threshold by 32%.

Snippet from The 2020 Prospect Digest Handbook: The bat speed is off-the-charts with impressive opposite-field power. And he showed a tremendously patient approach as well, walking in more than 15% of the plate appearances. He could very well wind up as a Three True Outcomes hitter if the bat doesn't progress.

Scouting Report: Baty showed some potentially concerning swing-and-miss issues during his debut, fanning in nearly 29% of his plate appearances, so the fact that he was pushed into High-A and spent considerable amount of time in Double-A while improving his K-rate is incredibly encouraging. Baty still hasn't tapped into his plus-raw power. And unlike a lot of power-hitting, lefty-swinging prospects, Baty doesn't show any platoon concerns. He has to potential to elevate his production to the superstar stratus.

Ceiling: 5.0-win player
Risk: Moderate
MLB ETA: 2022

3. Ronny Mauricio, SS

	Hit	Power	SB	Patience	Glove	Overall
	45	50/55	40	40	50	55

Born: 04/04/01	Age: 21	Bats: B	Top Comp: Ian Desmond
Height: 6-3	Weight: 166	Throws: R	

Season	Team	Age	Level	PA	1B	2B	3B	HR	SB	CS	BB%	K%	AVG	OBP	SLG	ISO
2018	NYM	17	R	212	36	13	3	3	1	6	4.72%	14.62%	0.279	0.307	0.421	0.142
2018	NYM	17	R	35	4	3	0	0	1	0	8.57%	25.71%	0.233	0.286	0.333	0.100
2019	NYM	18	A	504	97	20	5	4	6	10	4.56%	19.64%	0.268	0.307	0.357	0.089
2021	NYM	20	A+	420	57	14	5	19	9	7	5.71%	24.05%	0.242	0.290	0.449	0.207
2021	NYM	20	AA	33	8	1	0	1	2	0	6.06%	33.33%	0.323	0.364	0.452	0.129

Background: It seemed that there were two constants with the Mets since Jose Reyes' initial departure nearly a decade ago: #1. The shortstop position with the big league club was a seemingly endless revolving door and #2 The farm system always had a constant "heir apparent" at the position that never came to fruition. Francisco Lindor's arrival last offseason squelched the big league issue and also quieted the need for Mauricio, the last prospect standing, to fill the role. Handed a hefty $2.1 million deal off the international free agent market, Mauricio continued to open eyes during his debut in a couple rookie leagues in 2018, hitting an aggregate .273/.304/.410. He followed that up with an intriguing showing as an 18-year-old in Low-A in 2019, batting .268/.307/.357 in 116 games with Columbia. Last season, Mauricio spent the lion's share of the season with the Brooklyn Cyclones, hitting a disappointing .242/.290/.449 in 100 games. He also spent eight games with Binghamton as well.

Snippet from The 2020 Prospect Digest Handbook: The defense was a bit too spotty at times last season – and it remains to be seen as to whether he can stick as shortstop – but the bat should be no worse than league average. Smooth, easy swing. Plenty of bat speed, so there's a chance the power ticks up into the 20-homer territory. There's a noticeable ease at which he does everything on the field.

Scouting Report: Consider the following:

- Since 2006, only four 20-year-old bats met the following criteria in a season with one organization (min. 400 PA): 90 to 100 wRC+, sub-6.0% walk rate, and a strikeout rate of at least 21%.Those four hitters: Mickey Moniak, Cesar Puello, Sean Coyle, and – of course – Ronny Mauricio.

It's a pretty uninspiring collection of prospects: Moniak is a failed top prospect, Puello never panned out for the Mets, and Coyle flamed out for the Red Sox. But there is a bit of a silver lining for Mauricio: after starting the year out by hitting a lowly .216/.254/.412 over his first 50 contests, the 6-foot-3, 166-pound shortstop slugged a healthy .277/.332/.482 over his remaining 58 games (including his time in AA). Mauricio's lack of patience at the plate severely limits his offensive ceiling. And it ultimately cost him a place among the Top 100 prospects this year.

Ceiling: 3.0-win player
Risk: Moderate
MLB ETA: 2022

4. Mark Vientos, 3B/LF

Hit	Power	SB	Patience	Glove	Overall
45	60	35	45	50	55

Born: 12/11/99	Age: 22	Bats: R	Top Comp: Austin Riley
Height: 6-4	Weight: 185	Throws: R	

Season	Team	Age	Level	PA	1B	2B	3B	HR	SB	CS	BB%	K%	AVG	OBP	SLG	ISO
2018	NYM	18	R	262	41	12	0	11	1	0	14.12%	16.41%	0.287	0.389	0.489	0.202
2019	NYM	19	A	454	66	27	1	12	1	4	4.85%	24.23%	0.255	0.300	0.411	0.156
2021	NYM	21	AA	306	39	16	0	22	0	1	8.50%	28.43%	0.281	0.346	0.580	0.299
2021	NYM	21	AAA	43	5	2	0	3	0	1	16.28%	30.23%	0.278	0.395	0.583	0.306

Background: There *must* be something in the water the Mets are handing out to their top minor league bats because Vientos – like Francisco Alvarez, Brett Baty, and Khalil Lee – turned in finest professional season to date in 2021. A second rounder out of American Heritage High School in 2017, Vientos spent the majority of last season shredding Double AA pitching before earning a late season promotion up to AAA – where he maintained his killer production. In 82 total games, the 6-foot-4, 185-pound third baseman / left fielder slugged .281/.352/.581 with 18 doubles and a career-high 25 dingers. His overall production, according to *Weighted Runs Created Plus*, topped the league average mark by 46%, tied for the 42nd best among all minor leaguers with at least 300 plate appearances.

Snippet from The 2020 Prospect Digest Handbook: At his peak, Vientos looks like a starting caliber third baseman on a non-contending team.

Scouting Report: Consider the following:

- Since 2006, there have been 132 qualified hitters to post a wRC+ total between 140 and 150 in Double AA in a season with one organization. Only seven of those have been by players during their age-21 season: Logan Morrison, Triston Casas, Miguel Vargas, Kyle Blanks, Justin Williams, Josh Stephen, and Mark Vientos.

And now the bad news: only two of those hitters struck out in more than 27% of their plate appearances – Stephen and Vientos. Average eye and glove. Vientos' power really started to shine last season as he was on pace for 49 homeruns in a full 162-game season. According to *FanGraphs*, his average exit velocity was fairly impressive at 91 mph. The question is going to come down to his ability – or inability – to make consistent contact. It's hard to believe, but he's only entering his age-22 season, so there's time to improve upon his K-rate. Boom-bust potential and there likely isn't a level in between. If it does click, he could be an Austin Riley-type contributor.

Ceiling: 3.0-win player
Risk: Moderate to High
MLB ETA: 2022

5. Matt Allan, RHP

FB	CB	CH	Command	Overall
N/A	N/A	N/A	N/A	55

Born: 04/17/01	Age: 21	Bats: R	Top Comp: N/A
Height: 6-3	Weight: 225	Throws: R	

Background: Regarded as a near lock as an early first round talent heading into the 2019 draft, Allen, according to a variety of reports, was seeking a hefty bonus equivalent to Top 10 money. Scared off by the demands, as well as his commitment to the Florida Gators, Allan fell to the Mets in the third round and signed his name on the dotted line for a sizeable $2.5 million deal – which was roughly the money picks 23-25 signed for. The 6-foot-3, 225-pound right-hander tossed 10.1 low level innings during his debut and hasn't been heard of since. The 2020 season was lost to COVID-19, and he underwent the knife to repair a partial tear in his UCL in early May last year. Always take the big money when it's on the table, kids.

Scouting Report: With nothing new to report on his 2019, here's my analysis prior to the draft:

"The owner of two plus- to plus-plus pitches. Allen attacks hitters with a lethal fastball/curveball combination that was – simply – too overpowering for his current peers. The fastball sits in the mid-90s, touching 96 mph on several occasions, and his knee-buckling curveball hovers in the 79- to 81-mph range. Allen generates the premium velocity without much effort and – generally – commands the zone well. His third offering, an upper-80s changeup, profiles no worse than average. Allen has the build and arsenal to suggest a #2-type ceiling."

Ceiling: 3.0-win player
Risk: High
MLB ETA: 2022

6. Khalil Lee, OF

	Hit	Power	SB	Patience	Glove	Overall
	45	50	45	60	50	50

Born: 06/26/98	Age: 24	Bats: L	Top Comp: Ian Happ
Height: 5-10	Weight: 170	Throws: L	

Season	Team	Age	Level	PA	1B	2B	3B	HR	SB	CS	BB%	K%	AVG	OBP	SLG	ISO
2018	KCR	20	A+	301	45	13	4	4	14	3	15.95%	24.92%	0.270	0.402	0.406	0.135
2018	KCR	20	AA	118	18	5	0	2	2	2	9.32%	23.73%	0.245	0.330	0.353	0.108
2019	KCR	21	AA	546	92	21	3	8	53	12	11.90%	28.21%	0.264	0.363	0.372	0.109
2021	NYM	23	AAA	388	44	20	2	14	8	10	18.30%	29.64%	0.274	0.451	0.500	0.226

Background: For all intents and purposes, it was a big trade involving three clubs and seven players roughly a week before pitchers and catchers were supposed to start. The Mets acquired toolsy outfielder Khalil Lee, the Red Sox received Franchy Cordero, Josh Winckowski, Luis De La Rosa, Grant Gambrell, and Freddy Valdez; and the Royals got a fading former top prospect in Andrew Benintendi, who had a nice little bounce-back year in 2021. Lee, a third round pick out of Flint High School in 2016, has always flirted with a quasi-top prospect status. And he seemingly put it all together in New York's system last season: appearing in 102 games with the Syracuse Mets, the 5-foot-10, 170-pound outfielder slugged .274/.451/.500 with 20 doubles, two triples, and 14 homeruns. His overall production, per *Weighted Runs Created Plus*, topped the league average mark by 62%. Lee also appeared in 10 games with the big league club as well, hitting .056/.056/.111.

Snippet from The 2020 Prospect Digest Handbook: In terms of offensive upside think Shin-Soo Choo circa 2019 when he batted .265/.371/.455.

Scouting Report: Consider the following:

- Since 2006, only five 23-year-old AAA hitters posted at least a 155 wRC+ in a season with one organization (min. 350 PA): Brandon Nimmo, Adam Eaton, Daniel Vogelbach, Jose Miranda, and – of course – Khalil Lee.
- To put that into perspective: Eaton owns a career 95 wRC+ and had a string of six consecutive seasons of well above-average offensive production; Nimmo, of course, has been a consistently underrated outfielder for the Mets and owns a 126 wRC+; Vogelbach has been a better-than-average big league bat since 2019; and Miranda continues to bide his time in the Twins' system.

Now to be completely fair, Lee's peripherals stick out like a sore thumb among the group. Elite eye? Check? However, his K-rate *exploded* in 2021 to a career worst 29.6% with Syracuse, though that came with the added pop in the bat. Above-average runner who didn't steal nearly as much as he did with the Royals. Lee once looked like a potential Lorenzo Cain prototype due to his power-speed combo, but his defense is far from elite and he swings-and-misses way too much.

Ceiling: 2.0-win player
Risk: Moderate
MLB ETA: Debuted in 2021

7. J.T. Ginn, RHP

	FB	CB	SL	CH	Command	Overall
	55	50	60	50	50	45

Born: 05/20/99	Age: 23	Bats: R	Top Comp: Dakota Hudson
Height: 6-2	Weight: 200	Throws: R	

Season	Team	Age	Level	IP	TBF	K/9	K%	BB/9	BB%	K-BB%	ERA	FIP	xFIP	Pit/Bat
2021	NYM	22	A	38.2	148	8.15	23.65%	2.33	6.76%	16.89%	2.56	3.93	3.78	3.63
2021	NYM	22	A+	53.1	222	7.76	20.72%	2.03	5.41%	15.32%	3.38	3.00	3.90	3.53

Background: Ginn was originally taken in between a couple of high profile prospects in the latter part of the first round four years ago, Bo Naylor and Shane McClanahan, both of whom signed with their respective clubs for over $2 million. The 30th overall pick by the Dodgers that year, Ginn opted to take the collegiate route and signed his letter of intent with Mississippi State University. And was an immediate success for the SEC powerhouse. In 17 starts as a true freshman, the 6-foot-2, 200-pound right-hander averaged nearly 11 strikeouts and just two walks per nine innings of work. Then his baseball world came crashing down. After just one start and three innings into what would eventually be a COVID-shortened campaign, the former first round pick succumbed to elbow woes and underwent the knife for Tommy John surgery. The Mets selected him with the 52 overall selection and signed him to a deal worth $2.9 million. Fully recovered last season, the Mississippi native made 18 starts between St. Lucie and Brooklyn, averaging a pedestrian 7.9 strikeouts and just 2.2 walks per nine innings. He finished the year with an aggregate 3.03 ERA.

Scouting Report: A bit disappointed. At least based on the reports on how he looked prior to undergoing the knife. Ginn, reportedly, was touching as 97 mph with his heater. But last season he was sitting 92, 93 mph and took some noticeable effort to get up to 94. His best complimentary offering is a biting, plus slider. He added a curveball, which is just a slower, lesser effective version of slider. And he'll mix in an average changeup. And while he limited his walks, per the usual, his actual command was average at best – which is to be expected in a return from TJ. Backend starter unless the command and/or the heat upticks.

Ceiling: 1.5-win player
Risk: Moderate
MLB ETA: 2022

8. Calvin Ziegler, RHP

FB	SL	CH	Command	Overall
60	55	45/50	50	45

Born: 10/03/02	Age: 19	Bats: R	Top Comp: N/A
Height: 6-0	Weight: 205	Throws: R	

Background: TNXL Academy in Altamonte Springs, Florida, has become a bit of hotbed for baseball talent in recent years. The school is home to seven draft picks since 2017, three of them signing deals in excess of $300,000. Ziegler, a commit to Auburn University, was the Mets' first pick last June, 46th overall, and signed with the NL East organization for slightly under a million dollars. He did not play appear in a minor league game last year.

Scouting Report: Easy plus velocity, which is surprising given his 6-foot frame. Ziegler also shows a surprising feel for the strike zone, particularly with his fastball. He'll complement the offering, which will peak at 97 mph, with an above-average mid-80s slider, and a 90 mph changeup. Ziegler is maxed out from a physical standpoint, but he's a high upside arm with the potential to be a #4-type starting pitcher. The changeup will need to be fine tuned.

Ceiling: 1.5-win player
Risk: Moderate
MLB ETA: 2025

9. Dominic Hamel, RHP

FB	CB	SL	CH	Command	Overall
55	50	55	50	45	45

Born: 03/02/99	Age: 23	Bats: R	Top Comp: N/A
Height: 6-2	Weight: 206	Throws: R	

Background: The 2020 season was short – for obvious reasons – but Hamel made the most of it. The 6-foot-2, 206-pound right-hander from Dallas Baptist was named Collegiate Baseball's National Pitcher of the Week and Missouri Valley Conference Pitcher of the Week during mid-February. Last season the then-22-year-old hurler made 18 appearances for the Patriots, 16 of which were starts, throwing 91.2 innings with 136 strikeouts and just 34 free passes. He finished the year with a 4.22 ERA. The Mets drafted Hamel in the third round last July, 81st overall, signing him to a deal worth a smidgeon over $750,000. He made two brief appearances in the Florida Complex League, posting a 7-to-0 strikeout-to-walk ratio in three innings of work.

Scouting Report: Consider the following:

- Between 2011 and 2020, here's the list of pitchers from the Missouri Valley Conference to average at least 13 strikeouts per nine innings in a season (min. 75 IP): Dominic Hamel.

Let's continue:

- Between 2011 and 2020, here's the list of Division I pitchers to average at least 13 strikeouts per nine innings with a walk rate between 3.00 BB/9 and 3.99 BB/9: Zac Lowther, Joey Murray, Zach Thompson, and Drey Jameson.

A standard four-pitch mix that's highlighted by a fastball / slider combo that grades out as above-average. Hamel will show a slower curveball and a decent changeup. Hamel's the type of pitcher that would excel in Cleveland's farm system, so it'll be interesting to see how the Mets develop the third round pick. There's some sneaky mid-rotation upside.

Ceiling: 1.5-win player
Risk: Moderate
MLB ETA: 2024

10. Alex Ramirez, CF

	Hit	Power	SB	Patience	Glove	Overall
	40/45	40/55	55	50	50	45

Born: 01/13/03	Age: 19	Bats: R	Top Comp: N/A
Height: 6-3	Weight: 170	Throws: R	

Season	Team	Age	Level	PA	1B	2B	3B	HR	SB	CS	BB%	K%	AVG	OBP	SLG	ISO
2021	NYM	18	A	334	54	15	4	5	16	7	6.89%	31.14%	0.258	0.326	0.384	0.126

Background: Ranked as the 26th best prospect on the International Market by MLB.com two years ago. Ramirez, a toolsy 6-foot-3, 170-pound center fielder, signed with the Mets for $2.1 million. Hailing from Santo Domingo, Dominican Republic, Ramirez made his professional debut last season as the club *aggressively* pushed him straight into full season action at the ripe ol' age of 18. And he held his own against the older competition. In 76 games with the St. Lucie Mets, Ramirez batted a respectable .258/.326/.384 with 15 doubles, four triples, five homeruns, and 16 stolen bases (in 23 attempts). According to *Weighted Runs Created Plus*, his overall production was 4% below the league average mark.

Scouting Report: Consider the following:

- There's a pretty impressive list of 18-year-old hitters that posted a wRC+ between 90 to 100 in Low-A in a season with one organization (min. 300 PA): Cristian Pache, Franmil Reyes, Ronny Mauricio, Leody Taveras, Rougned Odor, Cole Tucker, Tommy Joseph, Anthony Gose, Alex Liddi, Francisco Pena, Jay Austin, Jack Suwinski, and Alex Ramirez.

And now the bad news:

- Here's the list of those players that fanned in at least 25% of their plate appearances: Alex Liddi, Jack Suwinski, and – unfortunately – Alex Ramirez.

Ramirez's month of July basically did him in as he posted monthly OPS totals of .777, .566, .789, and .716. But, unfortunately, the strikeout rate remained pretty steady during his debut season. Ronny Mauricio has long been lauded as the best bat speed in the system – until Ramirez came along. The swing is long, but it's ferocious and there's a little Gary Sheffield bat waggle in there too. And he does not get cheated. Despite some natural loft he still put the ball on the ground too frequently last year. The K-rate is going to have to improve as he matures, but there's a lot of potential with his premium athleticism.

Ceiling: 1.5-win player
Risk: Moderate
MLB ETA: 2025

11. Junior Santos, RHP

	FB	SL	CH	Command	Overall
	55	50	50	50	45

Born: 08/16/01	Age: 20	Bats: R	Top Comp: Buck Farmer
Height: 6-7	Weight: 244	Throws: R	

Season	Team	Age	Level	IP	TBF	K/9	K%	BB/9	BB%	K-BB%	ERA	FIP	xFIP	Pit/Bat
2018	NYM	16	R	45.0	173	7.20	20.81%	1.20	3.47%	17.34%	2.80	2.85	3.01	1.49
2019	NYM	17	R	40.2	197	7.97	18.27%	5.53	12.69%	5.58%	5.09	5.57	6.21	3.70
2021	NYM	19	A	96.0	429	7.41	18.41%	3.56	8.86%	9.56%	4.59	4.68	4.80	3.73

Background: A mountain of a man. Well, a mountain of a baby-faced 20-year-old. The Mets signed the redwood-esque right-hander to a deal worth $275,000 during the end of 2017 and debuted during the Dominican Summer League the following season. After showing a superb feel for the strike zone as a 16-year-old, Santos spent the 2019 season battling against the Appalachian League; he averaged 8.0 strikeouts and 5.5 walks per nine innings. Last season as baseball returned from the COVID year, Santos made 21 appearances for St. Lucie in Low-A – 16 of which were starts. The 6-foot-7, 244-pound hurler struck out 79 and walked 38 in 96.0 innings of work. He compiled a 4.59 ERA, 4.68 FIP, and a 4.80 xFIP.

Snippet from The 2020 Prospect Digest Handbook: Santos is still quite raw, and his lack of command was exposed against older competition. But it's difficult to see how he doesn't spend the majority of 2020 in the South Atlantic League.

Scouting Report: Consider the following:

- Since 2006, only nine 19-year-old hurlers met the following criteria in Low-A in a season with one organization (min. 75 IP): 17.5% to 19.5% strikeout percentage and a walk percentage 8% and 10%. Those nine arms: TJ House, Zach Davies, Jake Woodford, Antonio Cruz, Jacob Rasner, Josias De Los Santos, Richard Gallardo, Robert Hernandez, and Junior Santos.

A surprising strike-thrower because (1) he's 19-years-old battling against significantly older competition and (B) he's gargantuan. Clean arm action and simple, repeatable mechanics. Santos' heater will reach the mid-90s on occasion but settles in a few ticks lower. He complements the above-average offering with a pair of average offspeed pitches: a mid- to upper-80s changeup and a slurvy-type low 80s slider. If Santos isn't maxed out physically, he's close to it. One of the two offspeed pitches needs to mature to a 55-grade to push his ceiling into a backend starter. One final item: he finished the year on a strong note, posting a 45-to-18 strikeout-to-walk ratio in 57.1 innings of work.

Ceiling: 1.0- to 1.5-win player
Risk: Moderate
MLB ETA: 2024

12. Robert Dominguez, RHP

	FB	CB	CH	Command	Overall
	N/A	N/A	N/A	N/A	N/A

Born: 11/30/01	Age: 20	Bats: R	Top Comp: N/A
Height: 6-5	Weight: 195	Throws: R	

Season	Team	Age	Level	IP	TBF	K/9	K%	BB/9	BB%	K-BB%	ERA	FIP	xFIP	Pit/Bat
2021	NYM	19	CPX	12.0	60	7.50	16.67%	6.75	15.00%	1.67%	8.25	6.06	5.76	1.87

Background: One of the better potential steals on international scene a couple years ago. The Mets signed the flame-throwing – elder teenage – prospect for a bonus in the $100,000 range – according to Eric Longenhagen of FanGraphs. Roughly in a year's time the 6-foot-5, 195-pound right-hander crept up from the low-90s to touching 99 multiple times. Last season he made his professional debut for the club's Arizona Complex League. In 10 games, one of which was a start, Dominguez struck out 10 and walked nine in 12.0 innings of action. He tallied a horrific 8.25 ERA, 6.06 FIP, and a 5.76 xFIP.

Scouting Report: There's no game tape or videos of Dominguez floating about on the internet. But nearly every report available all summarizes Dominguez down to a few lines: plus to plus-plus fastball, an above-average or better curveball, and a changeup that...needs work. Really look forward to seeing Dominguez in action in 2022.

Ceiling: Too Soon to Tell
Risk: N/A
MLB ETA: N/A

13. Nick Plummer, OF

	Hit	Power	SB	Patience	Glove	Overall
	45	45	50	60	45	40

Born: 07/31/96	Age: 25	Bats: L	Top Comp: Ryan Sweeney
Height: 5-10	Weight: 200	Throws: L	

Season	Team	Age	Level	PA	1B	2B	3B	HR	SB	CS	BB%	K%	AVG	OBP	SLG	ISO
2018	STL	21	A	411	43	15	3	8	10	7	16.30%	31.87%	0.205	0.349	0.339	0.134
2019	STL	22	A+	356	29	15	2	5	3	3	13.20%	33.43%	0.176	0.312	0.294	0.118
2021	STL	24	AA	376	54	17	4	13	9	8	14.10%	28.72%	0.283	0.404	0.489	0.206
2021	STL	24	AAA	102	13	3	2	2	4	1	19.61%	17.65%	0.267	0.455	0.440	0.173

Background: Fun Fact Part I: 20 of the first 26 selections in the 2015 draft have made their respective big league debuts, including: Alex Bregman, Dansby Swanson, Andrew Benintendi, Trent Grisham, Kyle Tucker, Walker Buehler, and Tyler Stephenson. Unfortunately Nick Plummer, the 23rd overall pick that year, is among the small group to not appear in the bigs yet. Taken one selection before Walker Buehler, Plummer has been horrific throughout the majority of his career. Beginning in 2015 through 2019, he batted .228/.379/.344, missed all of 2016, .198/.353/.288, .205/.349/.339, and .176/.312/.294. He was awful. So his breakout in 2021 is all the more amazing. Appearing in 90 games in AA and another 27 contests in AAA, the 5-foot-10, 200-pound outfielder slugged .280/.415/.479 with 20 doubles, six triples, 15 homeruns, and 13 stolen bases. His overall production, per *Weighted Runs Created Plus*, topped the league average mark by a staggering 44%. The Mets signed him near the end of November to a one-year, Major League deal.

Scouting Report: Consider the following:

- Since 2006, only three 24-year-old Double-A hitters met the following criteria in a season with one organization (min. 350 PA): 138 to 148 wRC+, a walk percentage between 12% and 16%, and a strikeout percentage north of 25%. Those three hitters: Bobby Dalbec, Allan Dykstra, and Nick Plummer.

The production is otherworldly compared to the low bar he set previously. The patience at the plate is plus-plus, though it likely regresses as pitchers learn exploit his weakness/thump. I'm still not sold on the hit tool. And the power is merely average (unlike Bobby Dalbec). Throw in some fringy outfield defense and it doesn't paint an overall pretty picture for Plummer moving forward.

Ceiling: 1.0- win player
Risk: Moderate
MLB ETA: 2022

14. JT Schwartz, 1B

	Hit	Power	SB	Patience	Glove	Overall
	40/55	40/45	30	70	50	40

Born: 12/17/99	Age: 22	Bats: L	Top Comp: N/A
Height: 6-4	Weight: 215	Throws: R	

Season	Team	Age	Level	PA	1B	2B	3B	HR	SB	CS	BB%	K%	AVG	OBP	SLG	ISO
2021	NYM	21	A	100	11	5	0	0	2	0	13.00%	12.00%	0.195	0.320	0.256	0.061

Background: A four-year letter winner during his prep career at Corona Del Mar, Schwartz, a lefty-swinging first baseman departed the California-based high school with a .373/.455/.573 line. Along the way, the lanky 6-foot-4, 200-pound garnered a variety of awards and recognition, including:

- Ranked as the 29th best high school prospect in California by *Perfect Game*
- Ranked by *Perfect Game* as the 209th best prospect in the country
- 2017 *Perfect Game Rawlings* Underclass High Honorable Mention All-American
- 2017 *Collegiate Baseball* All-America Second Team

After redshirting his freshman season at UCLA, Schwartz looked quite comfortable during his abbreviated 2020 season, batting .328/.380/.391 with four doubles and a pair of stolen bases in 15 contests. And that just proved to be a harbinger of things to come. Appearing in a career best 44 games for the Bruins, the sweet swinging infielder slugged .396/.514/.628 with 12 doubles, one triple, and eight homeruns. He finished the year with an impeccable 28-to-37 strikeout-to-walk ratio. His .396 average ranked as the 17th best in the nation. His OBP, .514, is good enough for 13th. The Mets – wisely – selected Schwartz in the fourth round, 111th overall, and signed him to a deal worth $475,000. He appeared in the 25 games with St. Lucie, hitting a lowly .195/.320/.256 with a 12-to-13 strikeout-to-walk ratio.

Scouting Report: Per the usual, here's what I wrote prior to the draft:

"Consider the following:

- *Between 2011 and 2020, only two Pac12 hitters batted at least .380/.500/.600 in a season (min. 200 PA): Adley Rutschman and Andrew Vaughn, both of whom accomplished the feat twice.*

Let's take it one step further. Consider the following:

- *Between 2011 and 2020, there were 11 Division I hitters to bat .380/.500/.600 with a strikeout rate between 10% and 15% and a walk rate north of 16% (min. 200 PA): Adley Rutschman, Andrew Vaughn, Keston Hiura, Mike Papi, Peyton Burdick, Jameson Fisher, Taylor Davis, D.J. Peterson, Devlin Granberg, Casey Gillaspie, and Patrick Causa.*

Average power, above-average hit tool. Not a lot of speed. And he doesn't have a home to play. He's played some time at first and third bases, and left field during some summer league action. Above-average regular if he can move away for first base."

The debut is concerning. But I'm still a believer in the hit tool and his nose for the free pass.

Ceiling: 1.0-win player
Risk: Moderate
MLB ETA: 2025

15. Thomas Szapucki, LHP

	FB	CB	CH	Command	Overall
	50	55	50	40+	40

Born: 06/12/96	Age: 26	Bats: R	Top Comp: Steven Brault
Height: 6-2	Weight: 181	Throws: L	

Season	Team	Age	Level	IP	TBF	K/9	K%	BB/9	BB%	K-BB%	ERA	FIP	xFIP	Pit/Bat
2019	NYM	23	A	21.2	88	10.80	29.55%	4.15	11.36%	18.18%	2.08	3.21	3.43	4.11
2019	NYM	23	A+	36.0	158	10.50	26.58%	3.75	9.49%	17.09%	3.25	2.92	3.22	3.70
2021	NYM	25	AAA	41.2	193	8.86	21.24%	6.05	14.51%	6.74%	4.10	5.11	5.52	4.10

Background: A member of the club's Top 20 prospects for a decade – or at least that's what it *feels* like. New York originally selected the promising – albeit snake-bitten – southpaw out of William T. Dwyer High School in the fifth round all the way back in 2015. Since then it's been a long list of injury-shortened seasons: he tossed only 52 innings in 2016; he was limited to just 29 innings the following year, missed all of 2018, and came back to establish a career-best 62 innings in 2019. And, obviously, he missed all of 2020 due to COVID. Last year, his seventh in professional baseball, was much the same – except he did briefly ascend up to the big leagues for one appearance. In 10 appearances with Syracuse, the 6-foot-2, 181-pound lefty struck out 41, walked a whopping 28, and compiled a 4.10 ERA in 41.2 innings of action.

Snippet from The 2020 Prospect Digest Handbook: The question, of course, is whether Szapucki will be able to handle the rigors of a full season – which hasn't happened yet.

Scouting Report: There are few minor league pitchers I've watched more frequently over the years than Szapucki. With that being said, the repertoire looked disappointing. His fastball was 90- to 92-mph but lacked the life that I've seen in years past. His curveball, while still above-average, didn't have the typical sharp break. And the changeup, which shows a touch of sink, remains average. Couple that with his age – he'll be 26-years-old in 2022 – with his recent command issues and it doesn't look too promising for the oft-injured hurler. At this point he is what he is: an up-and-down spot-starter with some added value as a multi-inning relief arm – unfortunately.

Ceiling: 1.0-win player
Risk: Moderate
MLB ETA: Debuted in 2021

16. Jose Butto, RHP

	FB	CB	SL	CH	Command	Overall
	55	45/50	45/50	65	55	40

Born: 03/19/98	Age: 24	Bats: R	Top Comp: N/A
Height: 6-1	Weight: 202	Throws: R	

Season	Team	Age	Level	IP	TBF	K/9	K%	BB/9	BB%	K-BB%	ERA	FIP	xFIP	Pit/Bat
2018	NYM	20	R	32.2	133	8.54	23.31%	3.03	8.27%	15.04%	1.93	4.57	4.58	3.25
2018	NYM	20	A-	28.0	127	7.71	18.90%	3.54	8.66%	10.24%	6.11	6.16	4.39	3.75
2019	NYM	21	A	112.0	467	8.76	23.34%	2.49	6.64%	16.70%	3.62	3.43	3.47	3.74
2021	NYM	23	A+	58.1	239	9.26	25.10%	2.31	6.28%	18.83%	4.32	5.03	4.38	3.94
2021	NYM	23	AA	40.1	167	11.16	29.94%	2.01	5.39%	24.55%	3.12	4.01	3.48	3.83

Background: An older prospect unearthed on the international free agent market. Butto was practically ancient by today's standards, signing at the elderly age of 19-years-old. The 6-foot-1, 202-pound right-hander, who received a paltry four-figure sum, has already surpassed modest expectations as he spent a good portion of last season in Double-AA. Making 20 starts with Brooklyn and Binghamton, Butto posted an impressive 110-to-24 strikeout-to-walk ratio in only 98.2 innings of work. He finished his fourth professional season with an aggregate 3.83 ERA.

Scouting Report: On the short list of best changeups in Mets' system, likely the entire minor leagues, Butto's razzle-dazzle offering is straight out of an old Bugs Bunny cartoon. It's freakishly slow, thrown with tremendous arm speed. And the plus, sometimes plus-plus, offering plays up even better due to his above-average heater, which peaked out at 96 mph during a late July start. The long term problem for Butto, though, is his lack of even an average breaking ball. It appears he throws a curveball *and* a slider. And they're both 45s, at best. Butto could be a solid middle relief arm relying solely on his fastball/changeup combo.

Ceiling: 1.0-win player
Risk: Moderate
MLB ETA: 2022

17. Carlos Cortes, 2B/LF

Hit	Power	SB	Patience	Glove	Overall
40	55	40	55	50	40

Born: 06/30/97	Age: 25	Bats: L	Top Comp: N/A
Height: 5-7	Weight: 197	Throws: R	

Season	Team	Age	Level	PA	1B	2B	3B	HR	SB	CS	BB%	K%	AVG	OBP	SLG	ISO
2018	NYM	21	A-	202	36	5	2	4	1	0	8.42%	16.83%	0.264	0.338	0.382	0.118
2019	NYM	22	A+	526	77	26	3	11	6	5	9.89%	14.64%	0.255	0.336	0.397	0.142
2021	NYM	24	AA	346	37	26	1	14	1	2	10.12%	24.57%	0.257	0.332	0.487	0.230

Background: If you don't succeed, try, try, try again. And that's exactly what the Mets did. The organization selected the pint-sized prospect in the 20th round coming out of Lake Howell High School in 2016. But Cortes spurned the club's advances and opted to head to the University of South Carolina. After a solid junior campaign for the SEC school, Cortes, who batted .265/.385/.500, was drafted by the Mets in the third round in 2018. The 5-foot-7, 197-pound dynamo turned in a mediocre debut in short-season ball and more or less maintained status quo as he was aggressively pushed up to High-A in 2019. But last season the Florida native had a coming out party – thanks in large part due to rediscovering his power stroke. In only 79 games in at the minors' toughest challenge, AA, Cortes slugged .257/.332/.487 with 26 doubles, one triple, and 14 homeruns. His overall production, per *Weighted Runs Created Plus*, topped the league average threshold by 20%.

Scouting Report: Consider the following:

- Since 2006, five 23-year-old hitters that met the following criteria in Double-A in a season with one organization (min. 300 PA): 115 to 125 wRC+, a walk rate between 9% and 11%, and a strikeout rate between 23% and 26%. Those five hitters: Andruw Monasterio, Gavin LaValley, Kentrail Davis, Rhyne Hughes, and – of course – Carlos Cortes.

Cortes flashed above-average pop during his time at South Carolina, but last season was the first time he did so as a professional. His batted ball data, however, was less than supportive. Per *FanGraphs*, his average exit velocity was 88 mph with a low peak of 102. He also has a pair of obstacles standing in his way as well: his size (5-foot-7, 197-pounds) is always going to give talent evaluators pause and, more importantly, he can't hit left-handers. Cortes batted .187/.267/.308 against southpaws in 2019 and showed no improvement in 2021 as he hit .208/.247/.286 against them. He also some positional versatility, but it's not enough to make up for his platoon splits. Purely a bench option.

Ceiling: 0.5- to 1.0-win player
Risk: Moderate
MLB ETA: 2022

18. Jaylen Palmer, IF/OF

Hit	Power	SB	Patience	Glove	Overall
35/45	35/50	55	60	50	40

Born: 07/31/00	Age: 21	Bats: R	Top Comp: N/A
Height: 6-4	Weight: 208	Throws: R	

Season	Team	Age	Level	PA	1B	2B	3B	HR	SB	CS	BB%	K%	AVG	OBP	SLG	ISO
2018	NYM	17	R	100	21	4	1	1	5	2	8.00%	27.00%	0.310	0.394	0.414	0.103
2019	NYM	18	R	276	42	12	2	7	1	3	11.23%	39.13%	0.260	0.344	0.413	0.153
2021	NYM	20	A	291	49	13	4	2	23	5	13.40%	27.84%	0.276	0.378	0.386	0.110

Background: Holy Cross High School is far, *far* from a baseball hotbed – though the Flushing, New York, school did produce a pair of second round selections in the 1970s with John and Dave Valle (1972 and 1978). As for Palmer, the Mets handed the part-time infielder / part-time outfielder a nice little $200,000 bonus to convince him to sign as 22nd round selection in 2018. Last year was a tale of two seasons for the 6-foot-4, 208-pound prospect. Palmer began the year by hitting a respectable .276/.378/.386 with 13 doubles, four triples, two homeruns, and 23 stolen bases with the St. Lucie Mets in Low-A. His production with the club, per *Weighted Runs Created Plus*, was 14% better than the league average mark. And then...he was promoted to High-A. Palmer responded by cobbling together a lowly .189/.314/.336 triple-slash line in 39 games with Brooklyn.

Scouting Report: With respect to his work in Low-A, consider the following:

- Since 2006, only four 20-year-old hitters met the following criteria in a season with one organization (min. 275 PA): 110 to 120 wRC+, a walk rate north of 12%, and a strikeout rate above 27%. Those four hitters: Hudson Head, Johan Lopez, Andres Melendez, and Jaylen Palmer.

Palmer's a really interesting conundrum: he walks a metric ton of the time, but he also swings-and-misses *way* too much. The problem, of course, is that his sturdy 6-foot-4, 208-pound frame isn't showing any type of meaningful power yet. But on the other hand his average exit velocity was an impressive 91 mph last season. He puts the ball on the ground too frequently, but spreads it around the field. An enigma. And the Mets don't exactly have a track record of developing wild cards like Palmer. It should be noted that last season's struggle in High-A was the first time Palmer looked hopeless at the dish in his pro career.

Ceiling: 0.5-win player
Risk: Moderate
MLB ETA: 2025

19. Hayden Senger, C

Hit	Power	SB	Patience	Glove	Overall
40	40	30	45	55	40

Born: 04/03/97	Age: 25	Bats: R	
Height: 6-1	Weight: 210	Throws: R	Top Comp: Bobby Wilson

Season	Team	Age	Level	PA	1B	2B	3B	HR	SB	CS	BB%	K%	AVG	OBP	SLG	ISO
2018	NYM	21	A-	83	13	3	1	0	0	1	10.84%	27.71%	0.250	0.373	0.324	0.074
2018	NYM	21	R	41	9	4	0	1	0	0	9.76%	19.51%	0.400	0.488	0.600	0.200
2019	NYM	22	A	353	44	21	1	4	0	0	7.08%	18.13%	0.230	0.324	0.345	0.115
2021	NYM	24	A+	47	5	5	1	2	0	0	6.38%	34.04%	0.302	0.362	0.605	0.302
2021	NYM	24	AA	205	29	13	1	3	0	0	7.80%	30.24%	0.254	0.337	0.387	0.133

Background: Beyond Sam Bachman going to the Angels with the ninth overall pick last June, the University of Miami of Ohio hasn't churned out a lot of viable big league prospects. In fact, the Mid-American Conference school has had just 12 players drafted since 2010. And one of the school's late round selections, Hayden Senger, is slowly making his way up the minor league ladder. A 24th round pick that got a nice six-figure bonus ($125,000), Senger, the 710th player chosen in 2018, opened last season up with a quick tour through High-A before earning a promotion up to the minors' toughest challenge, Double-A, in late May. In total, the 6-foot-1, 210-pound backstop hit an aggregate .263/.341/.429 with 18 doubles, two triples, and five homeruns. Senger cobbled together a lowly .194/.375/.226 triple-slash line with Salt River in the Arizona Fall League as well.

Scouting Report: Not a real threat with the bat – even before last season. Senger's strikeout rate ballooned into full-blown red flag territory last season, fanning in more than his 30% of his plate appearances. Below-average hit tool. Modest walk rates. Not a ton of power. But he'll provide some above-average value behind the dish. Senger profiles strictly as a lower tier backup at the big league level. One silver lining: the Miami of Ohio product batted a more-than-respectable .285/.360/.437 over his first 43 games in AA before fading significantly over the final few weeks of the year.

Ceiling: 0.5-win player
Risk: Low to Moderate
MLB ETA: 2022

20. Nick Meyer, C

Hit	Power	SB	Patience	Glove	Overall
40	40	40	55	50	40

Born: 02/18/97	Age: 25	Bats: R	
Height: 6-1	Weight: 200	Throws: R	Top Comp:

Season	Team	Age	Level	PA	1B	2B	3B	HR	SB	CS	BB%	K%	AVG	OBP	SLG	ISO
2018	NYM	21	A-	149	26	4	1	0	2	1	6.04%	12.75%	0.226	0.275	0.270	0.044
2019	NYM	22	A+	229	32	4	1	1	12	2	6.99%	18.78%	0.182	0.250	0.225	0.043
2019	NYM	22	R	15	0	0	0	0	0	0	13.33%	26.67%	0.000	0.143	0.000	0.000
2021	NYM	24	AA	209	36	4	0	3	5	2	9.09%	18.66%	0.243	0.332	0.316	0.073
2021	NYM	24	AAA	48	9	3	0	0	1	2	10.42%	14.58%	0.286	0.362	0.357	0.071

Background: While not recognized as a traditional baseball hotbed, per se, Cal Poly has produced a few notable big leaguers and/or prospects including: Spencer Howard, Mitch Haniger, Bud Norris, Kevin Correia, Mike Krokow, and – easily – the school's most famous alumnus: the Wizard of Oz, a.k.a. Ozzie Smith. A sixth round pick out of the Big West Conference squad in 2018, Meyer appeared in 61 games for Mets affiliates in 2021: 51 contests with Binghamton and another 11 contests for Syracuse in AAA. The 6-foot-1, 200-pound mustachioed backstop hit a combined .251/.337/.324 with seven doubles and three homeruns. He also swiped six bags in nine attempts as well.

Scouting Report: Similar, yet quite difference from his counterpart Hayden Senger. Meyer, too, has a ceiling-limiting bat, though he doesn't strikeout nearly as much and walks a bit more frequently. There's next to no thump in his bat. And he won't win any Gold Glove Awards too. But he does a decent job limiting the opposition's running game. Another low end backup at the big league level.

Ceiling: 0.5-win player
Risk: Low to Moderate
MLB ETA: 2022

New York Yankees

Top Prospects

1. Anthony Volpe, SS

	Hit	Power	SB	Patience	Glove	Overall
	55/60	60	60	55	60	70

Born: 04/28/01	Age: 21	Bats: R	Top Comp: Xander Bogaerts
Height: 5-11	Weight: 180	Throws: R	

Season	Team	Age	Level	PA	1B	2B	3B	HR	SB	CS	BB%	K%	AVG	OBP	SLG	ISO
2019	NYY	18	R	150	15	7	2	2	6	1	15.33%	25.33%	0.215	0.349	0.355	0.140
2021	NYY	20	A	257	25	18	5	12	21	5	19.84%	16.73%	0.302	0.455	0.623	0.322
2021	NYY	20	A+	256	28	17	1	15	12	4	10.55%	22.66%	0.286	0.391	0.587	0.300

Background: There may be a time in the near future where the 2019 graduating class from Delbarton School will be recognized as one of the best in history – at least in terms of sheer baseball talent. The New Jersey-based baseball squad teamed 2019 first rounder Anthony Volpe *and* ace wunderkind Jack Leiter, whose strong (read: unbreakable) commitment to Vanderbilt caused him to fall in the draft. While the latter would go on to become the #2 overall selection in the 2021 July draft class, Volpe's production erupted last season and thrust him upwards among the best prospects in the entire sport. Handed a hefty $2,740,300 bonus as the 30th overall selection, Volpe put together a disappointing debut with New York's Appalachian League affiliate that year: he batted .215/.349/.355 with seven doubles, two triples, and a pair of dingers. Last season, though, the young middle infielder transformed into the second coming of Alex Rodriguez. He opened the by ripping through the Low-A competition to the tune of .302/.455/.623 and continued his dominance as he moved up to Hudson Valley in High-A (.286/.391/.587). In total, the 5-foot-11, 180-pound shortstop slugged an aggregate .294/.423/.604 with 35 doubles, six triples, 27 homeruns, and 33 stolen bases (in 42 total attempts). Per *Weighted Runs Created Plus*, his overall production topped the league average mark by 70%.

Snippet from The 2020 Prospect Digest Handbook: Fast hands and a short, quick, deliberate path to the ball – which is reminiscent of another Yankees shortstop. Volpe showed more pop than expected during his debut in the Appalachian League, posting a .140 Isolated Power. The New Jersey native also showed a patient approach at the plate, walking in more than 15% of his plate appearances. Defensively, he shows an average arm but soft hands and fluid hips. Volpe looks like a .280/.340/.420 type hitter with slightly better than average defense.

Scouting Report: Just a little bit of fun with his production last season:

- There were 377 hitters that received at least 400 plate appearances in the minor leagues. Of those 377, Volpe's aggregate production as measured by *Weighted Runs Created Plus*, 170, was the best.
- Only 20-years-old, the closest level of production from a 20-year-old is the Dodgers' Andy Pages, with a 152 wRC+.

So let's take a look at how Volpe's production stacks up against some recent peers. Consider the following:

- Since 2006, there have been 723 instances in which a 20-year-old received at least 250 plate appearances in a Low-A season. Volpe's production, 186 wRC+, is the best – by slightly more than 10 percentage points.
- In fact, here's the list of 20-year-olds with at least 160 wRC+, a sub-20% strikeout rate and a walk rate north of 16%: Mookie Betts and Anthony Volpe.

Now let's take a look at his production in High-A:

- Since 2006, only four 20-year-old hitters posted at least a 150 wRC+ with a double-digit walk rate with a K-rate between 19% and 23% (min. 250 PA): Christian Yelich, George Valera, Anthony Alford, and Anthony Volpe.

Needless to say, it was a season for the ages for Volpe. Above-average hit tool, plus power, plus speed, and a potentially plus glove at the most valuable infield position.

Ceiling: 7.0-win player
Risk: Moderate
MLB ETA: 2023

2. Jasson Dominguez, CF

	Hit	Power	SB	Patience	Glove	Overall
	50	65	50/35	50	45	60

Born: 02/07/03	Age: 19	Bats: B	Top Comp: Tyler O'Neill
Height: 5-10	Weight: 190	Throws: R	

Season	Team	Age	Level	PA	1B	2B	3B	HR	SB	CS	BB%	K%	AVG	OBP	SLG	ISO
2021	NYY	18	CPX	27	4	0	0	0	2	0	22.22%	22.22%	0.200	0.407	0.200	0.000
2021	NYY	18	A	214	33	9	1	5	7	3	9.81%	31.31%	0.258	0.346	0.398	0.140

Background: The way the hype machine was spinning last offseason there wouldn't have been too many people that would have correctly guess that Dominguez wouldn't be listed as the top prospect in the Yankees farm system heading into 2022. But here we are. And it's not necessary a result of Dominguez failing to live up to (unrealistic) expectations as it's about Anthony Volpe transforming into an otherworldly prospect. As for Dominguez, nicknamed the Martian, he opened his professional debut up in the Florida Complex League and after just seven games he was bumped up to Low-A for the remainder of the year. In 49 games with the Tampa Yankees, the 5-foot-10, 190-pound center fielder, who's built like a brick shithouse, batted a respectable .258/.346/.398 with nine doubles, one triple, and five homeruns. He also swiped seven bags in 10 attempts. Per *Weighted Runs Created Plus* Dominguez's production in Low-A was 5% better than league average. And just a reminder: New York signed the behemoth outfielder to a hefty $5.1 million.

Snippet from The 2020 Prospect Digest Handbook: Massive, massive raw power from both sides of the plate. The young switch-hitter's lightning quick bat, unlike anything I've seen from a 16-year-old, with a natural loft that all but guarantees a floor of 60-grade power with the ceiling of 40 homeruns in full season. And, truthfully, I keep circling back to his bat speed. It's almost breathtakingly fast.

Scouting Report: Consider the following:

- Since 2006, only three 18-year-olds posted a wRC+ between 100 and 110 with a strikeout rate of at least 27% in a Low-A season with one organization (min. 200 PA): Yorman Rodriguez, Alejandro Osuna, and – of course – Jasson Dominguez.

Well, that's not overly promising. So let's dive a little deeper. Consider the following:

- Dominguez got off to a solid start to his Low-A debut, hitting .271/.351/.418 over his first 46 contests. But a late season slump, in which he hit went 0-for-19 torpedoed his overall numbers.
- And with most young switch-hitters, Dominguez struggled significantly against left-handers, hitting a lowly .170/.237/.255 (compared to .288/.371/.446 vs. RHP).

Despite only entering his age-19 season, Dominguez is maxed out – to the extreme – physically. He's still showing plus to plus-plus bat speed, but there's definitely more swing-and-miss to his game than expected. He's was incredibly young for Low-A, so it's reasonable to expect the K-rate to regress some as he matures. There's superstar potential, but he does need to tone the swing down and I definitely expect him to slide over into a corner outfield position at some point in the next few years.

Ceiling: 4.5-win player
Risk: Moderate
MLB ETA: 2024

3. Oswald Peraza, SS

Hit	Power	SB	Patience	Glove	Overall
50	50	55	45	50+	60

Born: 06/15/00	Age: 22	Bats: R	Top Comp: Asdrubal Cabrera
Height: 6-0	Weight: 165	Throws: R	

Season	Team	Age	Level	PA	1B	2B	3B	HR	SB	CS	BB%	K%	AVG	OBP	SLG	ISO
2018	NYY	18	R	159	29	3	2	1	8	1	8.81%	25.79%	0.250	0.333	0.321	0.071
2019	NYY	19	A-	85	15	1	1	2	5	2	5.88%	10.59%	0.241	0.294	0.354	0.114
2019	NYY	19	A	208	43	5	0	2	18	5	7.69%	13.46%	0.273	0.348	0.333	0.060
2021	NYY	21	A+	127	19	10	0	5	16	1	9.45%	18.90%	0.306	0.386	0.532	0.225
2021	NYY	21	AA	353	66	16	2	12	20	8	6.52%	23.23%	0.294	0.348	0.466	0.172
2021	NYY	21	AAA	31	7	0	0	1	2	1	6.45%	16.13%	0.286	0.323	0.393	0.107

Background: Inked a contract with the historical franchise for $175,000 in 2016. The Venezuelan-born middle fielder entered last year with three respectable offensive seasons on his resume. Peraza batted .266/.363/.332 as a 17-year-old in the Gulf Coast League during his debut. He spent the following year as an 18-year-old in the Appalachian League, hitting .250/.333/.321. And he split time between Staten Island and Charleston in 2019, compiling an aggregate .263/.332/.340 with just six doubles, one triple, and four homeruns. But after missing the 2020 season due to the COVID shutdown, Peraza came back as an offensive force in 2021. The 6-foot, 165-pound shortstop shredded the High-A competition to the tune of .306/.386/.523, looked incredibly comfortable against the minors' toughest level (.294/.348/.466), and continued to hit in an eight-game cameo with Scranton/Wilkes-Barre. In total, Peraza slugged a combined .297/.356/.477 with career highs in doubles (26) and homeruns (18), and stolen bases (38). His overall production, per *Weighted Runs Created Plus*, topped the league average threshold by 26%.

Scouting Report: Consider the following:

- Since 2006, only three 21-year-old hitters posted a wRC+ total between 117 and 127 with a walk rate between 5.5% and 7.5% and strikeout rate between 18% and 24% in a Double-A season with one organization (min. 300 PA): Alex Kirilloff, Ryan Mountcastle, and – of course – the lone middle infielder, Oswald Peraza.

From a lightweight, slap-hitting shortstop to a middle-of-the-lineup run producer. It's been quite the change for Peraza over the past two seasons, hasn't it? And what's behind the massive swing in his approach? Groundball and flyball rates. Between 2018 and 2019, Peraza's groundball rates ranged from 50% to 59.4%. Last year, it was in the low 40%-range. The home ballparks for Somerset and Scranton/Wilkes-Barre tend to play neutral or slightly favorable to pitchers, so the massive spike in power seems to be repeatable. I don't think he's going to be a perennial 20-plus-homerun threat, but he could settle in somewhere between 15 and 18 dingers a year. Average to slightly better-than-average glove. Think: .280/.330/.430 as a big league ceiling.

Ceiling: 3.5-win player
Risk: Moderate
MLB ETA: 2022

4. Luis Gil, RHP

	FB	SL	CH	Command	Overall
	70	55/60	50	45	55

Born: 06/03/98	Age: 24	Bats: R	Top Comp: Sandy Alcantara
Height: 6-2	Weight: 185	Throws: R	

Season	Team	Age	Level	IP	TBF	K/9	K%	BB/9	BB%	K-BB%	ERA	FIP	xFIP	Pit/Bat
2018	NYY	20	R	39.1	162	13.27	35.80%	5.72	15.43%	20.37%	1.37	3.28	4.15	4.27
2019	NYY	21	A	83.0	350	12.14	32.00%	4.23	11.14%	20.86%	2.39	2.50	3.06	4.22
2019	NYY	21	A+	13.0	57	7.62	19.30%	5.54	14.04%	5.26%	4.85	3.69	4.83	4.25
2021	NYY	23	AA	30.2	130	14.67	38.46%	3.82	10.00%	28.46%	2.64	2.37	3.37	4.24
2021	NYY	23	AAA	48.2	212	12.39	31.60%	5.92	15.09%	16.51%	4.81	4.64	4.45	4.01

Background: Say what you will about the Yankees' massive payrolls and their ability to absorb the richest contracts in the game. But the front office, led by future Hall of Famer Brian Cashman, trade as well as anybody in the business. And if there wasn't enough evidence, just take a look at Luis Gil's addition to the storied franchise. Signed out of the Dominican Republic for a five-figure deal, New York acquired the then-20-year-old right-hander, fresh off of a shoulder issue, for nondescript outfielder Jake Cave. Fast forward a couples seasons and Gil has transformed into the best pitching prospect the organization has, as well as coming off of a stellar six-game debut in the big leagues. Standing a wiry 6-foot-2 and 185 pounds, Gil made a total of 20 appearances in the minor leagues last season, 17 of them coming via the start. Between his time with Scranton/Wilkes-Barre and Somerset, the hard-throwing right-hander struck out 117, walked 45, and compiled a 3.97 ERA in 79.1 innings. He made an additional six starts with the Yankees too, averaging 11.7 strikeouts and 5.8 walks per nine innings to go along with a 3.07 ERA.

Snippet from The 2020 Prospect Digest Handbook: Gil had a light's out, elite upper-90s fastball. But his secondary weapons were quite raw – raw enough that (A) there's not a ton of hope for future develops and (B) he eventually falls into a single-pitch relief role.

Scouting Report: Well, the offspeed weapons lurched forward from barely playable to above-average (slider) and average (changeup). And with regard to Gil's slider, there's enough velocity, shape, and movement that it may eventually creep into plus territory. With respect to his work in AAA last season, consider the following:

- Since 2006, only five 23-year-old hurlers struck out at between 30.5% and 32.5% of the hitters they faced in a Triple-A season with one org. (min. 40 IP): Jered Weaver, Dan Straily, Jose De Leon, Rogelio Armenteros, and Luis Gil.

You'll be hard-pressed to find a hurler that (A) generates the velocity and explosion that Gil's fastball has and (B) does it with as little effort as he does. There's definite upper-rotation caliber potential here, but the command has to at least get to a 45-grade. One more thought: ignoring three of his worst starts in the minors last season, Gil's walk rate declined all the way down to 3.8 BB/9. That's a great sign.

Ceiling: 3.0- to 3.5-win player
Risk: Moderate
MLB ETA: Debuted in 2020

5. Clarke Schmidt, RHP

	FB	CB	SL	CH	Command	Overall
	55	65	60	55	55	55

Born: 02/20/96	Age: 26	Bats: R	Top Comp: Marcus Stroman
Height: 6-1	Weight: 209	Throws: R	

Season	Team	Age	Level	IP	TBF	K/9	K%	BB/9	BB%	K-BB%	ERA	FIP	xFIP	Pit/Bat
2019	NYY	23	A+	63.1	271	9.81	25.46%	3.41	8.86%	16.61%	3.84	2.87	2.97	3.70
2019	NYY	23	AA	19.0	71	9.00	26.76%	0.47	1.41%	25.35%	2.37	2.01	2.47	3.66
2021	NYY	25	AAA	25.2	111	11.22	28.83%	2.81	7.21%	21.62%	2.10	3.95	3.31	4.02

Background: It's been a rough couple of years for the former University of South Carolina ace: Tommy John surgery shutdown his junior collegiate campaign after just nine starts and 60.1 innings of work. Schmidt would make back to regular season action – as a highly touted first round pick – the following year, though he would throw just 23.1 innings across eight different appearances. The 6-foot-1, 209-pound right-hander began the 2019 season on high note, fanning nine Lakeland Tigers on April 4th, but would hit the disabled list six starts later and miss more than a month of work. COVID, obviously, shutdown every minor leaguers' season in 2020. And a sprained elbow delayed Schmidt's return to the mound last season – which ultimately led him to throw just 44.1 innings between the minor and major leagues.

Snippet from The 2020 Prospect Digest Handbook: Schmidt has the build, repertoire, and pedigree to slide into a #4 spot at the big league level. And despite missing as much time as he has over the past couple of seasons, Schmidt showed a surprisingly strong feel for his offspeed pitches. In terms of ceiling, think: Mets' right-hander Marcus Stroman, who averaged 7.8 strikeouts and 2.8 walks per nine innings with a 3.22 ERA. Schmidt just needs to prove that he stay healthy.

Scouting Report: Talented, but oft-injured. That's the opening line, the entire plot, and the closing remarks on the book about Clarke Schmidt. And despite the laundry list of injuries, ailments, and woes, Schmidt hasn't lost anything on his impressive repertoire. His fastball, an above-average offering, sits in the 93 mph range. His curveball is one helluva snapdragon. His upper-80s slider doesn't feature a lot of movement, but it's late with a biting wrinkle that's difficult to hit. And his changeup is Zack Greinke-esque: hard, firm, diving. Injuries notwithstanding, Schmidt has the talent right now to be a league average starting pitcher. Hopefully, he can catch a break.

Ceiling: 2.5-win player
Risk: High
MLB ETA: Debuted in 2020

6. Everson Pereira, CF

Hit	Power	SB	Patience	Glove	Overall
40/45	55	55	50	45	50

Born: 04/10/01	Age: 21	Bats: R	Top Comp: N/A
Height: 6-0	Weight: 191	Throws: R	

Season	Team	Age	Level	PA	1B	2B	3B	HR	SB	CS	BB%	K%	AVG	OBP	SLG	ISO
2018	NYY	17	R	183	31	8	2	3	3	2	8.20%	32.79%	0.263	0.322	0.389	0.126
2019	NYY	18	A-	74	8	3	0	1	3	0	5.41%	35.14%	0.171	0.216	0.257	0.086
2021	NYY	20	CPX	11	0	2	0	1	0	0	27.27%	18.18%	0.375	0.545	1.000	0.625
2021	NYY	20	A	83	15	5	1	5	4	1	12.05%	25.30%	0.361	0.446	0.667	0.306
2021	NYY	20	A+	127	11	3	0	14	5	2	11.81%	29.92%	0.259	0.354	0.676	0.417

Background: The Yankees honed in on premium amateur talent available on the international market five years ago. And as part of the club's haul, the front office signed Everson Pereira, a native of Cabudare, Venezuela, to hefty seven figure bonus. $1.5 million, to be exact. A year later the organization aggressively pushed the then-17-year-old straight into the Advanced Rookie League for his debut. And Pereira didn't disappoint. He batted a respectable .263/.322/.389 with eight doubles, two triples, and a trio of homeruns. The club bumped him up to the New York-Penn League the following season, though his tenure with Staten Island was short lived: a collision with the outfield wall prematurely ended his sophomore campaign after 18 mostly disappointing games (.171/.216/.257). Last season Pereira got off to a late start and after a three-game tune-up in the Complex League, he shredded the Low-A competition and looked like the second coming of Kevin Maas after his promotion up to High-A. The Venezuelan-born outfielder hit a robust .303/.398/.686 with 10 doubles, one triple, and 20 homeruns. His production, per *Weighted Runs Created Plus*, was a whopping 78% better than the league average threshold.

Snippet from The 2020 Prospect Digest Handbook: It was more or less a lost season for the talented center fielder. So we'll just take a wait-and-see approach.

Scouting Report: Just for fun, here are Pereira's numbers prorated for a full 162-game season: 33 doubles, three triples, 66 homeruns, and 30 stolen bases. How Sosa-ian of him, no? Pereira went on a potential record breaking homerun pace after his promotion up to High-A, slugging 14 homeruns in only 27 games. He's never been a groundball hitter, so the power could very well be legitimate. Above-average batted ball data (89 mph average exit velocity with a peak of 108 mph). Good patience. Above-average speed. The lone pock mark is his swing-and-miss rate (29.9% in High-A) is fully in red flag territory. He's a bit miscast as a center fielder, but can fake it for the time being. The K-rates make him risky, but he's only entering his age-21 season.

Ceiling: 2.5-win player
Risk: Moderate to High
MLB ETA: 2024

7. Deivi Garcia, RHP

FB	CB	SL	CH	Command	Overall
55	60	65	50	40/45	50

Born: 05/19/99	Age: 23	Bats: R	Top Comp:
Height: 5-9	Weight: 163	Throws: R	

Season	Team	Age	Level	IP	TBF	K/9	K%	BB/9	BB%	K-BB%	ERA	FIP	xFIP	Pit/Bat
2018	NYY	19	A	40.2	170	13.94	37.06%	2.21	5.88%	31.18%	3.76	3.15	2.57	3.91
2018	NYY	19	A+	28.1	109	11.12	32.11%	2.54	7.34%	24.77%	1.27	1.96	2.77	3.82
2019	NYY	20	A+	17.2	73	16.81	45.21%	4.08	10.96%	34.25%	3.06	0.93	1.49	4.55
2019	NYY	20	AA	53.2	235	14.59	37.02%	4.36	11.06%	25.96%	3.86	2.20	2.45	4.22
2019	NYY	20	AAA	40.0	178	10.13	25.28%	4.50	11.24%	14.04%	5.40	5.77	5.18	4.23
2021	NYY	22	AAA	90.2	437	9.63	22.20%	6.75	15.56%	6.64%	6.85	6.72	5.94	4.24

Background: Taking a page out of – gulp – Manny Banuelos's book of disappointment. Everything was trending upward for the diminutive right-hander. He was a consensus Top 100 prospect. As a 19-year-old in 2018, he shot through three separate levels while averaging 12.8 strikeouts and just 2.4 walks per nine innings. He followed that up by averaging 13.3 strikeouts and 4.4 walks per nine innings across High-A, Double-A, and Triple-A. And he looked every bit the part of a big league starting pitcher – despite his small 5-foot-9, 163-pound frame – during his six-game cameo with New York as part of the club's COVID taxi squad: he fanned 33 and walked just six in 34.1 innings. Then…2021 happened. And, quite frankly, Garcia lost command of the strike zone as he struggled through the worst year of his professional career. In 24 games with Scranton/Wilkes-Barre, the hard-throwing righty struck out 97, but walked a whopping 67 in only 90.2 inning of work. And he coughed up six earned runs in 8.1 big league innings.

Snippet from The 2020 Prospect Digest Handbook: One more final thought: Garcia's command backed up a bit last season, but it still profiles as at least average.

Scouting Report: Where to even begin? Garcia's fastball is still quite good, ranging from the low- to mid-90s. And even on lower range of the spectrum it plays up because of the late, explosive life. He's traded in – for the most part – his big tilting, fall-off-the-table curveball for a more refined, late-snapping slider – a new pitch to his repertoire. It sits in the low 80s. And it's filthy, when he's finishing it. Fringy average changeup. He will bring back Uncle Charlie every now and then, though. Garcia's still primarily a two-pitch pitcher (fastball/slider). He needs to develop a third if he's going to succeed as a big league starter. Otherwise, he's starring down the Juan Cruz path of relief-dom.

Ceiling: 2.0-win player
Risk: Moderate to High
MLB ETA: Debuted in 2020

8. Trey Sweeney, SS

Hit	Power	SB	Patience	Glove	Overall
40/45	55	45	50	50	45

Born: 04/24/00	Age: 22	Bats: L	Top Comp: N/A
Height: 6-4	Weight: 200	Throws: R	

Season	Team	Age	Level	PA	1B	2B	3B	HR	SB	CS	BB%	K%	AVG	OBP	SLG	ISO
2021	NYY	21	A	129	13	4	4	6	3	1	13.95%	22.48%	0.245	0.357	0.518	0.273

Background: A standout at St. Xavier High School, Sweeney batted .389 and drove in 41 runs during his senior campaign. And the lefty-swinging shortstop / third baseman made the transition into the collegiate ranks without missing a beat. In 55 games with the Eastern Illinois Panthers, Sweeney hit .271/.342/.354 with nine doubles and a pair of homeruns. He spent the ensuing summer playing for the Lafayette Aviators in the Prospect League. And his offensive production *exploded.* He slugged .354/.453/.524 across 52 contests. Sweeney got off to an equally scorching start during the COVID-shortened 2020 season, batting .351/.439/.456 in 14 games. The 2021 season brought an even higher level of production: In 48 games for the Ohio Valley Conference squad, Sweeney battered the competition to the tune of .382/.522/.712 with 10 doubles, two triples, 14 homeruns, and a trio of stolen bases. Perhaps the best news: he finished the year with a sparkling 24-to-46 strikeout-to-walk ratio. New York drafted the lefty-swinging infielder with the 20th overall pick last July and signed him to deal worth $3 million. Sweeney spent the bulk of his debut with the Tampa Tarpons, hitting .245/.357/.518 with four doubles, four triples, and a six homeruns.

Scouting Report: Per the usual, here's what I wrote about Sweeney prior to the draft last season:

"Consider the following:

- *Between 2011 and 2020, only two OVC hitters have batted at least .360/.500/.700 in a season (min. 200 PA): Taylor Davis and Trenton Moses.*

Obviously, the level of competition – or lack of elite consistent competition – is concerning. But Sweeney has consistently been an elite bat against the levels he's faced since the summer of 2019. The hitting mechanics, particularly the timing leg kick and hands, need to revamped. The swing is intriguing: plus bat speed, natural loft, and 15- to 20-homerun power potential. He's likely going to move from short, so he's a man without a position. Sweeney looks like a project, but he could develop into a Hunter Dozier-type."

Ceiling: 1.5-win player
Risk: Moderate
MLB ETA: 2024

9. Luis Medina, RHP

FB	CB	CH	Command	Overall
80	60	45	40/45	45

Top Comp: Dellin Betances

Born: 05/03/99	Age: 23	Bats: R
Height: 6-1	Weight: 175	Throws: R

Season	Team	Age	Level	IP	TBF	K/9	K%	BB/9	BB%	K-BB%	ERA	FIP	xFIP	Pit/Bat
2018	NYY	19	R	36.0	184	11.75	25.54%	11.50	25.00%	0.54%	6.25	6.46	6.57	4.04
2019	NYY	20	A	93.0	427	11.13	26.93%	6.48	15.69%	11.24%	6.00	4.72	4.23	4.00
2019	NYY	20	A+	10.2	43	10.12	27.91%	2.53	6.98%	20.93%	0.84	1.90	2.36	4.07
2021	NYY	22	A+	32.2	133	13.78	37.59%	5.23	14.29%	23.31%	2.76	4.22	3.71	4.05
2021	NYY	22	AA	73.2	318	10.14	26.10%	5.01	12.89%	13.21%	3.67	4.25	4.21	3.99

Background: It's been a while since the club signed the hard-throwing hurler out of Nagua, Dominican Republic — seven years to be exact. And for Medina, a 6-foot-1, 175-pound right-hander, it's been a *long* seven years. He spent parts of three seasons in the foreign and stateside rookie leagues. And he wouldn't reach the true testing grounds of Double-A until the latter portion of 2021. Medina made a total of 22 appearances, 21 of which were starts, between High-A and Low-A, throwing a career-high 106.1 innings, posting a 133-to-60 strikeout-to-walk ratio to go along with a 3.39 ERA.

Snippet from The 2020 Prospect Digest Handbook: He looks like he's going to be Albert Abreu 2.0. His ceiling is predicated on the repertoire, but there's very little chance he actually achieves it.

Scouting Report: There are pitchers in baseball that throw as hard, maybe even a mile-per-hour or two harder, but I've yet to see a pitcher that throws as hard with as little effort as Medina. The 6-foot-1, 175-pound hurler's cheddar sits – easily, comfortably – in the 98- to 100-mph range, as a starter. He'll mix in a wicked, hard-biting curveball that opponents typically (A) beat into the ground or (B) stick their bat head out for an easy can-of-corn. His changeup is fringy, and it's clear that he slows his entire body down when he's throwing it. The command/control can be erratic at times, as well too. Medina has to come up with a viable third option – and I think the splitter should be an option – otherwise he's going to turn into one helluva backend reliever.

Ceiling: 1.5-win player
Risk: Moderate
MLB ETA: 2022

10. Ken Waldichuk, LHP

FB	CB	SL	CH	Command	Overall
55	55	55	50	45	45

Top Comp: Joey Lucchesi

Born: 01/08/98	Age: 24	Bats: L
Height: 6-4	Weight: 220	Throws: L

Season	Team	Age	Level	IP	TBF	K/9	K%	BB/9	BB%	K-BB%	ERA	FIP	xFIP	Pit/Bat
2019	NYY	21	R	29.1	115	15.03	42.61%	2.15	6.09%	36.52%	3.68	2.14	2.72	4.05
2021	NYY	23	A+	30.2	113	16.14	48.67%	3.82	11.50%	37.17%	0.00	1.45	2.59	4.29
2021	NYY	23	AA	79.1	340	12.25	31.76%	4.31	11.18%	20.59%	4.20	4.59	4.02	4.07

Background: Saint Mary's College of California has churned out eight big leaguers through their history: the underrated Von Hayes, All-Star right-hander and Cy Young award winner Corbin Burnes, Tony Gonsolin, Mark Teahen, Patrick Wisdom, Kyle Barraclough, James Mouton, and Broderick Perkins. Ken Waldichuk, barring an unfortunate turn of events, should be added to the list. A fifth round pick in 2019 out of the Moraga-based school, Waldichuk put together one of the most dominant stints you'll ever see during his seven game jaunt through High-A. In 30.2 innings with the Hudson Valley Renegades, the 6-foot-4, 220-pound southpaw struck out 55, walked just 13, and did not allow a run – unearned or earned. And he continued to dominate – though not to that extent – upon his promotion up to Double-A: 12.3 K/9, 4.3 BB/9 to go along with a 4.20 ERA. He finished his first full season in professional ball with 163 strikeouts, 51 walks, and a 3.03 ERA.

Scouting Report: Waldichuk's 163 punch outs tied for the fourth highest among all minor league hurlers last season. With regard to his work in Double-A, consider the following:

- Since 2006, only two 23-year-old Double-A pitchers posted a K% north of 30% with a walk percentage between 10% and 12% in a season with one organization (min. 75 IP): Paul Estrada and Ken Waldichuk.

Really quality repertoire highlighted by bat-breaking, heavy low-90s fastball. He'll add-and-subtract from the offering as well. He'll complement the above-average offering with a pair of above-average breaking balls: a curveball and slider, with the latter lacking consistency to be a plus-pitch. And he'll mix in a solid-average changeup as well. Effectively wild. There's some funk in his delivery that causes some inconsistencies with his release point. He's going to have one helluva time trying to crack New York's rotation, though.

Ceiling: 1.5-win player
Risk: Moderate
MLB ETA: 2022

11. Austin Wells, C

Hit	Power	SB	Patience	Glove	Overall
45	55	30	50	40/45	45

Born: 07/12/99	Age: 22	Bats: L	Top Comp: John Buck
Height: 6-2	Weight: 220	Throws: R	

Season	Team	Age	Level	PA	1B	2B	3B	HR	SB	CS	BB%	K%	AVG	OBP	SLG	ISO
2021	NYY	21	A	299	31	17	4	9	11	0	17.06%	20.74%	0.258	0.398	0.479	0.220
2021	NYY	21	A+	170	26	6	1	7	5	0	11.76%	32.35%	0.274	0.376	0.473	0.199

Background: When the New York Yankees are after someone they've set their sights on the club – typically – end up acquiring their services. At least at some point, unless they're Ken Griffey Jr. Case in point: Austin Wells (and Gerrit Cole too). Originally drafted by the Yanks coming out of Bishop Gorman High School in 2018, Wells bypassed the chance to join baseball's most storied franchise (as a 38th round pick), opting, instead, to go to the University of Arizona. After two stout years (well, 1.25 years thanks to COVID), Wells was sporting a .357/.476/.560 slash line and New York finally came calling again. The organization selected the lefty-swinging backstop in the opening round, 28th overall, and signed him to a deal worth $2.5 million. Last season Wells, who has bounced between catcher, first base, and a corner outfielder position at points in his career, remained at one defensive position (catcher) and hit an aggregate .264/.390/.476 with 23 doubles, five triples, and 16 homeruns between Tampa and Hudson Valley. He also spent the fall mashing for the Surprise Saguaros in the Arizona Fall League as well (.344/.456/.578).

Scouting Report: Consider the following:

- Since 2006, only three 21-year-old hitters posted a wRC+ between 135 and 145 with a walk rate north of 15% in a Low-A season with one organization (min. 275 PA): Max Ramirez, Dwanya Williams-Sutton, and Austin Wells.

Defensively, Wells was as smooth as walking on broken glass. Per Clay Davenport's defensive metrics, he was 14 runs *worse* than average – and that comes in just 70 games behind the dish. He also managed to throw out just 13% of would-be base stealers. Offensively, there's a nice little saber-slant to his approach at the plate: above-average patience and above-average power, but the concerning swing-and-miss tendencies make him a potential Three True Outcomes hitter. He did not show any platoon splits. Unless Wells' defensive production makes a complete reversal it's going to be difficult to not push him to first base or a full time designated hitter.

Ceiling: 1.5-win player
Risk: Moderate
MLB ETA: 2024

12. Brendan Beck, RHP

FB	CB	SL	CH	Command	Overall
55/60	55	55	55	50	45

Born: 10/06/98	Age: 23	Bats: R	Top Comp: N/A
Height: 6-2	Weight: 205	Throws: R	

Background: Fun Family Fact: the last time the New York Yankees selected a player from Stanford University was Tristan Beck, a 29th round pick who also happens to be the older brother of Brendan Beck. A 6-foot-2, 205-pound right-hander, Brendan was a stalwart for the Stanford Cardinal during his four-year career – though some poor luck during his junior campaign, as well as the limited COVID-impacted draft, forced him to go undrafted. Last season the then-22-year-old hurler struck out 143 hitters against just 26 walks to go along with a 3.15 ERA. Beck's 143 whiffs ranked fourth among all Division I hurlers, trailing only Jack Leiter, Kumar Rocker, and Andrew Abbott. New York selected him in the second round, 55th overall, and signed him to a deal worth $1.05 million. He did not make his pro debut last season.

Scouting Report: Consider the following:

- Between 2011 and 2020, there were only ten Division I hurlers that averaged at least 11.5 K/9 and less than 2.5 BB/9 in a season (min. 100 IP): Trevor Bauer, Logan Gilbert, Danny Hultzen, Casey Mize, David Peterson, Nick Sandlin, Adam Scott, Alek Manoah, and Reid Detmers.

An accomplished pitcher cut from a similar cloth as former first rounder Clarke Schmidt. Beck attacks hitters with a lively low-90s fastball that topped 96 mph in a game against Vanderbilt. He throws three above-average offspeed offerings as well: a low-80s slider, a mid-70s curveball, and an underrated, fading changeup. Throw in Beck's propensity for…uh hmmm…throwing strikes, and it's a recipe for some backend starting value. It's a fantastic little under-slot signing by the Yankees.

Ceiling: 1.5-win player
Risk: Moderate
MLB ETA: 2024

13. Oswaldo Cabrera, IF

	Hit	Power	SB	Patience	Glove	Overall
	45	50	55	45	55	45

Born: 03/01/99	Age: 23	Bats: B	Top Comp: N/A
Height: 5-10	Weight: 145	Throws: R	

Season	Team	Age	Level	PA	1B	2B	3B	HR	SB	CS	BB%	K%	AVG	OBP	SLG	ISO
2018	NYY	19	A	526	80	24	1	6	4	9	5.32%	12.55%	0.229	0.273	0.320	0.091
2019	NYY	20	A+	493	80	29	0	8	10	8	6.69%	21.30%	0.260	0.310	0.378	0.118
2021	NYY	22	AA	478	58	29	1	24	20	5	7.53%	24.69%	0.256	0.311	0.492	0.236
2021	NYY	22	AAA	36	7	2	1	5	1	0	13.89%	25.00%	0.500	0.583	1.133	0.633

Background: Prior to the 2021 season the book looked like it had all but been written on Oswaldo Cabrera. A small, light-hitting utility infielder out of Guarenas, Venezuela, Cabrera posted OPS totals of .628, .592, .687 between 2017 and 2019. Then – nearly out of the blue – the 5-foot-nothing, 140-pound infielder exploded during his stint in Double-A in 2021 as minor league baseball returned from the enforced COVID shutdown. In 109 games with the Somerset Patriots Cabrera slugged a hearty .256/.311/.492 with 29 doubles, one triple, and 24 homeruns. He also swiped 20 bags in 25 total attempts. Per *Weighted Runs Created Plus*, his overall production during his time in Double-A was 14% above the league average mark.

Scouting Report: Consider the following:

- Since 2006, only a pair of 22-year-old hitters met the following criteria in a Double-A season with one organization (min. 400 PA): 110 to 120 wRC+, a 6.5% to 8.5% walk rate, and a strikeout rate between 23% and 26%. Those two hitters: Junior Lake and Oswaldo Cabrera.

So…I'm not ready to buy into Cabrera's homerun binge in Double-A last season. But…while Somerset's home ballpark plays neutrally, it is incredibly prone to coughing up the long ball. Here's the kicker: Cabrera belted 15 homeruns at home and 14 dingers on the road. Plus, he's continued to show shrinking groundball rates. Above-average glove at third base, shortstop, or second base. The hit tool is a bit underwhelming. There's some super-sub potential here.

Ceiling: 1.5-win player
Risk: Moderate
MLB ETA: 2022

14. JP Sears, LHP

	FB	SL	CH	Command	Overall
	60	60	50	55	45

Born: 02/19/96	Age: 26	Bats: R	Top Comp: Ted Lilly
Height: 5-11	Weight: 180	Throws: L	

Season	Team	Age	Level	IP	TBF	K/9	K%	BB/9	BB%	K-BB%	ERA	FIP	xFIP	Pit/Bat
2018	NYY	22	A	54.0	215	9.00	25.12%	1.83	5.12%	20.00%	2.67	4.04	3.48	4.00
2019	NYY	23	A+	48.2	206	8.32	21.84%	2.96	7.77%	14.08%	4.07	3.92	3.93	3.78
2021	NYY	25	AA	50.2	211	12.61	33.65%	3.20	8.53%	25.12%	4.09	3.55	3.16	4.01
2021	NYY	25	AAA	53.1	204	10.97	31.86%	1.86	5.39%	26.47%	2.87	2.76	3.08	4.14

Background: A phenomenal strikeout artist during his collegiate career at The Citadel. Seattle originally drafted the favorite of mine in the 11th round of the 2017 draft. A few months later the Mariners dealt the little left-hander, along with righty Juan Then, in exchange for reliever Nick Rumbelow. The 5-foot-11, 180-pound hurler spent the 2018 season in Low-A and the following year in High-A. Finally, Sears crested over into the upper minors last season, splitting time between Somerset and Scranton/Wilkes-Barre. In total, he tossed 104.0 innings of work, averaging an impressive 11.8 strikeouts and just 2.5 walks per nine innings. He finished the year with 3.46 ERA.

Scouting Report: I've always had an analytical crush on Sears, even going back to his days at The Citadel. Last season the hard-throwing left-hander put together his finest showing to date, showcasing an above-average fastball sitting in the 93- to 95-mph, a plus slider, and an average changeup. Sears' breaking ball is especially difficult on left-handed hitters, almost death to them. He works methodically (read: slow) and exclusively from the stretch. There's some Ted Lilly to him, but he's almost guaranteed to get pigeonholed into a relief role.

Ceiling: 1.0- to 1.5-win player
Risk: Low to Moderate
MLB ETA: 2022

15. Yoendrys Gomez, RHP

	FB	CB	SL	CH	Command	Overall
	60	50	55	55	50	45

Born: 10/15/99	Age: 22	Bats: R	Top Comp: N/A
Height: 6-3	Weight: 175	Throws: R	

Season	Team	Age	Level	IP	TBF	K/9	K%	BB/9	BB%	K-BB%	ERA	FIP	xFIP	Pit/Bat
2018	NYY	18	R	38.2	161	10.01	26.71%	3.49	9.32%	17.39%	2.33	3.40	3.65	1.84
2019	NYY	19	A	29.2	124	8.49	22.58%	3.03	8.06%	14.52%	2.12	3.74	4.64	3.84
2019	NYY	19	A	26.2	119	8.44	21.01%	3.04	7.56%	13.45%	6.07	4.28	4.52	4.00
2021	NYY	21	A	23.2	96	11.03	30.21%	3.42	9.38%	20.83%	3.42	4.27	3.84	4.24

Background: Unlike a lot of the club's notable prospects signed off the international market, Gomez signed for a small pittance – comparatively speaking, of course. The big spending organization inked a deal with the wiry right-hander for just $50,000 in 2016. And in each of the ensuing seasons Gomez continues to make it look like larger and larger bargain. Last year was a bit of a rough one for the young hurler, at least in terms of health. He was delayed to start the year. The cause: "a sore arm." When he did make it back to Low-A with the Tarpons, Gomez was brilliant. In nine abbreviated starts he tossed 23.2 innings, averaging 11 strikeouts and 3.4 walks per nine innings to go along with a 3.42 ERA. His season ended prematurely in late July as he was placed on the COVID list.

Scouting Report: Three above-average or better offerings in his arsenal: a lively fastball that sits in the mid-90s and reaching as high as 98 mph, a late-tilting slider, and a tremendously fading, downward-biting changeup. He'll also mix a slow, loopy curveball as well. But here's the truth:

1. Gomez is entering his age-22 season ;
2. He's also entering his sixth season in the Yankees' organization;
3. He's thrown a grand total of 162.2 innings
4. And his career high for a season's workload is 56.1 innings;
5. And he's never been above A-ball.

That's an awful lot to overcome. And he's going to have to start making up for lost time in 2022.

Ceiling: 1.0 -to 1.5-win player
Risk: Moderate
MLB ETA: 2024

16. Anthony Garcia, 1B/RF

	Hit	Power	SB	Patience	Glove	Overall
	40/55	50/60	50/40	55	50	45

Born: 09/05/00	Age: 21	Bats: B	Top Comp: N/A
Height: 6-5	Weight: 204	Throws: R	

Season	Team	Age	Level	PA	1B	2B	3B	HR	SB	CS	BB%	K%	AVG	OBP	SLG	ISO
2018	NYY	17	R	23	1	1	0	0	0	0	8.70%	30.43%	0.095	0.174	0.143	0.048
2018	NYY	17	R	19	0	1	1	0	0	0	15.79%	42.11%	0.125	0.263	0.313	0.188
2018	NYY	17	R	175	19	6	3	10	3	0	10.29%	41.71%	0.244	0.320	0.513	0.269
2019	NYY	18	R	24	1	2	1	1	0	0	20.83%	37.50%	0.294	0.417	0.706	0.412
2021	NYY	20	CPX	85	12	1	0	8	10	1	21.18%	29.41%	0.318	0.459	0.697	0.379
2021	NYY	20	A	68	8	2	0	6	5	0	19.12%	36.76%	0.291	0.426	0.655	0.364

Background: Like a quote from a yearbook in the 70s, Garcia's trek through the low levels of the minor leagues has been an odd and strange journey. The herculean 6-foot-5, 204-pound prospect looked abysmal during his pro debut in 2018, hitting an aggregate .218/.300/.456 with a whopper of strikeout total, 88, in only 217 plate appearances (40.6% K-rate). New York bumped him up to the Appalachian League the following year, 2019, and the results were phenomenal, slugging .294/.417/.706 – though that's just in six games. That's all he played in that season. Last year, Garcia split time between the Florida Complex League and the Low-A, hitting an aggregate .306/.444/.678 with three doubles and 14 homeruns in only 39 games. His overall production, per *Weighted Runs Created Plus*, topped the league average production by a staggering 87%.

Scouting Report: Where to even begin? The lone reliable data set is from four years ago, when he was 17 and quite terrible. Since then, though, he's compiled 45 games of fantastic production, across two seasons, spanning three total years. For now, here's what we can gleam from that

45-game sample: big swing-and-miss issues (33.3% K-rate), very patient approach at the plate, massive power, and above-average speed. Built like an ideal middle-of-the-lineup hitter, tall, lean, strong; Garcia shows plenty of bat speed and some to spare. His swing and swing mechanics are very Anthony Rizzo-like. And when Garcia makes contact it's an explosion. He's very under-the-radar prospect and there's no in between: Garcia either ends up as massive star or he ends up punching out way too frequently. I like him a lot, though.

Ceiling: 1.5-win player
Risk: High
MLB ETA: 2024/2025

17. Alexander Vargas, SS

Hit	Power	SB	Patience	Glove	Overall
40/50	30/40	60	50	55/60	40

Born: 10/29/01	Age: 20	Bats: B	Top Comp: N/A
Height: 5-11	Weight: 148	Throws: R	

Season	Team	Age	Level	PA	1B	2B	3B	HR	SB	CS	BB%	K%	AVG	OBP	SLG	ISO
2019	NYY	17	R	173	23	5	5	1	13	0	8.09%	12.72%	0.219	0.301	0.335	0.116
2019	NYY	17	R	44	4	5	2	0	2	3	9.09%	13.64%	0.289	0.364	0.526	0.237
2021	NYY	19	CPX	174	30	7	1	3	17	8	11.49%	22.99%	0.273	0.362	0.393	0.120

Background: Recognized and touted on the international market for his defensive prowess and plus speed, the Yankees – once again – dipped into their deep pockets and signed the then-16-year-old shortstop to big $2.5 million deal. Vargas spent his debut season, 2019, mostly battling – and struggling – against the Gulf Coast League: he batted .219/.301/.335 with five doubles, five triples, one triple, and a perfect 13-for-13 in stolen bases. Last season the front office sent the 5-foot-11, 148-pound middle infielder to their Florida Complex League and the results were…well…what you'd expect out of speedy, defensive-minded shortstop. He hit .273/.362/.393 with seven doubles, one triple, and three homeruns. Per *Weighted Runs Created Plus*, his production topped the league average by 5%.

Scouting Report: Plus speed. And per Clay Davenport's defensive metrics, Vargas saved two runs above average in 42 games. Now the hitting: average patience, below-average hit tool, but he's at least flashing gap-to-gap power with enough pop to belt out eight or so homeruns in a full season. It's important to note that Vargas was 19-years-old last season, playing in the Complex League where recently signed high school draft picks pop up. And Vargas was essentially a league average bat. Like a lot of the club's other young hitters, Vargas' flyball rate dramatically increased from his output in 2019, going from 38.6% to 44.9%. He's tracking as a backup utility guy, at least for now.

Ceiling: 1.0-win player
Risk: Moderate
MLB ETA: 2023

18. Hayden Wesneski, RHP

FB	CB	SL	CH	Command	Overall
60	50	50	N/A	55	40

Born: 12/05/97	Age: 24	Bats: R	Top Comp: N/A
Height: 6-3	Weight: 210	Throws: R	

Season	Team	Age	Level	IP	TBF	K/9	K%	BB/9	BB%	K-BB%	ERA	FIP	xFIP	Pit/Bat
2019	NYY	21	R	28.1	125	9.53	24.00%	1.91	4.80%	19.20%	4.76	2.86	3.42	3.50
2021	NYY	23	A+	36.1	134	11.64	35.07%	2.23	6.72%	28.36%	1.49	2.72	3.07	3.62
2021	NYY	23	AA	83.0	344	9.98	26.74%	2.39	6.40%	20.35%	4.01	4.00	3.79	3.74
2021	NYY	23	AAA	11.0	46	9.82	26.09%	4.09	10.87%	15.22%	3.27	2.54	3.67	3.33

Background: Prior to the Orioles selection of Colton Cowser with the fifth overall pick last July, Sam Houston State University had only churned out a couple six round selections as their best draft picks for the better part of a decade. One of those sixth round picks: Hayden Wesneski, a 6-foot-3, 210-pound right-hander with some funk in his arm action. After a solid peripheral-based debut in the Appalachian League in 2019, Wesneski rocketed through Low-A, Double-A, and Triple-A during his first full season in the Yankees' organization. In a total of 25 appearances, 24 of which were starts, he threw 130.1 innings with 151 punch outs and just 36 free passes to go along with a 3.25 ERA. Wesneski averaged 10.4 strikeouts and just 2.4 walks per nine innings.

Scouting Report: An intriguing pitcher with an intriguing arsenal, but it's not really about the entire arsenal. It's about his two separate fastballs. One is a Brandon Webb-esque bowling ball of an offering with tumble and fade like a changeup. And the other, well, it's just pure gas. Unless the radar gun was wrong – and the eye test doesn't appear to be that off – he touched a scorching 100 mph. Curveball and slider are average. And I didn't see a changeup during the outing I was scouting. I do think he could be a valuable two-pitch reliever just using both versions of his fastball.

Ceiling: 1.0 win player
Risk: Moderate
MLB ETA: 2022

19. Josh Breaux, C

Hit	Power	SB	Patience	Glove	Overall
40/45	50/55	30	45	45	40

Born: 10/07/97	Age: 24	Bats: R	Top Comp: N/A
Height: 6-1	Weight: 220	Throws: R	

Season	Team	Age	Level	PA	1B	2B	3B	HR	SB	CS	BB%	K%	AVG	OBP	SLG	ISO
2018	NYY	20	A-	105	19	9	0	0	0	0	2.86%	19.05%	0.280	0.295	0.370	0.090
2019	NYY	21	A	216	31	10	0	13	0	0	6.94%	27.31%	0.271	0.324	0.518	0.246
2021	NYY	23	A+	276	34	12	0	17	0	0	7.97%	26.45%	0.252	0.308	0.504	0.252
2021	NYY	23	AA	106	10	8	0	6	1	0	3.77%	24.53%	0.240	0.274	0.500	0.260

Background: Still one of the greatest happenings involving the talented backstop took place on draft night: the ultimate "bro" Nick Swisher got to call out Josh Breaux (pronounced: bro) as the Yankees' second round selection in 2018. Since then the 6-foot-1, 220-pound backstop looked comfortable in Staten Island during his debut, and showed some offensive promise during his sophomore professional season with Charleston. Last season the McLennan Community College product opened the year up with Hudson Valley, hitting .252/.308/.504 before earning a promotion up to Somerset. Between both stops Breaux batted an OBP-deficient .249/.398/.503 with 20 doubles and 23 homeruns. His overall production, per *Weighted Runs Created Plus*, topped the league average mark by 8%.

Snippet from The 2020 Prospect Digest Handbook: Breaux looks like the bat first, power-oriented backstop, though he won't kill a team behind the dish. I still think he's going to continue to battle swing-and-miss issues as he progresses up the ladder. He's going to win a lot of homerun derbies throughout his professional career.

Scouting Report: Consider the following:

- Since 2006, only three 23-year-old hitters posted a wRC+ between 100 and 110 with a walk rate between 7% and 9% and a K-rate between 25.5% and 27.5% in a High-A season with one organization (min. 275 PA): Calvin Anderson, Nick Zammarelli III, and – of course – Josh Breaux.

Defensively speaking, Breaux is not as poor as Austin Wells, but he's not all that much better either. And like his fellow prospect counterpart he's barely throwing any would-be base stealers out (just 17% for his professional career). Above-average power with very little patience at the plate. And the hit tool is a bit subpar as well. Let's recap: poor glove, below average bat and walk rates, and above-average power. If it sounds like a Quad-A player, plays like a Quad-A player, and projects like a Quad-A player, then he must be a Quad-A player.

Ceiling: 1.0-win player
Risk: Moderate
MLB ETA: 2023

20. Brock Selvidge, LHP

FB	SL	CH	Command	Overall
50/55	50/55	55	45	40

Born: 08/28/02	Age: 19	Bats: R	Top Comp: N/A
Height: 6-3	Weight: 205	Throws: L	

Background: Chandler, Arizona-based Hamilton High School has produced 16 total draft picks. But here's where it gets interesting: eight of them signed for at least $150,000. And of those eight, four of them signed for at least a quarter-million dollars. The school's most famous alum: Cody Bellinger, who received a $700,000 bonus from the Dodgers as a fourth rounder in 2013. As for Brock Selvidge, the young right-hander was committed to Louisiana State University but bypassed the opportunity when the Yankees drafted him in the third round last July. Of course, handing the 18-year-old kid $1.5 million surely helps. That deal, by the way, was more than $800,000 above the recommended slot bonus.

Scouting Report: A standard three-pitch mix: a low-90s fastball, a slider that projects to grow some legs and reach an above-average grade, and a 55-grade diving, fading changeup. Mechanics are pretty clean, repeatable. At full maturation he projects to have three above-average offerings. It's a nice little draft pick and signing. Now it's time for the Yankees' player development program to eke out that projection.

Ceiling: 1.0-win player
Risk: Moderate
MLB ETA: 2025

Oakland Athletics

Top Prospects

1. Tyler Soderstrom, C/1B

Hit	Power	SB	Patience	Glove	Overall
55	55/60	30	50	50	60

Born: 11/24/01	Age: 20	Bats: L	Top Comp: Paul Konerko
Height: 6-2	Weight: 200	Throws: R	

Season	Team	Age	Level	PA	1B	2B	3B	HR	SB	CS	BB%	K%	AVG	OBP	SLG	ISO
2021	OAK	19	A	254	35	20	1	12	2	1	10.63%	24.02%	0.306	0.390	0.568	0.261

Background: The first round of the 1993 draft produced a ton of big league talent, including: Alex Rodriguez, Torii Hunter, Derrek Lee, Chris Carpenter, Billy Wagner, Jason Varitek, and Trot Nixon. But one player, almost no one remembers, was drafted ahead of the entire group sans Rodriguez. That player: Steve Soderstrom, a right-hander out of California State University chosen by the Giants with the sixth overall pick, who would sign a deal worth $750,000. Fast forward 17 years and there was another Soderstrom that heard his name in the first round – Tyler, Steve's high school-aged son. Taken by the Athletics with the 26th overall pick and signed for a hefty $3.3 million, the younger Soderstrom put together a dynamic, awe-inspiring debut with the Stockton Ports last summer. That is, until a back injury forced him to the injured list at the end of July. Prior to the injury, though, Soderstrom slugged a hearty .306/.390/.568 with 20 doubles, one triple, and 12 homeruns – as a 19-year-old in Low-A. His overall production, per *Weighted Runs Created Plus*, was a whopping 45% better than the league average threshold.

Scouting Report: Just for fun, here's Soderstrom's numbers prorated for a full 162-game season: 57 doubles, three triples, 34 homeruns. With respect to his actual production, consider the following:

- Since 2006, only three 19-year-old hitters met the following criteria in a Low-A season with one organization (min. 250 PA): 140 to 145 wRC+ total, a walk rate between 9% and 11%, and a strikeout rate between 22% and 25%. Those three hitters: Kyle Blanks, Caleb Grindl, and – of course – Mr. Tyler Soderstrom.

A low maintenance swing: short, simple, and quick. Soderstrom generates above-average, maybe even plus power, with a lot of natural loft. He stays compact and shows no platoon splits. It's concerning – needless to say – that a 19-year-old missed considerable time with a back injury, so hopefully that doesn't impact his future greatly. Defensively, he's a first baseman feigning the ability to play catcher. In terms of offensive upside, think .300/.380/.540.

Ceiling: 4.0-win player
Risk: Moderate
MLB ETA: 2024/2025

2. Nick Allen, 2B/SS

Hit	Power	SB	Patience	Glove	Overall
50	40	55	50	70	60

Born: 10/08/98	Age: 23	Bats: R	Top Comp: Brandon Crawford
Height: 5-8	Weight: 166	Throws: R	

Season	Team	Age	Level	PA	1B	2B	3B	HR	SB	CS	BB%	K%	AVG	OBP	SLG	ISO
2018	OAK	19	A	512	87	17	6	0	24	8	6.64%	16.60%	0.239	0.301	0.302	0.063
2019	OAK	20	A+	328	54	22	5	3	13	5	8.54%	15.85%	0.292	0.363	0.434	0.142
2021	OAK	22	AA	229	48	9	2	6	8	6	7.86%	20.09%	0.319	0.374	0.471	0.152
2021	OAK	22	AAA	151	25	8	0	0	4	1	7.28%	19.87%	0.243	0.302	0.301	0.059

Background: A fantastic job of scouting by the organization's front office. Oakland selected the undersized, twitchy middle-infield prospect in the third round five years ago. And since then, the light-hitting 5-foot-8, 166-pounder has developed into a legitimate Top 100 prospect. Allen, the 81st overall player chosen that year, put together a defensive-first, offensive punchless debut in the Arizona Summer League: he hit a lowly .254/.322/.326. And his follow up sophomore campaign was even worse as the franchise aggressively challenged him with his assignment to Low-A. In 121 games with the Beloit Snappers, the former $2 million bonus baby put together a paltry .239/.301/.302 showing. Then…something started to happen with Nick Allen, a transformation of sorts. He began to drive the ball with more authority, all the while the club continued to shoot him through the farm system. In 2019, now in High-A with the Stockton Ports, Allen slugged .292/.363/.434 with 22 doubles, five triples, and a trio of homeruns. Last summer, as minor league baseball returned to action from its COVID imposed break, Allen picked up right where he left off. In 50 games against the minors' toughest challenge, Double-A, Allen flashed tremendous offensive potential as he hit .319/.374/.471. His minor league season was temporarily placed on hold as he was rostered – and eventually starred – on Team USA, where he was named as the team's *Best Defensive Player*. After his return from Olympic action, Allen spent the remainder of the year in AAA, hitting a mediocre .243/.302/.301 across 39 games.

Snippet from The 2020 Prospect Digest Handbook: Elite levels of value on the defensive side of the ball, Allen's now transformed into not only a competent hitter, but a potential table-setter. Strong bat-to-ball skills with an average eye at the plate and plus speed, Allen's added enough gap-to-gap power to be a viable future big league hitter. The defense will carry him to The Show, anything else is just a cherry on top. Allen looks like a .270/.330/.390-type hitter during his peak at the big league level. He's going to win multiple Gold Gloves too.

Scouting Report: Nick Allen, the little 5-foot-8, 166-pound shortstop out of Park High School, is my favorite prospect in the minor leagues. And he's been that for several years now, even before his bat had an offensive pulse. Allen will draw the occasional walk, mix in strong contact skills, and flash doubles power with the rare homerun. He'll also swipe 20 bags or so in a full big league season, as well. Oakland currently has former All-Star Elvis Andrus under contract through 2022 with a vesting option for 2023; the option kicks in with 550 plate appearances, which is unlikely to happen. The front office shifted Allen from a full time shortstop to a part-time shortstop/second baseman, but that's likely in response to Andrus. There's no reason to expect him to play anywhere but shortstop at the big league level. Again, I think Allen's going to be a Gold Glove-winning shortstop with the offensive upside of a .270/.330/.390 hitter.

Ceiling: 4.0-win player
Risk: Moderate
MLB ETA: 2022

3. Zack Gelof, 3B

Hit	Power	SB	Patience	Glove	Overall
50	50	50	55	50	55

Born: 10/19/99	Age: 22	Bats: R	Top Comp: N/A
Height: 6-3	Weight: 205	Throws: R	

Season	Team	Age	Level	PA	1B	2B	3B	HR	SB	CS	BB%	K%	AVG	OBP	SLG	ISO
2021	OAK	21	A	145	21	8	1	7	11	2	13.10%	24.83%	0.298	0.393	0.548	0.250
2021	OAK	21	AAA	13	6	1	0	0	0	0	7.69%	15.38%	0.583	0.615	0.667	0.083

Background: Highly decorated coming out of Cape Henlopen High School in 2018, Gelof was awarded the Delaware Gatorade Player of the Year, as well as earning the distinction of the Delaware Baseball Coaches Player of the Year, after capping off a dominant amateur career in tremendous fashion: the 6-foot-3, 205-pound infielder batted a scorching .465 while leading the state in hits (35), runs (37), and homeruns (7). He also knocked in 17 runs and went a perfect 28-to-28 in the stolen base category as well. And not to be outdone: Gelof starred on the mound as well; he topped 26 innings with 34 punch outs and a tidy 1.30 ERA to go along with a 4-0 win-loss record. Cleveland took a late round flier on the talented prospect in the June draft that year. Gelof bypassed their offer and headed to Virginia. And he didn't miss a beat as he immediately stepped into the Cavaliers' lineup as a true freshman. Appearing in 56 games for the ACC powerhouse, he slugged .313/.377/.396 with 15 extra-base hits and 16 stolen bases. Gelof got off to a spectacular start to the COVID-shortened 2020 season as well, batting .349/.469/.746 in 18 games. He capped off his successful collegiate career by hitting .312/.393/.485 with career highs in doubles (18) and homeruns (9) in 2021. Oakland drafted him in the second round, 60th overall, and signed him to a deal worth $1,157,400 – the full slot value. The young third baseman ripped through the Low-A West League during his debut, slugging .298/.393/.548 in 32 games. He also appeared in a trio of Triple-A games as well; he promptly went 7-for-13 with a double.

Scouting Report: Per the usual, here's what I wrote about the second rounded immediately after the draft:

"Consider the following:

- *Between 2011 and 2020, only five ACC hitters met the following criteria in a season (min. 250 PA): .300/.380/.480 with a walk rate between 9% and 11% and a strikeout rate between 13% and 16%. Those five hitters: Devon Travis, Logan Warmoth, Preston Palmeiro, Matt Vierling, and Ben Breazeale.*
- *It's a mixed bag of results: Devon Travis had his moments as a solid big league infielder. Logan Warmoth was a first round pick by the Blue Jays in 2017 out of UNC, but has struggled in the mid- to upper-levels of the minor leagues. Matt Vierling made his big league debut in 2021 with the Phillies. Palmeiro is on the downward slope of his professional career. And Breazeale isn't playing affiliated ball anymore.*

Recent top hitting prospects out of Virginia, for whatever reason, have really struggled to prove themselves in professional ball. And Gelof may eventually follow suit. He's a non-traditional third baseman in the sense that he runs better than expected, but never showed above-average power – even in Virginia's cavernous ballpark – during his collegiate career. He plays a decent hot corner, but stiff hands and movements may relegate him to another position. At the plate, he starts from a wide base, which likely gets shortened in the Oakland organization. The Athletics have a history of developing these type of under-the-radar players and tapping into more power than expected. Looks like a bench option at this point."

After his explosive start to his professional career, I'm going to bump his ceiling up to a solid 55-grade.

Ceiling: 3.0-win player
Risk: Moderate
MLB ETA: 2022/2023

4. Pedro Pineda, CF

	Hit	Power	SB	Patience	Glove	Overall
	30/50	35/55	50	50	50/60	55

Born: 09/06/03	Age: 18	Bats: R	Top Comp: N/A
Height: 6-1	Weight: 170	Throws: R	

Season	Team	Age	Level	PA	1B	2B	3B	HR	SB	CS	BB%	K%	AVG	OBP	SLG	ISO
2021	OAK	17	DSL	40	5	1	1	0	3	2	12.50%	32.50%	0.200	0.300	0.286	0.086
2021	OAK	17	CPX	77	11	2	2	1	3	3	16.88%	36.36%	0.258	0.403	0.403	0.145

Background: Another example of the club's willingness to spend top dollar on the international amateur market. Oakland inked the toolsy, raw teenage center fielder to a massive $2.5 million deal in January 2021. And almost immediately the club sent him straight into rookie ball. Ranked as the 13th best prospect on the international scene last year by MLB Pipeline, Pineda struggled a bit in the Dominican Summer League to start his debut, batting a lowly .200/.300/.286 through 10 games. But things seemed to click for the 6-foot-1, 170-pound outfielder when he moved stateside to the Arizona Complex League. In 23 games, spanning 77 plate appearances, Pineda batted a respectable, red flag-pocked .258/.403/.403 with two doubles, two triples, and one homerun. His overall production, per *Weighted Runs Created Plus*, was 21% above the league average mark.

Scouting Report: Like a lot of the A's top prospect bats, Pineda swings and misses *a lot*. He whiffed in 32.5% of his plate appearances in the foreign rookie league and bumped that tally up a bit as he moved stateside (36.4%). He's a chaser, loves pitches high and low. But I think some of that corrects itself as he matures – especially given his level of competition last season. Quick bat. Athletic. He just "looks" like damn ballplayer. One more thought: I wouldn't be surprised to him win a Gold Glove or two at full maturity.

Ceiling: 3.0-win player
Risk: Moderate
MLB ETA: 2025

5. A.J. Puk, LHP

	FB	CB	SL	CH	Command	Overall
	65	N/A	70	50	50	50

Born: 04/25/95	Age: 27	Bats: L	Top Comp: Andrew Miller
Height: 6-7	Weight: 248	Throws: L	

Season	Team	Age	Level	IP	TBF	K/9	K%	BB/9	BB%	K-BB%	ERA	FIP	xFIP	Pit/Bat
2019	OAK	24	AAA	11.0	44	13.09	36.36%	2.45	6.82%	29.55%	4.91	5.52	4.25	3.61
2021	OAK	26	AAA	48.2	226	10.73	25.66%	3.51	8.41%	17.26%	6.10	6.05	4.79	3.80

Background: It bears repeating – only because I still can't quite wrap my own head around it, even after all these years – but the 2016 Florida Gators team was so remarkably talented. The roster included the likes of: A.J. Puk, Brady Singer, Jackson Kowar, Alex Faedo, Dane Dunning, Shaun Anderson, Kirby Snead, Scott Moss, Logan Shore, Pete Alonso, and Jonathan India. If that roster was a Michelangelo paint it would've been The Creation of Adam. As for Puk, well, the former sixth overall pick in 2016 draft seemed destined for stardom – a big, projectable, hard-throwing left-hander with a wicked repertoire. Then life, as it tends to do, got in the way. Less than two years into his professional career, the 6-foot-7, 248-pound southpaw missed the entirety of 2018 as he recovered from Tommy John surgery. Two years later he would miss the 2020 campaign dealing with a wonky shoulder, which would eventually require a surgical procedure termed "a debridement of his labrum and rotator cuff." Finally healthy – again – Puk made a total 41 appearances between Las Vegas and Oakland last season. The peripherals for both levels were similar: 10.7 K/9 and 3.5 BB/9 in Triple-A and 10.8 K/9 and 4.1 BB/9 with Oakland.

Snippet from The 2020 Prospect Digest Handbook: He's a potential bonafide ace – if, *if*, he can maintain a sub-4.0 walk rate.

Scouting Report: Prior to the 2021 season A's General Manager David Forst indicated that the plan was for Puk to continue down the path as a starting pitcher. A year later and that's still to be determined. Of course, two major arm surgeries tend to have that impact. The big left-hander's still showcasing a plus heater, sitting comfortably in the mid-90s; a wickedly devastating slider; and an average changeup. He'll also mix in a rare curveball, though I didn't see one during the games I scouted. Without the arm woes Puk seemed destined to be a front-of-the-rotation caliber starting pitcher. Now, though, he may be heading down the path of Andrew Miller.

Ceiling: 2.5-win player
Risk: Moderate
MLB ETA: Debuted in 2019

6. Max Muncy, SS

Hit	Power	SB	Patience	Glove	Overall
35/50	35/45	50	50	50	50

Born: 08/25/02	Age: 19	Bats: R	Top Comp: N/A
Height: 6-1	Weight: 180	Throws: R	

Season	Team	Age	Level	PA	1B	2B	3B	HR	SB	CS	BB%	K%	AVG	OBP	SLG	ISO
2021	OAK	18	CPX	34	4	0	0	0	1	0	8.82%	35.29%	0.129	0.206	0.129	0.000

Background: As soon as the Athletics snagged the wiry shortstop in the latter part of the first round, the blogosphere *blew* up – perhaps – with one of the most charming coincidences in recent memory. Muncy, who hails from Thousand Oaks High School, not only has the same name as Dodgers' two-time All-Star infielder, but also shares the same birthday as well. Both players were born on August 25th – though the teenage phenom is 12 years younger. The *LA Times'* Player of the Year recipient in 2021, Muncy, who led his squad to the Southern Section Championship, hit a scorching .469 (45 for 96) with 11 dingers, 49 RBIs, and 10 stolen bases. The Athletics drafted him in the opening round, 25th overall, and signed the talented shortstop for $2.85 million bonus, slightly above the recommended slot ($2,740,300). Muncy the Younger appeared in 11 games with the organization's Arizona Complex League affiliate, hitting a disappointingly bad .129/.206/.129.

Scouting Report: Per the usual, here's what I wrote about the teenage shortstop immediately after the draft:

"A natural born shortstop who (A) should have no problem sticking at the position and (B) shows a little bit of flair for the dramatic. Strong arm, but not elite. He'll make all the throws – accurately. Surprising pop for a wiry, thin-framed middle infielder. He projects to add some strength as he matures. Muncy shows a willingness to shoot the ball to the opposite field with his in-and-out swing and approach at the plate. He's not going to be a star, but he should settle in nicely at the big league level."

Ceiling: 2.0-win player
Risk: Moderate
MLB ETA: 2025

7. Brayan Buelvas, OF

Hit	Power	SB	Patience	Glove	Overall
40/45	50/55	50	50	45/50	50

Born: 06/08/02	Age: 20	Bats: R	Top Comp: N/A
Height: 5-11	Weight: 155	Throws: R	

Season	Team	Age	Level	PA	1B	2B	3B	HR	SB	CS	BB%	K%	AVG	OBP	SLG	ISO
2019	OAK	17	R	186	28	10	7	3	12	5	11.83%	24.73%	0.300	0.392	0.506	0.206
2019	OAK	17	R	88	13	5	1	0	4	4	9.09%	15.91%	0.244	0.330	0.333	0.090
2021	OAK	19	A	392	45	11	4	16	17	7	9.44%	24.23%	0.219	0.306	0.412	0.193

Background: Compared to some of the club's other higher profile players signed off the international free agent market, Buelvas's $100,000 bonus is a downright steal. Signed out of Monteria, Colombia, mid-summer of 2018, Buelvas looked incredibly comfortable – and quite good – against the Arizona Summer League competition during his debut the following season. He slugged .300/.392/.506 with 10 doubles, seven triples, and three triples, in only 44 games of action. Last season the A's bounced the then-19-year-old straight up to Low-A. And the results were…mixed. Appearing in 88 games with the Stockton Ports, the 5-foot-11, 155-pound outfield vagabond batted .219/.306/.412 with 11 doubles, four triples, and 16 homeruns. Per *Weighted Runs Created Plus*, his overall production was 12% *below* the league average threshold.

Snippet from The 2020 Prospect Digest Handbook: Buelvas's thump really started pounding loudly after his jump to the stateside rookie league. The swing-and-miss numbers – he fanned in nearly a quarter of his plate appearances – are a concern; though he whiffed only 18 times over his final 73 plate appearances. Above-average speed, a chance at 50-grade power, and a solid hit tool.

Scouting Report: It was an interesting season for the teenage outfielder. He showed incredible promise as speed /power oriented outfielder. His peripherals, too, were quite solid: he walked in 9.4% of his plate appearances and his potential problematic K-rate from rookie ball (24.7%) maintained status (24.2%) quo despite the big leap in competition. The problem, of course, is the hit tool basically stagnated. And it didn't really show any type of maturation as the season progressed either. Per *FanGraphs*, his average exit velocity was pretty impressive too: 89 mph. If the hit tool creeps up into the 45-grade territory he's a lock to be a starter. If it climbs up into average territory he may see a couple All-Star caliber seasons. Buelvas just "feels" like a guy that clicks in 2022.

Ceiling: 1.5- to 2.0-win player
Risk: Moderate to High
MLB ETA: 2024

8. Daulton Jefferies, RHP

FB	SL	CU	CH	Command	Overall
55	50	55	60	60	45

Born: 08/02/95	Age: 26	Bats: R	Top Comp: Josh Tomlin
Height: 6-0	Weight: 182	Throws: R	

Season	Team	Age	Level	IP	TBF	K/9	K%	BB/9	BB%	K-BB%	ERA	FIP	xFIP	Pit/Bat
2019	OAK	23	A+	15.0	57	12.60	36.84%	1.20	3.51%	33.33%	2.40	2.13	2.39	3.30
2019	OAK	23	AA	64.0	262	10.13	27.48%	0.98	2.67%	24.81%	3.66	3.19	3.17	3.84
2021	OAK	25	AAA	77.0	332	7.95	20.48%	1.29	3.31%	17.17%	4.91	4.95	4.94	3.45

Background: A former favorite collegiate arm of mine – from way back when, or at least it seems. And, unfortunately for the former early pick, his development was significantly delayed: he lost nearly two full seasons recovering from an early 2017 Tommy John procedure.

Finally healthy to start the 2019 season, Jefferies quickly made up for lost time as he made a brief five-game tour through High-A before earning a promotion up to the minors' toughest challenge, Double-A. And he sparkled. The former Cal product finished the year with averages of 10.6 strikeouts and 1.0 walks per nine innings. Oakland taxied the then-24-year-old during the COVID-impacted year, bringing him up for one brief, and quite unsuccessful, start. Last season, Jefferies spent the majority of the year with the Las Vegas Aviators, posting an impeccable 68-to-11 strikeout-to-walk ratio in 77.0 innings of work. He also appeared in another five contests with the A's, as well, averaging just 4.8 K/9 and 2.4 BB/9.

Snippet from The 2020 Prospect Digest Handbook: He's very reminiscent of a Tim Hudson-like competitor.

Scouting Report: Two years ago, I envisioned that he would have a stranglehold on a spot in Oakland's rotation, but that failed to materialize. Now Jefferies, the 37th overall pick in 2016, is entering his age-26 season with just 17 big league innings on his resume. He's one of the best pinpoint artists in professional baseball, commanding the zone with snipe-like precision. Above-average low 90s heater. An average slider. An above-average cutter. And a plus changeup. Since entering college the 6-foot, 182-pound right-hander has also never thrown 100 innings in a season. Josh Tomlin seems like a best case scenario at this point. One more note: he dealt with more arm injuries in 2021.

Ceiling: 1.5-win player
Risk: Moderate
MLB ETA: Debuted in 2020

9. Lawrence Butler, 1B/OF

Hit	Power	SB	Patience	Glove	Overall
30/40	55/60	55/50	55	50	45

Born: 07/10/00	Age: 21	Bats: L	Top Comp: N/A
Height: 6-3	Weight: 210	Throws: R	

Season	Team	Age	Level	PA	1B	2B	3B	HR	SB	CS	BB%	K%	AVG	OBP	SLG	ISO
2018	OAK	17	R	124	17	4	2	1	3	1	14.52%	34.68%	0.226	0.339	0.330	0.104
2019	OAK	18	A-	221	23	5	2	4	1	0	11.76%	40.72%	0.177	0.276	0.286	0.109
2021	OAK	20	A	396	47	20	4	17	26	4	13.89%	33.08%	0.263	0.364	0.499	0.236
2021	OAK	20	A+	54	11	4	0	2	3	1	7.41%	27.78%	0.340	0.389	0.540	0.200

Background: Georgia-based Westlake High School has been home to five draft picks in their history: Courteney Stewart (1994, 27th round), Eddie Rush (2005, 44th round), Rashad Brown (2012, 26th round), Myles Austin (2019, 20th round), and – of course – Lawrence Butler.

Taken in the sixth round four years ago and handed a deal worth $285,000, the lefty-swinging first baseman / outfielder put together a quiet explosion of offensive production during the 2021 season. In 102 games, most of which were spent in Low-A, the then-20-year-old slugged a robust .273/.367/.504 with 24 doubles, four triples, 19 homeruns, and 29 stolen bases (in 34 total attempts).

Scouting Report: Butler's offensive firepower that was displayed last season was more shocking considering his abysmal showing in 2018 (.226/.339/.330) and 2019 (.177/.276/.286). And, perhaps not surprising, Butler's cut from the Three True Outcomes mold: he walked nearly 14% of the time in Low-A, whiffed in slightly more than a third of the time, and was on pace for a 30-homer season. Butler's always swung-and-missed way too much, but last season's tally marks a career low. With respect to his work in Low-A, consider the following:

- Since 2006, there were only three 20-year-old hitters that met the following criteria in a Low-A season with one organization (min. 350 PA): a wRC+ total between 118 and 128, a walk rate north of 12% and a strikeout rate of at least 27%. Those three hitters: Brandon Nimmo, Garrett Whitley, and Lawrence Butler.

If I were betting man, Butler's the exact type of player that Oakland develops to its fullest extent. The arrow is definitely trending upward.

Ceiling: 1.5-win player
Risk: Moderate
MLB ETA: 2024

10. Jorge Juan, RHP

	FB	CB	CH	Command	Overall
	70	50/55	45	40/45	45

Born: 03/06/99	Age: 23	Bats: R	Top Comp: N/A
Height: 6-8	Weight: 200	Throws: R	

Season	Team	Age	Level	IP	TBF	K/9	K%	BB/9	BB%	K-BB%	ERA	FIP	xFIP	Pit/Bat
2018	OAK	19	R	43.0	194	10.05	24.74%	5.02	12.37%	12.37%	2.51	3.71	3.99	1.99
2019	OAK	20	R	33.1	166	9.72	21.69%	8.91	19.88%	1.81%	7.29	5.92	6.21	2.35
2021	OAK	22	A	21.0	82	13.29	37.80%	3.00	8.54%	29.27%	3.86	3.66	3.92	3.98

Background: From a sheer frame size point of view, there are very few professional ballplayers that can match Jorge Juan height – 6-foot-8 – and lean weight, which is *generously* listed at 200 pounds. Aesthetically, he looks closer to 220 or 230 pounds. Signed out of Payita, Dominican Republic, Juan wouldn't make his professional debut until he was 19-years-old, which is closer to AARP status for foreign signed players. The gargantuan right-hander spent a year in the foreign rookie leagues, and he struggled through another campaign in the stateside rookie leagues the following season. Last season, though, the organization decided to aggressively challenging the erratic flame-thrower. And the results weren't terrible. Opening the year with six appearances, four of which were starts, with the Stockton Ports, Juan struck out 31 against just seven free passes in only 21.0 innings of work. He was promoted up to High-A in early August for another final two (disastrous) starts. Juan finished the year with a 13.5 K/9 and 4.4 BB/9.

Scouting Report: There's no chance Juan develops into a starting pitcher. And it's a fallacy to even suggest it. He's (A) entering his age-23 season with (B) a total of 103.0 innings of professional ball on his resume and (C) lacks the command, (D) a second offspeed weapon, and (E) enough confidence to trust his slow stuff. But what he does look like, though, is a potential dominant backend relief option, showcasing a 70-grade fastball and a curveball that flashes above-average at times. Right now he's succeeding on pure velocity, which plays up due to his intimidating frame size.

Ceiling: 1.5-win player
Risk: Moderate to High
MLB ETA: 2023

11. Brent Honeywell Jr., RHP

	FB	CU/SL	SC/CH	Command	Overall
	55	50/55	65	55	45

Born: 03/31/95	Age: 27	Bats: R	Top Comp: N/A
Height: 6-2	Weight: 195	Throws: R	

Season	Team	Age	Level	IP	TBF	K/9	K%	BB/9	BB%	K-BB%	ERA	FIP	xFIP	Pit/Bat
2021	TBR	26	AAA	81.2	335	7.38	20.00%	2.64	7.16%	12.84%	3.97	4.78	4.78	3.71

Background: From my point of view, as purely as a fan of the game of baseball, Brent Honeywell Jr. is perhaps my favorite pitching prospect of all time – bar none. I looked forward to scouting and writing about the Walters State Community College hurler like he was a brother of mine. And from that perspective it's been hard to watch injury after injury wreck what was destined to be a phenomenal big league career. Honeywell Jr., a former second round pick, went four years between appearances. But you would be hard pressed to see any type of degradation in his robotic right arm. Last season, Honeywell made a total of 34 appearances, all but three coming in AAA with Durham. The 6-foot-2, 195-pound righty posted a 67-to-24 strikeout-to-walk ratio in 81.2 minor league innings and a 4-to-3 strikeout-to-walk ratio in 4.1 major league innings.

Snippet from The 2020 Prospect Digest Handbook: At this point, we can only hope Honeywell (A) gets past this snake-bitten couple of years and (B) returns to something close to his pre-injury ceiling. Fingers crossed for the now-25-year-old right-hander.

Scouting Report: With the depth of the once bountiful arsenal limited to just three pitches, Honeywell's making the most out of his repertoire. Above-average 93- to 95-mph heater. A cutter / slider type breaking ball that flashes above-average on occasional. And he's still snapping-off that helluva beautiful screwball that he's using as the razzle-dazzle change-of-pace. Oakland may have a spot in their rotation, so Honeywell may be given a crack at it. I'm always hopeful that Honeywell Jr. catches some lightning in a bottle.

Ceiling: 1.5-win player
Risk: Moderate to High
MLB ETA: 2022 /2023

12. Denzel Clarke, OF

Hit	Power	SB	Patience	Glove	Overall
40/45	60	55	50	50	45

Born: 05/01/00	Age: 22	Bats: R	Top Comp: N/A	
Height: 6-5	Weight: 220	Throws: R		

Season	Team	Age	Level	PA	1B	2B	3B	HR	SB	CS	BB%	K%	AVG	OBP	SLG	ISO
2021	OAK	21	CPX	22	3	2	0	1	1	2	13.64%	27.27%	0.316	0.409	0.579	0.263

Background: In a farm system chock full of raw, toolsy, pure athletes, it would difficult to find one who can top Clarke's athleticism and bloodlines. Clarke's mother, Donna, finished 17th in the 1998 Olympics for the women's heptathlon, and his cousins – Josh and Bo Naylor – are a couple of former first round draft picks. Oakland snagged the massive 6-foot-5, 220-pound outfielder in the fourth round last July, 127th overall, and signed him to an above-slot deal worth $700,000. After slugging .324/.445/.570 in 38 games for California State University, Northridge, Clarke maintained status quote as he batted .316/.409/.579 in seven games with Oakland's Arizona Complex League affiliate.

Scouting Report: As much raw power as any player in Oakland's organization and, perhaps, in all of the minor leagues. Clarke can absolutely destroy any inside pitch he turns on. Explosive bat speed – like jaw dropping, saliva-inducing. Plus speed. But like a lot of the young, inexperienced bats in the Oakland system, he's going to swing-and-miss a lot. He fanned in slightly more than 23% of the time as a junior for CS Northridge, and that's a number that's only going to creep up as he faces more advanced pitching. There's some poor man's Danny Tartabull-type potential here. If you speculate on prospect cards, Clarke maybe a penny stock to tuck away for a few years.

Ceiling: 1.5-win player
Risk: Moderate to High
MLB ETA: 2024

13. Michael Guldberg, CF

Hit	Power	SB	Patience	Glove	Overall
45/50	40/45	50	50	50+	45

Born: 06/22/99	Age: 23	Bats: R	Top Comp: N/A	
Height: 6-0	Weight: 171	Throws: R		

Season	Team	Age	Level	PA	1B	2B	3B	HR	SB	CS	BB%	K%	AVG	OBP	SLG	ISO
2021	OAK	22	A+	206	29	9	2	5	11	1	8.25%	17.48%	0.259	0.347	0.420	0.161

Background: You'll be hard-pressed to find more than a few hitters that were more dominant year-in and year-out as Guldberg during his three-year stretch at Georgia Tech. A wiry, less and then imposing center fielder, Guldberg slugged .368/.510/.579 in limited action as a true freshman. He followed that up by hitting .355/.441/.418 in full-time action for the Yellow Jackets the following year. And he looked like the second coming of Ted Williams before COVID wrecked what could have been a special junior campaign: through 16 games the 6-foot, 171-pound outfield batted a scorching .450/.521/.533. When the Athletics selected him in the third round two years ago and signed him to a deal worth $300,000, Guldberg left the school as a .374/.465/.459 hitter. In an injury-interrupted pro debut last season, the exceeding impressive collegiate prospect strung together a respectable .259/.347/.420 with nine doubles, two triples, five homeruns, and 11 stolen bases in only 48 games. His production, per *Weighted Runs Created Plus*, topped the league average mark by 12%.

Scouting Report: Just for fun, here's Guldberg's production prorated for a full 162-game season: 30 doubles, seven triples, 17 homeruns, and 37 stolen bases. With respect to how his production stacks up to his peers, consider the following:

- Since 2006, there were twelve 22-year-old hitters to meet the following criteria in a High-A season with one organization (min. 200 PA): 107 to 117 wRC+, a walk rate between 7.5% and 9.5%, and a strikeout rate between 17% and 19.5%. Those 12 hitters: Luis Barrera, Ryan Adams, Daniel Mayora, Hector Pellot, Michael Osinski, Daniel Amaral, Kurt Mertins, Kolbrin Vitek, Glynn Davis, Danny Mars, Ryne Birk, and – of course – Michael Guldberg.

There's an awful lot to dissect here. Let's attempt to paint a complete picture:

- Guldberg went from college ball straight into High-A.
- He spent half of his games playing in the Lansing Launching Pad and his home / road splits are evidence of that as well (.287/.398/.494 vs .230/.292/.345).
- He was quite solid in May (.286/.349/.481) and July (.304/.407/.478), and incredibly poor during the month of June (.071/.188/.107).

So...what's the end result? Well, he has a chance to develop an average hit tool. I'm not sold on the power just yet, especially given his propensity to shoot line drives in college. And the above-average speed should allow him to stay in center field. One more note: for a player lacking traditional over-the-fence thump Guldberg posted some seriously low GB-rates in 2021 (37.9%). There's a non-zero chance that he continues to exceed expectations and develops into a low end starting option. Otherwise, he's a fourth outfielder.

Ceiling: 1.0- to 1.5-win player
Risk: Moderate
MLB ETA: 2023

14. Jeff Criswell, RHP

FB	CB	SL	CH	Command	Overall
60	45/50	60	55	45	45

Born: 03/10/99	Age: 23	Bats: R	Top Comp: N/A
Height: 6-4	Weight: 225	Throws: R	

Season	Team	Age	Level	IP	TBF	K/9	K%	BB/9	BB%	K-BB%	ERA	FIP	xFIP	Pit/Bat
2021	OAK	22	A+	12.0	50	9.00	24.00%	3.00	8.00%	16.00%	4.50	4.11	4.20	3.68

Background: As much as it pains me to say so, but the University of Michigan (Go Bucks!) has become a baseball hotbed in the northern parts of the country. The Team Up North (TTUN) has produced eight players taken within the top five rounds of the draft over the past three seasons. Among those players no one was selected earlier than Jeff Criswell, the 58th overall pick two years ago. In fact, only one player from the Big10 school was drafted higher in the 21st century (Dave Parrish, 28th overall pick, 2000, New York Yankees). An undisclosed injury limited Criswell to five brief starts with the Lansing Lugnuts in 2021: he tossed just 12.0 innings, recording 12 strikeouts, and four walks to go along with a 4.50 ERA. Criswell made an additional six appearances with the Mesa Solar Sox in the Arizona Fall League, posting 32-to-12 strikeout-to-walk ratio in 22.2 innings of work.

Scouting Report: Plus fastball, above-average change, and a solid curveball when he's getting the traditional 12-6 break and not trying to sweep it away from right-hander hitters (and in to left-handers, obviously). His slider, though, is a game changer in terms of a second viable "out" pitch. Criswell has never been mistaken for Daulton Jefferies or his ability to command the strike zone like an artist with a paintbrush. And like a lot of the club's other top arms, He's quickly advancing in age. He's now entering his age-23 season with just 12.0 minor league innings on his resume. He needs to prove he can take the ball every fifth day and throw quality strikes. Otherwise, he's heading down the path of a reliever.

Ceiling: 1.0- to 1.5-win player
Risk: Moderate
MLB ETA: 2023

15. Robert Puason, SS

Hit	Power	SB	Patience	Glove	Overall
30/40	30/40	50	40	50	40

Born: 09/11/02	Age: 19	Bats: B	Top Comp: N/A
Height: 6-3	Weight: 165	Throws: R	

Season	Team	Age	Level	PA	1B	2B	3B	HR	SB	CS	BB%	K%	AVG	OBP	SLG	ISO
2021	OAK	18	A	337	49	12	1	3	3	1	7.12%	41.25%	0.215	0.282	0.291	0.076

Background: Oakland's never been afraid to take a large plunge on the international free agency market – though it's always a calculated risk. Like the time they inked teenage phenom Michael Ynoa, who received a massive $4.25 million deal, or when they signed Yoenis Cespedes as well. Fast forward a couple years and Oakland did it yet again: they came to terms with Dominican shortstop Robert Puason on a massive $5.1 million bonus. A raw, toolsy switch-hitting shortstop, Puason made his professional debut with the Stockton Ports last season, hitting a disappointingly awful .215/.282/.291 in 91 games with the club's Low-A affiliate. His overall production, per *Weighted Runs Created Plus*, was a mindboggling 44% *below* the league average mark.

Snippet from The 2020 Prospect Digest Handbook: Regarded as one of the top two prospects on the international scene last season; Puason, a 6-foot-3, 165-pound shortstop, physically looks like a ballplayer entering his early 20s. He's lean, yet muscular. Explosive and twitch with fluidity and flair, especially on the defensive side of the ball. Fast hands, but the swing's long and needs to be shortened – especially from the left side. From what I saw, Puason looked a bit overmatched in the Instructional League, but there's gobs of potential as a true five-tool threat in the coming years. One more final thought: he may outgrow shortstop and slide into a comfortable spot as a third baseman.

Scouting Report: Consider the following:

- Since 2006, there have been 83 different 18-year-old hitters that received at least 300 plate appearances in a season with one organization in Low-A. Of those 83 hitters, Puason's lowly 56 wRC+ total was the second worst, trailing only Philadelphia's Luis Garcia by one measly percentage point.

It was a long season for Puason, so much so, in fact, that (A) I'm shocked Oakland didn't demote the youngster down to the Complex League and (B) that his monthly OPS totals only crested over the .600 threshold once (June). Oh, and there's this little tidbit too: Puason, he of the massive bonus, whiffed in more than 41.2% of his plate appearances. In other words: he punched out 139 times in 337 plate appearances. It's true that he's only entering his age-19 season and has just one year of professional experience on his resume, but that data is so bad that it seems almost impossible to overcome.

Ceiling: 1.0-win player
Risk: Moderate
MLB ETA: 2025

16. Colin Peluse, RHP

	FB	SL	CH	Command	Overall
	55	55	50	50	40

Born: 06/11/98	Age: 24	Bats: R	Top Comp: N/A
Height: 6-3	Weight: 230	Throws: R	

Season	Team	Age	Level	IP	TBF	K/9	K%	BB/9	BB%	K-BB%	ERA	FIP	xFIP	Pit/Bat
2019	OAK	21	A-	24.0	104	9.75	25.00%	2.25	5.77%	19.23%	2.25	3.15	3.14	3.95
2021	OAK	23	A+	86.0	357	9.63	25.77%	2.30	6.16%	19.61%	3.66	3.95	4.13	3.89
2021	OAK	23	AA	15.0	57	10.20	29.82%	2.40	7.02%	22.81%	1.80	2.88	4.26	4.40

Background: Things seemed to be lining up nicely for the collegiate hurler heading into the 2020 season. Peluse was coming off of strong sophomore campaign for the Demon Deacons, averaging 6.8 strikeouts and just 2.8 walks per nine innings. And he flashed some promise during the summer with the Chatham Anglers as well, posting a 10-to-4 strikeout-to-walk ratio in seven innings of work. But Peluse's command backed up during his junior season and the uptick in punch outs wasn't enough to compensate. His draft stock tumbled and Oakland eventually called his name in the ninth round three years ago. Last season the 6-foot-3, 230-pound right-hander made 21 appearances across High-A and Double-A, throwing 101.0 innings with 109 strikeouts and just 26 free passes. He finished the year with a 3.39 ERA.

Scouting Report: Consider the following:

- Since 2006 only six 23-year-old hurlers met the following criteria in a High-A season with one organization (min. 80 IP): a strikeout percentage between 25% and 27% with a walk percentage between 5% and 7%. Those six hurlers: rick Fedde, Ryan Borucki, Brayan Villarreal, Darin Gorski, Yusniel Padron-Artiles, and – of course – Mr. Colin Peluse.

Peluse owns a solid three-pitch repertoire: a low- to mid-90s fastball, an above-average slider that will buckle the occasional knee, and an average changeup. He's a strike-thrower, but he's going to struggle keeping the ball in the park as he moves up through the minors (and eventually the majors). There's just not enough here to strongly suggest future starter. His repertoire does point to some type of relief path in the near future, especially when he gets closer to the big leagues.

Ceiling: 1.0-win player
Risk: Moderate
MLB ETA: 2022

17. Jordan Diaz, 1B/3B/LF

	Hit	Power	SB	Patience	Glove	Overall
	50	50	30	45	45	40

Born: 08/13/00	Age: 21	Bats: R	Top Comp: N/A
Height: 5-10	Weight: 175	Throws: R	

Season	Team	Age	Level	PA	1B	2B	3B	HR	SB	CS	BB%	K%	AVG	OBP	SLG	ISO
2018	OAK	17	R	186	30	11	2	1	0	2	10.22%	11.83%	0.277	0.371	0.390	0.113
2019	OAK	18	A-	300	46	17	1	9	2	2	6.00%	15.33%	0.264	0.307	0.430	0.166
2021	OAK	20	A+	365	58	24	1	13	2	3	6.85%	15.89%	0.288	0.337	0.483	0.195

Background: Signed out of Monteria, Columbia, five years ago. Diaz has taken a slow methodical path through the low levels of the minor leagues. He spent his (mostly) underwhelming debut in the Dominican Summer League in 2017, another full year in the Arizona Summer League, and the entirety of the 2019 campaign with the Vermont Lake Monsters. After the return to action last season, Oakland had the 5-foot-10, 175-pound infielder / outfielder bypass Low-A altogether and pushed him directly into High-A. And Diaz took full advantage of Lansing's favorable home ballpark. In a career-high 90 games, the defensive vagabond slugged .288/.337/.483 with 24 doubles, one triple, and 13 homeruns. He also swiped two bags in five attempts as well. His overall production, per *Weighted Runs Created Plus*, topped the league average threshold by a solid 21%.

Snippet from The 2020 Prospect Digest Handbook: He consistently makes contact, though his walk rates are slightly below-average. Like Franco, the young third baseman looks like a potential low end starting caliber third baseman, maybe a little more if the hit tool progresses better than expected. One word of warning: his production worsened as the year advanced.

Scouting Report: Consider the following:

- Since 2006, only five 20-year-old hitters met the following criteria in a High-A season with one organization (min. 300 PA): 115 to 125 wRC+, a strikeout rate below 17%, and a walk rate between 6% and 8%. Those five hitters: Austin Romine, Yolmer Sanchez, Juremi Profar, Moises Sierra, and Jordan Diaz.

Despite playing half of his game – or roughly half – at the friendly confines of Lansing, Diaz actually performed better on the road (.790 OPS vs. .851 OPS). The power continues to develop into an average skill and might even peak slightly above that level (he was on pace for 23 homeruns last season). He rarely swings-and-misses, but doesn't work the count all that well either. Defensively, he's not a great fit for third base and his bat doesn't profile nearly that well at first base. Oakland tends to get a ton of value out of their fringy hitting prospects, so it wouldn't be surprising to look up and see Diaz as a competent big league bat in a couple years.

Ceiling: 1.0-win player
Risk: Moderate
MLB ETA: 2023/2024

18. Garrett Acton, RHP

	FB	SL	CH	Command	Overall
	65	45	50/55	55	40

Born: 06/15/98	Age: 24	Bats: L	Top Comp: N/A
Height: 6-2	Weight: 215	Throws: R	

Season	Team	Age	Level	IP	TBF	K/9	K%	BB/9	BB%	K-BB%	ERA	FIP	xFIP	Pit/Bat
2021	OAK	23	A	36.1	148	13.13	35.81%	3.47	9.46%	26.35%	3.72	4.70	4.13	3.88
2021	OAK	23	A+	17.1	67	17.65	50.75%	2.08	5.97%	44.78%	3.63	2.79	1.68	4.22

Background: The 2020 season was a rough one for nearly every single person involved. The major leagues played in front of empty, cardboard cutout-filled stadiums. The minor leagues lost an entire year of development. And the amateur draft was cut to just five rounds. Oakland being Oakland swooped in and signed erratic University of Illinois closer Garrett Acton for no more than $20,000. Acton, a thick 6-foot-2, 215-pound right-hander, made his professional debut last season, splitting time between Stockton and Lansing. In a combined 34 relief appearances between the Low-A and High-A affiliates, Acton punched out a whopping 84 and walked only 18. For those counting at home: Acton averaged 14.6 strikeouts and just three walks per nine innings to go along with a 3.69 ERA.

Scouting Report: Plus fastball, questionable slider that lacks bite and floats to the plate, and an average changeup that shows enough fade at times that suggests it may get into above-average territory with some continued fine-tuning. Acton throws strikes, a lot of them quality strikes. It's imperative that a secondary pitch takes a leap forward in the coming year or two. If so, he could be a Craig Kimbrel-lite version.

Ceiling: 1.0-win player
Risk: Moderate
MLB ETA: 2023

19. Mason Miller, RHP

	FB	CB	SL	CH	Command	Overall
	70	45	55	45/50	45	40

Born: 08/24/98	Age: 23	Bats: R	Top Comp: N/A
Height: 6-5	Weight: 200	Throws: R	

Background: Not all roads to professional baseball are the same. And this was echoed to me by my old pitching coach once. And there's no better example of that than Mason Miller. The 6-foot-5, 200-pound right-hander spent parts of four seasons at Division III Waynesburg University. But after the 2020 season was wrecked by COVID-19, Miller used the additional service time to transfer to Division I school Gardner-Webb. He made 15 appearances last season for the Big South Conference school, posting a dominating 121-to-30 strikeout-to-walk ratio in only 92.2 innings of work. He compiled an 8-1 win-loss record to go along with a 3.30 ERA. Oakland drafted the flame-throwing righty in the third round, 97th overall, and signed him to a deal worth just a smidgeon less than $600,000. Miller made three brief appearances in the Arizona Complex League, fanning nine and walking a trio in 6.0 innings of work.

Scouting Report: Consider the following:

- Since 2011, only one Big South Conference pitcher averaged at least 11 strikeouts per nine innings in a season (min. 75 IP): Matt Fraudin, an undrafted hurler out of Miller's alma mater, Gardner-Webb.

Make no mistake about it: regardless of Miller's meek collegiate beginnings, the 6-foot-5, 200-pound right-hander owns a blazing plus-heater, which comfortably sits in the mid- to upper-90s. His best secondary pitch is a late-biting, horizontal-darting slider. He'll also mix in a pair of below-average / fringy off-speed offerings: a curveball and changeup, with the latter flashing the potential to move into 50-grade territory. There's definite reliever risk here unless the command improves or a third weapons develops.

Ceiling: 1.0-win player
Risk: Moderate
MLB ETA: 2024

20. Jonah Bride, 1B/2B/3B

Hit	Power	SB	Patience	Glove	Overall
50	45	35	60	50	40

Born: 12/27/95	Age: 26	Bats: R	Top Comp: N/A
Height: 5-10	Weight: 200	Throws: R	

Season	Team	Age	Level	PA	1B	2B	3B	HR	SB	CS	BB%	K%	AVG	OBP	SLG	ISO
2018	OAK	22	A-	229	36	17	0	3	3	2	10.48%	15.28%	0.287	0.376	0.421	0.133
2019	OAK	23	A+	466	80	18	4	10	2	0	9.44%	20.82%	0.279	0.371	0.418	0.139
2021	OAK	25	AA	334	48	11	2	9	2	0	17.07%	17.07%	0.265	0.407	0.424	0.159

Background: A consistent, albeit unspectacular, bat at the University of South Carolina. Bride was plucked in the late, late rounds of the 2018 draft. And, for the most part, he continued along his unremarkable trek in the minor leagues as well.

Bride batted .287/.376/.421 in 54 games in the New York-Penn League during his debut. He followed that up with a .279/.371/.418 triple-slash line the following year as he jumped all the way up to High-A. And last season, as minor league baseball returned to action, he batted a saber-friendly .265/.407/.424 with 11 doubles, two triples, and nine homeruns in 78 games in Double-A. Per *Weighted Runs Created Plus,* his overall production was 30% above the league average mark.

Scouting Report: The minor league equivalent to Kevin Youkilis, the Greek God of Walks. Bride squared off against the minors' most difficult challenge, AA, and came out with a perfect 57-to-57 strikeout-to-walk ratio in only 78 games of work. He doesn't possess anything more than slightly below-average power. But there's surely a place, at least at the end of the bench, for an OBP fiend with positional versatility like Bride.

Ceiling: 1.0-win player
Risk: Moderate
MLB ETA: 2022

Philadelphia Phillies

Top Prospects

1. Andrew Painter, RHP

	FB	CB	SL	CH	Command	Overall
	60	55	50/55	55	50/55	60

Born: 04/10/03	Age: 19	Bats: R	Top Comp: Justin Verlander
Height: 6-7	Weight: 215	Throws: R	

Background: The 6-foot-7, 215-pound, hard-throwing right-hander – likely – would have had his choice of any college, but Painter's recruitment process was rather abbreviated. The University of Miami, according to reports, offered him a scholarship prior to his freshman season at Calvary Christian. But the University of Florida came calling after a camp, which was enough to change his mind. A member of Team USA's 15U squad in 2018, Painter tied for the team lead in innings pitched (10.0 IP) while recording 13 punch outs, handing out just three free passes, and compiling 0.90 ERA. And, of course, he maintained that level of dominance during the remainder of his high school career. Painter won seven games and lost two to go along with a 1.43 ERA in 53.2 innings as his squad captured the 4A State Championship during his sophomore season. And prior to the pandemic shutdown, the behemoth hurler struck out 33 in 15 innings of work. The 2021 season was just another ordinary campaign of sheer dominance for Painter: in 11 starts, he completed three games, throwing 47 innings with 93 punch outs (17.8 K/9), 15 walks, and a miniscule 0.30 ERA. He finished his high school career with a combined 0.76 ERA in 138.2 innings, while averaging 15.6 K/9 and 2.72 BB/9. The Phillies drafted him with the 13th overall pick last June and signed him to a deal worth $3.9 million. Painter made four brief appearances with the organization's Florida Complex League, tossing six innings with 12 strikeouts and no walks.

Scouting Report: Per the usual, here's his pre-draft write up:

> "Four average or better offerings with underrated athleticism that allows easy repeatability of his mechanics. Painter's fastball sits – comfortably – in the mid-90s without a lot of effort. He'll mix in a pair of breaking balls: an above-average, upper-70s curveball and a solid, low-80s slider. There's some projection left in the slider that may push it into 55-grade territory. But it's Painter's changeup that differentiates him from most high school-aged power pitchers. It's a mid-80s offering with sink that's more polished than usual. It's almost sacrilege to say it, but he's reminiscent of young Justin Verlander in some ways."

Ceiling: 5.0-win player
Risk: Moderate to High
MLB ETA: 2022

2. Mick Abel, RHP

	FB	CB	CH	Command	Overall
	65	60	50	40/45	60

Born: 08/18/01	Age: 20	Bats: R	Top Comp: Zack Wheeler
Height: 6-5	Weight: 190	Throws: R	

Season	Team	Age	Level	IP	TBF	K/9	K%	BB/9	BB%	K-BB%	ERA	FIP	xFIP	Pit/Bat
2021	PHI	19	A	44.2	189	13.30	34.92%	5.44	14.29%	20.63%	4.43	4.52	4.11	4.38

Background: The front office hasn't generated a ton of value out their first round selections. In fact, their most successful first round pick between 2008 and 2012 was Jesse Biddle, who's tallied -0.7 *Wins Above Replacement* during his big league career. They made notable picks in the opening round the next two years, snagging J.P. Crawford and Aaron Nola in 2013 and 2014. They missed on Cornelius Randolph in 2015. Mickey Moniak, the top pick in the draft the following year, has been an utter disappointment. And the jury's still out on Adam Haseley and Alec Bohm. So there's a lot riding on the club's three most recent first rounders: Bryson Stott (2019), Mick Abel (2020), and Andrew Painter (2021). The 15th overall pick out Jesuit High School, Abel made his professional debut last season. In an injury-shortened campaign, the 6-foot-5, 190-pound right-hander made 14 starts for Clearwater, throwing 44.2 innings with 66 strikeouts and 27 walks to go along with a 4.43 ERA. He was shutdown in late July with shoulder tendonitis, according to reports.

Scouting Report: Consider the following:

- Since 2006, only five 19-year-old pitchers in Low-A have thrown at least 40 innings in a season while posting a strikeout percentage north of 33% and walking more than 13% of the hitters they faced: Tyler Glasnow, Cole Ragans, Jeremy Molero, Fabio Martinez, and – of course – young Mick Abel.

In one fell swoop it's easy to see (A) why Abel was a highly touted prep arm and (B) the sheer amount of risk associated with teenage arms. During an early July start against the Bradenton Marauders, the firebolt-slinging right-hander's fastball sat anywhere between 94 and 98 mph. He mixed in a plus slurvey-like curveball, and a firm 90 mph changeup. A few reports indicate Abel mixes in a slider and curveball, but it appeared they were one in the same. The command has some ways to go to get to average. The shoulder issue, which was termed as tendonitis, is concerning. Assuming it won't hamper him in the coming seasons, Abel looks like a viable mid-rotation caliber arm – unless the command ticks up. One final note: he trusts his breaking ball more than most teenagers.

Ceiling: 3.5-win player
Risk: Moderate to High
MLB ETA: 2024

3. Johan Rojas, CF

Hit	Power	SB	Patience	Glove	Overall
50	55	60	50	60	55

Born: 08/14/00	Age: 21	Bats: R	Top Comp: Starling Marte
Height: 6-1	Weight: 165	Throws: R	

Season	Team	Age	Level	PA	1B	2B	3B	HR	SB	CS	BB%	K%	AVG	OBP	SLG	ISO
2018	PHI	17	R	292	65	12	4	2	19	8	6.16%	12.67%	0.320	0.376	0.421	0.100
2019	PHI	18	R	84	12	6	5	0	3	2	10.71%	14.29%	0.311	0.393	0.527	0.216
2019	PHI	18	A-	172	27	5	6	2	11	4	2.91%	16.86%	0.244	0.273	0.384	0.140
2021	PHI	20	A	351	50	15	3	7	25	6	7.41%	19.66%	0.240	0.305	0.374	0.134
2021	PHI	20	A+	74	15	3	1	3	8	3	9.46%	10.81%	0.344	0.419	0.563	0.219

Background: Arguably the most intriguing prospect in the entire system. Rojas is a dichotomy – of sorts. On one hand he's just a couple summers removed from signing for a paltry $10,000. But on the other hand Phillies manager – and 15-year big league veteran – Joe Girardi heaped tons of praise on the raw-yet-toolsy center fielder. According to Matt Breen of *The Philadelphia Inquirer* in a late March article last year Girardi summed up his analysis of Rojas rather succinctly, "He's a plus-plus defender. He's a plus runner. He has the chance to be a special player. I believe so. I believe there's Gold Glove potential there." Now, some of that's the typical organizational hyperbole. But there's some truth to Girardi's assessment. Rojas opened last season in Low-A, hitting a disappointing .240/.305/.374 in 78 games. But after missing a couple weeks in late July / early August, the front office bumped him up to High-A. And he dominated, slugging .344/.419/.563 in 17 games.

Scouting Report: Let the level of intrigue quietly simmer, nearing a boiling point. After an absolutely abysmal start the year in which he batted an awful .184/.231/.281 through his first 26 games, Rojas' production *exploded*. He slugged a scorching .296/.368/.476 with 12 doubles, three triples, 10 homeruns, and 28 stolen bases (in only 34 attempts). And the analytics support Girardi's defensive assessment: according *Baseball Prospectus*, Rojas saved 3.6 FRAA in 96 games. The swing still needs a bit of work; it's a bit robotic as times. But it's simple. 20-homer potential? Check. Plus speed? Check. Rojas could be the club's best prospect within in a year.

Ceiling: 3.0-win player
Risk: Moderate
MLB ETA: 2023

4. Hans Crouse, RHP

FB	SL	CH	Command	Overall
55	55	55	50	55

Born: 09/15/98	Age: 23	Bats: L	Top Comp: Tanner Houck
Height: 6-4	Weight: 180	Throws: R	

Season	Team	Age	Level	IP	TBF	K/9	K%	BB/9	BB%	K-BB%	ERA	FIP	xFIP	Pit/Bat
2018	TEX	19	A-	38.0	151	11.13	31.13%	2.61	7.28%	23.84%	2.37	2.63	3.05	3.79
2018	TEX	19	A	16.2	76	8.10	19.74%	4.32	10.53%	9.21%	2.70	4.07	4.77	3.91
2019	TEX	20	A	87.2	367	7.80	20.71%	1.95	5.18%	15.53%	4.41	4.46	4.06	3.60
2021	TEX	22	AA	51.0	195	9.53	27.69%	3.35	9.74%	17.95%	3.35	3.87	4.62	4.15
2021	PHI	22	AA	29.2	122	11.53	31.15%	3.64	9.84%	21.31%	2.73	3.68	4.33	4.12

Background: A second round out of Dana High School in 2017. Crouse, who signed for $1.45 million, was in the midst of a breakout season before the Rangers dealt the lanky right-hander to Philly near the trade deadline last season. He was acquired along with veterans Kyle Gibson and Ian Kennedy, as well as cash, for Spencer Howard, Kevin Gowdy, and Josh Gessner. Crouse made a combined 20 minor league starts between both organizations last season, throwing 85.0 innings with 98 strikeouts and 34 walks to go along with a 3.28 ERA. The 6-foot-4, 180-pound righty made a pair of brief starts with the Phillies at the end of the season, throwing seven innings with just two punch outs and seven walks.

Snippet from The 2020 Prospect Digest Handbook: Given the emphasis on his changeup, as well as his 55-grade control/command, I'd expect Crouse's strikeout percentage to leap several degrees in 2020. Again, there's some potential #3 caliber status here.

Scouting Report: Consider the following:

- Since 2006, only two other 22-year-old Double-A arms met the following criteria in a season with one organization: 75 IP, a strikeout percentage between 28% and 31% and a walk percentage between 9% and 11%. Those two arms: Touki Toussaint and Mike Minor.

Twenty-two-year-old pitchers with (A) three above-average pitches and (B) success at Double-A are pretty rare. Crouse works exclusively from the stretch, which is becoming more en vogue these days. His fastball, during a late season Double-A start, was sitting in the 92-94 mph range and peaked at 95. His slider shows some hard, sweeping cutter-like movement. And his upper 80s changeup is deceiving, an equalizer. He throws plenty of strikes and may eventually see an uptick in command, going from average to above-average. Crouse has some #3/#4-type upside.

Ceiling: 2.5-win player
Risk: Low to Moderate
MLB ETA: Debuted in 2021

5. Bryson Stott, SS

Hit	Power	SB	Patience	Glove	Overall
50	50	50	50+	50	50

Born: 10/06/97	Age: 24	Bats: L	Top Comp: Hunter Dozier
Height: 6-3	Weight: 200	Throws: R	

Season	Team	Age	Level	PA	1B	2B	3B	HR	SB	CS	BB%	K%	AVG	OBP	SLG	ISO
2019	PHI	21	R	11	3	1	1	1	0	0	18.18%	0.00%	0.667	0.727	1.333	0.667
2019	PHI	21	A-	182	28	8	2	5	5	3	12.09%	21.43%	0.274	0.370	0.446	0.172
2021	PHI	23	A+	95	12	4	0	5	3	2	23.16%	23.16%	0.288	0.453	0.548	0.260
2021	PHI	23	AA	351	60	22	2	10	6	2	9.97%	22.22%	0.301	0.368	0.481	0.179
2021	PHI	23	AAA	41	9	0	0	1	1	0	19.51%	19.51%	0.303	0.439	0.394	0.091

Background: Only two players from the University of Nevada, Las Vegas were taken higher in the June amateur draft than Bryson Stott, the 14th overall pick in 2019. Matt Williams, member of the Hall of Very Good, was plucked out the school with the third overall pick in 1986, a few selections ahead of right-hander Kevin Brown and 500 Homerun Club member Gary Sheffield. And Donovan Osborne, the 13th pick by the St. Louis Cardinals in 1990 – who was snagged a few picks in front of Hall of Famer Mike Mussina. Stott, a lefty-swinging shortstop, blitzed through three levels during his second professional minor league season, going from High-A to Double-A to Triple-A. Stott slugged an aggregate .299/.390/.486 with 26 doubles, a pair of triples, 16 homeruns, and 10 stolen bases.

Snippet from The 2020 Prospect Digest Handbook: I was a little pessimistic about Stott's future heading into the draft – mainly the power, which showed up significantly better than I expected. There's some Hunter Dozier type production here.

Scouting Report: With regard to his largest single level stint in 2021 (Double-A), consider the following:

- Since 2006, only four 23-year-old hitters in Double-A met the following criteria in a season (min. 300 PA): post a wRC+ between 125 and 135, a walk rate between 9% and 11% and a strikeout rate between 20% and 24%. Those four hitters: Forrest Wall, Matt Curry, Jason Vosler, and – of course – Bryson Stott.

The Hunter Dozier comparison, which I noted two years ago, still seems close enough: Stott may trade some long balls in for some added notches on his batting average. He looks like a low end starter/bench option at this point. But as a quasi-silver lining for Phillies fans: three of the next four college shortstops taken after the former UNLV star – Will Wilson, Braden Shewmake, and Logan Davidson – have all been disappointments.

Ceiling: 2.0-win player
Risk: Moderate
MLB ETA: 2022

6. Logan O'Hoppe, C

Hit	Power	SB	Patience	Glove	Overall
45	55	30	45	45	50

Born: 02/09/00	Age: 22	Bats: R	Top Comp: James McCann
Height: 6-2	Weight: 185	Throws: R	

Season	Team	Age	Level	PA	1B	2B	3B	HR	SB	CS	BB%	K%	AVG	OBP	SLG	ISO
2018	PHI	18	R	124	27	10	1	2	2	1	8.06%	22.58%	0.367	0.411	0.532	0.165
2019	PHI	19	A-	177	16	12	2	5	3	0	6.78%	27.68%	0.216	0.266	0.407	0.191
2021	PHI	21	A+	358	54	17	2	13	6	3	8.38%	17.60%	0.270	0.335	0.459	0.189
2021	PHI	21	AA	57	12	1	0	3	0	0	1.75%	15.79%	0.296	0.333	0.481	0.185
2021	PHI	21	AAA	23	2	1	0	1	0	0	8.70%	17.39%	0.190	0.261	0.381	0.190

Background: Fun Fact Part I: St. John Baptist has produced four professional ballplayers. Fun Fact Part II: Two of those players, John Habyan and Joe Palumbo, made the big leagues. O'Hoppe, the fourth and latest St. John Baptist High School product, was unearthed in the late, late rounds of the 2018 draft. A 6-foot-2, 185-pound backstop out of New York, O'Hoppe, the 677th overall pick in 2018, earned a nice $215,000 bonus. After signing he simply put together one of the better professional debuts that summer, slugging a hefty .367/.411/.532 with 13 extra-base hits in the Gulf Coast League. His production cratered during his promotion up to short season the following year, but came roaring back in

2021 as he rocketed through three separate levels. O'Hoppe slugged an aggregate .270/.331/.458 with 19 doubles, two triples, 17 homeruns, and six stolen bases between High-A, Double-A, and Triple-A.

Scouting Report: Consider the following:

- Since 2006, here's the list of 21-year-old High-A hitters to post a wRC+ total between 105 and 115, a walk rate between 7% and 9%, and a strikeout rate between 15% and 20% (min. 350 PA): Max Kepler, Abiatal Avelino, Logan Watkins, Juan Portes, Orlando Martinez, Joe Rizzo, and Logan O'Hoppe.

One of the most underrated catching prospects in the minor leagues. O'Hoppe offers up some interesting, tantalizing potential as a power-oriented backstop who won't kill a team on defense. And, perhaps, the best news: he makes consistent contact. I think there's 20- to 25-homer pop brewing in the bat.

Ceiling: 2.0-win player
Risk: Moderate
MLB ETA: 2022

7. Francisco Morales, RHP

FB	SL	CH	Command	Overall
60	60	45	40	45

Born: 10/27/99	Age: 22	Bats: R	Top Comp: Kyle Crick
Height: 6-4	Weight: 185	Throws: R	

Season	Team	Age	Level	IP	TBF	K/9	K%	BB/9	BB%	K-BB%	ERA	FIP	xFIP	Pit/Bat
2018	PHI	18	A-	56.1	258	10.86	26.36%	5.27	12.79%	13.57%	5.27	4.37	3.77	3.82
2019	PHI	19	A	96.2	417	12.01	30.94%	4.28	11.03%	19.90%	3.82	3.51	3.23	3.96
2021	PHI	21	AA	83.0	390	11.93	28.21%	6.51	15.38%	12.82%	6.94	5.01	4.86	3.93

Background: Just another example of the organization reaching deep into their pockets and handing out a big six-figure bonus on the international free agent market. Morales, who signed on the dotted line for slightly more than $700,000 in 2016, turned in a promising debut the following summer as he posted a 44-to-20 strikeout-to-walk ratio in 41.1 innings of work in the Gulf Coast League. He spent the next two summers ripping through short season ball and Low-A while racking up promising strikeout totals mixed in with a touch of wavering control. The front office refused to pump the proverbial breaks on his development – despite missing the 2020 season thanks to COVID – and bumped him straight up to the minors' toughest challenge, Double-A, to begin the year. And the results were…not great. Morales continued to miss a tremendous amount of bats – he averaged nearly 12 punch outs per nine innings – but the command/control ballooned to an a career-high (6.5 BB/9). He made two final appearances with Lehigh Valley in Triple-A to cap off his fourth professional season.

Snippet from The 2020 Prospect Digest Handbook: There's some intriguing #3-type potential, maybe more if his changeup becomes a consistent weapon. One final thought: the front office is likely going to start aggressively challenging Morales next season.

Scouting Report: Morales' listed frame size – 6-foot-4 and 185-pounds – is (A) either wrong or (B) deceiving. Because the Venezuelan-born right-hander looks like he could play either tight or power forward. The big righty attacks hitters with a hyper-focused two-pitch mix: a mid-90s fastball with riding life and a knee-buckling slider with 12-6 break. He'll – *rarely* – mix in a rare, underdeveloped changeup as well. Along with lacking a consistent third offering, Morales lack of command almost immediately pushes him into some type of future relief role – unless he seems a major uptick in the next year or two.

Ceiling: 1.5-win player
Risk: Moderate
MLB ETA: 2022

8. Ethan Wilson, OF

Hit	Power	SB	Patience	Glove	Overall
45/50	45	45	50	50	45

Born: 11/07/99	Age: 22	Bats: L	Top Comp: Christin Stewart
Height: 6-1	Weight: 210	Throws: L	

Season	Team	Age	Level	PA	1B	2B	3B	HR	SB	CS	BB%	K%	AVG	OBP	SLG	ISO
2021	PHI	21	A	117	14	4	2	3	2	2	8.55%	21.37%	0.215	0.282	0.374	0.159

Background: A rarity in high school, at least to my knowledge, Wilson lettered in baseball five times during his career at Andalusia High School. The toolsy outfielder cracked the varsity team's lineup – for the first time – as an eighth grader. And the 6-foot-1, 210-pound corner outfielder also lettered in football four times and basketball twice. Wilson rattled off a senior season for the ages during his final campaign for the Alabama high school: he also tossed 2,388 yards and aired it out for 29 touchdowns while rushing for 783 yards and another 12 TDs while quarterbacking the football team. Impressive enough, sure, but he led the baseball team to a Class 4A state championship while hitting .529 with 10 homeruns and posting a 12-0 record with a 0.65 ERA and 112 strikeouts in 62 innings on the mound. And that just proved to be a harbinger of things to come. Wilson torched the competition during his freshman season at South Alabama, slugging a robust .345/.453/.686 with 16 doubles, four triples, and 17 homeruns. He was named 2019 Collegiate Baseball Co-Freshman of the Year, Sun Belt Conference Player of the Year, Sun Belt Freshman of the Year, and First-Team Freshman All-America (Collegiate Baseball, Baseball America, and National Collegiate Writers Association). Wilson's production took a noticeable downturn during his 18-game pre-pandemic sophomore season: .282/.329/.465. And he completed his junior campaign with a triple-slash line somewhere in between: he hit .318/.419/.528 with 13 doubles, four triples, and eight homeruns. The Phillies drafted him in the second round, 49th overall, and signed him to a deal worth slightly more than $1.5 million. He made his professional debut in Low-A, hitting a paltry .215/.282/.374 with four doubles, two triples, three homeruns, and two stolen bases.

Scouting Report: Per the usual, here's my pre-draft write-up:

"Let's take a look at Wilson's dynamic freshman season:

- *Between 2011 and 2020, there were only 28 instances in which a Division I hitter – in any conference – met the following criteria (min. 250 PA): hit .340/.440/.670 with a walk rate great than 12% and a sub-18% strikeout rate.*

Obviously, the production han'ts quite been back up to the level. But Wilson's been one of the better bats in college baseball in 2021. Consider how his production stacks up against recent Sun Belt hitters:

- *Between 2011 and 2020, only four Sun Belt Conference hitters batted .300/.400/.500 with a sub-10% strikeout rate and a double-digit walk rate (min. 225 PA): Tyler Hannah, Jeremy Patton, Logan Pierce, and Ryan Bottger.*

Obviously, it's not stellar company. But Wilson has a three-year (or two-plus-year) track record of success. Short and stocky, but not quite the typical power associated from a corner outfielder position. Wilson makes a uniform look good though. Not in love with the swing, it's a bit long and his toe tap might cause some timing issues in the professional ranks. Wilson looks like a tweener: the tools aren't enough to scream big league left fielder and his lack of positional versatility keeps him from a fourth outfielder role."

Ceiling: 1.5-win player
Risk: Moderate
MLB ETA: 2023/2024

9. Jordan Viars, 1B/LF

	Hit	Power	SB	Patience	Glove	Overall
	45/50	50/60	40	50	50	45

Born: 07/18/03	Age: 18	Bats: L	Top Comp: Matt Stairs
Height: 6-4	Weight: 215	Throws: L	

Season	Team	Age	Level	PA	1B	2B	3B	HR	SB	CS	BB%	K%	AVG	OBP	SLG	ISO
2021	PHI	17	CPX	64	8	1	0	3	2	0	17.19%	18.75%	0.255	0.406	0.468	0.213

Background: A University of Arkansas commit, Viars, according to reports, was an under-the-radar pick by the Phillies last June. Taken in the third round, 84th overall, and signed to an above-slot bonus worth $747,500. Viars was also the second Arkansas commit to be drafted in 2021 as well. After signing the first baseman / left fielder, who's built like a brick shithouse, turned in a solid debut showing in the Florida Complex League: he slugged .255/.406/.468 with one double, three homeruns, and two stolen bases in 22 games. He finished his debut with as a solid 12-to-11 strikeout-to-walk ratio. His overall production, per *Weighted Runs Created Plus*, topped the league average mark by 32%.

Scouting Report: Big time raw power, though he didn't flash much in-game pop during his debut, Viars has 25-homer potential. He's shown a willingness to work the count and an ability to shoot the ball the other way. Above-average bat speed. Viars could shoot up a lot of prospect lists in the next year or two.

Ceiling: 1.5-win player
Risk: Moderate
MLB ETA: 2025

10. Adam Leverett, RHP

FB	CB	CH	Command	Overall
55	50	60	50	45

Born: 09/19/98	Age: 23	Bats: L	Top Comp:
Height: 6-4	Weight: 190	Throws: R	

Season	Team	Age	Level	IP	TBF	K/9	K%	BB/9	BB%	K-BB%	ERA	FIP	xFIP	Pit/Bat
2019	PHI	20	A-	28.1	126	6.99	17.46%	4.13	10.32%	7.14%	4.45	4.71	4.05	3.60
2021	PHI	22	A+	40.1	158	10.26	29.11%	3.35	9.49%	19.62%	1.56	2.90	4.63	4.34
2021	PHI	22	AA	36.0	158	9.00	22.78%	3.25	8.23%	14.56%	5.50	4.65	4.59	3.98

Background: Since 2000 Gordon State College in Barnesville, Georgia, has produced a total of three draft picks: Grant Mullen, a 34th round pick in 2000, Datren Bray, a 19th round pick in 2018, and Adam Leverett, who was snagged in the 15th round three years ago. A wiry, yet strong 6-foot-4 and 190-pound right-hander, Leverett, who signed for a $150,000, rocketed through three separate levels during his second professional season, bouncing from High-A to Double-A and eventually up to Triple-A. In total he tossed 85.1 innings between the three levels, striking out 90, walking 31, and tallying a 3.48 ERA.

Scouting Report: The conversation starts, focuses on, and ends with Leverett's changeup. It's filthy. It's arguably my favorite pitch in the entire minor leagues. It dives. It fades. It has fantastic velo separation. And it's thrown with phenomenal arm speed. Not to be outdone, Lverett's fastball is an above-average offering that he locates well. And he'll mix in a tightly wound average curveball. There's some backend rotation potential here, especially if he sees an uptick in his curveball.

Ceiling: 1.5-win player
Risk: Moderate
MLB ETA: 2022

11. Griff McGarry, RHP

FB	SL	CH	Command	Overall
65	60	50	40/45	45

Born: 06/08/99	Age: 23	Bats: R	Top Comp: N/A
Height: 6-2	Weight: 190	Throws: R	

Season	Team	Age	Level	IP	TBF	K/9	K%	BB/9	BB%	K-BB%	ERA	FIP	xFIP	Pit/Bat
2021	PHI	22	A	11.0	46	18.00	47.83%	5.73	15.22%	32.61%	3.27	1.71	2.21	4.17
2021	PHI	22	A+	13.1	54	14.18	38.89%	4.73	12.96%	25.93%	2.70	2.19	3.85	4.15

Background: Fun Fact: Menlo School, McGarry's alma mater, produced one big league player – former Astros outfielder Kevin Bass, who finished seventh in the MVP voting in 1987 after posting a .311/.357/.486 slash line with 20 homeruns and 22 stolen bases. McGarry was a decorated two-way player for Menlo, earning several awards and recognitions including: MaxPreps California Small Schools Player of the Year, MaxPreps Small Schools First-Team All-American and First-Team All-State, Perfect Game First-Team All-Region. And the Texas Rangers eventually took a late round flier on the dynamic right-hander. Except…well…things didn't really pan out the way McGarry would've liked during his four-year career with the Virginia Cavaliers. McGarry, a 6-foot-2, 190-pound hurler, made 41 appearances for the ACC powerhouse, throwing just 126.2 innings with an impressive 178 strikeouts and a whopper of a walk total (129). But it was his work against Mississippi State during the College World Series that showcased his potential: 7.1 IP (including seven innings of no-hit ball), eight punch outs, and just two walks. The Phillies drafted the enigmatic, dynamic right-hander in the fifth round, 145th overall, and signed him to a deal worth $322,500. McGarry made eight appearances between Low-A and High-A during his professional debut, throwing 24.1 innings with a 2.96 ERA, 43 strikeouts, and 14 walks.

Scouting Report: Per the usual, my pre-draft write-up:

> "Absurdly talented. So much so, in fact, if his command was even a 45 he'd be a lock for a Top 10 or Top 15 selection. McGarry's fastball is explosive with late riding life, sitting – almost effortless – in the mid-90s and touching 97 mph with regularity. His slider is an 83- to 84-mph lethal swing-and-miss pitch. And he'll mix in a surprisingly solid mid-80s changeup. The problem, of course, is for four years McGarry couldn't hit the broadside of a barn. 45-grade command puts him as a #3/#4-type arm because that's how good the arsenal is. I'd take a third round flier on him and hope to harness the lightning oozing from his right arm. The Royals took Josh Staumont in the second round in 2015 and developed him into a late-inning arm – which could be a nice fallback for McGarry."

Ceiling: 1.0- to 1.5-win player
Risk: Moderate to High
MLB ETA: 2023/2024

12. Dominic Pipkin, RHP

	FB	CB	SL	CH	Command	Overall
	60	50	50/55	N/A	45	40

Born: 11/05/99	Age: 22	Bats: R	Top Comp: Zach McAllister
Height: 6-4	Weight: 160	Throws: R	

Season	Team	Age	Level	IP	TBF	K/9	K%	BB/9	BB%	K-BB%	ERA	FIP	xFIP	Pit/Bat
2018	PHI	18	R	29.2	116	5.46	15.52%	2.43	6.90%	8.62%	3.64	4.67	4.08	1.53
2019	PHI	19	A	71.2	331	5.53	13.29%	5.65	13.60%	-0.30%	5.15	5.37	5.62	3.72
2021	PHI	21	A+	58.0	255	9.93	25.10%	4.19	10.59%	14.51%	4.97	4.56	4.87	3.91

Background: Fun Fact: California based Pinole Valley High School is home to three big leaguers – Chris Singleton, Dale Sveum, and Nathan Haynes. Dominic Pipkin, a ninth round pick in 2018 by the Phillies, earned a hefty $800,000 bonus as the 257th overall pick. He turned in a mediocre debut showing in the Gulf Coast League that summer, averaging just 5.5 strikeouts and 2.4 walks per nine innings. Philly bounced the raw, projectable right-hander up to the South Atlantic League for the 2019 season and the results were...not good. He posted a 44-to-45 strikeout-to-walk ratio in 71.2 innings of work. After minor league ball returned to action last year, Pipkin turned in his finest professional showing to date: he struck out 64, walked 27, and posted a 4.97 ERA across 16 appearances (12 of them starts).

Scouting Report: Consider the following:

- Since 2006, here's the list of 21-year-old High-A pitchers to post a strikeout percentage between 24% and 26% and a walk percentage between 10% and 12% (min. 50 IP): Logan Webb, Luke Jackson, Sam Hentges, Chris Anderson, Bruce Pugh, Cody Scarpetta, Frank German, Luis Pena, Steve Johnson, and Dominic Pipkin.

A project, but less of a project than he was two years ago. Pipkin attacks hitters with a plus fastball. And after working without a reliable breaking ball early in his career, the hard-throwing righty has developed a potentially above-average slider. It's still inconsistent; at times the break is more like a tradition cutter; other times it shows more traditional movement. He also show (rarely) a decent, though not great curveball. He'll also mix in a changeup; though I didn't see it in a brief High-A appearance. Pipkin is still in tweener territory: he could creep up into a backend starter role or fall into a multi-pitch, multi-inning reliever.

Ceiling: 1.0-win player
Risk: Moderate
MLB ETA: 2023

13. Mickey Moniak, CF

	Hit	Power	SB	Patience	Glove	Overall
	45	50	40	45	45/50	40

Born: 05/13/98	Age: 24	Bats: L	Top Comp: Trevor Crowe
Height: 6-2	Weight: 195	Throws: R	

Season	Team	Age	Level	PA	1B	2B	3B	HR	SB	CS	BB%	K%	AVG	OBP	SLG	ISO
2018	PHI	20	A+	465	81	28	3	5	6	5	4.73%	21.51%	0.270	0.304	0.383	0.113
2019	PHI	21	AA	504	65	28	13	11	15	3	6.55%	22.02%	0.252	0.303	0.439	0.187
2021	PHI	23	AAA	409	49	15	8	15	5	2	7.58%	24.69%	0.238	0.299	0.447	0.208

Background: It's easy to point a finger at the Phillies' front office at their misstep in selecting Moniak as the top player taken in the 2016 draft. But is it really a blunder when the first round, now more than five years later, has produced very little in terms of big league value. Will Smith, who's tallied 6.6 bWAR, and Cal Quantrill, 4.9, are the lead producers at the big league level at this point. And only nine of the first 41 selections – all first rounders by the way – have totaled more than one win above replacement. By all accounts, an incredible worker both on and off the field Moniak's production has oscillated between mediocre to downright disappointing throughout his five-year professional career. And, unfortunately, for everyone involved last year was more of a valley rather than a peak. In 99 games with the club's Triple-A affiliate, the Lehigh Valley IronPigs, the 6-foot-2, 195-pound lefty-swinging center fielder batted a disappointing .238/.299/.447 with 15 doubles, eight triples, a career best 15 homeruns, and a pair of stolen bases. His overall production, per *Weighted Runs Created Plus*, was 9% *below* the league average threshold.

Snippet from The 2020 Prospect Digest Handbook: But he's a grinder, though. And there's something to be said for that. He's flawed, but he's the type of player to get everything out of talent. He's easy to root for. And he's constantly improving.

Scouting Report: Consider the following:

- Since 2006, only two 23-year-old Triple-A hitters met the following criteria in a season (min. 350 PA): 85 to 95 wRC+, a strikeout rate between 24% and 26%, and a walk rate between 7% and 10%. Those two players: Colin Moran and Mickey Moniak.

Moniak's a flawed player. The bat hasn't developed as expected. And, at best, it's a 45-grade tool. He doesn't take a ton of walks. He doesn't run frequently. And he's not an extraordinary defender either. But his power has crept up from below average to average. He's going to spend the rest of his professional career riding his lofty draft status between big league and minor league shuttles.

Ceiling: 1.0-win player
Risk: Moderate
MLB ETA: Debuted in 2020

14. Luis Garcia, 2B/SS

Hit	Power	SB	Patience	Glove	Overall
40/45	50	50	55	50	45

Born: 10/01/00	Age: 21	Bats: B	Top Comp: Brooks Conrad
Height: 5-11	Weight: 170	Throws: R	

Season	Team	Age	Level	PA	1B	2B	3B	HR	SB	CS	BB%	K%	AVG	OBP	SLG	ISO
2018	PHI	17	R	187	47	11	3	1	12	8	8.02%	11.23%	0.369	0.433	0.488	0.119
2019	PHI	18	A	524	66	14	3	4	9	8	8.40%	25.19%	0.186	0.261	0.255	0.069
2021	PHI	20	A	395	50	16	5	11	11	6	13.67%	23.54%	0.246	0.356	0.423	0.177
2021	PHI	20	A+	70	9	2	0	2	4	0	14.29%	27.14%	0.224	0.333	0.362	0.138

Background: Listed as the 7th best prospect by MLB Pipeline on the international free agent market during the 2017-18 signing period; the Phillies – as you guessed – handed Garcia a whopping $2.5 million bonus. And it looked like a bargain a year later as the toolsy switch-hitter slugged a scorching .369/.433/.488 with 11 doubles, three triples, and a dinger in only 43 games with the club's Gulf Coast League affiliate. Then the trademark Philadelphia Aggressive Promotion Schedule was put in place. Garcia jumped straight up to Low-A, as an 18-year-old, and looked completely overmatched: he hit a lowly .186/.261/.255 in 127 games. The front office cautiously sent the young middle infielder back down to Low-A and his production improved a bit: he batted .246/.356/.423 with 16 doubles, five triples, 11 homeruns, and 11 stolen bases in 87 games. His overall production, per *Weighted Runs Created Plus*, was 15% better than the league average. Garcia spent the last 16 games in High-A, mostly struggling.

Snippet from The 2020 Prospect Digest Handbook: It's still way too early to jump off of Garcia's bandwagon, but I certainly have one foot hanging off the ride.

Scouting Report: Consider the following:

- Since 2006, here's the list of 20-year-old Low-A hitters to post a wRC+ total between 110 and 120, a walk rate above 12% and a strikeout rate between 23% and 26% (min. 300 PA): Thomas Hickman, Boss Moanaroa, Brandon Diaz, and Luis Garcia.

Let's be frank: Garcia did a lot of damage during his final nine games in Low-A – he batted .526/.581/1.026 with three doubles, two triples, and four homeruns. Prior to the explosion he was batting .210/.329/.346 in 78 games. It's easy to dream upon the prospect that Garcia once looked like, but that seems like forever ago. He has some thump and speed as a middle infielder. But the hit tool is below-average at best. I'm officially jumping off the Luis Garcia bandwagon.

Ceiling: 1.5-win player
Risk: Moderate
MLB ETA: 2024

15. Jhailyn Ortiz, RF

Hit	Power	SB	Patience	Glove	Overall
40	70	40	50	45	40

Born: 11/18/98	Age: 23	Bats: R	Top Comp: Xavier Scruggs
Height: 6-3	Weight: 215	Throws: R	

Season	Team	Age	Level	PA	1B	2B	3B	HR	SB	CS	BB%	K%	AVG	OBP	SLG	ISO
2018	PHI	19	A	454	58	18	2	13	2	2	7.71%	32.60%	0.225	0.297	0.375	0.151
2019	PHI	20	A+	478	49	15	3	19	2	3	7.53%	31.17%	0.200	0.272	0.381	0.181
2021	PHI	22	A+	303	39	11	0	19	4	1	9.57%	28.38%	0.262	0.358	0.521	0.259
2021	PHI	22	AA	88	11	1	0	4	0	0	10.23%	30.68%	0.208	0.307	0.377	0.169

Background: The front office opened up their wallet and doled out a whopping $4 million to sign the slugging teenager during the 2015-16 international signing period. After showing some promise – as well as some potential swing-and-miss issues – as a 17-year-old in the Gulf Coast League in 2016, Ortiz turned a *lot* of heads with his explosive showing in the New York-Penn League the following year. Ortiz slugged .302/.401/.560 with 24 extra-base knocks in only 47 games with Williamsport. The Dominican Republic native struggled – *mightily* – over the next seasons, but the hulking corner outfielder regained his stroke in 2021 in his return to High-A. He belted out 11 doubles and 19 homeruns in 74 games with Jersey Shore. But his production, perhaps as expected, cratered upon his promotion up to Reading; he batted .208/.307/.377 in 21 games with the club's Double-A affiliate.

Scouting Report: Forgotten about in The 2020 Prospect Digest Handbook due to horrific back-to-back showings, Ortiz buffed some of the luster he lost on his prospect status. Consider the following:

- Since 2006, only three 22-year-old High-A hitters have posted a wRC+ between 128 and 138, a strikeout rate between 26% and 30%, and a walk rate below 10% (min. 250 PA): Xavier Scruggs, J.J. Matijevic, and – of course – Mr. Jhailyn Ortiz.

The power's a legit 70-grade. And if he made enough contact in a season he could probably barrel enough heaters for 50 dingers. The problem, however, is quite obvious: this was his second trip through High-A *and* he was two years older. Open stance. Not a lot of movement. And good bat speed. But he's a one dimensional guy that only does that one thing really well every couple of games.

Ceiling: 1.5-win player
Risk: Moderate
MLB ETA: 2022

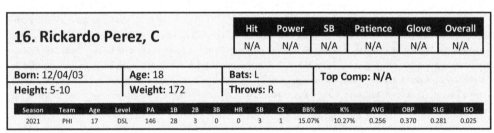

16. Rickardo Perez, C

	Hit	Power	SB	Patience	Glove	Overall
	N/A	N/A	N/A	N/A	N/A	N/A

Born: 12/04/03	Age: 18	Bats: L	Top Comp: N/A
Height: 5-10	Weight: 172	Throws: R	

Season	Team	Age	Level	PA	1B	2B	3B	HR	SB	CS	BB%	K%	AVG	OBP	SLG	ISO
2021	PHI	17	DSL	146	28	3	0	0	3	1	15.07%	10.27%	0.256	0.370	0.281	0.025

Background: Signed out Valencia, Venezuela, in early February 2021. Perez, according to a report from MLB.com, went through the same training / development program as current Phillies Top 10 prospect Francisco Morales. The young lefty-swinging backstop earned a hefty $1.2 million bonus. Listed as 5-foot-10 and 172 pounds, Perez spent the summer battling against the Dominican Summer League competition, batting a mediocre .256/.370/.281 with just a trio of doubles in 146 trips to the plate.

Scouting Report: Very long and lean and, according to MLB.com reports, Perez is loaded with tools on both sides of the ball. And despite the underwhelming professional debut showing Perez showed a willingness to work the count, make consistent contact, and threw out more than one-third of the potential base thieves. There is no available tape on Perez, but next summer the Phillies may aggressively push him stateside.

Ceiling: N/A
Risk: N/A
MLB ETA: N/A

17. Cristopher Sanchez, LHP

	FB	SL	CH	Command	Overall
	60	50	50	40	40

Born: 12/12/96	Age: 25	Bats: L	Top Comp: Genesis Cabrera
Height: 6-1	Weight: 165	Throws: L	

Season	Team	Age	Level	IP	TBF	K/9	K%	BB/9	BB%	K-BB%	ERA	FIP	xFIP	Pit/Bat
2018	TBR	21	R	43.0	197	7.12	17.26%	4.60	11.17%	6.09%	4.60	4.99	4.94	2.64
2019	TBR	22	A	40.1	162	8.26	22.84%	2.45	6.79%	16.05%	2.01	3.62	3.36	3.37
2019	TBR	22	A+	34.0	139	9.53	25.90%	3.44	9.35%	16.55%	1.85	2.60	3.08	3.63
2021	PHI	24	AAA	73.0	325	10.97	27.38%	5.92	14.77%	12.62%	4.68	3.69	4.03	3.96

Background: Built in a similar fashion as former Top 100 prospect – and current Cleveland starting pitcher – Triston McKenzie. Sanchez, who's listed at 6-foot-1 and 165 pounds, reached the pinnacle level of professional baseball in his seventh season. Originally a member of the Tampa Bay Rays, the Phillies acquired the lanky left-hander in 2019 for Curtis Mead. Last season Sanchez made 19 appearances in Triple-A, 17 of them coming in via the start, while fanning a whopping 89 and walking 48 in only 73.0 innings of work. The southpaw made seven appearances in the big leagues as well, throwing 12.2 innings with 13 strikeouts and seven walks.

Scouting Report: Consider the following:

- Since 2006, only three 24-year-old Triple-A pitchers have fanned at between 26% and 28% with a walk percentage north of 13% in a season (min. 70 IP): Anthony Castro, J.P. Martinez, and Cristopher Sanchez.

Lively mid-90s heater that plays up due to Sanchez's long arms. He'll show a couple of average offspeed offerings: a mid-80s slider and a mid-80s changeup, the latter being the better of the two options. He continues to struggle finding the strike zone, so it's a pipedream – especially at this point – for him to magically discover any type of reliable control. He could be a useful left arm out of the pen though – in low leverage situations.

Ceiling: 0.5- to 1.0-win player
Risk: Low to Moderate
MLB ETA: Debuted in 2020

18. Cristian Hernandez, RHP

	FB	CB	CH	Command	Overall
	50/55	45/50	50/55	40/45	40

Born: 09/23/00	Age: 21	Bats: R	Top Comp: Junior Guerra
Height: 6-3	Weight: 180	Throws: R	

Season	Team	Age	Level	IP	TBF	K/9	K%	BB/9	BB%	K-BB%	ERA	FIP	xFIP	Pit/Bat
2018	PHI	17	R	63.0	265	7.00	18.49%	1.43	3.77%	14.72%	2.57	2.98	3.04	1.56
2021	PHI	20	A	70.2	301	10.95	28.57%	3.69	9.63%	18.94%	3.69	4.79	4.18	3.71

Background: Not a highly touted prospect – even after a quietly stellar 2021 season – but Hernandez's production is forcing people to take notice. An under-the-radar, overlooked type of signing on the international market, the well-built 6-foot-3, 180-pound right-hander made his debut in the Dominican Summer League in 2018, throwing 63.0 innings of work to go along with a 2.57 ERA, 49 strikeouts, and just 10 walks. That production earned him a roster spot on the midsummer DSL All-Star squad. The Venezuelan-born hurler missed all of 2019, then didn't play – obviously – the following year due to the pandemic. Last season's action was the first time in three years that Hernandez toed the rubber in an actual game. He made 18 appearances for the Clearwater Threshers, 15 of which were starts, averaging a whopping 11.0 strikeouts and 3.7 walks per nine innings.

Scouting Report: Consider the following:

- Since 2006, only four 20-year-old pitchers have struck out between 27% and 29% with a walk percentage between 9% and 11% of the hitters they faced in Low-A (min. 60 IP): Wade Davis, Luis Pena, Connor Hoehn, and Cristian Hernandez

An interesting arm because (A) he's more projection than anything at this point and (B) the production was quite stellar, especially given the extended layoff. Hernandez adds and subtracts off his fastball, though it generally sits in the 90 and 92 mph range. His best secondary offering – and perhaps his best overall pitch – is a solid straight low-80s changeup thrown with fantastic arm speed. He'll also mix in a loopy, fringy curveball; he slows his body down when throwing it. He projects as more of an up-and-down arm for now.

Ceiling: 0.5- to 1.0-win player
Risk: Moderate
MLB ETA: 2024

19. Victor Vargas, RHP

	FB	SL	CH	Command	Overall
	45	50	50	50	40

Born: 09/03/00	Age: 21	Bats: R	Top Comp: N/A
Height: 6-1	Weight: 175	Throws: R	

Season	Team	Age	Level	IP	TBF	K/9	K%	BB/9	BB%	K-BB%	ERA	FIP	xFIP	Pit/Bat
2018	PHI	17	R	45.0	208	6.80	16.35%	2.20	5.29%	11.06%	6.00	5.53	4.00	1.43
2019	PHI	18	R	25.0	100	5.40	15.00%	1.44	4.00%	11.00%	1.44	3.31	3.20	1.56
2019	PHI	18	A-	14.2	60	6.75	18.33%	4.91	13.33%	5.00%	1.84	3.54	4.05	3.52
2021	PHI	20	A	49.2	209	9.79	25.84%	2.17	5.74%	20.10%	3.62	3.58	3.90	3.48
2021	PHI	20	A+	32.2	159	8.54	19.50%	4.68	10.69%	8.81%	10.47	6.58	5.77	3.60

Background: Signed out of Cartagena, Colombia, for a hefty $525,000 bonus during the 2017 summer. Vargas, like a lot of the club's other bonus babies, jumped straight into the Gulf Coast League. After a quick, albeit disappointing, jaunt through the rookie league, Vargas split time back in the Gulf as well as Williamsport the in 2019. Last season, the 6-foot-1, 175-pound right-hander made 22 appearances, 15 of them starts, mostly coming in Low-A. He tossed a career best 87.1 innings, recording 88 punch outs, 31 walks, and an aggregate 5.98 ERA.

Scouting Report: According to reports, Vargas's heater was clocked in the low 90s at the time of signing in 2017. Fast forward a couple years and his fastball was barely hard enough to break a pane of window. He was consistently sitting 87- to 89-mph in a mid-July start against Bradenton. He'll mix in a solid-average slider and a changeup that lacks enough velo separation too really matter unless he's locating it down and away. Vargas is strike-thrower, which is helping him succeed in the low levels. But his command is average. From a projection standpoint, there's not a left in the tank. The production and age, though, make him at least noteworthy.

Ceiling: 0.5- to 1.0-win player
Risk: Moderate
MLB ETA: 2023/2024

20. Erik Miller, LHP

	FB	CB	SL	CH	Command	Overall
	60	N/A	55	N/A	40	40

Born: 02/13/98	Age: 24	Bats: L	Top Comp: Justin Wilson
Height: 6-5	Weight: 240	Throws: L	

Season	Team	Age	Level	IP	TBF	K/9	K%	BB/9	BB%	K-BB%	ERA	FIP	xFIP	Pit/Bat
2019	PHI	21	A-	20.0	86	13.05	33.72%	3.15	8.14%	25.58%	0.90	2.15	2.60	4.00
2019	PHI	21	A	13.0	55	11.77	30.91%	4.15	10.91%	20.00%	2.08	2.49	3.55	3.58

Background: A big lefty out of Creve Coeur, Missouri; Miller spent three rather productive years with the Stanford Cardinals between 2017 and 2019. And after a frustratingly up-and-down junior campaign – he averaged 11 strikeouts and five walk s per nine innings in 16 starts – the Phillies took a flier on the big lefty in the fourth round. Miller tossed another 36.0 innings between the Gulf Coast, Williamsport, and Lakewood during his debut. Last season, with the pandemic impacted year in the rearview mirror, the southpaw was limited to just 12.2 innings as he spent the majority of the year on the disabled list. He posted a 16-to-11 strikeout-to-walk ratio.

Scouting Report: Raw. Wild. Aging. Miller, who is now entering his age-24 season, has just 48.2 professional innings under his belt. So it goes without saying that he remains largely unknown. His fastball will sit in the 93- to 95-mph range with riding life, showing some cutting/sinking action at times as well. It's heavy, so I'm guessing the spin rate is above-average. In his High-A start late in the year Miller was (A) really battling control issues and (B) choking off both of his breaking balls. His slider showed some wicked movement, but – again – he had no feel for it. Given his advanced age, lack of experience, and recent injuries it's pretty safe to say he's ticketed for a relief roll at some point in the very near future.

Ceiling: 0.5- to 1.0-win player
Risk: Moderate to High
MLB ETA: 2024

Pittsburgh Pirates

Top Prospects

1. Oneil Cruz, SS

Hit	Power	SB	Patience	Glove	Overall
50	55/60	60/50	50	50	60

Born: 10/04/98	Age: 23	Bats: L	Top Comp: Didi Gregorius
Height: 6-7	Weight: 210	Throws: R	

Season	Team	Age	Level	PA	1B	2B	3B	HR	SB	CS	BB%	K%	AVG	OBP	SLG	ISO
2018	PIT	19	A	443	69	25	7	14	11	5	7.67%	22.57%	0.286	0.343	0.488	0.201
2019	PIT	20	R	11	5	1	0	0	1	0	9.09%	9.09%	0.600	0.636	0.700	0.100
2019	PIT	20	A+	145	27	6	1	7	7	3	5.52%	26.21%	0.301	0.345	0.515	0.213
2019	PIT	20	AA	136	20	8	3	1	3	1	11.03%	25.74%	0.269	0.346	0.412	0.143
2021	PIT	22	AA	273	41	15	5	12	18	3	7.33%	23.44%	0.292	0.346	0.536	0.244
2021	PIT	22	AAA	29	5	1	0	5	1	0	27.59%	17.24%	0.524	0.655	1.286	0.762

Background: Originally signed by the Los Angeles Dodgers for a smidgeon under $1 million during the summer of 2015 – which seems so long ago at this point. The Dodgers flipped the gargantuan shortstop, along with right-hander Angel German to Pittsburgh for what amounted to 20.0 regular season and six postseason innings from Tony Watson. And since entering the Pirates' system Cruz has blossomed into one of the game's preeminent prospects. After a disappointing first stint in Low-A between both organizations in 2017, Pittsburgh sent the 6-foot-7, 230-pound teenager back down to the South Atlantic League for a do-over. This time, though, he proved up to the task. In 103 games with the West Virginia Power, Cruz slugged .286/.343/.488 with 46 extra-base knocks. He also torched the High-A competition and looked comfortable against Double-A pitching in 2019. Last season, Pittsburgh continued their slow-and-steady approach with the burgeoning star as they sent him back down to Double-A for additional seasoning. In an injury-interrupted 2021, Cruz hit .292/.346/.536 with 15 doubles, five triples, 12 homeruns, and 18 stolen bases in 62 games with Altoona. He also appeared in six games with the Indianapolis Indians, going 11-for-21. Per *Weighted Runs Created Plus*, his overall production topped the league average mark by a whopping 58%. A mild forearm strain forced him to miss roughly six weeks during the middle of the year.

Snippet from The 2020 Prospect Digest Handbook: Cruz is just beginning to tap into his massive, plus power potential. There's 30- to 35-homer thunder brewing in his bat. Above-average speed, OK-ish contact rates, above-average defense, and proven production against significantly older competition. Ke'Bryan Hayes is the long term answer at the hot corner. So Cruz will have to beat out former top prospect Cole Tucker for the starting shortstop gig. He could – and should – become a full fledged star, a potential face of the franchise. At his peak, Cruz looks like a .280/.350/.480-type hitter.

Scouting Report: Consider the following:

- Since 2006, only three 22-year-old hitters posted a 130 to 140 wRC+ with a 6.0% to 9.0% walk rate and a 22.5% to 24.5% strikeout rate in Double-A with one organization (min. 250 PA): Aaron Cunningham, Neftali Soto, and Oneil Cruz.

The elephant – or maybe giraffe – in the room, of course, is Cruz's 6-foot-7 frame. Per the invaluable *Stathead on Baseball Reference*, only four shortstops appeared in at least 100 games in a season who were 6-foot-4: Carlos Correa, Andy Fox, Cal Ripken Jr., and Corey Seager. However, there has never been a shortstop that was 6-foot-5 or taller to appear in at least 100 games at the position in a season. Cruz is two inches taller than that. Offensively speaking, the young Dominican showed improved contact rates, above-average speed with his long, galloping strides, and his in-game power continues to improve. Defensively, is average-ish at the infield's most important position. One more final thought: the lefty-swinging Cruz handles southpaws and right-handers equally well. He's still tracking like a .280/.350/.480-type hitter, though there's obviously more value if he can stick at shortstop instead of moving to the outfielder.

Ceiling: 5.0-win player
Risk: Moderate
MLB ETA: Debuted in 2021

2. Henry Davis, C

Hit	Power	SB	Patience	Glove	Overall
50	60	45/30	55	50	60

Born: 09/21/99	Age: 22	Bats: R	Top Comp: J.T. Realmuto
Height: 6-2	Weight: 210	Throws: R	

Season	Team	Age	Level	PA	1B	2B	3B	HR	SB	CS	BB%	K%	AVG	OBP	SLG	ISO
2021	PIT	21	A+	24	2	0	1	2	1	0	16.67%	33.33%	0.263	0.375	0.684	0.421

Background: A projected first round pick entering the 2021 season, Davis carried his breakout, COVID shortened sophomore showing into a dominant junior campaign for the Louisville Cardinals. A 6-foot-1, 220-pound backstop out of Bedford, New York, Davis was a four-year letterman at Fox Lane High School en route to earning some national recognition: *Perfect Game* ranked the young power hitter as the 231st best prospect in the 2018 Class, as well as naming him the New York Player of the Year. Undrafted as a prep player, Davis stepped into Louisville's lineup as a true freshman without missing a beat: in 45 games for the ACC powerhouse, he slugged .280/.345/.386 with five double, three homeruns, and a solid 18-to-13 strikeout-to-walk ratio.

Davis' production *exploded* during his shortened sophomore campaign, hitting a scorching .372/.481/.698 while fanning just four times in 52 plate appearances. And he was able to carry nearly an identical slash line through his final season in college. In a career high 50 games for Head Coach Dan McDonnell, Davis battered the competition to the tune of .370/.483/.663 with nine doubles, 15 homeruns, 10 stolen bases, and a stellar 31-to-24 strikeout-to-walk ratio. Pittsburgh drafted the promising catcher with the top pick last July, signing him to a deal worth $6.5 million, saving the club nearly $2 million to spend elsewhere. Davis appeared in just eight games during his debut, batting .308/.387/.808.

Scouting Report: Per the usual, my pre-draft write-up:

> *"A late addition to the potential #1 overall pick conversation, Davis has been the best backstop in college baseball – by a wide margin. Consider the following:*

> - *Between 2011 and 2019, only four ACC hitters have matched the following criteria (min. 175 PA): .360/.460/.630 with a double digit walk rate and a sub-14% strikeout rate. Those four hitters are James Ramsey, Will Craig (of defensive blunder fame), Seth Beer, and Adam Haseley – all of whom were first round selections that never truly panned out. Henry Davis' offensive production in 2021 would make him the fifth player in the group.*

> *Not overly promising, let's expand the criteria to all Division I hitters. Consider the following:*

> - *Between 2011 and 2019, only 13 DI hitters batted .360/.460/.630 with a walk rate between 11% and 15% and a strikeout rate between 10% and 14% (min. 175 PA): Pete Alonso, Josh Jung, Kody Hoese, Andrew Vaughn, D.J. Peterson, David Kerian, Grant Little, Effrey Valdez, Kevin Kaczmarski, Trenton Moses, Mason Katz, Andrew Moritz, and Cameron Cannon.*

> *An old school throwback that refuses to wear batting gloves at the plate, Davis has always shown an advanced approach at the plate – as evidenced by his stellar peripherals. The Louisville standout starts from a modified crouch and generates plus bat speed thanks to his core and lower body. He's a perennial 20-homerun threat. Defensively, he unfurls a howitzer on potential thieves with the accuracy to match. In terms of upside think: .270/.340/.450."*

Ceiling: 5.0-win player
Risk: Moderate
MLB ETA: 2023

3. Roansy Contreras, RHP

	FB	CB	SL	CH	Command	Overall
	60	60	50	55	60	60

Born: 11/07/99	Age: 22	Bats: R	Top Comp: Carlos Carrasco
Height: 6-0	Weight: 175	Throws: R	

Season	Team	Age	Level	IP	TBF	K/9	K%	BB/9	BB%	K-BB%	ERA	FIP	xFIP	Pit/Bat
2018	NYY	18	A	34.2	143	7.27	19.58%	3.12	8.39%	11.19%	3.37	4.48	4.50	3.78
2018	NYY	18	A-	28.2	107	10.05	29.91%	2.83	8.41%	21.50%	1.26	2.75	2.84	3.75
2019	NYY	19	A	132.1	536	7.69	21.08%	2.45	6.72%	14.37%	3.33	3.67	3.80	3.90
2021	PIT	21	AA	54.1	218	12.59	34.86%	1.99	5.50%	29.36%	2.65	2.74	2.93	3.74

Background: Signed by the Yankees for $250,000 in early July 2016, the wiry right-hander would make his unheralded debut the next season, splitting time between the foreign and domestic rookie leagues with modest results (5.7 K/9 and 2.9 BB/9). Contreras started to come into his own as an 18-year-old in 2018 as he shredded the New York-Penn League competition and mowed down the South Atlantic League hitters, averaging 8.5 strikeouts and just 3.0 walks per nine innings between affiliates. The Peralvillo, Dominican Republic, native would spend the entirety of the 2019 season working out of the Charleston RiverDogs' rotation, missing a handful of bats (7.7 K/9) as he continued to throw plenty of strikes (2.4 BB/9). After missing the 2020 season due to the COVID-imposed shutdown, the Yankees dealt the wiry 6-foot, 175-pound righty to the Pirates, along with Canaan Smith-Njigba, Miguel Yajure, and Maikol Escotto in exchange for a healthy Jameson Taillon. Contreras spent the majority of last season with Altoona in Double-A, though he did make one start with Indianapolis and another brief, three-inning appearance with the Pirates. He finished the minor league season with 82 strikeouts and just 13 walks in 58.0 innings of work. Like Oneil Cruz, Contreras missed several weeks due to a forearm strain. Following the season, the young right-hander made five starts with the Peoria Javelinas in the AFL, throwing 14.0 innings with 18 punch outs and four walks.

Snippet from The 2020 Prospect Digest Handbook: An interesting low lever arm developing for the Yankees – though I'd bet he's more likely ticketed as a trade chip rather than a member of the club's big league roster. Contreras attacks hitters with a loose-armed 93- to 94-mph fastball, an above-average curveball, which he'll vary the velocity and shape; and a changeup that flashes 55. The line between a solid backend starting pitcher and Jeanmar Gomez isn't extraordinarily large, but Contreras looks like a contender to take the multiple-inning relief route. The stuff's solid and he throws strikes. But there's not one true swing-and-miss offering.

Scouting Report: Though I predicted his impending status as a trade chip two years ago, his once-destined status as a #5-type starting pitcher looks to be underestimated by several margins. Contreras was the first pitcher I scouted in the 2021 season where I was actually in awe in his improved, oft-dominant repertoire. His fastball went from 94-mph all the way up to 97 mph last season. His curveball bumped up from above-average to plus. His changeup found consistency and went from flashing 55 to being a 55-grade offering. He also added a hard 89-mph slider/cutter as well. Perhaps the best part about Contreras emergence as a legitimate, across the board Top 100 prospect: he's throwing a larger number of quality strikes. He doesn't possess a true bonafide ace level ceiling, but he's going to settle in quite nicely as a strong #2.

Ceiling: 4.5-win player
Risk: Moderate
MLB ETA: Debuted in 2021

4. Liover Peguero, SS

	Hit	Power	SB	Patience	Glove	Overall
	50/55	40/50	60	50	60	60

Born: 12/31/00	Age: 21	Bats: R	Top Comp: N/A
Height: 6-1	Weight: 200	Throws: R	

Season	Team	Age	Level	PA	1B	2B	3B	HR	SB	CS	BB%	K%	AVG	OBP	SLG	ISO
2018	ARI	17	R	90	18	3	3	1	4	1	6.67%	13.33%	0.309	0.356	0.457	0.148
2018	ARI	17	R	71	13	0	0	0	3	2	7.04%	23.94%	0.197	0.254	0.197	0.000
2019	ARI	18	R	156	37	7	3	5	8	1	7.69%	21.79%	0.364	0.410	0.559	0.196
2019	ARI	18	A-	93	16	4	2	0	3	1	8.60%	18.28%	0.262	0.333	0.357	0.095
2021	PIT	20	A+	417	66	19	2	14	28	6	7.91%	25.18%	0.270	0.332	0.444	0.174

Background: Originally signed by Arizona for a shade under $500,000 five years ago. The DBacks would eventually flip the Dominican middle infielder, along with former first rounder Brennan Malone and international bonus money to the Pirates for Starling Marte and cash prior to the 2020 season. Prior to the lost COVID 2020 season, Peguero split time between the Pioneer and Northwest Leagues, batting an aggregate .326/.382/.485 in 60 games. Last season, like a lot of the club's better prospects, he was challenged with aggressive assignments by the Pirates' front office. And Peguero shined. Brightly. The then-20-year-old shortstop slugged .270/.332/.444 with 19 doubles, two triples, and 14 homeruns. He also swiped 28 bags. His production, per *Weighted Runs Created Plus*, topped the league average mark by 8%.

Snippet from The 2020 Prospect Digest Handbook: The offensive numbers in the opening portion of the year are a bit misleading. The Pioneer League tends to inflate numbers quite a bit. But…Peguero's batted ball data was nothing short of phenomenal. According to FanGraphs, the then-18-year-old posted an average exit velocity of 90 mph with a peak of 105 mph. Solid speed, glove, and a hit tool that could climb to a 55-grade. Arizona's front office seems determined to push Peguero aggressively through the system as long as he proves himself at a level over a reasonable amount of time. It wouldn't be shocking to see the Pirates take a similar approach. Very intriguing upside.

Scouting Report: As I speculated in The 2020 Handbook, the Pirates aggressively challenged the young shortstop. And his bat proved ready for the test. The power output is a bit misleading, though. The young infielder took full advantage of the Grasshoppers' incredibly hitter-friendly confines – particularly in the homerun department as he slugged 10 of his 14 dingers at home. There's a chance for an above-average hit tool, plus speed, and strong defensive contributions. The power is likely going to rest around the 15- to 17-homerun mark.

Ceiling: 4.0-win player
Risk: Moderate
MLB ETA: 2023/2024

5. Nick Gonzales, 2B/SS

	Hit	Power	SB	Patience	Glove	Overall
	55	50	50	50	55	60

Born: 05/27/99	Age: 23	Bats: R	Top Comp: Jake Cronenworth
Height: 5-10	Weight: 195	Throws: R	

Season	Team	Age	Level	PA	1B	2B	3B	HR	SB	CS	BB%	K%	AVG	OBP	SLG	ISO
2021	PIT	22	A+	369	53	23	4	18	7	2	10.84%	27.37%	0.302	0.385	0.565	0.262

Background: Perhaps not surprising given the pall of COVID hanging over a mostly lost season, the 2020 Draft opened up with seven straight collegiate picks with the Pirates making the last of those selections when the nabbed New Mexico State University star infielder Nick Gonzales. The only player chosen before the fourth round in school history, Pittsburgh signed the slugging second baseman / shortstop to a deal worth $5,432,400 – the full recommended slot value. A prolific hitter throughout his entire tenure with the Aggies, Gonzales batted .347/.425/.596 as a true freshman, followed it up with a scorching .432/.532/.773 slash line during his sophomore campaign, and looked unstoppable during his 16-game cameo as a junior (.448/.610/1.155). Last season, his first taste of pro ball, the front office pushed the 5-foot-10, 195-pound prospect straight up to High-A to begin his march towards The Show. In 80 games with the Greensboro Grasshoppers, Gonzales slugged .303/.385/.565 with 23 doubles, four triples, 18 homeruns, and seven stolen bases. Per *Weighted Runs Created Plus*, his production topped the league average threshold by a whopping 50%. The former New Mexico Star thumper also appeared in 19 games with the Peoria Javelinas, batting .380/.483/.549.

Scouting Report: Consider the following:

- Since 2006, only three 22-year-old hitters met the following criteria in High-A with one organization (min. 350 PA): 145 to 155 wRC+, a 26% to 28% strikeout rate, and a 9% to 12% walk rate. Those three hitters: future Hall of Famer Paul Goldschmidt, Brandon Wagner, and – of course – Nick Gonzales.

There are a couple important factors to consider:

1. Gonzales stepped right into High-A with essentially 16 games in between his sophomore and debut professional seasons.
2. He fractured a finger diving back to a base and missed – roughly – five weeks of action. Upon his return from the disabled list he batted a lowly .152/.222/.318 over his first 16 games. After that, though, he slugged .335/.430/.625 over his remaining 56 games.
3. The Greensboro Grasshoppers' home ballpark, First National Bank Field, is very friendly to hitters. And it shows in his home/road splits: .322/.393/.673 vs. .265/.373/.435

Gonzales flirted with some questionable swing-and-miss numbers throughout the season – he whiffed 27.4% of his total plate appearances – but he showed steady improvement as he adjusted to minor league pitching. He whiffed in 31.2% of his plate appearances in May, June, and July, but posted a 25.1% mark in August and September. Very solid toolkit and tracking to be an above-average big leaguer. Think: .290/.350/.450.

Ceiling: 4.0-win player
Risk: Moderate
MLB ETA: 2023

6. Quinn Priester, RHP		FB	CB	SL	CH	Command	Overall
		55/60	60	60	N/A	50/55	60

Born: 09/16/00	Age: 21	Bats: R	Top Comp: Mike Clevinger
Height: 6-3	Weight: 175	Throws: R	

Season	Team	Age	Level	IP	TBF	K/9	K%	BB/9	BB%	K-BB%	ERA	FIP	xFIP	Pit/Bat
2019	PIT	18	R	32.2	140	10.19	26.43%	2.76	7.14%	19.29%	3.03	2.92	2.96	1.81
2021	PIT	20	A+	97.2	407	9.03	24.08%	3.59	9.58%	14.50%	3.04	4.08	4.26	3.85

Background: Pittsburgh has been incredibly deft at drafting high school arms in the first round over the past several years – though getting them to sign is an entirely different dilemma. Since 2016, the club drafted Nick Lodolo, Shane Baz, Gunnar Hoglund, and Quinn Priester in the opening round, failing to sign Lodolo and Hoglund in 2016 and 2018. Priester, the 18th overall pick in 2019, signed for a hefty $3.4 million deal. A product of Cary-Grove High School, the 6-foot-3, 175-pound right-hander turned in an impressive debut as he made stops in the Gulf Coast and New York-Penn Leagues. Last season, the player development engine aggressively assigned the then-20-year-old straight up to High-A, despite throwing just four innings above rookie ball. And Priester proved to be not only up for the task, but also one of the game's better pitching prospects. In 20 starts with the Grasshoppers, the hard-throwing hurler punched out 98 and walked just 39 to go along with a 3.04 ERA, 4.08 FIP, and a 4.26 xFIP.

Snippet from The 2020 Prospect Digest Handbook: Showing easily repeatable, almost effortless mechanics; Priester attacks hitters with a deadly combination of a lively low- to mid-90s fastball and a sharp, late-breaking curveball – both grading out as plus pitches. His heater will show some solid arm side run at times as well. Reports indicate that he'll mix in a changeup at times, though he's mainly a two-pitch hurler at this point. As with a lot of young arms, his third pitch – the changeup – hasn't been used frequently.

Scouting Report: Consider the following:

- Since 2006, seven 20-year-old hurlers posted a 23% to 25% strikeout percentage with an 8.5% to 10.5% walk percentage in High-A with one organization (min. 75 IP): Kyle Muller, Troy Patton, Jesse Biddle, Johnny Barbato, Dan Cortes, Omar Poveda, and Quinn Priester.

Priester handled himself like a 10-year veteran as he navigated the waters of the hitter friendly confines of First National Bank Field, home to the Grasshoppers. Low- to mid-90s fastball, plus curveball, and a newly minted above-average / flashing plus slider. But over the course of a couple games, I never saw Priester's rumored changeup. There's more in the tank on the fastball; last season, particularly late in the year as it sat in the 93 mph range. There's the making of a very good #3-type hurler with some added helium if everything breaks the right way.

Ceiling: 4.0-win player
Risk: Moderate
MLB ETA: 2023

7. Michael Burrows, RHP			FB	CB	CH	Command	Overall
			65	60	50	50	60

Born: 11/08/99	Age: 22	Bats: R	Top Comp: N/A
Height: 6-2	Weight: 183	Throws: R	

Season	Team	Age	Level	IP	TBF	K/9	K%	BB/9	BB%	K-BB%	ERA	FIP	xFIP	Pit/Bat
2018	PIT	18	R	14.0	51	5.79	17.65%	2.57	7.84%	9.80%	0.64	3.66	4.02	1.25
2019	PIT	19	A-	43.2	193	8.86	22.28%	4.12	10.36%	11.92%	4.33	3.54	3.75	4.08
2021	PIT	21	A+	49.0	193	12.12	34.20%	3.67	10.36%	23.83%	2.20	3.28	4.36	4.27

Background: For all their flaws, particularly before the club's current GM Ben Cherington took over the captain's chair in 2019, the Pirates have done a fairly solid job of finding impressive talent well beyond the opening round of the draft. In the conversation as the organization's best late rounder in recent seasons, Pittsburgh unearthed the flame-throwing right-hander in the 11th round, 324th overall. The front office handed him a big $500,000 bonus to forgo his college career and join the organization. The 2018 draft pick made his debut that summer with in the Gulf Coast League, posting a barely-there 0.64 ERA with nine punch outs and four free passes in 14.0 innings of work. Burrows would spend the following season with West Virginia in the New York-Penn League, averaging 8.9 strikeouts and 4.1 walks per nine innings. Last year the 6-foot-2, 183-pound hurler jumped all the way up to High-A. And he dominated in an injury-shortened campaign. In 13 starts, spanning 49.0 innings, Burrows struck out 66 and walked just 20 to go along with a 2.20 ERA. He missed roughly two months with an oblique injury. He did pop up with the Peoria Javelinas in the Arizona Summer League, fanning 16 and walking five in 15.1 innings of work.

Scouting Report: Consider the following:

- Since 2006, only three 21-year-old hurlers posted a strikeout percentage north of 33% with a 9% to 11% walk percentage in High-A with one organization (min. 45 IP): Matt Moore, once viewed as the game's preeminent pitching prospect, Ben Hornbeck, and – of course – Michael Burrows, the former 11th round pick.

If he isn't my favorite minor league pitching prospect, he's awfully close to the top of the list at this point. Burrows brings a pair of wickedly overpowering plus pitches to the table: a mid-90s fastball that has as much late life as a greasy jalapeño popper rubbed in your eyes and his power, mid-80s curveball will haunt you like an ex-girlfriend. He'll mix in an upper-80s, almost too-firm changeup. There's reliever risk here. But if the changeup comes around, he's going to be a wipe big league arm. If I were to select one pitcher that comes from an unknown, under-the-radar to reach Shane Bieber territory it would be Michael Burrows.

Ceiling: 3.5-win player
Risk: Moderate to High
MLB ETA: 2023

8. Jared Jones, RHP			FB	CB	SL	CH	Command	Overall
			60	60	50	50	40/45	50

Born: 08/06/01	Age: 20	Bats: L	Top Comp: N/A
Height: 6-1	Weight: 180	Throws: R	

Season	Team	Age	Level	IP	TBF	K/9	K%	BB/9	BB%	K-BB%	ERA	FIP	xFIP	Pit/Bat
2021	PIT	19	A	66.0	302	14.05	34.11%	4.64	11.26%	22.85%	4.64	3.91	3.75	3.66

Background: Like a lot of the organizations owning early selections in the 2020 draft, the Pirates honed in on older, more experienced (read: with more reliable track records) players. The franchise selected a pair of college stars with the 7th and 31st overall picks (Nick Gonzales and Carmen Mlodzinski), but ventured into the prep ranks in the second round, grabbing hard-throwing right-hander Jared Jones – their lone high school pick in the five-round limited draft. Standing 6-foot-1 and 180 pounds, the club signed the La Mirada High School product to a deal worth $2.2 million – roughly $500,000 above the recommended slot bonus. The former University of Texas commit made his anticipated debut with the Bradenton Marauders last season, posting a staggering 103-to-34 strikeout-to-walk ratio in only 66.0 innings of work. For those counting at home: that's 14 whiffs every nine innings across 15 starts and three relief outings. He finished the year with a 4.64 ERA.

Scouting Report: Consider the following:

- Since 2006, only three 19-year-old hurlers posted at least a 33% strikeout percentage with a 9% to 12% walk percentage in Low-A with one organization (min. 60 IP): Grayson Rodriguez, the best pitching prospect in the game, Kyle Harrison, and – of course – Jared Jones.

A really, *really* promising arm that remains incredibly underrated – despite the dominant showing in 2021. Plus, mid-90s heater that sits – comfortably – in the 94- to 95-mph range. A wicked, hard biting 80-mph curveball. A decent little slider that sits in the mid-80s. And an average changeup. The command will likely climb into the 45-grade area in the next 12 to 24 months. The arsenal screams mid-rotation caliber arm, but he needs a more reliable third option if the command doesn't move into above-average territory.

Ceiling: 3.5-win player
Risk: Moderate
MLB ETA: 2023/2024

8. Tahnaj Thomas, RHP

	FB	CB	CH	Command	Overall
	80	60	55	40/45	60

Born: 06/16/99	Age: 23	Bats: R	Top Comp: N/A
Height: 6-4	Weight: 190	Throws: R	

Season	Team	Age	Level	IP	TBF	K/9	K%	BB/9	BB%	K-BB%	ERA	FIP	xFIP	Pit/Bat
2018	CLE	19	R	19.2	80	12.36	33.75%	4.58	12.50%	21.25%	4.58	4.32	3.42	2.24
2019	PIT	20	R	48.1	200	10.99	29.50%	2.61	7.00%	22.50%	3.17	3.67	3.49	3.92
2021	PIT	22	A+	60.2	281	9.20	22.06%	5.19	12.46%	9.61%	5.19	6.49	5.80	4.01

Background: It was the exact type of deal the perpetually rebuilding Pirates needed to make. They shipped off a serviceable, albeit flawed, big league bat in Jordan Luplow, as well as Max Moroff, in exchange for replacement level utility infielder Erik Gonzalez, right-hander Dane Mendoza, and lottery tick Tahnaj Thomas. And that gamble is beginning to payoff for Pittsburgh. Signed out of Freeport, Bahamas, for $200,000 by Cleveland in 2016, Thomas began to blossom in his first season in the Pirates' organization. In 48.1 innings with the Bristol Pirates, he averaged 11.0 strikeouts and 2.6 walks per nine innings. Last season, despite not throwing a single inning in full season ball prior to the year, Thomas was pushed all the way up to High-A. In 16 starts with the Grasshoppers, he posted a 62-to-35 strikeout-to-walk ratio in 60.2 innings. He finished the season with a 5.19 ERA, 6.49 FIP, and a 5.80 xFIP.

Snippet from The 2020 Prospect Digest Handbook: Explosive plus- to plus-fastball with riding, late life. A curveball that may eventually climb into 60-grade territory. And he'll mix in a changeup, though I didn't see one. Throw in some improving control / command and Thomas is quietly becoming a legitimate pitching prospect. The wiry right-hander may see another slight uptick in velocity as he gains experience and strength. This is a bit of an aggressive ranking, but he could eventually settle in as a mid-rotation caliber arm with the floor of a high-leverage relief arm.

Scouting Report: There's always been reliever risk with Thomas. And that was only reinforced after his up-and-down showing in High-A. Thomas' fastball was sitting – with *ease* – in the 97- to 100-mph range. He curveball went from a strong 55-grade to a hellacious, knee-buckling bender that haunts hitters' nightmares. And his changeup, which I didn't see in 2019, is an above-average, legitimate third weapon. The problem, of course, is command – though it's not as bad as his 5.2 BB/9 would suggest. After issuing 25 free passes in his first 25.1 innings, Thomas coughed up just 10 free passes over his remaining 35.1 innings. Very high ceiling, even higher risk.

Ceiling: 4.0-win player
Risk: High
MLB ETA: 2023/2024

9. Bubba Chandler, SS/RHP

	Hit	Power	SB	Patience	Glove	Overall
	40/50	30/55	40	50	50	45

	FB	CB	SL	CH	Control	Overall
	60	50/55	N/A	N/A	50	50

Born: 09/14/02	Age: 19	Bats: B	Top Comp: N/A
Height: 6-3	Weight: 200	Throws: R	

Season	Team	Age	Level	PA	1B	2B	3B	HR	SB	CS	BB%	K%	AVG	OBP	SLG	ISO
2021	PIT	18	CPX	37	3	1	0	1	0	0	13.51%	43.24%	0.167	0.324	0.300	0.133

Background: This isn't exactly your older brother's Pirates. And the oft-downtrodden franchise reminded everyone of that fact last July. After selecting Louisville backstop Henry Davis (and signed him to a well below slot deal), Anthony Solometo, and Lonnie White with their first three selections, Pittsburgh took a calculated gamble and picked two-sport phenom Bubba Chandler with the 72nd overall pick. Committed to the Clemson University as both a football *and* baseball player, the Pirates convinced the quarterback/pitcher/shortstop to bypass any collegiate glory for a hefty $3 million bonus – the equivalent money of a mid- to late- first round draft pick. Ranked as the 19th best quarterback in the country, Chandler, a four-star recruit, punched out 96 hitters in just 44.2 innings as a senior, posting a 1.25 ERA. According to reports, he also batted .411 with 41 runs, 35 RBIs, 12 doubles, and eight homeruns.

Scouting Report: First off, the organization intends on keeping their prized third rounder on both sides of the ball – a la Shohei Ohtani – at least at the beginning stages of his journey. But watching Chandler hit and pitch, it's immediately clear that his future's on the mound. It's not that he's a bad hitting prospect, but the swing is long – particularly from the left side and it needs a lot of seasoning. Also, it has too much of an uppercut. Unfortunately, I only saw limited game tape of Chandler pitch, but the talent is clear: plus fastball, two solid breaking balls, and a workable changeup. He did not toe the rubber in a Pittsburgh affiliate uniform, so watching him pitch will be a high priority in 2022.

Ceiling: 2.0-win player
Risk: Moderate
MLB ETA: 2024

11. Anthony Solometo, LHP

FB	SL	CH	Command	Overall
55	55	50	50/55	50

Born: 12/02/02	Age: 19	Bats: L	Top Comp: N/A
Height: 6-5	Weight: 220	Throws: L	

Background: Highly touted from an early age. Solometo, a massive 6-foot-5, 220-pound prep southpaw from New Jersey, committed to the University of North Carolina prior to his freshman year in high school. Fast forward a year later and the big lefty was dominating the high school competition: he posted a 1.59 ERA with a 5-2 ERA to go along with 64 punch outs in 44 innings. And following a COVID-shortened 2020 campaign, Solometo got off to another – typical – Solometo start: he didn't surrender a hit or run through his first 17.1 innings of work in 2021. He also struck out 64 hitters through his first 32.2 innings as well, giving up just one earned run, five hits, and five walks in the process. Pittsburgh selected the southpaw in the second round, 37th overall, and signed him to a deal worth $2,797,500.

Scouting Report: Per the usual, my pre-draft write-up:

> "While not in the Hideo Nomo category of funky windups, Solometo's herky-jerky, all legs and arms delivery isn't far behind. Beginning with an extraordinarily large step in his windup, the big lefty's curls his body away from the hitter – almost Luis Tiant-like – before unfurling an impressive arsenal from a low 3/4 slot. Low 90s fastball that will touch as high as 94 (according to reports), an above-average slider that plays up do his funk and arm slot, and a decent change up. And he doesn't alter his mechanical approach much from the stretch as well, so it'll be interesting to see how he adapts to professional base runners. There's some Kodi Medeiros-type feeling here with Solometo. Medieros had to move into the bullpen, despite his lofty draft status out of high school, due to his inability to get right-handers out."

Ceiling: 1.5- to 2.0-win player
Risk: Moderate
MLB ETA: 2025

12. Cody Bolton, RHP

FB	SL	CU	CH	Command	Overall
N/A	N/A	N/A	N/A	N/A	50

Born: 06/19/98	Age: 24	Bats: R	Top Comp: N/A
Height: 6-3	Weight: 230	Throws: R	

Season	Team	Age	Level	IP	TBF	K/9	K%	BB/9	BB%	K-BB%	ERA	FIP	xFIP	Pit/Bat
2018	PIT	20	A	44.1	179	9.14	25.14%	1.42	3.91%	21.23%	3.65	3.74	3.05	3.75
2019	PIT	21	A+	61.2	239	10.07	28.87%	2.04	5.86%	23.01%	1.61	1.96	2.46	3.85
2019	PIT	21	AA	40.0	167	7.43	19.76%	3.60	9.58%	10.18%	5.85	4.67	4.02	3.81

Background: A sixth round pick out of Tracy High School five years ago, Pittsburgh signed the promising wild card to a deal worth $300,000. Bolton began the slow-and-steady trek through the minor leagues as he made his debut in the Gulf Coast League that summer. He was limited to just nine starts, courtesy of an injury, with West Virginia in the South Atlantic League in 2018, averaging 9.1 strikeouts and just 1.4 walks per nine innings. Finally, though, the 6-foot-3, 230-pound right-hander put together a full, healthy season in 2019. Making stops between Bradenton and Altoona, the Virginia native tossed 101.2 innings, posting a 102-to-30 strikeout-to-walk ratio to go along with a tidy 3.28 ERA. Bolton looked poised to be one of the came's big risers in 2020, but it never happened courtesy of COVID. And he would miss his second straight season last year due to a torn medial meniscal tear in his knee, an injury that happened in mid-May and reports indicated he wouldn't report to baseball activities for four to six months.

Snippet from The 2020 Prospect Digest Handbook: Easily, easily the best pitcher you've never heard of. Bolton looks like a bonafide upper-part-of-the-rotation caliber arm in the making. I scouted a handful of his games last season. His fastball was sitting – *effortlessly* – in the 94- to 96-mph range and touching 98 mph several times. He features two types of breaking pitches, though they're quasi-similar. His slider is a wipeout swing-and-miss offering, sitting in the 87- to 88-mph neighborhood. He'll also feature a hard, low-90s cutter that he throws the same way as his slider that's lethal. Bolton, like Mitch Keller, throws a subpar, too firm changeup; though the former does show some promising fade and arm-side run. Bolton has the feel of a #2 / #3 type pitcher.

Scouting Report: Hopefully, Bolton can pick up where he left off two seasons ago.

Ceiling: 1.5- to 2.0-win player
Risk: Moderate to High
MLB ETA: 2022/2023

13. Ji-hwan Bae, 2B/CF

	Hit	Power	SB	Patience	Glove	Overall
	50/60	40	60	50	45	45

Born: 07/26/99	Age: 22	Bats: L	Top Comp: N/A
Height: 6-1	Weight: 185	Throws: R	

Season	Team	Age	Level	PA	1B	2B	3B	HR	SB	CS	BB%	K%	AVG	OBP	SLG	ISO
2018	PIT	18	R	152	27	6	2	0	10	4	9.87%	10.53%	0.271	0.362	0.349	0.078
2019	PIT	19	A	380	76	25	5	0	31	11	11.32%	20.26%	0.323	0.403	0.430	0.107
2021	PIT	21	AA	365	65	12	5	7	20	8	10.41%	22.74%	0.278	0.359	0.413	0.134

Background: Initially caught up in the Braves' international free agency scandal that would eventually result in the permanent ban of former GM John Coppolella. Pittsburgh swooped in and signed the lefty-swinging infielder to a deal worth $1.25 million. The 6-foot-1, 185-pound prospect showed some offensive promise as a 19-year-old in the South Atlantic League three years ago, hitting .323/.403/.430 in 86 games with the Greensboro Grasshoppers. Last season, as minor league baseball returned to its normal life, Bae was assigned to the minors' toughest challenge, Double-A. In 83 games with the Altoona Curve, Bae batted .278/.359/.413 with 12 doubles, five triples, seven homeruns, and 20 stolen bases. Per *Weighted Runs Created Plus*, his overall production was 14% better than the league average mark. Bae missed several weeks recovering from a Grade 1 MCL sprain in his knee resulting from a nasty collision in the outfield.

Snippet from The 2020 Prospect Digest Handbook: The potential to have a 60-grade hit tool and some defensive versatility. The Eiffel Tower-sized red flag, of course, has been Bae's lack of thunder in his bat. He's slugged exactly *zero* homeruns in 121 career minor league games.

Scouting Report: Consider the following:

- Since 2006, there were only four 21-year-old hitters to post a 110 to 120 wRC+, a 22% and 24% strikeout rate, and a 9% to 11% walk rate in Double-A with one organization (min. 350 PA): Nick Gordon, Bobby Bradley, Eguy Rosario, and Ji-hwan Bae.

After belting out a total of zero dingers in his first two seasons in professional baseball, Bae teed off for seven long balls in only 83 games at the minors' toughest challenge – Double-A. Above-average speed. Solid patience and contact rates. But the glove is a 45-grade at the keystone. The bat is the carrying tool here. If he can consistently bat near .300 he'll be a league average starting option.

Ceiling: 1.5-win player
Risk: Moderate
MLB ETA: 2022

14. Carmen Mlodzinski, RHP

	FB	CB	CH	Command	Overall
	60	60	55	45	45

Born: 02/19/99	Age: 23	Bats: R	Top Comp: N/A
Height: 6-2	Weight: 232	Throws: R	

Season	Team	Age	Level	IP	TBF	K/9	K%	BB/9	BB%	K-BB%	ERA	FIP	xFIP	Pit/Bat
2021	PIT	22	A+	50.1	213	11.44	30.05%	3.58	9.39%	20.66%	3.93	4.34	4.00	4.15

Background: Undrafted coming out of Hilton Head High School, Mlodzinski settled in nicely as a swing-man for the University of South Carolina: he posted a 43-to-21 strikeout-to-walk ratio in 45.2 innings of work. The club pushed him into the rotation full time during his sophomore season, but the tenure lasted just three starts before he hit the disabled list with a broken foot. After a strong showing in the Cape Cod with the Falmouth Falcons – he averaged 12.3 K/9 and just 1.2 BB/9 – Mlodzinski made four starts in the 2020 season before COVID prematurely ended it. Pittsburgh would select him in the opening round that summer, 31st overall, and signed him to a deal worth $2,050,00. Mlodzinski made his organizational debut last summer with the Greensboro Grasshoppers, throwing just 50.1 innings as he battled through a wonky shoulder. He finished his time with the High-A affiliate with a 64-to-20 strikeout-to-walk ratio and a 3.93 ERA. Mlodzinski made another seven relief appearances with the Peoria Javelinas in the Arizona Fall League, fanning nine and walking five in 11.0 innings.

Scouting Report: The Grasshoppers were absolutely loaded throughout the summer, featuring the likes of Henry Davis, Nick Gonzales, Lolo Sanchez, Braxton Ashcraft, Michael Burrows, Quinn Priester, Tahnaj Thomas, and – of course – Carmen Mlodzinski. A limited collegiate track record both in terms of success and health, Mlodzinski's showing in the Cape did more for his value than anything else. He sports a pair of plus offerings – a mid-90s fastball and a mid-80s power curveball that's often incorrectly labeled a slider. He also features a heavily pronated mid-80s changeup. Efficient mechanics with a long stride, the only thing stopping Mlodzinski's plod to a #4-type rotation spot is health – maybe command, too. Very solid gamble by the Pirates two years ago.

Ceiling: 1.5-win player
Risk: Moderate
MLB ETA: 2023/2024

15. Lonnie White Jr., CF

	Hit	Power	SB	Patience	Glove	Overall
	35/45	40/60	40/35	50	50	50

Born: 12/31/02	Age: 19	Bats: R	Top Comp: N/A
Height: 6-3	Weight: 212	Throws: R	

Season	Team	Age	Level	PA	1B	2B	3B	HR	SB	CS	BB%	K%	AVG	OBP	SLG	ISO
2021	PIT	18	CPX	33	4	2	0	2	0	0	6.06%	42.42%	0.258	0.303	0.516	0.258

Background: Not only did the Pirates – the once forever downtrodden franchise – convince Bubba Chandler to bypass collegiate football glory at a big time program, the club inked fellow two-sport star Lonnie White Jr., signing him away from a scholarship to play football at Penn State University. The 6-foot-3, 212-pound outfielder batted .395 with 16 extra-base hits and 25 RBIs during his final prep season. Pittsburgh drafted the Malvern Prep product in the second round, 64th overall, and signed him to a deal worth $1.5 million – roughly a half million dollars above the recommended slot bonus. White appeared in nine games with the club's Florida Complex League, batting .258/.303/.516 with two doubles and a pair of homeruns.

Scouting Report: As much power potential as any hitter in the club's farm system, including top overall pick Henry Davis. Plus bat speed. Incredibly fast hands. Tremendous rotation around the torso / spine. And White does it all effortlessly. He may struggle with contact – especially through the early parts of his career – and he's a bit rawer than the typical second rounder. Defensively, he's a long strider with a plus arm. There's All-Star caliber potential here, but there's a lot of risk. If White succeeds, it will be a true indictment of the club's development program.

Ceiling: 2.5-win player
Risk: High
MLB ETA: 2025

16. Brennan Malone, RHP

	FB	CB	SL	CH	Command	Overall
	N/A	N/A	N/A	N/A	N/A	45

Born: 09/08/00	Age: 21	Bats: R	Top Comp: N/A
Height: 6-4	Weight: 205	Throws: R	

Season	Team	Age	Level	IP	TBF	K/9	K%	BB/9	BB%	K-BB%	ERA	FIP	xFIP	Pit/Bat
2021	PIT	20	CPX	10.1	42	12.19	33.33%	4.35	11.90%	21.43%	5.23	4.15	3.46	1.81

Background: Part of the vaunted IMG Academy class that featured six players drafted in 2019, five of which eventually signed with their respect organizations. It was Malone, the broad-shoulder, NFL tight end-size right-hander that heard his name called first among the group. Selected with the 33rd overall pick that summer, the Diamondbacks signed the North Carolina native to a deal worth $2,202,200. Malone would make seven brief appearances between the Arizona Summer and Northwest Leagues, posting an 8-to-5 strikeout-to-walk in eight innings of work. And that, how they say, is that. The Diamondbacks sent their recent first round pick to the Pirates, along with Liover Peguero, for Gold Glove and All-Star outfielder Starling Marte at the end of August two years ago. Malone opened last season up with Bradenton Marauders of Low-A Southeast, making just three appearances before hitting the disabled list for roughly 2.5 months due to a severe lat strain. He would make it back to the mound for six brief rehab appearances at the end of the summer.

Snippet from The 2020 Prospect Digest Handbook: Huge, burly frame that looks like he should be playing professionally as a tight end or a linebacker. Malone attacks hitters with an impressive four pitch mix: his explosive fastball sits comfortably in the mid-90s with significant run on his two-seamer; his curveball shows solid 12-6 break; his slider, often times resembling a cutter, flashes plus; and his changeup should become an average weapon in his arsenal. Malone's an interesting prospect because his max effort and massive frame suggest a future reliever. Bu the has the potential to develop into a strong – pun intended – starting pitcher.

Scouting Report: Hopefully, the injury is firmly in the past for Malone.

Ceiling: 1.5-win player
Risk: Moderate
MLB ETA: 2024

17. Connor Scott, CF

	Hit	Power	SB	Patience	Glove	Overall
	45	40/50	50	50	55	45

Born: 10/08/99	Age: 22	Bats: L	Top Comp: N/A
Height: 6-3	Weight: 187	Throws: L	

Season	Team	Age	Level	PA	1B	2B	3B	HR	SB	CS	BB%	K%	AVG	OBP	SLG	ISO
2018	MIA	18	R	119	18	1	4	0	8	5	11.76%	24.37%	0.223	0.319	0.311	0.087
2018	MIA	18	A	89	13	2	0	1	1	3	11.24%	30.34%	0.211	0.295	0.276	0.066
2019	MIA	19	A	413	63	24	4	4	21	9	7.51%	22.03%	0.251	0.311	0.368	0.116
2019	MIA	19	A+	111	17	4	1	1	2	1	9.91%	23.42%	0.235	0.306	0.327	0.092
2021	MIA	21	A+	435	68	25	6	10	14	6	7.13%	21.15%	0.276	0.333	0.446	0.170

Background: The first pick under the Derek Jeter regime. Miami – and their new ownership group – selected the young center fielder out of H.B. Plant High School with the 13th overall selection four years ago. Sandwiched between the selections of Jordan Groshans and right-hander Logan Gilbert, Scott began his career on an inauspicious note: he batted a lowly .218/.309/.296 with just eight extra-base hits in 50 games between the Gulf Coast and South Atlantic Leagues. Scott's sophomore season was only slightly better as he split time between Clinton and Jupiter: he hit an aggregate .248/.310/.359 with 28 doubles, five triples, and five homeruns in 122 games. The 6-foot-3, 187-pound center fielder did, however, turn in his finest professional season to date in 2021 – though he returned back to High-A two years after making his debut at the level. In 96 games, the H.B. Plant High School product slugged .276/.333/.446 with 25 doubles and career highs in triples (six) and homeruns (10). He also swiped 14 bags in 20 attempts. Per *Weighted Runs Created Plus*, Scott's overall production topped the league average threshold by 12% - the best showing of his career. The Pirates acquired Scott, along with Kyle Nicolas and Zach Thompson in exchange for backstop Jacob Stallings.

Scouting Report: Consider the following:

- Since 2006, two 21-year-old hitters met the following criteria in High-A with one organization (min. 300 PA): 117 to 127 wRC+, 20% and 22% strikeout rate, and a 7% to 9% walk rate. Those two hitters: Eric Wood and Connor Scott.

The front office – rightly or wrongly – placed Scott on an aggressive, overly accelerated path the moment he stepped on a professional diamond. He made it to Low-A during his professional debut and spent significant time in High-A in his second season. And you have to wonder if the aggressive assignments have stunted his growth at some point. The power's creeping forward to the point where it likely gets to be an average skill. Good speed. 45-grade bat. The above-average defense likely pushes him between low end starter / bench outfielder.

Ceiling: 1.5-win player
Risk: Moderate
MLB ETA: 2023/2024

18. Endy Rodriguez, C

	Hit	Power	SB	Patience	Glove	Overall
	50	50/55	30	50	45	45

Born: 05/26/00	Age: 22	Bats: B	Top Comp: N/A
Height: 6-0	Weight: 170	Throws: R	

Season	Team	Age	Level	PA	1B	2B	3B	HR	SB	CS	BB%	K%	AVG	OBP	SLG	ISO
2018	NYM	18	R	96	8	4	1	2	1	0	15.63%	17.71%	0.197	0.333	0.355	0.158
2018	NYM	18	R	45	12	2	1	0	1	2	11.11%	20.00%	0.385	0.444	0.487	0.103
2019	NYM	19	R	90	11	10	1	0	4	0	11.11%	14.44%	0.293	0.393	0.453	0.160
2019	NYM	19	R	35	2	4	0	2	0	0	14.29%	14.29%	0.296	0.457	0.667	0.370
2021	PIT	21	A	434	65	25	6	15	2	0	11.52%	17.74%	0.294	0.380	0.512	0.218

Background: Arguably the least known cog in the massive three-team deal involving the Pirates, Padres, and Mets in mid-January last year. San Diego sent right-handed reliever David Bednar, Omar Cruz, Drake Fellows, and Hudson Head to the Pirates. Pittsburgh shipped righty Joe Musgrove, owner of a no-hitter last season, to the Friars. New York acquired southpaw Joey Lucchesi. And the Mets, of course, sent Endy Rodriguez to the Buccos. A native of Santiago, Dominican Republic, the switch-hitting backstop spent his first two professional seasons in the foreign and domestic rookie leagues. Last year, his first in the Pirates' organization, Rodriguez turned in his finest professional season to date as he moved into Low-A Southeast. In 98 games with the Bradenton Marauders, the 6-foot, 170-pounder slugged .294/.380/.512 with 25 doubles, six triples, and 15 homeruns. He also swiped a pair of bags – just for good measure. Per *Weighted Runs Created Plus*, his overall production topped the league average mark by 40%.

Scouting Report: Consider the following:

- Since 2006, only a pair of 21-year-old hitters posted the following criteria in Low-A with one organization (min. 350 PA): 135 to 140 wRC+, a double-digit walk rate, and a sub-20% strikeout rate. Those two hitters: Taylor Walls and – of course – Endy Rodriguez.

A solid offensive performer during the summer's opening two months – he hit .252/.337/.453 in May and June – Rodriguez, though, heated up as the summer did, slugging .333/.416/.554 in July through the end of September. Average power with more in the tank. Solid approach at the plate (including a good eye and contact skills), Rodriguez is an interesting low level bat-first backstop. There's some sleeper starting potential here, but he needs to show some improved performance behind the dish as well. The Pirates may look to accelerate his develop arc in 2022. Double-A isn't out of the question.

Ceiling: 1.5-win player
Risk: Moderate
MLB ETA: 2024

19. Kyle Nicolas, RHP

FB	CB	SL	CH	Command	Overall
55	50	55	50	45	45

Born: 02/22/99	Age: 23	Bats: R	Top Comp: N/A
Height: 6-4	Weight: 223	Throws: R	

Season	Team	Age	Level	IP	TBF	K/9	K%	BB/9	BB%	K-BB%	ERA	FIP	xFIP	Pit/Bat
2021	MIA	22	A+	59.2	259	12.97	33.20%	3.62	9.27%	23.94%	5.28	5.03	3.79	4.25
2021	MIA	22	AA	39.1	167	11.44	29.94%	5.72	14.97%	14.97%	2.52	3.99	5.01	3.90

Background: Bringing back the memories of the ill gotten #1 overall pick from the same college, Ball State University, the Pirates acquired another Cardinals ace right-hander, though it was in a deal with the Marlins. Taken in the second round in 2020 by Miami, Pittsburgh acquired the big right-hander, as well as former first rounder Connor Scott and right-hander Zach Thompson, in exchange for Gold Glove backstop Jacob Stallings. An erratic hurler throughout his first two years in college, as well as a pair of summer league stints, things seemed to click for Nicolas during his abbreviated junior campaign as he posted a 37-to-7 strikeout-to-walk ratio in only 23.0 innings of work. Last season, all of which was spent in Miami's farm system, the 6-foot-4, 223-pound righty averaged 12.4 strikeouts and 4.5 walks per nine innings across 21 appearances in High-A and Double-A. He finished the year with an aggregate 4.18 ERA.

Scouting Report: It was almost a guarantee that Nicolas' command was going to regress at some point in his minor league career. After all, he averaged 7.61 walks per nine innings as a freshman and sophomore. And the 45-grade command he showed last season feels about right. Nicolas showed a big time fastball during his collegiate days, touching as high 100 mph according to reports. However, across a couple starts I saw last season, the former second rounder was sitting 93- to 94-mph (with effort). Fringy average curveball. An above-average cutter-like slider. And a 50-grade changeup. There's a lot of reliever risk here. And, truthfully, there's not a lot of difference between Nicolas and Kyle Funkhouser.

Ceiling: 1.0- to 1.5-win player
Risk: Moderate
MLB ETA: 2022/2023

20. Calvin Mitchell, RF

Hit	Power	SB	Patience	Glove	Overall
40/45	50/55	35	45	55	40

Born: 03/08/99	Age: 23	Bats: L	Top Comp: N/A
Height: 6-0	Weight: 205	Throws: L	

Season	Team	Age	Level	PA	1B	2B	3B	HR	SB	CS	BB%	K%	AVG	OBP	SLG	ISO
2018	PIT	19	A	495	82	29	3	10	4	5	8.28%	22.02%	0.280	0.344	0.427	0.147
2019	PIT	20	A+	493	75	21	2	15	1	1	6.49%	28.80%	0.251	0.304	0.406	0.155
2021	PIT	22	AA	419	75	19	1	12	6	7	5.73%	16.95%	0.280	0.330	0.429	0.149
2021	PIT	22	AAA	21	4	1	0	0	0	0	0.00%	19.05%	0.250	0.286	0.300	0.050

Background: As the saying goes, hindsight is 20/20. Looking back at the second round of the 2017 draft and it's pretty clear that there wasn't a whole lot of big league talent taken. Of the 39 players chosen, just 15 have made the big leagues – which aren't terrible odds. But of those 15, twelve of them have tallied 0.0 wins above replacement or less. Calvin Mitchell, a 6-foot, 205-pound corner outfielder, was the 50th overall pick that June, signing a deal worth slightly less than $1.4 million. A product of Rancho Bernardo High School, Mitchell turned in a solid, albeit unremarkable debut in the Gulf Coast League that summer, hitting .245/.351/.52 in 43 games. But things seemed to click for the teenager the following year as he slugged .280/.344/.427 in 19 games with West Virginia in Low-A. His numbers regressed a bit as he moved into High-A in 2019. Last season though, Mitchell continued his roller coaster performances within another solid showing – this time coming in the minors' toughest league, Double-A. In 108 games with the Altoona Curve, the former prep star batted .280/.330/.429 with 19 doubles, one triple, and 12 homeruns. His overall production, per *Weighted Runs Created Plus*, topped the league average mark by six percent. Mitchell spent the final week of the year getting his feet wet in Triple-A.

Snippet from The 2020 Prospect Digest Handbook: Mitchell's still a borderline starting outfielder contender. He still has plenty of youth on his side and is set to enter Class AA.

Scouting Report: Consider the following:

- Since 2006, only a trio of 22-year-old hitters met the following criteria in Double-A with one organization (min. 350 PA): 100 to 110 wRC+, a 4.5% to 6.5% walk rate, and a 15% to 17% strikeout rate. Those three hitters: Ty France, John Drennen, and Calvin Mitchell.

As in years past, Mitchell's production steadily declined as the season progressed. His monthly OPS totals (starting in April): 1.043, .791, .709, .611, and .672. And after questioning whether he was wearing down or failing to make adjustments as the league caught an extended look at him, I'm now firmly in the latter option. Now the bad news: he can't hit lefties, struggling mightily against them in 2019 (.218/.266/.276) and 2021 (.200/.243/.284). He still hasn't fully tapped into his above-average in-game power potential, nor does he walk much. He's entering his age-23 season with some success in Double-A, so he's still on the fringe of prospect-dom, even with the red flags.

Ceiling: 1.0-win player
Risk: Moderate
MLB ETA: 2022/2023

San Diego Padres

Top Prospects

1. CJ Abrams, SS

Hit	Power	SB	Patience	Glove	Overall
50/60	35/45	60	50	60	60

Born: 10/03/00	Age: 21	Bats: L	Top Comp: Jimmy Rollins
Height: 6-2	Weight: 185	Throws: R	

Season	Team	Age	Level	PA	1B	2B	3B	HR	SB	CS	BB%	K%	AVG	OBP	SLG	ISO
2019	SDP	18	R	156	34	12	8	3	14	6	6.41%	8.97%	0.401	0.442	0.662	0.261
2021	SDP	20	AA	183	32	14	0	2	13	2	8.20%	19.67%	0.296	0.363	0.420	0.123

Background: The opening 12 picks in the 2019 draft have a chance to go down in history as a special collection of talent: Adley Rutschman, Bobby Witt Jr., Riley Greene, CJ Abrams, Nick Lodolo, Josh Jung, Shea Langeliers, and Brett Baty are all Top 100 consensus prospects – most of which reside among the Top 25 in all of baseball. Andrew Vaughn, the third overall selection that year, already has 127 big league games on his resume, and Toronto right-hander Alek Manoah, 11th pick that year, finished eighth in the Rookie of the Year voting – despite only throwing 111.2 innings. Abrams, a sweet, lefty-swinging shortstop, became the Padres' first sixth overall pick since the club selected Kevin McReynolds out of the University of Arkansas all the way back 1981 – 19 years before Abrams was even born. Well known on the scouting circuit for several years heading into the draft, Abrams has not only lived up to, but he's exceeded even the loftiest of expectations since stepping foot onto a professional diamond. Standing 6-foot-2 and 185-pounds, the young middle infielder looked like the second coming of Ted Williams during his debut in the Arizona Summer League three years ago, slugging an impressive .401/.442/.662 with 12 doubles, eight triples, and three homeruns. He also appeared in a pair of games in Low-A, as well. Despite losing a year of development due to the COVID-imposed shutdown *and* only appearing in two games above the domestic rookie leagues, the front office aggressively pushed the baby-faced shortstop straight into the minors' toughest challenge – Double-A. The results were impressive – he batted a rock solid .296/.363/.420 with 14 doubles and a pair of homeruns to go along with 13 stolen bases – and only a severe injury was able to slow him. A fractured left tibia and a sprained MCL, a result of a collision at second base, prematurely ended his year on June 30th. Per *Weighted Runs Created Plus*, Abrams overall production topped the league average mark by 12%.

Snippet from The 2020 Prospect Digest Handbook: The hit tool has the makings of a plus weapon to match his elite speed with average power.

Scouting Report: While the same size is a touch too small, a touch too unreliable, consider the following – just for fun:

- Since 2006, only two 20-year-old hitters posted a 107 to 117 wRC+ total, a 18% to21% strikeout rate, and a 7% to 9% walk rate in Double-A (min. 175 PA): Brett Lawrie and – of course – CJ Abrams. Lawrie, by the way, owned a career 100 wRC+ mark in 588 big league games.

A potential franchise cornerstone – in a franchise with several cornerstones already in place – Abrams projects to a dynamic table setter for the Padres for the better part of decade. Plus speed. Plus hit tool. Solid patience. Above-average to plus middle infield glove. The lefty-swinging Abrams also shows no weaknesses against fellow southpaws either. The lone knock – for the time being – is Abrams lack of pop, but his improving groundball rates and batted ball data suggest at least 45-grade power is brewing, perhaps peaking in the 12- to 15-homerun range. He's going to be a dynamo at second base or shortstop. Future star. His big league ceiling: .310/.370/.450.

Ceiling: 5.0-win player
Risk: Low to Moderate
MLB ETA: 2022

2. Robert Hassell III, CF

Hit	Power	SB	Patience	Glove	Overall
45/55	40/55	60	60	50	60

Born: 08/15/01	Age: 20	Bats: L	Top Comp: Christian Yelich
Height: 6-2	Weight: 195	Throws: L	

Season	Team	Age	Level	PA	1B	2B	3B	HR	SB	CS	BB%	K%	AVG	OBP	SLG	ISO
2021	SDP	19	A	429	77	31	3	7	31	6	13.29%	17.25%	0.323	0.415	0.482	0.159
2021	SDP	19	A+	87	9	2	1	4	3	0	10.34%	28.74%	0.205	0.287	0.410	0.205

Background: With the club's selection of Robert Hassell as the eighth overall pick in the 2020 draft, it marked the fifth consecutive time the front office owned a Top 8 pick in the July amateur draft – a streak, by the way, that would eventually be snapped in 2021. Hassell, a toolsy center fielder out of Independence High School, agreed to terms with the Padres on a hefty $4.3 million deal. The 6-foot-2, 195-pound prospect put on a five-tool show in Low-A West last season, his first taste of professional ball. In 92 games with the Lake Elsinore Storm, Hassell slugged .323/.415/.482 with 31 doubles, three triples, and seven homeruns. He also swiped 31 bags in 37 total attempts. Per *Weighted Runs Created Plus*, his overall production at the level was 39% above the league average. Hassell was promoted up to High-A at the end of the year, though he struggled against the more advanced pitching (.205/.287/.410).

Scouting Report: Just for fun, here's Hassell's production in Low-A prorated for a full 162-game season: 55 doubles, five triples, 12 homeruns, and 55 stolen bases. Not too shabby. With regard to his work at the level, consider the following:

- Since 2006, only three 19-year-old hitters posted a 135 to 145 wRC+, a sub-20% strikeout rate, and a double-digit walk rate in Low-A (min 400 PA): Christian Yelich, Jesse Winker, and – of course – the lone player drafted out of Tennessee-based Independence High School, Robert Hassell III.
- For those counting at home: Yelich owns a career 120 wRC+ mark and Winker's actually been better, at 132 wRC+.

Strong contact hitter who sprays the ball from foul line to foul line, shows an advanced feel for hitting, a terrific eye at the plate, and plus speed. He's also showing the trademarks of above-average power as well. Like lefty-swinging CJ Abrams, Hassell showed no bias against southpaws as well. Throw in a solid glove and the ability to stay in center field, and Hassell – like Abrams – looks like a potential superstar.

Ceiling: 5.0-win player
Risk: Moderate
MLB ETA: 2024

3. Luis Campusano, C

	Hit	Power	SB	Patience	Glove	Overall
	55	50/55	30	50	45	55

Born: 09/29/98	Age: 23	Bats: R	Top Comp: Willson Contreras
Height: 5-11	Weight: 232	Throws: R	

Season	Team	Age	Level	PA	1B	2B	3B	HR	SB	CS	BB%	K%	AVG	OBP	SLG	ISO
2018	SDP	19	A	284	61	11	0	3	0	1	6.69%	15.14%	0.288	0.345	0.365	0.077
2019	SDP	20	A+	487	90	31	1	15	0	0	10.68%	11.70%	0.325	0.396	0.509	0.185
2021	SDP	22	AAA	326	47	21	3	15	1	0	8.28%	20.25%	0.295	0.365	0.541	0.247

Background: With their first six selections in the 2017 draft, the Padres honed in on high end prep talent, like a heat-seeking missile. They nabbed big time lefty MacKenzie Gore with the third overall pick, and followed that up by grabbing prep backstop Luis Campusano 36 selections later. The front office, essentially, threw out the old adage about the only prospect that's more volatile than a young arm, is a young backstop. At the ripe ol' age of 22, Campusano, a product Cross Creek High School, made the leap from High-A in 2019 all the way up to Triple-A. And he did so without so much as missing a beat. In 81 games with the El Paso Chihuahuas, the stocky backstop slugged .295/.365/.541 with 21 doubles, three triples, and 15 homeruns. His overall production, per *Weighted Runs Created Plus*, topped the league average mark by 22%. In addition, he appeared in 11 games with the Friars, batting a lowly .088/.184/.088 in 38 plate appearances.

Snippet from The 2020 Prospect Digest Handbook: His offensive firepower wasn't the only development; his defense showed tremendous leaps forward as well.

Scouting Report: Consider the following:

- Since 2006, only three 22-year-old posted a 117 to 127 wRC+ with a 19% to 21% strikeout rate and a 8% to 11% strikeout rate in Triple-A with one org. (min. 300 PA): Wladimir Balentien, Ian Stewart, and Luis Campusano.

A consistent producer at a premium position – which is ideal because Campusano owns a 45-grade glove and rarely throws any potential base thieves out. Campusano owns an above-average bat, power that may creep into above-average territory, and strong contact skills. The most impressive part of Campusano's debut showing in Triple-A: after an absolutely atrocious start to the year, Campusano, who batted .215/.302/.323 over his first 25 games, slugged .332/.395/.645 over his remaining 56 contests. His production, during that period, topped the league average mark by a whopping 52%. In terms of a big league ceiling, think .280/.350/.490.

Ceiling: 2.5-win player
Risk: Moderate
MLB ETA: Debuted in 2021

4. MacKenzie Gore, LHP

	FB	CB	SL	CH	Command	Overall
	60	55	45/50	55	40/45	55

Born: 02/24/99	Age: 23	Bats: L	Top Comp: Scott Kazmir
Height: 6-2	Weight: 197	Throws: L	

Season	Team	Age	Level	IP	TBF	K/9	K%	BB/9	BB%	K-BB%	ERA	FIP	xFIP	Pit/Bat
2018	SDP	19	A	60.2	261	10.98	28.35%	2.67	6.90%	21.46%	4.45	3.25	3.16	3.84
2019	SDP	20	A+	79.1	288	12.48	38.19%	2.27	6.94%	31.25%	1.02	2.38	2.76	4.22
2019	SDP	20	AA	21.2	90	10.38	27.78%	3.32	8.89%	18.89%	4.15	4.19	3.82	4.32
2021	SDP	22	CPX	16.1	64	12.12	34.38%	2.20	6.25%	28.13%	1.65	2.69	3.95	1.97
2021	SDP	22	AAA	20.0	96	8.10	18.75%	5.40	12.50%	6.25%	5.85	6.03	6.31	4.00

Background: As minor league baseball returned to life after the COVID-imposed lost season, the eye test alone proved that there were unexpected down seasons, a few surprising ones, and – what it felt like – an uptick in pitching injuries. Most of which seemed predictable. One thing that no one outside of the Padres' organization could have predicted, though, was MacKenzie Gore's implosion in 2021. Not only the darling of one of baseball's best farm systems, but he was one of the best – if not *the best* – pitching prospect in the entire game. The third overall pick in 2017, Gore dazzled during his 2019 campaign, reaching Double-A for five solid starts at only 20-years-old. He finished the year by averaging 12.0 strikeouts and 2.5 walks per nine innings to go along with a sparkling 1.69 ERA. Heading into last season Gore seemed poised – at least from the outside – to play a major role in the Padres' push for a World Series title. Then he struggled in Triple-A, disappeared for two months in an effort to correct mechanical issues, and reappeared all the back in the rookie complex league. From there he would make three starts, get bounced up to High-A for a game, and then on to Double-A for two more starts. When the dust had finally settled on his first disappointing professional season – as well as amateur, likely – Gore had tallied just 50.1 innings, averaging 10.9 strikeouts and a whopping 5.0 walks per nine innings. He popped up in the Arizona Fall League as well, fanning eight and walking six in 11.1 innings.

Snippet from The 2020 Prospect Digest Handbook: He's a bonafide, legitimate budding ace who likely ascends to true ace-dom. In terms of ceiling, think an in-his-prime Zack Greinke when he averaged 9.5 K/9 and 2.0 BB/9 for the Royals in 2009.

Scouting Report: "Stuff-wise", Gore looked like a reasonable facsimile of his 2019 body of work. His fastball looked more explosive than in years past, with nearly every hitter showing difficulty getting around on it. He didn't have issues throwing his above-average curveball for strikes. But his final two offerings – a slider and changeup – didn't look as crisp as in years past. During one of his final starts of the year, Gore struggled with the slider and couldn't quite get a feel for it, but it did flash average at times – which is where I had in 2019. The changeup, previously his second plus offering, was downgraded to a 55. The repertoire was – and still is – very solid. The differentiator for Gore was his command and pitch-ability, both of which he struggled with in 2021. As he stands now, based on the late season game I scouted, he looks like a future #4, but there were glimpses of his former self that would shine through every now and then.

Ceiling: 3.0-win player
Risk: Moderate to High
MLB ETA: 2022

5. Euribiel Angeles, IF

	Hit	Power	SB	Patience	Glove	Overall
	55/60	35/40	50	50	55	50

Born: 05/11/02	Age: 20	Bats: R	Top Comp: N/A
Height: 5-11	Weight: 175	Throws: R	

Season	Team	Age	Level	PA	1B	2B	3B	HR	SB	CS	BB%	K%	AVG	OBP	SLG	ISO
2019	SDP	17	R	198	41	9	2	0	17	9	7.58%	9.60%	0.301	0.359	0.376	0.075
2021	SDP	19	A	405	93	22	6	3	18	6	7.90%	15.06%	0.343	0.397	0.461	0.119
2021	SDP	19	A+	86	14	4	0	1	1	1	9.30%	18.60%	0.264	0.369	0.361	0.097

Background: An under-the-radar signing out of Higuey, Dominican Republic, during the summer of 2018. San Diego inked the teenage infielder to a relatively sizeable deal, handing him $300,000. Angeles made his debut in the foreign rookie league the following year, batting a solid .301/.359/.376 with nine doubles and a pair of triples to go along with 17 stolen bases. San Diego sent the then-19-year-old infielder to Low-A West to begin 2021. And Angeles came out firing on all cylinders. In 87 games with the Lake Elsinore Storm, the 5-foot-11, 175-pound prospect slugged a scorching .343/.397/.461 with 22 doubles, six triples, and three homeruns. He also swiped 18 stolen bases in 24 attempts. His production in Low-A, according to *Weighted Runs Created Plus*, was 28% better than the league average mark. Angeles spent the last several weeks in High-A, hitting a solid .264/.369/.361 in 18 games. Angeles finished the year with an aggregate .329/.392/.445 slash line, belting out 26 doubles, six triples, and four dingers with 19 stolen bases.

Scouting Report: Consider the following:

- Since 2006, only four players posted 123 to 133 wRC+ with a sub-17.0% strikeout rate and a walk rate between 7% and 9% in Low-A with one organization (min. 350 PA): Mike Moustakas, Jorge Polanco, Manuel Margot, and – of course – Euribiel Angeles.
- For those counting at home: Moustakas owns a career 99 wRC+; Polanco is sporting a 109 wRC+ mark; and Margot is checking in at 87.

Ignoring his first couple weeks of the season, Angeles slugged a scorching .372/.428/.490 over his final 71 games in Low-A, good enough for a 145 wRC+. Angeles take a high-contact approach at the plate and doesn't project to hit for much power. But he's willing to take a walk, shows a solid glove at shortstop, second or third bases, and can run. There's some sneaky upside here.

Ceiling: 2.5-win player
Risk: Moderate
MLB ETA: 2023/2024

6. Samuel Zavala, CF

	Hit	Power	SB	Patience	Glove	Overall
	35/55	35/55	50	50	50	50

Born: 07/15/04	Age: 17	Bats: L	Top Comp: N/A
Height: 6-1	Weight: 175	Throws: L	

Season	Team	Age	Level	PA	1B	2B	3B	HR	SB	CS	BB%	K%	AVG	OBP	SLG	ISO
2021	SDP	16	DSL	235	33	16	6	3	11	7	13.62%	15.32%	0.297	0.400	0.487	0.190

Background: Thanks to a later birthday, Zavala hit the 2021 international free agency market and would make his debut a few months later as a 16-year-old. The 6-foot-1, 175-pound center fielder signed with San Diego for a hefty $1.2 million bonus. A native of Caracas, Venezuela, the twitchy teenager appeared in 55 games with the club's Dominican Summer League, slugging an impressive .297/.400/.487 with 16 doubles, six triples, and three homeruns. He also swiped 11 bags, though it did take 18 total attempts. His overall production, per *Weighted Runs Created Plus*, topped the league average mark by an extraordinary 44%.

Scouting Report: Consider the following:

- There were 190 qualified hitters in the Dominican Summer League in 2021. Zavala's 144 wRC+ ranked as the 22nd best total in the league.
- Comparatively speaking, there were three other 16-year-old hitters in the DSL. Zavala's 144 wRC+ paced the group. The runner-up, Baltimore's Samuel Basallo, tallied only a 109 wRC+.
- Going all the way back to 2006, here's the list of 16-year-old hitters to post a equal or top wRC+ mark than Zavala's: Orlando Arcia (144 wRC+), Alexander Mojica (182 wRC+), Rayner Santana (170 wRC+), and Michael De La Cruz (148 wRC+).

Really good looking swing with some potential to develop above-average thunder in his bat. It's short, compact, and quick to the plate. And despite his youth, Zavala showed a mature approach at the plate during his debut as well. There's a lot of intrigue here. He could shoot up several lists within in the next 12 months.

Ceiling: 2.5-win player
Risk: High
MLB ETA: 2025

7. Jackson Merrill, SS

	Hit	Power	SB	Patience	Glove	Overall
	40/50	30/45	50	45/50	55	50

Born: 04/19/03	Age: 19	Bats: L	Top Comp: N/A
Height: 6-3	Weight: 195	Throws: R	

Season	Team	Age	Level	PA	1B	2B	3B	HR	SB	CS	BB%	K%	AVG	OBP	SLG	ISO
2021	SDP	18	CPX	120	21	7	2	0	5	1	8.33%	22.50%	0.280	0.339	0.383	0.103

Background: Starring for Severna Park High School, Merrill was one of the few helium guys to float up to the opening night of the MLB Draft in 2021. Standing a wiry 6-foot-3 and 160 pounds heading into his junior campaign for the Maryland prep school, the lefty-swinging shortstop, according to a variety of reports, put on a ton of weight while focusing on adding strength during the offseason. The eventual first round pick, now tipping the scales as a more solid 195 pounds, batted a scorching .500 with 13 homeruns and 39 RBIs during his final amateur campaign. The *Capital Gazette* named Merrill the Maryland Player of the Year. San Diego signed him to a deal worth $1.8 million, saving the club nearly $800,000 based on the slot value for the 27th overall pick. Merrill appeared in 31 games in the Arizona Complex League affiliate, hitting .280/.339/.383 with seven doubles and a pair of homeruns.

Scouting Report: Per the usual, here's my post-draft write-up:

> *"Really love the swing. It's silky smooth with plenty of bat speed and enough natural loft to belt out 15 or so homeruns during his peak. Good opposite field power. Defensively, he's fluid and should have no issues staying at the position long term. It wouldn't be surprising to see Merrill's defense grades out as above-average."*

Ceiling: 2.5-win player
Risk: Moderate
MLB ETA: 2024

8. James Wood, CF

Hit	Power	SB	Patience	Glove	Overall
35/45	40/65	50/40	55	50	50

Born: 09/17/02	Age: 19	Bats: L	Top Comp: N/A
Height: 6-7	Weight: 240	Throws: R	

Season	Team	Age	Level	PA	1B	2B	3B	HR	SB	CS	BB%	K%	AVG	OBP	SLG	ISO
2021	SDP	18	CPX	101	24	5	0	3	10	0	12.87%	31.68%	0.372	0.465	0.535	0.163

Background: After selecting prep shortstop Jackson Merrill at the end of the first round last July, the Padres took another high ceiling teenager with their second pick. A product of baseball hotbed IMG Academy, massive outfielder James Wood was chosen in the second round, 62nd overall, and signed for a hefty $2.6 million. After joining the organization, the 6-foot-7, 240-pound center fielder slugged his way through the Arizona Complex League, posting a Ruthian .372/.465/.535 with five doubles and three homeruns. Per *Weighted Runs Created Plus*, his production topped the league average mark by a whopping 66%.

Scouting Report: Another of the raw, high ceiling prospects that the organization seems to focus on in recent years. Like 2019 second round pick Joshua Mears, James Wood is absolutely loaded with loud tools. The club's most recent second rounder owns some of the best power potential – and raw power – in the minor leagues. However, that comes at the price of gaudy strikeout numbers. Wood whiffed in nearly 32% of his plate appearances during his debut. Short compact swing, solid bat speed, but Wood seems to be susceptible to offspeed low and away. If he can chew several percentage points off of his whiff rate, Wood has the potential to be a legitimate middle-of-the-order thumper.

Ceiling: 1.5- to 2.0-win player
Risk: Moderate to High
MLB ETA: 2025

9. Eguy Rosario, IF

Hit	Power	SB	Patience	Glove	Overall
50	45	60	50	45	45

Born: 08/25/99	Age: 22	Bats: R	Top Comp: N/A
Height: 5-9	Weight: 150	Throws: R	

Season	Team	Age	Level	PA	1B	2B	3B	HR	SB	CS	BB%	K%	AVG	OBP	SLG	ISO
2018	SDP	18	A+	505	71	28	1	9	9	8	7.52%	23.56%	0.239	0.307	0.363	0.125
2018	SDP	18	AA	14	2	0	0	0	1	0	14.29%	35.71%	0.182	0.357	0.182	0.000
2019	SDP	19	A+	512	89	25	8	7	21	9	7.23%	20.12%	0.278	0.331	0.412	0.134
2021	SDP	21	AA	481	72	31	3	12	30	14	10.19%	22.66%	0.281	0.360	0.455	0.174

Background: Sometimes it just takes a while for a prospect to get going. Rosario, one of the longest tenured prospects in the San Diego system, signed all the way back at the end of the 2015 summer. Almost immediately the diminutive infielder made a fantastic impression; he slugged a scorching .346/.423/.472 in 60 games during his debut, most of which was spent in the foreign rookie league. The club pushed the then-17-year-old up to the Midwest League to begin the 2017, but after hitting a disappointing .206/.296/.278 through 50 games, he was demoted back down to the Arizona Summer League where he regained his stroke. Undeterred by the lack of success in Low-A, the front office – inexplicably – pushed Rosario straight up to High-A to begin 2018. And it went as one would expect – poorly. He batted .239/.307/.363. Unsurprisingly, Rosario found himself back in High-A for the 2019 season. This time, though, the results were significantly improved: .278/.331/.412. Last year, with the return of minor league action, Rosario put together his finest professional season since his debut – and it came at the most important level, Double-A. In 114 games with San Antonio, he slugged .281/.360/.455 with 31 doubles, three triples, and 12 homeruns. He also swiped 30 bags in 44 attempts. Per *Weighted Runs Created Plus*, his production topped the league average mark by 18%.

Scouting Report: Consider the following:

- Since 2006, only four 21-year-old hitters met the following criteria in Double-A with one organization (min. 350 PA): 113 to 123 wRC+, 9% to 11% walk rate, and a strikeout rate between 21% and 24%. Those four hitters: Nick Gordon, Ji-hwan Bae, Bobby Bradley, and Eguy Rosario.

Like a lot of prospects last season – especially in the San Diego system – Rosario got off to slow start as he made the leap up to Double-A; he batted .180/.254/.246 over his first 17 games, but slugged .298/.378/.490 the remainder of the year. The Dominican-born infielder is a bit of a vagabond, spending time at second and third bases, and shortstop. The glove's – typically – been below average and last season was no different. Rosario's only listed at 5-foot-9 and 150-pounds, but he's rock solid and maxed out physically. Strong lower half. Impressive bat speed. Last season, he shaved off several percentage points on his groundball rate and that coincided with a career best power surge. Low end starting material, unless the hit tool develops better than expected. Very good utility guy, though.

Ceiling: 1.5-win player
Risk: Moderate
MLB ETA: 2022

10. Victor Acosta, SS

	Hit	Power	SB	Patience	Glove	Overall
	40/50	40/45	60	50	45/50	50

Born: 06/10/04	Age: 18	Bats: B	Top Comp: N/A
Height: 5-11	Weight: 170	Throws: R	

Season	Team	Age	Level	PA	1B	2B	3B	HR	SB	CS	BB%	K%	AVG	OBP	SLG	ISO
2021	SDP	17	DSL	240	31	12	5	5	26	7	15.83%	18.75%	0.285	0.431	0.484	0.199

Background: Ranked by MLB Pipeline as the 19th overall prospect on the international market during 2020. San Diego ponied up a sizeable bonus – $1.8 million, to be exact – to sign the 5-foot-11, 170-pound middle infielder in early 2021. Hailing from El Limon, Dominican Republic, Acosta spent the last season making his professional debut with the organization's foreign rookie league affiliate. In 56 games, the teenage shortstop batted a respectable .285/.431/.484 with 12 doubles, five triples, and five homeruns. He also swiped 26 bags in 33 total attempts. Per *Weighted Runs Created Plus*, his overall production topped the league average threshold by a whopping 53% – the 13th best total among all qualified bats in the league that summer.

Scouting Report: Only four 17-year-old hitters topped Acosta's 153 wRC+ total in the Dominican Summer League last season: Cubs' Pedro Ramirez (155 wRC+), teammate Daniel Montesino (160 wRC+), Tigers' Cristian Santana (161 wRC+), and Reds' Carlos Jorge (174 wRC+). Showcased in one of the better produced free agent videos I've ever seen, Acosta is long and projectable. He shows a natural feel for hitting, though – mechanically speaking – there's work to be done. His weight transfer, prior to signing, was off. He was hitting purely off of his front foot and not utilizing his lower half at all from the left side. Good arm strength. Above-average or better speed. He'll shoot balls from gap-to-gap and should develop 15 or so homerun thump.

Ceiling: 2.0-win player
Risk: High
MLB ETA: 2025

11. Justin Lange, RHP

	FB	SL	CH	Command	Overall
	N/A	N/A	N/A	N/A	45

Born: 09/11/01	Age: 20	Bats: R	Top Comp: N/A
Height: 6-4	Weight: 220	Throws: R	

Season	Team	Age	Level	IP	TBF	K/9	K%	BB/9	BB%	K-BB%	ERA	FIP	xFIP	Pit/Bat
2021	SDP	19	CPX	22.0	102	11.86	28.43%	6.14	14.71%	13.73%	6.95	5.01	5.30	1.66

Background: Armed with two first round picks in the 2020 draft. San Diego honed in on a pair of prep players with high ceilings, first taking toolsy center fielder Robert Hassell with the eighth overall pick and then circled back around to select teenage right-hander Justin Lange with the 34th selection. San Diego signed the Texas-born hurler to a $2 million pact. Lange made his professional debut – albeit a rather brief one – in the Arizona Complex League, throwing 22.0 innings with 29 punch outs and 15 free passes. He compiled a 6.95 ERA, a 5.01 FIP, and a 5.30 xFIP.

Scouting Report: To the best of my knowledge, there's no game tape from Lange's abbreviated, 22.0-inning debut in the Complex League last summer. A variety of reports all indicate the same thing: Lange's fastball grew some legs during the offseason heading into his senior season, going from the low-90s to sitting mid- to upper-90s and touching triple-digits. He'll also mix in a slider (reportedly, above-average) and a fringy changeup. Also, at first glance, Lange really struggled with his control in 2021; he averaged 6.1 BB/9. However, of the 15 free passes he handed out, 11 of them came in a three-game span in only 8.2 innings.

Ceiling: 1.5-win player
Risk: Moderate to High
MLB ETA: 2025

12. Kevin Kopps, RHP

	FB	CU	Command	Overall
	50	70	50/55	40

Born: 03/02/97	Age: 25	Bats: R	Top Comp: N/A
Height: 6-0	Weight: 200	Throws: R	

Background: One of the most compelling stories in college baseball last season, Kopps' rise to SEC Pitcher of the Year, as well as *Collegiate Baseball* Pitcher of the Year, doesn't begin in 2021. No, it started all the way back in 2016. Rather unheralded coming out of George Ranch High School, the 6-foot, 200-pound right-hander redshirted his true freshman season. After a solid 2017 season – one in which he posted 40-to-18 strikeout-to-walk ratio in 49.0 innings of work – Kopps would miss the entirety of the following season as he recovered from Tommy John surgery. Fully recovered, and now 23 years old, the Texas native labored through a disappointing, pandemic-shortened season two years ago: he tallied an 8.18 ERA across 11 innings, striking out nine and allowing four walks. But, according to reports,

Kopps transformed himself as a pitcher. He tossed aside his four-seamer, opting instead for a two-seamer – which, in turn – improved his unearthly cutter/slider. And the results have been…mindboggling impressive. Kopps tossed 89.2 innings of work, a career best, posting an absolutely absurd 131-to-18 strikeout-to-walk ratio with a miniscule 0.90 ERA. He averaged, by the way, 13.1 strikeouts and just 1.8 walks per nine innings. Kevin Kopps, the overlooked, under-the-radar, surgically repaired right-hander was named the 2021 Golden Spikes award winner. San Diego used the 99th overall pick on him, signing him to well below-slot deal worth $300,000. By the end of his abbreviated professional debut, Kopps had already accrued time in Double-A. He finished the year with 22 punch outs, six walks, and a tidy 0.61 ERA in 14.2 innings.

Scouting Report: Per the usual, here's my pre-draft write-up on the dominating right-hander:

> "Primarily a two-pitch pitcher. Kopps consistently throws his fastball in the 91- to 93-mph range. But the story is, of course, his breaking ball. And depending upon whom you talk to, it's either a curveball…or a slider…or a cutter. But as Arkansas pitching coach Matt Hobbs says, he'll call it whatever Kopps calls it – which is a cutter. Whatever you call it, though, it's disgusting – practically unhittable. And arguably the single best offering in the entire draft class. Momentarily ignoring the elephant in the room – which is his age – Kopps looks like a late first/early second round pick. But due to his redshirt, combined with the medical redshirt due to Tommy John surgery, he's already 24-years-old. Whichever team selects Kopps, though, should promote him aggressively. He could be the first player in the class to make The Show. Consider the following:

> - Between 2011 and 2020, only four Division I pitchers have completed a season with a sub-1.00 ERA (min. 75 IP): Eric Lauer, Luke Heimlich, David Berg, and Ben Holmes. For the record: the best strikeout rate between the quarter is 10.8 K/9 (Lauer); Kopps' strikeout rate is a whopping 13.4 K/9.

> I would love to see Kopps given the chance to develop as a starting option, though his age and reliance on two pitches almost guarantees him a reliever path. Love this guy. Love watching him pitch. He could be a throwback to a consistent multi-inning bullpen arm.

I placed a late second / early third round grade on Kopps, by the way.

Ceiling: 1.0-win player
Risk: Low
MLB ETA: 2022

13. Joshua Mears, OF

	Hit	Power	SB	Patience	Glove	Overall
	35/40	60	50	50	50	40

Born: 02/21/01	Age: 21	Bats: R	Top Comp: Jeren Kendall
Height: 6-3	Weight: 230	Throws: R	

Season	Team	Age	Level	PA	1B	2B	3B	HR	SB	CS	BB%	K%	AVG	OBP	SLG	ISO
2019	SDP	18	R	195	28	4	3	7	9	1	11.79%	30.26%	0.253	0.354	0.440	0.187
2021	SDP	20	A	291	28	10	4	17	10	5	12.37%	39.18%	0.244	0.368	0.529	0.285

Background: Federal Way High School, based in Washington, hasn't produced many draft picks throughout the years. Since 1967, the prep school has had just nine players selected in the amateur draft. However, of those nine, two have spent considerable time in the big leagues – right-hander Dan Spillner and first baseman Travis Ishikawa – and their most recent selection, Joshua Mears, was a Top 50 pick two years ago. A raw, toolsy outfielder, Mears turned in a solid, sometimes impressive, debut in the Arizona Summer League three years ago: he hit .253/.354/.440 with four doubles, three triples, seven homeruns, and nine stolen bases. Last season the front office pushed him up to Lake Elsinore in Low-A West. In an-injury interrupted sophomore campaign, the 6-foot-3, 230-pound outfielder slugged .241/.368/.529 with 10 doubles, four triples, 17 homeruns, and 10 stolen bases (in 15 attempts). Per *Weighted Runs Created Plus*, his overall production was 31% above the league average mark. A right shoulder strain essentially cost the former second round pick an entire month.

Snippet from The 2020 Prospect Digest Handbook: Strong, like natural God-given strength with tree trunks for legs and a surprising amount of speed. There's a chance for 65-grade power. The problem for Mears, though, are the punch outs. He whiffed in more than 30% of his plate appearances last season. If he can keep that mark on the right side of 25% moving forward, he could be special.

Scouting Report: Consider the following:

- Since 2006, only three 20-year-old hitters posted a 125 to 135 wRC+ total with a punch out rate north of 30% in Low-A with one organization (min. 275 PA): Telvin Nash, Micker Adolfo, and Joshua Mears.

The overall numbers are fairly impressive, as is the toolkit. The problem, of course, is something I highlighted in *The 2020 Prospect Digest Handbook*: he doesn't make enough contact. Mears whiffed in more than 39% of his plate appearances in 2021 – a number so outrageous that it's the fourth highest strikeout rate among 20-year-olds in Low-A since 2006 (min. 275 PA). When he does make contact, though, it's some of the loudest, hardest in the entire minor leagues. And if I threw 5 mph harder in college, I would be playing baseball, not writing about it.

Ceiling: 1.0-win player
Risk: Moderate
MLB ETA: 2024/2025

14. Robert Gasser, LHP

	FB	SL	CH	Command	Overall
	55/50	55	50	50	40

Born: 05/31/99	Age: 23	Bats: L	Top Comp: N/A
Height: 6-1	Weight: 190	Throws: L	

Season	Team	Age	Level	IP	TBF	K/9	K%	BB/9	BB%	K-BB%	ERA	FIP	xFIP	Pit/Bat
2021	SDP	22	A	14.0	51	8.36	25.49%	1.29	3.92%	21.57%	1.29	3.73	4.13	3.75

Background: The southpaw took a long road to the professional ranks, spanning two separate DI programs and a stint with Delta Junior College in between. Gasser, a 6-foot-1, 190-pound hurler from El Dorado Hills, California, spent his freshman season splitting time between the University of Mexico's bullpen and rotation – though he spent the entire time getting battered. He finished the year with a massive 7.05 ERA while averaging 8.9 strikeouts and 4.6 walks per nine innings. Gasser transferred to JuCo Delta College and – simply put – dominated: in 102.0 innings of work, he struck out 139 and walked 45 to go along with a 2.38 ERA. He then transferred back into the Division I ranks, opting to attend the University of Houston. He worked out of the Cougars' bullpen in the abbreviated COVID-shortened 2020 season, but spent the entirety of 2021 in the club's rotation. In 14 starts, the lefty struck out 105, walked 25, and compiled a 2.63 ERA. San Diego selected him in the second round, 71st overall, and signed him to a deal worth $884,200. Gasser tossed another 15.0 innings during his debut, posting a 14-to-2 strikeout-to-walk ratio.

Scouting Report: Consider the following:

- Between 2011 and 2020, only four American Athletic Conference hurlers have average at least 10 strikeouts and fewer than 3.0 walks per nine innings in a season (min. 75 IP): Tim Cate, Seth Romero, Jonathan Bowlan, and Phoenix Sanders.
- For those counting at home: Romero was a first round pick in 2017; both Cate and Bowlan were second rounders, and Sanders, the outlier, was taken in the 10th round in 2017.

Funky lefty that short-arms the ball. Gasser's sneaky heater shows some solid arm side action. It's currently a 55-grade offering, but I'm not optimistic on its future and expect it to downgrade to a 50 due to the rigors of professional ball. Above-average slider and a solid, workable changeup. San Diego signed Gasser to the recommended slot bonus, but I would have placed a backend third round grade on him. I think he ends up working out of the pen within three years.

Ceiling: 1.0-win player
Risk: Moderate
MLB ETA: 2023/2024

15. Esteury Ruiz, 2B/OF

	Hit	Power	SB	Patience	Glove	Overall
	45	40	55	45	50	40

Born: 02/15/99	Age: 23	Bats: R	Top Comp: Luigi Rodriguez
Height: 6-0	Weight: 169	Throws: R	

Season	Team	Age	Level	PA	1B	2B	3B	HR	SB	CS	BB%	K%	AVG	OBP	SLG	ISO
2018	SDP	19	A	493	74	20	5	12	49	11	7.71%	28.60%	0.253	0.324	0.403	0.150
2019	SDP	20	A+	380	55	18	2	6	34	11	6.84%	26.58%	0.239	0.300	0.357	0.118
2021	SDP	22	AA	353	49	16	2	10	36	7	7.93%	20.68%	0.249	0.328	0.411	0.162

Background: Signed out of Azua, Dominican Republic, by the Royals for $100,000 all the way back in 2015. Roughly two years later Kansas City would package Ruiz, along with Matt Strahm, Travis Wood, and cash to San Diego for triumvirate of hurlers: Brandon Maurer, Trevor Cahill, and Ryan Buchter. Ruiz, for his part, was mostly disappointing and underwhelming during his first two full seasons in the Padres' organization: he cobbled together a .253/.324/.403 showing as a 19-year-old in Low-A in 2018 and hit a puny .239/.300/.357 the following season in High-A. Last season was much of the same for Ruiz – though it came at the minors' toughest level, Double-A. In 84 games with the San Antonio Missions, Ruiz batted .249/.328/.411 with 16 doubles, two triples, 10 homeruns, and 36 stolen bases. His overall production, per *Weighted Runs Created Plus*, was 2% *below* the league average mark.

Scouting Report: Consider the following:

- Since 2006, only three 22-year-old hitters posted a 95 to 105 wRC+ total with a punch out rate between 7% and 9% and a strikeout rate between 20% and 22% (min. 300 PA): Austin Dean, Jonathan Meyer, and Esteury Ruiz.

Several years back the Cleveland ball team, then known as the Indians, had a young, quasi-interesting outfielder by the name of Luigi Rodriguez. The Dominican outfielder was a compiler, a stat-sheet stuffer without having more than a limited ceiling. That's what Esteury Ruiz is – a stat-sheeting stuffing infielder / outfielder. Ruiz has an impressive toolkit – or at least, an interesting one. His positional versatility adds a bit of value, some hope that he carves out a big league bench option.

Ceiling: 1.0-win player
Risk: Moderate
MLB ETA: 2022

16. Brandon Valenzuela, C/1B

Hit	Power	SB	Patience	Glove	Overall
50	35/40	30	55	45	40

Born: 10/02/00	Age: 21	Bats: B	Top Comp: N/A
Height: 6-0	Weight: 170	Throws: R	

Season	Team	Age	Level	PA	1B	2B	3B	HR	SB	CS	BB%	K%	AVG	OBP	SLG	ISO
2018	SDP	17	R	243	40	7	2	1	2	1	16.05%	24.28%	0.253	0.379	0.323	0.071
2019	SDP	18	R	183	31	4	1	0	0	0	18.58%	17.49%	0.248	0.399	0.290	0.041
2021	SDP	20	A	378	71	21	3	6	3	2	11.64%	21.16%	0.307	0.389	0.444	0.137
2021	SDP	20	A+	65	10	1	0	1	1	0	23.08%	30.77%	0.245	0.415	0.327	0.082

Background: San Diego signed the switch-hitting catcher / part-time first baseman in early July 2017. Since then the young Mexican prospect spent a year in the Dominican Summer League, another full season in the Arizona Summer League, and finally made it to full season action in 2021. Standing just 6-feet and 170 pounds, Valenzuela appeared in 82 games with the Lake Elsinore Storm, slugging a robust .307/.389/.444 with 21 doubles, three triples, and six homeruns. He also swiped a trio of bags in five attempts. His overall production, per *Weighted Runs Created Plus*, topped the league average mark by 23%. Valenzuela also appeared in 15 games with the Fort Wayne TinCaps in High-A as well, hitting .245/.415/.327 in 65 trips to the plate.

Scouting Report: Consider the following:

- Since 2006, only three 20-year-old hitters posted a 118 to 128 wRC+ with a walk rate between 9% and 12% and a strikeout rate between 20% and 22% in Low-A with one organization (min. 350 PA): Thomas Neal, Chris Bostick, and Brandon Valenzuela.

An average defender behind the plate, though he doesn't strike fear into the opposition's base runners, Valenzuela shows a bit of offensive promise – particularly one from a premium position. Solid hit tool, above-average walk rates, decent bat-to-ball skills, and doubles power. There's likely not enough to develop into a full time starter, but there's a backup ceiling here.

Ceiling: 1.0-win player
Risk: Moderate
MLB ETA: 2024

17. Efrain Contreras, RHP

FB	CB	SL	CH	Command	Overall
N/A	N/A	N/A	N/A	N/A	40

Born: 01/02/00	Age: 22	Bats: R	
Height: 5-10	Weight: 210	Throws: R	

Season	Team	Age	Level	IP	TBF	K/9	K%	BB/9	BB%	K-BB%	ERA	FIP	xFIP	Pit/Bat
2018	SDP	18	R	43.0	171	9.21	25.73%	1.88	5.26%	20.47%	2.72	3.77	3.56	1.42
2018	SDP	18	R	19.1	74	11.64	33.78%	1.40	4.05%	29.73%	1.40	2.21	1.84	1.85
2019	SDP	19	A	109.2	455	9.93	26.59%	2.63	7.03%	19.56%	3.61	3.70	3.26	3.85

Background: A native of Ciudad Juarez, Mexico, the stocky right-hander sparkled during his first taste of full season action in 2019 – at the ripe ol' age of 19. In 25 appearances with Fort Wayne that season, 23 of which were starts, the 5-foot-10, 210-pound hurler averaged a rock solid 9.9 strikeouts and just 2.6 walks per nine innings. He compiled a 3.61 ERA, a 3.70 FIP, and an impressive 3.26 xFIP. Not bad for a teenager in the Midwest League. Unfortunately, for Contreras, though, his elbow started barking during the Fall Instructional League in 2020 and he would eventually succumb to Tommy John surgery. According to reports, he should be back on a professional mound in early 2022.

Snippet from The 2020 Prospect Digest Handbook: I caught a couple of Contreras' April starts, as well as his final start of the year. The difference: his fastball. Contreras' heater was sitting 91- to 92-mph early in the year and was sitting – comfortably – in the 93- to 94-mph range at season's end. He'll mix in an above-average 12-6 bending curveball; an upper 80s slider; and a 50-grade changeup.

Scouting Report: Nothing new to report. Hopefully the young right-hander doesn't have any setbacks. Fingers crossed.

Ceiling: 1.0-win player
Risk: High
MLB ETA: 2023

18. Reggie Lawson, RHP

FB	SL	CH	Command	Overall
N/A	N/A	N/A	N/A	40

Born: 08/02/97	Age: 24	Bats: R	Top Comp: N/A
Height: 6-4	Weight: 205	Throws: R	

Season	Team	Age	Level	IP	TBF	K/9	K%	BB/9	BB%	K-BB%	ERA	FIP	xFIP	Pit/Bat
2018	SDP	20	A+	117.0	523	9.00	22.37%	3.92	9.75%	12.62%	4.69	4.34	4.47	4.05
2019	SDP	21	AA	27.2	121	11.71	29.75%	4.23	10.74%	19.01%	5.20	4.14	3.58	4.31

Background: A second round pick out of Victor Valley High School all the way back in 2016. Lawson turned in back-to-back solid, peripherally-slanted showings in the Midwest and California Leagues in 2018 and 2019. As a baby-faced 19-year-old, the right-hander averaged 11.0 strikeouts and 4.3 walks per nine innings in 73.0 innings in Low-A. He followed that up with a 117-to-51 strikeout-to-walk ratio in 117.0 innings in High-A the following year. His stint in Double-A to start the 2019 season followed the same course: through his first 11.0 innings, he was sporting a 0.82 ERA with 14 punch outs and a pair of walks. Then his elbow flared up and he eventually succumbed to Tommy John surgery – which knocked him out for the remainder of 2019. He would then miss 2020, as would all the minor leaguers due to COVID. Lawson made it back to Double-A in 2021, though that lasted four starts before he was shutdown with what was termed as a "setback".

Snippet from The 2020 Prospect Digest Handbook: Lawson's overall numbers were skewed by a couple horrific, Freddy Krueger-esque starts: he allowed 31 earned runs in 14.2 innings across four starts throughout the year; otherwise; he coughed up just 30 earned runs in 102.2 innings (an ERA of 2.63). Lawson has the repertoire to slide comfortably into a slot in the middle of a big league rotation: his fastball shows exceptional life up in the zone; his curveball is a late-breaking, heavily tilted weapon; and his changeup flashes above-average.

Scouting Report: Before the elbow woes, Lawson was tracking as a backend starting pitcher. Assuming he can move past whatever the latest setback was, he'll likely end up shifting into a middle relief role. Fingers crossed he makes it back to full health.

Ceiling: 1.0-win player
Risk: Moderate to High
MLB ETA: 2023

19. Daniel Montesino, 1B/OF

Hit	Power	SB	Patience	Glove	Overall
30/50	45/55	50/40	50	45	45

Born: 02/12/04	Age: 18	Bats: L	Top Comp: N/A
Height: 6-0	Weight: 180	Throws: L	

Season	Team	Age	Level	PA	1B	2B	3B	HR	SB	CS	BB%	K%	AVG	OBP	SLG	ISO
2021	SDP	17	DSL	243	39	13	4	4	8	4	17.70%	21.81%	0.316	0.444	0.489	0.174

Background: Hailing from San Juan de los Morros, Venezuela, the Padres went all in on hulking teenage prospect in mid-January 2021. The club handed the 6-foot, 180-pound first baseman / corner outfielder $1 million to join the NL West franchise as they look to rebuild there once bountiful farm system. Montesino made his professional debut a few months later in the Dominican Summer League. In 56 games, the young Venezuelan slugged a robust .316/.444/.489 with 13 doubles, four triples, four homeruns, and eight stolen bases.

Scouting Report: Montesino just *looks* like a future run producer at the big league level. Lean but muscular. Well-built but not stocky. The Venezuelan first baseman / corner outfielder shows almost a picture-esque left-handed stroke. Plenty of bat speed. Good natural loft. Montesino already began tapping into his above-average, maybe even plus-power potential in the Dominican Summer League. His bat and pop will have to carry him through the minor leagues, because he won't be providing any value on the defensive side of the ball.

Ceiling: 1.0- to 1.5-win player
Risk: Moderate to High
MLB ETA: 2025

20. Victor Lizarraga, RHP

FB	CB	CH	Command	Overall
55	50/55	N/A	40	40

Born: 11/30/03	Age: 18	Bats: R	Top Comp: N/A
Height: 6-3	Weight: 180	Throws: R	

Season	Team	Age	Level	IP	TBF	K/9	K%	BB/9	BB%	K-BB%	ERA	FIP	xFIP	Pit/Bat
2021	SDP	17	CPX	30.0	130	10.50	26.92%	4.50	11.54%	15.38%	5.10	6.00	5.20	1.85

Background: The Padres went aggressively after top amateur talent on the international market during the 2020 signing period, inking hitters like Samuel Zavala, Victor Acosta, and Daniel Montesino. As for pitchers, the front office snagged one of the better prospects as well, signing Lizarraga to another $1 million deal. Born in San Diego, California at the end of 2003 (man, do I feel old), the 6-foot-3, 180-pound right-hander made his debut in the Arizona Complex League in 2021. Throwing just 30.0 innings, Lizarraga struck out 35 and walked 15 to go along with a 5.10 ERA, a 6.00 FIP, and a 5.20 xFIP.

Scouting Report: Above-average fastball that shows some extra giddy-up at the top of the zone. He'll complement the low-90s pitch with an average curveball that projects to be a 55. And, according to reports, he'll mix in an average changeup, though I didn't see it. Lizarraga's a little soft physically and needs to get in better shape, get stronger. He looks like a low level wild card at this point.

Ceiling: 1.0-win player
Risk: High
MLB ETA: 2025

San Francisco Giants

Top Prospects

1. Marco Luciano, SS

Hit	Power	SB	Patience	Glove	Overall
50/55	50/60	50/40	55	45/50	70

Born: 09/10/01 | **Age:** 20 | **Bats:** R | **Top Comp: Manny Machado**
Height: 6-2 | **Weight:** 178 | **Throws:** R |

Season	Team	Age	Level	PA	1B	2B	3B	HR	SB	CS	BB%	K%	AVG	OBP	SLG	ISO
2019	SFG	17	R	178	26	9	2	10	8	6	15.17%	21.91%	0.322	0.438	0.616	0.295
2019	SFG	17	A-	38	3	4	0	0	1	0	13.16%	15.79%	0.212	0.316	0.333	0.121
2021	SFG	19	A	308	39	14	3	18	5	5	12.34%	22.08%	0.278	0.373	0.556	0.278
2021	SFG	19	A+	145	22	3	2	1	1	0	6.90%	37.24%	0.217	0.283	0.295	0.078

Background: Scouting is a tough gig. No matter how long you've been around, players destined for greatness bust, and players destined for the scrapheap succeed. Whether it's the Pirates passing on Sandy Koufax after his tryout with the ballclub, or 22 teams passing on Mike Trout, or the Giants handing out $6 million to Lucius Fox, or several national pundits ranking Victor Mesa as the top international prospect in 2018, who ahead of Marco Luciano, Diego Cartaya, Noelvi Marte, Orelvis Martinez, and Francisco Alvarez to name few. Luckily for the Giants' brass, the massive swing-and-miss on Fox didn't create any doubt to chase Luciano and hand him a hefty $2.6 million bonus. A native of San Francisco de Macoris, Dominican Republic (perhaps, serendipitous), the 6-foot-2, 178-pound shortstop immediately created a buzz as he dug in against the Arizona Summer League, slugging a robust .322/.438/.616 with 21 extra-base hits as a spry 17-year-old. He also appeared in the Northwest League for a handful of games at the end of the year, as well. After losing a year of development time due to the COVID-imposed shutdown, the club's player development program refused to pump the brakes on Luciano's express train to stardom: he began the year off in Low-A West, as a 19-year-old. That tour lasted all of 70 games as he slugged a hearty .278/.373/.556 and then the front office shoved him up to High-A – where his bat finally cooled (.217/.283/.295). Luciano finished his second professional season with an aggregate .258/.344/.471 slash line, belting out 17 doubles, five triples, and 19 homeruns.

Snippet from The 2020 Prospect Digest Handbook: He flashed tremendous potential as a dynamic top-of-the-lineup bat with an extreme saber-slant. He walked in nearly 15% of his plate appearances during his debut. Mix in solid contact rates, above-average speed, strong defense at an up-the-middle position, and plus- to plus-plus power potential and there's *A LOT* to love about this kid. Per FanGraphs, Luciano's average exit velocity, 92 mph, last season was tied as the seventh best among all measured minor league hitters (304 total). Again, he was 17-years-old.

Scouting Report: Consider the following:

- Since 2006, only four 19-year-old hitters met the following criteria in Low-A with one organization (min. 300 PA): 133 to 143 wRC+ total, a double-digit walk rate, and a strikeout rate between 20% and 23%. Those four hitters: Trevor Story, Kyle Blanks, Delino DeShields, and – of course – Mr. Marco Luciano.

The – seemingly – large red flag that's pockmarked Luciano's 2021 season would be his abysmal showing in High-A. Except, well, it's not a concern at all. Luciano struggle for the first week-and-a-half with the Eugene Emeralds, hitting a paltry .105/.167/.263 across his first 42 plate appearances. But after that, though, he slugged .283/.345/.377 over his final 119 plate appearances. Luciano owns a patient approach at the plate and solid contact skills that belie his prodigious power potential. He'll swipe a handful of bags each season, but that's almost guaranteed to become a non-skill at full maturity. Defensively, he played a passable Derek Jeter version of shortstop.

Ceiling: 6.0-win player
Risk: Moderate
MLB ETA: 2023/2024

2. Luis Matos, CF

Hit	Power	SB	Patience	Glove	Overall
55	50/60	55	45	55	60

Born: 01/28/02 | **Age:** 20 | **Bats:** R | **Top Comp: Starling Marte**
Height: 5-11 | **Weight:** 160 | **Throws:** R |

Season	Team	Age	Level	PA	1B	2B	3B	HR	SB	CS	BB%	K%	AVG	OBP	SLG	ISO
2019	SFG	17	R	270	52	24	2	7	20	2	7.04%	11.11%	0.362	0.430	0.570	0.209
2019	SFG	17	R	20	6	1	0	0	1	1	5.00%	5.00%	0.438	0.550	0.500	0.063
2021	SFG	19	A	491	90	35	1	15	21	5	5.70%	12.42%	0.313	0.358	0.494	0.182

Background: Clearly not an organization that shies away from doling out big money on the international scene (see: Lucius Fox, Marco Luciano, etc…) and Matos, a tools laden center fielder from Venezuela, is just another example. Signed out of Valera for a relatively small sum, at least in comparison to his other highly-touted prospects, Matos received a deal worth $725,000. And he put on a fireworks display during his debut in the Dominican Summer League in 2019: he slugged .362/.430/.570 with 24 doubles, two triples, seven homeruns, and 20 stolen bases in only 55 games. San Francisco bumped him to the stateside rookie league for another five games (.438/.550/.500) to cap off his explosive first season in affiliated ball. Last season, the front office shoved the then-19-year-old, baby-faced outfielder straight up to the wolves of Low-A. And it was Matos' growling that forced the rest of the pack to take notice. In 109 games with the

San Jose Giants, the 5-foot-11, 160-pound dynamo hit .313/.358/.494 with 35 doubles, one triple, 15 homeruns, and 21 stolen bases (in 26 total attempts). Per *Weighted Runs Created Plus*, his overall production topped the league average by 21%.

Snippet from The 2020 Prospect Digest Handbook: Like a blade quickly and quietly moving through the air, Matos' swing looks almost effortless. Impressive bat speed and the type of lean, projectable frame that should only add layers of athleticism as he matures. Matos – basically – ran at will during his stint in the Dominican Summer League, but the thick lower half and large plodding steps has me doubting if he'll continue to do so as he matures. There's a chance for average or better tools across the board.

Scouting Report: Consider the following:

- Since 2006, only three 19-year-old hitters posted 115 to 125 wRC+ total with a sub-14% strikeout rate and a sub-7% walk rate in a Low-A season with one organization (min. 350 PA): Austin Romine and Luis Matos.

Loud tools across the board. Matos is doing everything and he's doing everything well. He's making consistent, hard contact. He's hitting for plenty of power. He's fast *and* efficient on the base paths. He's an above-average defender in center field. And he did so while playing half of his games in ballpark that slants toward pitchers. Elite, elite bat speed. He's going to be a player for a *long time*.

Ceiling: 5.0-win player
Risk: Moderate
MLB ETA: 2024

3. Joey Bart, C

	Hit	Power	SB	Patience	Glove	Overall
	50	60	30	45	50	60

Born: 12/15/96	Age: 25	Bats: R	Top Comp: J.T. Realmuto
Height: 6-2	Weight: 238	Throws: R	

Season	Team	Age	Level	PA	1B	2B	3B	HR	SB	CS	BB%	K%	AVG	OBP	SLG	ISO
2018	SFG	21	R	25	4	1	1	0	0	0	4.00%	28.00%	0.261	0.320	0.391	0.130
2018	SFG	21	A-	203	25	14	2	13	2	1	5.91%	19.70%	0.298	0.369	0.613	0.315
2019	SFG	22	A+	251	38	10	2	12	5	2	5.58%	19.92%	0.265	0.315	0.479	0.214
2019	SFG	22	AA	87	16	4	1	4	0	2	8.05%	24.14%	0.316	0.368	0.544	0.228
2021	SFG	24	AAA	279	49	15	0	10	0	0	7.53%	29.39%	0.294	0.358	0.472	0.179

Background: Looking back at the 2018 draft, less than four full years removed, and it's readily apparent the power level was off the charts: the top seven selections have already spent time in the big leagues, including 2021 N.L. Rookie of the Year winner Jonathan India; pick number nine bypassed the opportunity to play baseball and simply became one of the best quarterbacks in the NFL (Kyler Murray); and Grayson Rodriguez and Nolan Gorman are on the brink of stardom. And that's just barely scratching the service. But it was Bart, a dynamic athlete, that went #2 overall. Before the ink dried on the contract the 6-foot-2, 238-pound backstop was already being pegged as *the* heir apparent to Buster Posey's golden throne. No one in their wildest dreams would have thought (A) that Bart wouldn't have a strangled hold on the position by now, (B) that Posey would have had the resurgence that he did at the age of 34, (C) or that the future Hall of Famer would've walked away, saving the organization from making a very difficult decision. Last season Bart appeared in 67 games with the Sacramento River Cats, slugging a rock solid .294/.358/.472 with 15 doubles and 10 homeruns. His overall production, per *Weighted Runs Created Plus*, topped the league average mark by just 7%.

Snippet from The 2020 Prospect Digest Handbook: He's like the Adam Jones the catching. Low walk rates, 30-homer power potential, 55-grade hit tool.

Scouting Report: Bart was hitting a scorching .338/.400/.581 before getting recalled to San Francisco for the final time on July 10th. Then after going 2-for-5 against the Diamondbacks, he was demoted back down to Triple-A and his bat cooled – considerably. He hit a lowly .241/.310/.345 over his remaining 32 games (which included a stint on the disabled list with a quadriceps issue). Bart's been a good hitter, sometimes very good, but he hasn't reached the heights that were once projected for him. Now he's whiffing nearly 30% of the time. The power is above-average and he should have no issue belting out 25 homeruns in a season. Good defense, good arm. In terms of offensive ceiling, think: .265/.340/.480.

Ceiling: 4.0-win player
Risk: Moderate
MLB ETA: Debuted in 2020

4. Jairo Pomares, LF/RF

Hit	Power	SB	Patience	Glove	Overall
50/55	55/65	30	40	45	60

Born: 08/04/00	Age: 21	Bats: L	Top Comp: Yoenis Cespedes
Height: 6-1	Weight: 185	Throws: R	

Season	Team	Age	Level	PA	1B	2B	3B	HR	SB	CS	BB%	K%	AVG	OBP	SLG	ISO
2019	SFG	18	A-	62	9	3	0	0	0	0	1.61%	27.42%	0.207	0.258	0.259	0.052
2019	SFG	18	R	167	40	10	4	3	5	3	5.99%	15.57%	0.368	0.401	0.542	0.174
2021	SFG	20	A	224	38	22	0	14	0	0	6.70%	24.11%	0.372	0.429	0.693	0.322
2021	SFG	20	A+	104	15	5	1	6	1	0	0.96%	31.73%	0.262	0.269	0.505	0.243

Background: Every now and then the stars seem to align when an organization collects a vast amount of talent in one fell swoop. The Kansas City Royals added Brady Singer, Jackson Kowar, Daniel Lynch, Kris Bubic, Jonathan Bowlan, and Kyle Isbel with their first six selections in the 2018 draft (and that doesn't include Austin Cox or Jon Heasley either). The Cleveland Indians added three-fifths of their big league rotation in mid-rounds of the 2016 draft: Aaron Civale (third round), Shane Bieber (fourth round), and Zach Plesac (12th round). And the San Francisco Giants added a triumvirate of high end talent on the international scene during 2018, signing Marco Luciano, Luis Matos, and – of course – Jairo Pomares. A native of Sancti Spiritus, Cuba, Pomares put on an offensive clinic during his debut with the club's stateside rookie league affiliate in 2019, hitting .368/.401/.542 in 37 games in 2019. The front office pushed the then-20-year-old up to San Jose to begin last season. But that barely lasted 50 games before he moved onto more difficult competition. When the dust had finally settled, he was sporting an aggregate .334/.378/.629 production line with 27 doubles, one triple, and 20 homeruns. His overall production, per *Weighted Runs Created Plus*, topped the league average mark by a staggering 55%.

Snippet from The 2020 Prospect Digest Handbook: Big leg kick with a lightning quick bat that was touted for his power potential prior to signing with the club. Pomares has yet to fully tap into his over-the-fence pop, but showed a knack for consistently barreling up the baseball. If you're a believer in the power potential – which, personally, I am – than there's a starting caliber ceiling, likely more.

Scouting Report: Consider the following:

- Since 2006, only three 20-year-old hitters posted a wRC+ total of at least 175 in High-A with one organization (min. 200 PA): Anthony Volpe, the Yankees' top prospect; Alex Kirilloff, a consensus Top 100 prospect before losing his rookie eligibility in 2021; and – course – Jairo Pomares.

Named the franchise's 2021 Minor League Player of the Year, Pomares looked like the second coming of Babe Ruth during his 51-game stint in Low-A last season, slugging .372/.429/.693 – though his production cooled to league average territory after his promotion up to High-A. He's never going to be the type to work the count. He may end up posting some 30% strikeout rates in the coming years, but the power is legit. And he's hit with the type of authority that the average minor leaguer doesn't possess. Pomares actually got off to a great start with Eugene, hitting .301/.310/.566 over his first 21 games before scuffling over his remaining nine (.139/.139/.306). He's going to be a low OBP, 35-homerun threat whose overall value will fluctuate according to his batting averages.

Ceiling: 3.5-win player
Risk: Moderate
MLB ETA: 2023/2024

5. Kyle Harrison, LHP

FB	SL	CH	Command	Overall
60	55	50/55	40/45	55

Born: 08/12/01	Age: 20	Bats: R	Top Comp: Carlos Rodon
Height: 6-2	Weight: 200	Throws: L	

Season	Team	Age	Level	IP	TBF	K/9	K%	BB/9	BB%	K-BB%	ERA	FIP	xFIP	Pit/Bat
2021	SFG	19	A	98.2	440	14.32	35.68%	4.74	11.82%	23.86%	3.19	3.48	4.06	3.99

Background: Some people play the game. Other people play the game well. San Francisco's front office played the 2020 draft game well. The savvy regime selected hard-throwing left-hander Kyle Harrison in the third round, 85th overall. Viewed as a first round talent, the organization didn't have any qualms about ponying up late first round money – $2,497,500, to be exact – to get the deal done. A year later Harrison's looking like quite the bargain. In 23 starts with the San Jose Giants in Low-A West, the 6-foot-2, 200-pound southpaw averaged a whopping 14.3 strikeouts and 4.7 walks per nine innings to go along with a 3.19 ERA, a 3.48 FIP, and a 4.06 xFIP.

Scouting Report: Among all minor league arms in 2021, three of the top nine highest strikeout totals (A) came from San Francisco pitching prospects and (B) all pitched for the club's Low-A affiliate, the San Jose Giants. With respect to Harrison, could the following:

- Since 2006, only seven 19-year-old hurlers posted a strikeout percentage of at least 32% in Low-A with one organization (min. 75 IP): Clayton Kershaw, Jose Fernandez, Tyler Glasnow, Grayson Rodriguez, Joey Estes, Joey Cantillo, and – of course – Kyle Harrison, the former third round pick.
- Narrowing it a bit: the only two hurlers to fan at last 35% of the hitters they faced: Glasnow and Harrison.

Mid-90s velocity on his explosive fastball coupled with two above-average secondary offerings (changeup and slider). Harrison isn't your typical teenage power arm. He has full confidence in utilizing his quality offspeed pitches. The slider has tremendous horizontal movement. The changeup is firm, but there's enough velo separation to make it work. If the command ticks up to average he's a quality #2/#3 starting pitcher. He could pop in a big way in 2022. He's a bit of slinger, so platoon splits will have to be monitored (LHH batted .302/.432/.365 in 2021).

Ceiling: 3.0-win player
Risk: Moderate
MLB ETA: 2024

6. Will Bednar, RHP

	FB	CB	SL	CH	Command	Overall
	55	50	65	N/A	55	50

Born: 06/13/00	Age: 22	Bats: R	Top Comp: N/A
Height: 6-2	Weight: 229	Throws: R	

Background: Like a heavyweight prize fight where each boxer trades off haymaker for haymaker, Bednar went toe-to-toe with Ty Madden, one of the game's premier amateur hurlers, and came out on top. And when the dust had finally settled, the 6-foot-2, 229-pound right-hander combined with power-armed closer Landon Sims to set a College World Series record with 21 punch outs. A highly touted prospect coming out of Mars Area High School, Bednar, whose older brother David had a breakout season for the Pittsburgh Pirates last year, had his freshman season cut short for the Bulldogs in 2020: he made four appearances, throwing 15.1 innings with 21 strikeouts and 11 free passes. The 2021 season, in many ways, was his first – and only – exposure to college baseball. And he dominated. In 19 appearances, 16 of which were starts, Bednar tossed 92.1 innings, recording a mindboggling 139-to-26 strikeout-to-walk ratio to go along with a 9-1 record and a 3.12 ERA as his Mississippi State Bulldogs captured the college World Series. San Francisco drafted him with the 14th overall pick and signed him to a deal worth $3,647,500. Bednar made four appearances in the low levels, fanning six and walking one in seven innings.

Scouting Report: Per the usual, here's what I wrote about Bednar prior to the draft last July:

"Consider the following:

- *Between 2011 and 2020, only six SEC pitchers averaged at least 12 K/9 in a season (min. 75 IP): A.J. Puk, Casey Mize, Asa Lacy, Ethan Small, Zach Thompson, and Mason Hickman, who was the only player in the group not chosen in the first round.*

Not bad company to keep for the future first rounder. Bednar ticks off a lot of the important checkboxes: elite production against premier talent, multiple quality offerings, above-average command, workhorse, and – of course – incredibly underrated. Bednar's fastball sits – effortlessly – in the low 90s and can touch as high as 95 mph. His bread-and-butter offering is a gyro-spinning slider that's lethal on both lefties and righties. He'll also mix in an average curveball. And according to reports, he'll mix in an average changeup (I never saw one). Put him down as a quick moving #3/#4 type arm. Love him. Very safe."

Ceiling: 2.5-win player
Risk: Low to Moderate
MLB ETA: 2022

7. Heliot Ramos, CF

Hit	Power	SB	Patience	Glove	Overall
45	50/50	55	45	45	50

Born: 09/07/99 **Age:** 22 **Bats:** R **Top Comp:** Ramon Laureano
Height: 6-1 **Weight:** 188 **Throws:** R

Season	Team	Age	Level	PA	1B	2B	3B	HR	SB	CS	BB%	K%	AVG	OBP	SLG	ISO
2018	SFG	18	A	535	76	24	8	11	8	7	6.54%	25.42%	0.245	0.313	0.396	0.151
2019	SFG	19	A+	338	59	18	0	13	6	7	9.47%	25.15%	0.306	0.385	0.500	0.194
2019	SFG	19	AA	106	13	6	1	3	2	3	9.43%	31.13%	0.242	0.321	0.421	0.179
2021	SFG	21	AA	266	31	14	1	10	7	2	10.15%	27.44%	0.237	0.323	0.432	0.195
2021	SFG	21	AAA	229	41	11	2	4	8	2	6.55%	28.38%	0.272	0.323	0.399	0.127

Background: The second prep outfielder taken in the 2017 draft. San Francisco selected the 6-foot-1, 188-pound toolsy, but raw center fielder with the 19th overall pick that year, sandwiched between the Tigers' selection of Alex Faedo and the Mets' selection of David Peterson. Ramos began his career like every other toolsy, high profile teenage outfielder in the system (or at least that's how it *feels*): like a bat out of hell. He slugged .348/.404/.645 in 35 rookie league games. Young for his draft class, Ramos spent the 2018 season as an 18-year-old mostly struggling against the South Atlantic League competition. His production came roaring back the following season in High-A and he held his own for 25 games in Double-A. Last year, with the return of regular minor league action, Ramos labored through a disappointing return to Double-A before spending the second half nestled in the hitter-friendly Triple-A West. In total, the 6-foot-1, 188-pound outfielder hit an aggregate .254/.323/.416 with 25 doubles, three triples, 14 homeruns, and 15 stolen bases.

Snippet from The 2020 Prospect Digest Handbook: The lone pockmark (still): his borderline problematic strikeout rates. He whiffed in more than a quarter of his plate appearances in High Class A.

Scouting Report: Ramos' problematic strikeout rates reared its ugly head again last season as he whiffed in roughly 28% of his plate appearances in Double-A and Triple-A. The tools remain in place and, yes, he's still quite young – he's only entering his age-22 season – but Ramos has never really dominated a level for an extended period – sans his explosion in High-A three years ago. Otherwise, he's been good, not great. The batted ball data has typically been off the charts (average exit velocity is 90 mph).

Ceiling: 2.0-win player
Risk: Moderate
MLB ETA: 2022

8. Patrick Bailey, C

Hit	Power	SB	Patience	Glove	Overall
40/45	50/55	30	55	55	50

Born: 05/29/99 **Age:** 23 **Bats:** R **Top Comp:** Travis d'Arnaud
Height: 6-1 **Weight:** 210 **Throws:** R

Season	Team	Age	Level	PA	1B	2B	3B	HR	SB	CS	BB%	K%	AVG	OBP	SLG	ISO
2021	SFG	22	A	207	34	16	0	7	1	1	13.53%	22.71%	0.322	0.415	0.531	0.209
2021	SFG	22	A+	155	14	9	0	2	6	0	11.61%	27.74%	0.185	0.290	0.296	0.111

Background: When it comes to hitting prospects the Giants' front office brass loves toolsy international free agents and collegiate catching. The club has used first round selections on big time college backstops in two of the last four drafts, selection Georgia Tech star Joey Bart with the second overall pick in 2018 and then snagging N.C. State catcher Patrick Bailey with the 13th pick two years later. Projected as a slam dunk first rounder since his dynamic freshman season when he slugged .321/.419/.604, Bailey lived up to those expectations two years later when he signed a hefty $3.8 million deal. Last season the 6-foot-1, 210-pound prospect made his debut as he spent the majority of the year in Low-A and High-A. Bailey would hit an aggregate .265/.366/.429 with 25 doubles and nine homeruns in 82 contests, some of which was spent rehabbing in the rookie leagues as he was coming back from a concussion.

Scouting Report: The club aggressively assigned the former Wolfpack slugger to High-A to begin his professional career, but Bailey was woefully overmatched as he batted just .185/.290/.296 across his first 33 games (155 plate appearances). He hit the disabled list for a couple weeks, did a two-game tune-up in the Complex League, and was sent down to Low-A. Finally, his bat came alive. He slugged .326/.420/.561 with 17 doubles and nine dingers in 50 games. He's not likely going to be much more than a .250 hitter. But Bailey owns enough thump to slug 20 homeruns and post a .340 OBP. Throw in above-average defense and a strong throwing arm and he looks like a lock to be a solid caliber starting option for the Giants in a couple years.

Ceiling: 2.0-win player
Risk: Moderate
MLB ETA: 2024

9. Nick Swiney, LHP

FB	CB	CH	Command	Overall
50	60	65	45	45

Born: 02/12/99	Age: 23	Bats: R	Top Comp: N/A
Height: 6-3	Weight: 185	Throws: L	

Season	Team	Age	Level	IP	TBF	K/9	K%	BB/9	BB%	K-BB%	ERA	FIP	xFIP	Pit/Bat
2021	SFG	22	A	24.1	102	15.53	41.18%	4.44	11.76%	29.41%	0.74	2.26	3.20	4.10

Background: A full time reliever over his first two seasons at N.C. State University. The Wolfpack transitioned the lanky lefty into the rotation permanently during his junior campaign. And the 6-foot-3, 185-pound hurler got off to one helluva start to the 2020 campaign: through four starts, spanning 28.0 innings of work, Swiney struck out 42 and walked just six to go along with a 1.29 ERA. San Francisco selected him in the second round, 67th overall, and handed him an above-slot deal worth $1,197,500. The southpaw kicked off his career professional career in stellar fashion, pitching four innings of one-hit ball while fanning six and walking a pair against the Fresno Grizzlies. Then he hit the disabled list for nearly three months. The reason: a severe concussion that resulted from him knocking his noggin on the bus door. After a five-game detour through the Complex League during his rehab assignment, Swiney popped back up in Low-A in mid-August for six final appearances. During his time with San Jose, he posted a 42-to-12 strikeout-to-walk ratio in only 24.1 innings of work with a 0.74 ERA.

Scouting Report: Swiney owns an average-ish 89- to 93-mph fastball, but it's all about the offspeed, baby. Swiney's curveball shows late sweeping movement away from lefties and into righties. When he's spotting it correctly, it's nearly difficult for right-handed hitters to pull it and keep it in play. He also throws my favorite changeup in the minor leagues. It's slow with a bit of cutting action. It's Bugs Bunny-esque. The command waivered for Swiney last season and it's tough to pinpoint the reason: had it regressed back to his freshman and sophomore seasons at N.C. State? Or was it from all the time off? If he can keep the walk rate in the upper 3s / lower 4s he's a nice little backend option. I really enjoyed watching his carve up the opposition, very much so.

Ceiling: 1.5-win player
Risk: Moderate
MLB ETA: 2023/2024

10. Diego Rincones, LF/RF

Hit	Power	SB	Patience	Glove	Overall
50	45/50	30	50	45/50	45

Born: 06/14/99	Age: 23	Bats: R	Top Comp: Angel Pagan without the speed
Height: 6-0	Weight: 175	Throws: R	

Season	Team	Age	Level	PA	1B	2B	3B	HR	SB	CS	BB%	K%	AVG	OBP	SLG	ISO
2018	SFG	19	A-	277	59	15	0	7	0	0	3.61%	11.55%	0.315	0.357	0.455	0.140
2019	SFG	20	A	442	84	25	4	5	0	0	6.11%	12.67%	0.295	0.346	0.415	0.120
2019	SFG	20	A+	88	12	4	0	2	0	0	12.50%	9.09%	0.247	0.375	0.384	0.137
2021	SFG	22	A+	107	16	6	0	5	0	0	9.35%	17.76%	0.300	0.385	0.533	0.233
2021	SFG	22	AA	213	35	8	1	10	1	0	7.51%	17.37%	0.290	0.373	0.505	0.215

Background: Let me know if you've heard this one before: the Giants have this outfielder plucked off the international market making his way through the club's farm system with impressive numbers. Signed out of Cuidad Bolivar, Venezuela, the 6-foot, 175-pound corner outfielder turned in another Rincones-like showing in 2021. Splitting time between Eugene and Richmond, the ballclub's High-A and Double-A affiliates, the young Venezuelan slugged put together an aggregate .293/.377/.514 triple-slash line, belting out 14 doubles, one three-bagger, and a career best 15 long balls in only 76 games. His overall production, per *Weighted Runs Created Plus*, topped the league average mark by a whopping 40%.

Snippet from The 2020 Prospect Digest Handbook: Interesting prospect. If the power takes a step forward, he is instantly a starting contender.

Scouting Report: Consider the following:

- Since 2006, only four 22-year-old hitters posted a 135 to 145 wRC+ total with a walk rate between 6% and 9% and a strikeout rate between 16% and 19% in a Double-A season (min. 200 PA): Matt Adams, Brandon Laird, Kyle Waldrop, and Diego Rincones.

In terms of notable hitting prospects in the system, Rincones is the outlier in a lot of ways: he's not projectable, doesn't own a standout tool (let alone several), but he produces. And produces. And produces. In fact, beginning with his debut in 2016, Rincones has never posted a production line that's at least 10% *above* the average mark. He's still showing impressive bat-to-ball skills and that hasn't changed as he's developing power that's closely inching towards a 50-grade. Rincones is still tracking like a fourth outfielder, but he's going to make a very good case to be given a long look at holding down a permanent job.

Ceiling: 1.5-win player
Risk: Moderate
MLB ETA: 2022/2023

11. Hunter Bishop, OF

	Hit	Power	SB	Patience	Glove	Overall
	N/A	N/A	N/A	N/A	N/A	50

Born: 06/25/98 | **Age:** 24 | **Bats:** L | **Top Comp:** N/A
Height: 6-5 | **Weight:** 210 | **Throws:** R |

Season	Team	Age	Level	PA	1B	2B	3B	HR	SB	CS	BB%	K%	AVG	OBP	SLG	ISO
2019	SFG	21	R	29	1	3	0	1	2	0	31.03%	37.93%	0.250	0.483	0.550	0.300
2019	SFG	21	A-	117	13	1	1	4	6	2	24.79%	23.93%	0.224	0.427	0.400	0.176
2021	SFG	23	CPX	32	3	1	0	0	1	1	15.63%	31.25%	0.160	0.313	0.200	0.040
2021	SFG	23	A+	15	1	1	0	0	0	0	13.33%	26.67%	0.167	0.333	0.250	0.083

Background: Fun Fact Part I: Prior to San Francisco's selection of Hunter Bishop with the 10th overall pick in 2019, the last time an Arizona State player went that high was all the way in 2009 when Mike Leake was nabbed by the Cincinnati Reds with the eighth overall pick. Fun Fact Pact II: throughout the school's history, the Giants have selected a total of 23 Sun Devils. Fun Fact Part III: Only three of those 23 player have been taken in the opening round – Bishop (10th overall, 2019), Dan McKinley (49th overall, 1997), and Jacob Cruz (32nd overall, 1994). One of the most explosive college bats in 2019, Bishop had an up-and-down showing in the Northwest League during his debut, hitting .224/.427/.400 in 25 games. And it's been downhill from there. During the 2020 COVID shutdown, the 6-foot-5, 210-pound outfielder caught the virus that year and, according to reports, was a late arrival to the Giants' alternate site. And then last year a left shoulder issue limited him to just 16 games across three low levels. Bishop did make a return to the Arizona Fall League, hitting a respectable .262/.373/.381 with the Scottsdale Scorpions.

Snippet from The 2020 Prospect Digest Handbook: Bishop shows solid bat speed and enough loft in his swing to belt out 20 homeruns in a professional season. His swing-and-miss tendencies, despite the dramatic improvement, are still a bit concerning. But he should have no problems developing into a league average starting outfielder, particularly if he can stay in center field.

Scouting Report: There's nothing really tangible to report on thanks to the injury and subsequent setback. Two years ago I cautioned about Bishop's potentially damning swing-and-miss issues, and he punched out in nearly 40% of his plate appearances in the Fall League. Could it be a harbinger of things to come? Maybe. Could it simply be from the injury and layoff? Maybe. Will the left shoulder issue plague him in the coming year? Hopefully not, but who knows?

Ceiling: 2.5-win player
Risk: High
MLB ETA: 2024

12. Sean Hjelle, RHP

	FB	SL	CH	Command	Overall
	60	55	55	50+	45

Born: 05/07/97 | **Age:** 25 | **Bats:** R | **Top Comp:** Ryan Vogelsong
Height: 6-11 | **Weight:** 228 | **Throws:** R |

Season	Team	Age	Level	IP	TBF	K/9	K%	BB/9	BB%	K-BB%	ERA	FIP	xFIP	Pit/Bat
2018	SFG	21	A-	21.1	94	9.28	23.40%	1.69	4.26%	19.15%	5.06	4.63	3.39	3.72
2019	SFG	22	A	40.2	172	9.74	25.58%	1.99	5.23%	20.35%	2.66	3.02	2.67	4.01
2019	SFG	22	A+	77.2	325	8.58	22.77%	2.20	5.85%	16.92%	2.78	3.29	3.46	3.68
2019	SFG	22	AA	25.1	119	7.46	17.65%	3.20	7.56%	10.08%	6.04	3.33	3.59	3.73
2021	SFG	24	AA	65.2	274	9.46	25.18%	2.60	6.93%	18.25%	3.15	4.00	3.54	3.83
2021	SFG	24	AAA	53.1	248	5.91	14.11%	4.89	11.69%	2.42%	5.74	5.77	6.19	3.54

Background: When it comes to Sean Hjelle (pronounced: jelly) the conversation will always circle back around to his height. Standing a NBA center-esque 6-foot-11 and 228 pounds, Hjelle is – without question – the tallest player in professional baseball. A product of the University of Kentucky by way of the 2018 second round, Hjelle split time between Richmond and Sacramento last season, his fourth in the Giants' organization. In a combined 24 starts, the big right-hander struck out 104 and walked 48 to go along with a 4.31 ERA. For the year Hjelle averaged 7.9 strikeouts and 3.6 walks per nine innings.

Snippet from The 2020 Prospect Digest Handbook: Hjelle throws a surprising amount of strikes for a massively-framed pitcher. And he generally commands the strike zone with all four pitches well. He still looks like a #4/#5-type arm unless one of the breaking balls takes a step forward.

Scouting Report: Throughout the duration of his minor league career Hjelle's fastball has continued to creep up in velocity, little by little every season – or so it seems. Three years ago, pre-COVID shutdown, the massive right-hander was sitting 91- to 92-mph with his fastball. In his last start of his 2021 campaign, however, he was sitting 94 and touching 95 regularly. The former Wildcat seems to have scrapped the average curveball and he's hyper-focused on his improving his slider. The result: an above-average, sometimes bat-shattering breaking ball that will sit in the mid-80s with hard southern bite. Hjelle's changeup is an underrated third offering, showing significantly arm side run and a little bit of dive when he's finishing it. Currently the NL West Division Champs only have three starting pitchers slated for their rotation – Alex Wood, Logan Webb, and Anthony DeSlafani. Hjelle certainly seems to have the inside track on the #5 gig.

Ceiling: 1.5-win player
Risk: Moderate
MLB ETA: 2022

13. Ryan Murphy, RHP

	FB	CB	SL	CH	Command	Overall
	50	55	55	55	60	45

Born: 10/08/99	Age: 22	Bats: R	Top Comp: Mike Leake
Height: 6-1	Weight: 190	Throws: R	

Season	Team	Age	Level	IP	TBF	K/9	K%	BB/9	BB%	K-BB%	ERA	FIP	xFIP	Pit/Bat
2021	SFG	21	A	76.0	300	13.74	38.67%	2.13	6.00%	32.67%	2.96	3.85	3.18	4.04
2021	SFG	21	A+	31.1	117	13.79	41.03%	2.30	6.84%	34.19%	1.44	2.29	3.33	4.19

Background: An underrated, undersized player coming out of high school. Murphy, a 6-foot-1, 190-pound right-hander, had only one D1offer on the table: the University at Albany. Murphy, instead, went to former Division I school Le Moyne College.

After a stellar career with the Division II squad, San Francisco used their final selection in the 2020 draft to snag the craft right-hander. Fast forward a year and Murphy is forcing people to take notice. In 21 total starts between Low-A and High-A, the New York native struck out a whopping 164 versus only 26 free passes. He compiled a tidy 2.52 ERA while averaging an impressive 13.8 K/9 and only 2.2 BB/9.

Scouting Report: Just how good was Murphy last season? His 167 strikeouts were the third highest among all minor leaguers. Among all MiLB pitchers with at least 100 innings pitched in 2021, his strikeout percentage, 39.3%, and strikeout-to-walk percentage, 33.1%, trailed only uber-prospect Grayson Rodriguez. He didn't make many waves, but his second half surge was Bob Gibson-esque from a production standpoint: over his final 62.1 innings he posted a 1.59 ERA and struck out 104 hitters. Really enjoyable pitcher to watch from a pure fan standpoint. Murphy is very reminiscent of veteran right-hander Josh Tomlin. San Francisco's right-hander won't blow his 91 mph heater past a lot bats, but he can sure as hell pitch. Complementing – or perhaps offsetting – his average fastball with three above-average secondary weapons: a knuckle / spike curveball, a slider, and a very solid changeup. Murphy owns some of the best command in the minor leagues.

Ceiling: 1.5-win player
Risk: Moderate
MLB ETA: 2023

14. Matt Mikulski, LHP

	FB	SL	CH	Command	Overall
	55	55	50	45	45

Born: 05/08/99	Age: 23	Bats: L	Top Comp: N/A
Height: 6-4	Weight: 205	Throws: L	

Background: A solid, though far from spectacular prospect coming out of Lakeland High School in 2017, Mikulski compiled 73 punch outs and a tidy 1.08 ERA in 45.2 innings of work. *Perfect Game* listed him as a Preseason All-American in 2016, while also cracking the publication's Top 500 Recruits list as well. The 6-foot-4, 205-pound southpaw split time between Fordham's rotation and bullpen during his true freshman season: he made 17 appearances, five of which were starts, throwing 41.2 innings with 41 punch outs and 15 free passes. The following season, 2019, Mikulski made 14 starts and four relief appearances, throwing a career best 82 innings, averaging 9.8 strikeouts and 4.5 walks per nine innings. He spent the ensuing summer playing for the Brewster Whitecaps in the Cape Cod League, posting a 26-to-13 strikeout-to-walk ratio in 19.1 innings. After a mediocre four-game stretch in the COVID-shortened 2020 campaign, Mikulski established himself as of the game's best college arms in 2021: he tallied a 1.45 ERA across 68.1 innings, recording a whopping 124 strikeouts against just 27 walks. San Francisco selected him in the second round, 50th overall, and signed him to a deal worth $1.2 million. Mikulski made four brief appearances in the Complex League, fanning five and walking thee in five innings of work.

Scouting Report: Per the usual, here's what I wrote about the big lefty before the draft last summer:

"Consider the following:

- *Between 2011 and 2020, only five Atlantic 10 pitchers averaged at least 11 strikeouts per nine innings in a season (min. 50): Connor Gillispie (who accomplished it twice), Connor Lehmann, Cole Pletka, Miller Hogan, and Bobby Lucus. The best of the bunch was Pletka, who averaged 12.94 K/9 for Dayton in 2019.*

For the record: Mikulski averaged a staggering 16.33 punch outs per nine innings in 2021, which led all of Division I by a relatively wide margin. A couple of above-average pitches – fastball and a slider – combined with a decent changeup. Mikulski has tweaked his mechanics since his time in the Cape Cod League, opting to reduce a traditional arm path with the more en vogue shortened arm action. Back of the rotation caliber prospect, high floor, low ceiling."

Ceiling: 1.0- to 1.5-win player
Risk: Low to Moderate
MLB ETA: 2024

15. Ismael Munguia, CF

Hit	Power	SB	Patience	Glove	Overall
55	40	55	40	55	45

Born: 10/19/98	Age: 23	Bats: L	Top Comp: N/A
Height: 5-10	Weight: 185	Throws: L	

Season	Team	Age	Level	PA	1B	2B	3B	HR	SB	CS	BB%	K%	AVG	OBP	SLG	ISO
2018	SFG	19	A	147	25	1	3	1	2	0	4.08%	14.97%	0.226	0.261	0.301	0.075
2018	SFG	19	R	63	11	6	3	0	0	1	6.35%	9.52%	0.345	0.397	0.552	0.207
2019	SFG	20	A	427	83	22	5	1	13	5	5.62%	9.60%	0.286	0.343	0.376	0.090
2021	SFG	22	A+	357	78	22	3	9	15	5	3.64%	7.56%	0.336	0.366	0.502	0.165

Background: A 5-foot-10, 158-pound dynamo out of Chinandega, Nicaragua. The young center fielder has consistently performed with the bat at every stop along the way. As a 17-year, Munguia hit .274/.359/.363 during his debut in the Dominican Summer League. A year later he ripped through the domestic rookie league by slugging .331/.398/.458. In 2018, the front office bounced him back down to rookie league for another quick tune-up, but after 15 games he was pushed up to the South Atlantic League – which is the only time he failed to hit at a level (.226/.261/.301). Unsurprisingly, Munguia found himself back in Low-A for 2019. And he hit. And he hit well. In 100 games with Augusta he batted .286/.343/.376. Last season the then-22-year-old outfielder continued that trend as he moved up to High-A, slugging .336/.366/.502 with 22 doubles, three triples, and nine homeruns. He also swiped 15 bags in 20 attempts. Per *Weighted Runs Created Plus*, his overall production topped the league average mark by 30%.

Scouting Report: Consider the following:

- Since 2006, only three 22-year-old hitters posted a 125 to 135 wRC+ total with a sub-10% strikeout rate in High-A with one organization (min. 350 PA): Eric Sogard, Chesny Young, and – of course – Ismael "Toy Cannon" Munguia.

The lone knock on the little outfielder heading into the season was his lack of thump. Sure, he made consistent contact and played a solid center field, but he wasn't going to strike fear into the opposition slapping singles. Last year, in a home park that was *slightly* favorable for homeruns, Munguia knocked out nine longballs – three times his career total up to that point. 55-grade glove. 55-grade hit tool. 55-grade speed. 40-homerun pop . The low OBPs due to zero patience at the plate really chew into his value. Fourth/fifth outfielder.

Ceiling: 1.0- to 1.5-win player
Risk: Moderate
MLB ETA: 2023/2024

16. Mason Black, RHP

FB	SL	CH	Command	Overall
70	55	N/A	40/45	45

Born: 12/10/99	Age: 22	Bats: R	Top Comp: N/A
Height: 6-3	Weight: 230	Throws: R	

Background: Lehigh University, a Bethlehem, Pennsylvania, based college in the Patriot League, has produced just 14 draft picks in the school's history. The interesting part, to me at least, is that four of selections have occurred since 2019 – including two in 2021. San Francisco selected Black in the third round last July, the 85th overall pick, making him the second highest drafted player in

Lehigh history. Black made 13 starts for the Mountain Hawks during his junior campaign, throwing 72.1 innings with 95 strikeouts and 31 walks to go along with a 7-3 win-loss record and a 3.11 ERA. After signing with the franchise for $708,200, Black did not appear in a pro game.

Scouting Report: To the best of my knowledge, there's no publicly available game tape of Mason Black from last season's solid showing at Lehigh. ProspectLive has a tape from Black's time in the Cape Cod League with the Brewster Whitecaps during the 2019 summer. They're reporting his fastball was sitting in the 93- to 95-mph with an 80-mph breaking ball. It looks like a power curveball, but all updated reports suggest it's a slider. Either way, though, it looks to be an above-average offering with nice downward tilt. He also reportedly throws an average changeup as well. MLB.com is reporting that Black's heater touched 100 mph last season, so that's…nice.

Ceiling: 1.0- to 1.5-win player
Risk: Moderate
MLB ETA: 2024

17. Gregory Santos, RHP

FB	SL	Command	Overall
70	70	40/45	45

Born: 08/28/99	Age: 22	Bats: R	Top Comp: Joel Zumaya
Height: 6-2	Weight: 190	Throws: R	

Background: It was a year that started out with so much promise and ended with complete disappointment. Prior to the 2021 season the last time Santos toed a rubber was on July 7th, 2019, for the Augusta GreenJackets in the South Atlantic League. Fast forward through the lost COVID season and the now 21-year-old opened his 2021 campaign with the big league club, striking out a pair in one inning of work against the Marlins. Santos would make two more (disastrous) appearances in *The Show* before getting optioned back down to AAA. Ten appearances into his stay with the Sacramento River Cats the flame-throwing right-hander got popped for the synthetic steroid Stanozolol, which has anabolic and androgenic properties. He was promptly suspended for 80 games. He finished his minor league season with 15 strikeouts and nine walks in 15.2 innings. Santos did pop back up in the Arizona Fall League, where he recorded a 12-to-5 strikeout-to-walk ratio in 13.0 innings with the Scottsdale Scorpions.

Snippet from The 2020 Prospect Digest Handbook: Shoulder issues at any age are concerning at age, but Santos' comes very early in his career, lingered throughout the season, and eventually curtailed his 2019 after eight starts. Santos has the upside as a #4-type starting pitcher, but he could easily wind up in the bullpen in a few years.

Scouting Report: Everything ticked up for Santos last season: his fastball from plus to plus-plus and was averaging nearly 98 mph during his three-game stint with the Giants. And his slider went from flashing plus to a borderline plus-plus breaking ball. He always seem to be a long shot to stay in the rotation – even before the 2019 shoulder woes – so last season's transition shouldn't shock anyone. His command may never tick up enough to put him in a closer position, but he has the look of a solid seventh/eighth inning guy.

Ceiling: 1.0- to 1.5-win player
Risk: Moderate to High
MLB ETA: Debuted in 2021

18. Aeverson Arteaga, SS

Hit	Power	SB	Patience	Glove	Overall
30/45	45/50	50	50	45/50	40

Born: 03/16/03	Age: 19	Bats: R	Top Comp: N/A
Height: 6-1	Weight: 170	Throws: R	

Season	Team	Age	Level	PA	1B	2B	3B	HR	SB	CS	BB%	K%	AVG	OBP	SLG	ISO
2021	SFG	18	CPX	226	36	12	1	9	8	0	10.18%	30.53%	0.294	0.367	0.503	0.208

Background: Oh, hey, yet *another* one of the club's big international free agents that came out swinging like Babe *Freakin'* Ruth. San Francisco signed Arteaga to a million deal in 2019, the largest bonus the franchise handed out during that signing period. A 6-foot-1, 170-pound shortstop, Arteaga made his debut with the club's Arizona Complex League affiliate last summer. In 56 games, the Chirgua, Venezuela, native slugged .294/.367/.503 with 12 doubles, one triple, nine homeruns, and eight stolen bases. Per *Weighted Runs Created Plus*, his overall production topped the league average mark by 23%.

Scouting Report: And now the bad news: the teenage shortstop whiffed in 30% of his plate appearances last summer. Let's dive deeper, shall we? Over his first 45 games he posted a 26% K-rate – which is not great, but it's *better*. Over his final 13 games he whiffed 22 times in 52 plate appearances. The swing's OK, but it's not special. It needs to be cleaned up, simplified. Good bat speed, but it's chaos. And not controlled chaos. He might be a candidate to spend part of 2022 back in the Complex League, though that doesn't seem realistic at this point. Lottery ticket.

Ceiling: 1.0-win player
Risk: Moderate
MLB ETA: 2025

19. Seth Corry, LHP

	FB	CB	CH	Command	Overall
	60	65	50	30/45	45

Born: 11/03/98	**Age:** 23	**Bats:** L	**Top Comp:** N/A
Height: 6-2	**Weight:** 195	**Throws:** L	

Season	Team	Age	Level	IP	TBF	K/9	K%	BB/9	BB%	K-BB%	ERA	FIP	xFIP	Pit/Bat
2018	SFG	19	R	38.0	169	9.95	24.85%	4.03	10.06%	14.79%	2.61	3.70	3.93	1.91
2018	SFG	19	A-	19.2	87	7.78	19.54%	6.86	17.24%	2.30%	5.49	4.93	5.30	4.14
2019	SFG	20	A	122.2	508	12.62	33.86%	4.26	11.42%	22.44%	1.76	2.87	3.15	4.15
2021	SFG	22	A+	67.2	317	13.30	31.55%	8.38	19.87%	11.67%	5.99	5.25	5.64	4.11

Background: Not everything came up aces for Giants prospects – in particular their pitching prospects. Sailing a bit under the radar due to the general success of the big league club and the emergence of arms like Kyle Harrison and Ryan Murphy, Seth Curry, one of the bigger hurlers in the system heading into the year, was beyond pitiful in 2021. The hard-throwing lefty with a penchant for bloated walk rates, though typivally manageable, completely imploded in High-A. In 19 starts with the Eugene Emeralds, the 6-foot-2, 195-pound southpaw racked up 100 punch outs in only 67.2 innings. The problem: he walked 63. He spent the fall working in the Arizona Fall League with the Scottsdale Scorpions, though the results were largely the same: 11.2 innings pitched, 17 strikeouts, 12 walks.

Snippet from The 2020 Prospect Digest Handbook: Corry's control – not command, though – took some important strides in the second half of last season. He walked just 18 hitters over his final 68.2 innings of work. It's a very encouraging sign that could point to better things in the future. He's a volatile prospect because he'll either wind up as a solid league-average starting or a solid reliever depending upon the control.

Scouting Report: When he's on, he's *on*. When he's off, he's *way off*. The problem for Corry last season, though, is that he was rarely on and seemingly always off. His fastball was sitting easily, explosively in the mid-90s. His curveball is a thing a beauty, a gift from the baseball gods granted to the likes of Barry Zito or Sandy Koufax. The changeup's nothing to write home about. But none of that really matters, though, because he has the yips. And, unfortunately, it's of the Steve Blass variety. The expectations are low. And I hope he rebounds. But at this point, it almost seems insurmountable.

Ceiling: 1.5-win player
Risk: High
MLB ETA: 2025

20. Blake Rivera, RHP

	FB	CB	CH	Command	Overall
	55	60	N/A	50	40

Born: 01/09/98	**Age:** 24	**Bats:** R	**Top Comp:** N/A
Height: 6-4	**Weight:** 225	**Throws:** R	

Season	Team	Age	Level	IP	TBF	K/9	K%	BB/9	BB%	K-BB%	ERA	FIP	xFIP	Pit/Bat
2018	SFG	20	A-	19.0	91	6.63	15.38%	5.21	12.09%	3.30%	6.16	5.66	5.84	3.78
2019	SFG	21	A	73.0	317	10.73	27.44%	4.81	12.30%	15.14%	3.95	3.32	3.36	3.81
2021	SFG	23	CPX	10.1	41	12.19	34.15%	2.61	7.32%	26.83%	2.61	3.89	3.00	2.05
2021	SFG	23	A+	14.0	68	10.93	25.00%	3.21	7.35%	17.65%	6.43	4.91	4.28	3.37

Background: A fourth round pick out of Wallace State Community College back in 2018, signing an above-slot bonus worth $800K. Rivera seemed to coming into his own during the 2019 season with the Augusta GreenJackets; he posted an 87-to-39 strikeout-to-walk ratio in 73.0 innings of work. Then COVID hit and the entire minor leagues lost a season of development. Last season Rivera wouldn't return to the mound until early August, debuting with the club's Arizona Complex League affiliate for a handful of games before making his way up to High-A for another five appearances. He would post a 17-to-5 strikeout-to-walk ratio in 14.0 innings with the Eugene Emeralds.

Snippet from The 2020 Prospect Digest Handbook: Rivera's heater sits in the 94 mph range, but it's a soft 94 mph. There's a lot of natural cut where you can almost see his fingers sliding off the ball on the side instead of pulling backwards on the strings. It's just one of those offerings that *should* be a plus a pitch, but it just doesn't play as well as the velocity would suggest. Already entering his age-22 season, it's unlikely that the former JuCo star's control – let alone his command – develops enough to keep him in the rotation long term.

Scouting Report: Rivera's heater is still sitting the 93- to 94-mph range. And it still doesn't get many – or any – swings-and-misses on it. The curveball is still a 12-6 hammer-of-a-plus offering. I did not see his fringy average-ish changeup. He's always had the feel of a middle reliever in waiting and nothing he's done has changed my mind. He's racking up more than a punch out an inning, but the majority of that comes on the Uncle Charlie.

Ceiling: 0.5-win player
Risk: Moderate
MLB ETA: 2023

Seattle Mariners

Top Prospects

1. Julio Rodriguez, OF

Hit	Power	SB	Patience	Glove	Overall
55/60	50/60	55	55/60	55/60	70

Born: 12/29/00	Age: 21	Bats: R	Top Comp: Christian Yelich
Height: 6-3	Weight: 180	Throws: R	

Season	Team	Age	Level	PA	1B	2B	3B	HR	SB	CS	BB%	K%	AVG	OBP	SLG	ISO
2018	SEA	17	R	255	42	13	9	5	10	0	11.76%	15.69%	0.315	0.404	0.525	0.210
2019	SEA	18	A	295	46	20	1	10	1	3	6.78%	22.37%	0.293	0.359	0.490	0.198
2019	SEA	18	A+	72	19	6	3	2	0	0	6.94%	13.89%	0.462	0.514	0.738	0.277
2021	SEA	20	A+	134	22	8	2	6	5	1	10.45%	21.64%	0.325	0.410	0.581	0.256
2021	SEA	20	AA	206	45	11	0	7	16	4	14.08%	17.96%	0.362	0.461	0.546	0.184

Background: Looking back at the 2017 international free agent market only solidifies just how difficult it is to predict player development behind Wander Franco, the consensus #1 prospect available at the time. *MLB Pipeline* listed Julio Rodriguez as the 9th best prospect, behind the likes of: Daniel Flores, Jelfry Marte, Everson Pereira, Eric Pardinho, Raimfer Salinas, Luis Garcia, and Antonio Cabello. *Baseball America* had a slightly different list, listing Rodriguez as the 6th best teenager behind Flores, Ronny Mauricio, Pereira, and George Valera. Fast forward five years and it's clear that (A) Wander Franco is going to be a superstar and (B) Seattle's young outfielder has the potential – and minor league production – to follow suit. Standing a solid 6-foot-3 and 180 pounds, Rodriguez made his professional debut in the Dominican Summer League a year after joining the Mariners' organization, slugging a rock solid .315/.404/.525 in the offensive-friendly environment. The Mariners immediately placed him on an aggressive development schedule after that. Rodriguez spent time at Low-A and High-A the next season, batting .326/.390/.540 as an 18-year-old against the significantly older competition. As baseball returned from its COVID absence last season, the front office bounced the then-20-year-old back down to High-A for a tune-up before sending him to the minors' toughest challenge, AA, in late June. The Loma de Cabrera, Dominican Republic, native finished his third full season of professional action with a stellar .347/.441/.560 slash line, belting out 19 doubles, two triples, 13 homeruns, and 21 stolen bases (in 26 total attempts). Per *Weighted Runs Created Plus*, his overall production topped the league average mark by a monstrous 69%.

Snippet from The 2020 Prospect Digest Handbook: The Mariners' future face-of-the-franchise does everything else at an above-average or plus level. He's going to be a perennial .300/.370/.550 type hitter, though he likely slides over into right field permanently.

Scouting Report: Consider the following little tidbits:

- There were 853 different hitters that received at least 300 plate appearances in the minor leagues last season. Rodriguez's total offensive production, 169 wRC+, ranked second. He trailed only the Yankees' Anthony Volpe, who was playing a level under Rodriguez. And both were the same age (20), by the way.
- The next best offensive production by a 20-year-old or younger was 18-percentage points less than Rodriguez: St. Louis' Jordan Walker, who tallied a 151 wRC+.
- Rodriguez's 1.001 OPS was the ninth best among the same group.

Now let's take a look at how his production stacks up from a historical perspective. Consider the following:

- Since 2006, only three 20-year-old hitters posted a wRC+ of at least 160 and a sub-20% strikeout rate in a Double-A season with one organization (min. 200 PA): Eric Hosmer, Dilson Herrera, and Julio Rodriguez.
- Rodriguez, by the way, owns the best mark among the trio, by seven percentage points.

And if you're not willing to buy into Rodriguez's incredible production at the Double-A level last season just yet, how's this for a kicker? He hit .362/.461/.546 with Arkansas, which, according to *Baseball America's park factors*, is the single most pitcher-friendly home field in all three Double-A leagues. Not only does Rodriguez do everything, but he does everything *incredibly well*. He hits for average. He hits for power, though he's just starting to tap into his power potential. He has above-average speed. He makes consistent contact. He walks – a lot. And he's an above-average to potential plus defender in right field. There's zero indication that he's not going to ascend to the top five players in all of baseball. After he rolled out his new found plus patience at the dish, Rodriguez is tracking to be a .310/.400/.550-type hitter.

Ceiling: 6.0-win player
Risk: Moderate
MLB ETA: 2022

2. George Kirby, RHP

	FB	CB	SL	CH	Command	Overall
	65	55	60	60	60	70

Born: 09/04/98	Age: 24	Bats: R	Top Comp: Max Scherzer
Height: 6-4	Weight: 215	Throws: R	

Season	Team	Age	Level	IP	TBF	K/9	K%	BB/9	BB%	K-BB%	ERA	FIP	xFIP	Pit/Bat
2019	SEA	21	A-	23.0	89	9.78	28.09%	0.00	0.00%	28.09%	2.35	2.04	2.10	3.62
2021	SEA	23	A+	41.2	164	11.23	31.71%	1.73	4.88%	26.83%	2.38	2.44	3.07	3.80
2021	SEA	23	AA	26.0	110	9.69	25.45%	2.42	6.36%	19.09%	2.77	2.25	3.62	3.88

Background: With a name that sounds like he'd be the guy to do your taxes, George Kirby is providing plenty of other reasons to turn heads. A product of Elon University – which, let's be honest, sounds like an accounting school – Seattle drafted the 6-foot-4, 215-pound right-hander in the opening round, 20th overall, three years ago. After inking a deal worth $3,242,900, Kirby was practically unhittable during his debut with the Everett AquaSox, posting a 25-to-0 strikeout-to-walk ratio in 23.0 innings of work. Last season the front office – hoping to make up for the lost 2020 year – pushed Kirby up to High-A to begin the season. After nine mostly dominant starts, the hard-throwing right-hander, who also dealt with a bout of right should fatigue, moved up to Arkansas for his final six games. In total, Kirby tossed 67.2 innings of work, averaging a stellar 10.6 punch outs and just 2.0 walks per nine innings. He finished with a 2.53 combined ERA.

Snippet from The 2020 Prospect Digest Handbook: Kirby attacks hitters with four average or better offerings: his fastball sits comfortably in the low 90s without much effort and may have some additional growth as his lanky frame begins to fill out; his curveball is a tightly spun 12-6 bender; his slider shows cutter-like characteristics. One final thought: his changeup, when it's on, could be among the best in the draft.

Scouting Report: It was roughly two years in between the time I scouted Kirby, a favorite of mine coming out of Elon. And I have to be frank: I was absolutely blown away with how much his arsenal improved since entering Seattle's farm system. (Side note: The Mariners' front office does not get nearly the credit it deserves for its pitching analytics department; it's among the best in the game.) Kirby's heater grew from an above-average, low-90s offering to plus-plus upper-90s one. He features an above-average curveball and a "sit-your-butt-down" slider that's lethal. And his changeup remains among the best in the game. Plus command. Add it all up and there's a very high ceiling with the potential to ascend to true ace-dom. This is going to come across a bit skewed, and I certainly don't take this lightly: but if I were to pick a minor league pitcher that could ascend to the level of Max Scherzer, it'd be George Kirby.

Ceiling: 6.0-win player
Risk: Moderate
MLB ETA: 2022

3. Noelvi Marte, SS

	Hit	Power	SB	Patience	Glove	Overall
	45/50	50/55	55/50	55	55	60

Born: 10/16/01	Age: 20	Bats: R	Top Comp: Gleyber Torres
Height: 6-1	Weight: 181	Throws: R	

Season	Team	Age	Level	PA	1B	2B	3B	HR	SB	CS	BB%	K%	AVG	OBP	SLG	ISO
2019	SEA	17	R	299	50	18	4	9	17	7	9.70%	18.39%	0.309	0.371	0.511	0.202
2021	SEA	19	A	478	69	24	2	17	23	7	12.13%	22.18%	0.271	0.368	0.462	0.191
2021	SEA	19	A+	33	5	4	0	0	1	0	6.06%	33.33%	0.290	0.333	0.419	0.129

Background: There aren't too many organizations and big league farm systems that can boast (A) a player of similar or better potential than Marte or (B) the one-two hitting punch of Julio Rodriguez / Noelvi Marte for one season. Let alone for multiple years like the Mariners, who sported Jarred Kelenic and Rodriguez as their top duo in years past. A year after signing mega-prospect Rodriguez on the international free agency market, Seattle inked the toolsy shortstop to a deal worth slightly more than $1.5 million. Marte would make his debut the following season, 2019, in the foreign rookie league, batting .309/.371/.511 with 18 doubles, four triples, and nine homeruns. And despite losing a year to the COVID shutdown, as well as his relative youth, the front office aggressively pushed the then-19-year-old shortstop straight into Low-A to begin 2021. And Marte was tremendous. In 99 games with the Modesto Nuts, the 6-foot-1, 181-pound prospect slugged .271/.368/.462 with 24 doubles, two triples, and 17 homeruns. He also swiped 23 bags in 30 total attempts. His overall production, per *Weighted Runs Created Plus*, topped the league average threshold by 19%.

Scouting Report: Consider the following:

- Since 2006, only two 19-year-old hitters posted a wRC+ between 115 and 125 with a double-digit walk rate, and a strikeout rate between 21% and 24% in a Low-A season with one organization (min. 350 PA): Akil Baddoo and – of course – Noelvi Marte.
- Baddoo, of course, is coming off his rookie season in which he slugged .259/.330/.436 for the Detroit Tigers.

Diving into the month-by-month production, Marte's poor showing in July (.219/.270/.316) really tanked his overall numbers. He slugged .299/.398/.527 in May and June and then finished the year with a .281/.393/.486 showing in August and September. His numbers in Low-A are all that more impressive once his home ballpark is factored in: John Thurman Field, according to *Baseball America's* Park Factors, was the least hitter-friendly park in Low-A West last season. Patient approach. Solid contact rates. Above-average power potential. Above-average speed, though I expect it to regress down to average in the coming years. And an above-average glove. Add it all up and he looks like a potential All-Star at his peak.

Ceiling: 5.0-win player
Risk: Moderate
MLB ETA: 2023/2024

4. Emerson Hancock, RHP

	FB	CB	SL	CH	Command	Overall
	60	N/A	60	60	55	60

Born: 05/31/99	Age: 23	Bats: R	Top Comp: Stephen Strasburg
Height: 6-4	Weight: 213	Throws: R	

Season	Team	Age	Level	IP	TBF	K/9	K%	BB/9	BB%	K-BB%	ERA	FIP	xFIP	Pit/Bat
2021	SEA	22	A+	31.0	124	8.71	24.19%	3.77	10.48%	13.71%	2.32	3.91	4.15	4.25
2021	SEA	22	AA	13.2	55	8.56	23.64%	2.63	7.27%	16.36%	3.29	2.45	4.28	3.80

Background: Fun Fact Part I: Hancock's prep school alma mater, Cairo High School, is home to former big league Willie Harris, who appeared in over a thousand big league games. Fun Fact Part II: The hard-throwing right-hander became the second highest draft pick out of the University of Georgia, trailing only Jeff Plyburn, the fifth overall pick in 1980. Fun Fact Part III: with the consecutive first round selections of Logan Gilbert, George Kirby, and Emerson Hancock between 2018 through 2020, it was first time the organization selected hurlers in the opening round three straight years since 2006 through 2008 (Brandon Morrow, Phillippe Aumont, and Josh Fields). Hancock, who signed a deal with the organization for a hefty $5.7 million as the sixth overall pick two years ago, was limited to just 12 starts between Everett and Arkansas as he battled a non-structural shoulder issue. He posted a 43-to-17 strikeout-to-walk ratio in 44.2 innings of work.

Scouting Report: A long time fan of Emerson Hancock, pre-dating his junior campaign with the Georgia Bulldogs. Hancock is built in a similar fashion as fellow Mariners top pitching prospect George Kirby, both physically as well as repertoire-wise. Hancock posses a plus fastball, sitting in the mid-nineties and plays up ever further given his above-average command. Reports indicate he'll mix in a pair of breaking balls, though I only personally witnessed a plus slider. He seems to vary the break on the pitch, but its plus. He'll also throw a Zack Greinke power changeup as well, showing plenty of hard tumble. Hancock doesn't quite have the ceiling that Kirby does, but he's going to be a very good – sort of Robin to Kirby's Batman. Barring any significant injury, of course.

Ceiling: 4.0-win player
Risk: Moderate to High
MLB ETA: 2022/2023

5. Harry Ford, C

	Hit	Power	SB	Patience	Glove	Overall
	45/55	45/55	50/40	50/55	45/50	55

Born: 02/21/03	Age: 19	Bats: R	Top Comp: N/A
Height: 5-10	Weight: 200	Throws: R	

Season	Team	Age	Level	PA	1B	2B	3B	HR	SB	CS	BB%	K%	AVG	OBP	SLG	ISO
2021	SEA	18	CPX	65	6	7	0	3	3	0	13.85%	21.54%	0.291	0.400	0.582	0.291

Background: Fun Fact Part I: Prior to the 2021 season North Cobb High School in Kennesaw, GA, has produced six pro baseball players – C.J. Bressoud, Eric McQueen, Skip Shipp, Kyle Reese, Ronnie McGarity, and John Jiles. Fun Fact Part II: The earliest drafted player – at least until Ford's named was called in the opening round in 2021 – is McQueen, a fourteenth round pick by the Mets after his career at Georgia Tech wrapped up. Fun Fact Part III: Five of the six players were backstops. Ford, committed to Georgia Tech during the summer of 2019. Seattle selected the stocky, well-built prep backstop with the 12th overall pick last July, signing him to a deal worth $4,366,400. Ford appeared in 19 games with the organization's Arizona Complex League affiliate, slugging an impressive .291/.400/.582 with seven doubles and 10 dingers to go along with a 14-to-9 strikeout-to-walk ratio.

Scouting Report: Per the usual, here's my pre-draft write-up:

> *"One of the most athletic – either college or prep – prospects in the 2021 draft class. Ford, a [catcher], shows plus bat speed and matching 60-times, as well. He was reportedly clocked in the 6.4-range in the 60-yard dash. The 5-foot-10, 200-pound athlete shows natural loft that suggests 20- to 25-homerun power potential. Simplified stance with very few moving parts. Premium athlete that will likely move to another position to hasten his develop. Strong lower half. Fast*

hands. Defensively, it's not an overly quick release and the arm is average, maybe a tick better. One of my favorite prospects in the draft. I wouldn't be surprised to see a team like Kansas City jump all over him."

Ceiling: 3.0-win player
Risk: Moderate
MLB ETA: 2025

6. Adam Macko, LHP

	FB	CB	CH	Command	Overall
	55/60	65	45/50	40/45	55

Born: 12/30/00	Age: 21	Bats: L	Top Comp: Erik Bedard
Height: 6-0	Weight: 170	Throws: L	

Season	Team	Age	Level	IP	TBF	K/9	K%	BB/9	BB%	K-BB%	ERA	FIP	xFIP	Pit/Bat
2019	SEA	18	R	21.1	94	13.08	32.98%	4.64	11.70%	21.28%	3.38	3.80	3.95	2.84
2021	SEA	20	A	33.1	155	15.12	36.13%	5.67	13.55%	22.58%	4.59	3.33	4.10	3.84

Background: According to the invaluable *Baseball Reference*, only two players in baseball history have been born in Slovakia and made it to the big leagues: right-hander Jack Quinn, who's a borderline Hall of Famer, and right fielder Elmer Valo, who turned in a very solid, respectable 20-year career. Taken in the seventh round, 216th overall, in 2019, Adam Macko could be the third player born in the country and ascend up to the big leagues. After moving from Bratislava, the left-hander's family eventually settled in Albert, Canada. After a solid debut in 2019, Macko battled a shoulder injury / issue and missed several weeks last season. In total, he was limited to just nine starts, spanning 33.1 innings – though he managed to average a mindboggling 15.1 punch outs per nine innings (as well a 5.7 BB9).

Scouting Report: High ceiling southpaw, which is surprising given his draft status (seventh round, 2019) and unimpressive frame size (6-foot, 170 pounds). But there's some sneaky, sneaky mid-rotation caliber potential here. Macko is a slinger. His fastball sits in the low- to mid-90s with relatively ease. But it's his wicked knuckle curveball, referred by him as "spike" curveball in an article on FanGraphs by fantastic writer David Laurila, that separates him from a lot of the pack. He'll also mix in a changeup which projects as average. Macko's still incredibly raw, but there's some Erik Bedard-type potential here. He needs to further develop his changeup. And his command has to bump up at least to a 45. He also has to avoid the injury nexus as well – obviously.

Ceiling: 3.0-win player
Risk: High
MLB ETA: 2024/2025

7. Gabriel Gonzalez, RF

	Hit	Power	SB	Patience	Glove	Overall
	40/50	40/55	50/40	50	50	50

Born: 01/04/04	Age: 18	Bats: R	Top Comp: Jorge Soler
Height: 5-10	Weight: 165	Throws: R	

Season	Team	Age	Level	PA	1B	2B	3B	HR	SB	CS	BB%	K%	AVG	OBP	SLG	ISO
2021	SEA	17	DSL	221	28	15	4	7	9	3	9.50%	15.84%	0.287	0.371	0.521	0.234

Background: The early part of last year the Mariners added a bevy of high end international talent, including the likes of third baseman Starlin Aguilar, outfielder Juan Cruz, outfielder Victor Labrada, and a little bit lesser known Gabriel Gonzalez. Barely cracking *Baseball America's* Top 30 International Prospect list, Gonzalez, ranked as #30, agreed to join the organization for a deal worth slightly more than a million dollars. The 5-foot-10, 165-pound right fielder made his debut in the foreign rookie league last season. Appearing in 54 games, the teenage Venezuelan slugged a hearty .287/.371/.521 with 15 doubles, four triples, and seven homeruns. He also swiped nine bags in 12 total attempts. His overall production, per *Weighted Runs Created Plus*, topped the league average mark by 41%.

Scouting Report: Gonzalez outperformed his two fellow high profile Dominican Summer League counterparts – Starlin Aguilar and Juan Cruz – by sizeable amounts. Considering the offensively-friendly environment, Gonzalez performed well, showing no major red flags. He whiffed in a modest amount of his plate appearances (15.8%). He walked a decent amount time (9.5%), which is preferred so as to not overly inflate his production at such a low minor league level. He showed power and speed. During his time in the Dominican Summer League, when Gonzalez connected it sounded like a shotgun blast. Good bat speed, not elite. There's quite a bit of potential here, but he's years away.

And he needs to get stronger, lean out some as well. Just for comparison's sake, consider the following:

Player	Age	Level	PA	AVG	OBP	SLG	K%	BB%	wRC+
Julio Rodriguez	17	DSL	255	0.315	0.404	0.525	15.7%	11.8%	161
Gabriel Gonzalez	17	DSL	221	0.287	0.371	0.521	15.8%	9.5%	141

Ceiling: 2.0-win player
Risk: Moderate to High
MLB ETA: 2025

8. Brandon Williamson, LHP

	FB	CB	SL	CH	Command	Overall
	60	55	55	50	50	45

Born: 04/02/98	**Age:** 24	**Bats:** R	**Top Comp:** Drew Pomeranz
Height: 6-6	**Weight:** 210	**Throws:** L	

Season	Team	Age	Level	IP	TBF	K/9	K%	BB/9	BB%	K-BB%	ERA	FIP	xFIP	Pit/Bat
2019	SEA	21	A-	15.1	61	14.67	40.98%	2.93	8.20%	32.79%	2.35	1.57	1.86	4.15
2021	SEA	23	A+	31.0	124	17.13	47.58%	2.90	8.06%	39.52%	3.19	3.11	2.09	4.26
2021	SEA	23	AA	67.1	285	12.56	32.98%	3.07	8.07%	24.91%	3.48	3.24	3.84	3.99

Background: The big left-hander made the most out of his only season at Texas Christian University after transferring from North Iowa Area Community College. In 16 starts for the Horned Frogs, the 6-foot-6, 210-pound southpaw struck out 89 and walked 36 to go along with a 4.19 ERA in 77.1 innings of work. Seattle selected him in the second round, 59th overall, and handed him a deal worth $925,000. The southpaw put on a dominant debut showing in the Northwest League, posting a 25-to-4 strikeout-to-walk ratio in only 15.1 innings. Last season Williamson – like a lot of organization recent collegiate draft picks – split time between the Everett AquaSox and the Arkansas Travelers. He tossed 98.1 innings, recording a whopping 153 strikeouts and just 33 free passes to go along with a 3.39 ERA and an even better 3.20 FIP.

Snippet from The 2020 Prospect Digest Handbook: Williamson still has a little bit of project left as he begins to fill out his lanky frame. Brian Tallet-type lefty.

Scouting Report: From a skills standpoint: Williamson hardly resembles the pitcher I scouted two years ago. His fastball ticked up from an above-average to plus-offering. His horizontal darting slider and his big curveball grade out as above-average pitches. And his changeup's a workable fourth weapon in his surprisingly deep arsenal. With regard to his production, consider the following tidbits:

- Last season there were 547 minor league hurlers that eclipsed the 75-inning threshold. Williamson's strikeout rate, 14.0 K/9, ranked as the seventh best total. His strikeout percentage, 37.4%, ranked as the eighth best. And his strikeout-to-walk percentage, 29.3%, was good enough for seventh.
- Since 2006, only three 23-year-old Double-A pitchers posted a strikeout percentage between 32% and 34% with a walk percentage between 7% and 9% in a season with one organization (min. 60 IP): Brandon Beachy, Ryne Nelson, and Brandon Williamson.

Lefties with three above-average pitches (and a fourth average one) with solid command don't exactly grow on trees. I'm really turning into a fan of the organization's pitching development program, and I think the club's going to eke the most out of Williamson. There's some #4-type upside. Maybe more if everything breaks the right way.

Ceiling: 1.5-win player
Risk: Moderate
MLB ETA: 2022

9. Alberto Rodriguez, RF

	Hit	Power	SB	Patience	Glove	Overall
	45/50	50	50/40	50	55	45

Born: 10/06/00	**Age:** 21	**Bats:** L	**Top Comp:** N/A
Height: 5-11	**Weight:** 180	**Throws:** L	

Season	Team	Age	Level	PA	1B	2B	3B	HR	SB	CS	BB%	K%	AVG	OBP	SLG	ISO
2018	TOR	17	R	263	43	9	1	5	21	6	12.17%	20.91%	0.254	0.350	0.368	0.114
2019	TOR	18	R	195	36	13	1	2	13	2	9.74%	16.41%	0.301	0.364	0.422	0.121
2021	SEA	20	A	431	64	30	5	10	13	7	11.83%	22.04%	0.295	0.383	0.484	0.189
2021	SEA	20	A+	28	4	1	0	0	2	0	7.14%	25.00%	0.208	0.321	0.250	0.042

Background: The front office played the game perfectly, to a "T". The organization signed their former first rounder selection Taijuan Walker to an incredibly team-friendly one year, $2 million deal in mid-February 2020. A little more than six months later the club flipped him to Toronto in exchange for Dominican outfielder Alberto Rodriguez. Last season, his first full year in Seattle's increasing savvy organization, the 5-foot-11, 180-pound prospect spent the majority of the campaign with the Modesto Nuts. In 93 games, spanning 431 plate appearances, Rodriguez batted .295/.383/.484 with 30 doubles, five triples, and 10 homeruns. He also swiped 13 bags, though he was thrown out seven times. Per *Weighted Runs Created Plus*, his overall production topped the league average mark by 27%. He also spent the final seven games of his season in High-A as well.

Scouting Report: Consider the following:

- Since 2006, only four 20-year-old hitters met the following criteria in a Low-A season with one organization (min. 350 PA): a 122 to 132 wRC+, a walk rate between 11% and 13%, and a strikeout percentage between 21% and 24%. T hose four hitters: Travis Harrison, Max George, Brandon Valenzuela, and – of course – Alberto Rodriguez.

Rodriguez is reminiscent of a young Rusty Greer, a short, compact swing with some power and speed. The young outfield is adept at recognizing breaking pitches, particularly low, but he does loved elevated fastballs. No platoon splits. And he can play the hell out of right field. There may be an outside shot he reaches a low end starting production level, but he's going to have to carry a similar level of production for the next two years.

Ceiling: 1.0- to 1.5-win player
Risk: Moderate
MLB ETA: 2024/2025

10. Zach DeLoach, OF

	Hit	Power	SB	Patience	Glove	Overall
	40/45	50	40	55	50	45

Born: 08/18/98	Age: 23	Bats: L	Top Comp: N/A
Height: 6-1	Weight: 205	Throws: R	

Season	Team	Age	Level	PA	1B	2B	3B	HR	SB	CS	BB%	K%	AVG	OBP	SLG	ISO
2021	SEA	22	A+	285	44	23	2	9	6	3	11.23%	22.11%	0.313	0.400	0.530	0.217
2021	SEA	22	AA	216	25	10	2	5	1	2	12.96%	26.85%	0.227	0.338	0.384	0.157

Background: It was a curious path to the professional ranks for the Texas A&M product. DeLoach turned in a solid true freshman campaign in 2018: .264/.355/.374. And he continued to mash in the Northwoods League

during the ensuing summer as well (.323/.409/.495). But something happened with the Ivring, Texas, native during his sophomore campaign as he struggled – mightily – to the tune of .200/.318/.294 with just eight extra-base hits. Something clicked as he moved into the Cape Cod League, slugging a scorching .353/.428/.541 in 37 games with the Falmouth Commodores. And DeLoach got off to a tremendous start to the 2020 year too: he batted .421/.547/.789 with a spectacular 3-to-14 strikeout-to-walk ratio through 18 games. Seattle drafted him in the second two years ago. Last season the 6-foot-1, 205-pound outfielder picked up in High-A right where he left off: he hit .313/.400/.530 with 23 doubles, two triples, and nine homeruns in only 58 games. But like fellow 2020 draft pick Kaden Polcovich, DeLoach looked overmatched and underprepared when he moved into Double-A; he hit a lowly .227/.338/.384.

Scouting Report: DeLoach actually got off to a solid start in Double-A, hitting .269/.367/.436 through his first 21 games. But a late season collapse tanked his numbers at the level; he .191/.329/.309 over his final 18 games. The lefty-swinging outfielder showed average power with the potential to peak at 20 dingers in a full professional season. But the fact is simple: DeLoach has the basic toolkit as a lot of failed high round college outfielders, like Brad Snyder, Michael Choice, etc... And his struggles in the Arizona Fall League don't help assuage that gut feeling.

Ceiling: 1.0- to 1.5-win player
Risk: Moderate
MLB ETA: 2023

11. Edwin Arroyo, SS

	Hit	Power	SB	Patience	Glove	Overall
	35/45	30/40	50	50	50	45

Born: 08/25/03	Age: 18	Bats: B	Top Comp: N/A
Height: 6-0	Weight: 175	Throws: R	

Season	Team	Age	Level	PA	1B	2B	3B	HR	SB	CS	BB%	K%	AVG	OBP	SLG	ISO
2021	SEA	17	CPX	86	11	2	0	2	4	1	11.63%	30.23%	0.211	0.337	0.324	0.113

Background: Uniquely talented as a ballplayer. Not only is the young infielder a switch-hitting, but he's also an ambidextrous thrower. Born in Arecibo, Puerto Rica, Arroyo became the first player drafted out of

Arecibo Baseball Academy when the Mariners selected him in the second round, 48th overall, and signed him to a deal worth $1,650,000. He appeared in 21 games in the Arizona Complex League after joining the organization, hitting a disappointing .211/.337/.324 with a pair of doubles and homeruns. Per *Weighted Runs Created Plus*, his overall production was 16% below the league average mark. Arroyo spent the winter playing in the Puerto Rican Winter League, batting a solid .296/.367/.370 in 13 games.

Scouting Report: Arroyo's a potentially premium athlete – as evidenced by his work on the mound as an amateur southpaw. The swing from the left side looks more complete than from the right side. I just don't know if he's going to (A) hit or (B) hit for any type of meaningful power. As noted by nearly every draft publication, he was one of the class's youngest players – and he's only entering his-18 season. Defensively, he's got enough to stick at shortstop, but he won't win any Gold Gloves there.

Ceiling: 1.0- to 1.5-win player
Risk: Moderate
MLB ETA: 2025/2026

12. Kaden Polcovich, IF/CF

Hit	Power	SB	Patience	Glove	Overall
40/45	50/55	50	55	50	45

Born: 02/21/99	Age: 23	Bats: B	Top Comp: N/A
Height: 5-10	Weight: 185	Throws: R	

Season	Team	Age	Level	PA	1B	2B	3B	HR	SB	CS	BB%	K%	AVG	OBP	SLG	ISO
2021	SEA	22	A+	272	32	12	4	10	16	3	17.28%	23.53%	0.271	0.415	0.505	0.234
2021	SEA	22	AA	149	11	4	0	2	4	1	10.74%	27.52%	0.133	0.242	0.211	0.078

Background: Fun Fact Part I: Seattle has drafted five players from Oregon State University. Fun Fact Part II: Of those five players, four of them – Mat Mangini, Tyler Blandford, Donovan Walton, and Kaden Polcovich – were drafted since 2007; the lone outlier, Dave Mlicki, was taken in 1989. Seattle selected the switch-hitting infielder / outfielder in the third round, 78th overall, two years ago and handed him a deal worth $575,000. Last season the 5-foot-10, 185-pound prospect opened the year up on a tear in High-A, slugging a robust .271/.415/.505 with 12 doubles, four triples, and 10 homeruns in 58 games. And then he was promoted up to Double-A, the most challenging test in the minors. He failed – wildly. In 36 games with Arkansas he hit a lowly .133/.242/.211 with just six extra-base knocks.

Scouting Report: Consider the following:

- Since 2006, only three 22-year-old High-A hitters posted a 142 to 152 wRC+ total with a walk rate north of 14% and a strikeout rate between 23% and 26% in a season with one organization (min. 270 PA): Aaron Judge, Mickey Hall, and Kaden Polcovich.

There's a lot going on here. Polcovich was otherworldly during his High-A stint and his Double-A production made Mario Mendoza look like Babe Ruth. But here's what we know definitively about the young switch-hitter: above-average patience, a little bit of speed, above-average pop, and a solid infield glove. At the plate Polcovich does not get cheated. At all. Great bat speed. Big time uppercut. He's looking to one thing with the baseball. And it's not put it on the ground. I'm willing to give him a do-over on the horrific showing in Double-A, but he's going to have to come out swinging – and connecting – when he returns to the level in 2022.

Ceiling: 1.0- to 1.5-win player
Risk: Moderate to High
MLB ETA: 2023

13. Matt Brash, RHP

FB	CB	SL	CH	Command	Overall
55	55	55	N/A	45	40

Born: 05/12/98	Age: 24	Bats: R	Top Comp: N/A
Height: 6-1	Weight: 170	Throws: R	

Season	Team	Age	Level	IP	TBF	K/9	K%	BB/9	BB%	K-BB%	ERA	FIP	xFIP	Pit/Bat
2021	SEA	23	A+	42.1	183	13.18	33.88%	5.31	13.66%	20.22%	2.55	4.03	4.14	4.09
2021	SEA	23	AA	55.0	222	13.09	36.04%	3.76	10.36%	25.68%	2.13	2.53	3.25	4.08

Background: The Mariners and the Padres have been two of the more active teams on the trade market over the past few years. And they've gotten together on a few occasions as well. Seattle dealt right-handed reliever Taylor Williams to the San Diego for a Player To Be Named Later – who was eventually determined to be Matt Brash, a fourth round pick out of Niagara University in 2019. Last season the 6-foot-1, 170-pound righty made a total of 20 appearances, all but one of which was a start, between Everett and Arkansas. Brash tossed 97.1 innings of work, averaging an impressive 13.1 strikeouts and 4.4 walks per nine innings. He finished the year with a 2.31 ERA.

Scouting Report: Consider the following:

- Since 2006, only two 23-year-old hurlers posted at least a 35% K% and at least a 10% BB% in a Double-A season with one organization (min. 50 IP): Paul Estrada and – of course – Matt Brash.

Brash is an interesting hurler: he's primarily a three-pitch pitcher, and one of those offerings isn't a changeup. Instead he offers up a pair of breaking balls – a late sweeping slider and a traditional 12-6 downward biting curveball. Brash's fastball, like both feature offspeed pitches, is an above-average offering. He's a max effort guy and Seattle has a bevy of starting candidates that are better suited for flipping a lineup over multiple times a game, so he's probably looking at future relief gig.

Ceiling: 1.0-win player
Risk: Moderate
MLB ETA: 2022

14. Connor Phillips, RHP

	FB	CB	SL	CH	Command	Overall
	60	50	50/55	50	40/45	40

Born: 05/04/01	Age: 21	Bats: R	Top Comp: N/A
Height: 6-2	Weight: 190	Throws: R	

Season	Team	Age	Level	IP	TBF	K/9	K%	BB/9	BB%	K-BB%	ERA	FIP	xFIP	Pit/Bat
2021	SEA	20	A	72.0	322	13.00	32.30%	5.50	13.66%	18.63%	4.75	3.52	4.56	4.03

Background: Phillips, according to reports, was a late 2019 "pop up" guy at Magnolia West, a Texas-based High School. The Blue Jays took a late round flier on the hard-throwing right-hander that year, drafting him in the 35th round. But Phillips attended McLennan Community College in Waco, Texas. A year later and – viola – Seattle comes calling in the second round, 64th overall, and handed him a deal worth slightly more than a million bucks. Phillips, by the way, was the first JuCo player drafted that year. Last season the 6-foot-2, 190-pound right-hander made 17 starts, 16 of which were with Modesto in Low-A, throwing a total of 76.0 innings with 111 strikeouts and 46 free passes – or an average of 13.1 K/9 and 5.4 BB/9.

Scouting Report: Phillips fits the mold of the new Seattle pitcher: he throws gas and a couple solid breaking balls. Phillips, though, is no George Kirby or Emerson Hancock; he doesn't have a firm grip on the strike zone. And I'm not hopeful that the command bumps past a 45. Phillips loves to pitch inside, particularly to left-handed hitters. The curveball's a little loopy and needs to be firmed up. The slider's inconsistent, but it flashes 55 at times. The break and depth alternates from a cutter to a more traditional slider. The changeup is nothing to write home about. There's definite reliever risk with Phillips.

Ceiling: 1.0-win player
Risk: Moderate
MLB ETA: 2022

15. Juan Then, RHP

	FB	SL	CH	Command	Overall
	60	50	55	50	40

Born: 02/07/00	Age: 22	Bats: R	Top Comp: Juan Cruz
Height: 6-1	Weight: 175	Throws: R	

Season	Team	Age	Level	IP	TBF	K/9	K%	BB/9	BB%	K-BB%	ERA	FIP	xFIP	Pit/Bat
2018	NYY	18	R	50.0	195	7.56	21.54%	1.98	5.64%	15.90%	2.70	3.22	3.23	1.48
2019	SEA	19	A-	30.1	119	9.49	26.89%	2.67	7.56%	19.33%	3.56	2.86	3.40	3.92
2019	SEA	19	A	16.0	61	7.88	22.95%	2.25	6.56%	16.39%	2.25	3.68	4.03	4.05
2021	SEA	21	A+	54.1	250	9.77	23.60%	3.15	7.60%	16.00%	6.46	5.84	4.47	3.76

Background: Originally signed by Seattle in the opening days of July 2016. The Mariners would eventually deal the wiry right-hander, as well as southpaw strikeout artist JP Sears, to the Yankees in exchange for reliever Nick Rumbelow in mid-November 2017. A year-and-a-half later Seattle would re-acquire the hard-throwing Dominican for power-hitting first baseman / designated hitter Edwin Encarnacion in mid-June 2019. For the time being Then is part of the Mariners, but we'll see how long that lasts. Last season the 6-foot-1, 175-pound hurler made only 14 starts – he missed the majority of July and the early part of August – with the Everett AquaSox, throwing just 54.1 innings with 59 strikeouts and just 19 free passes. He finished the year with a 6.46 ERA, a 5.84 FIP, and a 4.47 xFIP. Then made an additional four appearances with the Peoria Javelinas in the Arizona Fall League as well, striking out 16 and walking in 13 innings.

Snippet from The 2020 Prospect Digest Handbook: Like a lot of the lower level arms in the system Then is an intriguing wild card. He's a bit reminiscent in stature and stuff to former Cubs top prospect Juan Cruz.

Scouting Report: Then's still pumping mid-90s heat that'll touch the upper-90s on occasional. It's explosive, late-lifed, and overpowers the inexperienced hitters in the low levels. His best "go-to" offspeed pitch is the power changeup with hard tumble. The offering's made a lot of progress in the past few years and borders on plus territory at times. He'll also mix in a hard slider, though it's average and doesn't miss many bats. Then's eventually going to end up in the bullpen where he'll be serviceable middle relief arm. With respect to his work in High-A last, consider the following:

- Since 2006, only five 21-year-old pitchers met the following criteria in a High-A season with one organization (min. 50 IP): 22.5 to 24.5% strikeout percentage, 6.5% to 8.5% walk percentage, and a ground ball rate between 44% and 48%. Those five hurlers: Reynaldo Lopez, Brock Burke, Andrew Faulkner, Jon Moscot, and Juan Then.

There's definite big league value, but he's more of strike-thrower and not a pitcher. He needs to refine / improve his breaking ball.

Ceiling: 1.0-win player
Risk: Moderate
MLB ETA: 2023

16. Michael Morales, RHP

	FB	CB	CH	Command	Overall
	50/55	50/55	55/60	45	40

Born: 08/13/02	Age: 19	Bats: R	Top Comp: N/A
Height: 6-2	Weight: 205	Throws: R	

Background: Fun Fact Part I: East Pennsboro High School, located in Enola, Pennsylvania, has produced a total of two draft picks in its history – Matt Farner, a supplemental first round pick by the Blue Jays in 1993, and Michael Morales, a third round pick by the Mariners last July. Fun Fact Part II: The first round of the 1993 draft is famous for including Alex Rodriguez, Bill Wagner, Torii Hunter, Jason Varitek, Derek Lee, Chris Carpenter, and Trot Nixon. Fun Fact Part III: Farner was selected just nine picks before the Phillies drafted third baseman Scott Rolen. Seattle drafted Morales with the 83rd overall pick last year, signing him to a deal worth $1.5 million. That over-slot bonus was equivalent to roughly the 50th overall pick. And there appears to be good reason for it too. According to *Baseball America*, the Mariners' scouting director, Scott Hunter, was quoted: "I don't' want to put this much pressure on him, but there are some comparisons from our guys that this is what Walker Buehler looked like in high school – an 88-92 (mph) guy with a ton of strikes, can really spin a breaking ball." Don't worry, kid, no pressure.

Scouting Report: All projection at this point. If everything breaks the right way – and he avoids any major injuries and pitfalls – Morales has a chance to develop three above-average or better pitches. His fastball sits in the low 90s and touches a tick higher. His curveball shows good shape, spin. Both project to be solid 55-grades. But it's his changeup that's really impressed. It's a heavy fading offering with screwball like run. Tremendous movement through pronation. Morales still has plenty of room to fill out. He's the type of guy that could really grow in the Mariners' increasingly pitching development savvy front office.

Ceiling: 1.0-win player
Risk: Moderate
MLB ETA: 2025

17. Levi Stoudt, RHP

	FB	CB	SL	CH	Command	Overall
	55	45	50/55	60	45	40

Born: 12/04/97	Age: 24	Bats: R	Top Comp: N/A
Height: 6-1	Weight: 195	Throws: R	

Season	Team	Age	Level	IP	TBF	K/9	K%	BB/9	BB%	K-BB%	ERA	FIP	xFIP	Pit/Bat
2021	SEA	23	A+	64.0	263	9.42	25.48%	4.08	11.03%	14.45%	3.52	4.65	4.83	3.93
2021	SEA	23	AA	17.2	74	9.68	25.68%	4.08	10.81%	14.86%	2.55	4.16	5.10	3.61

Background: Fun Fact Part I: Throughout the its history Bethlehem, Pennsylvania-based Lehigh University has produced a total of 14 draft picks. Of those 14, eight have come since 2015. Fun Fact Part II: Stoudt, the 97th player chosen in 2019, is the third highest player taken in the school's history, trailing only Matt McBride (2006, 75th overall) and Mason Black (2021, 85th overall). Stoudt made his professional debut in 2021, immediately being pushed up to the Everett AquaSox in High-A. After 12 mostly solid starts, the hard-throwing right-hander was bumped up to the minors' toughest challenge, AA, for three final starts. In total, Stoudt tossed 81.2 innings, racking up 86 punch outs and 37 free passes to go along with a 3.31 ERA.

Scouting Report: After being selected in the third round by the Mariners Stoudt immediately underwent Tommy John surgery for a wonky elbow. And he looked fully healed during his debut in 2021. Mid-90s fastball backed up by an easy plus-changeup. Stoudt throws a pair of breaking balls: a slow, loopy-ish curveball and a better slider that will flash above-average at times. Soudt was more of a strike-thrower during his collegiate days, so there's some hope that will continue to improve as he moves further away from Tommy John surgery. Stoudt is tracking like a middle reliever that relies on the fastball/changeup combo with a slider to keep hitters honest.

Ceiling: 1.0-win player
Risk: Moderate
MLB ETA: 2023

18. Victor Labrada, CF

Hit	Power	SB	Patience	Glove	Overall
40/45	40	60	50	45	40

Born: 01/16/00	Age: 22	Bats: L	Top Comp: N/A
Height: 5-9	Weight: 165	Throws: L	

Season	Team	Age	Level	PA	1B	2B	3B	HR	SB	CS	BB%	K%	AVG	OBP	SLG	ISO
2021	SEA	21	A	243	39	16	3	1	22	9	13.99%	24.69%	0.294	0.407	0.418	0.124
2021	SEA	21	A+	227	34	7	3	6	10	6	8.37%	27.75%	0.246	0.314	0.399	0.153

Background: A member of the Pan-American-winning Cuba's U-18 National Team. Labrada, according to various reports, captained the squad. Then, at 18-years-old, the speedy center fielder appeared in 33 games with the Industriales de La Habana in the Cuban National Serie, slugging a robust .360/.429/.640 with two doubles, one triple, and a dinger. Seattle signed the 80-grade speedster to a deal worth $350,000 three years ago. Last season the 5-foot-9, 165-pound outfielder split time between Modesto and Everett. In 99 total games, Labrada hit .270/.362/.408 with 23 doubles, six triples, seven homeruns, and 32 stolen bases (in 47 attempts). Per *Weighted Runs Created Plus*, his overall production was 9% above the league average threshold.

Scouting Report: It was a tale of two seasons for Labrada. He was a saber-slanted, speedy, slashing, top-of-the-lineup setting outfielder during his time with Modesto, batting .284/.407/.418. And then following his promotion to High-A he stopped walking as much, stopped running as frequently, and his K-rate went from borderline concerning to red flag territory. The lefty-swing Labrada was also exposed by southpaws as well, hitting .232/.361/.304 against them (compared to .279/.363/.432 vs. RHP). The Cuban import also struggled defensively as well. Per Clay Davenport's metrics, he was eight runs below average.

Ceiling: 1.0-win player
Risk: Moderate
MLB ETA: 2023

19. Taylor Dollard, RHP

FB	CB	SL	CH	Command	Overall
50	50	50	50	55	40

Born: 02/17/99	Age: 23	Bats: R	Top Comp: Ljay Newsome
Height: 6-3	Weight: 195	Throws: R	

Season	Team	Age	Level	IP	TBF	K/9	K%	BB/9	BB%	K-BB%	ERA	FIP	xFIP	Pit/Bat
2021	SEA	22	A	37.2	162	14.10	36.42%	2.39	6.17%	30.25%	3.35	2.66	3.04	3.91
2021	SEA	22	A+	67.1	297	9.89	24.92%	1.87	4.71%	20.20%	6.15	4.99	4.49	3.73

Background: Fun Fact: California Polytechnic State University, San Luis Obispo produced a few notable big leaguers, though none more recognizable than Ozzie Smith, the Wizard of Oz. But others include: right-hander Mike Krukow and Mitch Haniger. Seattle selected Taylor Dollard in the fifth round, 137th overall, two years ago and signed him to a deal worth $406,000. Dollard, a 6-foot-3, 195-pound right-hander, made a total of 18 starts between Modesto and Everett last season, posting an impressive 133-to-24 strikeout-to-walk ratio to go along with an unsightly 5.14 ERA in 105.0 innings of work.

Scouting Report: Consider the following:

- Since 2006 nine 22-year-old hurlers met the following criteria in a High-A season with one organization (min. 60 IP): 23% to 25% strikeout percentage with a sub-5% walk rate. Those nine hurlers: Wade LeBlanc, Trent Thornton, Jonathan Bowlan, Rookie Davis, Connor Lunn, Tyler Wilson, Terance Marin, Max Povse, and Taylor Dollard.

An old school throwback to pitching. Dollard attacks hitters with offspeed stuff first, which will speed up his below-average heater. 45-grade fastball. Slow loopy curveball – quasi-reminiscent of Roy Oswalt's. A solid average slider. And a decent changeup. I don't see a fifth round talent here. He could be a Ljay Newsome-type of arm.

Ceiling: 1.0-win player
Risk: Moderate
MLB ETA: 2023

20. Isaiah Campbell, RHP

	FB	CB	SL	CH	Command	Overall
	N/A	N/A	N/A	N/A	N/A	40

Born: 08/15/97	Age: 24	Bats: R	Top Comp: N/A
Height: 6-4	Weight: 230	Throws: R	

Season	Team	Age	Level	IP	TBF	K/9	K%	BB/9	BB%	K-BB%	ERA	FIP	xFIP	Pit/Bat
2021	SEA	23	A+	19.1	78	9.31	25.64%	2.79	7.69%	17.95%	2.33	4.50	4.21	4.01

Background: A member of Arkansas's baseball program for four seasons – though one full year was lost to a surgical procedure to remove bone spurs in his right elbow. Campbell, who took a redshirt in 2017, came back strong in 2018 and 2019 as he convinced the Mariners he was worthy of a second round selection. Last season the 6-foot-4, 230-pound right-hander made his debut. But that only lasted five solid outings with the Everett AquaSox before he was shutdown with elbow issues and subsequently missed the remainder of the year. He finished his first taste of pro ball with 20 punch outs and six free passes in 19.1 innings of work. He compiled a 2.33 ERA.

Scouting Report: Here's what we know:

- Campbell's entering his age-24 season.
- He's thrown a total of 19.1 innings since the end of 2019.
- He's has a history – by that I mean one surgical procedure on his right elbow – and missed the overwhelming majority of 2021 with another major elbow issue.

At best, Campbell's two years away from being big league ready – which puts him at age-26. It's hard to imagine the club not pushing him into a relief role to try and mitigate health issues and expedite his move to the big leagues.

Ceiling: 1.0-win player
Risk: Moderate to High
MLB ETA: 2023

St. Louis Cardinals

Top Prospects

1. Nolan Gorman, 2B/3B

Hit	Power	SB	Patience	Glove	Overall
50	60	40	50	60	70

Born: 05/10/00	Age: 22	Bats: L	Top Comp: Chase Utley
Height: 6-1	Weight: 210	Throws: R	

Season	Team	Age	Level	PA	1B	2B	3B	HR	SB	CS	BB%	K%	AVG	OBP	SLG	ISO
2018	STL	18	R	167	28	10	1	11	1	3	14.37%	22.16%	0.350	0.443	0.664	0.315
2018	STL	18	A	107	10	3	0	6	0	2	9.35%	36.45%	0.202	0.280	0.426	0.223
2019	STL	19	A	282	31	14	3	10	2	0	11.35%	28.01%	0.241	0.344	0.448	0.207
2019	STL	19	A+	230	31	16	3	5	0	1	5.65%	31.74%	0.256	0.304	0.428	0.172
2021	STL	21	AA	195	34	6	0	11	4	0	9.23%	26.67%	0.288	0.354	0.508	0.220
2021	STL	21	AAA	328	54	14	1	14	3	0	6.10%	19.21%	0.274	0.320	0.465	0.191

Background: Likely not a coincidence, but Sandra Day O'Connor High School has been home to four draft picks, two coming in 2018 and the other pair being selected in 2008. Gorman, easily the best product to come out of the Phoenix, Arizona, school, was drafted with the 19th overall pick in 2018. The lefty-swinging third baseman was selected between a pair of high profile collegiate players, Brady Singer and Trevor Larnach, both of whom already made their big league debuts, and signed for a hefty $3.2 million bonus. And since signing with the perennial National League powerhouse Gorman has deposited a ton of baseballs over the fence – including 25 in 2021. Splitting time between Springfield and Memphis, St. Louis's AA and AAA affiliates, the 6-foot-1, 210-pound infielder slugged an aggregate .279/.333/.481 with 20 doubles, one triple, and 25 homeruns. He also went a perfect 7-for-7 in the stolen base department as well. Per *Weighted Runs Created Plus*, his overall production topped the league average threshold by 15%.

Snippet from The 2020 Prospect Digest Handbook: Gorman's one of the more underrated defenders – as well as being one of the best defensive infielders – in the minor leagues. There's the potential to earn a few Gold Gloves at the major league level. Last year I remarked how Gorman's ceiling resides in the .250/.340/.540 neighborhood. Throw in some plus-defensive value and all of a sudden you're staring down the ceiling of a Matt Chapman.

Scouting Report: The young third baseman spent the majority of time with Memphis in Triple-A East in 2021; so let's take a look at how his production stacks up against his peers. Consider the following:

- Since 2006, only three 21-year-olds met the following criteria in AAA in a season with one organization (min. 300 PA): a wRC+ between 100 and 110, a sub-20% strikeout rate, and a K-rate below 8%. Those three hitters: Corey Seager, Manuel Margot, and – of course –Nolan Gorman.
- And just for fun: Seager is career .297/.367/.504 big league hitter, owning a wRC+ total of 132, and Margot is sporting a career .251/.306/.388 with an 87 wRC+ total.

Prior to last offseason Gorman looked like a lock to man St. Louis's third base gig for at least a decade. But the front office acquired future Hall of Famer Nolan Arenado from Colorado for peanuts. So where does that leave Gorman and his elite glove? Second base, of course. Plus in-game power. Improving contact skills to the point where his K-rate dropped from 31.7% in High-A in 2019 all the way down to 19.2% in AAA last year. The lone pockmark on an otherwise impeccable resume: his struggles against southpaws in 2021, the first time in his professional career he's been impotent against lefties. He batted .191/.250/.278 in 124 plate appearances vs. LHP. Assuming that it's just a blip, which it should be, Gorman is going to be a star. Oh, one more thing: per FanGraphs, his batted ball data is out of this world. His average exit velocity was 91 mph with a peak of 109 mph. He's going to put a .300/.360/.560 triple-slash line at some point in his big league career.

Ceiling: 6.0-win player
Risk: Moderate
MLB ETA: 2022

2. Jordan Walker, 3B

Hit	Power	SB	Patience	Glove	Overall
45/55	50/60	55/45	50	40/50	60

Born: 05/22/02	Age: 20	Bats: R	Top Comp: Corey Hart
Height: 6-5	Weight: 220	Throws: R	

Season	Team	Age	Level	PA	1B	2B	3B	HR	SB	CS	BB%	K%	AVG	OBP	SLG	ISO
2021	STL	19	A	122	19	11	1	6	1	0	14.75%	17.21%	0.374	0.475	0.687	0.313
2021	STL	19	A+	244	41	14	3	8	13	2	6.15%	27.05%	0.292	0.344	0.487	0.195

Background: Since the inception of the draft, Georgia-based Decatur High School has produced just four draft picks: Dwight Bryant, the 388th overall player in 1975; David Fowlkes, a fifth rounder by Cleveland in 1976; Trumon Jefferson, a 39th round selection by the Rangers in 2011; and – of course – Jordan Walker, the 21st overall pick in 2020. Standing an imposing 6-foot-5 and 220 pounds, the massive third baseman had one of the biggest showings in 2021. The baby faced slugger torched the Low-A competition to the tune of .374/.475/.687 through 27 games and continued to dominate following a promotion up to High-A at the end of June. He would bat .292/.344/.487 in 55 games with Peoria. In total, Walker battered the older competition to the tune of .317/.388/.548

with 25 doubles, four triples, 14 homeruns and 14 stolen bases (in 16 attempts). Per *Weighted Runs Created Plus*, his overall production topped the league average by a mindboggling 51% - tied for the 18th best showing among all MiLB hitters with at least 350 plate appearances.

Scouting Report: No teenager with at least 350 plate appearances was more lethal at the plate last season than the Cardinals' former first round pick. With respect to his work in High-A, consider the following:

- Since 2006, only three 19-year-old hitters met the following criteria in a High-A season with one organization (min. 225 PA): 120 to 130 wRC+, a strikeout rate of at least 24%, and a single digit walk rate. Those three hitters: Gabriel Arias, Hudson Potts, and – of course – Mr. Jordan Walker.

In terms of comparisons, it's less than promising. Potts has been abysmal in three trips through AA; though Arias looked quite promising in his season with Cleveland's AAA affiliate last year (.284/.348/.454) as a 21-year-old. I don't think Walker takes the Potts development path, though. The Cardinals' young infielder showed an incredible feel for the strike zone *and* strong contact skills during his abbreviated stint in Low-A at the beginning of the year. His k-rate through his first 33 games in High-A was a reasonable 24.5%. Over his final 22 contests he whiffed 31% of the time. He either (A) tired down the stretch or (B) the league figured him out. If it's the latter, I'm betting on Walker making the necessary adjustments. Like Nolan Gorman, he's going to shift away from the hot corner, though Walker's likely headed for a corner outfield spot. In terms of big league production, think: .280/.350/.490

Ceiling: 5.0-win player
Risk: Moderate
MLB ETA: 2024

3. Matthew Liberatore, LHP			FB	CB	SL	CH	Command	Overall
			55	60	55	50	55	60

Born: 11/06/99	Age: 22	Bats: L	Top Comp: Danny Duffy
Height: 6-4	Weight: 200	Throws: L	

Season	Team	Age	Level	IP	TBF	K/9	K%	BB/9	BB%	K-BB%	ERA	FIP	xFIP	Pit/Bat
2018	TBR	18	R	27.2	108	10.41	29.63%	3.58	10.19%	19.44%	0.98	2.86	3.34	1.94
2019	TBR	19	A	78.1	332	8.73	22.89%	3.56	9.34%	13.55%	3.10	3.18	3.59	3.38
2021	STL	21	AAA	124.2	520	8.88	23.65%	2.38	6.35%	17.31%	4.04	4.26	4.15	3.66

Background: it doesn't happen too often – or barely ever – but Liberatore could be the rare pitching prospect that reaches his full potential *after* leaving Tampa Bay's organization. Originally drafted out of Mountain Ridge High School with the 16th overall pick in 2018, St. Louis acquired the talented southpaw, Edgardo Rodriguez, and a 2020 supplemental second round pick for eventual 2021 AL Rookie of the Year Randy Arozarena and Jose Martinez. Liberatore, a close friend of fellow Cardinals top prospect Nolan Gorman, was aggressively assigned to AAA last year – at the ripe ol' age of 21. In 22 appearances with Memphis, 18 of which were starts, the 6-foot-4, 200-pound left-hander struck out 123 and walked 33 in a career best 124.2 innings of work. He finished the year with a 4.04 ERA, 4.26 FIP, and a 4.15 xFIP.

Snippet from The 2020 Prospect Digest Handbook: St. Louis has generally done well in cultivating young arms and Liberatore could begin to move quickly once the training wheels are removed. A year after prognosticating a potential #2 ceiling, I'm more inclined to bump him down to a true #3, unless some extra velocity develops and/or above-average control/command.

Scouting Report: Consider the following:

- Since 2006, only three 21-year-old hurlers struck out between 23% and 25% in a season in AAA with one organization (min. 100 IP): Noah Syndergaard, Bryse Wilson, and Liberatore.

Owner of three above-average pitches and poise well beyond his years. Liberatore's heater sits in the 92- to 94-mph range, but has reached several ticks higher on occasion. His curveball is a legitimate, bonafide swing-and-miss plus offering that tops out at 2800 RPMs. He'll also showcase – primarily to left-handers – an above-average slider and a firm changeup. Liberatore's a strike-thrower that mixes speeds well. He's not destined to become an upper echelon pitcher, but should settle in for St. Louis as a very strong mid-rotation arm.

Ceiling: 3.5-win player
Risk: Low to Moderate
MLB ETA: 2022

4. Ivan Herrera, C

Hit	Power	SB	Patience	Glove	Overall
45	50	35	60	50	55

Born: 06/01/00   **Age:** 22   **Bats:** R   **Top Comp:** Carson Kelly

Height: 5-11   **Weight:** 220   **Throws:** R

Season	Team	Age	Level	PA	1B	2B	3B	HR	SB	CS	BB%	K%	AVG	OBP	SLG	ISO
2018	STL	18	R	130	28	6	4	1	1	1	8.46%	15.38%	0.348	0.423	0.500	0.152
2019	STL	19	A	291	53	10	0	8	1	1	12.03%	19.24%	0.286	0.381	0.423	0.137
2019	STL	19	A+	65	15	0	0	1	0	0	7.69%	24.62%	0.276	0.338	0.328	0.052
2021	STL	21	AA	437	54	13	0	17	2	3	13.73%	21.97%	0.231	0.346	0.408	0.176

Background: More of a testament to his Hall of Fame endurance than anything else, but there's been several catching prospects that have been tabbed as Yadier Molina's heir apparent. The two that immediately come to mind: Carson Kelly, a sturdy backstop who was dealt to Arizona as part of the package for Paul Goldschmidt, and Andrew Knizner. The latest potential long term solution to the Cards' catching position: baby-faced backstop Ivan Herrera. Hailing from Panama, Panama, the pudgy 5-foot-11, 220-pound prospect consistently put together impressive showing after impressive showing since his debut in 2017 – at least until 2021 rolled around. He batted .335/.425/.441 in 2017, slugged .336/.415/.483 the following season, and hit .284/.374/.405 in 2019. Last season he spent the year toiling away in the minors' toughest level: Class AA. In 98 games with Springfield Herrera hit a respectable .231/.346/.408 with 13 doubles and 17 homeruns. His overall production topped the league average threshold by 4%, per *Weighted Runs Created Plus*.

Snippet from The 2020 Prospect Digest Handbook: There's a solid possibility that Herrera develops into a 50-grade hit tool with 20-homerun thump with a solid enough glove to stay behind the dish.

Scouting Report: Consider the following:

- Since 2006, only four 21-year-old hitters met the following criteria in a season in AA with one organization (min. 400PA): 100 to 110 wRC+, a strikeout rate between 20% and 23%, and a walk rate of at least 12% Those four hitters: Trent Grisham, Delino DeShields Jr., Lucius Fox, and Ivan Herrera.

Herrera showed some pretty impressive batted ball data last season, according to *FanGraphs*. His average exit velocity was an average-ish 87 mph but his peak exit velocity was 110 mph, tied for the 19th highest mark. After a bit of an adjustment period, Herrera finished the year on a high note, slugging .256/.335/.518 over his final 43 games with Springfield. He's tracking to be a .250/.340/.450-type hitter with average-ish defense.

Ceiling: 2.5-win player
Risk: Moderate
MLB ETA: 2022

5. Michael McGreevy, RHP

FB	CB	SL	CH	Command	Overall
55	55	55	50	55	50

Born: 07/08/00   **Age:** 21   **Bats:** R   **Top Comp:** N/A

Height: 6-4   **Weight:** 215   **Throws:** R

Background: A two-way star for San Clemente during his prep years, McGreevy had a couple interesting colleges pursuing him, including: UC Irvine, Nevada, and Oregon. The 6-foot-4, 215-pound right-hander opted to attend UC Santa Barbara, whose notable alums include 2015 former fourth overall pick Dillon Tate, Michael Young, Barry Zito, and – of course – Shane Bieber. McGreevy spent his freshman year pitching exclusively out of the bullpen for the Gauchos, throwing 60.1 innings with 53 strikeouts, 13 walks, and a tidy 1.94 ERA. He spent the COVID-shortened 2020 campaign transitioning into the club's rotation, making four dominant starts en route to totaling a 1.32 ERA with 26 punch outs and seven walks. And the beach loving righty carried that momentum into an incredible junior season: 101.2 innings, 115 strikeouts, just 11 free passes, a 2.92 ERA, and a 9-2 win-loss record. St. Louis selected him in the opening round last July, 18th overall, and signed him to a deal worth $2.75 million. McGreevy tossed 7.2 innings during his professional debut, allowing a whopping 14 hits while fanning seven and walking a pair.

Scouting Report: Per the usual, here's my pre-draft write-up on the young righty:

> "Consider the following:

- Between 2011 and 2020, only three Big West hurlers have averaged at least 10 strikeouts and fewer than 2.0 walks per nine innings in a season (min. 75 IP): Connor Seabold, Ben Brecht, and – my all-time favorite college player – Clayton Andrews.

McGreevy attacks hitters with a 92-93-mph fastball that will peak a couple ticks above that at times, an above-average upper 12-6 curveball, an above-average 83 mph slider, and a workable changeup. He's not overpowering, but gets the most out of his talent and arsenal due to his superb feel for the strike zone. He's a safe, low risk college arm that should move quickly through the minor leagues. He's been linked to the Indians in recent mock drafts, and that seems like a logical choice given their propensity for developing similar arms."

Ceiling: 2.5-win player
Risk: Moderate
MLB ETA: 2023/2024

6. Alec Burleson, LF/RF

Hit	Power	SB	Patience	Glove	Overall
50	55	35	50	50	50

Born: 11/25/98	Age: 23	Bats: L	Top Comp: Stephen Piscotty
Height: 6-2	Weight: 212	Throws: L	

Season	Team	Age	Level	PA	1B	2B	3B	HR	SB	CS	BB%	K%	AVG	OBP	SLG	ISO
2021	STL	22	A+	49	7	1	0	4	1	0	12.24%	30.61%	0.286	0.367	0.595	0.310
2021	STL	22	AA	282	51	10	0	14	2	0	6.74%	20.92%	0.288	0.333	0.488	0.200
2021	STL	22	AAA	172	25	7	0	4	0	1	9.88%	15.70%	0.234	0.310	0.357	0.123

Background: It feels like every year a Cardinals minor leaguer – or three – *explodes* and rockets up prospect lists. Enter: Alec Burleson, a second round pick in 2020 out of East Carolina University. A stout, power-packed bat throughout his collegiate career, Burleson left the American Athletic Conference squad as a career .341/.387/.496 hitter. Less than a year later the 6-foot-2, 212-pound corner outfielder was digging in against Triple-A pitching. Burleson ripped through High-A to start the year, batting .286/.367/.595 in 11 games. He continued to produce against the minors' toughest challenge, AA, for 63 games, slugging .288/.333/.488. And he finally slowed during his 45-game stint with Memphis in AAA. In total, the former Division I bomber hit .270/.329/.454 with 18 doubles, 22 homeruns, and three stolen bases. Per *Weighted Runs Created Plus*, his overall production topped the league mark by 8%.

Scouting Report: Consider the following:

- Since 2006, only two 22-year-old hitters met the following criteria in a Double-A season with one organization (min. 250 PA): 110 to 120 wRC+, a strikeout rate between 20% and 22%, and a sub-7% walk rate. Those two hitters: Orlando Mercado and – of course – Alec Burleson.

Above-average power that likely tops out with 25 or so homeruns in a full season. Burleson achieved a rather amazing feat during his sprint through St. Louis' farm system last season: his strikeout rate declined at every stop along the way. No massive platoon splits. Burleson is a typical Cardinals draft pick: he's going to pop up in the big leagues, without much fanfare, and hit .270/.335/.450 in 400 plate appearances a season for eight years.

Ceiling: 2.0-win player
Risk: Moderate
MLB ETA: 2022

7. Masyn Winn, SS

Hit	Power	SB	Patience	Glove	Overall
40/50	35/40	60	55	50	45

Born: 03/21/02	Age: 20	Bats: R	Top Comp: Ruben Tejada
Height: 5-11	Weight: 180	Throws: R	

Season	Team	Age	Level	PA	1B	2B	3B	HR	SB	CS	BB%	K%	AVG	OBP	SLG	ISO
2021	STL	19	A	284	41	15	3	3	16	2	14.08%	21.13%	0.262	0.370	0.388	0.127
2021	STL	19	A+	154	23	4	2	2	16	3	3.90%	25.97%	0.209	0.240	0.304	0.095

Background: Kingwood High School is familiar with high-priced amateur talent: the Texas-based school has produced two first round picks, and a pair of second rounders as well. And, on a side note, the school can claim four big leaguers among their alumnus, though they've all totaled a negative Wins Above Replacement: Micah Bowie, Jeff Austin, Ryan Jorgensen, and Lance Pendleton. Two years ago St. Louis selected Kingwood shortstop Masyn Winn in the second round, 54th overall, and signed him to a hefty

$2.1 million deal. The 5-foot-11, 180-pound shortstop began the year on a high note, hitting .262/.370/.388 as a 19-year-old in Low-A. The front office bumped him up to High-A at the end of July and his production cratered; he hit a lowly .209/.240/.304.

Scouting Report: Consider the following:

- Since 2006, only a pair of 19-year-old hitters met the following criteria in Low-A in a season with one organization (min. 275 PA): 107 to 117 wRC+, a walk rate north of 12%, and a strikeout rate between 19% and 22%. Those two hitters: All-Star and Silver Slugger award winner Eric Hosmer and, of course, Masyn Winn.

Winn is not Hosmer, though the latter has developed into more of a slap-hitting middle infielder at this point in his career. Winn's season was a tale of two stories: he was a patient, top-of-the-line type table-setter in Low-A and an OBP-deficient, swing-at-everything hack in High-A. A lot of Winn's value is tied up into two different facets: (1) his patient approach at the plate and (2) his plus speed on the base paths. He's never going to win a gold glove, but he should have no problem manning the position. Winn also flashed an upper-90s heater as an amateur, though he tossed just one inning as pro last year.

Ceiling: 1.5- win player
Risk: Moderate
MLB ETA: 2024/2025

8. Malcom Nunez, 3B

Hit	Power	SB	Patience	Glove	Overall
50	45/55	45	50	45/50	45

Born: 03/09/01	Age: 21	Bats: R	Top Comp: Jesus Aguilar
Height: 5-11	Weight: 205	Throws: R	

Season	Team	Age	Level	PA	1B	2B	3B	HR	SB	CS	BB%	K%	AVG	OBP	SLG	ISO
2018	STL	17	R	199	37	16	2	13	3	0	13.07%	14.57%	0.415	0.497	0.774	0.360
2019	STL	18	R	146	20	11	0	2	3	2	8.90%	21.92%	0.254	0.336	0.385	0.131
2019	STL	18	A	77	12	1	0	0	0	0	6.49%	19.48%	0.183	0.247	0.197	0.014
2021	STL	20	A+	151	24	10	2	3	5	2	7.28%	17.88%	0.285	0.351	0.453	0.168
2021	STL	20	AA	224	41	5	0	6	2	1	9.38%	19.64%	0.257	0.330	0.371	0.114

Background: A high profile signing out of La Habana, Cuba several years ago, Nunez, who received a hefty $300,000 bonus, looked the part of a big, stocky middle-of-the-lineup thumper during his debut in the Dominican Summer League in 2018. In 44 games that summer the 5-foot-11, 205-pound third baseman slugged a scorching .415/.497/.774 with 16 doubles, two triples, and 13 homeruns. His overall production, per *Weighted Runs Created Plus*, topped the league average threshold by a whopping 138%. And then the bottom fell out. The front office bumped the Cuban import straight up to Peoria the following season, but after batting a paltry .183/.247/.197 in 21 games, he was demoted down to the Appalachian League – where he batted a mediocre .254/.336/.385. Like Lloyd Christmas, Nunez "totally redeemed" himself in 2021. Splitting time between Peoria, now St. Louis's High-A affiliate, and Springfield, he hit an aggregate .268/.339/.404 with 15 doubles, two triples, and nine homeruns. Per *Weighted Runs Created Plus*, his overall production topped the league average mark by 3%.

Snippet from The 2020 Prospect Digest Handbook: There's a ton of talent here, strictly as a potential power-hitter, but he looked far rawer than what I thought he was a year ago. I'd put Nunez's ceiling in the Jesus Aguilar territory.

Scouting Report: Consider the following:

- Since 2006, only three 20-year-old hitters met the following criteria in a Double-A season with one organization (min. 200 PA): an 85 to 95 wRC+, a strikeout rate between 19% and 21%, and a single-digit walk rate. Those three hitters: Tommy Joseph, Leody Taveras, and Malcom Nunez.
- Tommy Joseph was a league average hitter during his two-year big league career, belting out 43 homeruns in 249 games. And Taveras, a speedy center fielder, was widely recognized – across the board – as a Top 100 prospect for multiple seasons.

I still think Nunez develops into a Jesus Aguilar-type of hitter, someone capable of putting together a .270/.340/.470 line. Per *FanGraphs'* data, Nunez's average exit velocity was a stellar 90 mph last season. He shows an average glove at third base, though I think he eventually slides across the diamond. There's the potential to put together one of those patented *Cardinals prospects* seasons and shoot up the prospect charts.

Ceiling: 1.5-win player
Risk: Moderate
MLB ETA: 2022

9. Tink Hence, RHP

	FB	CB	SL	CH	Command	Overall
	55	50	55/60	50/55	50	45

Born: 08/06/02	Age: 19	Bats: R	Top Comp: N/A
Height: 6-1	Weight: 175	Throws: R	

Background: Watson Chapel High School has been home to three draft picks since 2018: Gionti Turner, who got $125,000 from the Guardians as a 27th round pick in 2018; Kaleb Hill, who was chosen 12 rounds later by Cleveland; and – of course – Tink Hence. The 63rd overall pick in 2020, Hence agreed to join the St. Louis organization for a slightly above-slot $1,115,000. Hence wouldn't make his debut until last season. In eight brief appearances with the organization's Florida Complex League affiliate, the 6-foot-1, 175-pound right-hander struck out 14 and walked a trio in eight innings of work. He compiled a 9.00 ERA along the way.

Scouting Report: One of the more fascinating facts about Hence's debut in the rookie league: the wiry right-hander struck out six and didn't allow a hit or walk over his first three appearances, and through his first four appearances he sported a 9-to-0 strikeout-to-walk ratio. He's skinny and needs to pack on some serious poundage, but he's shown an intriguing four-pitch mix prior to his debut. Very, very loose arm. There's some potential upside as a backend starter.

Ceiling: 1.5-win player
Risk: Moderate
MLB ETA: 2025

10. Ryan Holgate, RF

	Hit	Power	SB	Patience	Glove	Overall
	40/45	50	30	50	50	45

Born: 06/08/00	Age: 22	Bats: L	Top Comp: N/A
Height: 6-2	Weight: 193	Throws: L	

Season	Team	Age	Level	PA	1B	2B	3B	HR	SB	CS	BB%	K%	AVG	OBP	SLG	ISO
2021	STL	21	A	129	17	2	0	3	0	0	10.08%	35.66%	0.193	0.279	0.289	0.096

Background: Originally taken by the Minnesota Twins in the late, late rounds of the 2018 draft coming out of Davis High School in 2018, Holgate, a well-built outfielder, put together a solid showing at the University of Arizona as a true freshman the following the season. Appearing in 53 games with the Wildcats, the 6-foot-2, 193-pound slugger batted .240/.378/.437 with eight doubles, two triples, and seven homeruns. Holgate's production took a noticeable leap forward during the ensuing summer in the Northwoods League as he hit .297/.392/.554 for the La Crosse Loggers. The native Californian, like so many others, got off to a torrid start during the 2020 season, slugging a scorching .377/.459/.547 in 15 contests before the season came to a premature COVID-induced end. Last season, Holgate, appearing in a career best 63 games for the Pac12 squad, developed into one of college baseball's most explosive bats: he mashed .351/.421/.576 with career highs in doubles (20), homeruns (11) and stolen bases (3). The Cardinals drafted him in the second round, 70th overall, and signed him to a deal worth $875,000, slightly below-slot. Unfortunately, the corner outfielder hit a putrid .193/.279/.289 in 30 games with the Palm Beach Cardinals in Low-A.

Scouting Report: Per the usual, my pre-draft write-up:

> *"Consider the following:*

> - *Between 2011 and 2020, here's the list of PAC12 hitters to hit at least .340/.410/.560 with double digit homeruns and a single-digit walk rate in a season (min. 275 PA): J.J. Matijevic, a 2017 second round pick out of Arizona, and Garrett Mitchell, a first round selection out of UCLA in 2020.*

> *Gobs of raw power that he was just beginning to tap into in game-play in 2021, Holgate should have no problem slugging 20 to 25 longballs in a full professional season. Not the most patient of hitters, Holgate may battle some swing-and-miss tendencies as he approaches the middle rungs of the minor leagues. Holgate looks like a potential Ryan Ludwick-type bat, capable of hitting .260/.320/.440."*

Ceiling: 1.5- win player
Risk: Moderate
MLB ETA: 2024

11. Dionys Rodriguez, RHP

	FB	SL	CH	Command	Overall
	55	60	50	50	45

Born: 09/03/00	Age: 21	Bats: L	Top Comp: N/A
Height: 6-0	Weight: 188	Throws: R	

Season	Team	Age	Level	IP	TBF	K/9	K%	BB/9	BB%	K-BB%	ERA	FIP	xFIP	Pit/Bat
2018	STL	17	R	21.0	109	9.43	20.18%	10.71	22.94%	-2.75%	6.43	6.31	6.41	2.04
2019	STL	18	R	26.0	118	11.08	27.12%	6.58	16.10%	11.02%	5.88	3.87	3.76	2.12
2021	STL	20	A	69.2	288	11.37	30.56%	2.84	7.64%	22.92%	3.36	3.37	3.81	4.02

Background: Just the latest example of one of "popup prospects" the Cardinals' system seems to burp up each season. Rodriguez, a thick-bodied right-hander from Pedro Brand, Dominican Republic, spent the 2018 and 2019 seasons toiling away in the foreign rookie league, showcasing promising swing-and-miss stuff with zero feel for the strike zone. Last season, perhaps shockingly, the front office bounced the 6-foot, 188-pound hurler up to Palm Beach. And Rodriguez hit the ground running. Making 22 appearances, 12 of which were starts, Rodriguez struck out a whopping 88 and walked just 22 in 69.2 innings of work. He finished his first full season in professional ball with a 3.36 ERA, 3.37 FIP, and a 3.81 xFIP.

Scouting Report: Quite good – particularly for his age, past performances, and level of competition – Rodriguez, though, is exactly the type of arm that carves up the lower levels of the minor leagues: he's a strike-thrower with multiple above-average or better offerings. Rodriguez challenges hitters with a lively low- to mid-90s fastball, a wipeout plus slider, and a decent little changeup. He's – likely – generously listed as 6-foot. Meaning: he's going to have to fight out the potential to get pushed into a relief role. With respect to his work in 2021, consider the following:

- Since 2006, only four 20-year-old hurlers met the following criteria in a season in Low-A with one organization (min. 60 IP): a strikeout percentage between 29% and 33% and a walk percentage between 6.5% and 8.5%. Those four hurlers: Trevor May, Robert Stephenson, Taj Bradley, and Dionys Rodriguez.

One more final thought: Rodriguez, who can really spin it, could jump up pretty quickly if he can repeat his performance in High-A in 2022. He's a potential helium guy.

Ceiling: 1.5-win player
Risk: Moderate
MLB ETA: 2024

12. Zack Thompson, LHP

	FB	CB	SL	CH	Command	Overall
	55	60	50	50	40	50

Born: 10/28/97	Age: 24	Bats: L	Top Comp: N/A
Height: 6-2	Weight: 215	Throws: L	

Season	Team	Age	Level	IP	TBF	K/9	K%	BB/9	BB%	K-BB%	ERA	FIP	xFIP	Pit/Bat
2019	STL	21	A+	13.1	61	12.83	31.15%	2.70	6.56%	24.59%	4.05	2.03	2.46	4.18
2021	STL	23	AAA	93.0	444	7.94	18.47%	5.52	12.84%	5.63%	7.06	6.15	5.66	3.84

Background: An enigmatic arm during his first two seasons at the University of Kentucky, Thompson racked up plenty of strikeouts and walks. But the 6-foot-2, 215-pound southpaw put it all together during his junior campaign in 2019 as he averaged 13.0 strikeouts and just 3.4 walks per nine innings. The Cardinals selected the left-hander in the opening round, 19th overall, and signed him to a deal worth $3 million. After continuing his dominance during his brief debut that year, Thompson's command – and performance – regressed to his earlier collegiate form. In 22 appearances with the organization's AAA affiliate, the Memphis Redbirds, Thompson struck out only 82 and walked a whopping 57. He tallied a 7.06 ERA, a 6.15 FIP, and a 5.66 xFIP. He continued to struggle in 17.1 innings in the Arizona Fall League following the year as well, striking out 22 and walking 15.

Snippet from The 2020 Prospect Digest Handbook: Thompson looks like a good #3 at his peak.

Scouting Report: Low 90s, above-average fastball, plus curveball that may be one of the finest in the minor leagues, a vanilla slider and changeup. The question, of course, is whether Thompson's command comes back to his 2019 form or whether he'll battle with the strike zone from here on out. The potential to be a #4-type arm is still present. But Thompson seemed to be battling himself on the mound, both emotionally and mentally, when he would lose the strike zone. He could be starring down a relief role in a year-plus.

Ceiling: 1.5- to 2.0-win player
Risk: High
MLB ETA: 2022

13. Juan Yepez, 1B/3B/LF

	Hit	Power	SB	Patience	Glove	Overall
	50	50	30	55	45	40

Born: 02/19/98	Age: 24	Bats: R	Top Comp: Wilmer Flores
Height: 6-1	Weight: 200	Throws: R	

Season	Team	Age	Level	PA	1B	2B	3B	HR	SB	CS	BB%	K%	AVG	OBP	SLG	ISO
2018	STL	20	A	106	26	10	2	1	4	1	9.43%	13.21%	0.415	0.462	0.596	0.181
2018	STL	20	A+	242	33	12	0	2	2	1	4.96%	21.49%	0.208	0.257	0.288	0.080
2019	STL	21	A	101	14	7	0	4	2	1	10.89%	23.76%	0.284	0.366	0.500	0.216
2019	STL	21	A+	115	20	4	0	4	1	0	8.70%	18.26%	0.275	0.351	0.431	0.157
2019	STL	21	AA	59	8	2	0	2	0	0	8.47%	23.73%	0.231	0.288	0.385	0.154
2021	STL	23	AA	77	8	4	0	5	0	0	11.69%	16.88%	0.270	0.387	0.571	0.302
2021	STL	23	AAA	357	41	25	0	22	1	3	11.76%	19.33%	0.289	0.382	0.589	0.299

Background: There were 377 minor league hitters that made at least 400 trips to the plate in 2021. Of those 377, Juan Yepez, a stocky corner infielder / outfielder, was tied for the ninth best offensive showing. Suffice to say, it was a *wildly* successful year for the Venezuelan-born prospect. Hailing from Caracas, Yepez appeared in 111 total games between Memphis and Springfield (all but 19 coming with the former), slugging an aggregate .286/.383/.586 while tying a career high with 29 doubles and easily setting a new best with 27 dingers. Per *Weighted Runs Created Plus,* his overall production topped the league average mark by a staggering by 54%. And Yepez's scorching bat didn't cool as he moved into the Arizona Fall League either. In 23 games with the Glendale Deseret Dogs, he batted .302/.388/.640.

Scouting Report: Consider the following:

- Since 2006, only three 23-year-old hitters met the following criteria in AAA in a season with one organization (min. 350 PA): a wRC+ total of at least 150, a strikeout rate below 20%, and a walk rate of at least 10%. Those three hitters: Brandon Nimmo, Daniel Vogelbach, and Juan Yepez.

Pretty good batted ball data coming from Yepez last season: *FanGraphs* has his average exit velocity as 90 with a peak of 107. The interesting – or downright fascinating – aspect about his breakout 2021 season: he transformed the type of hitter he was, going from a high contact, low walk rate, groundball hitter into a patient, high contact power hitter. Yepez has never really had a defensive home, though he tends to bounce between left field and first and third bases. He could be a low end starter on a non-contending team, capable of hitting .260/.330/.440.

Ceiling: 1.0- win player
Risk: Low to Moderate
MLB ETA: 2022

14. Joshua Baez, CF

	Hit	Power	SB	Patience	Glove	Overall
	40/45	50/60	50	50	50	40

Born: 06/28/03	Age: 19	Bats: R	Top Comp: N/A
Height: 6-4	Weight: 220	Throws: R	

Season	Team	Age	Level	PA	1B	2B	3B	HR	SB	CS	BB%	K%	AVG	OBP	SLG	ISO
2021	STL	18	CPX	95	6	3	1	2	5	0	14.74%	29.47%	0.158	0.305	0.303	0.145

Background: Exactly two players have been drafted out of Dexter School in Brookline, MA: Johnny Magliozzi, a 3th round pick by the Rays in 2011, and Joshua Baez, a highly touted outfielder selected in second round by the Cardinals last season. Taken with the 54th overall and signed to a deal worth slightly more than $2.2 million, Baez is far from short on confidence. In a post-draft article on MLB.com, the 6-foot-4, 220-pound center fielder had this to say: "A lot of people talk about how I'm kind of like Mike Trout. I'm like, I just want to be better than Mike Trout and just want to be the face of the game one day." Call me pessimistic, but I don't think this quote is going to age very well. Someone should send Baez to the school of Crash Davis. The raw outfielder appeared in 23 games with the club's Florida Complex League affiliate, hitting a non-Mike Trout-esque .158/.305/.303 with three doubles, one triple, and a pair of homeruns.

Scouting Report: Plus arm strength from the outfield – as well as the mound where he, reportedly, would touch the mid- to upper-90s on occasion. Baez has plus bat speed, but it's undone – at times – by a hitch in his swing and a penchant for swinging at pitches below the zone. I don't love the swing, there's some holes that may be too much to overcome. The tools are there to be an impact player. But he's raw. And he needs a lot of work to get there. It's a very atypical Cardinals type draft pick. And I wouldn't be surprised if he ends up back on the mound at some point to increase his chances at the big leagues.

Ceiling: 1.0-win player
Risk: Moderate
MLB ETA: 2025

15. Brendan Donovan, IF/OF

Hit	Power	SB	Patience	Glove	Overall
45	40	55	55	50	40

Born: 01/16/97	Age: 25	Bats: L	Top Comp: Tommy Pham
Height: 6-1	Weight: 195	Throws: R	

Season	Team	Age	Level	PA	1B	2B	3B	HR	SB	CS	BB%	K%	AVG	OBP	SLG	ISO
2018	STL	21	A-	18	1	1	1	0	0	0	5.56%	38.89%	0.188	0.222	0.375	0.188
2019	STL	22	A	480	70	26	3	8	4	2	13.13%	18.96%	0.266	0.377	0.405	0.139
2021	STL	24	A+	109	20	6	0	2	7	1	9.17%	13.76%	0.295	0.385	0.421	0.126
2021	STL	24	AA	219	44	10	1	4	8	5	11.42%	17.81%	0.319	0.411	0.449	0.130
2021	STL	24	AAA	131	21	5	0	6	4	2	11.45%	17.56%	0.288	0.389	0.495	0.207

Background: According to Baseball Reference, there have been a few dozen big leaguers that were born in Germany, the most notable include: Glenn Hubbard, Max Kepler, Craig Lefferts, Edwin Jackson, Ron Gardenhire, Pretzels Getzien, and Will Ohman. Brendan Donovan, a seventh round pick out of the University of South Alabama in 2018, could add his name to the list in 2022. Born in Wurzburg, Germany, the infielder/outfielder, defensive jack-of-all-trades rocketed through the Cardinals' system last year, spending time in High-A, Double-A, and Triple-A. In total, the 6-foot-1, 195-pound utility man slugged .304/.399/.455 with 21 doubles, one triple, and 12 homeruns. He also swiped 19 bags in 27 attempts. Per *Weighted Runs Created Plus*, his overall production topped the league average mark by 34%.

Scouting Report: Consider the following:

- Since 2006, there have been five 24-year-old hitters in Double-A that have met the following criteria in a season with one organization: 130 to 140 wRC+, a walk rate between 10.5% and 12.5%, and a strikeout rate between 16% and 19%. Those five hitters: Lorenzo Cain, Steve Tolleson, Zelous Wheeler, Chris Nowak, and Brendan Donovan.

The 2021 season wasn't the first time Donovan showed some promise with the stick. He posted a .266/.377/.405 triple-slash line in Low-A three years ago, good enough for a 131 wRC+. He's consistently shown an above-average eye at the plate, and subsequently a strong nose for first base, good speed, and gap power. St. Louis has a track record of getting the most of underrated prospects, like: Tommy Pham, Tommy Edman, and Edmundo Sosa.

Ceiling: 1.0-win player
Risk: Moderate
MLB ETA: 2022

16. Angel Rondon, RHP

FB	CB	SL	CH	Command	Overall
50	50	50	50	50	40

Born: 12/01/97	Age: 24	Bats: R	Top Comp: Jesse Chavez
Height: 6-1	Weight: 205	Throws: R	

Season	Team	Age	Level	IP	TBF	K/9	K%	BB/9	BB%	K-BB%	ERA	FIP	xFIP	Pit/Bat
2018	STL	20	A-	29.0	121	7.14	19.01%	2.17	5.79%	13.22%	3.72	4.17	3.78	3.88
2018	STL	20	A	59.0	247	8.69	23.08%	2.59	6.88%	16.19%	2.90	4.16	3.69	3.36
2019	STL	21	A+	45.0	179	9.40	26.26%	3.40	9.50%	16.76%	2.20	3.35	3.42	3.92
2019	STL	21	AA	115.0	481	8.77	23.28%	3.29	8.73%	14.55%	3.21	3.97	4.31	3.73
2021	STL	23	AAA	76.2	339	7.98	20.06%	2.58	6.49%	13.57%	4.58	5.11	4.61	3.86

Background: A steal unearthed on the international market six years ago, Rondon and Cardinals agreed to deal worth just $25,000. Since then, the 6-foot-1, 205-pound right-hander ripped through the Dominican Summer League, held his own in the stateside rookie leagues, and showed a ton of promise as a 20-year-old with Peoria in 2018. In 10 starts, the Dominican-born hurler struck out 57 and walked 17 in 59.0 innings of work. Rondon split time between Palm Beach and Springfield the following year, averaging an impressive 8.9 strikeouts and 3.3 walks per nine innings in a career best 28 starts. Last season Rondon sandwiched a pair of Major League starts in between 19 appearances in Triple-A. In total, he struck out 68 and walked 22 in 76.2 minor league innings. And he tossed another pair of innings with St. Louis in early June, fanning one and walking another.

Snippet from The 2020 Prospect Digest Handbook: As long as he can throw 160+ innings a decent ball, he'll provide value to the organization.

Scouting Report: Consider the following:

- Since 2006, only three 23-year-old pitchers met the following criteria in a season with one organization in Triple-A (min. 75 IP): a strikeout percentage 19% and 21% with a walk percentage between 5.5% and 7.5%. Those three hurlers: Liam Hendriks, Duane Underwood Jr., and Angel Rondon.

Like Hendriks and Underwood Jr., Rondon is headed towards a relief gig in the big leagues. He's larger and leaner than his 6-foot-1, 205-pound frame would suggest. And you'd swear there was more in the tank, though that's likely not a possibility given his age. Rondon's fastball will sit in the 93-94 mpg range. It appears Rondon shows two distinct curveballs, based on the signals relayed from the catcher – a power curveball and a slow slider. The change looks better than in years past. Rondon is still a strike-thrower, instead of a command guy. He's going to be a solid middle-relief option for the Cardinals for the foreseeable future.

Ceiling: 0.5- to 1.0-win player
Risk: Low to Moderate
MLB ETA: Debuted in 2021

17. Austin Love, RHP

	FB	SL	CH	Command	Overall
	55	50	55	50	40

Born: 01/26/99	Age: 23	Bats: R	Top Comp: N/A
Height: 6-3	Weight: 232	Throws: R	

Background: St. Louis honed in on collegiate talent early and often in the draft last July, using 18 of their 21 picks on them. The club's third round selection, Austin Love, was the second college pitcher the organization drafted. Standing a stocky 6-foot-3 and 232 pounds, Love was dominant during his final season at the University of North Carolina: making a career-high 16 appearances, as well as one out of the bullpen, he averaged an impressive 11.4 strikeouts and just 2.8 walks per nine innings. The club signed the 90th overall selection to a $600,000. Love made seven appearances as a pro, posting a 13-to-1 strikeout-to-walk ratio in eight innings of work.

Scouting Report: Consider the following:

- Between 2011 and 2020, only four ACC pitchers averaged at least 11 strikeouts and less than 3.0 walks per nine innings in a season (min. 75 IP): Reid Detmers, Marcus Stroman, Brendan McKay, and Danny Hultzen. Love's production in 2021 would add his name to the list.

Unfortunately for the former Tar Heel, his repertoire isn't as impressive as his aforementioned ACC counterparts. Love features a low 90s heater, which will touch a tick or two higher one occasion, a low- to mid-80s average slider, and an above-average changeup. He's a strike-thrower. And it's very likely the club aggressively pushes Love through the farm system in 2022. He's lacking a true swing-and-miss weapon, so he's likely headed for a relief role at some point. One more thing to note: he's entering his age-23 season, so time is ticking.

Ceiling: 0.5- to 1.0-win player
Risk: Moderate
MLB ETA: 2023/2024

18. Connor Thomas, LHP

	FB	SL	CH	Command	Overall
	45	50	55	60	40

Born: 05/29/98	Age: 24	Bats: L	Top Comp: Aaron Loup
Height: 5-11	Weight: 173	Throws: L	

Season	Team	Age	Level	IP	TBF	K/9	K%	BB/9	BB%	K-BB%	ERA	FIP	xFIP	Pit/Bat
2019	STL	21	A-	15.2	68	9.77	25.00%	0.57	1.47%	23.53%	4.02	1.61	2.33	3.40
2019	STL	21	A	27.1	111	6.26	17.12%	2.96	8.11%	9.01%	3.62	4.00	3.55	3.43
2021	STL	23	AA	20.1	88	10.62	27.27%	1.33	3.41%	23.86%	4.87	5.20	3.14	3.70
2021	STL	23	AAA	101.2	436	8.14	21.10%	2.66	6.88%	14.22%	3.10	3.93	3.61	3.75

Background: The little southpaw put together quite the collegiate career at Georgia Tech: he made 38 appearances for the ACC squad across parts of three seasons, averaging 8.7 strikeouts and just 1.6 walks per nine innings. St. Louis selected the crafty hurler in the fifth round three years ago and signed him to a deal worth $340,000. After a solid debut with State College and Peoria in 2019, it took Thomas all of four Double-A starts last year before earning a promotion up to AAA. Thomas made 26 total appearances, 18 of which were starts, posting an impressive 116-to-33 strikeout-to-walk ratio. He finished the year with a 3.39 ERA, a 4.14 FIP, and a 3.53 xFIP.

Scouting Report: Sort of a dying breed of a pitcher: Thomas relies on guile and changing speeds, rather than an explosive repertoire. Below-average fastball, a slurvy slider, and an above-average changeup. All packaged together with above-average or better command. The life span for similar pitchers nowadays is pretty short.

He's likely going to slide into a single inning relief role at some point in his big league career. With respect to his work in AAA last year, consider the following:

- Since 2006, only five 23-year-old hurlers met the following criteria in AAA in a season with one organization (min. 100 IP): a strikeout percentage between 20% and 22% with a walk percentage between 6% and 8%. Those five pitchers: Carlos Carrasco, Jason Hammel, Brian Flynn, Duane Underwood Jr., and Connor Thomas.

Ceiling: 0.5-win player
Risk: Low to Moderate
MLB ETA: 2022

19. Ludwin Jimenez, RHP

FB	CB	CH	Command	Overall
50	N/A	50/55	45	40

Born: 08/09/01	Age: 20	Bats: R	Top Comp: N/A
Height: 6-2	Weight: 165	Throws: R	

Season	Team	Age	Level	IP	TBF	K/9	K%	BB/9	BB%	K-BB%	ERA	FIP	xFIP	Pit/Bat
2018	STL	16	R	63.1	264	9.81	26.14%	2.56	6.82%	19.32%	3.55	3.23	2.91	1.83
2019	STL	17	R	51.0	225	9.00	22.67%	4.24	10.67%	12.00%	4.59	4.62	3.85	1.88
2019	STL	17	R	20.0	80	5.85	16.25%	3.15	8.75%	7.50%	3.15	4.19	4.10	1.63
2021	STL	19	A	77.1	373	10.36	23.86%	5.94	13.67%	10.19%	6.17	5.02	5.12	4.06

Background: A member of the St. Louis organization since 2018. Jimenez spent that season with the club's Dominican Summer League affiliate where he posted a 69-to-18 strikeout-to-walk ratio in 63.1 innings of work. The front office bounced him between three different levels the following year. And last season, as minor league baseball returned from the lost year of COVID, the 6-foot-2, 165-pound string bean made 23 appearances in Low-A, averaging 10.4 strikeouts and 5.9 walks per nine innings. He compiled an unsightly 6.17 ERA.

Scouting Report: Consider the following:

- Since 2006, five 19-year-old hurlers met the following criteria in a season in Low-A with one organization (min. 75 IP): a strikeout percentage between 23% and 25% with a walk percentage of at least 11%. Those five hurlers: Jonathan Niese, Tyler Matzek, Freddy Tarnok, J.C. Sulbaran, and Ludwin Jimenez.

Projection more than production at this point. Jimenez's heater hasn't really progressed in the last couple of years. It's sitting in the 90 mph range and topped 91 mph in an early season start against Bradenton. His changeup, though, is a genuine differentiator at this point in his career. Tremendous arm speed, velocity separation, and fade due to pronation. It's projecting as an above-average offering, though it may eventually get into plus territory. Reports indicate Jimenez will mix in a curveball, though he was exclusively fastball/changeup when I saw him. Very raw but he has some ingredients to develop into a nice little pitching prospect.

Ceiling: 0.5-win player
Risk: Moderate
MLB ETA: 2025

20. Luken Baker, 1B

Hit	Power	SB	Patience	Glove	Overall
40	55	30	50	50	40

Born: 03/10/97	Age: 25	Bats: R	Top Comp: N/A
Height: 6-4	Weight: 280	Throws: R	

Season	Team	Age	Level	PA	1B	2B	3B	HR	SB	CS	BB%	K%	AVG	OBP	SLG	ISO
2018	STL	21	A	156	28	9	0	3	0	0	10.26%	19.87%	0.288	0.359	0.417	0.129
2019	STL	22	A+	496	64	32	1	10	1	1	10.48%	22.58%	0.244	0.327	0.390	0.146
2021	STL	24	AA	391	40	20	0	26	0	0	9.72%	26.34%	0.248	0.322	0.530	0.282

Background: Fun fact about Mr. Baker: we share a birthday. Injuries robbed Baker of significant playing time during his tenure with the Horned Frogs of Texas Christian University. After establishing himself as one of the best bats in the college game as a true freshman, Baker, who slugged .379/.3483/.577 in 67 games, only managed to appeared in 78 games over his final two campaigns with the Big12 Conference school. St. Louis took a second round flier on the behemoth, Boog Powell-esque first baseball four years ago. And the results have been mixed. Baker turned in a solid debut showing in 2018 as he split time between rookie ball and the Midwest League, batting an aggregate .319/.386/.460. But he struggled – significantly – with the club's aggressive assignment up to High-A the following season (.244/.327/.390). Last year, Baker appeared in 91 games with the Springfield Cardinals in Double-A Central, posting a .248/.322/.530 slash line with 20 doubles and 26 homeruns. His production at the game's most difficult challenge, per *Weighted Runs Created Plus*, was 21% above the league average mark. He also appeared in a pair of games with the club's Triple-A affiliate as well.

Snippet from The 2020 Prospect Digest Handbook: In short, outside of his hot month of August – where he batted .346/.413/.654 with four bombs – Baker was pretty terrible for the majority of the season. He's walking an above-average amount of time with 20- to 25-homer power potential. But the limited collegiate experience – combined with the body woes – seems like it's finally caught up to him. Poor Man's Paul Goldschmidt, maybe 70% of Goldschmidt.

Scouting Report: If he's not the largest man in professional baseball, then he's *awfully* close. Two years in The 2020 Prospect Digest Handbook, Baker was tipping the scales at a rather portly 265 pounds. Last year he was up to 280 pounds. That's problematic in itself. The power, as expected, came roaring back for Baker in 2021 as he slugged 26 dingers. And he's still walking a solid amount of the time, but the hit tool hasn't developed in the past couple of years. Strictly an up-and-down fill-in / Quad-A bat.

Ceiling: 0.5-win player
Risk: Moderate
MLB ETA: 2022

Tampa Bay Rays

Top Prospects

1. Shane Baz, RHP

FB	CB	SL	CH	Command	Overall
65	50	60	50	60	60

Born: 06/17/99	Age: 23	Bats: R	Top Comp: Corbin Burnes
Height: 6-2	Weight: 190	Throws: R	

Season	Team	Age	Level	IP	TBF	K/9	K%	BB/9	BB%	K-BB%	ERA	FIP	xFIP	Pit/Bat
2018	PIT	19	R	45.1	207	10.72	26.09%	4.57	11.11%	14.98%	3.97	3.90	4.04	3.82
2019	TBR	20	A	81.1	342	9.63	25.44%	4.09	10.82%	14.62%	2.99	3.66	3.85	4.07
2021	TBR	22	AA	32.2	120	13.50	40.83%	0.55	1.67%	39.17%	2.48	1.96	1.86	3.94
2021	TBR	22	AAA	46.0	178	12.52	35.96%	2.15	6.18%	29.78%	1.76	3.32	2.98	3.93

Background: How does that old saying go? The only certainties in life are death, taxes, and the Rays fleecing the rest of Major League Baseball in trades. It was a deal that was destined to fall into one of two categories: #1 Tampa Bay winning or #2 Pittsburgh losing. Instead, though, it somehow hit *both* checkboxes – the Rays won in astounding fashion and it forced the Pirates back into their rebuild several seasons prematurely. At the trade deadline four seasons ago the two clubs got together for a mega-swap as Tampa Bay agreed to send Chris Archer and his team-friendly deal to the Buccos for a trio of prospects: Austin Meadows, Tyler Glasnow, and former first rounder Shane Baz. All three of those aforementioned minor leaguers the Rays would receive would eventually become consensus Top 10 prospects in baseball. Only adding insult to injury, Tampa Bay signed their former ace to a deal just 2.5 years later. As for Baz, Pittsburgh selected the hard-throwing prep right-hander in the opening round, 12th overall, in 2017. The Concordia Lutheran High School product was mostly underwhelming during his abbreviated debut as he posted a 19-to-14 strikeouts-to-walk ratio in 23.2 innings in the Gulf Coast League. The following season Baz spent time with both organizations' Appalachian League affiliates, averaging 10.1 strikeouts and 5.0 walks per nine innings. Things continued to trend in the right direction in 2019 as he showed improved control (4.1 BB/9) and missed plenty of bats (9.6 K/9) as he posted a 2.99 ERA as a 20-year-old in the Midwest League. Last season, though, Baz transformed from promising arm to bonafide burgeoning ace. In 17 starts between the top two levels of the minors', the Texas-born hurler posted an absurd 113-to-13 strikeout-to-walk ratio in only 78.2 innings of work. He finished the MiLB season with a 2.06 ERA and a 2.76 FIP. Baz also won a Silver Medal during the middle of the summer with Team USA. And he continued to dominate big league hitters during his three-start cameo with the Rays as well, fanning 18 and walking just three to go along with a 2.03 ERA.

Snippet from The 2020 Prospect Digest Handbook: Unharnessed lightning. Or straight filth. Whichever you prefer, though both perfectly describe Baz's high octane repertoire. There's some Mike Clevenger-type potential here, but the control/command may force him towards the #3/#4-type potential. He's not far from being – widely – regarded as a Top 100 prospect. He's poised to spend half of 2020 in Class AA.

Scouting Report: Consider the following:

- Since 2006, only four 22-year-old hurlers posted a strikeout percentage north of 35% in Triple-A with one organization (min. 45 IP): Craig Kimbrel, Matt Moore, Tommy Hanson, and Shane Baz.

Upper-90s heat. Plus slider that he throws with complete confidence and trust, at any point in a plate appearance. Average low-80s curveball. And a rare, upper-80s average change-of-pace. Baz always had the *potential* to become an elite pitching prospect. Last season, though, his control improved by leaps and bounds, allowing him to become one of the best in the game. The fastball / slider combo ranks as one of the best in the minor leagues. His curveball or changeup will need further development as Major League hitters will come accustomed to the two-pitch repertoire. There's legitimate #1 potential, but he needs a more reliable third weapon.

Ceiling: 5.0-win player
Risk: Moderate
MLB ETA: 2022

2. Cole Wilcox, RHP

FB	SL	CH	Command	Overall
60	60	55/60	55/60	60

Born: 07/14/99	Age: 22	Bats: R	Top Comp: N/A
Height: 6-5	Weight: 232	Throws: R	

Season	Team	Age	Level	IP	TBF	K/9	K%	BB/9	BB%	K-BB%	ERA	FIP	xFIP	Pit/Bat
2021	TBR	21	A	44.1	174	10.56	29.89%	1.02	2.87%	27.01%	2.03	2.40	2.84	3.60

Background: The big righty took an atypical path from the SEC to Tampa Bay. Or, maybe, it's a typical move by the Rays. Either way, though, he's one of the better arms in the minor leagues. Drafted by the Padres in the third round two years ago, the Friars signed Wilcox to a *massive* $3.3 million deal – a record for a third round selection, by the way. Roughly six months later San Diego shipped the former Georgia ace to Tampa Bay, along with former top prospect Francisco Mejia, consensus top prospect Luis Patino, and Blake Hunt, in exchange for 2018 AL Cy Young winner Blake Snell. Wilcox, a former swing-man for the Bulldogs during his first season, looked otherworldly during his 2020 campaign as he posted a 32-to-2 strikeout-to-walk ratio in only 23.0 innings of work. Last season, he got off to similar start with the Charleston RiverDogs in Low-A East, averaging 10.6 strikeouts and just 1.0 walk per nine innings through 10 starts. Then he hit the disabled list and eventually underwent Tommy John surgery in mid-September.

Scouting Report: incredibly talented and the potential to have three plus pitches *and* plus command. After watching Wilcox shred through the Low-A competition, it's abundantly clear why the Padres handed out the massive bonus two years ago, as well as why the Rays went after the burgeoning ace in the trade. Mid-90s fastball with fantastic, heavy natural arm-side run. Plus slider. And a disappearing, heavy sinking changeup. Assuming there isn't any ill effects from the TJ surgery, Wilcox could be a legitimate, genuine, bonafide ace. LOVE him.

Ceiling: 4.5-win player
Risk: Moderate to High
MLB ETA: 2023/2024

3. Josh Lowe, OF

Hit	Power	SB	Patience	Glove	Overall
45	55	65	55	55	60

Born: 02/02/98	Age: 24	Bats: L	Top Comp: Steven Souza
Height: 6-4	Weight: 205	Throws: R	

Season	Team	Age	Level	PA	1B	2B	3B	HR	SB	CS	BB%	K%	AVG	OBP	SLG	ISO
2018	TBR	20	A+	455	61	25	3	6	18	6	10.33%	25.71%	0.238	0.322	0.361	0.123
2019	TBR	21	AA	519	68	23	4	18	30	9	11.37%	25.43%	0.252	0.341	0.442	0.190
2021	TBR	23	AAA	470	65	28	2	22	26	0	12.98%	26.17%	0.291	0.381	0.535	0.244

Background: Part one of the more disappointing first rounds in recent draft years. Tampa Bay selected the prep outfielder with the 13th overall pick, sandwiched between Jay Groome and Will Benson, in 2016. Lowe split time between Tampa Bay's Gulf Coast and Appalachian League affiliates during his debut, batting a saber-friendly .249/.374/.405 in 54 games. The 6-foot-4, 205-pound prospect struggled through the next two seasons as he moved through the Midwest and Florida State Leagues. But the front office continued to challenge their former first rounder and sent him to the minors' toughest level, Double-A, in 2019. And he more than held his own. In 121 games with the Montgomery Biscuits, Lowe slugged .252/.341/.442 with 23 doubles, four triples, 18 homeruns, and 30 stolen bases. Last season, as minor league ball returned to action, the Pope High School product put together their finest showing to date: in 111 games with the Durham Bulls, he hit .291/.381/.535 with career highs in doubles (28) and homeruns (22). He also went a perfect 26-for-26 in the stolen base department. Per *Weighted Runs Created Plus*, his overall production topped the league average mark by 42%.

Snippet from The 2020 Prospect Digest Handbook: Lowe helped alleviate my biggest concern: his strikeout rate held firm, despite moving up into the make-it-or-break-it level. There's plenty of more power in the bat as he's just scratching the surface, something along the lines of 25- to 30-homer thump. Solid patience. Above-average glove work. Plus-speed that he utilizes efficiently on the base paths.

Scouting Report: Consider the following:

- Since 2006, only three 23-year-old hitters met the following criteria in Triple-A with one organization (min. 350 PA): 137 to 147 wRC+, a double-digit walk rate, and a strikeout rate north of 23%. Those three hitters: Brett Phillips, Brandon Wood, and Josh Lowe.

Lowe always showed the potential of a saber-tilted hitter with a below-average hit tool. And despite the .291 average last season, the former first rounder isn't expected to reach that level in the big leagues. 45-grade bat. 50-power that may eventually creep into above-average territory. Plus speed that he continues to employ on the base paths with impressive efficiency. Above-average glove, but it's better in a corner outfield spot. Steven Souza offensive potential with a better glove.

Ceiling: 3.5-win player
Risk: Moderate
MLB ETA: Debuted in 2021

4. Curtis Mead, 1B/3B

Hit	Power	SB	Patience	Glove	Overall
60	50	40	50	50	60

Born: 10/26/00	Age: 21	Bats: R	Top Comp: Martin Prado
Height: 6-2	Weight: 171	Throws: R	

Season	Team	Age	Level	PA	1B	2B	3B	HR	SB	CS	BB%	K%	AVG	OBP	SLG	ISO
2019	PHI	18	R	175	27	12	2	4	4	3	7.43%	13.14%	0.285	0.351	0.462	0.177
2021	TBR	20	A	211	39	21	1	7	9	2	7.11%	14.22%	0.356	0.408	0.586	0.230
2021	TBR	20	A+	233	35	15	1	7	2	2	8.15%	16.31%	0.282	0.348	0.466	0.184
2021	TBR	20	AAA	14	3	2	0	1	0	0	0.00%	21.43%	0.429	0.429	0.786	0.357

Background: In a very Rays-like move, the ultra savvy front office sent erratic southpaw Cristopher Sanchez to the Phillies for Australian infielder Curtis Mead in mid-November two years ago. A member of Philadelphia's organization after signing in 2018, Mead first popped up on teams' radars as a spry, smooth swinging 16-year-old torching the Australian Baseball League to the tune of .373/.411/.471. Prior to joining Tampa

Bay's organization Mead batted a rock solid .285/.351/.462 in 44 games in the Gulf Coast League. Last season, the 6-foot-2, 171-pound infielder slugged .321/.378/.533 with 38 doubles, two triple, 15 homeruns, and 11 stolen bases (in 15 total attempts) across stops in Low-A, High-A, and Triple-A. Per *Weighted Runs Created Plus*, his overall production topped the league average mark by a whopping 41%. He continued to perform during his extended look in the Arizona Fall League as well, slugging .313/.360/.530 in 20 games.

Scouting Report: Consider the following:

- Since 2006, only four 20-year-old hitters met the following criteria in High-A with one organization (min. 225 PA): 112 to 122 wRC+, a 7% to 10% walk rate, and a strikeout rate between 15.5% and 17.5%. Those four hitters: Blake DeWitt, Tyler Wade, Alen Hanson, and Curtis Mead.

Despite spending half of his time in two pitcher-friendly ballparks, Mead put together his finest season to date. There's a chance for a plus-hit tool, 20-homerun power, and phenomenal contact rates. Throw in an overall solid approach at the plate and a good glove at the hot corner, and Mead has the makings of a quality, sometimes borderline All-Star big leaguer. In terms of big league ceiling, think: .300/.360/.470.

Ceiling: 3.5-win player
Risk: Moderate
MLB ETA: 2022/2023

5. Taj Bradley, RHP

	FB	SL	CH	Command	Overall
	60	55	50	55	55

Born: 03/20/01	Age: 21	Bats: R	Top Comp: N/A
Height: 6-2	Weight: 190	Throws: R	

Season	Team	Age	Level	IP	TBF	K/9	K%	BB/9	BB%	K-BB%	ERA	FIP	xFIP	Pit/Bat
2018	TBR	17	R	23.0	116	9.39	20.69%	4.70	10.34%	10.34%	5.09	4.61	4.90	1.79
2019	TBR	18	R	51.0	215	10.06	26.51%	3.35	8.84%	17.67%	3.18	3.80	4.26	4.09
2021	TBR	20	A	66.2	249	10.94	32.53%	2.70	8.03%	24.50%	1.76	3.45	3.65	3.81
2021	TBR	20	A+	36.2	148	10.31	28.38%	2.70	7.43%	20.95%	1.96	3.79	4.24	3.70

Background: Stone Mountain, Georgia, based Redan High School has produced several notable players throughout its history, including: Brandon Phillips, a second round pick by the Expos in 1999; Chris Nelson, the ninth overall pick by the Rockies in 2004; former consensus Top 10 prospect Dominic Brown, a 20th round pick by the Phillies in 2006; and, of course, Taj Bradley, a fifth round pick by the Rays in 2018. Handed a hefty $747,500 over-slot bonus as the 150th overall player chosen that year, Bradley showed some promise during his abbreviated debut in the Gulf Coast League as he averaged 9.4 strikeouts and 4.7 walks per nine innings as a 17-year-old. The front office took the cautious approach and bumped the hard-throwing teenager up to the rookie advanced league the following season. And it proved to be the correct approach. He posted a 57-to-19 strikeout-to-walk ratio in 51.0 innings with the Princeton Rays. Last season, though, the organization began to place their foot on the gas pedal as Bradley split time between Charleston and Bowling Green – both stops being equally dominant. He made a total of 23 appearances, only one of which came in relief, between the Low-A and High-A affiliates, striking out 123 and walking just 31 in 103.1 innings of work. He finished the year with a sparkling 1.83 ERA and a 3.57 FIP.

Snippet from The 2020 Prospect Digest Handbook: Unharnessed lightning. Or straight filth. Whichever you prefer, though both perfectly describe Baz's high octane repertoire. There's some Mike Clevenger-type potential here, but the control/command may force him towards the #3/#4-type potential. He's not far from being – widely – regarded as a Top 100 prospect. He's poised to spend half of 2020 in Class AA.

Scouting Report: Consider the following comparison between two 20-year-old hurlers in Low-A:

Season	Name	Team	Level	Age	IP	K/9	BB/9	K%	BB%
2008	Neftali Feliz	TEX	A	20	82.0	11.63	3.07	32.72%	8.64%
2021	Taj Bradley	TBR	A	20	66.2	10.94	2.70	32.53%	8.03%

Bradley attacks hitters with a lively, plus mid-90s fastball, a biting low- to mid-80s slider, and a solid changeup that shows some arm side sink/fade. The former University of South Carolina commit showed significant progress in his ability to command the strike zone in 2021. Solid mid-rotation caliber arm with the floor of a high leverage, fastball / slider combo reliever.

Ceiling: 3.0-win player
Risk: Moderate
MLB ETA: 2023/2024

6. Vidal Brujan, IF/OF

Hit	Power	SB	Patience	Glove	Overall
50	40	60	55	50	50

Born: 02/09/98	Age: 24	Bats: B	Top Comp: Gregor Blanco
Height: 5-10	Weight: 180	Throws: R	

Season	Team	Age	Level	PA	1B	2B	3B	HR	SB	CS	BB%	K%	AVG	OBP	SLG	ISO
2018	TBR	20	A	434	90	18	5	5	43	15	11.06%	12.21%	0.313	0.395	0.427	0.114
2018	TBR	20	A+	114	21	7	2	4	12	4	13.16%	13.16%	0.347	0.434	0.582	0.235
2019	TBR	21	A+	196	39	8	3	1	24	5	8.67%	13.27%	0.290	0.357	0.386	0.097
2019	TBR	21	AA	233	39	9	4	3	24	8	8.58%	15.02%	0.266	0.336	0.391	0.126
2021	TBR	23	AAA	441	58	31	1	12	44	8	11.11%	15.42%	0.262	0.345	0.440	0.177

Background: I've been touting the Rays' farm system since I've been writing about prospects – which, believe it or not, has been nearly a decade at this point. It's (A) the best run organization, (B) evaluates talent better than any organization, and (C) their player development program is among the best as well. Case in point: Vidal Brujan. A light-hitting middle infielder out of San Pedro de Macoris, Dominican Republic, Tampa Bay deftly signed Brujan to a paltry – even by their standards – $15,000 deal in 2014. After two solid showings in the foreign and domestic rookie leagues, Brujan *exploded* as he moved into full season action in 2018 as he slugged .320/.403/.459 with 41 extra-base hits in 122 games with Bowling Green and Charlotte. Brujan's production took a step back the following season as he returned to High-A and eventually moved up to Double-A. Last season the 5-foot-10, 180-pound switch-hitter appeared in 103 games with the Durham Bulls of Triple-A, batting .262/.346/.440 with career highs in doubles (31) and homeruns (12) to go along with 44 stolen bases. Per *Weighted Runs Created Plus*, his overall production topped the league average mark by 11%. He also appeared in 10 big leagues games as well.

Snippet from The 2020 Prospect Digest Handbook: One the big "helium" guys in the minor leagues this offseason, Brujan's shooting up a ton of prospect lists – which is surprising because (A) his production line regressed noticeably from his breakout campaign in 2018 and (B) a lot of the underlying skills weren't as sharp; his walk rate decline, his power shrank a bit.

Scouting Report: Consider the following:

- Since 2006, three 23-year-old hitters posted the following criteria in Triple-A with one organization (min. 350 PA): 105 to 115 wRC+, a 14% to 16% strikeout rate, and a 10% to 12% walk rate. Those three hitters: Desmond Jennings, Gregor Blanco, and Vidal Brujan.
- For those counting at home: Jennings finished his career with a 103 wRC+ total, and Blanco tallied a 93 wRC+.

He's not going to be an impact bat, but that doesn't mean he won't be valuable big league player. Brujan once looked destine to develop a plus hit tool but it's tracking more like a 50, maybe 50-plus, offering. He showed more power last season than at any point in his career, but Triple-A tended to inflate a lot of power output in 2021. But there's a glaring red flag that has been overlooked the past couple of seasons, though: his inability to hit southpaws. In terms of big league ceiling think: .260/.340/.390. There's more risk here than most people what to admit.

Ceiling: 2.5-win player
Risk: Moderate
MLB ETA: Debuted in 2021

7. Seth Johnson, RHP

FB	CB	SL	CH	Command	Overall
65	50	55	45/50	50	50

Born: 09/19/98	Age: 23	Bats: R	Top Comp: N/A
Height: 6-1	Weight: 200	Throws: R	

Season	Team	Age	Level	IP	TBF	K/9	K%	BB/9	BB%	K-BB%	ERA	FIP	xFIP	Pit/Bat
2019	TBR	20	R	10.0	39	6.30	17.95%	1.80	5.13%	12.82%	0.00	2.71	3.55	1.56
2021	TBR	22	A	93.2	397	11.05	28.97%	3.17	8.31%	20.65%	2.88	3.71	3.71	3.96

Background: Armed with a trio of first round picks in 2019, Tampa Bay spread the wealth around as they selected college shortstop Greg Jones with the 22nd overall pick, prep right-hander J.J. Goss 14 picks later, and closed out their opening round with college hurler Seth Johnson. The highest player drafted out of Campbell University, Johnson, who signed a deal worth $1.7 million, turned in an impressive debut showing as he spent time in the Gulf Coast and Appalachian Leagues, posting a 16-to-3 strikeout-to-walk ratio in 17.0 innings of work. Last year, with the return of minor league action, Johnson spent the entirety of his first full professional campaign with the Charleston RiverDogs in Low-A East, averaging 11.0 K/9 and 3.2 BB/9. He compiled a 2.88 ERA, 3.71 FIP, and a 3.71 xFIP.

Snippet from The 2020 Prospect Digest Handbook: Impressive athleticism that readily apparent in controlled mechanics. Because of his limited experience on the mound, as well as his youth, Johnson has significantly more projection as compared to the typical three-year collegiate arm.

Scouting Report: Consider the following:

- Since 2006, only five 22-year-old hurlers met the following criteria in High-A with one organization (min. 75 IP): 28% to 30% strikeout percentage and a 7.5% to 9.5% walk percentage. Those five hurlers: Steven Matz, Alex Meyer, Matt Bower, Adrian Florencio, and – of course – former Campbell ace Seth Johnson.

As noted in the 2020 Handbook, Johnson's fastball not only bumped up several ticks, but it firmly sits in 65-grade territory. He was sitting – comfortably – at 98 mph during one of his final starts of 2021. Average 12-6 curveball. Above-average tightly wound slider. And a firm – almost too firm – changeup that still projects to get to average. It's a bit surprising the club didn't bump the former first rounder up to High-A, particularly as he dominated the competition over his last 43.0 innings (he posted a 0.84 ERA with a 59-to-10 strikeout-to-walk ratio). He's rawer than expected for a former college arm, though he made a late transition to pitching. There's solid backend starting caliber potential. Expect the Rays to start to shove Johnson through the minors in 2022.

Ceiling: 2.5-win player
Risk: Moderate
MLB ETA: 2023/2024

8. Brendan McKay, 1B/LHP

	Hit	Power	SB	Field	Overall
	N/A	N/A	N/A	N/A	40

	FB	CB	CU	CH	Control	Overall
	N/A	N/A	N/A	N/A	N/A	55

Born: 12/18/95	**Age:** 26	**Bats:** L	**Top Comp: N/A**
Height: 6-2	**Weight:** 220	**Throws:** L	

Season	Team	Age	Level	IP	TBF	K/9	K%	BB/9	BB%	K-BB%	ERA	FIP	xFIP	Pit/Bat
2018	TBR	22	A	24.2	85	14.59	47.06%	0.73	2.35%	44.71%	1.09	1.01	0.87	3.84
2018	TBR	22	A+	47.2	192	10.20	28.13%	2.08	5.73%	22.40%	3.21	2.51	2.88	3.89
2019	TBR	23	AA	41.2	156	13.39	39.74%	1.94	5.77%	33.97%	1.30	1.67	1.83	3.83
2019	TBR	23	AAA	32.0	122	11.25	32.79%	2.53	7.38%	25.41%	0.84	2.56	3.41	3.78

Background: There's only one certainty when it comes to prospects (and prospecting): nothing is certain when it comes to prospects. Can't miss prospects miss all the time. Generational talent – as well as production – flame out every year without reaching the full level of their potential. McKay was supposed to be what Shohei Ohtani was in 2021: a dynamic middle-of-the-lineup force and a bonafide upper-rotation-caliber starting pitcher when the Rays selected the former Louisville Cardinal star with the fourth overall pick in 2017. Except McKay hasn't really hit across parts of four minor league seasons. And he missed all of 2020 and 2021 with serious shoulder woes. The 6-foot-2, 220-pound southpaw / first baseman underwent shoulder surgery two years ago, spending the majority of last season rehabbing from the injury. *Then* he went under the knife for thoracic outlet syndrome decompression surgery in late November – though he's expected to be able to resume throwing around the start of Spring Training.

Snippet from The 2020 Prospect Digest Handbook (Pitcher): McKay commands the strike zone as well as any prospect in the minor leagues, showing the consistent ability to throw his entire repertoire for quality strikes. The problem for the big left-hander, though, is the arsenal seemed to regress a bit from the previous year. McKay was throwing – *easily* – in the mid-90s with a sharp, late-tilting curveball. Last season, though, he was 91- to 93-mph during the minor leagues (though he averaged 93 mph in the big leagues) with a slightly inconsistent curveball. The cutter remains a borderline plus-offering and has become a real equalizer. Despite the small dip in velocity, McKay still has the makings of a very good #3-type arm.

Snippet from The 2020 Prospect Digest Handbook (Hitter): The in-game power has – and will always be – a plus weapon. And he continues to show an incredibly patient approach at the plate. But the swing-and-miss issues that first popped up in High Class A two years ago continued their upward trend in 2019. He fanned in slightly more than 30% of his minor league plate appearances. Hitting a baseball at the professional level is the single most difficult skill to master in all of professional sports. And that's not taking into account the fact that McKay's developmental time is split between pitching and hitting. I don't think the K-rates will be an issue long term, but I do wonder how long the Rays – with a loaded lineup – will allow McKay to work on both sides of the ball.

Scouting Report: The success rate for thoracic outlet syndrome surgery is far less successful than, say, Tommy John surgery. McKay was already staring down the path of a starting pitcher due to his lack of success with the bat, but even that future is murkier given the health woes. He showed a bevy of solid secondary offerings, so even if he loses a few ticks on the heater he should be able to survive as a backend starter.

Ceiling: 3.0-win player
Risk: High
MLB ETA: Debuted in 2019

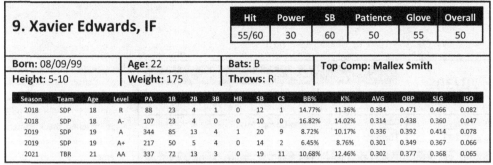

9. Xavier Edwards, IF

	Hit	Power	SB	Patience	Glove	Overall
	55/60	30	60	50	55	50

Born: 08/09/99	Age: 22	Bats: B	Top Comp: Mallex Smith
Height: 5-10	Weight: 175	Throws: R	

Season	Team	Age	Level	PA	1B	2B	3B	HR	SB	CS	BB%	K%	AVG	OBP	SLG	ISO
2018	SDP	18	R	88	23	4	1	0	12	1	14.77%	11.36%	0.384	0.471	0.466	0.082
2018	SDP	18	A-	107	23	4	0	0	10	0	16.82%	14.02%	0.314	0.438	0.360	0.047
2019	SDP	19	A	344	85	13	4	1	20	9	8.72%	10.17%	0.336	0.392	0.414	0.078
2019	SDP	19	A+	217	50	5	4	0	14	2	6.45%	8.76%	0.301	0.349	0.367	0.066
2021	TBR	21	AA	337	72	13	3	0	19	11	10.68%	12.46%	0.302	0.377	0.368	0.065

Background: In one of the few trades that may not bounce the Rays' way. Tampa Bay sent infielder Jake Cronenworth, the eventual runner-up to the Rookie of the Year award, and fading outfielder Tommy Pham to the Padres for Hunter Renfroe, minor league vagabond Esteban Quiroz, and former first rounder Xavier Edwards. The 38th overall pick in 2018, sandwiched between Cadyn Grenier and Jake McCarthy, Edwards has quickly and efficiently moved through the minor leagues during his first few seasons in pro ball. As a spry 18-year-old, the switch-hitting infielder spent the majority of his debut in the Northwest League. He appeared in nearly 50 games in High-A the following year. And he spent the entirety of last season handling the tough competition of Double-A. In 79 games with the Montgomery Biscuits, the 5-foot-10, 175-pound prospect batted .302/.377/.368 with 13 doubles, three triples, and 19 stolen bases. Per *Weighted Runs Created Plus*, his overall production topped the league average mark by 13%.

Snippet from The 2020 Prospect Digest Handbook: Tremendous bat-to-ball skills, solid patience. But the power is almost non-existent at this point; he's slugged just one homerun in his young career. Mallex Smith's 2018 season with the Rays seems like a reasonable ceiling; he batted .296/.367/.406.

Scouting Report: Consider the following:

- Since 2006, three 21-year-old hitters posted the following criteria in Double-A with one organization (min. 300 PA): 108 to 118wRC+, a 10% to 14% strikeout rate, and a 8% to 11% walk rate. Those three hitters: Hank Conger, Henry Alejandro Rodriguez, and Xavier Edwards.

A unicorn of sorts, at least in today's game. Edwards takes a slashing, high contact approach at the plate with above-average speed and a strong glove up the middle. The red flag, though, remains unchanged: he's slugged just one dinger in 247 career minor league games. And his near 50% groundball rate doesn't offer up much in terms of future power projection.

Ceiling: 2.0-win player
Risk: Moderate
MLB ETA: 2022

10. Carson Williams, SS

	Hit	Power	SB	Patience	Glove	Overall
	45/50	45	50	50	50	50

Born: 06/25/03	Age: 19	Bats: R	Top Comp: N/A
Height: 6-2	Weight: 180	Throws: R	

Season	Team	Age	Level	PA	1B	2B	3B	HR	SB	CS	BB%	K%	AVG	OBP	SLG	ISO
2021	TBR	18	CPX	47	6	4	1	0	2	2	12.77%	27.66%	0.282	0.404	0.436	0.154

Background: The highest drafted player to come out of Torrey Pines High School since the Braves drafted – though failed to sign – hard-throwing right-hander Chad Hutchinson with the 26th overall selection all the way back in 1995. A two-way star for the California-based prep school, Williams was scouted as both a pitcher with a blazing fastball, as well as a frontline shortstop prospect. The 6-foot-2, 180-pound athlete's heater reportedly kisses the upper 90s. And he compiled a .495 batting average during his senior season, belting out 10 doubles and 11 homeruns while swiping a whopping 34 bases. On the mound he struck out 28 and walked just three without surrendering a run in 15 innings of work. Tampa Bay drafted the prep star in the opening round, 28th overall, and signed him to a deal worth $2.3475 million, slightly below the recommended slot of $2.4939 million. Williams appeared in 11 games with the Rays' Florida Complex League affiliate, hitting a solid .282/.404/.436 with four doubles, one triple, and a pair of stolen bases.

Scouting Report: Per the usual, here's my draft write-up on the talented shortstop:

"Fundamentally solid on the defensive side of the ball with plenty of arm strength – of course – to make all the difficult throws. Williams may not be an elite shortstop, but he should have no issues sticking at the position. Offensively speaking, he's used to swinging a wood bat and looks to take regular BP with one as well as used it during the 2020 summer/fall. Nice easy swing with above-average, not elite, bat speed. He needs to get stronger to take advantage of the natural loft in his swing. He won't be a blue-chip prospect but has the chance to be a solid overall ballplayer."

Ceiling: 2.0-win player
Risk: Moderate
MLB ETA: 2025

11. Cooper Kinney, 2B/3B

Hit	Power	SB	Patience	Glove	Overall
50	50/55	45	50	50	50

Born: 01/27/03	Age: 19	Bats: L	Top Comp: N/A
Height: 6-3	Weight: 200	Throws: R	

Season	Team	Age	Level	PA	1B	2B	3B	HR	SB	CS	BB%	K%	AVG	OBP	SLG	ISO
2021	TBR	18	CPX	47	8	1	1	0	2	0	21.28%	19.15%	0.286	0.468	0.371	0.086

Background: After snagging prep shortstop Carson Williams with their first Day 1 selection, the Tampa Bay Rays reached back down into the prep ranks and selected – wait for it – shortstop Cooper Kinney. A product of Baylor School in Chattanooga, Tennessee, Kinney agreed to a deal with the organization for $2.145 million, $3,100 below the recommended slot bonus. Kinney, who was coached by his father Mike, earned Tennessee's Mr. Baseball Award, as well as garnering the state's Gatorade Player of the Year. He put together a scorching .480/.539/.990 during his senior campaign, belting out 19 doubles and 10 homeruns. The lefty-swinging second / third baseman appeared in 11 games with the organization's Florida Complex League affiliate, hitting .286/.468/.371 with one doubles, one triple, and two stolen bases. He also compiled a 9-to-10 strikeout-to-walk ratio, as well.

Scouting Report: Per the usual, here's my draft write-up:

> *"Per the Rays' Scouting Director, Rob Metzler, the lefty-swinging infielder will work at second and third bases in the professional ranks, not shortstop. Defensively, Kinney shows soft hands and enough twitch to handle the keystone. At the plate, the young prospect does not get cheated, showcasing phenomenal bat speed with an upper cut swing. Quick hands. Smooth swing. The power has a chance to be above-average."*

Ceiling: 2.0-win player
Risk: Moderate
MLB ETA: 2025

12. Carlos Colmenarez, SS

Hit	Power	SB	Patience	Glove	Overall
30/50	30/50	50	50	50	50

Born: 11/15/03	Age: 18	Bats: L	Top Comp: N/A
Height: 5-10	Weight: 170	Throws: R	

Season	Team	Age	Level	PA	1B	2B	3B	HR	SB	CS	BB%	K%	AVG	OBP	SLG	ISO
2021	TBR	17	DSL	114	21	2	1	0	7	6	7.02%	26.32%	0.247	0.319	0.289	0.041

Background: Armed with a ton of bonus pool money to spend in the 2020-21 International Free Agent signing period – $6,431,000, to be exact – Tampa Bay went out and signed a couple high profile prospects: Venezuelan middle-infielder Carlos Colmenarez and Dominican outfielder Jhonny Piron. Ranked as the fourth best prospect available by MLB Pipeline, the Rays handed Colmenarez, a native of San Felipe, a massive $3 million bonus in mid-January 2021. The lefty-swinging shortstop made his anticipated professional debut with the club's Dominican Summer League affiliate a few months later, batting a disappointing .247/.319/.289 with just two doubles and a triple in 26 games. Per *Weighted Runs Created Plus*, his overall production was a whopping 21% below the average.

Scouting Report: Really good looking swing with a plenty of bat speed and a natural loft in his swing that projects for average or better power. A broken hamate injury – which has a tendency to sap a hitter's power – pushed his debut in the foreign rookie league back to late August. The delayed start coupled with the injury render his pitiful production meaningless at this point. Defensively, he's smooth with a touch of flash and should have no issues sticking at the position. It wouldn't be shocking to see the front office push the now-18-year-old up to the Complex Leagues for the 2022 season.

Ceiling: 2.0-win player
Risk: Moderate
MLB ETA: Debuted in 2021

13. J.J. Goss, RHP

	FB	SL	CH	Command	Overall
	N/A	N/A	N/A	N/A	50

Born: 12/25/00	Age: 21	Bats: R	Top Comp: N/A
Height: 6-3	Weight: 185	Throws: R	

Season	Team	Age	Level	IP	TBF	K/9	K%	BB/9	BB%	K-BB%	ERA	FIP	xFIP	Pit/Bat
2019	TBR	18	R	17.0	71	8.47	22.54%	1.06	2.82%	19.72%	5.82	2.92	2.77	1.69
2021	TBR	20	CPX	10.1	44	10.45	27.27%	0.00	0.00%	27.27%	6.10	1.82	3.41	1.61

Background: Cypress Ranch High School had an incredible pitching staff during the 2018 season, featuring Ty Madden, Matthew Thompson, and J.J. Goss. Madden, who was originally drafted by the Royals in the 34th round that season, headed to the University of Texas and went to the Tigers at the back of the first round last July. Thompson was drafted by the White Sox in 2019, 45th overall, and signed for a hefty $2.1 million. And, of course, Goss was drafted by the Rays with the 36th pick in 2019 as well, signing for $2,042,900. The 6-foot-3, 185-pound right-hander made nine brief appearances in the Gulf Coast League during his debut, posting a 16-to-2 strikeout-to-walk ratio in 17.0 innings of work. After minor league life returned to normal in 2021, Goss dealt with a shoulder impingement and missed the majority of the year. He made four brief appearances in the Complex League at the end of the year, striking out 12 and walking seven in 10.1 innings of work. He compiled a 6.10 ERA, though four of his seven earned runs were coughed up in one game.

Snippet from The 2020 Prospect Digest Handbook: Tall and thin, which suggests there may be a little more in the tank once he begins to fill out. Goss attacks hitters with a low-90s fastball, peaking in the 94-mph range which projects as a plus-offering at full maturity. He'll also show a mid-80s change that shows the makings of a potential above-average offering. But it's his late-tilting slider that separates Goss from the rest of his talented peers. Also of note: Goss showed a decent 12-6 curveball prior to his senior season, though he seems to have shelved it in favor of throwing the slider exclusively.

Scouting Report: Shoulder issues can be tricky, just ask Nick Bitsko, but hopefully it's in the past for Goss. I'm looking forward to scouting him in 2022.

Ceiling: 1.5- to 2.0-win player
Risk: Moderate to High
MLB ETA: 2024

14. Kyle Manzardo, 1B

	Hit	Power	SB	Patience	Glove	Overall
	55	45/50	30	50	50	45

Born: 07/18/00	Age: 21	Bats: L	Top Comp: N/A
Height: 6-1	Weight: 205	Throws: R	

Season	Team	Age	Level	PA	1B	2B	3B	HR	SB	CS	BB%	K%	AVG	OBP	SLG	ISO
2021	TBR	20	CPX	50	8	5	0	2	0	0	8.00%	12.00%	0.349	0.440	0.605	0.256

Background: Washington State University has churned out a surprising number of big league talent, including: borderline Hall of Famers John Olerud and Ron Cey, as well as Aaron Sele, Scott Hatteberg, big lefty – and former BA player – Mark Hendrickson, Adam Conley, and – of course – Kyle Manzardo. A lefty swinging first baseman, Manzardo was a consistent, albeit mediocre, contributor for the Pac12 squad during his freshman season in 2019: in 52 games with the Cougars he hit .272/.335/.364 with 11 doubles and a pair of dingers. After a successful jaunt through the West Coast League, Manzardo returned with a vengeance during his abbreviated sophomore campaign, slugging .435/.500/.694 with 10 extra-base hits in only 16 games. And the 6-foot-1, 205-pound undersized first baseman carried that momentum into an explosive junior season. In 47 games, he batted .365/.437/.640 with career highs in doubles (19) and homeruns (11) while posting a 29-to-25 strikeout-to-walk ratio. Tampa Bay drafted him in the second round, 63rd overall, and signed him to a below slot deal worth $747,000, saving the organization roughly $300,000. He appeared in 13 Complex League games, batting .349/.440/.605 with five doubles and two homers.

Scouting Report: Per the usual, here's my draft write-up:

"Consider the following:

- Between 2012 and 2020, only three Pac12 hitters met the following criteria in a season (min. 200 PA): .350/.425/.625 with a sub-15% strikeout rate and a walk rate between 10% and 17%. Those three hitters: Adley Rutschman, Andrew Vaughn, and Cameron Cannon. Two top picks (Rutschman and Vaughn) and Cannon, a second round pick by the Red Sox in 2019 who blitzed through High Class A in the first half of 2021.

In a lot of ways Manzardo's a very typical Rays-type-pick. He's not overly big, but performed well. He's maxed out physically, but does a little bit of everything. He'll flash some above-average power, mix in a handful of walks, and make consistent contact. He's not going to be a star, but he has a shot at being a lot end starting option at first base."

Ceiling: 1.5-win player
Risk: Moderate
MLB ETA: 2023

15. Tommy Romero, RHP

	FB	SL	CH	Command	Overall
	50	55	50	55	45

Born: 07/08/97	Age: 24	Bats: R	Top Comp: Mike Fiers
Height: 6-2	Weight: 225	Throws: R	

Season	Team	Age	Level	IP	TBF	K/9	K%	BB/9	BB%	K-BB%	ERA	FIP	xFIP	Pit/Bat
2018	SEA	20	A	44.0	180	11.05	30.00%	3.07	8.33%	21.67%	2.45	2.48	2.95	3.94
2018	TBR	20	A	84.0	343	8.25	22.45%	3.86	10.50%	11.95%	3.21	4.55	4.09	3.93
2019	TBR	21	A+	119.1	463	7.77	22.25%	2.72	7.78%	14.47%	1.89	3.00	3.58	4.13
2021	TBR	23	AA	48.0	191	14.06	39.27%	1.88	5.24%	34.03%	1.88	1.78	2.14	4.04
2021	TBR	23	AAA	62.1	244	10.11	28.69%	3.03	8.61%	20.08%	3.18	3.68	4.16	3.95

Background: Originally drafted by the Mariners in the 15th round out of Eastern Florida State College in 2017. The Rays acquired the right-hander, along with Andrew Moore, in exchange for veterans Alex Colome and Denard Span in late-May four years ago. Last season, Romero continued to mow down every minor league hitter standing in his way. Splitting time between Double-A and Triple-A, the 6-foot-2, 225-pound righty struck out 145, walked just 31, and tallied a 2.61 ERA in 110.1 innings of work. He finished the year with an aggregate 2.85 FIP. For his minor league career, he's averaging 9.5 strikeouts and just 3.0 walks per nine innings.

Scouting Report: Consider the following:

- Since 2006, only three 23-year-old hurlers posted a 27.5% to 29.5% strikeout percentage with a 7.5% to 9.5% walk percentage in Triple-A with one organization (min. 60 IP): Mitch Keller, Lucas Sims, and Tommy Romero.

One of the more underrated hurlers in the minor leagues. Not in terms of "stuff", but in terms of production vs. level of competition. Romero sports a three-pitch mix: a low-90s fastball, a hard slider (which is often referred to incorrectly as a curveball), and a mid-80s changeup. Velocity-wise, Romero's fastball is in average territory, but it generates a lot of swings-and-misses at the top of the zone, where he lives, and he commands it exceptionally well. The slider is an above-average weapon. There's a solid middle relief floor with the ceiling as a #4/#5.

Ceiling: 1.0- to 1.5-win player
Risk: Moderate
MLB ETA: 2022

16. Greg Jones, SS

	Hit	Power	SB	Patience	Glove	Overall
	50	50	60	50	55	45

Born: 03/07/98	Age: 24	Bats: B	Top Comp: N/A
Height: 6-2	Weight: 175	Throws: R	

Season	Team	Age	Level	PA	1B	2B	3B	HR	SB	CS	BB%	K%	AVG	OBP	SLG	ISO
2019	TBR	21	A-	218	46	13	4	1	19	8	10.09%	25.69%	0.335	0.413	0.461	0.126
2021	TBR	23	A+	257	41	7	3	13	27	2	11.28%	29.18%	0.291	0.389	0.527	0.236
2021	TBR	23	AA	60	7	1	1	1	7	0	6.67%	35.00%	0.185	0.267	0.296	0.111

Background: One of the bigger helium guys in the 2019 draft class. Jones, who was coming off of a mediocre sophomore season in which he batted .278/.412/.370, put together a scorching .341/.491/.543 in 63 games with UNC Wilmington. Tampa Bay selected the 6-foot-2, 175-pound shortstop in the opening round three years ago, signing him to a deal worth $3,024,500. The North Carolina native continued to rake during his debut in the New York-Penn League as well, batting .335/.413/.461 in 48 games with the Hudson Valley Renegades. Last season, after losing the 2020 year due to the COVID-imposed shutdown, Jones opened his sophomore campaign up with 56 games in High-A. And he continued to rake, slugging .291/.389/.527 with seven doubles, three triples, 13 homeruns, and 27 stolen bases. Tampa Bay bumped him up to Double-A for the remaining few weeks of the year – though he looked quite overmatched (.185/.267/.296).

Snippet from The 2020 Prospect Digest Handbook: The hit tool was better than I suspected, though the power remains firmly in the below-average category – especially for a hitter that puts the ball on the ground more than 50% of the time. I'm still concerned a bit by the strikeout rate – which was an issue during his freshman campaign. He whiffed in more than a quarter of his plate appearances during his debut. And that's as a pedigreed, early draft pick squaring off against an age-appropriate level of competition. In terms of ceiling, I would put it at .280/.330/.400 with 30 doubles, 35 stolen bases, and above-average defense.

Scouting Report: The production in High-A was phenomenal – at least at first glance. He walked, flashed 20-homerun power, ran well and at will, and played a solid shortstop. The problem, of course, is something that I highlighted in *The 2020 Prospect Digest Handbook*: his concerning swing-and-miss issues. He fanned in 29.2% of his plate appearances in High-A and punched out an extraordinary 21 times in 60 trips to the plate in Double-A. The bottom line: Jones is entering his age-24 season with a massive red flag. If something doesn't turn around in 2022, he's staring at future utility infielder-dom.

Ceiling: 1.0- to 1.5-win player
Risk: Moderate
MLB ETA: 2023

17. Ian Seymour, LHP

	FB	CB	SL	CH	Command	Overall
	50	55	50	55	45	45

Born: 12/13/98	Age: 23	Bats: L	Top Comp: Ryan Yarbrough
Height: 6-0	Weight: 210	Throws: L	

Season	Team	Age	Level	IP	TBF	K/9	K%	BB/9	BB%	K-BB%	ERA	FIP	xFIP	Pit/Bat
2021	TBR	22	A	35.1	135	15.03	43.70%	3.31	9.63%	34.07%	2.55	3.01	3.02	4.26
2021	TBR	22	A+	10.0	42	17.10	45.24%	1.80	4.76%	40.48%	1.80	3.07	3.06	3.64
2021	TBR	22	AAA	10.0	37	8.10	24.32%	3.60	10.81%	13.51%	0.00	2.76	5.25	4.16

Background: Virginia Polytechnic Institute and State University – also known Virginia Tech – has been no stranger to the professional game, having 88 players selected during the draft process and sending 17 of those to the big leagues. But it was 18 years before a player (Joe Saunders, 12th overall, 2002) got selected earlier than Ian Seymour, who heard his named called by the Rays with the 57th overall pick. A 6-foot, 210-pound left-hander, Seymour quietly put together a dominant career with the Hokies, averaging 10.8 strikeouts and 3.3 walks per nine innings. Last season, his first taste of professional action, the southpaw shredded Low-A in 10 appearances, looked unhittable in two starts with Bowling Green in High-A East, and in a bit of a serendipitous turn of events, capped off his breakout season with a pair of starts in Triple-A. His late season promotion up to the minors' final level only occurred last minute to cover for Shane Baz, who was dealing with food poisoning. In total, Seymour tossed 55.1 innings with 87 punch outs, 19 free passes, and an aggregate 1.95 ERA and a 2.98 FIP.

Scouting Report: In a lot of ways Seymour is the prototypical lefty with a little bit of funk in his windup, almost quasi-Madison Bumgarner. Solid repertoire, though it's a bit unremarkable. He features a low-90s fastball, an above-average 10-4 breaking curveball, a horizontally darting slider, and a fantastic, 55-grade changeup, easily his best overall offering. Seymour shows complete confidence in his changeup, throwing it ahead in the count, behind in the count, to lefties, to righties. He commands it better than any of his other pitches.

Ceiling: 1.0- to 1.5-win player
Risk: Moderate
MLB ETA: 2022

18. Ryan Spikes, IF

	Hit	Power	SB	Patience	Glove	Overall
	35/45	40	50	50	50	40

Born: 03/13/03	Age: 19	Bats: R	Top Comp: N/A
Height: 5-9	Weight: 185	Throws: R	

Season	Team	Age	Level	PA	1B	2B	3B	HR	SB	CS	BB%	K%	AVG	OBP	SLG	ISO
2021	TBR	18	CPX	47	6	3	0	1	4	1	12.77%	27.66%	0.250	0.362	0.400	0.150

Background: Lilburn, Georgia, based Parkview High School has churned out an impressive amount of talent throughout the years, including big leaguers Jeff Francoeur, who once graced the cover of *Sports Illustrated* with the title *The Natural*, and A's slugging first baseman Matt Olson. The prep school has also produced a bevy of big bonus babies as well, like: Brandon Jacobs ($750,000), Jarrett Freeland ($324,500), Josh Hart ($1,450,000), and Ryne Inman ($100,000). The high school's latest top prospect: Ryan Spikes, the 100th player chosen last July. Signed to a deal worth a smidgeon over $1,000,000, Tampa Bay convinced him to bypass his commitment to the University of Tennessee and join the perennial AL East powerhouse. The 5-9, 185-pound infielder batted a solid .250/.362/.400 in 11 games with the club's Florida Complex League affiliate.

Scouting Report: Like all premium infielders in the prep ranks, Spikes spent his high school career as a slick fielding shortstop, though his small 5-foot-9, 180-pound frame almost assures a permanent move to the keystone. Good arm, solid glove. Spikes has a simple swing with average bat speed and 40-grade power – though he was noticeably stronger in 2021 than the previous year. Not only did he battle some swing-and-miss issues as during his abbreviated debut, but Spikes looked like he may struggle against quality breaking balls as well.

Ceiling: 1.0-win player
Risk: Moderate
MLB ETA: 2025

19. Jonathan Aranda, IF/OF

	Hit	Power	SB	Patience	Glove	Overall
	55	50	35	50	50	40

Born: 05/23/98	Age: 24	Bats: L	Top Comp: N/A
Height: 5-10	Weight: 173	Throws: R	

Season	Team	Age	Level	PA	1B	2B	3B	HR	SB	CS	BB%	K%	AVG	OBP	SLG	ISO
2018	TBR	20	R	144	23	8	4	1	0	1	8.33%	12.50%	0.286	0.357	0.437	0.151
2018	TBR	20	A-	32	6	0	0	0	0	0	6.25%	6.25%	0.200	0.250	0.200	0.000
2019	TBR	21	A	246	40	13	2	3	1	1	12.20%	17.48%	0.275	0.359	0.398	0.123
2019	TBR	21	A+	19	4	0	0	0	0	0	10.53%	5.26%	0.235	0.316	0.235	0.000
2021	TBR	23	A+	89	19	3	0	4	1	0	10.11%	14.61%	0.351	0.449	0.554	0.203
2021	TBR	23	AA	322	55	19	5	10	4	2	10.25%	19.57%	0.325	0.410	0.540	0.215

Background: Coming out of Tijuana, Mexico, the Rays signed the smallish unheralded infielder during the 2015-16 signing period. And for the majority of his career, Aranda – and his prospect status – remained largely unchanged: he was unremarkable. From 2016 through 2019, his best season OPS total was just .742. Last year, though, something seemed to click for the lefty-swinging infielder. He torched the High-A East competition to the tune of .351/.449/.554 in 21 games and barely slowed as he spent the remaining 79 games with the Montgomery Biscuits. In total, the 5-foot-10, 173-pound infielder slugged .331/.419/.543 with career highs in doubles (22), triples (5), and homeruns (14). Per *Weighted Runs Created Plus*, his overall production topped the league average mark by 64%.

Scouting Report: Consider the following:

- Since 2006, only four 23-year-old hitters met the following criteria in Double-A with one organization (min. 300 PA): at least a 160 wRC+ with a double-digit walk rate and a strikeout rate between 18% and 22%. Those four hitters: Paul Goldschmidt, Chase Headley, Vince Belnome, and little Jonathan Aranda.
- For those counting at home: Goldschmidt's closing in on a potential Hall of Fame career and owns a 141 wRC+ total in the big leagues. Headley finished his 12-year career with a 107 wRC+ mark. And Belnome eventually made his way into the Rays' organization and appeared in four games with the club in 2014.

Aranda has always been high a contact, moderate walk rate hitter throughout his career. And in that regard, nothing for him changed during his massive 2021 breakout season. The big differentiator, though, was his non-existent power transforming into a solid-average tool. The Rays have moved Aranda around the diamond throughout his career – he appeared at every position on the infield sans catcher and pitcher, as well as left field – so he seems destined to be a super-utility guy.

Ceiling: 1.0-win player
Risk: Moderate
MLB ETA: 2022

20. Sandy Gaston, RHP

	FB	CB	CH	Command	Overall
	70	60	50	30	40

Born: 12/16/01	Age: 20	Bats: R	Top Comp: N/A
Height: 6-3	Weight: 200	Throws: R	

Season	Team	Age	Level	IP	TBF	K/9	K%	BB/9	BB%	K-BB%	ERA	FIP	xFIP	Pit/Bat
2019	TBR	17	R	27.0	129	10.33	24.03%	9.00	20.93%	3.10%	6.00	4.91	4.94	2.20
2021	TBR	19	A	30.1	135	11.27	28.15%	6.53	16.30%	11.85%	3.86	5.00	5.21	4.10
2021	TBR	19	CPX	19.2	76	14.64	42.11%	5.95	17.11%	25.00%	3.20	3.69	3.68	2.47

Background: Ranked by MLB Pipeline as the 16th overall prospect on the international market in 2018. The Cuban import signed with the Rays at the ripe ol' age of 16. Since then, the flame-throwing right-hander has had a rollercoaster pro career. Gaston would make his stateside debut with the organization's Gulf Coast League affiliate in 2019, throwing 27.0 innings while racking up plenty of strikeouts (31) and a bevy of walks (27) to go along with a 6.00 ERA. Last season, after missing the 2020 year due to the COVID-imposed shutdown, the 6-foot-3, 200-pound hurler split time between the Florida Complex League and Low-A East. He totaled 50.0 innings of work, striking out 70 and walking 35 to go along with an aggregate 3.60 ERA.

Scouting Report: One of the more potent fastballs in all of the minor leagues. Gaston's heater sits in the 96- to 98-mph range with explosive life. He'll mix in a plus, wickedly snapping low-80s curveball, as well as a low-90s changeup. The problem, of course, is that Gaston makes early-movie Luke LaLoosh look like Greg Maddux. The control – forget about command – is so poor it's like LaLoosh and Rick Vaughn's early-movie control divided in half. It'll be the baseball miracle of baseball miracle's if Tampa Bay can coax some additional strikes out of Gaston.

Ceiling: 1.0-win player
Risk: Moderate
MLB ETA: 2024

Texas Rangers

Top Prospects

1. Jack Leiter, RHP

	FB	CB	SL	CH	Command	Overall
	60	60	55	55	50/55	70

Born: 04/21/00	Age: 22	Bats: R	Top Comp: Max Scherzer
Height: 6-1	Weight: 205	Throws: R	

Background: A surefire first round pick coming out of Delbarton School if not for his rock-solid commitment to Vanderbilt. With bloodlines that run deep – his father, of course, is two-time All-Star left-hander Al Leiter, and both his uncle and cousin player in the big leagues as well – the younger Leiter got off to a torrid start to his freshman campaign with Commodores in 2020: in four appearances, three of which were starts, the fireballing right-hander posted a 22-to-8 strikeout-to-walk ratio in 15.2 innings of work for the SEC powerhouse. And that – *truly* – proved to be a harbinger of things to come. In his first start of the 2021 season, the 6-foot-1, 205-pound silky smooth hurler fanned eight and surrendered just one hit against Wright State near the end of February. And that string of dominance continued as he held opponents to just one earned run or fewer in each of his next seven starts – including games against Oklahoma State; a 16-strikeout, one walk no-hit affair against South Carolina, Missouri, LSU, and Georgia. Tennessee finally got to the burgeoning ace during his ninth start, plating three runs against him in 6.1 innings of work. Leiter was a bit shaky over his next two starts against Mississippi St. and Florida before righting the ship for four dominant starts against Ole Miss, Kentucky, Ole Miss (again), and Georgia Tech. Leiter ended the year with 18 starts, 110.0 innings of work, a whopping 179 strikeouts, 45 free passes, and a tidy 2.13 ERA. Texas drafted the collegiate ace with the second overall pick last July, signing him to a deal worth $7,922,000.

Scouting Report: Per the usual, here's my pre-draft analysis on Leiter:

> "First things first, let's dive into the numbers. Consider the following:

> - Between 2011 and 2020, here's the list of SEC pitchers to average at 12 strikeouts per nine innings (min. 75 IP): A.J. Puk, Casey Mize, Asa Lacy, Ethan Small, Zach Thompson, and Mason Hickman, who was the lone player chosen beyond the first round.

> Leiter's current strikeout rate, 14.8 K/9, is the best among the group. Now let's expand to all Division I arms. Consider the following:

> - Between 2011 and 2020, here's the list of Division I hurlers to average at least 14 strikeouts every nine innings with a sub-4.0 walk rate (75IP): Drey Jameson, Ethan Small, and Noah Song.

> Again, Leiter production belongs in the group. Prior to the 2019, here's a snippet of the scouting report I put together for the young righty:

> > "Polished and poised well beyond his years – something to be expected for a ballplayer coming from a lineage of big leaguers. Leiter attacks hitters with a low-90s fastball that he generally commands well. But it's his pair of secondary offerings – a hellacious 12-6, knee-buckling curveball and an above-average slider – that easily separates him from his peers. The curveball, a mid- to upper-70s offering, is one of the better breaking balls in the entire draft class. He'll also mix in a fringy low-80s changeup that shows average potential."

> So let's update that a bit, shall we?

> Leiter's heater has moved from an above-average to plus offering, going from the low 90s to sitting in the mid-90s and touching triple digits on occasion. His curveball is still one hellacious knee-buckler, the slider is a firm above-average offering. And his changeup has bumped up into the 55-grade territory. Perhaps the most impressive part about Leiter: I watched his early season dominant no-hitter, and he was essentially just using his fastball. He has a chance to be a dominant ace, along the lines of a Max Scherzer, if the command ticks up. I would expect him to be in the big leagues by end of 2022 for a September cup of coffee."

Ceiling: 6.0-win player
Risk: Moderate
MLB ETA: 2023

2. Josh Jung, 3B

Hit	Power	SB	Patience	Glove	Overall
50	55	40	50	55	60

Born: 02/12/98	Age: 24	Bats: R	Top Comp: Manny Machado
Height: 6-2	Weight: 214	Throws: R	

Season	Team	Age	Level	PA	1B	2B	3B	HR	SB	CS	BB%	K%	AVG	OBP	SLG	ISO
2019	TEX	21	R	19	7	1	1	1	0	0	10.53%	15.79%	0.588	0.632	0.941	0.353
2019	TEX	21	A	179	31	13	0	1	4	1	8.94%	16.20%	0.287	0.363	0.389	0.102
2021	TEX	23	AA	186	33	8	1	10	2	2	6.99%	22.58%	0.308	0.366	0.544	0.237
2021	TEX	23	AAA	156	24	14	0	9	0	0	11.54%	21.79%	0.348	0.436	0.652	0.304

Background: There's going to be quite the rivalry in the Jung household come midseason 2022. Josh's younger brother, Jace, who also attends Texas Tech, might usurp his lofty draft status. Josh was the eighth overall player chosen in 2019. And Jace is a potential #1 overall pick after his dominating 2021 season. As for his part, the elder Jung is living up to – and perhaps even exceeding – his draft expectations. Splitting time between Frisco and Round Rock last year, the 6-foot-2, 214-pound third baseman slugged a scorching .326/.398/.592 with 22 doubles, one triple, and 19 homeruns. He also stole a pair of bags for good measure as well. His overall production for the year topped the league average mark by a whopping 52%, per *Weighted Runs Created Plus*, which was tied for the 21st best mark among all hitters with at least 300 PAs.

Snippet from The 2020 Prospect Digest Handbook: At his peak, he looks like a .280/.340/.480 type hitter [of big league hitter].

Scouting Report: Jung got off to a late start to the year – he didn't play his first game until June – so his time at each level was exceptionally long: he appeared in just 43 games in Double-A and 35 games in Triple-A. But the production, though, remained among the best in professional baseball. Solid patience at the plate. Above-average thump combined with strong contact skills. However, per FanGraphs data, Jung's average exit velocity was pedestrian 87 mph. The .280/.340/480-type ceiling is still tracking.

Ceiling: 4.0-win player
Risk: Moderate
MLB ETA: 2022

3. Cole Winn, RHP

FB	CB	SL	CH	Command	Overall
60	55	55	60	50	60

Born: 11/25/99	Age: 22	Bats: R	Top Comp: Noah Syndergaard
Height: 6-2	Weight: 190	Throws: R	

Season	Team	Age	Level	IP	TBF	K/9	K%	BB/9	BB%	K-BB%	ERA	FIP	xFIP	Pit/Bat
2019	TEX	19	A	68.2	298	8.52	21.81%	5.11	13.09%	8.72%	4.46	4.38	4.35	4.09
2021	TEX	21	AA	78.0	296	11.19	32.77%	3.00	8.78%	23.99%	2.31	3.15	3.90	4.03

Background: Sandwiched in between a pair of more recognizable pitchers in the middle of the first round four years later. Winn, the 15th overall pick, was taken one pick after Logan Gilbert and before Matthew Liberatore. Despite a lesser known name among casual fans, Winn's quietly establishing himself as one of the best pitching prospects in baseball. After holding his own as a 19-year-old in Low-A in 2019, the 6-foot-2, 190-pound right-hander ripped through the minors' toughest challenge, Double-A, for 19 starts before finishing off his dominant season with a pair of games in AAA. In total, he logged 86.0 innings, striking out 107 and walking just 31.

Snippet from The 2020 Prospect Digest Handbook: Given the emphasis on his changeup, as well as his 55-grade control/command, I'd expect Crouse's strikeout percentage to leap several degrees in 2020. Again, there's some potential #3 caliber status here.

Scouting Report: Consider the following:

- Since 2006, here's the list of 21-year-old Double-A arms to post a strikeout percentage of at least 30% with a walk percentage less than 9% in a season (min. 75 IP): Grayson Rodriguez and Cole Winn. That's it.
- Let's take it one step further: here's the list of 21-year-old Double-A pitchers to strikeout out at least 32% of the hitters they faced in season (min. 75 IP): Grayson Rodriguez and Cole Winn.

Plus fastball and changeup combination – which would be enough to guarantee him a spot at the back of a rotation – but Winn mixes in two above-average breaking balls as well. His power slider shows late downward tilt that he locates low-and-away from right-handers exceptionally well. And he'll flash a 55-grade 12-6 yacker of a curveball too. He's still refining his command, but it's taken several leaps forward. He's going to be a #3-type guy with some potential to uptick if the command continues to improve.

Ceiling: 4.0-win player
Risk: Moderate
MLB ETA: 2022

4. Luisangel Acuna, 2B/SS

	Hit	Power	SB	Patience	Glove	Overall
	50/55	50	60	50	50	50

Born: 03/12/02	**Age:** 20	**Bats:** R	**Top Comp:** Jonathan Villar
Height: 5-10	**Weight:** 181	**Throws:** R	

Season	Team	Age	Level	PA	1B	2B	3B	HR	SB	CS	BB%	K%	AVG	OBP	SLG	ISO
2019	TEX	17	R	240	53	11	3	2	17	6	14.17%	10.83%	0.342	0.438	0.455	0.114
2021	TEX	19	A	473	80	15	3	12	44	11	10.36%	23.26%	0.266	0.345	0.404	0.138

Background: Ron Acuna was never a serious big league prospect. Sure, he finished with a nice enough, batting average-inflated MiLB slash line (.282/.330/.364), but he never really flashed enough loud tools to really turn heads. Ron's son, Ronald, however, is a different story. And Ron's younger son, Luisangel – who is sometimes known as Jose – is tracking as a better prospect than his old man too. The Rangers signed the younger Acuna for a rather sizeable deal, $425,000, during the 2018 signing period and sent him to the Dominican Summer League the following season. And he ripped through the league's pitching like a shark's fin in water: in 51 games, the 5-foot-10, 181-pound middle infielder slugged .342/.438/.455 with 11 doubles, three triples, and a pair of dingers. Last season, the front office aggressively challenged the then-19-year-old by pushing him straight into Low-A. And the results were…promising. In 111 games with the Down East Wood Ducks, Acuna the Younger batted .266/.345/.404 with 15 doubles, three triples, 12 homeruns, and 44 stolen bases (in 55 attempts). His overall production, per *Weighted Runs Created Plus*, topped the league average mark by 5%.

Scouting Report: Consider the following:

- Since 2011, here's the list of 19-year-old hitters to post a wRC+ total between 100 and 110 with a walk rate between 9% and 12% and a strikeout rate between 22% and 24% (min. 400 PA): Joe Benson, Daryl Jones, and Luisangel Acuna.

While the production comparisons don't offer up a ton a ton of future hope – Benson was once a Top 100 prospect and Jones appeared in the 2009 Futures Games – Acuna's ceiling is considerably higher. After starting the year off on a sour note (he hit a paltry .165/.280/.291 over his first 22 games), Acuna slugged a healthy .281/.354/.406 over his remaining 94 contests. There's the potential for an above-average hit tool, plus speed, and 15- to 20-homerun pop from a middle infield position.

Ceiling: 2.5-win player
Risk: Moderate to High
MLB ETA: 2024

5. Justin Foscue, 2B

	Hit	Power	SB	Patience	Glove	Overall
	50	50	40	45	45/50	50

Born: 03/02/99	**Age:** 23	**Bats:** R	**Top Comp:** Brandon Lowe/Nick Solak
Height: 6-0	**Weight:** 205	**Throws:** R	

Season	Team	Age	Level	PA	1B	2B	3B	HR	SB	CS	BB%	K%	AVG	OBP	SLG	ISO
2021	TEX	22	CPX	13	1	1	0	1	1	0	7.69%	30.77%	0.273	0.385	0.636	0.364
2021	TEX	22	A+	150	11	11	1	14	1	1	10.67%	26.00%	0.296	0.407	0.736	0.440
2021	TEX	22	AA	104	14	7	0	2	0	1	7.69%	27.88%	0.247	0.317	0.387	0.140

Background: Mississippi State threw a ton of at bats at Foscue during his freshman season in 2018, allowing the then-19-year-old to walk up to the plate 216 times – even though the results were modest, at best. But Foscue's offensive production *exploded* during his sophomore campaign with the SEC powerhouse, slugging .331/.395/.564 with 22 doubles and 14 long balls. And he maintained status quo for his 16-game, pre-COVID shutdown campaign the following year as well. Texas would eventually expend the 14th pick in the draft on the second baseman. Foscue made his professional debut last season, hitting an aggregate .275/.371/.590 with 19 doubles, one triple, and 17 homeruns in just 62 games during his injury-marred year.

Scouting Report: Like his counterpart Josh Jung, Foscue didn't come close to logging a full season of action in 2021. But just for fun, here's Foscue's stats prorated for a full 162-game season: 50 doubles, three triples, and 44 homers. Not too shabby… On the other hand, the majority of Foscue's production occurred during his 33-game stint with Hickory in High-A and his numbers took a noticeable downward turn in Double-A as well. Foscue is a quasi-hybrid of the Rangers' Nick Solak and Tampa Bay's Brandon Lowe. Expect Foscue to be a .270/.330/.450-type of bat.

Ceiling: 2.0-win player
Risk: Moderate
MLB ETA: 2022/2023

6. Aaron Zavala, 3B/RF

	Hit	Power	SB	Patience	Glove	Overall
	55	40/45	50	55	50	50

Born: 06/23/00	Age: 22	Bats: L	Top Comp: Adam Eaton
Height: 6-0	Weight: 193	Throws: R	

Season	Team	Age	Level	PA	1B	2B	3B	HR	SB	CS	BB%	K%	AVG	OBP	SLG	ISO
2021	TEX	21	CPX	26	5	1	0	0	2	0	11.54%	26.92%	0.273	0.385	0.318	0.045
2021	TEX	21	A	67	11	4	0	1	7	0	14.93%	19.40%	0.302	0.433	0.434	0.132

Background: Highly decorated coming out of South Salem High School, Zavala was named: Oregon 6A Player of the Year in 2018, *USA Today's* All-USA Oregon Team, and Greater Valley Conference Player of the Year. The 6-foot, 193-pound infielder/outfielder looked comfortable in the box for the Pac12 powerhouse during his true freshman season in 2019: he batted .273/.356/.338 with nine doubles and a pair of stolen bases in 43 games. The lefty-swinging Zavala's production took a massive leap forward during his COVID-shortened campaign the following year, slugging .418/.493/.491 in 15 games for the Ducks. And the OBP Machine carried that momentum over into a career 2021 season. Appearing in 55 games, Zavala slugged .392/.525/.628 with 14 doubles, three triples, nine homeruns, and 11 stolen bases. He finished the year with an impressive 31-to-50 strikeout-to-walk ratio. Texas snagged him in the second round, 38th overall, and signed him to a well below-slot deal worth $830,000. Zavala appeared in 22 games with the club's Arizona Complex League and Low-A squads, hitting an aggregate .293/.419/.400.

Scouting Report: Per the usual, here's my pre-draft write-up:

"Consider the following:

- *Between 2011 and 2020, here's the list of Pac12 hitters to slug at least .380/.500/.600 in a season (min. 200 PA): Adley Rutschman (twice) and Andrew Vaughn (twice).*

Zavala, of course, met the aforementioned criteria during his under-the-radar dominant 2021 season. An on-base machine that can play a couple positions, run a bit, and flash average-ish power. Sounds like a promising big league prospect. Zavala's a little miscast as a right fielder because he doesn't have the traditional thump, but could carve out a career as a super-utility guy. Good arm. Lightning quick bat that's geared towards line drives and plenty of doubles. There's some Adam Eaton to Zavala's game."

Ceiling: 2.0-win player
Risk: Moderate
MLB ETA: 2023

7. Evan Carter, CF

	Hit	Power	SB	Patience	Glove	Overall
	45/50	45/50	55	60	50	50

Born: 08/29/02	Age: 19	Bats: L	Top Comp: Brandon Nimmo
Height: 6-4	Weight: 190	Throws: R	

Season	Team	Age	Level	PA	1B	2B	3B	HR	SB	CS	BB%	K%	AVG	OBP	SLG	ISO
2021	TEX	18	A	146	14	8	1	2	12	4	23.29%	19.18%	0.236	0.438	0.387	0.151

Background: Elizabethton High School has been home to exactly two professional ballplayers: Ricky Carriger, a right-hander taken by the Braves in the 11th round of the 1975 draft, and Evan Carter, a center fielder selected by the Rangers in the second round two years ago. Handed a hefty $1.25 million deal, Carter made his professional debut with the Down East Wood Ducks in Low-A. In an injury-shortened season, Carter batted an OBP-driven .236/.438/.387 with eight doubles, one triple, two homeruns, and 12 stolen bases (in 16 attempts). His overall production, per *Weighted Runs Created Plus*, topped the league average mark by 38%. A back injury cropped up and prematurely ended his season in mid-June.

Scouting Report: Just for fun, here's Carter's numbers prorated for a full 162-game season: 41 doubles, five triples, 10 homeruns, and 61 stolen bases. Yeah...that'll play, kid. Carter has a little Brandon Nimmo in him – both owning incredible patience at the plate. The Rangers' young center fielder walked in more than 23% of his plate appearances and posted a sub-20% K-rate as well. It's an aggressive statement but Carter could find his way into the Top 100 as early as 2023.

Ceiling: 2.0-win player
Risk: Moderate to High
MLB ETA: 2024

8. Ezequiel Duran, IF

	Hit	Power	SB	Patience	Glove	Overall
	45	55	55	45	50	45

Born: 05/22/99	Age: 23	Bats: R	Top Comp: Rougned Odor
Height: 5-11	Weight: 185	Throws: R	

Season	Team	Age	Level	PA	1B	2B	3B	HR	SB	CS	BB%	K%	AVG	OBP	SLG	ISO
2018	NYY	19	R	235	30	8	2	4	7	0	3.83%	27.66%	0.201	0.251	0.311	0.110
2019	NYY	20	A-	277	34	12	4	13	11	4	9.03%	27.80%	0.256	0.329	0.496	0.240
2021	NYY	22	A+	297	42	15	6	12	12	7	9.43%	23.91%	0.290	0.374	0.533	0.243
2021	TEX	22	A+	174	22	7	0	7	7	2	6.90%	33.91%	0.229	0.287	0.408	0.178

Background: It was a tough pill to swallow, not only for Joey Gallo but also for Rangers fans, when the club sent the long time fan favorite to the Yankees for a package of four minor leaguers: Ezequiel Duran, Glenn Otto, Josh Smith, and Trevor Hauver near the trade deadline last July.

Texas also included Joely Rodriguez to complete swap. Hailing from San Juan de la Manguana, Dominican Republic, the offensive-minded infielder began to open eyes as a 20-year-old playing for Staten Island three years ago: he slugged .256/.329/.496 with 12 doubles, four triples, and 13 homeruns for New York's short-season affiliate. Duran spent the entirety of last year in High-A, hitting an aggregate .267/.342/.486 with 22 doubles, six triples, 19 homeruns, and 19 stolen bases between both organizations' affiliates. His overall production, per *Weighted Runs Created Plus*, topped the league average mark by 18%.

Snippet from The 2020 Prospect Digest Handbook: In terms of ceiling, he looks like a late career Ian Kinsler.

Scouting Report: Consider the following:

- Since 2006, only four 22-year-old High-A hitters met the following criteria in a season (min. 400 PA): wRC+ total between 113 and 123, a strikeout rate north of 27%, and a sub-10% walk rate. Those four hitters: Jesse Franklin, Taylor Sparks, Ibandel Isabel, and – of course – Mr. Ezequiel Duran.

Similar to current Rangers prospect Bubba Thompson in a lot of ways. Duran flashes an impressive combination of power and speed from an up-the-middle position, but it's hampered by his problematic contact issues. The silver lining: when he does make contact it's typical loud and hard. Per FanGraphs data, Duran's average exit velocity was an impressive 92 mph with a peak of 109 mph. And to put that into terms: top prospects like Bobby Witt Jr., Marco Luciano, Julio Rodriguez, and Joey Bart showcased the same average and peak exit velocities as well. Duran's a boom-bust guy. And there's really no in between either. Double-A in 2022 will likely determine which path he's headed down.

Ceiling: 1.5-win player
Risk: Moderate
MLB ETA: 2023

9. Thomas Saggese, IF

	Hit	Power	SB	Patience	Glove	Overall
	50	50	50	55	50	45

Born: 04/10/02	Age: 20	Bats: R	Top Comp: Cavan Biggio
Height: 5-11	Weight: 175	Throws: R	

Season	Team	Age	Level	PA	1B	2B	3B	HR	SB	CS	BB%	K%	AVG	OBP	SLG	ISO
2021	TEX	19	A	288	35	14	3	10	11	3	14.58%	29.51%	0.256	0.372	0.463	0.207

Background: California-based Carlsbad High School can claim that seven of their alums have made it to professional ranks, and two of those players even played in the big leagues: four-time All-Star third baseman Troy Glaus and 11-year veteran Greg Dobbs. The school's most recent alum, Thomas Saggese, may add his name to the big league list as well. Unearthed in the fifth – and final – round of the 2020 draft, the Rangers handed the twitchy infielder an $800,000 bonus – the fourth highest for any player chosen that round. Despite no minor league season that year, the Rangers aggressively pushed the mid-round pick straight up to Low-A last season to begin his career. And it was totally the right move. Appearing in 73 games with the Down East Wood Ducks, Saggese slugged a hearty .256/.372/.463 with 14 doubles, three triples, 10 homeruns, and 11 stolen bases. His overall production, per *Weighted Runs Created Plus*, was 27% better than the league average threshold.

Scouting Report: Consider the following:

- Since 2006, only four 19-year-old hitters in Low-A met the following criteria in a season (min. 250 PA): wRC+ between 122 and 132, a walk rate of at least 10% and a strikeout rate greater than 27%. Those four hitters: Khalil Lee, Braxton Davidson, Alex De Jesus, and Thomas Saggese.

The 29% k-rate is concerning, yes, but let's take a look at his production. During the first 30 games of his 2021 season – and remember he didn't play much in high school or any in pro ball last season due to COVID – Saggese batted a lowly .217/.327/.413 with a hefty 38% punch out rate.

Beginning on July 15th through the end of the year he slugged .287/.394/.509 while whiffing in just a quarter of his plate appearances. I'm betting big on the latter numbers. There's some low end starting potential here, but it's years away.

Ceiling: 1.5-win player
Risk: Moderate
MLB ETA: 2024

10. Owen White, RHP

FB	CB	CH	Command	Overall
60	55	45	50	45

Born: 08/09/99	Age: 22	Bats: R	Top Comp: Zach McAllister
Height: 6-3	Weight: 199	Throws: R	

Season	Team	Age	Level	IP	TBF	K/9	K%	BB/9	BB%	K-BB%	ERA	FIP	xFIP	Pit/Bat
2021	TEX	21	A	33.1	135	14.58	40.00%	3.24	8.89%	31.11%	3.24	2.69	2.92	3.96

Background: The Rangers went with highly touted high school arms with their first two selections in the 2018 draft, first taking Cole Winn with the 15th overall pick then snagging White 40 selections later. Unfortunately for White, he's on the Cole Ragans development path. White missed all of 2019 recovering from Tommy John surgery. Then he had to sit out the following year due to the COVID shutdown. And then he missed the majority of last season due to a fractured hand. The 6-foot-3, 199-pound right-hander made eight starts with Down East in Low-A, averaging an impressive 14.6 strikeouts and 3.2 walks per nine innings. He made an additional four starts with the Surprise Saguaros in the Arizona Fall League as well, posting a 19-to-9 strikeout-to-walk ratio in 19.1 innings of work.

Scouting Report: If you really think about it, prior to White's debut in 2021 his last meaningful baseball game was played three years earlier – as a high school kid. And despite the long layoff, his feel for the strike zone was surprisingly sound. He attacks hitters with a straight mid-90s fastball, an above-average curveball, and a changeup that requires work. There's some reliever risk given his lack of a solid third option. It's important to remember his lack of development time. If the changeup ticks up to average White looks like a backend innings gobbler.

Ceiling: 1.5-win player
Risk: Moderate
MLB ETA: 2024

11. A.J. Alexy, RHP

FB	CB	SL	CH	Command	Overall
60	60	50	50	45	45

Born: 04/21/98	Age: 24	Bats: R	Top Comp: Luke Jackson
Height: 6-4	Weight: 195	Throws: R	

Season	Team	Age	Level	IP	TBF	K/9	K%	BB/9	BB%	K-BB%	ERA	FIP	xFIP	Pit/Bat
2018	TEX	20	A	108.0	452	11.50	30.53%	4.33	11.50%	19.03%	3.58	3.18	3.69	3.96
2019	TEX	21	A+	19.1	85	10.71	27.06%	6.05	15.29%	11.76%	5.12	4.00	4.30	4.59
2021	TEX	23	AA	50.1	198	10.19	28.79%	3.75	10.61%	18.18%	1.61	3.74	4.36	4.23
2021	TEX	23	AAA	14.2	57	11.66	33.33%	3.68	10.53%	22.81%	1.84	4.34	4.28	4.26

Background: The 11th round of the 2016 draft turned out to be a spending spree of sorts for Major League clubs. Twelve of the 30 selections received at least a $150,000 bonus. And two players – prep third baseman Chad McClanahan and prep right-hander Cameron Planck – received seven figure bonuses. Alexy, a long-limbed, wiry righty, was handed the fifth highest bonus in the round: $597,500. Texas acquired the promising youngster, along with Willie Calhoun and Brendon Davis, for ace Yu Darvish at the trade deadline five years ago. Last season the 6-foot-4, 195-pound right-hander put together his finest professional season to date – by a wide margin. Throwing 65 innings between AA and AAA, Alexy posted a 76-to-27 strikeout-to-walk ratio to go along with a Bob Gibson-esque 1.66 ERA across 10 starts and six relief appearances. The former late round bonus baby made another five appearances with the big league club as well, posting a 17-to-17 strikeout-to-walk ratio in 23.0 innings of work.

Snippet from The 2020 Prospect Digest Handbook: He has the floor of a dominant, dominant high leverage, late-inning reliever – something along the lines of Luke Jackson's showing for the Braves in 2019.

Scouting Report: With respect to Alexy's production in AA last season, consider the following:

- Since 2006, only six 23-year-olds AA arms have struck out between 28% and 30% with a walk percentage between 10% and 12% in a season (min. 50 IP): Carlos Marmol, Conner Menez, Cole Sands, Ian Gibaut, Alejandro Chacin, and A.J. Alexy.

Alexy's fastball hovers in the 93- to 95-mph range with some added life at the top of the zone. It's relatively straight but he – typically – commands it well. He'll complement the 55-grade offering with a trio of offspeed pitches: a mid- to upper-70s curveball with hellacious bend; a low 80s slider, which is a new weapon in his arsenal; and an inconsistent, albeit solid, changeup. Alexy still has some Luke Jackson upside in the bullpen.

Ceiling: 1.5-win player
Risk: Moderate
MLB ETA: Debuted in 2021

12. Ronny Henriquez, RHP		FB	SL	CH	Command	Overall
		60	55	55	55	45

Born: 06/20/00	Age: 22	Bats: R	Top Comp: Jose Urena
Height: 5-10	Weight: 155	Throws: R	

Season	Team	Age	Level	IP	TBF	K/9	K%	BB/9	BB%	K-BB%	ERA	FIP	xFIP	Pit/Bat
2018	TEX	18	R	58.0	219	12.26	36.07%	1.24	3.65%	32.42%	1.55	1.64	1.60	1.93
2019	TEX	19	A	82.0	357	10.87	27.73%	2.96	7.56%	20.17%	4.50	3.12	3.21	3.94
2021	TEX	21	A+	24.0	96	10.13	28.13%	3.00	8.33%	19.79%	3.75	3.85	4.46	3.70
2021	TEX	21	AA	69.2	291	10.08	26.80%	2.20	5.84%	20.96%	5.04	4.86	4.02	3.85

Background: In terms of returns on investment, the Rangers couldn't have envisioned Henriquez developing as well as he has since signing him on the dotted line for a paltry $10,000 during the summer of 2017. A wiry right-hander built in the Pedro Martinez-mold, Henriquez checks in at a less-than-imposing 5-foot-10 (which seems to be generously listed) and only 155 pounds. Regardless, though, Henriquez turned in another solid showing in 2021. Splitting time between High-A and Double-A, the diminutive – oft-times dominating – righty posted a 105-to-27 strikeout-to-walk ratio in 93.2 innings of work. He finished the year with a combined 4.71 ERA to go along with a 5-7 win-loss record.

Snippet from The 2020 Prospect Digest Handbook: Similarly with any small hurler, Henriquez is will have to continually prove he can withstand the rigors of grabbing the ball every fifth day. But there's some #3/#4-type potential brewing in his right arm.

Scouting Report: With respect to Henriquez's production in AA last season, consider the following:

- Since 2006, only four 21-year-old Double-A arms whiffed between 26% and 28% and walked fewer than 8% of the hitters they faced (min. 60 IP): John Danks, Brett Cecil, Logan Allen, and Ronny Henriquez.

The lone right-hander among the group, Henriquez is also the sole power arm among the trio. Henriquez's heater will sit, comfortably, in the 94-95-mph range. He'll showcase an above-average slider that generates a ton of swings when he's locating it just below the strike zone. And his upper-80s changeup is a legit plus offering. Henriquez is going to have to continue to fight the good fight when it comes to answering the bell on whether he can withstand the rigors of grabbing the ball every day. There's #4/#5-type ceiling with a solid relief floor.

Ceiling: 1.5-win player
Risk: Moderate
MLB ETA: 2022

13. Yerry Rodriguez, RHP		FB	SL	CH	Command	Overall
		55	60	55	45	45

Born: 10/15/97	Age: 24	Bats: R	Top Comp: Wily Peralta
Height: 6-2	Weight: 198	Throws: R	

Season	Team	Age	Level	IP	TBF	K/9	K%	BB/9	BB%	K-BB%	ERA	FIP	xFIP	Pit/Bat
2018	TEX	20	R	38.1	158	12.91	34.81%	0.70	1.90%	32.91%	3.52	1.93	2.11	1.82
2018	TEX	20	A-	24.2	102	9.85	26.47%	1.82	4.90%	21.57%	1.82	3.15	2.84	3.44
2019	TEX	21	A	73.2	283	10.38	30.04%	2.57	7.42%	22.61%	2.08	3.12	3.04	3.79
2021	TEX	23	AA	51.1	213	11.05	29.58%	3.68	9.86%	19.72%	2.63	3.30	4.14	4.08
2021	TEX	23	AAA	30.1	138	10.98	26.81%	3.56	8.70%	18.12%	8.01	4.92	4.69	4.05

Background: Another one of the club's bargain finds on the international market. The Rangers signed the hard-throwing right-hander for a rather paltry sum of $60,000 seven years ago. After that it took Rodriguez a couple years before he found his footing as a professional. He spent parts of two seasons in the Dominican Summer League, split a year between a stateside rookie league and short-season ball, and finally made it up to full season action in 2019. Last season, though, Rodriguez started to make up for lost time: he made 14 starts with Frisco in Double-A Central and another 13 appearances with Round Rock in Triple-A. In total, the 6-foot-2, 198-pound righty tossed a career high 81.2 innings, recording 100 punch outs and issuing 33 free passes. He compiled an aggregate 4.63 ERA.

Snippet from The 2020 Prospect Digest Handbook: Rodriguez looks like a potential backend starting pitcher with the floor of a high leverage setup reliever.

Scouting Report: With respect to Rodriguez's production in AA last season, consider the following:

- Since 2006, only six 23-year-old Double-A arms posted a strikeout percentage between 29% and 31% with a walk percentage between 9 and 11% in a season (min. 50 IP): Dinelson Lamet, Konnor Pilkington, Travis Ott, Humberto Sanchez, Alejandro Chacin, and – of course – Yerry Rodriguez.

The sprained UCL that hampered Rodriguez a couple years ago doesn't appear to be an issue. Rodriguez throws an easy 93 mph fastball, a hard-tilting slider, and a fading changeup – the latter flashing above-average a few times a game. Beyond physical differences, there's not a lot of difference between, say, Rodriguez and Ronny Henriquez. Rodriguez seemed to tire down the stretch, which was helped by the club pushing him into a multi-inning relief arm with Round Rock. Backend rotation arm with a floor as an above-average reliever.

Ceiling: 1.0- to 1.5-win player
Risk: Moderate
MLB ETA: 2022

14. Bubba Thompson, OF

	Hit	Power	SB	Patience	Glove	Overall
	45	50	55	45	50	40

Born: 06/09/98	Age: 24	Bats: R	Top Comp: Nick Williams
Height: 6-2	Weight: 197	Throws: R	

Season	Team	Age	Level	PA	1B	2B	3B	HR	SB	CS	BB%	K%	AVG	OBP	SLG	ISO
2018	TEX	20	A	363	65	18	5	8	32	7	6.34%	28.65%	0.289	0.344	0.446	0.157
2019	TEX	21	A+	228	21	8	2	5	12	3	9.21%	31.58%	0.178	0.261	0.312	0.134
2021	TEX	23	AA	470	70	23	9	16	25	8	6.17%	25.74%	0.275	0.325	0.483	0.207

Background: From one of my favorite under-the-radar guys to looking helpless a year later, Thompson, a 2017 first round selection, quietly redeemed himself with a solid showing in Double-A in 2021. The former 26th overall pick, who batted .178/.261/.312 in 57 High-A games in 2019, hardly resembled the same player with the Frisco RoughRiders last year. In 104 games with the Double-A Central squad, the 6-foot-2, 197-pound outfielder slugged .275/.325/.485 23 doubles, nine triples, 16 homeruns, and 25 stolen bases. His overall production, per *Weighted Runs Created Plus*, was 12% better than the league average.

Snippet from The 2020 Prospect Digest Handbook: Assuming he can shake the injuries and the poor 2019 season – which is far from a certainty – he looks like a Nick Williams-esque type performer. Williams, a former Rangers farmhand, owns a .254/.313/.420 career big league line.

Scouting Report: Consider the following:

- Since 2006, here's the list of 23-year-old Double-A hitters that posted a wRC+ between 107 and 117 with a K-rate between 25% and 27% and a walk rate below 7% (min. 400 PA): Markey Shorey and Bubba Thompson. Shorey, by the way, washed out of affiliated ball just two seasons later.

The tools are…still intact. Power. Speed. But the flaws don't add up to anything more than…Nick Williams, who's a .251/.312/.415 career big league hitter in 294 games. Thompson's lack of patience at the plate only exacerbates his below-average hit tool – which, of course, limits his ceiling considerably. Just like Williams.

Ceiling: 1.0-win player
Risk: Moderate
MLB ETA: 2022

15. Maximo Acosta, SS

	Hit	Power	SB	Patience	Glove	Overall
	40/45	45	50	40	45	40

Born: 10/29/02	Age: 19	Bats: R	Top Comp: N/A
Height: 6-1	Weight: 187	Throws: R	

Season	Team	Age	Level	PA	1B	2B	3B	HR	SB	CS	BB%	K%	AVG	OBP	SLG	ISO
2021	TEX	18	CPX	68	10	2	2	1	7	2	4.41%	22.06%	0.246	0.279	0.393	0.148

Background: Lauded as one of the more advanced bats on the international free agency market three years ago. The Rangers went all out and signed the toolsy shortstop for a hefty $1.65 million deal. The Caracas, Venezuela, native made his professional debut last season – sort of. Acosta's debut was cut short after just 17 games and 68 plate appearances. The cause: thoracic outlet syndrome surgery. Prior to the premature ending Acosta was batting .246/.279/.393 with two doubles, two triples, one homerun, and seven stolen bases. His overall production, per *Weighted Runs Created Plus*, was 30% below the league average mark.

Scouting Report: Assuming there will be no long term ill effects from the thoracic outlet syndrome surgery, Acosta never shied away from taking healthy cuts. In some video clips prior to the injury, Acosta seemed to love pitches at the top of the strike zone. There's a lot of movement through his swing, going from an upright position to a slight crouch.

Ceiling: 1.0-win player
Risk: Moderate
MLB ETA: 2025

16. Justin Slaten, RHP

	FB	CB	SL	CH	Command	Overall
	45+	50	50	60	45	40

Born: 09/15/97	Age: 24	Bats: R	Top Comp: Jimmy Nelson
Height: 6-4	Weight: 222	Throws: R	

Season	Team	Age	Level	IP	TBF	K/9	K%	BB/9	BB%	K-BB%	ERA	FIP	xFIP	Pit/Bat
2019	TEX	21	A-	15.1	75	12.33	28.00%	4.11	9.33%	18.67%	6.46	3.98	3.39	3.96
2021	TEX	23	A+	82.1	366	12.02	30.05%	3.39	8.47%	21.58%	6.01	5.05	4.27	4.16

Background: A third round pick out of the University of New Mexico, Slaten became the earliest drafted arm out of the school since the Pirates selected Kevin Andersh with the 15th overall pick in 1984. The 6-foot-4, 222-pound right-hander had one of the more interesting – and likely frustrating – seasons in 2021. In 20 games with the Hickory Crawdads, 19 of which were starts, Slaten averaged 12.0 strikeouts and just 3.4 walks per nine innings. The bad news: he put up a 6.01 ERA, 5.05 FIP, and a decent 4.27 xFIP.

Scouting Report: Consider the following:

- Since 2006, only three 23-year-old High-A arms posted a strikeout percentage north of 29% with a walk percentage between 7.5% and 9.5% in a season (min. 75 IP): Hector Neris, Anthony Veneziano, an Justin Slaten.

Really, really fascinating pitcher and it's easy to understand why the Rangers burned a third round selection on him as well. Fifty-five grades across the board for his repertoire: a lively fastball, a really strong slider, and a nice little change of pace. But Slaten doesn't trust his stuff enough which forces him to rely too heavily on his heater. The former New Mexico ace posted a 10.65 ERA across his first eight games and then settled in with a 4.14 ERA over his final 58.2 innings. There's backend potential, but he's got to trust the secondary weapons more. Period.

Ceiling: 0.5- to 1.0-win player
Risk: Moderate
MLB ETA: 2023

17. Cole Ragans, LHP

	FB	CB	SL	CH	Command	Overall
	45+	50	50	60	45	40

Born: 12/12/97	Age: 24	Bats: L	Top Comp: Eric Stults
Height: 6-4	Weight: 190	Throws: L	

Season	Team	Age	Level	IP	TBF	K/9	K%	BB/9	BB%	K-BB%	ERA	FIP	xFIP	Pit/Bat
2021	TEX	23	A+	44.1	173	10.96	31.21%	2.84	8.09%	23.12%	3.25	3.52	4.01	4.17
2021	TEX	23	AA	36.1	166	8.17	19.88%	4.95	12.05%	7.83%	5.70	6.34	5.93	3.87

Background: Fun Fact Part I: Nine of the top 30 players chosen in the 2016 draft have yet to make the big leagues. Fun Fact Part II: Eight of those players were from the high school ranks. Fun Fact Part III: Four of those eight high school kids were pitchers – Riley Pint, Jay Groome, Forrest Whitley, and – of course – Cole Ragans. The 30th overall selection that year, Ragans has had a tough go of it in the professional ranks. He flashed some incredible promise as a 19-year-old in short-season ball in 2017, average nearly 14 strikeouts per nine innings. But he missed all of 2018, 2019, and – of course – 2020. COVID shutdown notwithstanding, the main culprit – Tommy John surgery. More specifically: *two* Tommy John surgeries. Finally healthy last season, Ragans quickly made up for lost time. The then-23-year-old southpaw split time between High-A and Double-A, throwing 80.2 innings with 87 punch outs and 34 free passes. He finished the year with a 4.35 ERA.

Scouting Report: The fastball never really ticked up as expected. And the two TJ surgeries didn't help at all. Ragans' heater hovers in the 90-91 mph range. It's a below-average offering, particularly by today's max effort standards. His curveball is slow and loopy. The slider is mid-80s with some decent lateral movement. But it's his plus, low-80s changeup that can – potentially – push him into some type of big league opportunity. He struggled with his command in Double-A during the latter part of 2021, so it needs to see an uptick. Otherwise, he's headed to the bullpen.

Ceiling: 0.5-win player
Risk: Moderate
MLB ETA: 2022

19. Tekoah Roby, RHP

FB	CB	CH	Command	Overall
55	50	55	50/55	40

Born: 09/18/01	Age: 20	Bats: R	Top Comp: N/A
Height: 6-1	Weight: 185	Throws: R	

Season	Team	Age	Level	IP	TBF	K/9	K%	BB/9	BB%	K-BB%	ERA	FIP	xFIP	Pit/Bat
2021	TEX	19	A	22.0	90	14.32	38.89%	2.86	7.78%	31.11%	2.45	2.75	3.33	4.00

Background: Pine Forest High School in Pensacola, Florida, was a little bit of a baseball hotbed during the latter part of the 1990s to the early 2000s: B.J. Robbins, Jake Jacobs, Chad Rogers, Erik Thompson, Cliff Dancy, Darren Byrd, and Tim Spooneybarger all spent some time in the minor leagues (not including Spooneybarger's three-year big league career. But the school went 15 years in between graduating a player to the minor leagues. Enter: Tekoah Roby, a 6-foot-1, 185-pound right-hander. Taken in the third round and signed for $775,000 bonus two years ago, Roby was limited to just half a dozen starts with the Down East Wood Ducks last season before a sprained elbow knocked him out for the remainder of 2021. He tossed just 22.0 innings during debut, fanning 35 and walking just seven.

Scouting Report: Not really your typical early round prep arm. Roby showcases an above-average fastball, which he commands exceptionally well given his age, a loopy, get-me-over curveball, and an above-average changeup, which is thrown with good arm speed. One of the things that stick out from Roby's abbreviated debut is ability to throw quality strikes, not just strikes. He's still quite the project. His curveball needs to tick up at least half of a grade. But he has the makings of a #5-type arm.

Ceiling: 0.5-win player
Risk: Moderate
MLB ETA: 2025

20. Cameron Cauley, SS

Hit	Power	SB	Patience	Glove	Overall
40/45	30/40	60	50	50	40

Born: 02/06/03	Age: 19	Bats: R	Top Comp: N/A
Height: 5-10	Weight: 170	Throws: R	

Season	Team	Age	Level	PA	1B	2B	3B	HR	SB	CS	BB%	K%	AVG	OBP	SLG	ISO
2021	TEX	18	CPX	103	16	4	4	0	10	1	7.77%	30.10%	0.255	0.311	0.383	0.128

Background: The first high school prospect taken by the Rangers last June. Cauley, the club's third round selection, capped off his impressive prep career in fashion: he batted .450 with six dingers, 35 RBIs, and 52 stolen bases while leading the Barbers Hill Eagles to their first state championship. A Texas Tech commit, the 5-foot-10, 170-pound shortstop appeared in 24 games with the organization's Arizona Complex League squad, batting .255/.311/.383 with four doubles, four triples, and 10 stolen bases. His overall production, per *Weighted Runs Created Plus*, was a staggering 18% *below* the league average mark.

Scouting Report: The plus speed is evident in every faucet of the game. Cauley owns the fluidity, arm strength, and agility to remain at shortstop where he profiles to be at least an average defender. Offensively, he has trouble with hard stuff up in the zone. It's a simple swing without a lot of pop or thump. He needs to get stronger, learn how to drive the ball more efficiently. He looked lost against soft stuff down in the zone.

Ceiling: 0.5-win player
Risk: Moderate
MLB ETA: 2025

Toronto Blue Jays

Top Prospects

1. Gabriel Moreno, C

Hit	Power	SB	Patience	Glove	Overall
60	50/55	30	50	60	70

Born: 02/14/00	**Age:** 22	**Bats:** R	**Top Comp:** Buster Posey
Height: 5-11	**Weight:** 160	**Throws:** R	

Season	Team	Age	Level	PA	1B	2B	3B	HR	SB	CS	BB%	K%	AVG	OBP	SLG	ISO
2018	TOR	18	R	66	10	5	0	2	1	0	4.55%	19.70%	0.279	0.303	0.459	0.180
2018	TOR	18	R	101	22	12	2	2	1	1	3.96%	6.93%	0.413	0.455	0.652	0.239
2019	TOR	19	A	341	52	17	5	12	7	1	6.45%	11.14%	0.280	0.337	0.485	0.205
2021	TOR	21	AA	145	29	9	1	8	1	2	9.66%	15.17%	0.373	0.441	0.651	0.278
2021	TOR	21	AAA	10	1	0	0	0	0	0	0.00%	20.00%	0.111	0.200	0.111	0.000

Background: Beyond teenage arms, backstops are notorious for their incessant flameouts — *especially* teenage backstops. But Toronto's become a bit of a pipeline for top catching prospects in recent years. Danny Jansen, a 16th round pick out of West High School in 2013, was a consensus Top 100 prospect and has turned into a serviceable big league catcher. Rotund youngster Alejandro Kirk, a personal favorite of mine, is coming off of a rookie season in which he batted a respectable .242/.328/.436 in 60 games as a 22-year-old. And then there's Gabriel Moreno, the best of the trio and a potential budding superstar. Signed out of Barquisimeto, Venezuela, for barely nothing – his bonus was only $25,000, to be exact – Moreno looked a bit overwhelmed during his debut in the Dominican Summer League in 2017, hitting a lowly .248/.274/.296 in 32 games. Undeterred, the front office aggressively pushed him state to the Gulf Coast League, but that only last briefly as he slugged a Ruthian .413/.455/.652 in 23 games before he was bumped up to Bluefield. Moreno spent the ensuing summer, 2019, squaring off against the significantly older Midwest League: he hit .280/.337/.485 with 34 extra-base hits in only 82 games. And like a simmering pot, the 5-foot-11, 160-pound backstop's offensive production reached a boiling point in 2021 – until a fractured thumb, courtesy of an errant pitch, prematurely ended it. Before the injury he was battering the competition to the tune of .373/.441/.651. In Double-A. As a 21-year-old catcher. Moreno returned to action for a handful of games at the end of the year before shredding the Arizona Fall League competition (.329/.410/.494).

Snippet from The 2020 Prospect Digest Handbook: There's definite starting caliber potential here with the ceiling of a .270/.330/.450 type hitter.

Scouting Report: After ranking the young backstop as the club's fifth best prospect two years ago, Moreno's left little doubt who the big cheese is in the farm system now. The young Venezuelan catcher does it all – minus running: hits for average, hits for power, he owns a howitzer for an arm, and he's an absolute brick wall behind the dish. Oh, yeah, his patience at the dish has been trending in the right direction since the start of his career, going from well below average to slightly better-than-average. He's a perennial All-Star and a franchise cornerstone – as long as he can (A) withstand the rigors of catching without breaking down and (B) avoid serious injuries.

Ceiling: 7.0-win player
Risk: Moderate
MLB ETA: 2022

2. Orelvis Martinez, 3B/SS

Hit	Power	SB	Patience	Glove	Overall
45/50	50/60	35	50	45/50	60

Born: 11/19/01	**Age:** 20	**Bats:** R	**Top Comp:** Eduardo Escobar
Height: 6-1	**Weight:** 188	**Throws:** R	

Season	Team	Age	Level	PA	1B	2B	3B	HR	SB	CS	BB%	K%	AVG	OBP	SLG	ISO
2019	TOR	17	R	163	19	8	5	7	2	0	8.59%	17.79%	0.275	0.352	0.549	0.275
2021	TOR	19	A	326	36	22	4	19	4	1	10.12%	26.07%	0.279	0.369	0.572	0.293
2021	TOR	19	A+	125	11	4	0	9	0	1	8.00%	22.40%	0.214	0.282	0.491	0.277

Background: In a talent-laden international free agent class in 2018 – which included the likes fellow top prospects Diego Cartaya and Marco Luciano – it was Orelvis Martinez's deal with Toronto that ranked as the second highest handed out, trailing only Miami's not-so-great $5 million investment in Victor Victor Mesa. Martinez received a hefty $3.5 million deal, by the way. The 6-foot-1, 188-pound third baseman / shortstop was immediately placed on the fast track by the Jays' savvy front office as he debuted in the Gulf Coast League in 2019. In 40 games in the stateside rookie league, he hit a respectable .275/.352/.549 with eight doubles, five triples, and seven homeruns. Last season, Toronto pushed the young Dominican infielder up to Dunedin in Low-A. And he responded by slugging .279/.369/.572 with 22 doubles, two triples, and 19 homeruns in only 71 games. His overall production with their affiliate, per *Weighted Runs Created Plus*, topped the league average mark by a whopping 49%. Martinez spent the last month-plus battling – and mostly flailing away – at the High-A West league pitching.

Snippet from The 2020 Prospect Digest Handbook: Really impressive power for a teenage bat, regardless of the level. Martinez may develop 25- to 30-homer thump in the coming years. And he combines that with surprisingly strong contact skills. Martinez also showed a willingness to walk as well. Defensively speaking, he's solid. Martinez has some above-average starting caliber potential. Perhaps even peaking as a borderline All-Star. Short quick swing with impressive bat speed due to his strong, twitchy wrists. He doesn't get cheated either.

Scouting Report: Consider the following:

- Since 2006, only two 19-year-old hitters met the following criteria in Low-A with one organization: 145 to 155 wRC+ total, a strikeout rate between 24% and 28%, and a walk rate between 8% and 11%. Those two hitters: Travis Snider and Orelvis Martinez. Snider, of course, is a former longtime top prospect of the Jays with a history of dominant MiLB seasons that never quite figured it out at the big league level.

Martinez's strikeout rate in Low-A, 26.1%, isn't a concern given (A) his age, (B) his level of competition, and (C) the fact that it's declined noticeably during his 27-game cameo In High-A. The young baby-faced Dominican infielder shows a solid approach at the plate, above-average power, and an average glove. Like Jordan Groshans, he's almost assuredly getting moved to the hot corner with Bo Bichette entrenched at shortstop. Making Martinez's numbers in Low-A all that more impressive: according to *Baseball America's* park factors, Dunedin is heavily slanted towards pitchers.

Ceiling: 4.0-win player
Risk: Moderate
MLB ETA: 2024

3. Jordan Groshans, 3B/SS

	Hit	Power	SB	Patience	Glove	Overall
	50/55	50/55	30	55	50	60

Born: 10/10/99	Age: 22	Bats: R	Top Comp: Kyle Seager
Height: 6-3	Weight: 205	Throws: R	

Season	Team	Age	Level	PA	1B	2B	3B	HR	SB	CS	BB%	K%	AVG	OBP	SLG	ISO
2018	TOR	18	R	48	6	1	0	1	0	0	4.17%	16.67%	0.182	0.229	0.273	0.091
2018	TOR	18	R	159	31	12	0	4	0	0	8.18%	18.24%	0.331	0.390	0.500	0.169
2019	TOR	19	A	96	20	6	0	2	1	1	13.54%	21.88%	0.337	0.427	0.482	0.145
2021	TOR	21	AA	316	51	23	0	7	0	0	10.76%	19.30%	0.291	0.367	0.450	0.158

Background: The 2018 draft class will inevitably go down as one of the stronger ones in recent memory. The first seven picks – Casey Mize, Joey Bart, Alec Bohm, Nick Madrigal, Jonathan India, Jarred Kelenic, and Ryan Weathers – have already spent time in the big leagues, as have Logan Gilbert, Brady Singer, Trevor Larnach, and Nick Hoerner, among others. That doesn't include current top prospects like Grayson Rodriguez, Matthew Liberatore, Triston Casas, and – of course – Jordan Groshans. The first prep shortstop taken off the board that year, Groshans turned in a dynamic debut as he split time between the Gulf Coast and Appalachian Leagues, batting an aggregate .296/.353/.446 with 13 doubles and five homeruns in only 48 games. The 6-foot-3, 205-pound third baseman / shortstop got off to another scorching start in 2019, ripping through the Midwest League to the tune of .337/.427/.482 but a stress injury to his navicular bone in the left foot prematurely ended his sophomore campaign. Last year the Magnolia High School product – once again – was limited due to an injury, this time a sore back that delayed the start of the season, but he managed to squeeze in 75 games – a new career high. Playing in the minors' most important level, AA, Groshans stroked .291/.367/.450 with 23 doubles and seven homeruns. Per *Weighted Runs Created Plus*, his overall production topped the league average mark by 24%. For his career, he's sporting a .300/.372/.453 triple-slash line through 146 games.

Snippet from The 2020 Prospect Digest Handbook: But Groshans is flashing an impressive skill set that may end up with two above-average tools (hit and power) and a couple strong 50-grades in his glove and speed.

Scouting Report: Consider the following:

- Since 2006, only three 21-year-old hitters met the following criteria in Double-A with one organization (min. 300 PA): 120 to 130 wRC+, a walk rate between 8% and 11%, and a strikeout rate between 18% and 21%. Those three hitters: Chris Lubanski, Jonathan Galvez, and – of course – Jordan Groshans.

Understandably so, Groshans got off to a bit of a slow start to the year – remember he's not only making the leap from Low-A but he's totaled just 71 minor league games prior to the season – but he picked things up in early June and slugged .308/.380/.482 the remainder of the year. Groshans hasn't started tapping into his above-average power, but it's coming. Regardless of his defensive ability, he's not going to stick at shortstop as long as Bo Bichette is around, so third base is his for the taking.

Ceiling: 4.0-win player
Risk: Moderate
MLB ETA: 2022

4. Nate Pearson, RHP

	FB	CB	SL	CH	Command	Overall
	70	55	70	50	50	60

Born: 08/20/96	Age: 25	Bats: R	Top Comp: Lance McCullers Jr.
Height: 6-6	Weight: 250	Throws: R	

Season	Team	Age	Level	IP	TBF	K/9	K%	BB/9	BB%	K-BB%	ERA	FIP	xFIP	Pit/Bat
2019	TOR	22	A+	21.0	75	15.00	46.67%	1.29	4.00%	42.67%	0.86	1.64	1.07	4.23
2019	TOR	22	AA	62.2	244	9.91	28.28%	3.02	8.61%	19.67%	2.59	2.90	3.12	4.01
2019	TOR	22	AAA	18.0	69	7.50	21.74%	1.50	4.35%	17.39%	3.00	4.07	4.45	4.16
2021	TOR	24	AAA	30.2	129	12.91	34.11%	3.82	10.08%	24.03%	4.40	3.85	3.95	4.25

Background: The hard-throwing righty's old stomping ground, the College of Central Florida, has created a bit of pipeline to the minor leagues, sending seven players to the professional ranks via the amateur draft. The highest chosen player: big Nate Pearson, a 6-foot-6, 250-pound hurler with a hellacious fastball. The 28th overall pick in 2017, Pearson immediately began vaulting up prospect lists with each passing triple-digit fastball. And he put an exclamation point on it with his exceptional showing in 2019. Splitting time across three separate levels, the Florida native struck out 119 and walked just 27 to go along with a 2.30 ERA in 101.2 innings of work. Pearson was on Toronto's taxi squad during the COVID season two years ago, making five appearances, four of which were starts. Last season, he bounced between AAA and the big league, as well as an extended period on the disabled list with a core injury. He threw 30.2 minor league innings, averaging 12.9 strikeouts and 3.8 walks per nine innings. He tossed another 15 frames in Toronto, posting a 20-to-12 strikeout-to-walk ratio.

Snippet from The 2020 Prospect Digest Handbook: An abnormally strong feel for the strike for a pitcher with a premium arsenal. Person, who works entirely from the stretch, pounded the zone with the regularity of a crafty, 15-year veteran. He has a legitimate chance to ascend to a bonafide, true #1 starting pitcher.

Scouting Report: What will Toronto do with the firebolt-slinging right-hander? Is he a starter or a reliever? He was a member of Buffalo's rotation, and he made one start with the Jays, before hitting the DL. But once he returned he was a full-time reliever – though it's likely they were trying to limit his usage from further aggravating the core issue. In article in *The Toronto Star* by Gregor Chisholm on December 21, 2021, Blue Jays General Manager was quoted as saying, "If there's a way to create a bridge from here, where he's getting exposed to longer outings, and being built up, it may mean he's not always in the a starting role…Maybe there's an extended outing way to do that, whether that be starting, pitching out of the 'pen, or some combination of the two." I think it's too early to push him into a single-inning relief role. The stuff is still legit: 80-grade fastball, plus slider, above-average curveball, and a decent changeup. The only question is his inability to command the zone in his brief outings in the big leagues.

Ceiling: 3.5-win player
Risk: Moderate to High
MLB ETA: Debuted in 2020

5. Gunnar Hoglund, RHP

	FB	CB	SL	CH	Command	Overall
	N/A	N/A	N/A	N/A	N/A	55

Born: 12/17/99	Age: 22	Bats: L	Top Comp: N/A
Height: 6-4	Weight: 220	Throws: R	

Background: A highly touted prep prospect coming out of Fivay High School in 2018. Hoglund, a 6-foot-4, 220-pound right-hander, was incredibly dominant during his senior season for the Florida-based school, posting a 0.27 ERA to go along with a perfect 7-0 win-loss record. He also batted .385 at the dish as well. Hoglund, who capped off his prep career with a staggering 310 punch outs on the mound, was eventually taken by the Pirates in the opening round, 36th overall, of the 2018 draft. The two sides failed to come to an agreement and the hard-throwing hurler opted to attend Ole' Miss. The Florida-native had an up-and-down freshman year for the Rebels, posting an unsightly 5.29 ERA across 68 innings, though he managed to fan 53 and walk just 14. Hoglund had a bit of a coming out year during his abbreviated 2020 campaign, averaging 14.5 punch outs and just 1.5 walks per nine innings in four starts for the SEC school. And he was able to carry that momentum into a dominant – albeit Tommy John-shortened 2021 season. Prior to undergoing the surgical knife, he fanned 98, walked just 17, and tallied a 2.87 ERA in 11 starts. Toronto took a calculated risk and selected Hoglund with the 19th overall pick last July, signing him to a deal worth $3,247,500.

Scouting Report: Per the usual, here's my pre-draft write-up:

"Ignoring the injury momentarily, consider the following:

- Between 2011 and 2020, only three SEC starting pitchers averaged at least 12 strikeouts and fewer than three walks per innings in a season (min. 50 IP): Casey Mize, Ethan Small, and Mason Hickman.

Obviously, Hoglund's abbreviated 2021 season places him among the group. Prior to the injury, Hoglund, according to reports, showcased a low 90s fastball, an above-average slider and changeup, and a decent curveball. He had the look and production to go within the Top 15 picks of the draft before the elbow issues, but a team in the latter part of the 20s will likely take a gamble."

Ceiling: 3.0-win player
Risk: Moderate to High
MLB ETA: 2024

6. Otto Lopez, 2B/SS/CF

Hit	Power	SB	Patience	Glove	Overall
55	35	60	45	55	45

Born: 10/01/98	Age: 23	Bats: R	Top Comp: Ryan Theriot
Height: 5-10	Weight: 160	Throws: R	

Season	Team	Age	Level	PA	1B	2B	3B	HR	SB	CS	BB%	K%	AVG	OBP	SLG	ISO
2018	TOR	19	R	34	5	5	2	0	1	0	0.00%	14.71%	0.364	0.382	0.636	0.273
2018	TOR	19	A-	206	38	7	4	3	13	6	12.62%	10.19%	0.297	0.390	0.434	0.137
2019	TOR	20	A	492	115	20	5	5	20	15	6.91%	12.80%	0.324	0.371	0.425	0.101
2021	TOR	22	AA	314	64	24	1	3	7	3	8.92%	19.75%	0.331	0.398	0.457	0.126
2021	TOR	22	AAA	194	37	8	3	2	15	1	6.70%	13.40%	0.289	0.347	0.405	0.116

Background: An older prospect when he signed with Toronto during the summer of 2016 – or at least in terms of the typical international free agent age. Lopez was an elderly 17-years-old. The Dominican-born infielder wouldn't make his professional debut until the following season, but the player development engine decided to bypass the foreign rookie league and push him directly into the Gulf Coast League: he responded with a productive .275/.361/.360 slash line in 51 games. Lopez, a 5-foot-10, 160-pound middle infielder / part-time center fielder, spent the majority of the following season with Vancouver in the old Northwest League, batting .297/.390/.434. And he finally moved into full season action in 2019. He, of course, continued to hit: .324/.371/.425 with 20 doubles, five triples, and five homeruns. As minor league action returned to normal in 2021, after the COVID-imposed shutdown, Lopez upped the ante even further – in the minors' most important test, AA. In 70 games with New Hampshire, he slugged .331/.398/.457 with 24 doubles, one triple, and three homeruns. Toronto bumped him up to Triple-A in early August for another 43 games (.289/.347/.405).

Snippet from The 2020 Prospect Digest Handbook: Lopez still looks like a utility-type guy with the same caveat: if the power continues to creep forward as will his prospect ceiling. Strong bat-to-ball skills. Above-average speed, though he doesn't use it efficiently. And a solid glove.

Scouting Report: Consider the following:

- Since 2006, only five 22-year-old hitters met the following criteria in Double-A with one organization (min. 300 PA): 130 to 140 wRC+ total, 18% to 21% strikeout rate, 8% to 11% walk rate. Those five hitters: Colin Moran, Jerry Sands, Yusniel Diaz, Brandon Laird, and – of course – Otto Lopez.

One step closer to his utility role in the big leagues, especially now that he's accruing some valuable time in the outfield. Lopez is a slashing speedster with modest patience and very little power. Beyond his limiting frame size, the 5-foot-10, 160-pound infielder/outfielder puts the ball on the ground all too frequently (approximately 53% in 2021) to have a shot at any surge in the power department. One more thought: Lopez posted a 134 wRC+ in A-, a 132 wRC+ in A-ball, and a 136 wRC+ in AA.

Ceiling: 1.5-win player
Risk: Low to Moderate
MLB ETA: Debuted in 2021

7. Sem Robberse, RHP

FB	CB	SL	CH	Command	Overall
55	55	50/55	50/55	45/55	45

Born: 10/12/01	Age: 20	Bats: R	Top Comp: Jordan Balazovic
Height: 6-1	Weight: 160	Throws: R	

Season	Team	Age	Level	IP	TBF	K/9	K%	BB%	BB/9	K-BB%	ERA	FIP	xFIP	Pit/Bat
2019	TOR	17	R	10.1	41	7.84	21.95%	0.00	0.00%	21.95%	0.87	2.05	2.62	1.44
2021	TOR	19	A	57.2	239	9.52	25.52%	3.12	8.37%	17.15%	3.90	3.63	3.90	3.78

Background: Fun Fact Part I: According to the invaluable *Baseball Reference*, there have been 12 players born in the Netherlands to make the big leagues. Fun Fact Part II: of those 12 players, only two of them would establish themselves as above-average or better regulars – Hall of Famer Bert Blyleven and shortstop Didi Gregorius. The Zeist, Netherland, native spent parts of two years working in the Dutch Major League, at the ages of 16 and 17. He would throwing a total of 84 innings, fanning 74, walking 16, and compiling an aggregate 1.82 ERA. After signing with Toronto during the summer of 2019, Robberse made five brief appearances with the club's Gulf Coast League affiliate, posting a 9-to-0 strikeout-to-walk ratio in 10.0 innings. Last season the 6-foot-1, 160-pound right-hander made a total of 21 appearances, 19 of which were starts, between Dunedin and Vancouver. The then-19-year-old tossed 88.2 innings, racking up 90 strikeouts and 38 walks to go along with a 4.36 ERA and a 4.18 FIP.

Scouting Report: A tremendous job of unearthing the right-hander by the club's scouting department. In spite of the solid showings in 2019 and 2021, Robberse remains incredibly projectable – even as he's entering his age-20 season. He owns two present above-average offerings – a low- to mid-90s fastball and a curveball – with two others that may eventually creep into 55-grade territory (changeup and slider). He's a strike-thrower more than a command guy, but – again – that's trending in the right direction as well. Robberse has the starter's kit for a solid #4 / #5 arm. Consider the following:

- Since 2006, only seven 19-year-old hurlers met the following criteria in Low-A with one organization (min. 50 IP): 24.5% to 26.5% strikeout percentage and a 7.5% to 9.5% walk percentage. Those seven arms: Randall Delgado, Jake Thompson, Kelvin De La Cruz, Victor Vodnik, Ian Clarkin, Alfredo Garcia, and Sem Robberse.

Ceiling: 1.5-win player
Risk: Moderate
MLB ETA: 2024

8. Kevin Smith, 3B/SS

Hit	Power	SB	Patience	Glove	Overall
45	55	50	45	60	45

Born: 07/04/96	Age: 25	Bats: R	Top Comp: Danny Espinosa
Height: 6-0	Weight: 190	Throws: R	

Season	Team	Age	Level	PA	1B	2B	3B	HR	SB	CS	BB%	K%	AVG	OBP	SLG	ISO
2018	TOR	21	A	204	31	23	4	7	12	1	8.33%	16.18%	0.355	0.407	0.639	0.284
2018	TOR	21	A+	371	65	8	2	18	17	5	6.20%	23.72%	0.274	0.332	0.468	0.194
2019	TOR	22	AA	468	47	22	2	19	11	6	6.20%	32.26%	0.209	0.263	0.402	0.193
2021	TOR	24	AAA	410	49	27	4	21	18	3	11.22%	23.66%	0.285	0.370	0.561	0.276

Background: Solid contributor for the Maryland Terrapins during his three-year collegiate career, Smith left the Big 10 Conference school as a .267/.331/.455 hitter. Toronto selected him in the fourth round, 129th overall, in 2017. After signing with the organization quickly, Smith put together a solid debut in the Appalachian League that summer, hitting .271/.312/.466 in 61 games. The following year he ripped through Low-A (.355/.407/.639) and handled himself well enough in a second half promotion up to High-A (.274/.332/.468). And then things fell apart for the former Terp. Squaring off against the minors' most important test, AA, Smith failed – massively. In 116 games with New Hampshire in 2019, the 6-foot, 190-pound infielder hit a lowly .209/.263/.402 with 22 doubles two triples, and 19 homeruns. Last season Smith rediscovered his swing while he moved up to the final minor league stop, AAA. In 94 games with the Buffalo Bisons, he put together a .285/.370/.561 slash line, belting out 27 doubles, four triples, and 21 homeruns. Per *Weighted Runs Created Plus*, his overall production topped the league average mark by 44%. Smith also appeared in 18 big league hitting, batting a putrid .094/.194/.188.

Scouting Report: Consider the following:

- Since 2006, only two hitters posted a 140 to 150 wRC+ with a 10% to 12% walk rate, and a 22.5% to 24.5% strikeout rate in Triple-A with one organization (min. 350 PA): Aaron Judge and Kevin Smith.

Did. Not. See. That. Coming. Throughout his amateur career, even against the Big 10 competition, Smith has always been hampered by a 45-grade hit tool. But the Jays have been able to pull more out the bat than expected, sans his disastrous 2019 showing. Likewise, he's always flashed a plus glove and above-average power. Smith is going to get relegated to some type of backup gig – especially if Santiago Espinal performs well at third base in 2022 – but there's some low end starting potential here.

Ceiling: 1.5-win player
Risk: Moderate
MLB ETA: Debuted in 2021

9. Miguel Hiraldo, 2B/3B

Hit	Power	SB	Patience	Glove	Overall
45/50	40/50	55/45	50	50	45

Born: 09/05/00	Age: 21	Bats: R	Top Comp: Gordon Beckham
Height: 5-11	Weight: 170	Throws: R	

Season	Team	Age	Level	PA	1B	2B	3B	HR	SB	CS	BB%	K%	AVG	OBP	SLG	ISO
2018	TOR	17	R	239	44	18	3	2	15	6	9.62%	12.55%	0.313	0.381	0.453	0.140
2018	TOR	17	R	40	5	4	0	0	3	0	2.50%	30.00%	0.231	0.250	0.333	0.103
2019	TOR	18	R	256	43	20	1	7	11	3	5.47%	14.06%	0.300	0.348	0.481	0.181
2021	TOR	20	A	453	60	26	4	7	29	5	11.26%	24.50%	0.249	0.338	0.390	0.141

Background: Cut from a similar mold as all the other infield prospects the team has signed off the international market in recent years. Hiraldo garnered a hefty $750,000 bonus from the Jays during the summer of 2017. The second / third baseman would make his debut the following year with a strong showing in the Dominican Summer League, hitting .313/.381/.453 before earning a 10-game cameo in the Gulf Coast at the end of the year. Prior to the COVID shutdown, Hiraldo spent the majority of the season in the Rookie Advanced League; he would bat .300/.348/.481 with 20 doubles, one triple, and seven homeruns in 56 games. Last season, as MiLB action returned, the 5-foot-11, 170-pound infielder spent the entirety of the year battling against the Low-A Southeast competition, hitting a mediocre .249/.338/.390 with 26 doubles, four triples, and seven homeruns. He also swiped 29 bags in 34 attempts. His overall production was exactly league average, 100 wRC+, per *Weighted Runs Created Plus*.

Snippet from The 2020 Prospect Digest Handbook: Impressive power that could peak in 20-homer territory in the coming years. Throw in some average defense and Hiraldo already has the makings of a legitimate prospect. The best part about Hiraldo, though, is his ability to consistently square up the baseball. He's poised to be one of the bigger breakouts in 2020.

Scouting Report: Consider the following:

- Since 2006, only three 20-year-old hitters posted a 95 to 105 wRC+ total with a strikeout rate between 23.5% to 25.5% and a walk rate between 9% and 12% in Low-A with one organization (min. 400 PA): Matt West, Luis Mateo, and Miguel Hiraldo.

Hiraldo had an up-and-down year for Dunedin in 2021. He was solid in May (.270/.333/.404), July (.277/.381/.479), and September (.263/.333/.421), but struggled in June (.216/.336/.330) and August (.222/.293/.321). Among all the club's young infielders plucked from the international scene, Hiraldo has the best present power and it's still projecting to be a 45- to 50-grade tool. Above-average speed. Decent glove. He falls into the utility backup role like so many others in the organization.

Ceiling: 1.5-win player
Risk: Moderate
MLB ETA: 2023/2024

10. Estiven Machado, 2B/SS

Hit	Power	SB	Patience	Glove	Overall
N/A	N/A	N/A	N/A	N/A	N/A

Born: 10/04/02	**Age:** 19	**Bats:** B
Height: 5-10	**Weight:** 170	**Throws:** R

Top Comp: N/A

Background: Signed off the international market for a hefty $775,000 during the summer of 2019. Machado was limited to just one plate appearance during his debut last season due to a severe hamstring injury.

Scouting Report: Very, very flashing on the defensive side of the ball. Smooth, quick, twitchy movements. Really good looking swing from both sides of the plate. When Machado makes contact it's audibly loud, like a firecracker. Above-average runner. I think there's some Brandon Phillips-type potential here. But with basically no game data to go off of, Machado remains an unknown. He looks like a player though.

Ceiling: Too Soon to Tell
Risk: Too Soon to Tell
MLB ETA: Too Soon to Tell

11. C.J. Van Eyk, RHP

FB	CB	SL	CH	Command	Overall
55	60	50/55	50	40/45	45

Born: 09/15/98	Age: 23	Bats: R	Top Comp: Zac Gallen
Height: 6-1	Weight: 198	Throws: R	

Season	Team	Age	Level	IP	TBF	K/9	K%	BB/9	BB%	K-BB%	ERA	FIP	xFIP	Pit/Bat
2021	TOR	22	A+	80.1	353	11.20	28.33%	4.37	11.05%	17.28%	5.83	4.55	4.58	3.89

Background: A New York-based organization took a late round flier on Van Eyk coming out of George M. Steinbrenner High School – though it wasn't the New York team that Mr. Steinbrenner owned. Van Eyk, of course, bypassed the Mets' interest and headed to Florida State University. After a stellar three-year career – he averaged 11.5 strikeouts and 4.2 walks per nine innings – Toronto drafted the 6-foot-1, 198-pound right-hander in the second round, 42nd overall, in the 2020 draft. The two sides agreed to a deal worth slightly less than $1.8 million. Van Eyk made 19 starts with the Vancouver Canadians in High-A West last season, throwing 80.1 innings with 100 strikeouts and 39 walks. He finished the year with a 5.83 ERA, a 4.55 FIP, and a 4.58 xFIP.

Scouting Report: Consider the following:

- Since 2006, only three 22-year-old hurlers met the following criteria in High-A with one organization (min. 75 IP): 27% to 29% strikeout percentage with a 10% to 12% walk percentage. Those three hurlers: Sean Manaea, Kyle Bradish, and Cornelius Johannes Van Eyk.

Very solid four-pitch repertoire highlight by a lively 93 mph fastball. Van Eyk complements the above-average heater with a plus, 12-6 downward biting curveball that falls off the table, a slider that projects to be above-average, and a firm changeup. Even going back to his collegiate days, Van Eyk's never displayed a solid grasp of the strike zone (his lowest walk rate was 3.7 BB/9, which happened during his sophomore campaign). He needs to show some type of tangible improvement in the next year or so. If that happens, he looks like a #4-type arm. If not, well, he could be service fastball/curveball combo relief arm.

Ceiling: 1.5-win player
Risk: Moderate to High
MLB ETA: 2023/2024

12. Adam Kloffenstein, RHP

FB	CB	SL	CH	Command	Overall
50/55	55	50/55	45	40/45	45

Born: 08/25/00	Age: 21	Bats: R	Top Comp: Cam Bedrosian
Height: 6-5	Weight: 243	Throws: R	

Season	Team	Age	Level	IP	TBF	K/9	K%	BB/9	BB%	K-BB%	ERA	FIP	xFIP	Pit/Bat
2019	TOR	18	A-	64.1	259	8.95	24.71%	3.22	8.88%	15.83%	2.24	3.73	3.46	3.85
2021	TOR	20	A+	101.1	466	9.50	22.96%	5.42	13.09%	9.87%	6.22	5.16	5.09	3.80

Background: The Blue Jays staff spent a lot of time at Texas-based Magnolia High School heading into the 2018 draft. They selected shortstop Jordan Groshans with the 12th overall selection that year from the prep school, signing him to a below-slot deal worth $3.4 million. Two rounds later Toronto snagged Groshan's teammate Adam Kloffenstein – except the big right-hander received nearly $2 million above the recommended slot to sign. Built like an NFL tightend at 6-foot-5 and 243 pounds, Kloffenstein spent the entirety of 2021 battling – with mix results – the High-A West competition with the Vancouver Canadians. In a career-high 23 starts, the big righty posted a mediocre 107-to-61 strikeout-to-walk ratio in 101.1 innings of work. He finished the year with a 6.22 ERA, a 5.16 FIP, and a 5.09 xFIP.

Snippet from The 2020 Prospect Digest Handbook: Kloffenstein fastball was touching the mid-90s last season; his curveball showed flashes of above-average; his slider's a swing-and-miss pitch; and his changeup is quietly strong. Throw in a solid feel for the strike zone and Kloffenstein has the makings of a #4-type starting pitcher. He's poised to be one of the bigger breakouts in 2020.

Scouting Report: Consider the following:

- Since 2006, there have been twelve 20-year-old pitchers to post a strikeout percentage between 22% and 24% in High-A (min. 100 IP): Jack Flaherty, Brad Hand, Antonio Senzatela, Brett Oberholtzer, Troy Patton, Ricardo Sanchez, Peter Lambert, Reggie Lawson, Kyle Smith, Gabby Hernandez, Dan Cortes, and – of course – Adam Kloffenstein.
- Only two of those hurlers posted a walk rate of at least 10%: Ricardo Sanchez and Adam Kloffenstein, the latter being 3-percentage points higher.

Kloffenstein hardly resembled the same pitcher from two years ago. His fastball backed up a few ticks, now sitting in the 90 mph range. His slider was inconsistent, though it would flash above-average on rare occasion. And his change, now thrown rarely, is below-average. His 40-

grade command from two years ago showed no signs of improvement either. Add it all up – especially combined with his production – and Kloffenstein's prospect status has dulled quite bit. Instead of tracking like a #4-type starting pitcher, he's in the #6 / spot-starter path with the floor of a middle reliever.

Ceiling: 1.0- to 1.5-win player
Risk: Moderate
MLB ETA: 2024

13. Eric Pardinho, RHP

	FB	CB	SL	CH	Command	Overall
	N/A	N/A	N/A	N/A	N/A	50

Born: 01/05/01	Age: 21	Bats: R	Top Comp: N/A
Height: 5-10	Weight: 155	Throws: R	

Season	Team	Age	Level	IP	TBF	K/9	K%	BB/9	BB%	K-BB%	ERA	FIP	xFIP	Pit/Bat
2018	TOR	17	R	50.0	203	11.52	31.53%	2.88	7.88%	23.65%	2.88	3.75	3.33	3.65
2019	TOR	18	A	33.2	136	8.02	22.06%	3.48	9.56%	12.50%	2.41	3.21	3.65	3.83

Background: Once upon a time in the not-so-distant past, Pardinho was the pitching pearl of Toronto's bountiful farm system. He was a big time bonus baby from the international market – the club invested $1.4 million to sign him – and he showed poise beyond his years as the organization pushed him to the Appalachian League – *as a 17-year-old.* And he continued that momentum into the Midwest League the following year…until his elbow began creek and ache. He would eventually undergo Tommy John surgery in February 2020. And if things worked according to plan, the 5-foot-10, 155-pound right-hander would have been on the rehab circuit in early 2021. That didn't happen. In fact, Pardinho made two brief appearances with the club's Arizona Complex League affiliate before shutting it down with more elbow issues in early July.

Snippet from The 2020 Prospect Digest Handbook: Despite some impressive numbers in Low Class A as an 18-year-old last season, Pardinho, who averaged eight strikeouts and 3.5 walks per nine innings, didn't seem to fully trust his healed elbow. In a late-July start Pardinho's fastball was touching 94 with a surprising amount of ease and fluidity. A couple weeks later his heater was sitting in the 87- to 88-mph range. Pardinho is the type of pitcher to add and subtract velocity from his fastball, but it certainly needs to be monitored. Above-average fastball and curveball. A 50-grade changeup. And a slider that flashes above-average at times. Assuming the wonky elbow is firmly in the past, there's a solid chance Pardinho pokes his head up in Class AA at some point in 2020. One more thought: he's physically maxed out so the velocity's not likely going to climb much higher..

Scouting Report: Nothing new to report on beyond the elbow woes. Fingers crossed the kid catches a break because he looked like a special talent during the first two years of his career.

Ceiling: 2.0-win player
Risk: Extremely High
MLB ETA: 2024

14. Maximo Castillo, RHP

	FB	SL	CH	Command	Overall
	55	50	50	55	40

Born: 05/04/99	Age: 23	Bats: R	Top Comp: Cory Lidle
Height: 6-2	Weight: 256	Throws: R	

Season	Team	Age	Level	IP	TBF	K/9	K%	BB/9	BB%	K-BB%	ERA	FIP	xFIP	Pit/Bat
2018	TOR	19	A	131.1	568	7.88	20.25%	2.88	7.39%	12.85%	4.52	4.04	3.81	3.58
2019	TOR	20	A+	130.1	523	7.87	21.80%	1.93	5.35%	16.44%	2.69	3.09	3.37	3.87
2021	TOR	22	AA	102.0	441	7.85	20.18%	3.09	7.94%	12.24%	4.85	4.45	4.78	3.78

Background: In terms of signing bonuses doled out on the international free agent market, the $10,000 deal Castillo was handed barely registers a blip on any radar, but the portly right-hander is proving to be quite the bargain. A native of Caracas, Venezuela, the 6-foot-2, 256-pound hurler first made it up to full season action as a 19-year-old in 2018, recording a solid 115-to-42 strikeout-to-walk ratio in 131.1 innings with Lansing. Castillo spent the following year frustrating the Florida State League hitters as he averaged 7.9 strikeouts and just 1.9 walks per nine innings to go along with a 2.69 ERA in 24 starts. Last season, the bulky prospect got his first taste of Double-A. And the results were…mediocre. Castillo struck out 89 and walked 35 in 102.0 innings across 20 starts and one relief appearance with the New Hampshire Fisher Cats. He finished the year with a 4.85 ERA, 4.45 FIP, and a 4.78 xFIP.

Snippet from The 2020 Prospect Digest Handbook: He lacks a dominant swing-and-miss secondary option, though the pinpoint accuracy helps to compensate some. He's going to have to monitor his weight moving forward as well.

Scouting Report: Consider the following:

- Since 2006, seven 22-year-old hurlers posted a strikeout percentage between 21% and 23% with a walk percentage between 7% and 9% in Double-A with one organization (min. 100 IP): James Houser, Yennsy Diaz, Jose Rodriguez, Brooks Pounders, Bear Bay, Devin Jones, and Maximo Castillo.

The basic building blocks of successful pitching are built on a few different skills. Castillo's owns two of those: durability / innings eater and strike-thrower. Beyond that the hefty righty is pretty run-of-the-mill. He'll run his fastball up to the mid-90s with decent regularity and it sits comfortably in the 92- to 93-mph range. He'll throw a laterally-darting slider and a sinking power changeup that's only a few ticks slower than his heater. Castillo lacks a traditional out pitch and even his fastball plays down a half grade. But there is tremendous value in pitchers that can chew through innings and keep the team in the game. And that's exactly what Maximo Castillo does.

Ceiling: 1.0-win player
Risk: Low to Moderate
MLB ETA: 2022

15. Leo Jimenez, 2B/SS

Hit	Power	SB	Patience	Glove	Overall
45/55	30	30	55	50	40

Born: 05/17/01	Age: 21	Bats: R	Top Comp: N/A
Height: 5-11	Weight: 160	Throws: R	

Season	Team	Age	Level	PA	1B	2B	3B	HR	SB	CS	BB%	K%	AVG	OBP	SLG	ISO
2018	TOR	17	R	150	23	8	2	0	0	0	10.67%	11.33%	0.250	0.333	0.341	0.091
2019	TOR	18	R	245	49	13	2	0	2	1	8.57%	17.14%	0.298	0.377	0.377	0.079
2021	TOR	20	CPX	20	3	2	0	0	1	0	15.00%	5.00%	0.385	0.600	0.538	0.154
2021	TOR	20	A	242	44	8	0	1	4	1	21.07%	14.46%	0.315	0.517	0.381	0.065

Background: Another one of the intriguing low- to mid-level middle infield prospects the Jays seem to be collecting. Jimenez agreed to join the Canadian franchise during the summer of 2017 for a rather sizeable $825,000. After a bit of a mediocre debut in the Gulf Coast League – he hit .250/.333/.341 as a 17-year-old – Jimenez made some waves the following year in the Appalachian League. In 56 games with the Bluefield Blue Jays, the 5-foot-11, 160-pound second baseman / shortstop batted .298/.377/.377 with 13 doubles and a pair of triples, His overall production, per *Weighted Runs Created Plus*, topped the league average mark by 15%. Last season, in an injury-interrupted campaign, Jimenez put his best Eddie Stanky impression on display as he hit .315/.517/.381 in 54 games. His overall production topped the league average mark by a mindboggling 68%. Jimenez appeared in 15 games with the Mesa Solar Sox in the Arizona Fall League, batting .237/.412/.342

Snippet from The 2020 Prospect Digest Handbook: Unless Jimenez's power develops better than expected, he profiles best as a solid up-the-middle utility bat.

Scouting Report: Consider the following:

- Since 2006, only four 20-year-old hitters posted a walk rate north of 18% in Low-A (min. 200 PA): Anthony Volpe, the Yankees' top prospects, Travis Denker, Josh Johnson, and Leo Jimenez.

Jimenez underwent a very interesting transformation at the dish over the past couple of seasons. After posting average-ish walk rates during his first two years in the Jays' organization, the 5-foot-11, 160-pound middle infielder posted an absurd 21.1% walk rate in Low-A. His walk-to-strikeout rate was nearly 3-to-2 last season. There's still nonexistent power – though he did slug his first four-bagger – and he's not running enough to compensate for the lack pop. Still looking as a contact-over-power utility infielder.

Ceiling: 1.0-win player
Risk: Moderate
MLB ETA: 2025

16. Manuel Beltre, SS

Hit	Power	SB	Patience	Glove	Overall
30/50	30/45	50	50	50	40

Born: 06/09/04	Age: 18	Bats: R	Top Comp: N/A
Height: 5-9	Weight: 155	Throws: R	

Season	Team	Age	Level	PA	1B	2B	3B	HR	SB	CS	BB%	K%	AVG	OBP	SLG	ISO
2021	TOR	17	DSL	238	26	10	3	2	10	4	17.65%	13.87%	0.225	0.391	0.346	0.121

Background: Another high profile prospect the front office inked on the international market. The bonus: a hefty $2.35 million. According to the Canadian website, SportsNet.ca, the 5-foot-9,

155-pound infielder was "bought out of a commitment to Florida International University." Beltre made his professional debut in the Dominican Summer League last year – and it was mostly disastrous. In 53 games with the club's foreign rookie league affiliate, he batted a putrid .225/.391/.346 with just 10 doubles, three triples, and a pair of homeruns. He also swiped 10 bags in 14 total attempts. Per *Weighted Runs Created Plus*, still topped the league average mark by a surprising 19%.

Scouting Report: Once considered one of the better bats on the international scene due to his "advanced" feel for hitting, Beltre failed to live up to those expectations during his debut. Good looking swing with solid bat speed that should be no worse than above-average in the coming years. I'm willing to give him a mulligan on the disappointing debut, but he needs to show a lot of improvement during his sophomore professional campaign. One more thought: Of Beltre's 238 plate appearances last summer, 229 of them came against older pitchers.

Ceiling: 1.0-win player
Risk: Moderate
MLB ETA: 2025

17. Irv Carter, RHP

	FB	SL	CH	Command	Overall
	55	50/55	N/A	45	40

Born: 10/09/02	**Age:** 19	**Bats:** R	**Top Comp: N/A**
Height: 6-4	**Weight:** 210	**Throws:** R	

Background: Twenty years ago there was a private school in my town that featured a trio of pitchers on their varsity team that would pump some serious gas. One of them was clocked as high as 92 mph. Another one, the best pitcher of the group, would regularly sit 88- to 89-mph. A third guy would sit in the 80s with a hellacious curveball. They also had a couple other arms that would regularly touch 83 mph or 84 mph as well. Back then, in a cold northeast Ohio city, you would be hard pressed to find a deeper collection of hard-throwing hurlers. (They barely finished .500 on the season, by the way.) Well, Calvary Christian High School had a little something like that going on. Except, you know, *way better*. The Phillies selected the Fort Lauderdale, Florida, based school's ace, Andrew Painter, with the 10th overall pick. Four rounds later Toronto went way over slot to sign right-hander Irv Carter, the 152nd player chosen. And, for what it's worth, the prep school's shortstop, Alex Ulloa, was drafted by the Astros in the fourth round as well – though the sides failed to come to an agreement.

Scouting Report: Fast arm. High release point. Max effort delivery. According to game tape available by Prospect's Live, Carter's fastball would sit in the low- to mid-90s. He'll mix in a low-80s slider and a low-80s changeup. 55-grade fastball. The slider projects to be above-average. There's some reliever risk here.

Ceiling: 1.0-win player
Risk: Moderate
MLB ETA: 2025

18. Ricky Tiedemann, LHP

	FB	SL	CH	Command	Overall
	55	45/50	55	45	40

Born: 08/18/02	**Age:** 19	**Bats:** L	**Top Comp: N/A**
Height: 6-4	**Weight:** 220	**Throws:** L	

Background: Fun Fact Part I: Golden West College, a JuCo based in Huntington Beach, California, has churned out a surprising number of draft picks throughout its history – 75, to be exact. Fun Fact Part II: only two players, Kevin Elster and Craig Paquette, would go on to have extended big league careers, though. Fun Fact Part III: Tiedemann became the highest drafted player (in the June/July amateur draft) when the Blue Jays used the 91st overall pick last year. Prior to joining the Jays, the 6-foot-4, 220-pound southpaw made seven starts with the Golden West Rustlers, throwing 38.0 innings with a 60-to-15 strikeout-to-walk ratio with a 3.55 ERA. The Jays signed him to a deal worth $644,800 and he did not make his official professional debut last year.

Scouting Report: Tiedemann's shortened his arm path significantly over the years, going from a longer, more traditional path with a high three-quarter release to a low-slot, short-arm, slinging one. It adds some deception to his arsenal. 55-grade fastball with arm-side run. He owns two offspeed pitches – a slider and changeup with the later being an above-average offering. The former is fringy. Combined with Tiedemann's low slot and lack of a third pitch, I think he's looking at a life of relief-dom. Mechanically speaking, he looks like Brad Hand. Overdraft.

Ceiling: 1.0-win player
Risk: Moderate
MLB ETA: 2025

19. Samad Taylor, IF/OF

Hit	Power	SB	Patience	Glove	Overall
45	50	60	50	45	40

Born: 07/11/98	Age: 23	Bats: R	Top Comp: N/A
Height: 5-10	Weight: 160	Throws: R	

Season	Team	Age	Level	PA	1B	2B	3B	HR	SB	CS	BB%	K%	AVG	OBP	SLG	ISO
2018	TOR	19	A	530	57	32	7	9	44	16	10.75%	18.68%	0.228	0.319	0.387	0.159
2019	TOR	20	A+	384	39	20	3	7	26	10	12.76%	27.86%	0.216	0.325	0.364	0.147
2021	TOR	22	AA	374	60	17	1	16	30	8	11.23%	29.41%	0.294	0.385	0.503	0.209

Background: A product of California-based Corona High School, Cleveland originally drafted the sweet-swinging infielder / outfielder in the tenth round all the way back in 2016. After just parts of two seasons in the Guardians farm system, Taylor was flipped – along with reliever Thomas Pannone – to Toronto for veteran side-arming right-handed reliever Joe Smith. Taylor would struggle through back-to-back disappointing seasons with Lansing (.228/.319/.387) and Dunedin (.216/.325/.364) in 2018 and 2019. But the 5-foot-10, 160-pound prospect righted the ship in 2021 as he moved up to the most challenging minor league test – Double-A. In 87 games with the New Hampshire Fisher Cats, Taylor turned in a career high .294/.385/.503 with 17 doubles, one triple, and a personal best 16 homeruns. He also swiped 30 bags in 38 attempts. Per *Weighted Runs Created Plus*, his production topped the league average mark by 41%.

Scouting Report: Consider the following:

- Since 2006, only two 22-year-old hitters posted a wRC+ between 135 and 145 with a strikeout rate of at least 28% in Double-A with one organization (min. 350 PA): Wilkin Ramirez and Samad Taylor.

Early in his career Taylor was a hit-over-power guy with strong contact skills. But over his past two seasons – 2019 and 2021 – Taylor has sold out, going for more power in exchange for bloated strikeout rates. He whiffed in nearly 28% of his appearances in 2019 and posted a 29.4% mark in 2021. If he could find a happy balance between his past and present skills, he'd be a promising Top 10 prospect in Toronto's farm.

Ceiling: 1.0-win player
Risk: Moderate
MLB ETA: 2025

20. Gabriel Martinez, OF

Hit	Power	SB	Patience	Glove	Overall
N/A	N/A	N/A	N/A	N/A	N/A

Born: 07/24/02	Age: 19	Bats: R	Top Comp: N/A
Height: 6-0	Weight: 170	Throws: R	

Season	Team	Age	Level	PA	1B	2B	3B	HR	SB	CS	BB%	K%	AVG	OBP	SLG	ISO
2019	TOR	16	R	245	34	13	2	2	8	9	8.57%	10.61%	0.239	0.317	0.347	0.108
2021	TOR	18	CPX	125	25	8	0	0	7	2	16.80%	14.40%	0.330	0.448	0.410	0.080
2021	TOR	18	A	13	3	1	0	0	0	1	7.69%	30.77%	0.333	0.385	0.417	0.083

Background: The first recorded professional appearance by Gabriel Martinez happened in the Venezuelan Winter League in 2018-19. He went 1-for-1 in two brief appearances with the Aguilas del Zulia. A handful of months later he was playing for Toronto's Dominican Summer League affiliate, though the results were far less impressive. In 58 games, the then-16-year-old outfielder hit a paltry .239/.317/.347 with 13 doubles, two triples, and a pair of homeruns to go along with eight stolen bases (in 17 attempts). Last season the front office pushed the then-18-year-old up to the Florida Complex League. This time, though, he looked for more prepared he slugged .330/.448/.410 with eight doubles in 31 games. He spent the last few days of his sophomore professional season with Dunedin, going 4-for-12 with a double. Overall, Martinez finished the year with an aggregate .330/.442/.411 with nine doubles and seven stolen bases.

Scouting Report: To the best of knowledge, there's no available game tape of Martinez, a native of Maracaibo, Venezuela. Statistically speaking, he saw significant improvement between his two professional stints. Patient approach at the plate with a contact oriented swing. Above-average runner. He could be very interesting to watch in 2021 as he's likely ticketed for Dunedin for a full year.

Ceiling: Too Soon to Tell
Risk: Too Soon to Tell
MLB ETA: Too Soon to Tell

Washington Nationals

Top Prospects

1. Keibert Ruiz, C

Hit	Power	SB	Patience	Glove	Overall
55	50	30	50	45	60

Born: 07/20/98	Age: 23	Bats: B	Top Comp: Carlos Ruiz
Height: 6-0	Weight: 225	Throws: R	

Year	Org.	Level	PA	1B	2B	3B	HR	SB	AVG	OBP	SLG	BB%	K%	SwStr%	wRC+
2018	LAD	AA	415	75	14	0	12	0	0.268	0.328	0.401	6.27%	7.95%	6.82%	100
2019	LAD	AA	310	57	9	0	4	0	0.254	0.329	0.330	9.03%	6.77%	5.08%	88
2021	LAD	AAA	231	30	18	0	16	0	0.311	0.381	0.631	9.96%	11.69%	6.35%	143
2021	WSN	AAA	85	13	6	0	5	0	0.308	0.365	0.577	8.24%	7.06%	6.33%	146

Background: It was – quite simply – the biggest trade in Washington Nationals history: the club agreed to send future Hall of Famer Max Scherzer and his expiring contract, as well as infielder Trea Turner, perhaps a long shot future HoF'er – all the way across the country to the Dodgers for a quartet of prospects: Josiah Gray, Gerardo Carrillo, Donovan Casey, and – of course – Keibert Ruiz. A long time member of the Top 100 Club, Ruiz first began opening eyes as a baby-faced 16-year-old dominating the Dominican Summer League when he batted .300/.340/.387. After reaching – and succeeding in – Double-A just three seasons later, the stocky backstop's status dulled a bit as he struggled in a return to the Texas League in 2019. Last season, his seventh in professional baseball, Ruiz rediscovered his sweet-swinging stroke, hitting a combined .310/.377/.616 between both organizations' Triple-A squads. He also batted a collective .273/.333/.409 in 29 games in the big leagues.

Snippet from The 2020 Prospect Digest Handbook: There's an artificially concerning trend in Ruiz's production line: his production line has declined in each of the past of three seasons.

Scouting Report: The good news:

- Since 2006, only three 22-year-old hitters have posted at least a 140 wRC+ with a sub-15% strikeout rate in Triple-A in a season (min. 250 PA): Elijah Dukes, the troubled former Top 100 prospect, and silky smooth first baseman James Loney. Dukes and Loney, by the way, finished their respective big league careers with wRC+ totals of 103 and 105.
- Taking this one step further, here's the list of big league catchers to post a wRC+ between 100 and 109 during the 2020 season (min. 300 PA): Willson Contreras, J.T. Realmuto, Max Stassi, Carson Kelly, Luis Torrens, and Eric Haase.

Catchers with average or better offensive prowess are worth their weight in gold – especially one that consistently makes contact. Ruiz's long projected power finally took a step forward last season. Perhaps what's even more encouraging: it actually looks like a sustainable, repeatable skill as he's now elevating the ball at the highest clip in his career. Now the bad news: Ruiz has gained some noticeable girth over the past couple of seasons. In The 2020 Prospect Digest Handbook Ruiz's weight was listed as 200 pounds. This year he's tipping the scales at 225. Just something to keep an eye in the coming years.

Ceiling: 4.5-win player
Risk: Low to Moderate
MLB ETA: Debuted in 2019

2. Cade Cavalli, RHP

FB	CB	SL	CH	Command	Overall
65	60	60	55	45	60

Born: 08/14/98	Age: 23	Bats: R	Top Comp: Dylan Cease
Height: 6-4	Weight: 230	Throws: R	

Year	Org.	Level	IP	W	L	SV	ERA	FIP	xFIP	WHIP	K/9	K%	BB/9	BB%	SwStr%
2021	WSN	A+	40.2	3	1	0	1.77	1.63	2.21	0.89	15.71	44.94%	2.66	7.59%	19.91%
2021	WSN	AAA	24.2	1	5	0	7.30	4.54	4.92	1.86	8.76	19.83%	4.74	10.74%	11.89%
2021	WSN	AA	58.0	3	3	0	2.79	3.02	3.84	1.28	12.41	32.92%	5.43	14.40%	15.36%

Background: A talented, albeit enigmatic, hurler during his first two seasons at the University of Oklahoma, Cavalli, who saw some serious time as a two-way player, put it all together during his COVID-shortened 2020 season: in just four starts, the big bodied right-hander ripped off 37 punch outs against just five free passes in only 23.2 innings of work. Washington snagged the hard-throwing Sooner with the 22nd pick and set him loose on the minor leagues a year later. Cavalli donned the Wilmington Blue Rocks' jersey for his first seven starts of the season, seemingly twirling gem after gem while averaging nearly 16 strikeouts and barely over 2.5 free passes per nine innings. The front office bumped up the 6-foot-4, 230-pound right-hander up to Double-A. And while he continued to miss a ton of bats at the game's biggest minor league challenge – he averaged 12.4 K/9 – his control/command faltered to the tune of 5.4 BB/9. Cavalli capped off his mercurial top prospect with a six-game cap in Triple-A with the Rochester Red Wings. He finished the year with 123.1 innings, a minor league leading 175 strikeouts, 60 walks, and a 3.36 ERA.

Scouting Report: Consider the following:

- Since 2006, only four 22-year-old pitchers have struck out at least 32% and walked more than 12% of the hitters they faced in Double-A (min. 50 IP): Cristian Javier, Josh Staumont, Dan Smith, and – of course – Cade Cavalli.

A projectable right-hander without a ton of wear-and-tear on his right wing – he was limited to just over 100 innings during his collegiate career – Cavalli's command is likely to improve as he matures. The 6-foot-4, 230-pound former Big12 star will uncork an effortless mid- to upper-90s heater that's tough to get around on, a pair of plus breaking balls, and a quietly solid changeup that hovers in the 90 mph range. His curveball, the preferred offspeed weapon of choice, is a big 12-6 hammer with tight downward tilt. And he'll mix in a tightly-spun, firm cutter-like slider. Loose arm. Fluid mechanics. If the command upticks to average Cavalli has a chance to reach a Dylan Cease-type level. One final note: It's likely not a coincidence that Cavalli, who battled health issues in high school and in college, remained healthy as he moved away from a two-way gig.

Ceiling: 5.0-win player
Risk: Moderate
MLB ETA: 2022

---

3. Brady House, SS

	Hit	Power	Speed	Field	Overall
	45/55	60	50/45	50	60

Born: 06/04/03	Age: 19	Bats: R
Height: 6-4	Weight: 215	Throws: R

Season	Team	Age	Level	PA	1B	2B	3B	HR	SB	CS	BB%	K%	AVG	OBP	SLG	ISO
2021	WSN	18	CPX	66	12	3	0	4	0	0	10.61%	19.70%	0.322	0.394	0.576	0.254

Background: Lumped into the quartet of premium prep shortstops, House, along with Marcel Mayer, Jordan Lawlar, and Kahlil Watson, were all drafted within the top 16 picks of the 2021 draft. It's something that's been projected for the House for more than half-of-a-decade. The youngster cracked the U-12 National Team after batting .536 and starring on the mound for his middle school team. Four years later the University of Tennessee got a verbal commitment from House, who was recognized as the country's #1 recruit from the 2021 class. The 6-foot-3, 210-pound prospect slugged .445 with five homeruns and 21 RBIs as a sophomore for Winder-Barrow High School; he followed that up with a scorching .653 batting average through 15 games before the COVID-19 shutdown. Last season House dropped eight dingers, tied for seventh in the state of Georgia to go along with a state-leading 50 runs scored, and his .571 batting average is tied for fifth. Washington snagged House in the first round, 11th overall, and signed him to a deal worth $5,000,000 – nearly $500,000 above the recommender slot bonus.

Scouting Report: Pre-draft analysis:

"Bigger than his notable prep counterparts, House looks larger than his listed 6-foot-3 and 210-pounds and should continue to fill out as he matures – which, unfortunately, likely means a move away from shortstop. Big time bat speed, perhaps tops in the draft class, with plenty of natural loft that could result in 25 or so homeruns down the line. House has enough forearm and wrist strength to shoot bad balls to the gaps. There are some concerns about his inability to lay off of and/or fight off offspeed pitches low in the zone – though he's shown a propensity to fight them off in high school. There's some Carlos Correa-type potential. On the mound, his fastball routinely reaches the mid-90s."

Ceiling: 4.0-win player
Risk: Moderate
MLB ETA: 2022

---

5. Cole Henry, RHP

	FB	CB	CH	Command	Overall
	60	60	50/55	50	50

Born: 07/15/99	Age: 22	Bats: R	Top Comp: Michael Wacha
Height: 6-4	Weight: 215	Throws: R	

Year	Org.	Level	IP	W	L	SV	ERA	FIP	xFIP	WHIP	K/9	K%	BB/9	BB%	SwStr%
2021	WSN	A+	43.0	3	3	0	1.88	2.86	3.32	0.79	13.19	38.65%	2.30	6.75%	17.43%

Background: The lanky right-hander sparkled during his abbreviated tenure at Louisiana State University: he tallied a 3.03 ERA while averaging 11.1 strikeouts and just 2.8 walks per nine innings – though his career with the Tigers was limited to just 77.1 innings of work. Washington snapped up the then-20-year-old youngster in the second round two years ago, signing him to a deal worth $2 million. Henry, like his fellow high round 2020 draft counterpart, Cade Cavalli, made his professional debut in 2021. The 6-foot-4, 215-pound hurler started the campaign off on a bit of a disappointing note: he was coughed up a quartet of runs in a five-inning appearance against the Aberdeen IronBirds. But the former Tiger looked brilliant over his next four starts before hitting the DL for an extended stint with a wonky elbow. After a couple tune-up games in the rookie league, Henry made another quartet of dominant starts in High-A. He finished the year with a dazzling 1.88 ERA across 43.0 innings of action in Advanced A, averaging 13.2 punch outs and just 2.3 walks per nine innings.

Scouting Report: Like Cavalli, Henry's battled some health issues throughout his career: a wonky elbow forced him out of action for a couple months in 2021; he also battled COVID and then dealt with a stress reaction in his upper arm, as well as another elbow issue as a freshman with LSU. But when he's healthy he's...damn near brilliant. The big righty attacks hitters with a mid-90s fastball that sits comfortably in the 94- to 95-mph range and touched as high as 98 mph in a start late in the season. He complements the plus pitch with an equally devastating 12-6 hammer-of-a-curveball. He'll also mix in a surprisingly solid changeup, which shows nice arm side run and promising arm speed. Henry has some #3/#4-type potential, though he needs to stay healthy.

Ceiling: 2.5-win player
Risk: Moderate
MLB ETA: 2022

5. Jackson Rutledge, RHP

FB	CB	SL	CH	Command	Overall
70	50	65	45	50	50

Born: 04/01/99	Age: 23	Bats: R	Top Comp: Nick Pivetta
Height: 6-8	Weight: 245	Throws: R	

Year	Org.	Level	IP	W	L	SV	ERA	FIP	xFIP	WHIP	K/9	K%	BB/9	BB%	SwStr%
2019	WSN	A	27.1	2	0	0	2.30	2.54	3.44	0.91	10.21	29.25%	3.62	10.38%	16.30%
2021	WSN	A	22.0	1	2	0	5.32	3.70	4.16	1.32	10.64	26.53%	3.68	9.18%	14.02%

Background: It's been a wild couple of years for the former first round selection. Rutledge, the 17th overall pick in 2019, began his collegiate career donning an Arkansas Razorbacks uniform, but after riding the pine for the entire month of May that season the 6-foot-8, 245-pound behemoth announced his transfer to JuCo school San Jacinto. And, of course, he was absurdly dominant: he whiffed a whopping 134 in only 82.2 innings of action. Rutledge's pro debut was limited to just over 37 innings of work across the three lowest stateside levels. And – unfortunately – the big righty failed to surpass that meager total after not playing during the COVID season. Once again splitting time in three levels, Rutledge fanned 41 and walked 20 to go along with a car crash-esque 7.68 ERA. The Rockwood Summit High School alumni dealt with a cranky shoulder for several months and hit the disabled list briefly later in the season as well.

Snippet from The 2020 Prospect Digest Handbook: If the command ticks up toward a 50-grade he becomes a potential #2-type arm. If not, he has the floor as a hard-throwing, sometimes erratic #4.

Scouting Report: If you catch him on a good game you'd swear he'd be nearly as unhittable as Bob Gibson; the gigantic Nationals prospect pumps seeds consistently in the upper 90s and snaps off wickedly evil sliders in the mid- to upper-80s. But those good days didn't come nearly as frequently as the club – or Rutledge, for that matter – would've liked in 2021. The former Razorback-turned-JuCo-star rounds out his arsenal with an average curveball and blasé changeup. He commanded the zone well during the latter part of his campaign. But he, like Cole Henry, needs to prove he can take the ball every fifth day. It goes without saying that there's some reliever, two-pitch wipe out risk in play.

Ceiling: 2.5-win player
Risk: Moderate
MLB ETA: 2022

6. Armando Cruz, SS

Hit	Power	SB	Patience	Glove	Overall
35/45	30/40	50/55	50	60	50

Born: 01/16/04	Age: 18	Bats: R	Top Comp: Elvis Andrus
Height: 5-10	Weight: 160	Throws: R	

Year	Org.	Level	PA	1B	2B	3B	HR	SB	AVG	OBP	SLG	BB%	K%	SwStr%	wRC+
2021	WSN	DSL	197	31	8	1	1	11	0.232	0.292	0.305	8.12%	13.71%	20.45%	73

Background: Never shy about spending big money on the international market, the club inked the talented teenage shortstop to a franchise-tying $3.9 million deal. The pact ties equals amount the club handed to Yasel Antuna.

Scouting Report: Like a peacock sporting its feathers during mating season; Cruz is a flashy, silky smooth defender with the potential to earn a couple Gold Gloves in his career. Fluid movements with a strong arm and soft hands, there's no concern about his ability to handle the position as his 5-foot-10, 160-pound frame fills out. He has that certain pizzazz on the defensive side of the ball that can't be taught. It borderlines on cockiness – which I like. The swing, as expected, needs some work. He shows average bat speed and willingness to shoot the ball the other way, but he's robotic and stiff.

Ceiling: 2.0-win player
Risk: Moderate
MLB ETA: 2026

7. Daylen Lile, OF

Hit	Power	SB	Patience	Glove	Overall
55	40/45	45	55	50	45

Born: 11/30/02	Age: 19	Bats: L	Top Comp: Jon Jay
Height: 6-0	Weight: 195	Throws: R	

Year	Org.	Level	PA	1B	2B	3B	HR	SB	AVG	OBP	SLG	BB%	K%	SwStr%	wRC+
2021	WSN	CPX	80	12	2	0	0	2	0.219	0.363	0.250	18.75%	25.00%	30.54%	84

Background: A product of Trinity High School in Louisville, Kentucky, Lile was one of the most prolific prep bats during the 2021 season. According to reports, the 6-foot, 195-pound outfielder batted .550 with 12 doubles, 12 triples, 18 homeruns, and 11 stolen bases. He scored a whopping 70 runs and knocked in another 61. The University of Louisville commit was taken by Washington in the second round, 47th overall, and signed him to an above-slot bonus worth $1.75 million. Lile turned in a disappointing, albeit brief, debut in the Florida Complex League, batting .219/.363/.250 with a pair of doubles and stolen bases.

Scouting Report: Short, quick stroke and a natural loft that allows him to shoot balls to the gap and – perhaps – will develop into average power as his wiry frame fills out. He has trouble getting on top of pitches at the top of the zone. Very compact at the plate. And he's likely going to be slapped with the "professional hitter" label at some point in his career. There's a chance he develops into a corner outfielder with a 55- grade hit tool, solid walk rates, and slightly below average power. Average arm, nothing to write home about. Poor man's Carl Crawford.

Ceiling: 1.5-win player
Risk: Moderate
MLB ETA: 2026

8. Mitchell Parker, LHP

FB	CB	CH	Command	Overall
55	55	50	45	45

Born: 09/27/99	Age: 22	Bats: L	Top Comp: Joe Saunders
Height: 6-4	Weight: 225	Throws: L	

Year	Org.	Level	IP	W	L	SV	ERA	FIP	xFIP	WHIP	K/9	K%	BB/9	BB%	SwStr%
2021	WSN	A	57.1	3	7	0	4.08	4.08	3.52	1.19	13.34	34.84%	3.30	8.61%	15.18%
2021	WSN	A+	44.1	1	5	0	5.89	3.63	4.25	1.65	11.98	28.50%	3.45	8.21%	13.35%

Background: Washington went fishing into the pitching pond frequently during the COVID-shortened, five-round 2020 draft: the organization snagged arms with their first, second, fourth, and sixth picks. Parker, the last of the club's picks that season, was originally taken by the Cubs in the 28th round coming out of Manzano High School in 2018. After a year at JuCo San Jacinto, the Rays selected the big lefty one round sooner. And, of course, Parker headed back to the Houston area school for another crack at improving his command, as well as his draft stock. In six starts, the 6-foot-4, 225-pound southpaw struck out 64 and walked 18 in only 30.1 innings of work. Parker made his professional debut last season, splitting time between Fredericksburg and Wilmington. He tossed a combined 101.2 innings of work, averaging 12.7 strikeouts and 3.4 walks per nine innings to go along with a 4.87 ERA.

Scouting Report: Typical lefty with a little bit of funk or twang in his delivery and some long arm action. Parker doesn't overpower hitters, nor is he up there chucking meatballs. He features a better than average fastball with a bit of life on the offering when he humps up at times. His curveball's a nice lil' yacker with some late movement. And the changeup is workable. The command isn't overly sharp, but it's steadily improved over the past couple of seasons. He's a backend rotation filler unless the fastball ticks up or he continues to sharpen the command.

Ceiling: 1.5-win player
Risk: Moderate
MLB ETA: 2023

9. Andy Lara, RHP

FB	CB	CH	Command	Overall
50/55	55	45	50/55	45

Born: 01/06/03	Age: 19	Bats: R	Top Comp: Johan Oviedo
Height: 6-4	Weight: 180	Throws: R	

Year	Org.	Level	IP	W	L	SV	ERA	FIP	xFIP	WHIP	K/9	K%	BB/9	BB%	SwStr%
2021	WSN	CPX	39.2	3	2	0	4.54	4.55	4.12	1.21	10.66	28.14%	2.95	7.78%	36.99%

Background: Considered by some to be one the top pitching prospects on the international scene during the 2019 signing period. Washington, never shy about doling out big money, handed the man-child a hefty $1.25 million bonus. And like a lot of the club's more recognizable pitching prospects, Lara didn't make his professional debut until last season. Beginning the year by squaring off against the Florida Complex League competition, the then-18-year-old hurler tallied an impressive 47-to-13 strikeout-to-walk ratio in 39.2 innings of work. The Venezuelan-born hurler capped off his debut with a two-game stint in A-ball. Lara finished the year with 52 strikeouts and 21 walks per nine innings to go along with a 4.66 ERA.

Snippet from The 2020 Prospect Digest Handbook: It's not difficult to imagine that if Lara was entering the 2021 draft that he wouldn't be an early- to mid-first round selection.

Scouting Report: Unimpressive. At least during the A-Ball game I watched at the end of the year. Lara's fastball was sitting 90-91 but he could ramp it up to 94 mph when he felt like it. His above-average curveball would sit in the low 80s with promising shape and depth. And his changeup – at least the few that I saw – was, well, disappointing. It was straight, showed enough velo separation, but generally underwhelming. Lara likely wouldn't have cracked the first round had he been in the 2021 draft, probably settling a round or three later.

Ceiling: 1.5-win player
Risk: Moderate
MLB ETA: 2022

10. Gerardo Carrillo, RHP

FB	SL	CH	Command	Overall
60	55	50	40	40

Born: 09/13/98	Age: 23	Bats: R	Top Comp: Mychal Givens
Height: 5-10	Weight: 170	Throws: R	

Year	Org.	Level	IP	W	L	SV	ERA	FIP	xFIP	WHIP	K/9	K%	BB/9	BB%	SwStr%
2017	LAD	R	48.1	5	2	0	2.79	3.57	3.66	1.20	5.96	15.24%	2.61	6.67%	24.62%
2018	LAD	A	49.0	2	1	0	1.65	3.93	4.01	1.02	6.80	18.97%	2.76	7.69%	11.60%
2019	LAD	A+	86.0	5	9	0	5.44	4.49	4.93	1.60	9.00	21.23%	5.34	12.59%	12.10%
2021	LAD	AA	59.1	3	2	0	4.25	5.37	4.62	1.31	10.62	26.22%	4.40	10.86%	13.10%
2021	WSN	AA	37.0	0	5	0	5.59	5.49	5.00	1.65	9.24	21.47%	5.11	11.86%	10.51%

Background: Hidden behind a couple of more well-known prospects, Keibert Ruiz and Josiah Gray, Carrillo was the third of four prospects the organization received in the Max Scherzer-Trea Turner mega-swap with the Dodgers near the trade deadline. A wiry right-hander built in the Pedro Martinez-mold: Carrillo stands a less than imposing 5-foot-10 and 170-pounds. The Mexican-born hurler split time between both organizations' Double-A affiliates, throwing a career high 96.1 innings, recording 108 punch outs and 50 free passes. He also plunked a Rick Vaughn-esque 23 hitters – or roughly an average of one HBP every four innings. He tallied a 4.76 ERA and a 3-7 win-loss record.

Scouting Report: Carrillo features a heavy, riding plus fastball that shows some cut or sink at times. The slinging right-hander will mix in a interesting slider. At first glance it doesn't look overly dominant but it generates a *ton* of awkward swings and/or some knee-buckling takes. Carrillo will also show a decent little changeup that may eventual spill over into above-average territory. The five-year minor league vet shows a lot of confidence in his secondary weapons. With regard to his work last season, consider the following:

- Between 2006 and 2020, only eight 22-year-old pitchers in Double-A fanned between 23% and 26% and walked between 9% and 12% of the hitters they faced in a season (min. 75 IP): Alex Torres, Frankie Montas, Jorge Lopez, Wily Peralta, Zack Wheeler, Daniel Haigwood, Juan Carlos Sulbaran, and Kodi Medeiros.

Carrillo's not long for the rotation, but he has the makings – potentially – of a very useful, sometimes high leverage setup arm.

Ceiling: 1.0-win player
Risk: Low to Moderate
MLB ETA: 2022

11. Joan Adon, RHP

FB	SL	CH	Command	Overall
60	55	N/A	45	40

Born: 08/12/98	Age: 23	Bats: R	Top Comp: Alex Colome
Height: 6-2	Weight: 242	Throws: R	

Year	Org.	Level	IP	W	L	SV	ERA	FIP	xFIP	WHIP	K/9	K%	BB/9	BB%	SwStr%
2017	WSN	R	28.0	2	1	1	3.54	3.12	3.05	1.18	9.96	26.50%	2.89	7.69%	39.64%
2019	WSN	A	105.0	11	3	0	3.86	4.25	4.29	1.30	7.71	20.13%	3.77	9.84%	11.44%
2021	WSN	A+	87.0	6	4	0	4.97	4.06	4.63	1.25	9.41	24.40%	3.31	8.58%	12.61%

Background: Signed out of Santo Domingo, Dominican Republic, for a five-figure bonus in early July in 2016. Adon's quietly forcing his way up prospect charts, going from a non-descript $50,000 bonus baby to cracking the big league roster five years later. Last season Adon put the progress in hyper-drive as he hopped, skipped, and jumped his way from High-A to Double-A to Triple-A, and then squeezing in one successful start in Washington against the vaunted Boston Red Sox. In total, the broad-shoulder, fire-bolt slinging right-hander struck out 122 minor league hitters, to go along with just 40 walks in 105 innings. He compiled a 4.97 ERA in a career-high tying 21 starts.

Snippet from The 2020 Prospect Digest Handbook: There's really nothing extraordinary about Adon: it's a decent repertoire; he throws a decent amount of strikes and misses some bats; and he handled his promotion to Low Class A well. There's not a lot that separates Adon from mediocre pitching prospects like long time vagabond Keury Mella.

Scouting Report: At this point in his career Adon's mainly a two-pitch pitcher: he'll feature a lively mid-90s fastball, topping out at 96 during his final minor league in 2021, and he complements the plus offering with an above-average , 12-6 slider that acts more like a power curveball. I failed to see his changeup and he tossed just six of them during his 94-pitch debut with the nationals. Unless the changeup ticks up *and* he begins to trust it more, Adon isn't long for the rotation. He could pitch some high leverage innings in the big leagues.

Ceiling: 1.0-win player
Risk: Low to Moderate
MLB ETA: Debuted in 2021

12. Aldo Ramirez, RHP

	FB	CB	CH	Command	Overall
	55/60	55	50	50/55	40

Born: 05/06/01	Age: 21	Bats: R	Top Comp: Wily Peralta
Height: 6-0	Weight: 191	Throws: R	

Year	Org.	Level	IP	W	L	SV	ERA	FIP	xFIP	WHIP	K/9	K%	BB/9	BB%	SwStr%
2018	BOS	R	23.0	1	2	0	0.39	2.67	3.03	0.57	6.65	20.00%	1.17	3.53%	32.14%
2019	BOS	A-	61.2	2	3	0	3.94	3.34	2.95	1.22	9.19	24.05%	2.34	6.11%	12.06%
2021	BOS	A	31.0	1	1	0	2.03	3.10	3.52	1.13	9.29	24.62%	2.32	6.15%	11.39%

Background: Another prospect the club acquired during their mid-season selloff. Ramirez, who was acquired for post-season hero Kyle Schwarber, was discovered by the Red Sox after appearing in five games for the Rieleros de Aguascalientes in 2018 as a wiry 17-year-old. The 6-foot, 191-pound right-hander spent the following season flashing some strong promise as an 18-year-old in the New York-Penn League, posting a 63-to-16 strikeout-to-walk ratio in 61.2 innings of work. And he continued that trend as he made the jump up to full season action last season, but an elbow injury shut him down in late June. Roughly a month later the Nationals gambled and acquired the youngster as the sole return for Schwarber. Ramirez made it back to the mound in late August, throwing another four games for Washington's Florida Complex League squad.

Snippet from The 2020 Prospect Digest Handbook: There is a reasonable chance that Ramirez develops three above-average or better offerings in the coming years.

Scouting Report: Two years ago Ramirez's heater was sitting – comfortably – at 92 mph. Early last season his fastball spike to the mid 90s, touching as high as 96 mph. His curveball, now up to 80 mph, continues to be an above-average secondary weapon. But the changeup, which flashed above-average, looked a bit disappointing. Assuming the elbow doesn't flare up in the coming years, Ramirez has the makings of a backend starter – but he's going to have to prove his frame can handle the rigors of grabbing the ball every fifth game.

Ceiling: 1.0-win player
Risk: Moderate
MLB ETA: 2023/2024

13. Yasel Antuna, SS

	Hit	Power	SB	Patience	Glove	Overall
	45	50	45	50	40/45	40

Born: 10/26/99	Age: 22	Bats: B	Top Comp: Yu Chang
Height: 6-0	Weight: 195	Throws: R	

Season	Team	Age	Level	PA	1B	2B	3B	HR	SB	CS	BB%	K%	AVG	OBP	SLG	ISO
2018	WSN	18	A	362	49	14	2	6	8	7	8.84%	21.82%	0.220	0.293	0.331	0.111
2021	WSN	21	A+	457	53	26	1	12	4	4	10.07%	21.88%	0.227	0.307	0.385	0.158

Background: Just another example of how difficult scouting actually is: the Nationals handed Antuna, a 16-year-old shortstop at the time, the largest international signing bonus in club history, $3.9 million – surpassing the previous high of $1.5 million. The front office handed another young shortstop, Luis Garcia, a third of Antuna's bonus. Five years later Garcia was spending his second season in Washington and, well, Antuna is flailing away at low level minor league pitching. Hailing from Peravia, Dominican Republic, Antuna appeared in 106 games with the Wilmington Blue Rocks last season, batting a meager .227/.307/.385 with 26 doubles, one triple, and 12 homeruns. His overall production, per *Weighted Runs Created Plus*, was 12% *below* the league average mark.

Snippet from The 2018 Prospect Digest Handbook: Antuna's likely going to have to shift to third base. Like last season, just give it time.

Scouting Report: Consider the following:

- Since 2006, here's the list of 21-year-old hitters in High-A to post an *Weighted Runs Created Plus* between 85 and 95 with a strikeout rate between 19% and 23% in a season (min. 450 PA): Ryan Wheeler, Lee Haydel, Keury De La Cruz, Jonah Arenado, and – of course – Yasel Antuna.

So, Antuna is still at shortstop – for now. But the *real* news is Antuna's production after the first two months of the year: over his last 77 games (341 PA), the Dominican-born infielder slugged .268/.344/.430 with 23 doubles, one triple, and eight homeruns. That's the making of a real prospect. He's not going to be a star. Well, he's probably not going to a starter either. But there's some backup potential here.

Ceiling: 1.0-win player
Risk: Moderate
MLBETA: 2023

14. Tim Cate, LHP

	FB	CB	CH	Command	Overall
	50	60	50	50	40

Born: 09/30/97	Age: 24	Bats: L	Top Comp: Hector Santiago
Height: 6-0	Weight: 185	Throws: L	

Season	Team	Age	Level	IP	TBF	K/9	K%	BB/9	BB%	K-BB%	ERA	FIP	xFIP	Pit/Bat
2018	WSN	20	A-	31.0	138	7.55	18.84%	2.90	7.25%	11.59%	4.65	3.39	3.86	3.51
2018	WSN	20	A	21.0	93	8.14	20.43%	2.57	6.45%	13.98%	5.57	5.14	3.78	3.22
2019	WSN	21	A	70.1	279	9.34	26.16%	1.66	4.66%	21.51%	2.82	2.34	2.72	3.51
2019	WSN	21	A+	73.1	302	8.10	21.85%	2.33	6.29%	15.56%	3.31	3.07	3.04	3.52
2021	WSN	23	AA	96.2	435	7.54	18.62%	3.44	8.51%	10.11%	5.31	4.66	4.64	3.74

Background: The Nationals track record in the draft is…spotty at best. And, perhaps, nothing better exemplifies than the club's 2018 class. Mason Denaburg, their first round pick, has pretty much been injured since day one. The conversion of Reid Schaller, their third round pick, from reliever to starter failed and he finally cracked a Double-A roster during his age-24 season. Jake Irvin and Gage Canning, their fourth and fifth round picks, are nondescript – at best. And Tim Cate, owner of one of the minor league's finest curveballs, is deathly close to joining the rest of the bunch. A second round pick out of Connecticut, Cate limped – *badly* – through his first crack at the minors' toughest challenge: Double-A. In 21 starts with the Harrisburg Senators the lefty posted a mediocre 81—to-37 strikeout-to-walk ratio and a 5.31 ERA in 96.2 innings of work.

Snippet from The 2020 Prospect Digest Handbook: Cate's becoming an anomaly of sorts as a soft-tossing hurler, so he'll have to continue to fight the good fight.

Scouting Report: A Kansas City Royals type of prospect because Cate can really spin a doozy of a curveball. But beyond the plus offering there's really nothing else that screams *future big leaguer*. His fastball is average, maybe even slightly below given the current game today. His changeup is nothing to write home about. And his command is fringy average. Add it all up and there's not a whole lot of hope for the former Connecticut ace.

Ceiling: 1.0-win player
Risk: Moderate
MLB ETA: 2022

15. Seth Romero, LHP

	FB	SL	CH	Command	Overall
	55	55	50	50	40

Born: 04/19/96	Age: 26	Bats: L	Top Comp: Andrew Miller
Height: 6-3	Weight: 225	Throws: L	

Year	Org.	Level	IP	W	L	SV	ERA	FIP	xFIP	WHIP	K/9	K%	BB/9	BB%	SwStr%
2017	WSN	R	28.0	2	1	1	3.54	3.12	3.05	1.18	9.96	26.50%	2.89	7.69%	39.64%
2019	WSN	A	105.0	11	3	0	3.86	4.25	4.29	1.30	7.71	20.13%	3.77	9.84%	11.44%
2021	WSN	A+	87.0	6	4	0	4.97	4.06	4.63	1.25	9.41	24.40%	3.31	8.58%	12.61%

Background: I have to frank: I'm not sure which one's longer – Romero's discipline infractions or his stints on the disabled list. Romero's latest health issue was non-baseball related: he reportedly fell down a flight of stairs and broke his hand during the offseason and underwent surgery. The 6-foot-3, 225-pound southpaw made 11 brief starts across nearly every minor league level, throwing 35.2 innings with 55 strikeouts and 15 walks .

Snippet from The 2020 Prospect Digest Handbook: Who the hell knows what to expect from Romero?

Scouting Report: Like a Greek tragedy, Romero has – at one time – showcased two plus pitches – an explosive, get-on-ya-quick fastball and a slider-from-hell – and an above-average changeup, but…well…stupid mistakes and bad luck have robbed a lot of precious development time. Romero's heater, which sat in the 93- to 95-mph range, was clocking higher than his brief MLB appearance in 2020, but it just seemed…hittable.

His trademark wipeout slider lacked the tilt from years past as well. And his change was downgraded to average. The front office seems content to let him try and figure out how to be a professional starting pitcher but I'm thinking he ends up as a wicked lefty reliever, maybe in the same vain as Ander Miller.

Ceiling: 1.0-win player
Risk: Moderate to High
MLB ETA: Debuted in 2020

16. Alfonso Hernandez, LHP

FB	SL	CH	Command	Overall
45	55	50	55	40

Born: 08/03/99	Age: 22	Bats: L	Top Comp: Aaron Loup
Height: 5-11	Weight: 198	Throws: L	

Season	Team	Age	Level	IP	TBF	K/9	K%	BB/9	BB%	K-BB%	ERA	FIP	xFIP	Pit/Bat
2018	WSN	18	R	33.2	138	8.29	22.46%	2.14	5.80%	16.67%	2.14	2.71	3.53	1.70
2018	WSN	18	A-	13.0	54	6.92	18.52%	4.15	11.11%	7.41%	2.77	3.79	4.67	3.41
2019	WSN	19	A-	32.1	127	9.19	25.98%	1.39	3.94%	22.05%	2.51	1.82	2.59	3.77
2019	WSN	19	A	18.0	76	8.00	21.05%	3.00	7.89%	13.16%	5.00	2.71	4.19	3.36
2021	WSN	21	A	32.0	137	9.56	24.82%	3.38	8.76%	16.06%	2.81	4.38	4.60	3.85
2021	WSN	21	A+	70.1	297	10.88	28.62%	2.69	7.07%	21.55%	3.97	4.92	4.32	4.03

Background: An overlooked arm, even in a weak farm system, Hernandez quietly turned in a fantastic little season in 2021. Hailing from Barcelona, Venezuela, the 5-foot-11, 198-pound lefty began the post-COVID season in Low-A with the Fredericksburg Nationals, striking out 34 and walking just 12 in 32.0 innings of work. Hernandez earned a promotion up to Wilmington in mid-June and he continued to hold his own. In 17 appearances with the Blue Rocks the stocky lefty tossed 70.1 innings with 85 punch outs and 21 walks. He set career a career high in 2021 by averaging 10.5 strikeouts per nine innings.

Scouting Report: Consider the following:

- Since 2006, only four 21-year-old pitchers fanned between 26% and 28% and walked between 6% and 8% of the hitters they faced in a High-A season (min. 60 IP): Kris Bubic, Wade Davis, Jared Lansford, and Alfonso Hernandez.
- For those counting at home: Bubic is a former first round selection; Davis was taken in the third round; and Lansford was a second round draft pick.

Hernandez isn't a traditional prospect in the modern day sense. His left fingers aren't breathing fire. His wrist isn't snapping off ungodly breaking balls. And he's not ripping off fading changeups with Pedro Martinez-type pronation. Instead, the little lefty chucks up 89- 91 mph heaters, a slick little slider that hitters have difficulty picking up, and decent little changeup with some cutting action. What separates Hernandez from the pack is his above-average command, which allows his mediocre repertoire to play up.

Ceiling: 1.0-win player
Risk: Low to Moderate
MLB ETA: 2023

17. Jeremy De La Rosa, CF

Hit	Power	SB	Patience	Glove	Overall
35/45	50	50	50	50	40

Born: 01/16/02	Age: 20	Bats: L	Top Comp: Courtney Hawkins
Height: 5-11	Weight: 160	Throws: L	

Season	Team	Age	Level	PA	1B	2B	3B	HR	SB	CS	BB%	K%	AVG	OBP	SLG	ISO
2019	WSN	17	R	99	14	1	2	2	3	2	12.12%	29.29%	0.232	0.343	0.366	0.134
2021	WSN	19	A	358	47	12	4	5	7	8	8.38%	34.08%	0.209	0.279	0.316	0.107

Background: There's raw. And then there's Jeremy De La Rosa raw. Signed off the internal market in 2018 for $300,000, the toolsy outfielder was thrust directly into the stateside rookie league a year later. And the then-17-year-old struggled – mightily. He batted a lowly .232/.343/.366 with a double, two triples, and a pair of dingers. The front office continued their aggressive promotion schedule, bumping De La Rosa straight up to Low-A for 2021. And predictably so, the results were pretty meager. In 87 games with the Fredericksburg Nationals, the 5-foot-11, 160-pound teenager hit .209/.279/.316 with 12 doubles, four triples, five homeruns, and seven stolen bases. His overall production, per *Weighted Runs Created Plus, was a staggering* 35% below the league average threshold.

Scouting Report: Consider the following:

- Since 2016, only seven 19-year-old hitters have met the following criteria in Low-A in a season with one organization (min. 300 PA): a post *Weighted Runs Created Plus* of 70 or less with a strikeout rate north of 30%. Those seven hitters: Steven Moya, Quentin Holmes, Ed Howard, D.J. Davis, Julian Leon, Marten Gasparini, and – of course – Mr. Jeremy De La Rosa.

The good news: ignoring De La Rosa momentarily, one of the struggling players spent a few brief seasons in the big leagues (Moya) and another one is a recent top draft pick (Howard). But the bad news is pretty glaring: regardless of the potentially loud tools, De La Rosa's climb to the big leagues, let alone a meaningful career, is a long shot – at best. The silver lining, though, is that in his last 30 games with the Low-A squad he slugged .272/.331/.412. He's probably better suited for a return trip to Low-A, but it wouldn't be surprising to see the Nationals continue to aggressively challenge him by promoting him up to High-A to start 2022.

Ceiling: 1.0-win player
Risk: Moderate
MLB ETA: 2024

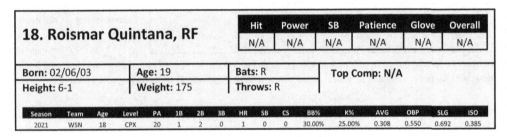

18. Roismar Quintana, RF

	Hit	Power	SB	Patience	Glove	Overall
	N/A	N/A	N/A	N/A	N/A	N/A

Born: 02/06/03	Age: 19	Bats: R	Top Comp: N/A
Height: 6-1	Weight: 175	Throws: R	

Season	Team	Age	Level	PA	1B	2B	3B	HR	SB	CS	BB%	K%	AVG	OBP	SLG	ISO
2021	WSN	18	CPX	20	1	2	0	1	0	0	30.00%	25.00%	0.308	0.550	0.692	0.385

Background: Another one of the club's bonus babies on the international free agent market. Washington handed the toolsy right fielder a deal slightly north of $800,000 during the 2019 summer. Quintana, a native of Caracas, Venezuela, made his professional debut last season, appearing in seven games for the club's Florida Complex League. He went 4-for-13 with a pair of doubles and a dinger. He finished the year with six walks and five strikeouts.

Scouting Report: There are no videos of Quintana existing on the internet – at least, as far as I can tell. Various scouting reports on the toolsy outfielder all include similar verbiage: raw, potential above-average thunder, projectable. Likely won't get a good feel until early spring when, I'm guessing, Quintana appears in Low-A.

Ceiling: N/A
Risk: N/A
MLB ETA: N/A

19. Branden Boissiere, 1B

	Hit	Power	SB	Patience	Glove	Overall
	55	40	40	50	50	40

Born: 03/23/00	Age: 22	Bats: L	Top Comp: Ryan Sweeney
Height: 6-1	Weight: 205	Throws: L	

Season	Team	Age	Level	PA	1B	2B	3B	HR	SB	CS	BB%	K%	AVG	OBP	SLG	ISO
2021	WSN	21	A	98	11	5	0	1	1	0	10.20%	25.51%	0.200	0.299	0.294	0.094

Background: Stout performer during his three-year career at the University of Arizona, Boissiere, a well-built 6-foot-1, 205-pound first baseman, was snagged in the third round last June. The Riverside, California, native turned in one of the better showings as a true freshman in 2019: he batted .336/.430/.464 with nine extra-base hits in 39 games for the Pac12 squad. His production took a bit of nosedive during the ensuing summer in the Northwoods League: he hit .270/.387/.362 In 51 games for the Willmar Stingers. Boissiere rediscovered his stroke prior to the COVID-shutdown, slugging .327/.356/.455. Last season, the then-21-year-old put together his finest showing to date: he battered the competition to the tune of .369/.451/.506 with 12 doubles, four doubles, and five homeruns. He finished the year with a 49-to-38 strikeout-to-walk ratio.

Scouting Report: A simple picturesque lefty swing that's more fitted for an up-the-middle position rather than a run producing one. Good bat speed. Short and compact. The question, of course, is whether the former Wildcat will hit for average power? And Boissiere didn't alleviate any of those concerns during his 25-game cameo with Fredericksburg Low-A: he slugged one long ball in 98 plate appearances – though the lefty-swinging first baseman tattooed an offering from a southpaw.

Ceiling: 1.0-win player
Risk: Moderate
MLB ETA: 2023/2024

20. Mason Denaburg, RHP	FB	CB	CH	Command	Overall
	N/A	N/A	N/A	N/A	40

Born: 08/08/99	Age: 22	Bats: R	Top Comp: N/A
Height: 6-4	Weight: 195	Throws: R	

Year	Org.	Level	IP	W	L	SV	ERA	FIP	xFIP	WHIP	K/9	K%	BB/9	BB%	SwStr%
2019	WSN	R	20.1	1	1	0	7.52	5.23	5.42	1.82	8.41	18.81%	6.20	13.86%	22.04%

Background: A little of maybe not-so-fun trivia, at least for Nationals fans: Denaburg was taken by the club with the 27th overall pick in 2018 – two picks after the Diamondbacks took high school infielder Matt McLain. Fast forward three years and McLain, who spurned Arizona's contact, was drafted with the 17th overall pick by the Reds *and* he's already (A) played in more professional games and (B) at a higher level than his former first round counterpart. Needless to say, it's been a rough couple of seasons for Denaburg. A University of Florida commit, the 6-foot-4, 195-pound right-hander has battled (A) bicep issues in high school, (B) underwent shoulder surgery in 2019, (C) didn't pitch in 2020, and (D) missed all of last year recovering from Tommy John surgery.

Snippet from The 2020 Prospect Digest Handbook: At this point he's a complete wild card – an expensive, supremely talent wild card, but a wild card nonetheless.

Scouting Report: Well, there's literally nothing else to report on. And, to be frank, there's two things keeping Denaburg among the club's Top 20 prospects: #1 his lofty draft status and #2 a weak Washington farm system.

Ceiling: 1.0-win player
Risk: High – like, *really high*
MLB ETA: The Magic 8 Ball says check again later.

Made in United States
North Haven, CT
04 June 2022

19832967R00226